SO-AEU-631

Successful
Writing
at Work

Successful Writing at Work

Fourth Edition

Philip C. Kolin
University of Southern Mississippi

D. C. Heath and Company
Lexington, Massachusetts   Toronto

Address editorial correspondence to:

D. C. Heath and Company
125 Spring Street
Lexington, MA 02173

Acquisitions Editor: Paul Smith
Developmental Editor: Linda Bieze
Production Editor: Renée M. Mary
Designer: Jan Shapiro
Art Editor: Diane Grossman
Production Coordinator: Charles Dutton
Permissions Editor: Margaret Roll

Published simultaneously in Canada.

Published in the United States of America.

International Standard Book Number: 0-669-29714-3.

Library of Congress Catalog Number: 92-85308.

10   9   8   7   6   5   4   3   2   1

To
Eric, Kristin, and Erica
Sharron
Julie and Loretta
and
MARY

Preface

Successful Writing at Work is a comprehensive introductory text designed for use in technical, business, professional, and occupational writing courses. As in the first three editions, the approach in this Fourth Edition remains practical, emphasizing that communication skills are essential for career advancement and that writing is a vital part of almost every job. The Fourth Edition even more strongly emphasizes that writing is a problem-solving activity that helps workers meet the needs of their employers, coworkers, customers, and clients. *Successful Writing at Work* presents multiple situations and problems that students as business and technical writers will have to address and asks them to consider the rhetorical options available for solving these problems. As in other editions, the Fourth Edition gives students detailed guidelines for creating clear, well-organized, and readable writing. It contains a wide range of writing examples drawn from such varied sources as student papers and reports, business correspondence and proposals, and magazine and journal articles.

Consistent with this view of writing in the workplace, the Fourth Edition places great emphasis on writing as a process. Students will find clear and concise explanations of the *hows* as well as the *whys* of writing for the world of work. *Successful Writing at Work* helps students develop the crucial skills of brainstorming, researching, drafting, revising, editing, proofreading, and formatting various business and technical documents—correspondence, instructions, question-naires, summaries, and reports.

As in prior editions, the Fourth Edition continues to emphasize audience analysis. Memos, letters, proposals, questionnaires, and reports are considered from the points of view of the intended audience(s); that is, personnel directors, employers, coworkers, customers, and so forth. Students are regarded as professionals seeking advancement at different phases of a business career. For example, students are addressed as employees who must meet the needs of employers and customers with specific problems and requests in Chapter 7, as job candidates looking for a position in Chapter 8, as assistants who have to summarize an article or a report for a superior in Chapter 11, and as business people who must write a persuasive proposal to win a contract in Chapter 15.

The organization of the Fourth Edition reflects the student's own progress in writing for the world of work. The text moves logically from consideration of basic concepts in writing (audience, tone, message, purpose) in Chapter 1 to the overall process of writing (brainstorming, drafting, revising), presented in Chapter 2, in which these concepts play a vital role. Chapters 3 through 5 on paragraphs, sentence structure, and word choice give students a solid foundation on which to apply their skills of generating ideas, drafting, and revising their work. The text then moves sequentially from shorter assignments (letters and memos) in Chapters 6 through 8 to more complex forms of business writing (instructions, questionnaires, proposals, and reports) in Chapters 9 through 18.

As in the three previous editions, the Fourth Edition is rich in practical applications, useful both to readers who have no on-the-job experience and to those with years of experience. Another strong feature found in the Fourth Edition is the abundance of exercises at the end of each chapter. These exercises give students numerous opportunities to practice a variety of skills from analyzing the strengths and weaknesses of diverse memos, letters, and reports to generating ideas, researching topics, organizing information, drafting, revising, editing, creating and incorporating visuals, and working as part of a collaborative writing team.

New Material in the Fourth Edition

The Fourth Edition has been improved and expanded to make it a more effective tool for the instructor and a more comprehensive and helpful resource for the student. New examples and exercises have been added throughout to make the discussion of occupational writing more useful and current. Much more information on computers and communication technologies, for example, has been included.

The following new features have been designed to help instructors and students use the Fourth Edition:

- New "Revision Checklists" help students to become more aware of writing as a process, something to be revised, reworked, and double-checked before submitting a final copy to readers. These end-of-chapter checklists serve as both summaries and quality control checkpoints.
- The process of writing in general receives even greater emphasis. An added section in Chapter 3 shows the evolution of a collaboratively written memo on recycling from early drafts to final copy. Additional guidelines, examples, and exercises in Chapters 6, 8, 16, and 17 assist students in drafting and revising memos, letters, and reports. Expanded coverage in Chapter 2 on using a word processor further highlights the writing process.
- More marginal annotations on a variety of documents assist students to see how a piece of writing is organized, worded, and formatted to meet the needs of the intended audience.
- New examples and readings focus on recent communication technologies: fax machines in Chapter 2; formatting options available from different kinds of software in Chapters 8 and 13; the modern technological office in Chapter 11; and E-mail in Chapter 7 and voice mail in Chapter 18. Additionally, examples from health care (MRI), banking (ATM's), and engineering technology (robotics) provide students with further perspectives on the changing worlds of business and industry.
- Collaborative writing at work receives contemporary emphasis throughout; a new section on "The Group Writing Process" in Chapter 2 gives practical suggestions on how students can succeed by working as a team. New and revised examples of memos, letters, and reports are discussed in light of collaborative writing; and a new case study in Chapter 15 illustrates how a proposal can be generated and prepared through collaborative effort.

- Coverage of writing for ESL readers (for whom English is not their first language but who will make up an increasingly larger proportion of the writer's audience) sharpens and expands the discussions of audience analysis. The needs of such readers are introduced in an expanded section on audience analysis in Chapter 1, and the topic is developed more fully in a new section of Chapter 6, "Writing for International Readers." The writer's need to develop "international English" is further discussed through new examples of memos and a sales letter.
- Additional coverage of sexist language, spelling practices, and word choice—with more examples—enhances Chapter 5.
- The order of Chapters 7 and 8 has been reversed from the Third Edition to stress the principles and practice of effective correspondence.
- Revised and expanded coverage of business correspondence in Chapter 7 includes new sections on "Correspondence in the Electronic Office" and "Adapting Your Style for E-Mail and Fax Messages" and even more examples of sales letters, and correspondence dealing with refusing and granting credit.
- Greatly expanded sections on job letters and résumé style and format in Chapter 8 assist job seekers of widely differing backgrounds and experience. Six different examples of resumes (including the highly used bullet résumé) and additional suggestions for students who are re-entering the workplace or changing careers make this strong chapter even more effective.
- Updated and greatly expanded sections dealing with on-line catalogs, computer searches, data bases, and other electronic reference works enhance Chapter 9.
- Much more information and practical advice on the use of computers in the workplace appears throughout, especially in preparing the list of works cited in Chapter 10, in tallying responses from questionnaires in Chapter 12, and in writing short and long reports in Chapters 16 and 17.
- Chapter 13 features additional updated material on computer graphics with new examples of computer clip art, computer-generated graphs, and three-dimensional graphics.
- A flexible and greatly enlarged instructor's guide is available in an 8 1/2"× 11" format. It includes a much expanded classified bibliography of materials on teaching and doing research on occupational writing, additional teaching tips, answers to exercises, transparency masters; 25 additional models of memos, letters, questionnaires, proposals; a long report on AIDS and the health care worker; and case studies. All these documents are suitable for copying and distributing to students for added practice in revising their writing.
- Examples of key documents, such as letters, résumés, and reports are available in a set of 25 transparencies for classroom discussion.

An Overview of the Chapters

A brief overview of the Fourth Edition will show how these new materials have been integrated. Section I deals with the overall writing process. Chapter 1, setting the stage for all occupational writing, identifies the basic concepts of audience analysis, purpose, message, style, and tone, and relates these concepts to on-the-job writing.

Chapters 2, 3, 4, and 5 continue this important unit on the basic elements of effective writing. Chapter 2, on the writing process at work, introduces students to prewriting strategies, drafting, revising, and editing their written work. Chapter 3 explains in detail how to generate effective paragraphs, with special emphasis on the needs of readers in business and industry. Chapter 4, on sentences, gives guidelines on how to create clear and economical sentences, with emphasis on seeing revisions as a key to success. Chapter 5, on words, prepares students to make appropriate choices for their message.

Section II deals with business correspondence. Chapter 6 introduces the nuts and bolts of letter writing and focuses on selecting the appropriate format (including a section on the AMS letter format), language, and tone. Chapter 7 examines the rhetorical strategies writers must employ to produce a variety of business correspondence—complaint, adjustment, order, sales, and collection letters—with new material on selecting the most effective organizational strategies for good or bad news letters, including refusing and granting credit. Chapter 8, covering the job search, takes students through the process of preparing a placement file, writing a résumé and organizing it by skill area and/or chronology, writing a letter of application, anticipating interviewers' questions and accepting or declining a job. For greater teaching flexibility, instructors will find four different letters of application and six résumés from applicants with varying degrees of experience—to help new and veteran job seekers alike.

Section III provides students with the techniques they need to gather and summarize information. Chapter 9 takes students on a guided tour of the computerized library, shows them how to locate printed and audiovisual materials and how to profit from searching various computer databases and electronic reference works, and provides them with an expanded and updated annotated appendix of useful reference works. Chapter 10 is devoted to several styles of documentation—and particularly to the MLA parenthetical method. A sample student research paper, "Stress and the Computer Programmer," illustrates this method of documentation. In Chapter 11 students will learn how to write clear and concise summaries and abstracts. Chapter 12, on questionnaires, shows how to construct reliable questions, select informants, organize responses, and write a questionnaire survey report. Chapter 13 supplies practical advice on designing visuals, explains how to coordinate visuals with written commentary, discusses and illustrates a variety of visuals students can use in their work, and concludes with a greatly expanded and illustrated section on computer graphics.

In Section IV students are asked to apply the skills they learned in Section III to more complex writing assignments. Chapter 14 covers writing accurate instructions and selecting the most appropriate language and visuals. Chapter 15 focuses on three common types of proposals: an internal proposal for an employer, a sales proposal (solicited and unsolicited) for customers, and a research proposal written for a teacher. A proposal on installing an ATM at a branch of a large bank is new to the Fourth Edition. Chapter 16 outlines the principles common to all short reports and then discusses specific types, with detailed coverage of test and laboratory reports. Instructors will also find the discussion of unusual occurrence reports especially detailed. Finally, students are cautioned about the legal implications of what they write and are shown how to avoid some legal pitfalls.

To make it more accessible to students, Chapter 17 on long reports has been revised for this edition to emphasize even more the process of writing such a report. In this chapter students are encouraged to see a long report as the culmination of all their work in the course or on a major project at work. The individual parts of such a report are discussed in detail, with a student-written model report, "The Positive Effects of Robots in American Industry," used as an illustration. Together with the report on "Stress and the Computer Programmer" in Chapter 10, instructors have two complete, fully documented student research papers to use in teaching the long report.

Chapter 18, which stresses the importance of audience analysis in oral communication, offers common-sense advice on handling briefings and on generating, organizing, and delivering formal speeches and includes a new speech outline on the benefits of using voice-mail.

Acknowledgments

I am grateful to the many friends who gave me the benefit of their suggestions as I prepared the Fourth Edition of *Successful Writing at Work*. At the University of Southern Mississippi, they include Cliff Burgess, Lisa Chiang, Jeanne Ezell, David Goff, Paul McCarver, Harry McCraw, Prakash Ramnath, David Wheeler, and Irmegard Wolfe. I also thank Colby Kullman of the University of Mississippi, David H. Roberts of Samford University, and LaNelle Daniel of Northwest Community College, Powell, Wyoming.

Several individuals from business and government also gave me valuable assistance for which I am very thankful. They include Joycelyn Woolfolk at the Federal Reserve Bank in Atlanta, Michael Sappington of the Bank of Mississippi, Sgt. Mannie Hall of the U. S. Army, Brad Robinson of Washington, D. C., and Virginia Pagliaro at Krames Communications.

I am deeply indebted to the following instructors who offered many valuable suggestions as they reviewed *Successful Writing at Work*: Donald F. Andrews, Chattanooga State Technical Community College; William J. Bean, Bethune-Cookman College; Albert G. Black, California State University at Long Beach; Eugene R. Cunnar, New Mexico State University; Robert F. Denton, Northern Illinois University; George Haber, New York Institute of Technology; Peggy Hartshorn, Franklin University; Marlys Hoon, Kirkwood Community College; Terri Johnson, Moraine Park Technical Institute; Dan Jones, University of Central Florida; Susan Allison McCormack, Miami University at Hamilton; Mickey C. Minnerly, St. Louis Community College at Florissant Valley; John Pennington,

Valdosta State College; Mary R. Scotto, Kean College of New Jersey; Skaidrite Stelzer, University of Toldeo; David L. Stewart, DeVry Institute of Technology; Anne Talley, Phillips Junior College; James A. Von Schilling, Northampton Community College; and Thomas L. Warren, Oklahoma State University.

My thanks to my editors at D. C. Heath for their assistance and friendship—Paul A. Smith, Linda Bieze, and Renée Mary. For their professional advice, I also thank Walter Cunningham, Mary Fraser, Jacquelyn Marchant, and Keith Sullivan at D. C. Heath. I am indebted, as well, to Anne Stascavage for her organizational, keyboarding, and proofreading skills.

Finally, I thank Sharron L. King, R. N. for her love and inspiration.

P. C. K.

Contents

Part I: Backgrounds   1

Chapter I: Getting Started: Writing and Your Career   3

Four Keys to Effective Writing   4
  Identifying Your Audience   4
  Establishing Your Purpose   10
  Formulating Your Message   11
  Selecting Your Style and Tone   12
Characteristics of Job-Related Writing   14
  Providing Practical Information   14
  Giving Facts, Not Impressions   14
  Providing Visuals to Clarify and Condense Information   15
  Giving Accurate Measurements   17
  Stating Responsibilities Precisely   18
  Persuading and Offering Recommendations   18
Collaborative Writing in the Workplace   20
  Benefits of Collaborative Writing   21
How This Book Will Work for You   22
Exercises   22

Chapter 2: The Writing Process at Work   27

What Writing Is and Isn't   27
Five Elements of the Writing Process   28
  Researching   28
  Prewriting   29
  Drafting   32
  Revising   37
  Editing   38
The Group Writing Process   39
  Organization of Writing Groups   39
  Establishing Group Responsibilities   41
  Problems to Avoid in Group Writing   42
Computers and the Writing Process   43
  How Computers Improve Collaborative Writing   46
Five Basic Points on Using a Word Processor   49
Revision Checklist   49
Exercises   50

Chapter 3: Writing: Paragraphs 55

The Importance of Paragraphs **55**
Paragraphs in the Writing Process **56**
   Case Study: Revising One Writer's Paragraphs **57**
   Case Study: Revising Collaboratively Written Paragraphs **60**
Four Types of Paragraphs **64**
   Supporting Paragraphs **64**
   Introductory Paragraphs **67**
   Transitional Paragraphs **68**
   Concluding Paragraphs **68**
Generating Topic Sentences **69**
Three Characteristics of an Effective Paragraph **71**
   Unity **71**
   Coherence **73**
   Completeness **76**
The Appearance of Paragraphs **78**
Patterns of Paragraph Organization **80**
   Examples Pattern **81**
   Description Pattern **81**
   Time Pattern **81**
   Space Pattern **82**
   Comparison/Contrast Pattern **82**
   Definition Pattern **83**
   Classification Pattern **83**
   Cause-to-Effect Pattern **84**
   Effect-to-Cause Pattern **85**
   Combination of Patterns **85**
The Paragraph: An Overview **86**
Revision Checklist **86**
Exercises **87**

Chapter 4: Writing: Sentences 94

Sentences and the Writing Process **94**
Clear Sentences and Your Career **95**
   Readers' Chief Complaints About Bad Sentences **95**
What This Chapter Can Do for You **96**
Constructing and Punctuating Sentences **96**
   The Difference Between Phrases and Clauses **96**
   Sentence Fragments **97**
   The Comma Splice **98**
   Four Ways to Correct Comma Splices **99**
   How Not *to Correct Comma Splices* **100**
Using the Appropriate Voice: Active or Passive **100**
   When to Use the Active Voice **100**

Advantages of Using the Active Voice   **101**

When to Use the Passive Voice   **102**

Using Parallelism   **103**

Writing Sentences That Say What You Mean   **104**

Logical Sentences   **105**

Sentences Using Contextually Appropriate Words   **105**

Sentences with Well-Placed Modifiers   **106**

Correct Use of Pronoun References in Sentences   **107**

Seven Guidelines for Writing Readable Sentences   **108**

1. *Write Sentences That Tell Who Does What to Whom or What*   **108**

2. *Arrange Information Logically Within Your Sentences*   **109**

3. *Avoid Needlessly Complex or Lengthy Sentences*   **110**

4. *Combine a Series of Short, Choppy Sentences*   **110**

5. *Use Strong, Active Verbs Rather Than Verb Phrases with Verbs Disguised as Nouns*   **111**

6. *Avoid Piling Up Modifiers in Front of a Noun*   **111**

7. *Avoid Unnecessary* That/Which *Clauses*   **112**

Revision Checklist   **112**

Exercises   **113**

Chapter 5: Writing: Words   117

Spelling Words Correctly   **118**

Matching the Right Word with the Right Meaning   **123**

Selecting Precise Words   **127**

Cutting Out Unnecessary Words   **129**

Eliminating Sexist Language   **134**

Avoiding Jargon and Slang   **135**

Jargon   **135**

Slang   **137**

Revision Checklist   **138**

Exercises   **139**

Part II: Correspondence   145

Chapter 6: Letter Writing: Some Basics   147

The Importance of Letters   **147**

The Process of Writing a Letter   **148**

Typing/Printing and Proofreading Letters   **149**

Letter Formats   **150**

Parts of a Letter   **154**

Date Line   **155**

Inside Address   **155**

Salutation   **157**

Subject Line   **157**

Body of the Letter   **159**

Complimentary Close   **159**

Signature   **159**

Reference Initials   **160**

Enclosure(s) Line   **160**

Copy or Copies Distributed   **160**

Addressing an Envelope   **161**

Outside Address   **161**

Return Address and Special Instructions   **162**

Making a Good Impression on Your Reader   **163**

The Process of Achieving the "You Attitude": Four Guidelines   **164**

Using the Most Effective Language in Your Letters   **169**

Writing for International Readers   **175**

Four Guidelines to Communicate with ESL Readers   **175**

Respecting the Cultural Traditions of Your ESL Readers   **177**

Revision Checklist   **180**

Exercises   **181**

Chapter 7: Types of Business Correspondence   187

Correspondence in the Electronic Office   **188**

Adapting Your Style for E-Mail and Fax Messages   **188**

Memos   **190**

Functions of Memos   **190**

Memo Format   **190**

Memo Protocol and Company Politics   **195**

Memo Style and Tone   **195**

Strategies for Organizing a Memo   **196**

Order Letters   **197**

Inquiry Letters   **199**

Special Request Letters   **199**

Sales Letters   **201**

Getting the Reader's Attention   **206**

Calling Attention to the Product's Appeal   **208**

Showing the Customer the Product's Application   **209**

Ending with a Specific Request for Action   **211**

Customer Relations Letters   **211**

Planning Your Customer Relations Letters   **212**

Being Direct or Indirect   **212**

Types of Customer Relations Letters   **215**

Thank-You Letters   **215**

Congratulation Letters   **216**

Follow-up Letters   **219**

Complaint Letters   **223**
Adjustment Letters   **226**
Refusal of Credit Letters   **233**
Collection Letters   **237**
Revision Checklist   **242**
Exercises   **243**

Chapter 8: How to Get a Job: Résumés, Letters, Applications, Interviews, and Evaluations   250

Analyzing Your Strengths and Restricting Your Job
Search   **251**
Preparing a Dossier   **252**
Looking in the Right Places for a Job   **256**
Preparing a Résumé   **258**
The Process of Writing Your Résumé   **258**
How Much Should You Include on a Résumé?   **261**
What Should You Exclude from a Résumé?   **263**
Parts of a Résumé   **265**
Organizing Your Résumé by Function or Skill Areas   **271**
The Appearance of Your Résumé   **274**
Writing a Letter of Application   **281**
How the Letter and Résumé Differ   **281**
Résumé Facts You Exclude from a Letter of Application   **281**
Finding Information About Your Prospective Employer   **281**
Drafting the Letter of Application   **283**
Filling Out a Job Application   **290**
Going to an Interview   **292**
Preparing for an Interview   **292**
Questions to Expect at an Interview   **295**
Interview Do's and Don't's   **297**
The Follow-up Letter   **297**
Accepting or Declining a Job   **299**
Employment Evaluations   **301**
Revision Checklist   **302**
Exercises   **303**

Part III: Gathering and Summarizing Information   309

Chapter 9: Finding and Using Library Materials   311

The Process of Doing Research   **312**
The Library and Its Sections   **313**
Books   **313**
The Library Catalog   **313**
The Stacks   **319**

Periodical Holdings and Indexes   321
The Readers' Guide to Periodical Literature   321
Specialized Indexes   324
Using the Computer in Your Library Research   326
Compact Disks   327
On-Line Searches   328
Suggestions on Using Computerized Searches   329
Finding a Periodical in Your Library   330
Reference Books   331
Encyclopedias   331
Dictionaries   331
Abstracts   332
Handbooks, Manuals, and Almanacs   333
Government Documents   333
The Popular Press   335
Vertical File Materials   336
Indexes to Newspapers   336
NewsBank   337
Audiovisual Materials   337
Microfilm   338
Microfiche   339
Note-Taking   339
How to Prepare Bibliography Notes   340
How to Prepare Information Notes   341
To Quote or Not to Quote   342
Revision Checklist   345
Appendix: Some Helpful Reference Works   346
Indexes   346
Encyclopedias   347
Dictionaries   349
Abstracts   350
Exercises   352

Chapter 10: Documenting Sources   356

The Whys and Hows of Documentation   356
Why Is Documentation Important?   357
What Must Be Documented   357
Documentation in the Writing Process   357
Parenthetical and Footnote Documentaton   358
Preparing the Works Cited Page   360
How to Alphabetize the Works in Your Reference List   365
Documenting Within the Text   366
Documenting in Scientific and Technical Writing   370
The Author-Date Method   371
The Ordered References Method   372

Sample Research Paper Using MLA
In-Text Documentation   372
Revision Checklist   387
Exercises   387

Chapter 11: Summarizing Material   390

The Importance of Summaries   390
Contents of a Summary   393
   What to Include in a Summary   393
   What to Omit in a Summary   393
The Process of Preparing a Summary   394
Evaluative Summaries   405
   Evaluating the Content   405
   Evaluating the Style   406
   Minutes   408
   What to Include in Minutes   409
Abstracts   413
   The Differences Between a Summary and an Abstract   413
   Writing the Informative Abstract   413
   Writing the Descriptive Abstract   414
   Where Abstracts Are Found   414
The Usefulness of Summaries   415
Revision Checklist   416
Exercises   417

Chapter 12: Preparing a Questionnaire and Reporting the Results   426

The Usefulness of Questionnaries   426
   *Mail Questionnaires Versus Personal
   Interview Questionnaires*   427
   A Questionnaire's Two Audiences   428
Choosing a Restricted Topic   429
Writing the Questions   430
   Relevant Questions   430
   Two Basic Types of Questions   431
   Reliable and Valid Questions   435
Two Sample Questionnaires   441
Writing Effective Instructions   443
Presenting an Attractive Questionnaire   444
Selecting Respondents   446
   Systematic Random Sampling   446
   Stratified Random Sampling   447
   Quota Sampling   447

Tabulating Responses   450
   Tallying by Hand   450
   Tallying by Computer   451
Writing Effective Questionnaire Reports   454
   Rules for Writing Numbers   454
   Explaining What the Numbers Mean   459
   Using Direct Quotations   460
   Writing a Recommendation   460
Revision Checklist   467
Exercises   468

Chapter 13: Designing Visuals   473

The Usefulness of Visuals   473
Choosing Effective Visuals   475
The Graphic Artist's Desk   478
Writing About Visuals   479
Tables   482
Figures   485
   Graphs   485
   Circle Charts   489
   Bar Charts   490
   Pictograms   494
   Organizational Charts   496
   Flow Charts   498
   Maps   500
   Photographs   502
   Drawings   504
Computer Graphics   508
   Two Types of Graphics Software Packages   510
   The Capabilities of Computer Graphics   512
Revision Checklist   514
Glossary   515
Exercises   516

Part IV: Instructions, Proposals, and Reports   521

Chapter 14: Writing Clear Instructions   523

The Importance of Instructions   523
The Variety of Instructions: A Brief Overview   524
Assessing and Meeting Audience Needs   525
Selecting the Right Words   528
Using Visuals Effectively   530
   Guidelines for Using Visuals with Your Instructions   532
The Four Parts of Instructions   534

The Introduction **534**
List of Equipment and Materials **540**
The Steps in Instructions **542**
The Conclusion **546**
Instructions: Some Final Advice **548**
Revision Checklist **552**
Exercises **552**

Chapter 15: Proposals 555

Writing Successful Proposals **555**
Proposals Are Persuasive Plans **556**
Proposals Frequently Are Collaborative Efforts **556**
Types of Proposals **558**
Solicited and Unsolicited Proposals **558**
Internal and External Proposals **559**
Guidelines for Writing a Successful Proposal **560**
Internal Proposals **561**
Your Audience and Office Politics **565**
The Organization of an Internal Proposal **566**
Sales Proposals **568**
The Audience and Its Needs **568**
Organizing a Sales Proposal **571**
Proposals for Research Papers and Reports **576**
Writing for Your Teacher **576**
Organization of a Proposal for a Research Paper **576**
Preparing Proposals: A Final Reminder **581**
Revision Checklist **581**
Exercises **582**

Chapter 16: Short Reports 588

Why Short Reports Are Important **588**
Types of Short Reports **589**
How to Write Short Reports **589**
Periodic Reports **592**
Sales Reports **594**
Progress Reports **598**
How to Begin a Progress Report **600**
How to Continue a Progress Report **600**
How to End a Progress Report **600**
Trip Reports **603**
Common Types of Trip Reports **604**
How to Gather Information for a Trip Report **606**
Test Reports **610**
Incident Reports **615**
Protecting Yourself Legally **615**

Parts of an Incident Report   **616**
Main Points to Remember About Short Reports   **620**
Revision Checklist   **620**
Exercises   **621**

Chapter 17: Long Reports   624

How a Long Report Differs from a Short Report   **624**
The Process of Writing a Long Report   **627**
Parts of a Long Report   **629**
Front Matter   **629**
Text of the Report   **632**
Back Matter   **636**
The Model Long Report in This Chapter   **637**
A Final Word About Long Reports   **637**
Revision Checklist   **657**
Exercises   **658**

Chapter 18: Oral Reports   661

Informal Briefings   **661**
Formal Speeches   **663**
Analyzing Your Audience   **663**
Speaking for the Occasion   **664**
Ways of Presenting a Speech   **664**
Preparing the Parts of a Speech   **665**
The Speech Outline   **669**
Using Visuals   **669**
Rehearsing a Speech   **676**
Delivering a Speech   **676**
Speech Evaluation Form   **678**
Revision Checklist   **681**
Exercises   **682**

Backgrounds

Getting Started: Writing and Your Career

What skills have you learned in school or on the job this year? Perhaps you have learned techniques of health care in order to become a nurse, respiratory therapist, or dental hygienist. Maybe you have received training in law enforcement to prepare yourself for work with a crime-detection unit or a traffic-control department. Possibly you have studied or worked in industrial technology, agriculture, computer science, hotel and restaurant management, or forestry. Or maybe you have improved skills needed to be an executive secretary, salesperson, office manager, computer programmer, or accountant. Whatever your area of accomplishment, the practical know-how you have acquired is essential for your career.

You need an additional skill, however, to ensure a successful career: you must be able to write clearly about the facts, procedures, and problems of your job. Writing is a part of every job. In fact, your first contact with a potential employer is through your letter of application, which determines a company's first impression of you. And the higher you advance in an organization, the more writing you will be doing. Promotions are often based on a person's writing skills.

The Associated Press reported in late 1992 that "most American businesses say workers need to improve their writing . . . skills." The same report cited a survey of 402 companies that identified writing as "the most valued skill of employees." Still, the employers polled in this survey indicated that 80 percent of their employees need to improve their writing skills. Clearly, writing is an essential skill important to everyone in business—employers and employers alike.

Offices and other workplaces contain numerous reminders of the importance of writing, such as "in" and "out" boxes, file cabinets, typewriters, word processors, printers, and fax machines. Why? Writing keeps business moving. It allows individuals working for a company to communicate with one another and with the customers and clients they must serve if the company is to stay in business. These written communications take the form of memos, letters, summaries, instructions, questionnaires, proposals, and reports. This book will show you, step by step, how to write these and other job-related communications easily and well.

Chapter 1 presents some basic information about writing and offers some questions you can ask yourself to make the writing process easier and more effective. This chapter also describes the basic functions of on-the-job writing and will introduce you to one of the most important requirements in the business world—collaborative writing.

Four Keys to Effective Writing

Effective writing on the job is carefully planned, thoroughly researched, and clearly presented. Whether you send a routine memo to a coworker or a special report to the president of the company, your writing will be more effective if you ask yourself four questions.

1. *Who* will read what I write? (Identify your *audience.*)
2. *Why* should they read what I write? (Establish your *purpose.*)
3. *What* do I have to say to them? (Formulate your *message.*)
4. *How* can I best communicate? (Select your *style* and *tone.*)

The questions *who? why? what?* and *how?* do not function independently; they are all related. You write (1) for a specific audience (2) with a clearly defined purpose in mind (3) about a topic your readers need to understand (4) in language appropriate for the occasion. Once you answer the first question, you are off to a good start toward answering the other three. Now let us examine each of the four questions in detail.

Identifying Your Audience

Knowing *who* makes up your audience is one of your most important responsibilities as a writer. In fact, it is important to analyze your audience throughout the composing process. Look for a minute at the American Heart Association posters reproduced in Figures 1.1, 1.2, and 1.3. The main purpose of all three posters is the same: to discourage individuals from smoking. The essential message in each poster—smoking is dangerous to your health—is also the same. But note how the different details—words, photographs, situations—have been selected to appeal to three different audiences.

The poster in Figure 1.1 emphasizes smoking problems that are especially troublesome to a teenager: red eyes, bad breath, discolored teeth, and unattractive hair. The smiling teen pictured without a cigarette appears to have avoided these problems. The message at the top of the poster plays on two meanings of the word *heart:* (1) smoking can cause heart disease and (2) smoking can be a deterrent to romance. Teenagers are particularly sensitive to the second meaning.

The poster in Figure 1.2 (p. 6) is aimed at an audience of pregnant women and appropriately shows a woman with a lit cigarette. The words at the top and bot-

FIGURE 1.1   No-smoking poster aimed at teenagers.

© Reprinted with permission of the American Heart Association.

tom of the poster appeal to a mother's sense of responsibility as the reason to stop smoking, a reason to which pregnant women would be most likely to respond.

Figure 1.3 (p. 7) is directed toward fathers and appropriately shows a small child seated on his father's lap. The situation depicted appeals to a father's wish for happiness for his child. The words in the poster warn that a father who smokes may die prematurely and make his child's life unhappy.

The copywriters for the American Heart Association have chosen appropriate details—words, pictures, and so on—to convince each audience not to smoke. With their careful choices, they successfully answered the question "How can we best communicate with each audience?" As an indication of their skill, note that details relevant for one audience (teenagers, for example) could not be used as effectively for another audience (fathers).

These three posters illustrate some fundamental points you need to keep in mind when writing for an audience.

- Members of each audience differ in backgrounds, experiences, needs, and opinions.
- How you picture your audience will determine what you say to them.

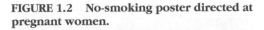

FIGURE 1.2   No-smoking poster directed at pregnant women.

© Reprinted with permission of the American Heart Association.

- Viewing something from the audience's perspective will help you to select the most relevant details for that audience.

Some Questions to Ask About Your Audience

You can form a fairly accurate picture of your audience by asking yourself some questions *before* you write. For each audience for whom you write, consider the following questions.

1. Who is my audience? What is the reader's job title? There's a big difference between writing to a vice-president for industrial relations and writing to a coworker. What specific duties does my audience have to perform? What kind of education, job experience, and interests does my audience have?

2. How well does my audience understand English? Are all my readers native speakers of English, or will my readers have lesser competence in understanding the English language? Because many businesses are multinational and have customers outside the United States, you need to be sensitive to the needs of an ESL (English as a second language) audience when you write to them. For these readers you need to write international English that communicates clearly and that

FIGURE 1.3   No-smoking poster appealing to fathers.

© Reprinted with permission of the American Heart Association.

does not offend them. See pages 175–180 for guidelines about using effective international English.

3. How many people will make up my audience? Is it just one individual (the nurse on the next shift, the desk sergeant) or many (all the users of a product manufactured by my company)? If I write a letter to a customer, will my boss also want to see and approve it? As a general rule, the more diverse your audience is, the less technical your discussion must be.

4. How much does my audience already know about what I am writing about? Are you writing to people who are familiar with all the technical procedures you know? Or are you addressing an employer or customer who, however intelligent, is not an expert in your field and cannot be expected to know technical details and language? Will your reader know as much about a problem or an issue as you do? Most often you will be writing to people who do not know as much about your job as you do. Such readers need more background information, more definitions of terms, and more explanatory visuals than a technically trained audience would. You may have to provide easy-to-understand comparisons and nontechnical summaries for these readers.

5. What is my audience's reason for reading my work? Is it a part of my readers' routine duties, such as a progress report? Are they looking for answers to special problems? Do they want to find a list of benefits from me that another writer or company cannot offer? Will they want to have complete details, or do they prefer a summary of the main points? What is it that the boss wants from me—information alone, some analysis and conclusions drawn from that information, or recommendations?

6. What is my audience's attitude toward me and my work? Am I writing to readers who are friendly and eager to receive my work—for example, my memo to my boss saying that sales are up? Will my reader be skeptical—for example, a customer whose business I want to attract by selling him or her a new piece of equipment or service? Is my reader antagonistic—for example, a disappointed customer whose request I must refuse? What are the reasons the reader is skeptical or antagonistic? Such readers will want more detailed or more logical explanations than sympathetic readers do. It is important to address directly the reasons for their disbelief or complaints.

7. What do I want my audience to do after reading my work? Should they store it for future reference, review it and send it to another office or individual, or act on it at once? Do I want the reader to use my work to purchase something from me or my company, approve my plan for a change within our company, agree with a decision I have made, or gather additional information for me? Have I made clear what I expect next from my reader?

As your answers to these questions will show, you may have to communicate with many different audiences on your job. If you work for a large organization that has numerous departments, you may have to write to such diverse readers as accountants, office managers, personnel directors, engineers, public relations specialists, marketing specialists, computer programmers, and individuals who install, operate, and maintain equipment. In addition, you will need to communicate effectively with customers about your company's products and services. Each group of readers will have different expectations and requirements; you need to understand these differences if you want to supply relevant information.

The advertisement in Figure 1.4 concisely illustrates how the writer for a manufacturer of heavy-duty equipment identified the priorities of five different audiences and selected appropriate information to communicate with them. For the owner or principal executive, the writer appropriately stresses financial benefits: the machine is a "money maker" and is compatible with other equipment, so additional equipment purchases are unnecessary. A production engineer is more interested in other information. For this reader, the writer emphasizes "state-of-the-art" transmissions, productivity, and upkeep. To appeal to operators, the writer focuses on how easy it is to run the machine—the pressurized cab keeps out environmental problems that interfere with the job. A maintenance worker is concerned about such things as "lube points" and "test ports," not costs or operational comforts. The writer has selected appropriate information about making this worker's job easier and quicker. For the production supervisor, the writer has

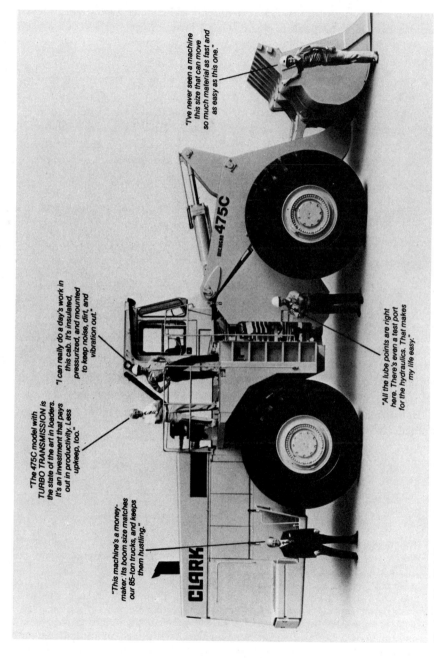

FIGURE 1.4   An advertisement aimed at the needs of five different audiences.

Courtesy of the Clark Company. Reprinted with permission.

emphasized the speed and efficiency the machine offers. The lesson of this ad is clear: give each reader the details that he or she needs to accomplish a given job.

In some cases you are not able to identify all the members of your potential audience. Just assume that you have a general audience and keep your message as simple as possible—nontechnical and straightforward.

Establishing Your Purpose

By knowing *why* you are writing, you will communicate better and find writing itself to be an easier process. The reader's needs and your goal in communicating will help you to formulate your purpose. It will help you to determine exactly what you can and must say. With your purpose clearly identified, you are on the right track. As you start to write, state clearly your goal in communicating. Don't worry about the way it sounds. It is more important at this stage to work on ideas.

> I want new employees to know how to log on to the computer.

Think over what you have written. Rewrite your purpose statement until it states precisely why you are writing and what you want your readers to do or to know.

> I want to teach new employees the security code for logging on to the company computer.

Since your purpose controls the amount and order of information you include, state it clearly at the beginning of every letter, memo, or report. Such an overview will help the reader to follow and act on your communication.

> This memo will acquaint new employees with the security measures they must take when logging on to the company computer.

> The following report will give you a detailed account of my progress to date on completing my research study this semester.

In the opening purpose statement below, note how the author clearly informs the reader what the report will and will not cover.

> As you requested at last month's organizational meeting, I have conducted a study of our policies for renting our safe deposit boxes. This report describes, but does not evaluate, our current procedures.

The following preface to a pamphlet on architectural casework details contains a model statement of purpose suited to a particular audience.

> This publication has been prepared by the Architectural Woodwork Institute to provide a source book of conventional details and uniform detail terminology. For this purpose a series of casework detail drawings, . . . representative of the best industry-wide practice, has been prepared and is presented here. By supplying both architect and woodwork manufacturer with a common authoritative reference, this work will enable architects and woodworkers to communicate in a common technical language. . . . It is hoped that besides serving as a basic reference for architects and architectural drafters, it will be an effective training tool for the beginning drafter-architect-in-training. It should also be a valuable aid to the project manager in coordinating the work of many drafters on large projects.[1]

---

[1] Reprinted by permission of Architectural Woodwork Institute.

After reading the preface, readers will have a clear sense of why they should use the sourcebook and what to do with the material they find in it.

Formulating Your Message

Your message is the sum of *what* facts, responses, and recommendations you put into writing. A message includes the *scope* and *details* of your communication. The details are those key points you think readers need to know to perform their jobs. Scope refers to how much information you give readers about those key details. Some messages will consist of one or two sentences: "Do not touch; wet paint." "Order #756 was sent this afternoon by Federal Express. It should arrive at your office by March 21." At the other extreme, messages may extend over twenty or thirty pages. Messages may carry good news or bad news. They may deal with routine matters, or they may handle changes in policy, special situations, or problems.

Keep in mind that you will adapt your message to fit your audience. For technical audiences such as engineers or technicians, you may have to supply a complete report with every detail noted or contained in an appendix. For other readers—busy executives, for example—you would be wrong to include such technical details. A short discussion or summary of the financial or managerial significance of these details is what this group of readers would want to have.

Consider the message of the following excerpt from a section of "Tips on Communication" included in a metropolitan telephone book. The message provides factual information about a change in mailing policies, informing the general public about acceptable and unacceptable sizes of first- and third-class mail.

Size Standards for Domestic Mail

Nonstandard Mail

The following material is considered nonstandard mail. First-class mail weighing one ounce or less and single piece third-class mail weighing two ounces or less which

1. exceeds any of the following:
   (a) Height of $6\frac{1}{8}$ inches.
   (b) Length of $11\frac{1}{2}$ inches.
   (c) Thickness of $\frac{1}{4}$ inch.
2. has a height-to-length ratio which does not fall between 1 : 13 and 1 : 25 inclusive.

A surcharge will be assessed on each piece of nonstandard mail in addition to the applicable postage and fees.

Minimum Sizes

All mail must be at least .007 of an inch thick and mail which is $\frac{1}{4}$ inch or less in thickness must be

1. at least $3\frac{1}{2}$ inches in height and at least 5 inches long.
2. rectangular.

The preceding message is appropriate for a general audience, readers who are given neither less nor more information than is required. However, employees of the U.S. Postal Service or individuals working in the mail rooms of large companies or in mail-order houses need more detailed instructions. Because of their specialized work, these individuals would consult the more technical and elaborate *Postal Service Manual.*

Selecting Your Style and Tone

Style is *how* something is written rather than what is written. Style helps to determine how well you communicate with an audience, how well it understands and receives your message. It involves the choices you make about the construction of your paragraphs, the length and patterns of your sentences, and the choice of your words. (Chapters 3, 4, and 5 discuss each of these elements of style in detail.) For now, keep in mind that you will have to adapt your style to take into account different messages, different purposes, and different audiences. Your words, for example, will certainly vary with your audience. If all your readers are specialists in your field, you may safely use the technical language and symbols of your profession. Your audience will be familiar with such terminology and will expect you to use it. Nonspecialists, however, will be confused and annoyed if you write to them in the same way. The average consumer, for example, will not know what a *potentiometer* is; but by writing "volume control on a radio" you will be using words that the general public can understand.

Tone in writing, like tone of voice, expresses your attitude toward a topic and toward your audience. In general, your tone can range from formal and impersonal (a scientific report) to informal and personal (a letter to a friend or a how-to article for a consumer). Tone, like style, is indicated in part by the words you choose. For example, saying that someone is "interested in details" conveys a more positive tone than saying the individual is a "nitpicker." The word *economical* is more positive than *stingy* or *cheap.* The tone of your writing is especially important in occupational writing, for it reflects the image you project to your readers and thus determines how they will respond to you, your work, and your company. Depending on your tone, you can appear sincere and intelligent or angry and uninformed. Of course, in all of your written work, you need to sound professional and knowledgeable about the topic and genuinely interested in your readers' opinions and problems. The wrong tone in a letter or a proposal might cost you a customer.

The following two descriptions of *heparin,* a drug used to prevent blood clots, illustrate two different styles and tones. The first description appears in a reference work for physicians and is written in a highly technical style with an impersonal tone.

HEPARIN SODIUM INJECTION, USP
STERILE SOLUTION
Description: Heparin Sodium Injection, USP is a sterile solution of heparin sodium derived from bovine lung tissue, standardized for anticoagulant activity.

Each ml of the 1,000 and 5,000 USP unites per ml preparations contains: Heparin sodium 1,000 or 5,000 UPS unites; 9 mg sodium chloride; 9.45 mg benzyl alcohol added as preservative. Each ml of the 10,000 USP units per ml preparations contains: heparin sodium 10,000 units; 9.45 mg benzyl alcohol added as preservative.

When necessary, the pH of Heparin Sodium Injection, USP was adjusted with hydrochloric acid and/or sodium hydroxide. The pH range is 5.0–7.5.

Clinical pharmacology: Heparin inhibits reactions that lead to the clotting of blood and the formation of fibrin clots both *in vitro* and *in vivo.* Heparin acts at multiple sites in the normal coagulation system. Small amounts of heparin in combination with antithrombin III (heparin cofactor) can inhibit thrombosis by inactivating activated Factor X and inhibiting the conversion of prothrombin to thrombin.

Dosage and administration: Heparin sodium is not effective by oral administration and should be given by intermittent intravenous injection, intravenous infusion, or deep subcutaneous (intrafrat, i.e., above the iliac crest or abdominal fat layer) injection. **The intramuscular rout of administration should be avoided because of the frequent occurrence of hematoma at the injection site.**[2]

The writer has made the appropriate stylistic choices for the audience, the purpose, and the message. Physicians reading the description will understand and need the technical vocabulary the writer uses; these physicians will also require the sophisticated and lengthy explanations in order to prescribe heparin correctly. The author's authoritative, impersonal tone is coldly clinical, which, of course, is also appropriate because the purpose is to convey the accurate, complete scientific facts about this drug, not the writer's or reader's opinions or beliefs. The author sounds both knowledgeable and appropriately objective.

The following description of heparin, on the other hand, is written in a nontechnical style and with an informal, caring tone. This description is similar to those found on information cards given to patients about the drugs they are receiving in a hospital.

Your doctor has prescribed for you a drug called *heparin.* This drug will prevent any new blood clots from forming in your body. Since heparin cannot be absorbed from your stomach or intestines, you will not receive it in a capsule or tablet. Instead, it will be given into a vein or the fatty tissue of your abdomen. After several days, when the danger of clotting is past, your dosage of heparin will be gradually reduced. Then another medication you can take by mouth will be started.

The writer of this description also made the appropriate choices for the purpose and for the readers. Familiar words rather than technical ones are suitable for nonspecialists such as patients. Note also that this audience does not need elaborate descriptions of the origin and composition of the drug. The tone is both personal and straightforward because the purpose is to win the patient's confidence and to explain the essential functions of the drug, a simpler message than the one for physicians.

The trend today in occupational writing is to make letters, reports, and proposals more natural and personal and less impersonal, formal, or stuffy. But adopting a personal tone does not mean that you should address the reader in a chummy or disrespectful way. Quite the contrary, a business letter or report needs to be personal and professional at the same time.

---

[2] Copyright © 1991 *Physicians' Desk Reference,* published by Medical Economics Company, Inc., at Oradell, New Jersey 07649.

Characteristics of Job-Related Writing

Job-related writing characteristically serves six basic functions: (1) to provide practical information, (2) to give facts rather than impressions, (3) to provide visuals to clarify and condense information, (4) to give accurate measurements, (5) to state responsibilities precisely, and (6) to persuade and offer recommendations. These six functions tell you what kind of writing you will produce after you successfully answer the *who? why? what?* and *how?* just discussed.

Providing Practical Information

On-the-job writing requires a practical here's-what-you-need-to-do-or-to-know approach. One such practical approach is *action oriented.* In this kind of writing, you instruct the reader to do something—assemble a ceiling fan, test for bacteria, perform an audit, or take an inventory. Another practical approach of job-related writing is to have someone understand something—why a procedure was changed, what caused a problem or solved it, how much progress occurred on a job site, or why a new piece of equipment should be purchased. Examples of such practical writing are a letter sent from a manufacturer to customers to explain a product recall or a memo sent to employees telling them about changes in their group health insurance policy.

The following description of Energy Efficiency Ratio combines both the action-oriented and knowledge-oriented approaches of practical writing.

> Whether you are buying window air-conditioning units or a central air-conditioning system, consider the performance factors and efficiency of the various units on the market. Before you buy, determine the Energy Efficiency Ratio (EER) of the units under consideration. The EER is found by dividing the BTUs (units of heat) that the unit removes from the area to be cooled by the watts (amount of electricity) the unit consumes. The result is usually a number between 5 and 12. The higher the number, the more efficiently the unit will use electricity. You'll note that EER will vary considerably from unit to unit of a given manufacturer, and from brand to brand. As efficiency is increased, you may find the purchase price is higher; however, operating costs will be lower. Remember, a good rule to follow is to choose the equipment with the highest EER. That way you'll get efficient equipment and enjoy operating economy.[3]

Giving Facts, Not Impressions

Occupational writing is concerned largely with those things that can be seen, heard, felt, tasted, or smelled. The writer uses *concrete language* and specific details (discussed on pages 169–174). The emphasis is on facts rather than on the writer's feelings or guesses. The following discussion by a group of scientists about the sources of oil spills and their impact on the environment is an example of writing with objectivity. It describes events and causes without anger or tears. Imagine how much emotion could have been packed into this paragraph by the residents of the coastal states who have watched such spills come ashore.

---

[3] Reprinted by permission of New Orleans Public Service, Inc.

The most critical impact results from the escapement of oil into the ecosystem, both crude oil and refined fuel oils, the latter coming from sources such as marine traffic. Major oil spills occur as a result of accidents such as blowout, pipeline breakage, etc. Technological advances coupled with stringent regulations have helped to reduce the chances of such major spills; however, there is a chronic low-level discharge of oil associated with normal drilling and production operations. Waste oils discharged through the river systems and practices associated with tanker transports dump more significant quantities of oils into the ocean, compared to what is introduced by the off-shore oil industry. All of this contributes to the chronic low-level discharge of oil into world oceans. The long-range cumulative effect of these discharges is possibly the most significant threat to the ecosystem.[4]

Providing Visuals to Clarify and Condense Information

Visuals are indispensable partners of words in conveying information to your readers. On-the-job writing makes frequent use of visuals such as tables, charts, photographs, diagrams, and drawings to clarify and condense information. Thanks to various computer software packages, visuals can be created easily and inserted into your writing. The use of visuals—including computer visuals—is discussed in detail in Chapter 13. Visuals play an important role in the workplace. As a poster or as an illustration in an employee handbook, Figure 1.5 helpfully reminds readers about correct lifting procedures and thereby prevents injuries.

FIGURE 1.5   Use of a visual to convey information.

© National Safety Council, Chicago.

---

[4] *The Offshore Ecology Investigation,* Galveston: Gulf Universities Research Consortium, 1975: 4.

TABLE 1.1   Commercial TV Stations in Operation, 1965–1990

Year	Total	VHF	UHF
1965	586	487	99
1966	598	491	107
1967	620	497	123
1968	648	504	144
1969	675	506	169
1970	690	508	182
1971	696	511	185
1972	699	510	189
1973	700	511	189
1974	705	513	192
1975	711	513	198
1976	710	513	197
1977	728	517	211
1978	727	516	211
1979	732	516	216
1980	746	517	229
1981	752	519	233
1982	772	524	248
1983	802	526	276
1984	870	536	334
1985	904	539	365
1986	922	541	381
1987	982	547	435
1988	1,017	541	476
1989	1,440	544	548
1990	1,469	563	552

Supplied by the Federal Communications Commission.

Visuals are extremely useful in making detailed relationships clear to readers. A great deal of information about the growth and diversity of commercial TV stations is condensed into Table 1.1. Consider how many words a writer would need in order to supply the data contained in the table. Note, too, how easily the numbers can be read when they are arranged in columns. It would be far more difficult to decipher them if they were printed like this: Commercial TV stations in operation: 1965, Total 586, VHF 487, UHF 99; 1966, Total 598, VHF 491, UHF 107, and so forth.

In addition to the visuals already mentioned, the following graphic devices (created quickly with the help of a computer) within your letters and reports will make your writing easier to read and follow.

- Headings, such as **Four Keys to Effective Writing** or **Characteristics of Job-Related Writing**
- Subheadings to divide major sections into parts, such as "Providing Practical Information" or "Giving Facts, Not Impressions"

- Numbers within a paragraph, or even a line, such as (1) this, (2) this, and (3) also this
- Different types of s p a c i n g
- CAPITALIZATION
- *Italics* (easily made by a word processing command or indicated in typed copy by <u>underscoring</u>)
- **Boldface** (darker type for emphasis)
- *Scripting* (simulating handwriting)
- Asterisks * to * separate * items * or to * note key items
- Lists with "bullets" (raised dots or other symbols like the squares before each entry in this list)

Keep in mind that such visual devices must be used carefully and with moderation. They should never be used just for decoration or to dress up a letter or report. Used properly, they can help you to organize, arrange, and emphasize your material. They make your work easier to read and recall. For example, headings in a memo, letter, or report make your organizational plan visible to readers and help them preview your ideas. Use bullets or numbers when you have many related points; by setting your points in a list, you make it easier for readers to follow and compare them.

Giving Accurate Measurements

Much of your work will depend on measurements—acres, bytes, calories, centimeters, degrees, dollars and cents, grams, percentages, pounds, square feet, units. Readers will look carefully at these measurements. Numbers are clear and convincing. An architect depends on specifications to accomplish a job; a nurse must record precise dosages of medications; a sales representative keeps track of the number of customers visited; and an electronics technologist has to monitor antenna patterns and systems. The following discussion of mixing colored cement for a basement floor would be useless to readers if it did not supply accurate quantities.

> The inclusion of permanent color in a basement floor is a good selling point. One way of doing this is by incorporating commercially pure mineral pigments in a topping mixture placed to a 1-inch depth over a normal base slab. The topping mix should range in volume between 1 part portland cement, 1 1/4 parts sand, and 1 1/4 parts gravel or crushed stone and 1 part portland cement, 2 parts sand and 2 parts gravel or crushed stone. Maximum size gravel or crushed stone should be 3/8 inch. Mixing of cement and pigment is done before aggregate and water are added and must be very thorough to secure uniform dispersion and the full color value of the pigment. The proportion varies from 5 to 10 percent of pigment by weight of cement, depending on the shade desired. If carbon black is used as a pigment to obtain grays or black, a proportion of from 1/2 to 1 percent will be adequate. Manufacturers' instructions should be followed closely and care in cleanliness, placing, and finishing must be regarded as essential. Colored topping mixes are available from some suppliers of ready mixed concrete.[5]

---

[5] Reprinted by permission from *Concrete Construction Magazine,* World of Concrete Center, 426 South Westgate, Addison, Illinois 60101.

Stating Responsibilities Precisely

Job-related writing, since it is directed to a specific audience, must make absolutely clear what it expects of, or can do for, that audience. Misunderstandings waste time and cost money. Directions on order forms, for example, should indicate how and where information is to be listed and how it is to be routed and acted on. The following directions are taken from different job-related communications, showing readers how to perform different tasks.

- Include agency code numbers in the upper-right corner.

- Items 1 through 16 of this form should be completed by the injured employee or by someone acting on his or her behalf, whenever an injury is sustained in the performance of duty. The term *injury* includes occupational disease caused by the employment. The form should be given to the employee's official superior within 48 hours following the injury. The official superior is that individual having responsible supervision over the employee.

- The Journal Tape from each cash register is to be removed on a daily basis. Record the register number and date on the exterior of the Journal Tape as it is removed. Place each day's Journal Tapes, along with the corresponding day's Cashier's Balance Sheets and bank deposit records, in a small bag, i.e., 10 lb. bag. Record the date on the face of this bag, and staple it closed.[6]

Other kinds of job-related writing deal with the writer's responsibilities rather than the reader's. For example, "Tomorrow I will have a meeting with the district sales manager to discuss (1) July's sales, (2) the possibility of expanding our Madison home market, and (3) next fall's production schedule. I will send you a report of our discussion by August 5, 1994." In a letter of application for a job, writers should conclude by asking for an interview and clearly inform a prospective employer when they are available for an interview—for example, weekday mornings, only on Monday and Tuesday afternoons, or any time after February 15.

Persuading and Offering Recommendations

Much writing in the business world is directed to employers, customers, and clients to persuade them to buy a product or service or to adopt a certain plan of action. In fact, the very first job-related writing you do will likely be a persuasive letter of application to obtain a job interview with a potential employer. Then, once on the job, you may be required to write persuasive sales letters, reports, proposals, brochures, and even advertisements.

Effective persuasive writing involves using all the skills you will learn about audience analysis, tone, organization, research, and the overall process of drafting and revising your work. In much job-related writing you will have to convince readers that you (and your company) can save them time and money, increase efficiency, reduce risks, and improve their image. At the same time you may have to

---

[6] Reprinted by permission from *A&P Store Management Manual*, NCR 2125.

FIGURE 1.6   An advertisement using arguments based on cost, time, efficiency, safety, and convenience to persuade a potential customer to use a service.

GENERAL MEDICAL WILL STOP THE UNNECESSARY TRANSPORTING OF YOUR INMATES.

- We'll bring our X-ray services to your facility, 7 days a week, 24 hours a day.
  We can reduce your X-ray costs by a minimum of 28%.
  X-ray cost includes radiologists's interpretation and written report.
  Same day service with immediate results telephoned to your facility.
- Save correctional officers' time, thereby saving your facility money.
- Avoid chance of prisoner's escape and possible danger to the public.
- Avoid long waits in overcrowded hospitals.
- Reduce your insurance liabilities.
- Other Services Available: Ultrasound, Two Dimensional Echocardiogram, C.T. Scan, EKG, Blood Lab and Holter Monitor.

General Medical Is Your On-Site Medical Problem Solver

General Medical Services Corp
A subsidiary of

FMI

Federal Medical Industries, Inc. O.T.C.
950 S.W. 12th Avenue, 2nd Floor Suite, Pompano, Florida 33069
(305) 942-1111   FL WATS: 1-800-654-8282

show readers why you are better than your competitors. Writing persuasive letters, proposals, and reports requires that you have a clear sense of your audience's needs, priorities, preferences, and even dislikes. You will have to conduct research, provide logical arguments, and supply concrete examples or appropriate data. Notice how the advertisement in Figure 1.6 offers a persuasively worded list of reasons—based on cost, time, safety, efficiency, and convenience—to convince correctional officials that they should use General Medical's services rather than those of a hospital or clinic.

Much job-centered writing also requires you to be highly persuasive when you make a recommendation to your employer. In many of your memos and reports you will have to evaluate various options and products for your employer. Your reader will expect you to offer clear-cut, logical, convincing reasons for your choice. The reader will want to know why and how you arrived at your recommendation.

Below is the conclusion to one writer's report on why it is better for a company to lease a truck than to purchase one.

After studying the pros and cons of buying or leasing a company truck, I recommend that we lease it for the following reasons.

1. We will not have to expend any of our funds for a down payment.
2. Our monthly payments for leasing the vehicle will be at least $50 less than the payments we would have to make if we purchased the truck.
3. All major and minor maintenance (up to 36,000 miles) is included as part of our monthly leasing payment.

4. Insurance (theft and damage) is also part of our monthly leasing payment.
5. We have the option of trading in our truck every 16 months for a newer model.

Note the persuasive tone and logical presentation of information this writer has used.

Collaborative Writing in the Workplace

You can expect to spend much of your time on the job working as part of a team. That includes your written work, too. You will need to develop skills both as an individual writer working alone and as a member of a collaborative writing team. One survey estimates that in the world of work 90 percent of all business people spend some time writing as a part of a collaborative team.[7] *Collaborative writing* might be defined as a group of individuals—usually three to five—combining their efforts to prepare a single document for which each of them is responsible. Collaborative writing means sharing authorship and sharing responsibility. It means working together for the common good, maybe even the survival, of your department, company, or agency.

There are many types of collaborative writing activities. Perhaps the simplest results when a fellow student or coworker offers some suggestions about your work or an employer critiques a draft of a memo or letter as in Figure 2.6 (see p. 46). Collaboration can be more extensive, of course. Many types of documents are routinely coauthored by a group; long reports in business are prepared by groups or are at least reviewed by key readers who evaluate and suggest changes. Part of a report, for example, might be drafted by one individual and then reviewed and critiqued by the entire group. Or the entire group may try its collective hand at drafting a section of the report. Training manuals or policy handbooks are routinely produced collaboratively with participation by management, attorneys, technicians, and safety experts.

A proposal (see pp. 556–558) is another document often prepared by a group of individuals from varying backgrounds and with different job functions—engineers, accountants, quality-control experts, and marketing specialists—each supplying his or her expertise to solve the common problems faced by the group. Similarly, an environmental impact statement might be coauthored by wildlife experts, law enforcement officials, and community leaders.

When you are a part of a collaborative team, you can expect to play many roles. In the world of work your audience is far more varied than it is in school, where you write for your teacher. Also, your audience may know far less about a topic than you do and expects to be informed by you. On the job you need to consider how a variety of readers, each with different requirements and contributions to make, will respond to your work. As a member of a writing team, you may be called on to be a researcher, a writer, an editor, a critic, or an illustrator. Your

---

[7] Lisa Ede and Andrea Lunsford, *Singular Texts/Plural Authors: Perspectives on Collaborative Writing* (Carbondale, IL: Southern Illinois University Press, 1990), p. 71.

work will be evaluated by many readers, and you will be asked to evaluate someone else's work. You will need to be open to suggestions and receptive to exchanging ideas with others. Chapter 2 (pages 39–42) supplies more information about the various roles individuals play in the collaborative writing process.

Benefits of Collaborative Writing

Collaborative writing offers a company and the individual employee many benefits. Some of these advantages include the following.

1. Since no one individual has all the answers, a collaborative writing team profits from the diverse expertise and talents of its individual members. One member may have strengths in computer programming, another in writing, and a third in computer graphics. Their combined skills would be greater than any one employee may possess. Human resources and employee productivity thus are increased when a company draws on the skills of individuals joined in a group.

2. Collaboration helps the team to develop better problem-solving skills and critical thinking than would be possible with one individual. Four heads are better than one. Thanks to their collective planning and decision making, the group can cover more territory, evaluate more solutions, and survey more opinions than the individual could. Working as a team, they can share a variety of ideas.

3. Feedback from so many diverse individuals is invaluable to the group effort. Members of the group can offer helpful critiques of each other's suggestions and written work. Constructive dialoguing can clarify issues, sort out appropriate from inappropriate solutions, and lead to useful recommendations for a customer or an employer. Even a difference of opinion can be healthy. Disagreements do not always have to be heated; they can be challenging and constructive. Differences of opinion among group members can bring out much useful information. The group can evaluate viewpoints that might not have been factored into their original planning. Disagreements can also help a team to identify weaknesses in their work—gaps, errors, inconsistencies, contradictions. And disagreements, when productive, assist the team to find better, more effective ways to organize, draft, and design their document.

4. Collaboration can be team building. An individual who feels like part of a group working toward a shared goal can acquire a strong sense of group identity and loyalty. By sharing information and offering suggestions, the team member will feel that he or she is helping others while assisting himself or herself at the same time. Moreover, by working together, team members can have a sense that they have a say in company policy and are influencing decisions that affect each of them.

5. Collaboration offers psychological benefits, too. Working as part of a team, the individual can be relieved of some job-related stress. He or she does not have to bear the entire burden alone. Knowing that there are others to discuss ideas with and that others are working on the same project can be reassuring. A division of labor makes deadlines less fearsome.

How This Book Will Work for You

This book is based on the belief that writing substantially influences your career. Effective writing can help you to obtain a job, to perform your duties more successfully, and to be promoted for your efforts. Guidelines and examples found in this book emphasize the progress you can make in your career by acquiring effective writing skills. Specifically, *Successful Writing at Work* will

- explain the writing process and show you how planning, drafting, revising, and editing can help you to produce a variety of essential job-related communications.
- describe the function and format of these job-related communications.
- teach you how to supply an audience with the information it must have.

The book is organized to coincide with your own progress in writing. After Chapter 2 explores the process of writing, Chapters 3, 4, and 5 present other elements of writing you must master if you are to advance in your profession. This book also discusses the basics you should know in order to write a business letter (Chapter 6) and then turns to the strategies to be used with the specific types of correspondence you will write for your employer (Chapter 7). Chapter 8 focuses on how to write a letter of application and résumé. In your job you will be responsible for gathering, documenting, and summarizing information (Chapters 9–12). And most important, you will have to report your findings both in writing (Chapters 13–17) and orally (Chapter 18). In your writing course this term, you can evaluate step by step your progress toward fulfilling professional goals.

Another useful feature of this book is that it frequently represents the view of the audience (prospective employer, customer, supervisor, questionnaire respondent, proposal evaluator) receiving the work you write. Each type of communication is discussed in terms of what readers will be looking for. In Chapter 7, for example, your readers are customers or agencies from whom you are ordering merchandise or to whom you have supplied merchandise or services. In Chapter 8 a letter of application and comments appropriate at an interview are discussed in the light of what personnel directors seek when they recruit new employees. In Chapter 11, which deals with summaries, your reader is a busy executive who does not have the time to read a two-hundred page report and will rely on your two-hundred-word summary of it instead. Each of these readers represents a different challenge. The insights you will gain from this book about readers' needs should prove extremely useful both on the job and off. With these insights, you will be able to prepare yourself psychologically for writing assignments in business and industry. You will also learn how to manage your own writing resources to your best advantage.

Exercises

1. What is your chosen career field? Make a list of the kinds of writing you think you will encounter or have already encountered in this career.

2. Make a list of the kinds of writing you have done in a history or English class or for a laboratory or shop course.

3. Compare your lists for Exercises 1 and 2. How do the two types of writing differ?

4. Bring to class a set of printed instructions, a memo, a sales letter, or a brochure. Comment on how well the printed material answers the following questions.
 a. Who is the audience?
 b. Why was the material written?
 c. What is the message?
 d. Are the language and ideas appropriate for the audience, the purpose, and the message? Why?

5. Cut out a newspaper ad that contains a drawing or photograph. Bring it to class together with a paragraph (75–100 words) of your own describing how the message of the ad is directed to a particular audience and commenting on why the illustration was selected for that audience.

6. Pick one of the following topics and write two descriptions of it. In the first description use technical vocabulary. In the second, use language suitable for the general public.

a. spark plug	**i.** muscle	**q.** calculator
b. blood pressure cuff	**j.** protein	**r.** Nintendo game
c. carburetor	**k.** compact disc player	**s.** AIDS
d. computer chip	**l.** word processor	**t.** thermostat
e. camera	**m.** bread	**u.** trees
f. legal contract	**n.** money	**v.** food processor
g. electric sander	**o.** fishing reel	**w.** earthquake
h. cement	**p.** soap	**x.** recycling

7. Accomplish Exercise 6 above as a collaborative writing project.

8. Select one article from a daily newspaper and one article from either a professional journal in your major field or one of the following journals: *Advertising Age, American Journal of Nursing, Business Marketing, Business Week, Computer, Computer Design, Construction Equipment, Criminal Justice Review, Food Service Marketing, Journal of Forestry, Journal of Soil and Water Conservation, National Safety News, Nutrition Action, Office Machines, Park Maintenance, Scientific American, Today's Secretary.* State how the two articles you selected differ in terms of audience, purpose, message, style, and tone.

9. Assume that you work for Appliance Rentals, Inc., a company that rents TVs, microwave ovens, stereo components, etc. Write a persuasive letter to the members of a campus organization or civic club urging them to rent an appropriate appliance or appliances. Include details in your letter that might have special relevance to members of this specific organization.

10. Explain how the advertisement on page 24 illustrates the techniques of occupational writing described in this chapter. Specifically comment on how the ad reveals that the copywriter successfully analyzed the intended audience. Pay attention to advertising copy (words), the images of people and equipment (visuals), and the situation depicted. Also explain how the ad illustrates the five characteristics of on-the-job writing.

11. Read the following article and identify its audience (technical or general), purpose, message, style, and tone.

Microwaves

Much of the world around us is in motion. A wave-like motion. Some waves are big like tidal waves and some are small like the almost unseen footprints of a waterspider on a quiet pond. Other waves can't be seen at all, such as an idling truck sending out vibrations our bodies can feel. Among these are electromagnetic waves. They range from very low frequency sound waves to very high frequency X-rays, gamma rays, and even cosmic rays.

Energy behaves differently as its frequency changes. The start of audible sound—somewhere around 20 cycles per second—covers a segment at the low end of the electromagnetic spectrum. Household electricity operates at 60 hertz (cycles per second). At a somewhat higher frequency we have radio, ranging from shortwave and marine beacons, through the familiar AM broadcast band that lies between 500 and 1600 kilohertz, then to citizen's band, FM, television, and up to the higher frequency police and aviation bands.

Even higher up the scale lies visible light with its array of colors best seen when light is scattered by raindrops to create a rainbow.

Lying between radio waves and visible light is the microwave region—from roughly one gigahertz (a billion cycles per second) up to 3000 gigahertz. In this region the electromagnetic energy behaves in special ways.

Microwaves travel in straight lines, so they can be aimed in a given direction. They can be *reflected* by dense objects so that they send back echoes—this is the basis for radar. They can be *absorbed,* with their energy being converted into heat—the principle behind microwave ovens. Or they can pass *through* some substances that are transparent to the energy—this enables food to be cooked on a paper plate in a microwave oven.

Microwaves for Radar

World War II provided the impetus to harness microwave energy as a means of detecting enemy planes. Early radars were mounted on the Cliffs of Dover to bounce their microwave signals off Nazi bombers that threatened England. The word *radar* itself is an acronym for *RA*dio *D*etection *A*nd *R*anging.

Radars grew more sophisticated. Special-purpose systems were developed to detect airplanes, to scan the horizon for enemy ships, to paint finely detailed electronic pictures of harbors to guide ships, and to measure the speeds of targets. These were installed on land and aboard warships. Radar—especially shipboard radar—was surely one of the most significant technological achievements to tip the scales toward an Allied victory in World War II.

Today, few mariners can recall what it was like before radar. It is such an important aid that it was embraced universally as soon as hostilities ended. Now, virtually every commercial vessel in the world has one, and most larger vessels have two radars: one for use on the open sea and one, operating at a higher frequency, to "paint" a more finely detailed picture, for use near shore.

Microwaves are also beamed across the skies to fix the positions of aircraft in flight, obviously an essential aid to controlling the movement of aircraft from city to city across the nation. These radars have also been linked to computers to tell air traffic controllers the altitude of planes in the area and to label them on their screens.

A new kind of radar, phased array, is now being used to search the skies thousands of miles out over the Atlantic and Pacific oceans. Although these advanced radars use microwave energy just as ordinary radars do, they do not depend upon a rotating antenna. Instead, a fixed antenna array, comprising thousands of elements like those of a fly's eye, looks everywhere. It has been said that these radars roll their eyes instead of turning their heads.

High-Speed Cooking

During World War II Raytheon had been selected to work with M.I.T. and British scientists to accelerate the production of magnetrons, the electron tubes that generate microwave energy, in order to speed up the production of radars. While testing some new, higher-powered tubes in a laboratory at Raytheon's Waltham, Massachusetts plant, Percy L. Spencer and several of his staff engineers observed an interesting phenomenon. If you placed your hand in a beam of microwave energy, your hand would grow pleasantly warm. It was not like putting your hand in a heated oven that might sear the skin. The warmth was deep-heating and uniform.

Spencer and his engineers sent out for some popcorn and some food, then piped the energy into a metal wastebasket. The microwave oven was born.

From these discoveries, some 35 years ago, a new industry was born. In millions of homes around the world, meals are prepared in minutes using microwave ovens. In many processing industries, microwaves are being used to perform difficult heating or drying jobs. Even printing presses use microwaves to speed the drying of ink on paper.

In hospitals, doctors' offices, and athletic training rooms, that deep heat that Percy Spencer noticed is now used in diathermy equipment to ease the discomfort of muscle aches and pains.

Telephones without Cable

The third characteristic of microwaves—that they pass undistorted through the air—makes them good messengers to carry telephone conversations as well as live television signals—without telephone poles or cables—across town or across the country. The microwave signals are beamed via satellite or by dish reflectors mounted atop buildings and mountaintop towers.

Microwaves take their name from the Greek *mikro* meaning very small. While the waves themselves may be very small, they play an important role in our world today: in defense; in communications; in air, sea, and highway safety; in industrial processing; and in cooking. At Raytheon the applications expand every day.

Raytheon Magazine Winter 1981: 22-23. Reprinted by permission.

The Writing Process at Work

In Chapter 1 you learned about the different functions of writing for the world of work and also explored some basic concepts all writers must master. To be a successful writer, you need to identify your audience's needs, make sure your message meets those needs, and use the most appropriate style and tone for that message. Understanding the importance of audience, message, style, and tone is a major part of being a successful writer. Just as significant to your success is knowing how effective writers actually create their work for their audiences. This chapter will give you some practical information about the strategies and techniques careful writers use when they work. These strategies and techniques are a vital part of what is known as the *writing process.* This process involves such matters as how writers gather information, how they get their ideas down into written form, and how they organize and revise what they have written to make it suitable for their audiences.

What Writing Is and Isn't

As you begin your study of writing for the world of work, it might be helpful to identify some notions about what writing is and what it is not. Writing is not something mysterious done according to a magical formula known only to a few. Even if you have not done much writing before, you can learn how effective writing works. Nor is writing simply a hit-or-miss affair, left up to chance. Successful writing requires hard, thoughtful effort. It is not done well by simply going through an ordered set of steps as if you were painting by number. You cannot sit down for 15 minutes and expect to write the perfect memo, letter, or short report straight through. Writing does not proceed in some predictable way, where introductions are always written first and conclusions last. Also, it is equally misleading to think that once you put something on paper it is there to stay forever and in that exact place in your letter or report.

Writing is a fluid process; it is dynamic, not static. It enables us to discover and evaluate our thoughts. It happens over a period of time and evolves through many changes. It means making a number of judgment calls. In fact, all careful writing involves rewriting and revising. Even experienced writers do not get it right the first time. An effective writer is a *re*writer. A rough draft is never a final copy. Writing grows unevenly, sometimes in bits and pieces and sometimes in great spurts. It changes as the writer's thoughts and information change, and as the writer's view of the material changes.

Five Elements of the Writing Process

The writing process involves five elements: (1) researching, (2) prewriting, (3) drafting, (4) revising, and (5) editing. Keep in mind, though, that these elements are not mutually exclusive. Do not expect to complete each of them just once or in that exact order. For example, research goes on throughout the process of preparing your written work, as does revision, since revising means *re*examining and improving what you have written. Effective writers add to or delete from their work, coming up with new information or crossing out irrelevant ideas. They also shift paragraphs, sentences, and words around. A careful writer often retraces steps or skips from one section to another to make a piece of work more complete, accurate, and appropriate for an audience.

You will see part of the process one writer engaged in to prepare a piece of on-the-job writing in Figures 2.2 (p. 32) through 2.5. (p. 36). These figures show the successive drafts involved when William Tisch was asked to write a short report for his boss, Melissa Hill. As the office manager for the company, Melissa was concerned about the costs and efficiency in sending information to customers and asked William to investigate ways of improving communications. His report recommends purchasing a fax machine to increase the flow of information to customers.

Researching

Before you start to compose any letter, memo, or report, do some research. Depending on the size of your assignment, your research can be simple or elaborate. Yet whatever the size of the job, researching will help you to obtain the necessary information your audience expects. Take a few minutes to write down what you know about the topic or problem and what you need to know. Don't think you will be wasting or losing time by not starting to write the report or letter immediately. Actually, you will waste more time if you do not find out as much as possible about your topic (and your audience's interest in it).

You might double-check with your employer, client, or teacher to make sure you have the right idea about length (for example, one page or ten?), format (memo or letter?), scope (all office practices or just one particular procedure?), and audience (expert or general?) for your work. Find out if your document will be routed to individuals in other departments. Knowing where your letter or report is headed will help you to gather information and say the right things for your audience. It might also be necessary to interview people outside your company, such as lab researchers or customers. Prepare for such conferences or interviews so that you will ask the right questions of the most appropriate people. In addition, writers in the business world often interact with their readers. Whenever feasible, try to speak to your readers to identify their needs and to target possible problems. You may also need to do library research (such as reading current periodicals), draft a questionnaire, or draw on personal observations and experiences.

Recall that research is not confined just to the start of the writing process; it goes on throughout. As you start to tackle your subject, take a little extra time during this formative period to think about the information you have gathered so you can most effectively adapt it for your audience.

In preparing his report for Melissa Hill, William Tisch realized he had to do some research. To make a recommendation, he had to find out something about different kinds of communication technologies. As he read articles in various business journals and magazines, he soon realized that fax machines were receiving a great deal of very favorable attention. As he read more and more about fax machines, he realized they offered some very strong benefits for his company. He visited a few fax dealers in his city and, after seeing some demonstrations, became convinced that purchasing a fax machine was a feasible and economically wise choice. The results of all this research would be reflected in his final report.

Prewriting

At this stage in the writing process your goal is to get something—anything—down on paper. For most writers who are fearful of writer's block, getting started is the hardest part of the job. But you will feel more comfortable and confident once you list your thoughts on paper. It is always easier to clarify and criticize something you can see. Knowing that you have researched your topic should also make getting started less painful because you have something to say and build on.

Still, getting started is not easy. A number of widely used prewriting strategies, though, can help you to find the right material for your audience and to restrict your message to them. Use any one of the following techniques alone or in combination.

1. Clustering. In the middle of a sheet of paper, write the word or phrase that best describes your topic. Then start writing any words or phrases that come to mind about this topic. As you write, circle each word or phrase and then connect it to the word from which it sprang. Take a look at the clustered grouping in Figure 2.1 (p. 30) to see how one writer used this prewriting strategy to get started on a report encouraging a manager to switch to flex time. (Flex time is a system in which employees may work on a flexible time schedule within certain limits.) The resulting diagram is still an incomplete picture of the final report, but it does give the writer a rough sense of some of the major divisions of the topic and where they may belong in the report.

FIGURE 2.1   Clustering on the topic of flex time.

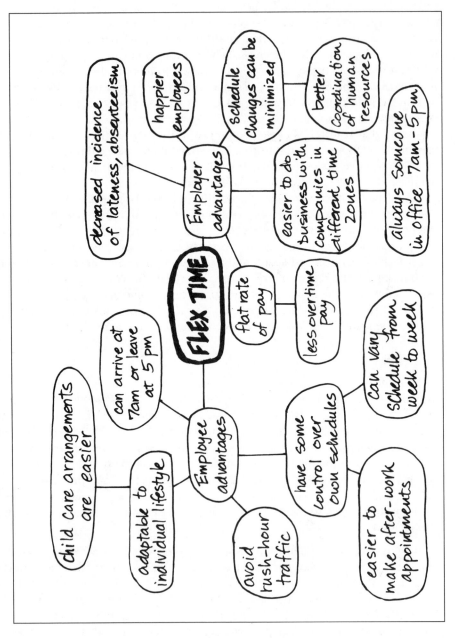

2. Brainstorming. At the top of a sheet of paper describe your topic in a word or phrase and then list any information you found out about that topic—in any order and as quickly as you can. Brainstorming is like thinking aloud except that you are recording your comments on paper. As you brainstorm, don't stop to delete, rearrange, or rewrite anything and don't dwell on any one item. Don't worry about spelling, punctuation, grammar, or whether you are using words and phrases instead of complete sentences. Keep going with the flow of ideas. The result may well be an odd assortment of details, comments, and opinions. After 10 to 15 minutes, stop and take a short break. When you come back to your list, you will want to make some changes. Some of your points will be irrelevant, so strike them. You may add some ideas, or combine or rearrange others as you start to develop them in more detail. Your list is not final by any means; you have just begun to mine the raw ore.

Figure 2.2 shows William Tisch's initial brainstormed list. After he began to revise it, he realized that some of the items were not relevant for his audience (6, 8, and 13) and that others were pertinent but needed to be adapted for his reader (5). He also recognized that some items were repetitious (1, 2, and 11). Further investigation revealed that his company could purchase a fax machine for far less than his initial high guess of $1,200. As he continued to work on his list, other relevant points came to mind that were not on his original list—that a fax can transmit and receive messages after 5:00 P.M. when phone rates are lower, that it is small and portable, and that it is compatible with a personal computer.

3. Outlining. A prewriting outline can be brief and very informal—for no one's eyes but yours. You might simply jot down some major points with a few subpoints to identify the major sections and subsections of your paper and to begin to discover relationships between them. Don't worry about a formal outline style with Roman or arabic numerals and parallel subdivisions. (Of course, at some later stage, you may have to prepare a formal outline for your employer or coworkers, especially for a longer, more complex project.) Many writers use an outline as a quick way to sketch in their ideas. The outline becomes a handy, convenient form into which writers can plug their ideas. As with a brainstormed list, leave your outline to cool for a while. When you return you can juggle points and add and delete others. Note that William Tisch organized his revised brainstormed list into an outline in Figure 2.3 (p. 33) as a further stage of his prewriting activities.

In addition to these techniques, there are a few others worth trying. You may find that asking and answering a series of questions (who, what, where, how, when, why) about your topic is a good way to get started. Or you might even try some *freewriting* (just plunging into a very early, unplanned draft) helpful. Freewriting is nonstop writing that will get you started and help build your confidence. Your goal is to fill the paper by exploring any ideas that come to you about your topic. When you freewrite, you do not worry about style, paragraphs, spelling, or punctuation. Just write fast and focus on your topic and the audience that needs to know about it.

The important point is that there is no one right way to get started. If you are not sure which way works best for you, experiment with a few of these techniques.

FIGURE 2.2   William Tisch's initial, unrevised brainstormed list.

> *Everything I can think of on how a*
> *fax machine could help our business*
>
> 1. *lots of small and big businesses are buying*
>   *fax machines*
> 2. *Two million of them used in 1992*
> 3. *inexpensive models — $700 to about $1,200*
>   *(more with attachments)*
> 4. *will scan anything, reproduce signatures,*
>   *blueprints, photographs*
> 5. *fast work — 9.6 Kbps*
> 6. *used a lot in Japan — M.D.s send prescriptions*
>   *to pharmacies via fax*
> 7. *would drastically reduce our cost for overnight*
>   *mail service*
> 8. *circuit boards, memory chips — real advance in*
>   *digital technology*
> 9. *would give us a record of everything we*
>   *send/receive*
> 10. *set up of a fax is quick*
> 11. *by 1994, 4.3 million will be installed*
> 12. *fax — part of a complete communication system*
> 13. *relationship to telex?*
> 14. *dual language capability — English/anything*
> 15. *no typist needed to transcribe*
> 16. *wouldn't interfere with office routines*
> 17. *Zap Fax is a good model to choose*

Drafting

When you draft, you convert the words and phrases from your outlines, brain-stormed lists, or clustered groups into paragraphs. Think of your prewriting jot-tings as the material out of which the basic building blocks (paragraphs) of your drafts will come. During drafting, as elsewhere in the writing process, you will see

FIGURE 2.3   William Tisch's rough outline made after revising his brainstormed list.

```
    I. Convenience

       A. Transmits over phone lines

       B. Easy to install and operate

       C. All we need is a phone

       D. Small, portable model that fits on a desk

       E. Can send anything--signatures, art, letters, reports

       F. Fits into our work routines

       G. Zap Fax is a good choice

   II. Time/Efficiency

       A. Fast speed--15-18 seconds per page

       B. Quick return of documents in less than a day, very good
          for invoice checking

       C. Quick turnaround of paperwork

       D. Will save time--no need to recopy everything

  III. Money

       A. Save on delivery service charges

       B. Can transmit when phone rates are lowest--after
          5:00 P.M.

       C. Initial cost of fax cheap

       D. Eliminates (or drastically cuts down on) misunderstood
          phone orders
```

some overlap as you look back over your lists or outlines to create your rough draft(s).

Keep in mind that drafting is still preliminary to the creation of your final copy. Don't expect to wind up with a polished, complete copy of your paper after working on only one draft. In most cases, you will have to work through many drafts, but each draft should be less rough than the preceding one, moving you

FIGURE 2.4   One of many drafts of William Tisch's report.

TO: Melissa Hill, Office Manager

FROM: William Tisch

DATE: November 2, 1994

RE: Improving Communications

    As you requested, I have been investigating a variety of ways that we might increase our efficiency and lower the costs of communicating with our customers. The most beneficial and immediate solution I propose is to purchase a fax (facsimile) machine. More and more of our clients have these machines in their offices, factories, and stores, and they are increasingly becoming a part of many companies' communication systems. With a fax machine, we can send our messages almost instantaneously all over the country, and at cheaper rates than we now pay for conventional delivery services. We will realize many advantages.

    A fax machine is easy to operate and to set up. All we need is the fax machine and a telephone line. Among the number of fax machines I have seen, most are small (about the size of a typewriter) and are portable. They easily fit on a desk. The Zap Fax is a good choice for us. The fax machine sends copies of letters, memos, reports, graphs, blueprints, and artwork over the ordinary phone lines. It is easy to learn to use a fax machine. Using one will not interfere with any existing office routines, and in fact will improve our communications. Many companies in our area sell fax machines.

    Fax machines work efficiently and speedily. They can scan and send a copy of a one-page letter in less than 18 seconds. In even less time they can send a copy of a blueprint or contract. Sending such documents by fax means that we can have a rapid turnaround of paperwork with our clients. In fact, a client can receive a copy of an invoice or an order form and complete it and have it back to us in less than an hour for easy processing on our part. The fax will also save us secretarial time since we won't have to have someone transcribe a document on either end of a message. The fax prints it exactly. We might therefore cut down on all those embarrassing typos we have seen lately.

    The greatest benefit a fax machine has for our company is the amount of money it will save us over time. A small fax machine runs about $700–800, or a little higher with a paper cutter. We spend that amount of money in less than six months on overnight delivery service. So, it should be easy to recoup the initial cost. Moreover, operating a fax machine is also economical. The cost of sending a single letter and piece of artwork over a fax during peak telephone rates (about $.96) is still less than sending it by Nationwide Express or Direct Overnight Service. And we can save even more if we transmit our message after 5:00 when the phone rates are lower. The fax is like an answering machine.

ever closer toward your final copy. Figure 2.4 shows only one of the many drafts that William Tisch prepared. Note that he has added an introduction and conclusion that were not included in his outline (Figure 2.3). These are necessary parts of Tisch's report if he is to accomplish his purpose in writing to his reader. Moreover, Tisch recognized that his draft was still not ready for his boss to see, so he showed it to a coworker for suggestions. Finally, Tisch did not consider his outline as final, so he revised it as necessary during the drafting stage.

The purpose of drafting is to get your main points down in the most logical order for your readers, so at this stage you need to pay careful attention to content and organization. You will make many changes in both areas as you draft your way toward the most satisfactory and satisfying version of your paper. Working on one of his drafts (Figure 2.4), Tisch realized that he had placed one of the most important considerations for his audience (savings) last. In his final version, shown in Figure 2.5 (p. 36), he moved this section to the beginning of his memo because he realized that Melissa Hill would be most interested in costs. As you draft, new and even better ideas will come to you, especially as you continue to research your topic and your audience's needs. You will also discard ideas that you once thought were usable but now appear irrelevant or repetitious. Keep in mind that if you are stuck, don't be afraid to go back and brainstorm, cluster, outline, or even do more research on a difficult part of your work. The writing process is not a linear, straightforward push; it is a back-and-forth, give-and-take activity.

As you work on your drafts, ask yourself these key questions.

- Is this the best way to start?
- Am I giving my readers too much or too little information?
- Does this point belong where I have it or does it more logically follow or precede something somewhere else?
- Did I forget to tell my readers something they need to know?
- Am I repeating myself?
- Have I contradicted myself?
- Have I ended appropriately for my audience?

Don't forget that effective drafting means making some big decisions about what you say and where you say it. Following are some more suggestions to help your drafting go more smoothly.

- Select a comfortable place to write. Use a pen, typewriter, or word processor—whatever gives you the most satisfying feeling about creating.
- Triple or even quadruple space between lines (if you use a pen or typewriter) to leave enough room to make changes.
- In an early draft, write the easiest part first, regardless of where it may finally end up. Some writers feel more comfortable drafting the body or middle of their work first.
- Then, as you work on a later draft, write straight through. Do not worry about spelling, punctuation, or the way a sentence sounds. Save these concerns for the stages to follow.
- Allow enough time between drafts so that you can evaluate your work with fresh eyes and a clear mind.

FIGURE 2.5   The final copy of William Tisch's report.

TO: Melissa Hill, Office Manager

FROM: William Tisch *W. T.*

DATE: November 2, 1994

RE: Improving Our Communication Cost and Efficiency

As you requested, I investigated some ways to increase efficiency and lower costs of communication with our customers. The most practical solution is to buy a fax (facsimile) machine. A fax scans the image of a document-- including contracts, photographs, blueprints--and transmits a copy over regular telephone lines all over the country or world instantaneously. In the U.S., more than one million companies own a fax. Since many of our clients have a fax, doing business with them should be easier.

The greatest benefit of a fax is the money it will save us. A small fax costs about $700–800, or slightly higher with a paper cutter. We spend that amount in less than six months on overnight delivery services. The cost of sending a letter and artwork over a fax at peak telephone rates (approx. $.96) is far less than sending it by Nationwide Express ($8.75). We can save even more by transmitting messages after 5:00 when phone rates are lower. The fax also takes messages 24 hours a day like an answering machine.

A fax works speedily and efficiently. It can send a one-page letter in less than 18 seconds. Sending such documents by fax promises a rapid turnaround of paperwork. A client can receive, complete, and return an order or invoice in less than an hour. By reproducing a message exactly, a fax will help to cut down on mistakes with orders taken over the phone. A fax will also give us a written record of our transaction. And by reproducing a message exactly, the fax will save us secretarial time used for transcriptions and help eliminate clerical errors.

A fax system is easy to install. All we need is the fax machine and a telephone. We can choose from among many small models marketed in our area. The Zap Fax, for example, is about the size of a typewriter, can fit on a desk, and is portable. It's easy to learn to use a fax, and it will not interfere with office routines. In fact, a fax can be made compatible with a personal computer to further improve our communications.

I recommend that we buy a fax immediately. It will improve communicating with our customers and also save us money.

■ Get frequent "outside" opinions. Show a draft to a fellow student, coworker, or maybe an employer for comment. A new pair of eyes will see things you missed.

During the drafting stage you will also want to consider what visuals you might use to help your readers and where to locate or how to construct these visuals.

Revising

Revision is an essential stage in the writing process; it requires more than giving your work a quick glance to check the spelling of a couple of words. Do not be tempted to skip the revision stage just because you have written the required number of words or sections or because you think you have put in too much time already. Revision is done *after* you produce a draft that you think conveys the appropriate message for your audience. Because revision is so important, allow enough time to do it carefully. Avoid drafting and revising in one sitting. If possible, wait at least a day before you start to revise. In the meantime you might ask a coworker or friend familiar with your topic to comment on your work.

When you revise, you *re*see, *re*think, and *re*consider your entire document. You ask questions about the major issues of content, organization, and tone. Revision means going back and repeating earlier steps you have taken in the writing process. It means asking the questions you already have asked during the planning and drafting stages. In the process you will discover gaps and things to change and correct in your draft. Revision gives you a second chance to get things right for your audience and to clarify your purpose in writing to them. At the revision stage you will ask the same questions about your audience that we studied in Chapter 1 (pages 6–8) and apply those questions to the draft you are reevaluating. As in the drafting stage, you once again will inspect your draft to make sure that it meets the audience's needs and takes into account their attitudes toward you and your work. After all, the audience's reason for reading your work and their background and job titles will determine the three big issues that you should be concerned with when you revise—content, organization, and tone. Plan to read your revised work more than once.

Like prewriting or drafting, revision is not done well in one big push. It evolves over a period of time. When effective writers revise their work, they go through their drafts several times to check for content, organization, and tone. Note the large number of changes William Tisch made between his draft in Figure 2.4 and the final, revised copy of his memo in Figure 2.5.

Here are some key questions to ask about these large topics as you revise your work.

Content

1. Is it accurate? Are my facts (figures, names, dates, costs, references, statistics) correct?
2. Is it relevant for my audience and purpose? Have I included information that is unnecessary, too technical, not appropriate? Does every detail belong in this communication with my reader(s)?

3. Have I included sufficient information for my readers' purpose? Have I given enough evidence to explain things adequately and to persuade my readers? (Too little information will make readers skeptical about what you are describing or proposing, and so they will question your conclusions.) Are my details complete or is there something I left out? Do I need to clarify or explain more for my readers' purpose? Have I left my readers hanging anywhere? Have I included all necessary information?

Organization

1. Is the arrangement of my information clear and straightforward? Is it easy to follow?
2. Have I clearly identified my main points and made it clear to my readers that these are the main points? Have I provided clear topic sentences (see Chapter 3) that tell readers what they can expect to find out and why?
3. Is everything proportionate to my purpose and my readers' needs, or have I spent too much (or too little) on one section? Do I repeat myself? What can be cut?
4. Is everything in the right, most effective order? Do I need to regroup sections or paragraphs of my document? Should anything be switched or moved toward the beginning or toward the end of my document?
5. Have I grouped like items together in the same part of my report or letter, or have I scattered details that really need to be collected in one paragraph or one section?
6. Is my work logical? Do my conclusions follow from the evidence I present? Are my recommendations valid and based on the conclusions I draw?

Tone

1. How do I sound to my readers? Am I professional and sincere, or do I come across as arrogant or unreliable? Do any of my words or expressions make me seem as though I might be hard to work with?
2. How will my readers think I perceive them? Will they think I believe they are honest and intelligent, or have I used words and details that may make them suspect I question their judgments and professionalism or that I am talking down to them?

Editing

Editing means getting the final copy ready for your audience. This last stage in the writing process might be compared to quality control. It is done only after you are completely satisfied that you have made all the big decisions about content and organization—that you have said what you have to, where and how, for your audience. When you edit, you check your work for style, grammar, punctuation, and you proofread. Here are some questions to keep in mind at this stage of the writing process.

1. Is my work readable? Are my sentences too long? Should I divide one long sentence into two? Can my readers get my message the first time they read my

sentences, or will they have to reread them? (If they have to reread, your sentences are not clear.) Are any of my sentences repetitious and unnecessary? Does each paragraph have a clear topic sentence?

2. Do my sentences flow easily from one to another? Does one sentence prepare the reader for the next? Are my sentences in the right order in the paragraph?

3. Is my writing concise and direct? Have I used several (needless) words when one word is enough? Have I used words my reader will be familiar with, or have I used jargon?

4. Are my sentences punctuated correctly? Have I checked to correct such errors as sentence fragments, wrong subject-verb agreement, faulty pronoun references, and dangling modifiers?

5. Are all my words spelled correctly? Have I spelled a word (or name) two different ways?

6. Have I supplied headings where they will help readers?

7. Have I proofread the entire document—making sure I did not transpose letters (*hte* for *the*) or leave a letter or an entire word out?

Don't skip or rush through the editing process, thinking that once your ideas are down you have done your work. Spelling, punctuation, and grammar matter a great deal to readers. If you make mistakes here, they will think that your ideas, your research, and your organization also are faulty. Chapters 3, 4, and 5 will help you know what to look for when you edit your paragraphs, sentences, and words, and pages 149–150 provide helpful tips on how to proofread your work effectively.

After you have made all these editing checks, you are ready to type or print the final, reader-ready copy. You will then have effectively completed the writing process and increased your chances for success.

The Group Writing Process

The writing process that we have just described also applies to collaborative writing. Groups have to take into account the same strategies and confront the same problems individual writers do. Like the individual writer, collaborative writing teams need to brainstorm, plan, research, draft, revise, and edit. Like the individual writer, the writing team can move through the writing process successfully only by identifying their audience, following a common goal, defining the problem, and deciding on the best ways to solve that problem.

Organization of Writing Groups

The success or failure of a collaborative writing team depends on how effectively the group interacts. Essential to group interaction is group organization. The group has to decide such fundamental issues as who is to do what, when, how often, and in what order. How a group is organized will depend, of course, on the scope and complexity of the document, the individuals available to work on it, and management's requirements. A shorter assignment (say, a memo) will not require the same type of group organization and participation as would a long pro-posal. Management's participation in and instructions to a group affect the way it functions, too. A boss may ask your group to determine a problem and then pro-vide possible solutions. Or your boss may identify the problem for your group, even supply a list of probable causes and solutions, and ask your group to investi-gate these causes/solutions and recommend the most appropriate course of action.

You are likely to encounter one of the following three possible organizational models in the world of work.

1. Sequential. Each individual in the group is assigned a specific, nonoverlap-ping responsibility—from brainstorming to revising—for a separate section of a proposal, report, or other document. There is a clear-cut, rigid division of labor. If four people are on the team, each will be responsible for his or her parts of the document. For example, one may write the introduction, another may write a sec-tion of the body of the report, and so forth. Members of the team may discuss their individual progress and even select one of them as a coordinator to oversee the general progress of the work. They may even exchange their work for group review and commentary. When each team member is finished with his or her sec-tion, the coordinator then will assemble the individual parts to form the report.

2. Functional. The division of labor in this organizational model is assigned not according to parts of a document but by skill or job function of the individual members of the team. For example, a four-person team may be headed by a team leader who schedules and conducts meetings, checks on individuals in the group, issues progress reports to management, solves problems by proposing alterna-tives, and generally coordinates everyone's efforts. The team also may appoint an individual to serve as a researcher responsible for gathering data from library research, interviewing, and testing. This researcher gathers and classifies informa-tion and then prepares notes on the information. The researcher then turns over his or her work to another member of the team, the designated writer/editor, responsible for preparing outlines and drafts and circulating them to make changes and revisions suggested by the group. The fourth member of the group—a graphics or visuals expert—obtains and prepares all visuals, specifying why, how, and where visuals should be placed in the report. This person may suggest that a visual replace a section of the text. This organizational scheme fosters much more group interaction than does the sequential model.

3. Integrated. According to this plan, all members of the team are engaged in planning, researching, drafting, and revising. Each member participates in every stage of the document's creation and design, and the group goes back to each stage as often as it needs. This model offers the most group interaction. There is no division of tasks by job title or document. The team drafts the document word for word, or each member prepares a draft and the group then selects the best version collectively. The group may vote to combine two members' work or to use parts from all members. Each member is then actively involved in revising the document. Visuals experts work with writers and researchers to organize and enhance the presentation of the document.

Perhaps the most frequently used organizational model is the sequential, where each team member is assigned a section to prepare and is encouraged to finish it as quickly as possible. The other two models—the functional and integrated—are used less often in the workplace but are becoming more popular.

Establishing Group Responsibilities

Collaborative writing does not work miracles effortlessly. Being a member of a team requires a lot of hard work. It is not a substitute for individual work. Don't view team membership as a way to escape work or dodge responsibility. You cannot be invisible in a group, nor can you be swept along on someone else's coattails. Collaboration works only if the members of the team observe the following fundamentals of group dynamics.

1. Do not think of the team as a group of separate individuals. This can lead to hard feelings and a loss of productivity. Nor should individuals think of themselves as the most important, or indispensable, member of the team. Everyone's task is necessary to group effort and success. A unified team can accomplish more than a collection of disgruntled individuals.

2. Understand and share the same goals and priorities. Unless the members of the group have a shared vision and common objective, they will go off in different directions. It is helpful for group members to establish their goals right from the start of their work and to set up priorities.

3. Set up the times, places, and length of group meetings. The more the group meets early in the project, the better. Each member will thereby have an opportunity to ask questions or share comments before the research and drafting starts.

4. Agree on the way in which the group is to be organized. Is there to be a group leader or recorder? Who will be responsible for assigning tasks?

5. Establish a precise list of duties for members, but first allow time for a discussion of individual talents and skills. The division of labor should be fair and reflect the diverse talents of the group members. Don't underestimate or overestimate the amount of time necessary for each member's (or the whole group's) tasks. Each member should perform the specific duties assigned to him or her, whether it is gathering data, drafting and revising, editing or preparing visuals, or a combination of these activities.

6. Adhere faithfully to an agreed-on timetable. The group should estimate a realistic time necessary to complete various stages of their work, and then prepare a schedule based on that estimate. Everyone in the group should be aware of short-term and long-range deadlines. Specify the order in which goals are to be accomplished, and make sure each member knows what his or her role is in the entire process. The group, either collectively or through its leader/recorder, also should build some fail-safe time into the schedule. Prepare for a possible delay at one stage—say, research is not completed because materials are not available, or someone fails to complete a task on time because of illness.

7. Provide clear and precise feedback to members of your group. Nothing is more frustrating to a writer than to have a reader/editor offer general or superficial comments—for example, "needs improvement," "lacks focus," "does not flow." You can help the writer(s) of the draft by supplying specific criticism of what is wrong, incomplete, and misleading. Then offer some clear advice on where and how to fix things. Also, do not think you are doing yourself or the group a favor by simply responding "OK" or "Looks good" on a draft. Skimming helps no one. If something is effective, state why, but be honest. Holding back valid criticism will hurt the group as much as skimming a document will.

Problems to Avoid in Group Writing

Regardless of the organizational model you follow, you need to be aware of certain difficulties in collaborative writing. These difficulties result when the group does not follow the guidelines outlined in the writing process itself. Here are a few pitfalls to watch out for.

1. Losing sight of the audience's needs and the group's main goals in meeting them. As we saw in Chapter 1 (pages 4-10), the audience's needs determine the writer's content, language, organization, and tone. So, too, with collaborative writing groups. When a group acts without considering the audience's reasons for reading its work, there is a danger of including irrelevant or inappropriate information. That danger is greatest when a team member works alone or does not stay current with what other members are doing. Similarly, when a group loses sight of the big picture—or the audience's primary needs—and focuses on lesser topics, it can go astray. Not taking into account the audience's requirements, the group may do an insufficient amount of research or include too many unnecessary technical details. Or it may omit information about a valid option the reader needs to know.

2. Not allowing sufficient time for each stage of the process. A group that is too eager to get started writing may cut corners in researching, drafting, or revising. Skimping at the beginning of their work, group members may find that they have written a report that is wrong for the audience and that they must start all over again. It is not a simple and easy matter to go from an outline to a first draft. The group needs to explore large issues (big Roman numerals on the outline) before transforming these into sections of their draft. The group should consider overall organization, likely things to omit, and the relevance of all topics and subtopics before jumping into drafting. Another pitfall in group writing is assuming that a first draft (something finally in prose/paragraph form) is very close to the final copy. Group members must recognize that large organizational changes and shifts occur throughout the drafting stage. A similar stumbling block that groups experience is mistaking spell checking, correcting grammar, and polishing for revising. Again, revision deals with large issues of structure and content. Many of these problems occur because groups do not allot ample time for group discussion and review of each other's work.

3. Including too much or too little information. One of the most misleading assumptions about collaborative writing is believing that everything the group has shared or discovered must be included in the final document. The urge to "include everything from everybody" is false democracy and leads to bad writing. A group that includes everything runs the risk of offering readers a report full of repetitious, contradictory, and/or potentially irrelevant details. Such thinking makes minor points equal with—or even more important than—major ones. Keeping the readers' needs in mind, the group should exercise caution and select only information that will help the readers. By recognizing the goals they have to fulfill, the group should establish and act on priorities—any information that does not pertain to these priorities, as determined by the readers' requirements, should be discarded. Be careful, too, of loading one section of a report down while scanting another.

4. Having an inconsistent style or tone of voice. If each part of a report has been written by a separate member of the team, the danger is great that there will be as many styles and tones of voice as there are writers. One section of the report may be clear and concise while another could be foggy and wordy. One section may be filled with technical jargon while another may avoid such words altogether. One writer may go overboard with documentation—filling his or her work with detailed and excessive references to research; another writer may merely summarize one or two main research studies. Such inconsistency is inevitable when the writing of a report is divided among different writers.

Not all members of the team will have equal writing skills. By taking an inventory of their collective skills, the group should identify and then assign one of them to the job of revising and editing the document so that, although prepared by four or five people, it reads in a consistent style, as if it were written by one individual. This writer/editor also should review the final copy to make sure it is consistent in tone (see pages 12-13) and format. The writer/editor then becomes the document's quality-control officer.

5. Not finishing on time or having an incomplete document. Meeting deadlines is the group's most important duty. These include deadlines for various stages of their work, as well as for different sections of the report or proposal, and, of course, the most important deadline of all—the date the work must be submitted to the boss or customer. Deadlines are missed when some group members are not involved in the planning stages and discussion sessions and consequently miss vital dates. Deadlines also are missed when group members do not clearly understand their individual assignments and therefore duplicate what someone else has been asked to do.

Computers and the Writing Process

The computer is an essential tool in the workplace. Almost every type of business relies heavily on computers to generate, store, retrieve, and transmit information. Based on computer technology, the automated office today is likely to have word processors, microcomputers, teleconferencing equipment, fax machines, and even voice synthesizers that recognize and translate sounds into writing.

Computers increase efficiency, save time, lower costs, and streamline the process of receiving and sending messages.

Knowing how to use a word processor is a requirement for most jobs. Employees either have word processors at their desks or have access to them. Gone are the days when you could do everything in longhand or on a typewriter and then turn over a rough copy to a secretary to edit and produce the finished product. Since you will most likely have access to a word processor, your employer will expect you to create, revise, and print a professional-looking document.

There are a variety of computers on the market, but common to all of them are an illuminated display screen (or monitor), a keyboard, a memory component using a computer chip, and a printer. These parts are known as the *hardware;* the various programs used to give instructions to the computer are known as the *software.* Various software programs will allow you to perform word processing, create graphics, and do accounting ledgers.

The word processor has been misleadingly called a typewriter with a memory. It is more than that; with a typewriter you are stuck with what you type on a given sheet of paper, and if you do not like it you have to start over. With a word processor you can make a large number of changes on a thin, flexible magnetic disk or on the computer's hard disk. The word processor saves what you want to keep while it makes room on the disk for any additions, deletions, or corrections. You are spared the drudgery of retyping a page each time you make a change or a mistake.

With the computer, the appropriate software, and a printer, you can make the following changes anytime and anywhere in your document:

- insert or delete words, sentences, paragraphs
- move around lines or entire paragraphs
- search for and replace a word or phrase
- copy part of something in the document or in another document stored in the computer
- design and insert visuals
- use boldface or italic print; change the size of lettering; center headings and put information into columns
- set tabs and margins
- check and verify spelling and punctuation
- identify wordiness, sexist language, overused words

Since you can watch all these changes on your screen, you will be able to visualize the writing process at work. You are thus able to interact with the text you are creating on the screen. And at any stage in the process you can *scroll* your document—roll the text up or down on the screen—to view different parts of the document.

The word processor assists you in every phase of the writing process by making it easier to complete. The computer is an invaluable help in your research. In fact, depending on your company's computer capabilities, you might be able to do some of your research right at your computer terminal. If your company stores documents on disks, you will want to check appropriate ones as part of your research. That means calling up memos from your boss and coworkers, examining previous correspondence with a customer, and studying company brochures, reports, catalogs, or budgets. By familiarizing yourself with the history of correspondence with a particular customer, you will be better informed to offer the kinds of service that the customer wants. In-house research can give you the necessary edge to succeed.

Many reference works—indexes, encyclopedias, abstracts—are available on-line (see Chapter 9). Again, depending on your company's computer facilities and software, you might be able to access these reference works at your own terminal. Even if your office does not offer these works on-line, chances are that your library does. Using these electronic reference works will make researching material for a proposal or report much easier. You can also use your computer to take notes from your research, thus saving time and making sure that your notes are safely stored for future use.

When you are prewriting, a word processor can help you to move items in your outline or brainstormed list quickly to organize them into categories. You might even use some of the software packages designed to generate and organize information so you can identify ideas easily.

When you draft your document, the word processor can help you get some writing on the monitor screen quickly. In doing this, the word processor keeps pace with the speed of your thought process and also allows you to concentrate on your writing rather than on the more technical aspects of creating a document. You will not have to worry about the time-consuming drudgery of having to return a typewriter carriage after every line or of retyping successive drafts. You do not have to stop to check spelling or punctuation since you can return to these matters later. And if you run into a snag on any draft, you do not have to stop to fix it and lose momentum. With a single stroke on the keyboard, the word processor will flag items that you want to return to or need more information about. During drafting and revising, some writers in fact move back and forth between a hard copy (the paper copy run off by the printer) and the text on the screen.

When you are revising, the word processor assists you in refining and refocusing your thoughts. Using a word processor can actually encourage you to make revisions since they can be accomplished easily and quickly. Again, you will be relieved of the burden of retyping or recopying what you want to save each time you make a change or spot an omission or an error. Since you can rearrange words, sentences, and paragraphs, or even the appearance of material, you can experiment with a number of versions of your work without having to type each separately. Some software packages even allow you to split your monitor screen into two or four parts (*windows*) to view different versions of a text or several pages of the text simultaneously. From that perspective you will be able to select the best version of a paper or format for your audience and also to see how a revision on one page might affect another page of your text. A word processor also allows you to print a clean copy at any stage; it is always easier to catch errors on a clean copy than on a marked-up one. Your printer will allow you to create multiple copies, too.

A computer can assist you during the editing phase as well. A number of software programs are available to help you edit and proof your final copy. Some of these programs will flag mistakes in grammar, punctuation, spelling, and word choice. Although such software programs are unquestionably useful, they do have some drawbacks. See pages 118–119 for a few of the problems involved in using such programs.

Undoubtedly, the word processor is a wonderful tool that will help you to increase and improve your writing. But it will not do your writing for you. You may use a software package to help organize your ideas, although you must first do research to discover what ideas are relevant for your audience. The word processor will enable you to produce more writing, but you are the one who must select the right words with the appropriate tone and put them into readable sentences and logically organized paragraphs. As we saw, the word processor can greatly assist you in making revisions, but again you must decide what must be revised and how. And never be lulled into thinking that a clean, professionally printed document will hide or make up for incorrect content or poor writing.

How Computers Improve Collaborative Writing

The word processor was created with the needs of the business world in mind. It becomes an invaluable link in any collaborative writing venture; all you have to do is share your disk with a coworker, who can make changes on the disk and then return it to you. And if the boss asks you to change a word or two in the middle of a letter, add a new paragraph, or reverse the order of some paragraphs after seeing your "final" copy, you do not have to do the whole thing over. You can make these changes quickly and have a revised copy ready in no time. Figure 2.6 shows a letter an employee drafted on a word processor and on which her boss made a number of changes in wording, format, and content. Using the appropriate software, the employee was able to create the revised letter seen in Figure 2.7 (p. 48). If she had mailed the first draft, her reader most likely would not have been impressed with the company's professionalism and would have thought twice about placing an order. The revised final version of the letter is much more effective in its presentation of the material, in its individualized address, and in its formatting. Good writers benefit from constructive criticism of their drafts and know how to make effective changes during the revision process. In this example the employee benefited from the criticism of her boss. The final copy in Figure 2.7 is the result of the suggested revisions.

Recent advances in computer software packages make it even easier for members of a collaborative writing team to do their work. Although word processing capabilities vary from office to office, there are software network systems that allow a group to circulate, read, and comment on written work without ever leaving their personal computers. The writer(s), for example, can put a document on-line and thereby allow other members of the team to pull up that text on their screens. Using appropriate commands to delete, to insert, or to provide commentary, members of the team can provide feedback to each other and to the writer(s). The writer(s) can then retrieve group comments and revisions and incorporate them as necessary.

FIGURE 2.6   A draft of a letter prepared on a word processor and edited by an employer.

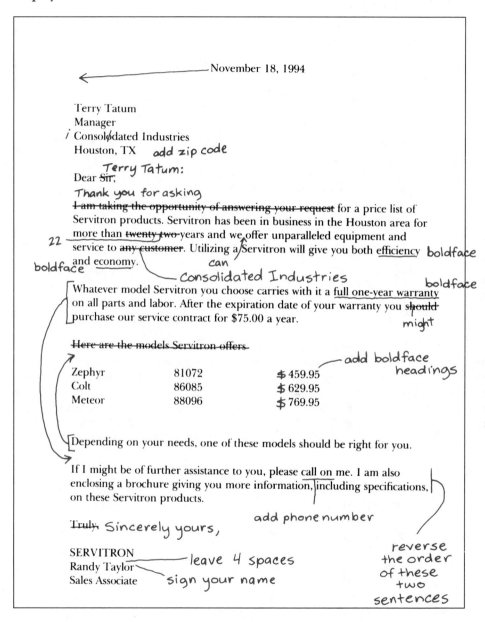

Computers also make long-distance conferencing possible. A writer can enter a document—an outline or a section of a report—on-line, and then other members of the team located in regional or main offices miles away can call it up to read, evaluate, and revise. The computer and appropriate word processing software thereby increase group participation in creating a document.

FIGURE 2.7   The edited, final copy of Figure 2.6.

November 18, 1994

Terry Tatum
Manager
Consolidated Industries
Houston, TX 77005-0096

Dear Terry Tatum:

Thank you for asking for a price list of Servitron products. Servitron has been in business in the Houston area for more than 22 years and we can offer unparalleled equipment and service to Consolidated Industries. Using a Servitron will give you both efficiency and economy.

Depending on your needs, one of these models should be right for you.

Model Name	Number	Price
Zephyr	81072	$459.95
Colt	86085	$629.95
Meteor	88096	$769.95

Whatever model Servitron you choose carries with it a full one-year warranty on all parts and labor. After the expiration date of your warranty you might purchase our service contract for $75.00 a year.

I am also enclosing a brochure giving you more information, including specifications, on these Servitron products. If I might be of further assistance to you, please call me at (904) 555-1689 or fax me at (904) 555-7321.

Sincerely yours,

SERVITRON

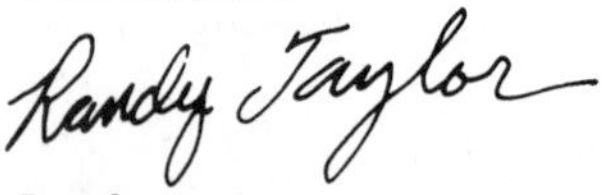

Randy Taylor

Randy Taylor
Sales Associate

Five Basic Points on Using a Word Processor

Throughout this book you will find a number of suggestions on how a word processor can help you to write better. But here are five basic points to help you escape some computer users' nightmares.

1. Give yourself adequate time to learn to operate your word processor and any software packages your employer uses. Read the manuals. A few hours of trial and error testing is time well spent.
2. Press the SAVE command every 10-15 minutes or you risk wiping out hours of hard work. Some word processors do so automatically.
3. Make a hard (paper) copy as a backup so that if an electrical storm knocks out the power or you make a keyboard error you will have a written record of your work. Also make a daily backup disk copy of your file.
4. Keep your disks away from magnetized surfaces (e.g., microwave ovens) and heat because these can destroy what you have recorded.
5. Make sure you store disks in a clean area. Do not touch the exposed part of a disk—that is what the computer reads.

✓ Revision Checklist

You need to ask yourself the following questions to make sure you have successfully completed the various stages of the writing process.

1. Have I researched my topic carefully to obtain enough information to answer all my readers' questions? Did I use such appropriate means as library research, on-line data search, interviews, questionnaires, personal observations, or a combination of methods?
2. Before I began writing, did I determine how much and what kind of information I would need to complete my writing task?
3. Did I spend enough time prewriting—brainstorming, outlining, clustering, or a combination of these techniques? Have I produced enough substantial material from which to shape a draft?
4. Has my work gone through enough drafts for me to decide upon major points in my message to my readers? Have I been willing to make major changes and deletions if necessary in my drafts?
5. Did I revise my drafts carefully so that I successfully answered any questions my readers may have about content, organization, or tone?
6. Have I made time to edit my work so that my style is clear and concise and that my sentences are correctly punctuated? Did I check my words to make sure they are spelled correctly and are appropriate for my audience?

7. If I am working in a group, do I fully understand my specific responsibilities for researching, drafting, revising, or editing? Am I clearly aware of my other obligations to the group?
8. Most crucial, do I know all the timetables for the group as a whole and my individual deadlines?
9. Have I investigated the research, drafting, revising, and editing benefits available to me through my computer at work or home?

Exercises

1. Below is an initial brainstormed list on stress in the workplace.

   leads to absenteeism
   high costs for compensation for stress-related illnesses
   proper nutrition
   numerous stress-reduction techniques
   good idea to conduct interviews to find out levels, causes, and extent of stress in the workplace
   low morale caused by stress
   higher insurance claims for employees' physical ailments
   myth to see stress leading to greater productivity
   various tapes used to teach relaxation
   environmental factors—too hot? too cold?
   teamwork intensifies stress
   counseling
   work overload
   setting priorities
   wellness campaign
   savings per employee add up to $2,500 per year
   skills to relax
   learning to get along with coworkers
   need for privacy
   interpersonal communication
   employee's need for clear policies on transfers, promotion
   stress management workshops very successful in California
   physical activity to relieve stress
   affects management
   breathing exercises

   Revise this brainstormed list, eliminating any repetition and combining any related items.

2. Prepare a suitable outline from your revised list in Exercise 1 for a report to a decision maker on the problems of stress in the workplace and the necessity of creating a stress management program.

3. From the revised brainstormed list in Exercise 1, write a short memo to a decision maker about the problems and possible solutions related to stress in the workplace.

4. Write a short report (2–3 pages) to the manager of the small company you work for to convince her to establish a system of flex time. Prepare an outline based on the clustered items in Figure 2.1 (p. 30). Add, delete, or rearrange anything in this clustered grouping to complete your outline. Submit your final outline along with your report to your instructor.

5. Compare the draft of William Tisch's report in Figure 2.4 (p. 34) with the final copy of his report in Figure 2.5 (p. 36). What kinds of changes did he make? Were they appropriate and effective for his audience and purpose? Why or why not?

6. Assume you have been asked to write a short report (similar to William Tisch's in Figure 2.5) to a decision maker (the manager of a business you work for or have worked for; the director of your campus union, library, or security force; a city official) about one of the following topics.

a. computer facilities   **f.** public transportation
b. telephone service   **g.** sporting events/activities
c. security lighting   **h.** training programs
d. food service   **i.** morale
e. insurance plans   **j.** hiring more part-time student workers

Do some research and planning about one of these topics and the audience for whom it is intended by writing your answers to the following questions.

- What is my precise purpose in writing to my audience?
- What do I know about the topic?
- What information will my audience expect me to know?
- Where can I obtain relevant information about my topic to meet my audience's needs?

7. Using one or more of the prewriting strategies discussed in this chapter (clustering, brainstorming, outlining, freewriting), generate a group of items for the topic you chose in Exercise 6. Do your prewriting activities for about 15–20 minutes, or until you have about 10–15 items. At this stage do not worry about how appropriate these items are or even if some of them overlap. Just get some thoughts down on paper.

8. Go through the list you prepared in Exercise 7 and eliminate any items that are inappropriate for your topic or audience or any items that overlap. Try to see how many of them you might expand or rearrange into categories or subcategories. Then create an outline similar to the one in Figure 2.3 (p. 33).

9. Using your outline in Exercise 8, prepare some drafts of your memo report. Submit at least two drafts to your instructor.

10. Revise your drafts as much as necessary to create the final copy of your report.

11. In a few paragraphs, explain to your instructor the changes you made between your early drafts and your revised drafts. Explain why you made them. Concentrate on large changes—adding and moving paragraphs—as well as matters of style and tone.

12. In another memo—addressed to your instructor—explain what major problems you encountered at various phases of working on your report. Also point out what prewriting, drafting, and revising strategies worked especially well for you.

13. Below are very early drafts of memos that employees/employers have sent to their bosses or fellow workers. Revise and edit each draft, referring to the revising and editing checklists on pages 37–39. Turn in your revision and the final, reader-ready copy. As you revise, keep in mind that you may have to delete and add information, rearrange the order of information, and make the tone suitable for the reader.

a. TO: All workers
   FROM: B.J. Blackwell
   SUBJECT: Parking
   DATE: September 29, 1994

   The parking violations around here have gotten
   very very bad. And the administration is provoked
   and wants some action taken. I don't blame them. I
   have been late for meetings several times in the
   last month because inconsiderate folks from other
   divisions have parked their cars in our zone. That
   just is not fair, and so I must not be the only one
   who is upset. No wonder the management finds things
   so bad they have asked me to prepare this memo.

   A big part of the problem it seems to me is that
   employees just cannot read signs. They park in the
   wrong zones. They also park in visitors' spots. The
   penalties are going to be stiff. The administration,
   or so I was led to believe, is thinking of fining
   any employee who does not obey the parking policies.
   I know for a fact that I saw someone from the
   research department pull right into a visitor
   parking area last week just because it was 8:55 and
   he did not want to be late for work. That gives our
   business a bad name. People will not want to do
   business with us if they cannot even find a parking
   spot in the area that the company has reserved for
   them.

   Ms. Watson has laid the law down to me about all
   this and told me to let each and every one of you

know that things have to improve. One of the other
big problems around here is that some employees
have even parked their cars in loading zones,
and security had to track them down to move.

As part of the administration's new policy, each
employee is going to be issued a company parking
policy and will have to come in and sign for it
verifying that he or she received it. I think things
really have gotten out of hand and that some drastic
action has to be taken. We will all have to shape up
around here.

b. TO: Betty Jones, Director
FROM: Tom Cranford
RE: Vacation request for vacation from June 12-24
DATE: April 21, 1994

I have been a highly productive employee and so I
do not think that it is out of line for me to make
this request. I have put in overtime and even done
others' work in the department while they were away.
So, I think that it is fair and just, and I can see
no reason why I should not be allowed to take my
vacation during the last two weeks of June.

Let me explain some of the reasons. I could have
others watch my desk and do the work. I have helped
them out, too, and they know it. I have been
remarkably dependable. I have been readily
accessible whenever their vacations have come
around, and so I know it can be done.

I fully realize that this is the busiest time of
the year for our company and that vacations are not
usually granted during this season. But I do have
personal reasons which I think should be honored/
respected. Peak business times are major. I
understand this, and I do hope an exception will be
made in my case. After all, I do have the on-the-job
training that other companies would reward. Thanks
very much.

c. TO: All Employees
FROM: George Holmes
DATE: February 21, 1994
RE: Travel

Every company has its policies regarding travel
and vouchers. Ours strike me as important and fairly

straightforward. Yet for the life of me I cannot
fathom why they are being ignored. It is in
everyone's best interest. When you travel, you are
on company time, company business. Respect that,
won't you. Explain your purpose, keep your receipts,
document your visits, keep track of meals,

If you see more than one client per day, it
should not be too hard or too much to ask you to
keep a log of each, separate, individual visit.
After all, our business does depend on these people,
and we will never know your true contributions on
company trips unless you inform us (please!) of whom
you see, where, why, and how much it costs you. That
way we can keep our books straight and know that
everything is going according to company policy.

Please review the appropriate pages (I think they
are pages 23-25) about travel procedures. Thanks. If
you have questions, give me a call, but check your
procedures book or with your office/section manager,
first. That will save everyone more time. Good luck.

14. Find a piece of writing—a memo, letter, pamphlet, or short report—that you
believe was not carefully drafted or revised. In a short memo, point out to
your instructor what is wrong with this piece of writing—e.g., not logically
organized, inappropriate tone, incomplete or too technical information.
Attach a copy of the poor example to your memo.

15. Revise the poor piece of writing you analyzed in Exercise 14. Submit your
improved version to your instructor.

Writing: Paragraphs

This chapter will discuss paragraphs within the writing process. Specifically, it will show you how to generate, draft, organize, and revise your paragraphs. A paragraph is the basic building block for any piece of writing. If you master the art of writing paragraphs, you should be able to handle any kind of business or technical writing. A *paragraph* is (1) a group of related sentences (2) arranged in a logical order (3) supplying readers with detailed, appropriate information (4) on a single important topic. Each of these points is discussed in detail in this chapter.

The Importance of Paragraphs

Paragraphs give readers the necessary navigational clues to understand your work. The following three functions of paragraphs are equally important.

1. Paragraphs divide your message into segments. They break complex messages into smaller, more understandable segments for readers. Imagine what a piece of writing would look like without indentations or white spaces to divide it into paragraphs. Without the paragraph breaks, readers would not know where to find key statements and would wonder where one part of a message began and another stopped. Furthermore, an unbroken piece of writing is intimidating to readers; paragraph breaks provide pauses to help refresh your reader.

2. Paragraphs group related details for readers' benefit. Think of a paragraph as an information block. Each block treats only one main idea at a time; that is, it usually contains a general statement and sufficient details to explain that statement. Within each information block you provide readers with only the relevant details they will need to understand that portion of your message. By collecting all related details in one paragraph, you make it easier for readers to understand them in terms of the main idea.

3. Paragraphs link ideas to make your work easier to understand. Paragraphs are not written in isolation. Each paragraph should flow smoothly and logically into the next, linking the different information blocks that make up your message. Transitions (discussed on pages 73-75), especially at the beginning and end of your paragraphs, hook one part of your message to another. In this way, paragraphs show how the different parts of your message are connected and related to each other, how one part "fits" into the next. Paragraphs also help readers to link ideas by saying to them: you have finished one part of the message; now stop to consider what you have read before starting the next section.

Paragraphs in the Writing Process

Paragraphing is a vital activity in the writing process. But writing clear and logical paragraphs is not easy, and it certainly cannot be done in one draft. Our thoughts do not conveniently sort themselves into orderly, ready-made paragraphs. Instead, we have to revise and regroup our ideas, expanding some and subordinating or eliminating others. This process of sorting our thoughts into meaningful chunks of information for readers is what writing paragraphs is all about.

As we saw in Chapter 2, in the writing process you will move from finding your ideas to expressing them for your readers. When you are working on a brainstormed list or an outline, you will not be concerned with paragraph breaks or structure. And even when you are working on your first or second draft, you may not be primarily occupied with how individual paragraphs look. During the early drafting stage, you do begin to pour information into paragraph-like shapes, but you may have to go through a number of drafts before you actually start to identify the initial shape, content, and flow of your paragraphs.

Writers can use several methods to discover their paragraphs. Some, for example, write straight through and then draft and redraft their paragraphs. Others move back and forth from outlines to drafts, or between a brainstormed list (or other prewriting plan) and various drafts. Going through a number of drafts will help you to start identifying the overall sequence of the paragraphs in your letter, memo, or report. You will be deciding what information you need to give readers and where to put it. Try to get your basic plan down during the drafting stage, but do not worry about getting it into final shape. The draft is like a blueprint of your work—not the final, finished product. During the next stage—revising—you will transform the blueprint of your paragraphs into their more final and complete shape.

Before you move on to revising your paragraphs, take a break. Some breathing room will give you more objectivity when you return. After the break you will know better what to look for. Keep in mind that when you leave your drafting you are primarily a writer; when you return you are both a critical reader/editor and a refreshed writer. In the meantime, you may obtain the reactions of a colleague, a supervisor, or other members of your collaborative writing team.

When you revise your work for the order, content, and organization of your paragraphs, you will be transforming a rough draft into a work more acceptable to your audience and more appropriate for your message to them. As you work on various revisions, expect to make many changes. You might reverse paragraphs or combine them. You should expect to read your work many times to revise it effectively. One hurried reading will not give you enough time to spot the weaknesses in your paragraphs. You will want to check each paragraph during revision and then check the entire sequence of paragraphs that make up your memo, report, or letter. You should study the relationship of individual sentences to each other within a given paragraph as well as the relationship of one paragraph to another. For example, you might find yourself crowding too much information into one paragraph and then splitting that paragraph into two or even three separate ones in a later revision. Or you may do just the reverse and substantially add to a short paragraph in a later revision to answer specific questions a reader may have at this point.

The way writers revise varies. If you are preparing your work on a word processor, it will be easy to add or delete a paragraph or a sentence or move paragraphs or sentences around without having to rekey/retype the entire document. You will also be able to print different revisions of your work to test them or share them (again) with members of your collaborative writing team. Some writers print each paragraph on a separate page to work on them more easily. If you do not use a word processor, you might "cut and paste"—move paragraphs and sentences around by manually cutting them out and pasting them in more appropriate places in your work. Whether you cut and paste or use a word processor, keep in mind that revising paragraphs is like working on a canvas. You have to be able to see how things are shaping up in order to know if they will turn out the way you need them to for your audience.

Case Study: Revising One Writer's Paragraphs

A few paragraphs from the beginning of a writer's early draft appear on p. 57. The writer, an employee at Seacoast Lab, was asked by her supervisor to prepare a short report for the general public on the lab's most recent experiments. These paragraphs represented the writer's first attempt at putting her ideas into paragraphs on the topic for the audience.

As she worked on her ideas and thought about the audience's needs, the writer realized that these early paragraphs presented some problems she would have to solve at the revision stage. As she started to revise, she asked herself several questions about the content and order of her paragraphs. Answering these questions in turn led her to make a number of major changes.

The writer realized that her first paragraph lacked focus. It was not carefully organized, jumping back and forth between drag on a ship and on an airplane. Consequently, she decided to delete information about planes since Seacoast Lab

---

Early Draft

Drag is an important concept in the world of science and technology. It has many implications. Drag occurs when a ship moves through the water and eddies build up. Ships on the high seas have to fight the eddies, which results in drag. In the same way, an airplane has to fight the winds at the various altitudes at which it flies; these winds are very forceful, moving at many knots per hour. All of these forces of nature are around us. Sometimes we can feel them, too. We get tired walking against a strong wind. The eddies around a ship are the same thing. These eddies form various barriers around the ship's hull. They come from a combination of different molecules around the ship's hull and exert quite a force. Both types of molecules pull against the ship. This is where the eddies come in.

Scientists at Seacoast Lab are concerned about drag. Dr. Karen Runnels, who joined Seacoast about three years ago, is the chief investigator. She and her team of highly qualified experts have constructed some fascinating multilevel water tunnels. These tunnels should be useful to ship owners. Drag wastes a ship's fuel.

---

did not work in this area. In working on the development of this paragraph, she also decided that the information on the effect of drag on a ship was so important that it deserved a separate paragraph. So she removed the details on that topic from this long first paragraph and started to develop them separately. In the process, she discovered that her explanation of molecules, eddies, and drag was unclear and would need to be reorganized. As she continued reading on the topic, she came across an interesting analogy that would be appropriate for her audience, so she included it, proving that additional ideas can come to you even as you revise your work. Working on this explanation, she had to decide how to organize her information. After some deliberation, the topic suggested she follow the pattern "How does drag work?" So, she developed her paragraph as a cause-effect (drag is the cause, and the effect is how it works).

So much for a new second paragraph. But the writer was left with the job of finding an opening for her short report. She wanted to start with something that would both introduce the topic and encourage the audience to continue reading. Buried in the original paragraph from her last draft was an idea she found worth developing—that we cannot always see the forces of nature but we can feel them. So rather than beginning with a wooden statement about the scientific concept of drag (which she realized over several revisions did not have to be scientifically defined for the audience), she began with a readily understood example about an individual walking against the wind. Through continued revision she created two useful, carefully organized paragraphs out of one long opening paragraph. And she kept the reader's needs in mind throughout this process.

Working on her original second paragraph from her last draft, the writer realized that it said very little about the lab's experiments with drag. In fact, what she had initially written might even confuse readers about how and why the tunnels were useful. Once the writer put herself in the reader's place, however, she asked the question that helped her to develop the paragraph on "What specific things are they doing at Seacoast Lab to reduce drag?" Generating a precise starting sentence from this question made all the difference. Focusing now on the lab's "ways to reduce drag on ships," she found a restricted idea that guided her in choosing specific examples about experiments at Seacoast. Instead of leaving in interesting but unnecessary information (e.g., that Dr. Runnels has been at the lab for three years), the writer sought concrete illustrations and appropriately explained their significance to her audience. She also discovered that the last sentence in her original second paragraph did not belong in the new revised paragraph on experiments. The cost of drag was much more appropriately placed in her new opening paragraph.

The final effort of the writer's work is found below. Through revising, she transformed two poorly organized and incomplete paragraphs into the following three carefully separated yet logically connected paragraphs.

Revised Version of Draft

We cannot see or hear many of the forces around us, but we can certainly detect their presence. Walking or running into a strong wind, for example, requires a great deal of effort and often quickly leaves us feeling tired. When a ship sails through the water, it also experiences these opposing sources known as <u>drag</u>. Overcoming drag causes a ship to reduce its energy efficiency, which leads to higher fuel costs.

It is not easy for a ship to fight drag. As the ship moves through the water, it drags the water molecules around its hull at the same rate the ship is moving. Because of the cohesive force of these molecules, other water molecules immediately outside the ship's path get pulled into its way. All these molecules become tangled rather than simply sliding past each other. The result produces an eddy, or small circling burst of water around the ship's hull, that intensifies the drag. Dr. Charles Hester, a noted engineer, explains it using an analogy: "When you put a spoon in honey and pull it out, half the honey comes

out with the spoon. That's what is happening to ships.
The ship is moving and at the same time dragging the
ocean with it."

At Seacoast Lab, scientists are working to find
ways to reduce drag on ships. Dr. Karen Runnels, the
principal investigator, and a team of researchers have
constructed water tunnels to simulate the movement of
ships at sea. The drag a ship encounters is measured
from the tiny air bubbles emitted in the water tunnel.
Dr. Runnels's team has also developed the use of
polymers, or long carbon chain molecules, to reduce
drag. These polymers act like a slimy coating for the
ship's hull to help it glide through the water more
easily. When asbestos fibers were added to the polymer
solutions, the investigators measured a 90 percent
reduction in drag. The team has also experimented with
an external pump attached to the hull of the ship,
which pushes the water away from the ship's path.

Case Study: Revising Collaboratively Written Paragraphs

Figures 3.1, 3.2, and 3.3 show the evolution of a memo informing employees that
their company was beginning a recycling program. Alice Schuster, the vice-president of Fenton Industries, a large manufacturing company, asked two employees
in the personnel department—Abigail Chappel and Manuel Garcia—to prepare a
memo ("a few paragraphs" is how Schuster put it) to be sent to all Fenton employees. Schuster had an initial conference with Chappel and Garcia and stressed that
in their memo they had to convey Fenton's commitment to conservation and that,
in order to share this commitment, the employees had to practice recycling.
Chappel and Garcia thus had the job of convincing coworkers of the importance
of recycling and educating them about doing it. Chappel and Garcia also had the
difficult job of writing for two audiences simultaneously—the boss, whose name
would not appear on the memo, and the Fenton work force.

Figure 3.1 is the first draft that Chappel and Garcia cowrote and then presented to the manager of the personnel department—Wells McCraw—for his comments and suggestions for changes. As you can see from McCraw's remarks,
written in ink, he was not pleased with their first attempt and asked them to
change many things. As a careful reader (conscious of the audience for the
memo), McCraw focused on the way in which Chappel and Garcia's paragraphs
were structured. He found their paragraphs to be rambling and repetitious—the
writers were unable to stick to the point. Specifically, he found that they included
too much information in one paragraph and not enough in others. He also
directed their attention to factual mistakes, irrelevant and even contradictory comments, and material they needed to include but had not. McCraw also gave them
some advice on using helpful visual devices (see Chapter 1, pages 15-17) to make
their information more accessible to readers.

FIGURE 3.1   Early draft of the Chappel and Garcia memo.

FENTON INDUSTRIES

TO: All Employees
FROM: Abigail Chappel; Manuel Garcia
RE: Starting a Recycling Program
DATE: February 10, 1994

FI

This ¶ is too long

Too many topics — costs, protecting the environment

Keep it short — say what we are doing and why

Delete — not relevant to our purpose

An in-house study has shown that Fenton sends approximately 26,000 pounds of paper to the landfill. The landfill charge for this runs about $2,240, which we could save by recycling. Fenton Industries is conscious of our responsibility to save and protect the environment. Accordingly, starting March 1 we will begin a paper recycling program. Our program, like many others nationwide, seeks first of all to employ the latest degradable technology to safeguard the air, trees, and water in our community. It has been estimated that of the 250 million tons of solid waste, three quarters of goes to landfills. These landfills across the country are becoming dangerously overcrowded. Such a practice wastes our natural resources and endangers our air and drinking water. For example, it takes 10 trees to make one ton of paper, or roughly the amount of paper Fenton uses in four weeks. If we could recycle that amount of paper, we would save those trees. [Recycling old paper into new paper involves less energy than making paper from new trees.] Moreover, waste sent to landfills can, once broken down, leach, seep into our water supply, and contaminate it. The dangers are great.

start off with this key idea

word "it" left out

Check your facts; I think it is closer to 16 – 17

Add the fact about our saving trees in this ¶

Start ¶ with this point

By recycling, we will not be sending so much to the Springfield Landfill and so help alleviate a dangerous condition there. We will keep it from overflowing. Fenton will also be contributing to transforming waste products into valuable reusable materials. Recycling paper in our own office shows that we are concerned about the environmental clutter. By having a paper recycling program we will establish our company's reputation as an environmentally conscious industry and enhance our company's image.]

No cap

Delete — makes us look bad

¶ too short

Fenton is primarily concerned with recycling paper. The 200 old phone books that otherwise would be tossed away can get our recycling program off to a good start.

When? How? Implications for saving/ costs?

Give some examples

We encourage you to start thinking about the kinds of paper around your office / workspace that needs to be earmarked for recycling. When you start to think about it, you will see how much paper we as a company use.

FIGURE 3.1 (Continued)

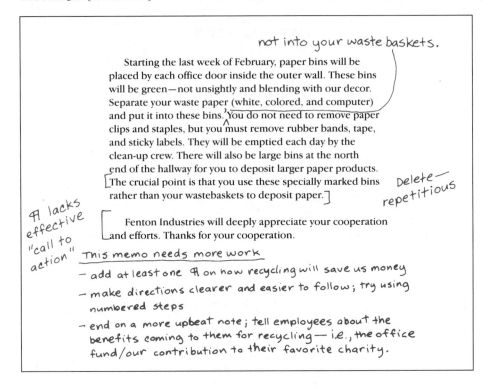

not into your waste baskets.

Starting the last week of February, paper bins will be placed by each office door inside the outer wall. These bins will be green—not unsightly and blending with our decor. Separate your waste paper (white, colored, and computer) and put it into these bins. You do not need to remove paper clips and staples, but you must remove rubber bands, tape, and sticky labels. They will be emptied each day by the clean-up crew. There will also be large bins at the north end of the hallway for you to deposit larger paper products. [The crucial point is that you use these specially marked bins rather than your wastebaskets to deposit paper.]

Delete— repetitious

Fenton Industries will deeply appreciate your cooperation and efforts. Thanks for your cooperation.

¶ lacks effective "call to action"

This memo needs more work
— add at least one ¶ on how recycling will save us money
— make directions clearer and easier to follow; try using numbered steps
— end on a more upbeat note; tell employees about the benefits coming to them for recycling — i.e., the office fund/our contribution to their favorite charity.

Figure 3.2, showing the next stage in Chappel and Garcia's work, is the revised version of the draft found in Figure 3.1. The authors incorporated McCraw's suggestions as well as some changes of their own. They did this through several revisions over a two-day period. It was this revision that they submitted to Vice-President Schuster, who also made some suggestions, as indicated by her comments on the memo. Schuster's comments—all valid—show how different readers can assist writers in meeting their objectives. Following Schuster's suggestions and continuing to revise the memo on their own, Chappel and Garcia submitted the final, revised memo found in Figure 3.3 (p. 65) to Alice Schuster a few days later. This final copy received Schuster's approval and was then sent to the Fenton staff.

FIGURE 3.2 Revision of the Chappel and Garcia memo.

FENTON INDUSTRIES

TO: All Employees
FROM: Abigail Chappel; Manuel Garcia
RE: Starting a Recycling Program
DATE: February 10, 1994

FI

To save money and protect our environment, Fenton Industries will begin a waste paper recycling program on March 1. Recycling has become an environmental necessity. It has been estimated that three quarters of the 250 million tons of solid waste dumped annually in America could be recycled. Our program will employ the latest recycling technology to safeguard trees, air, and water.

say strengthen or continue

¶ needs more information

This new program will ~~establish~~ Fenton's reputation as an environmentally conscious company. Fenton now uses one ton of paper every four weeks. This represents 17 trees that can be saved just by recycling our paper waste. Recycling also means that we will send less waste to the landfill, alleviating problems of overfill and reducing the potential for contamination of the water supply. Waste sent to large landfills can leach and seep into water systems. By recycling paper, Fenton will also reduce the risk of long-term environmental pollution.

Add that we no Longer use styrofoam and that our suppliers use only biodegrad-able products

Recycling will also save us money. Right now Fenton pays $180 per month to dump 2,000 pounds (one ton) of paper waste at the landfill. However, scrap paper is worth $100 per ton. Recycling will generate $100 each month in new revenue while eliminating the $180 dumping expense.

This sentence more logically goes in ¶ 3

Ultimately, the success of our project depends on being aware of the variety of office paper suitable for recycling. Paper products that can be recycled include newspapers, scrap paper, computer printouts, letters, envelopes (without windows), shipping cartons, old phone books, and uncoated paper cups.

Put in itemized or bulleted list to stand out better

Recycling 200 or so old phone books each year alone will save 22 cubic yards of landfill space (or close to $100) and will generate $25 in scrap paper income for our company. The old 1993 phone books, which will be replaced by new 1994 ones on March 1, will give us an excellent opportunity to start recycling.

Do not start new ¶ here; keep as part of previous ¶

Here are some easy-to-follow directions to make our recycling efforts effective:

Boldface these words

1. Starting the last week in February, <u>paper bins will be placed</u> ~~on~~ <u>inside each office door. Put all waste paper into</u> these bins, which will be emptied by maintenance.

FIGURE 3.2 (Continued)

2. Place larger paper products—such as bulky cartons or phone books—in the green bigger paper bins at the end of each main corridor.

3. Put white, colored, computer printout, and newspapers into separate marked bins. Remove all rubber bands, tape, and sticky notes.

Thanks for your cooperation. To show our appreciation for your help, 50 percent of all proceeds from the recycled paper will go into the general office fund and the other 50 percent will be given to the office's favorite charity. The benefits of our new recycling program will more than outweigh the inconvenience it may cause.

↳Add another sentence to this ¶ on how a safer environment will benefit our company and the employees, too

Thanks to their collaboration and the careful readings by McCraw and Schuster, Chappel and Garcia were able to revise their work successfully. Note how in the process of revising their work they had to make major changes in their paragraphs from an early draft through several revisions to the final copy. The types of changes Chappel and Garcia made—shortening, expanding paragraphs, adding and deleting information, and refocusing their approach to meet the needs of their audience—are the types of revisions you and/or your collaborative writing team can expect to make as well. Effective paragraph structure and organization were at the heart of Chappel and Garcia's assignment.

Four Types of Paragraphs

As we saw earlier in the Seacoast Lab report and in the memo on recycling, paragraphs are not all alike. Generally speaking, you will use four types of paragraphs: **supporting, introductory, transitional,** and **concluding**. Each differs in length, purpose, and position in your work. Each meets your readers' needs in a specific way. The following section describes each type of paragraph, explains how to write it, and provides examples.

Supporting Paragraphs

You will write more supporting paragraphs than any other type. Supporting paragraphs are the workhorses of letters and reports. They carry information that supports the purpose and message of your writing. Also called *middle* or *body paragraphs,* they appear between the introduction and conclusion of your work to provide explanations, evidence, directions, descriptions, or commentary.

A supporting paragraph expresses one central idea, with each sentence contributing to the overall meaning of that idea. The supporting paragraph does this by giving readers a *topic sentence,* which states the central idea, and *supporting information,* which explains the topic sentence.

FIGURE 3.3   Final copy of the Chappel and Garcia memo.

FENTON INDUSTRIES

TO: All Employees
FROM: Abigail Chappel; Manuel Garcia
RE: Starting a Recycling Program
DATE: February 10, 1994

To save money and protect our environment, Fenton Industries will begin a waste paper recycling program on March 1. For the program to succeed, all of us need to recycle paper. Recycling has become an environmental necessity. It has been estimated that three quarters of the 250 million tons of solid waste dumped annually in America could be recycled. Our program will employ the latest technology to safeguard trees, air, and water.

This new program will strengthen Fenton's reputation as an environmentally conscious company. Three years ago, we stopped using Styrofoam products and asked suppliers to use biodegradable materials for all our shipping containers. Fenton now uses one ton of paper every four weeks. This represents 17 trees that can be saved just by recycling our paper waste. Recycling also means that we will send less waste to the Springfield landfill, alleviating problems of overfill and reducing the potential for contamination of the water supply. Waste sent to large landfills can leach and seep into water systems.

Recycling will also save us money. Right now Fenton pays $180 per month to dump 2,000 pounds (one ton) of paper waste at the landfill. However, scrap paper is worth $100 per ton. Recycling will thereby generate $100 each month in new revenue while eliminating the $180 dumping expense. Recycling 200 or so old phone books each year will save us an additional 22 cubic yards of landfill space (or close to $100) and will generate $25 of scrap paper income for our company.

Ultimately, the success of our project depends on all of us being aware of the variety of office products suitable for recycling. Paper products that can be recycled include

- newspapers
- letters and envelopes
  (without cellophane windows)
- old phone books
- uncoated paper cups

- scrap paper
- computer printouts
- junk mail (only black print on
  white paper)
- shipping cartons

The old 1993 phone books, which will be replaced by the new 1994 ones on March 1, will give us an excellent opportunity to start recycling.

Here are some easy-to-follow directions to make our recycling efforts effective:

1. Starting the last week in February, **paper bins** will be placed **inside each office door.** Put all waste paper into these bins, which will be emptied daily by maintenance.
2. Place **larger paper products**—such as bulky cartons—in the **green** bigger paper bins at the end of each main corridor.

FIGURE 3.3 (Continued)

---

3. Put white, colored, computer printout, and newspapers into separate marked
bins. Remove all rubber bands, tape, and sticky notes.

Thanks for your cooperation. To show our appreciation for your help, 50 percent
of all proceeds from the recycled paper will go into the general office fund and the
other 50 percent will be given to the office's favorite charity. The benefits of our new
recycling program will more than outweigh the inconvenience it may cause. A safer
environment—and a more cost-effective way to run our company—benefit us all.

The topic sentence is the most important part of the paragraph for readers. It
tells readers what your paragraph is about. More specifically, a topic sentence

- helps you generate sentences that will logically follow in that paragraph.
- shows how you restricted your topic.
- summarizes the content of a paragraph.
- forecasts the kinds of information readers can expect to find in the paragraph.
- explains why you included or excluded certain details.

Your topic sentence is a pledge to readers that all the other sentences in the paragraph will support it. You will learn more about writing topic sentences on pages
69-71.

Supporting information includes data to convince readers that what you say
about the central idea is accurate and complete. These data can include a range of
information—facts about costs, dates, employees, changes in policies, summaries
of your reading, comments obtained through interviews of questionnaires—or
your interpretation of such facts.

The following is an example of a carefully constructed supporting paragraph.
It contains a clear topic sentence (highlighted in color) as well as adequate and
relevant supporting details.

> Fat is an important part of everyone's diet. It is nutritionally present in the basic
> food groups we eat—meat and poultry, dairy products, and oils—to aid growth or
> development. The fats and fatty acids present in these foods ensure proper metabo-
> lism, thus helping to turn what we eat into the energy we need. These same fats and
> fatty acids also act as carriers for important vitamins like A, D, E, and K. Another
> important role of fat is that it keeps us from feeling hungry by delaying digestion. Fat
> also enhances the flavor of the food we eat, making it more enjoyable.

This paragraph contains only one central idea—fat is an important part of everyone's diet. It does not stray from this central topic; every statement refers to the
role of fat in the diet. The topic sentence both summarizes and forecasts what
readers can expect to learn in the paragraph. The rest of the paragraph uses relevant information (fats are nutritional, ensure proper metabolism, carry vitamins,
delay digestion, flavor food) to support the topic sentence.

FIGURE 3.4   A T-shaped paragraph.

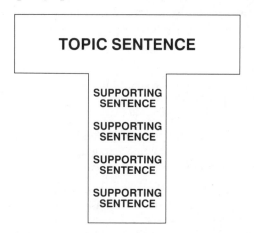

To picture the structure of a well-made supporting paragraph, visualize a capital T as in Figure 3.4. The topic sentence is like the crossbar (or top) of the capital T; the individual sentences supporting the topic sentence are like the vertical column of the T.

Note how the paragraph about fat in the diet can be visually redesigned to reveal its T-shape.

Fat is an important part of everyone's diet.

provides nutrition

ensures metabolism

carries vitamins

delays hunger

flavors food

The T-shape is just one of many structural shapes paragraphs may take. In other patterns, the topic sentence may come halfway through or at the end of the paragraph or be implied instead of stated. But in business or technical writing, it is customary and desirable to have the topic sentence come first. On pages 69–71 you will learn more about why topic sentences should be placed first.

Introductory Paragraphs

Your introductory (or opening) paragraph serves several important functions. It tells your readers what they can expect to find in your letter or report and, like a preview of coming attractions, also sets the tone for your work. Note how the writer's opening paragraph for the Seacoast Lab report (page 59) invites reader interest through a friendly, nontechnical tone and how the opening paragraph in the Chappel-Garcia memo on recycling (Figure 3.3) clearly states the importance of the topic for employees and what their employer wants them to do.

The introductory paragraph to a memo, a letter, or a short business report is generally brief (two to four sentences) and comes to the point at once. Note how the following introductory paragraph previews what the report will cover. The paragraph also makes a helpful connection for the reader by referring to her previous request.

> Our sales department has compiled the data you recently requested on third-quarter sales. The following brief report provides you with the specific information you need on (1) retail, (2) wholesale, and (3) foreign sales.

A number of introductory paragraphs might be used in a longer report. In the following example, note how the first paragraph establishes the topic and the second describes what readers can expect to learn about that topic.

> The U.S. government is the world's largest buyer of goods and services. One of the major responsibilities of the Small Business Administration (SBA) is to see that small businesses obtain a fair share of this vast government market.
> This manual explains how the government buys goods and services, how most businesses sell to the government, and how the SBA helps small business owners sell to federal purchasing agencies and their prime contractors.

Transitional Paragraphs

Transitions move the reader from one idea to another. You can provide transitions through individual words (see Table 3.1 [p. 74]) or through sentences at the beginning or end of a paragraph. Another way is to write transitional paragraphs to take readers from one section of a letter, memo, or report to another. (They are also called *linking paragraphs* because of this function.) As the following examples show, transitional paragraphs are generally very brief—one or two sentences. Note that transitional words and phrases are italicized.

> *Up to this point* we have considered the engineering advantages of the Rudex system. *Now* we will turn to the financial benefits it offers us.

> The *above process* will so saturate materials with solution that they may be too wet to use properly. *The following instructions* will show you how to dry and recomb the materials.

> The same kind of popularity generated by *the earlier subdivision* can be found at the new construction site. *Below* are some examples.

Concluding Paragraphs

Like introductory paragraphs, concluding ones can be brief—usually only a few sentences. Concluding paragraphs can perform one or all of the following three functions.

1. They can summarize the main points by recapping the key points of your message without giving any new information.

> In summary, the main features of the plan ask the city to reroute traffic on Clinton Avenue, to install a traffic signal on the corner of Adams and Fourth Streets, and to change Concord Place into a one-way thoroughfare.

2. They can draw conclusions by interpreting or emphasizing the significance of the information you have presented.

> In conclusion, then, the soundest investment opportunities for our firm lie in Continental Driftwood securities. They offer the lowest rate of capital, supply the highest interest yield, and have the most stable financial history.

3. They can make recommendations by calling for a specific action.

> After studying the responses of customers to our recent survey, I recommend that we do the following by the last week in May:
>
> - extend our store hours on Friday night from 8:00 P.M. to 9:00 P.M.
> - open on Saturday morning at 8:30 A.M. instead of 9:30 A.M.
> - close at 6:00 P.M. rather than 7:00 P.M. on Monday, Tuesday, Wednesday, and Thursday nights

Remember that you need a concluding paragraph to avoid ending a letter or report abruptly. Concluding paragraphs give readers a sense of completion, of having stopped officially and satisfyingly. You can give readers this sense of completion by using such phrases or words as *finally, in conclusion, in summary,* or *last of all* in the concluding paragraph.

Generating Topic Sentences

As we saw on pages 64–67, the topic sentence is the most important sentence in your paragraph. Carefully worded and restricted, it helps you to generate and control the kinds of information you need to include in that paragraph. An effective topic sentence also helps your readers to grasp your main idea quickly.

How can you create an effective topic sentence? As with other types of writing, you must work in stages. Usually you will start with brainstorming to collect ideas and facts; then you will draft a topic sentence to explain or summarize these details. You may have to discard some ideas or facts as you revise the topic sentence several times. In other words, you will work back and forth, adjusting the content of the paragraph, then the topic sentence, then the content again, and so on. Recall how the writer of the Seacoast Lab report (pages 59–60) generated her topic sentences over various drafts. Note, too, how Abigail Chappel and Manuel Garcia revised the topic sentences in their memo (see Figures 3.1–3.3) with each other's help as well as with the assistance of personnel manager Wells McCraw and their boss, Alice Schuster. Again, keep in mind that writing is a process. Your topic sentence, like your paper, evolves from rough early stages that only you see to a completed restricted statement. As you draft and revise, pay close attention to the following three guidelines, which will help you produce an effective topic sentence for each paragraph.

1. Make sure you provide a topic sentence. In their rush to supply readers with facts—measurements, working principles, descriptions—some writers forget to include a topic sentence to explain what all the details mean. As it stands, the following paragraph lacks a topic sentence and thus deprives readers of the writer's reason for discussing the mechanics of a wind turbine.

> Sensors found on each machine detect wind speed and direction and other important details such as ice loading and potential metal fatigue. The information is fed into a small computer (microprocessor) in the nacelle (or engine housing). The microprocessor automatically keeps the blades turned into the wind, starts and stops the machine, and changes the pitch of the tips of the blades to increase power under varying wind conditions. Should any part of the wind turbine suffer damage or malfunction, the microprocessor will immediately shut the machine down.

With the addition of a suitable topic sentence, "The MOD-2 wind turbine is designed to be operated completely by computer," readers can more clearly identify the central topic and understand what the details have in common. To make sure you include a topic sentence for every paragraph, ask yourself if the first sentence in the paragraph explains or clarifies everything else in that paragraph. If it does, chances are you have an effective topic sentence. If it doesn't, see if one of the other sentences in your paragraph can be modified (expanded or restricted) to form a topic sentence.

2. Put your topic sentence first. Place your topic sentence at the beginning—not the middle or end—of your paragraph. Because the beginning sentence occupies an emphatic place, readers are sure to give it their attention. In some business and technical writing, the topic sentence at the beginning of each paragraph is even underscored or boldfaced to help busy readers grasp main points quickly. By seeing that main point up front, readers are not kept in doubt or suspense. Burying the key idea in the middle or near the end of the paragraph makes it harder for readers to act on your information, as illustrated by the following poorly written paragraph.

> In the last two years the cost of insurance on the trucks has increased almost 17 percent. We are now paying $2,300 to the Rawlins Agency whereas in March of 1994 we had a bill of $1,935. Although it will be impossible to predict the price of gasoline for even one season, let alone a single year, certainly it will go up, too. Also, we have been receiving many orders from customers who live outside a 40-mile radius of Bloomington, which makes our policy of providing free delivery even more costly. Whenever one of the delivery trucks is in the shop for repair, we can expect a bill of at least $150, if this year's rates continue. Another major expense is the cost of drivers' overtime. Two of them have logged more than 35 hours of overtime in the last month, amounting to $750.

Eager to assemble all the facts about the firm's delivery trucks, the writer did not consider the reader's need to have the reason for these facts in the first sentence of the paragraph. The writer's main reason for compiling the facts is buried in the fourth sentence of the paragraph—the company's present policy of supplying free delivery to customers is costly and should be changed. If the writer had begun with that fact, the reader would then have been better prepared to follow and interpret the figures about the costs of operating the trucks.

3. Make sure your topic sentence is restricted. If restricted, a topic sentence identifies only one central idea. A broad or unrestricted topic sentence does not zero in on a single idea. Instead, it encourages the writer to stray from one central topic into the territory of numerous other topics. The result is a paragraph that lacks direction and focus. Here are two examples of overly broad topic sentences.

1. Computers have changed the ways we do business.
2. Working conditions are important.

Either of these two sentences, if used as a topic sentence, would fail to give readers a clear understanding of the central idea the paragraph will develop. In the first sentence the writer goes astray by using the vague word *ways,* which can apply to almost any computer application in business—producing copy, making graphics, scanning records, storing information. After several revisions, the writer discovered a topic sentence that focused on a more precise use of the computer in a particular business context.

The new Aldridge 200 has improved our efficiency in billing customers.

As a topic sentence, sentence 2 above is even more misleading than the first. The phrase "working conditions" suggests many different topics (legal, physical, social, psychological, and environmental conditions) and does not specify for whom or why such conditions are important. An appropriate revision might read as follows:

The increase in rate of overtime pay will boost our employees' morale.

A broad topic sentence leads to a shaky, incomplete paragraph for two reasons. On the one hand, the paragraph will not contain enough information to support the topic sentence. On the other hand, a broad topic sentence will not be able to summarize or forecast accurately the information available in the paragraph.

It is important to remember that broad topic sentences are part of the process of writing a restricted topic sentence. The first time you write a topic sentence, it is likely to be too broad. A broad topic sentence is one starting point for a restricted topic sentence. The next step is to revise, rework, and rephrase the sentence until it is restricted. If you have a restricted topic sentence, your paragraph will be far less likely to contain irrelevant or unnecessary information.

Three Characteristics of An Effective Paragraph

Effective paragraphs have **unity, coherence,** and **completeness**. In the following section, each of these characteristics is described, together with techniques you can follow to achieve these characteristics in your paragraphs.

Unity

A unified paragraph sticks to one topic without wandering from it. Every sentence and every detail in the paragraph supports, explains, or proves the central idea stated in the topic sentence. A unified paragraph includes only relevant information and excludes unnecessary or irrelevant comments. However, a unified paragraph offers readers more than just pertinent details. It assures them that the appropriate information they need is included in that paragraph and not lodged elsewhere. For example, in a progress report a paragraph on the work you have already completed should not include details about work you hope to accomplish during the next report period. These are two separate topics and hence deserve separate paragraphs.

Let's say you are writing a report for an insurance company about the increasing popularity of recreational vehicles (RVs). You might include sections (and paragraphs) about the variety of RVs, their costs, the training and licensing of dealers, and the amount of taxes RV owners pay. You might want to include a section on the convenience and advantages of RVs to show why they are popular. In fact, one of your supporting paragraphs in such a section might have the following topic sentence: RVs offer owners the comforts of a home on wheels. Which of the following points from a writer's brainstormed list would support that central idea?

---

1. RVs can come equipped with showers.
2. Ad valorem taxes on RVs have increased 13 percent in the last three years.
3. Some RVs come equipped with microwave ovens.
4. RVs get fairly decent mileage on the highway—around 16 miles per gallon.
5. Dealers can customize any van to suit an owner's taste.
6. The number of RV dealerships in the state has doubled over the last six years.
7. RVs often have large swivel chairs—captain's chairs—comparable to recliners.
8. Financing is an important part of the dealer's job.
9. RVs carry their own air-conditioning units equipped with thermostat control for steady-state cooling.
10. Some RVs offer built-in desks.
11. RVs come in many forms—vans, motor homes, trailers, slide-in pickup trucks.
12. RVs can be small and compact (sometimes even crowded) or large and spacious.

Only points 1, 3, 7, 9, and 10 would be relevant for a paragraph whose central idea was on the comforts of home that RVs offered buyers. The writer would be able to discover this by having a clear idea of the topic and by evaluating all of the brainstormed points in light of the topic. The advice is clear—the more control you have over your topic, the easier it will be to decide what is appropriate to develop it.

The other points in the list would destroy the unity of that paragraph because they are not directly related to the topic sentence. Point 2 raises a comparison between homes and RVs—they both require the owner to pay taxes—but information on a tax increase would hardly support the idea of home comfort in an RV. Point 4 expresses an advantage of owning an RV but not a relevant one. A house does not travel by gasoline. Points 5, 6, and 8 would belong in a paragraph on RV dealers. Point 5 appears to be relevant, but note that the emphasis in it is on the dealer's ability, not the RV's comparison with a home. Point 11 belongs in a separate paragraph because it does not support the topic. And as it is currently worded, point 12 contradicts the idea expressed in the topic sentence. The writer needs to stress the comforts an RV offers; saying that some RVs are crowded does not support that idea.

Coherence

A paragraph is coherent when all its sentences flow smoothly and logically to and from each other. Sentences in a paragraph need to serve as the links of a chain. By showing the connections, you will help readers understand the precise relationship a sentence has with the one preceding it. By making clear the relationships that exist between sentences, you help to make clear the relationship that exists between your ideas.

Four Ways to Achieve Coherence

You can clarify relationships between your sentences (and paragraphs) by using transitional words and phrases, by repeating key words and ideas, by using pronouns and demonstrative adjectives, and by using parallel grammatical structures.

1. Use transitional words and phrases. One of the easiest ways to achieve coherence in a paragraph is to use transitional words and short phrases like those included in Table 3.1 (p. 74). They are also called *connective words* to emphasize their function of joining or connecting ideas together. Note how these words are arranged according to the types of relationships they signal to readers. For example, when readers see words like *also, furthermore, in addition,* the message the writer conveys is, "Go ahead; you are on the right track." Words used to contrast ideas—*however, on the other hand, in contrast*—prepare readers for this message: "Go in the opposite direction from the one you have been following." And transitional words and phrases signaling that your work is coming to an end—*finally, in short, to summarize*—tell readers "Prepare to stop; here comes a wrap-up." Be careful how you use these transitional devices. They should be logical and natural.

A paragraph without such transitional words and phrases lacks coherence, as the following example demonstrates.

> Advertising a product on the radio has some advantages over using television. Radio rates are much cheaper. A one-time 60-second spot on television can cost $750. Advertisers can purchase nine 30-second spots on the radio. The production costs are low on radio. Advertisers can pay extra for models and voice-overs. Radio offers advertisers immediate scheduling. Ads appear the same week a contract is signed. Television

TABLE 3.1   Transitional, or Connective, Words and Phrases

Addition	also	first, second, third	next
	and	in addition	too
	besides	many	what's more
	furthermore	moreover	
Cause/Effect	and so	consequently	on account of
	accordingly	due to	since
	as a result	hence	therefore
	because of	if	thus
Comparison/ Contrast	but	in contrast	on the other hand
	conversely	in the same way	similarly
	equally	likewise	still
	however	on the contrary	yet
Condition	although	of course	
	even though	provided that	
	granted that	to be sure	
	if	unless	
Conclusion	at last	in short	
	finally	in summary	
	in conclusion	on the whole	
	to conclude	to put into perspective	
Emphasis	above all	indeed	to repeat
	after all	in fact	unquestionably
	again	in other words	
	as a matter of fact	of course	
	as I said	obviously	
	for emphasis	surely	
Illustration	for example	in particular	
	for instance	specifically	
	in effect	that is	
	in other words	to illustrate	
Place	across from	here	where
	alongside of	in front of	wherever
	at this point	next to	
	behind	there	
	below		
Time	afterwards	earlier	presently
	at length	later	soon
	at the same time	meanwhile	then
	at times	next	until
	beforehand	now	when
	currently	once	while
	during		

stations are booked up months in advance. Radio gives advertisers a greater opportunity to reach potential buyers. Radio follows listeners everywhere—in their homes, at work, and in their cars. Television is popular. Television cannot do that.

Readers will find this paragraph hard to follow because the writer did not point out relationships (especially contrasts) between advertising on radio and advertising on television. To remedy the problem, effective transitional words and phrases must be added. Note how smoothly and logically the revised version reads, thanks to such transitions (in italics).

> Advertising a product on the radio has many advantages over using television. *For one thing,* radio rates are much cheaper. *For example,* a one-time 60-second spot on local T.V. can cost $750. *For that money,* advertisers can purchase nine 30-second spots on radio. *Equally attractive* are the low production costs for radio advertising. *In contrast,* television advertising often includes extra costs for models and voice-overs. *Another* advantage radio offers advertisers is immediate scheduling. *Often* the ad appears during the same week a contract is signed. *On the other hand,* television stations are *frequently* booked up months in advance, so it may be a long time *before* an ad appears. *Furthermore,* radio gives advertisers a greater opportunity to reach their potential buyers. *After all,* radio follows listeners everywhere—in their homes, at work, and in their cars. *Although* it is very popular, television cannot do that.

2. Repeat key words or ideas. Restating key words or ideas in a paragraph provides continuity for readers by keeping important ideas constantly before them. Key words link different parts of the paragraph for readers and show how the paragraph is put together. The following paragraph effectively repeats the key words *fringe benefits* or *benefits* for readers.

> *Fringe benefits* are an important part of recruiting and retaining qualified employees. In a highly competitive job market, such *benefits* rather than salary may determine if a talented professional accepts or declines a job. Traditionally, *fringe benefits* were limited to basic hospital and surgical insurance and to pension plans. But today they also extend to dental and optical riders on company insurance policies. Other more lucrative *fringe benefits* include the financial rewards companies offer loyal employees—for example, profit-sharing options to buy stock at reduced rates and generous bonuses for diligent sales activities.

Notice how the writer's lively use of transitional words (*also, but, for example*) prevents the four references to *fringe benefits* from becoming dull or redundant. The reader is made aware of the controlling sense of fringe benefits in the paragraph without being overwhelmed by the repetition of the phrase.

3. Use pronouns and demonstrative adjectives. The use of personal pronouns (*he, she, him, her, they,* and so on) also contributes to the coherence of a paragraph. When readers connect the pronoun with its antecedent (the noun to which it refers), they tie sentences and ideas together. Demonstrative adjectives (*this, that, these, those*) also help readers to link related pieces of information. As their name implies, these adjectives emphasize and distinguish specific objects or features for readers. In the paragraph that follows, the connections that pronouns and demonstrative adjectives make between sentences are graphically emphasized through boxes and lines.

Traffic studies are an important tool for store owners looking for a new location. These studies are relatively inexpensive and highly accurate. They can tell owners how much traffic passes by a particular location at a particular time and why. Moreover, they can help owners to determine what particular characteristics these individuals have in common. Because of their helpfulness, these studies can save owners time and money and possibly prevent financial ruin. They should be done before any contemplated move.

4. Use parallel grammatical structures. Writers can provide a great deal of coherence by using parallel grammatical structures. When readers see how ideas are related grammatically, they can more easily see how they are related logically. (See pages 103–104 for a discussion of parallel grammatical structures.) Note the use of parallelism in the following paragraph.

> Orientation sessions accomplish four useful goals for trainees. First, they introduce trainees to key personnel in accounting, data processing, maintenance, and security. Second, they give trainees experience logging into the data base system, selecting an appropriate menu, editing core documents, and getting off the system. Third, they explain to trainees the company policies affecting the way supplies are ordered, used, and stored. Fourth, they help trainees understand their responsibilities in such sensitive areas as computer security and use.

In this paragraph parallelism is at work on a number of levels. The four sentences about the four goals start in the same way grammatically (". . . they introduce/give/explain/help trainees . . .") to help readers categorize the information. Within individual sentences, the repetition of *present participles* (logg*ing*, select*ing*, edit*ing*, gett*ing*) and of *past participles* (order*ed*, us*ed*, stor*ed*) helps the writer to summarize information and to see the related nature of the activities being explained. Note that the transitional words *first, second, third, fourth* convey a sense of parallelism as well as of sequence.

Completeness

Completeness means that your paragraph provides a well-developed and satisfying information block for your reader. In a complete paragraph you provide readers with a restricted topic sentence and sufficient information to clarify, analyze, support, defend, or prove the central idea expressed in your topic sentence.

A complete, carefully developed paragraph is an information block—containing the following types of supporting information for readers:

- names of specific individuals
- dates and times
- examples of a term, plan, situation
- measurements—size, shape, designs, temperatures, and so on

- costs and other figures
- descriptions
- statistical details
- reasons or explanations
- quotations from interviews or questionnaires

You gather these facts from your research and through your prewriting strategies, such as brainstorming and outlining (see pages 31-33).

Individually, these facts might not mean much to readers. But when linked in your paragraph, they provide the support readers need. Readers need these specific supporting details to understand a concept, perform a task, or evaluate a plan you are proposing. Without such supporting details, your paragraph will be underdeveloped, undernourished, incomplete.

One sure sign of an incomplete paragraph is that it leaves readers with questions, not answers. "Have I missed something?" "Is that the whole story?" "How did the writer arrive at that conclusion?" "Why is X better than Y?" "What proof has the writer given to make me accept his or her point of view?" For instance, the following skimpy paragraph is incomplete because it lacks the specific details necessary to explain and prove the assertion made in the topic sentence.

> Farmers can turn their crops and farm wastes into useful, cost-effective fuels. Much grown on the farm can be converted to energy. This energy can have many uses and save farmers a lot of money in operating expenses.

The writer did not consider the readers' needs. Farmers would expect to find examples of energy-rich fuels and specific farm uses of these fuels. Instead the farmer is left with the following questions: "What specific materials lend themselves to energy use?" "How can crops and farm wastes be turned into energy?" "What are some specific uses of this new energy?"

In the revised version that follows, the writer answers these questions through specific examples and explanations.

> Farm crops and wastes can be turned into fuels to save farmers money on their operating costs. Alcohol can be distilled from grain, sugar beets, potatoes—even from blighted crops. Converted to gasohol (90 percent gasoline, 10 percent alcohol), this fuel can be used to run such farm equipment as irrigation pumps, feed grinders, and tractors. Similarly, through a biomass digestion system, farmers can produce methane from animal or crop wastes. This methane can be an important source of the natural gas used for heating and cooking. Finally, cellulose pellets, derived from plant materials, are an important solid fuel that can save farmers money in heating barns.

How will you know if your paragraph is complete? Chances are that a series of skimpy shoestring paragraphs lack necessary supporting data. Some word processing packages will count the words in each of your paragraphs. Such tabulating can be most helpful. A short paragraph (20-30 words) might signal underdevelopment; a long paragraph (200 words) could indicate that you have packed two paragraphs into one or that your topic needs to be restricted more. But measuring length alone is not the only way to determine if a paragraph is developed sufficiently. Even a paragraph of four or five sentences can be incomplete if it contains a series of generalities and does not provide factual details. A paragraph is complete when it leaves no confusion in the reader's mind about what you intended, how the reader is supposed to respond, and why such a response is both necessary and appropriate.

The Appearance of Paragraphs

Readers appreciate well-designed paragraphs and will respond more favorably to you and your message if you construct them carefully. You should have a clear idea of what your paragraphs will look like near the end of the revision stage of your work. The appearance of your paragraphs is especially important in the business world, where an excessively long paragraph is as unappreciated as a series of skimpy ones. Your paragraphs should look professional and inviting. With the help of a word processor you can quickly change the size and shape of your paragraphs. But more than format changes are required to write appropriately constructed paragraphs. The following guidelines on the appearance of your paragraphs and the writing skills involved will help you to write readable and complete paragraphs.

1. Avoid excessively long paragraphs. Long paragraphs, especially long opening paragraphs, turn readers off. A full-page paragraph jammed with information is not user friendly and will cause readers to conclude that your work is too technical and that it will require a lot of hard work to get through. Long paragraphs tend to repeat the same idea (although in slightly different words) or to include information that belongs in another paragraph. Another cause of excessively long paragraphs may be overly broad topic sentences. By narrowing your topic sentence, you will shorten and tighten the paragraph.

Perhaps an excessively long paragraph signals that you have two or even three other paragraphs packed into one oversize block, as the writer for Seacoast Lab discovered (pages 59–60). Similarly, Abigail Chappel and Manuel Garcia had to revise an excessively long opening paragraph in Figure 3.1 to make it tighter and more unified for their message to Fenton employees. When you suspect this, mark off parts of the long paragraph into smaller sized sections and see if each of these can be separately developed.

Keep in mind that a paragraph is the right length and size when it contains only the details readers need to understand the main point of the paragraph. Anything that does not directly support the topic sentence would make the paragraph too long.

2. Avoid stringing together a series of short paragraphs. An entire letter or report made up of one- and two-line paragraphs does not make the reader's job easier. On the contrary, making each sentence or two into a new paragraph may frustrate your reader. Such shoestring paragraphs suggest that your subject is trivial or that you could not find enough information about it. If your paragraphs are too short because of lack of supporting details, include additional relevant facts for readers (see the earlier section on paragraph completeness, pages 76–78). A string of short paragraphs may also tell you that you have chopped a complete paragraph into unnecessary smaller ones. Try to find a topic sentence in your

FIGURE 3.5   Use of visual clues to show emphasis and organization.

Audio Interference and Remedies

INTERFERENCE TO AUDIO DEVICES (TELEPHONE, STEREOS, AM/FM RADIOS)

Telephones, electronic organs, stereo/hi-fi equipment, or AM/FM radios can be susceptible to interference. The source of interference will determine the effect on your audio device. For instance, if the equipment is picking up a nearby radio transmitter, you may hear the voice of the operator. When electrical interference is present, you may hear a sizzling or popping sound.

If you are receiving interference from a nearby radio transmitter, you should contact the operator and provide the Radio Operator Guidelines section of this handbook.

1. Generally, internal modification of your equipment must be made to eliminate the interference.
2. For **safety** reasons, it is recommended that any modification be made by a qualified service representative. The service representative should make the modifications in the home while the interference is occurring, in order to locate the point at which the interfering signal is entering the equipment.

Telephone Interference

Transmissions from a nearby radio transmitter can be picked up by your telephone system. The interference could enter the system at the following points:

1. drop wire leading to the house
2. telephone wiring inside the house
3. in the telephone instrument itself

Customer Owned Telephones

If you own your telephone and interference is occurring, the dealer or manufacturer should be contacted to assist you with modifications that will eliminate the interference.

Note: All telephone equipment must meet FCC registration standards and any internal filtering or modifications must be made by the manufacturer of the equipment or by other companies authorized by the FCC to do so.

Some states permit a telephone company to charge customers for service visits when they determine that the equipment is customer-owned.

Federal Communications Commission, *How to Identify and Resolve TV Interference Problems.* 2nd ed. Washington, D.C.: U.S. Government Printing Office, 1982.

short paragraphs to see whether they might be combined into one paragraph under that central idea.

3. Use visual clues to show emphasis and organization. Headings make organization visible and prepare readers for the information found in a group of related paragraphs. Headings also emphasize the major ideas of a memo or report. Within paragraphs, use italics, boldface type, bullets, and numbering to emphasize points as well as to break them down into smaller, easier-to-understand units. Figures 3.3 and 3.5 show examples of these visual clues.

However, a short paragraph does not always signal that your idea is underdeveloped. Not every paragraph you write must be a traditional, supporting paragraph containing five to six sentences. A great deal of business writing uses short paragraphs for variety and for the readers' needs. As we saw, special function paragraphs—such as introductory, transitional, and concluding paragraphs—are short and to the point. A short concluding paragraph summarizing the main point of a memo or report is all that busy readers want in the world of work. Furthermore, longer, supporting paragraphs sometimes are inappropriate in business correspondence. For example, a sales letter can use fully developed but shorter paragraphs to make a point or to establish an ongoing pattern where longer paragraphs would be inappropriate for the audience's needs. See, for example, the sales letter in Figure 7.10 (page 204). You might also review the draft and revision of Abigail Chappel and Manuel Garcia's memo on recycling (Figures 3.1 and 3.2) to see how they shortened some of their paragraphs.

4. Make your paragraphs visually attractive. Readability is enhanced when you use relatively compact segments of prose with plenty of white space surrounding them. Paragraphs of 6 to 8 lines, with 40 to 60 spaces per line, are easiest to read. White space on the page makes readers feel comfortable and shows that you have not crowded ideas together. Thanks to word processors, you may be able to experiment with the most pleasing format for your readers. More specific guidelines on spacing will be found in Chapter 6 (pages 149–161).

If possible, you might also try varying the length of your paragraphs to create a pleasant visual effect. As mentioned earlier, a series of long paragraphs is hard for readers to digest, while a string of short, skimpy paragraphs can be annoying and jarring. When you use a combination of long and short paragraphs, you stand a better chance of holding the reader's interest. Generally, your first and last paragraphs will be shorter than your supporting paragraphs.

Patterns of Paragraph Organization

As you have seen, information in a paragraph should be unified, coherent, and complete. That information must also be presented in a logical and orderly sequence. Without organization each paragraph would be simply a list of unrelated ideas, which would not explain how the ideas are related. To explain the relationship of the ideas within a paragraph, you will have to choose an appropriate pattern of organization. The ones you select will depend on three things about the writing assignment: (1) the nature of your message, that is, the topic you are writing about, (2) the purpose of your work, and (3) the needs of your audience. In a short letter or memo, you may be able to develop your ideas using only one or two patterns for all the paragraphs. However, in a longer report you may use many patterns, and you may also combine patterns.

In the following pages, examine how paragraphs can be organized by means of these commonly used patterns: examples, description, time, space, comparison and contrast, definition, classification, and cause and effect.

Examples Pattern

To use the examples pattern, begin your paragraph with your restricted topic sentence and then offer examples proving or explaining that statement. (You may find it easier to generate your topic sentence *after* you think of a list of examples.) In the following paragraph, the author wants to prove that owning and operating an automobile is an escalating expense. To do that, the author found examples of the costs a driver will encounter over the life of the car.

> The cost of owning and operating a motor vehicle is of major significance as Americans experience increasing demands on their incomes. It costs more than $14,300 to purchase a car. If the car is driven 120,000 miles over a period of 12 years, the total cost to the owner will be $35,853 as the following expenses show. During the 12 years it will cost about $8,604 (excluding taxes) for some 7,059 gallons of gasoline. To maintain and repair the car, the owner can expect to pay another $6,232. Insurance will run about $3,991. Expenses for parking and tolls will be about $939. And, finally, the driver can expect to pay $1,787 in taxes.[1]

Description Pattern

Use the description pattern to explain what something—a tool, a site, any object—looks like. Start your paragraph with a topic sentence that identifies what you will describe. Then provide a part-by-part practical description giving readers precise details about size, shape, color, function, or other relevant information. Your description may also emphasize any special features. The following paragraph describes the appearance and function of a golf ball.

> A golf ball has three interrelated parts that make it function effectively—the center, the threads, and the cover. The center of the golf ball, a liquid of clay, glycerine, and water, gives the ball its bounce. This small but compact center is like a ball within a ball. Wound around the center of the golf ball are hundreds of tiny rubber threads. When the ball is hit by a golf club these threads at first contract and then expand to give the ball its velocity. The cover, two hemispherical shells made of thermoplastic, contains indentations, or dimples, that affect the way the ball spins in flight. Without them, the ball would not travel as far or as fast.

Time Pattern

A paragraph organized by a temporal pattern discusses events in the order in which they occurred. This pattern is very versatile. You might use a chronological sequence to summarize events for a progress report or to analyze how a certain problem developed. For instance, you might use this pattern to outline the steps in a physical process such as continental drift or radiation. Or you might employ the temporal pattern to give instructions on how to do something. Note how the following paragraph arranges information about women's participation in the U.S. labor force chronologically.

> Over the last 50 years, the number of women in the U.S. labor force has steadily increased. In fact, since the end of World War II, women have accounted for about 60 percent of the net growth of the American labor force. According to the Bureau of

---

[1] U.S. Department of Transportation, *Cost of Owning and Operating Automobiles and Vans.*

Labor Statistics, in 1950 slightly less than 34 percent of all American women were employed outside the home. By 1960 that number was 38 percent. In 1970 the percentage of women in the labor market had increased to 43.4 percent. And by 1980 one woman out of two, or 51.6 percent, was a member of the U.S. labor force. It is estimated that by the year 2000 as many as 80 percent of all American women will be employed in business and industry.

A chronological pattern is also essential when readers have to follow instructions in a strict order. To point out that sequence, label each step.

> To clean a storage tank, follow these steps exactly. First, ventilate the tank to release noxious fumes. Second, wash out the tank with water to dispel flammable vapors and to further reduce the chances of an explosion. Third, remove any sludge or deposits with Anixyl 345 or Metathine 45XT. Finally, allow the tank to air for at least 36 hours.

Space Pattern

A paragraph with a spatial pattern of development arranges information according to a particular view of an object or its location. Consider the many perspectives or views possible—from top to bottom, from bottom to top, from inside to outside, from outside to inside, from front to back, from back to front, from left to right, or from right to left. Choose a view that is most appropriate for your topic and your reader. In the paragraph below, the writer arranges the types of protective clothing worn by industrial workers from helmets to shoes, or from top to bottom. This head-to-toe order helps readers follow the information in a familiar sequence; the writer does not jump from goggles to overalls to helmets.

> Protective clothing is available for every part of the industrial worker's body. Hard hats protect the worker's head from the impact of falling objects when the individual is handling stock. Caps and hair nets keep the worker's hair from catching in machinery. Face shields, safety goggles, glasses, and similar kinds of clothing guard the worker's eyes from splashing chemicals or flying debris. Protective vests, jackets, aprons, and overalls shield the worker's body from cuts or bruises from heavy or rough-edged stock. The worker's hands are protected from the same kinds of injuries with special gloves. Finally, safety shoes and boots shield the worker's feet from being injured by falling stock.[2]

Comparison/Contrast Pattern

This pattern for organizing the ideas can show readers the similarities (comparisons) and the differences (contrasts) between objects, plans, locations, or the like. In a single paragraph you show either similarities or differences or both. You can also use this pattern to explain an unfamiliar concept or object by comparing it to one known to readers. When you use this pattern, always identify in the topic sentence the points or objects you are comparing or contrasting. The following paragraph both compares and contrasts two types of home mortgages.

> Before making a loan application, prospective home buyers need to know the two most popular types of mortgage: the conventional mortgage and the adjustable-rate mortgage (ARM). The conventional mortgage gives buyers a fixed rate of interest over the life of the loan, for example, $8\frac{1}{2}$ percent for 30 years. The ARM, however, has inter-

---

[2]U.S. Department of Labor, *Concepts and Techniques of Machine Safeguarding.*

est rates that vary as the rate of interest paid on Treasury Bills varies. For example, an ARM may begin at $7\frac{1}{2}$ percent but in a year or two either escalate or decrease by 2 percent or more. With a conventional loan, monthly mortgage payments are fixed. With an ARM, on the other hand, they can change each year, depending on the financial market. A conventional loan may be more expensive for home buyers to obtain than would be an ARM. Lending institutions generally demand higher discount points (costs to rent the money) for fixed-rate mortgages than for ARMs. Therefore, home buyers will have to decide between the stable but initially higher rate of a conventional mortgage and the fluctuating, initially lower rate of an ARM.

Or you can use a separate paragraph for each subject of the comparison and contrast.

> The traditional office exists in a one-to-one environment: each manager has a secretary. Each secretary has nonspecialized functions—typing, filing, copying, scheduling, answering telephones, and doing correspondence with an electric typewriter and a copier, resulting in much retyping and duplication of effort. The manager waits for the secretary, and the secretary waits for the manager. The situation always generates more paperwork. The traditional solution is to hire more people, use more overtime, or miss more deadlines.
>
> The automated office, however, is no longer a one-to-one arrangement. One secretary supports several managers and oversees several people, each with a different specific function. Managers use automation (telephone, dictation equipment) to create or implement ideas. The secretary, using automated equipment such as word processors or voice mail, distributes information largely through electronic means (terminals). In this contemporary office, the skills of existing personnel, particularly those performing secretarial functions, are used most effectively.[3]

Definition Pattern

When you use the definition pattern, you organize your paragraph around what a term or concept means. Definition is especially useful in on-the-job writing because of the many technical words you may have to explain to customers or to professionals outside your field. Some of the elements that may appear in a definition paragraph, depending on the situation, include: (a) what the term means; (b) where and when the term originated; (c) what its applications or characteristics are; and (d) what examples or illustrations of the term will help readers to understand it. Note how the following paragraph on flex time uses many of these techniques.

> Flex time refers to a policy of replacing the traditional fixed work hours with a more flexible schedule set by employees within certain prescribed limits. These limits typically include a *core time* and *flexible time*. During core time, such as 9:30 A.M. to 3:00 P.M., all employees are required to be at work. Flexible time is a period before or after core time when employees can exercise their option to start or leave work. Flexible time is usually between 7:00 A.M. and 9:30 A.M., and 3:00 P.M. and 6:00 P.M.[4]

Classification Pattern

To classify is to sort *related* objects (types of wrenches or types of microcomputers) into mutually exclusive groups according to a consistent principle. In

---

[3] Adapted from *USAF Medical Service Digest* Nov.–Dec. 1982: 15–16.
[4] *Supervisory Management* Feb. 1984: 38.

libraries, the Dewey decimal system classifies all books into one of ten large branches of knowledge. The same objects can usually be classified according to several different principles as long as the classification is done systematically and logically. For example, items on a shopping list can be arranged in one of several ways; in one classification, you may list items according to how essential they are to you: essential—items that are needed immediately (milk, bread); less essential—items needed at some time in the future (more soap, more dog food); and luxuries—items you can live without (snack foods, extra cookies). Or using a different classification, you may list items on your shopping list according to how many calories they contain: high calorie (chocolates), medium calorie (bread, milk), and low calorie (lettuce). Or yet another shopper may classify items according to their location in the supermarket in order to avoid retracing steps.

For on-the-job writing, the classification pattern is especially helpful when you have to identify or evaluate different products, sites, or plans for an employer. The following paragraph classifies for a store manager different types of burglar alarms.

> An appropriate burglar alarm system can help protect the merchant. Basically, the merchant can choose from two type of alarms. The central alarm alerts a security or police agency but does not warn the burglar. The local alarm, usually a siren or bell, goes off at the site of the break-in. Whether the alarm is central or local, the merchant has a wide choice of alarm-sensing devices. Among them are radar motion detectors, invisible photo beams, detectors that work on ultrasonic sound, and vibration detectors. Also, there is supplemental equipment such as an automatic phone dialer. This device phones the police and the store owner to give them verbal warning when an alarm is breached.[5]

Cause-to-Effect Pattern

In a cause-to-effect pattern, the paragraph starts with why something occurred (the cause) and then tells readers what resulted (the effect). This pattern is useful as the structure for a letter of complaint, an investigative report, or a proposal. In writing a proposal you try to convince readers that if your plan (the cause) is adopted, certain good things will follow (the effects). With this pattern you can describe any problem or decision and then trace its effects. In the following paragraph the writer begins with the causes of the employees' problems (the improperly positioned video display terminals, or VDTs) and then lists some of the effects of that action (glare, backache, decreased productivity).

> When new VDTs were put in a month ago, they were installed incorrectly. They were placed too low, at the wrong angle, and in the wrong lighting conditions. As a result, our employees have experienced a number of problems. They have complained of an annoying glare from the reflection of room lighting on the screen. In addition to experiencing eyestrain, employees have had low backaches because they have to slump in their chairs to focus on the screens, which were not tilted up and not placed high enough on the desks. Consequently, our employees' efficiency dropped 15–20 percent during the last month.

---

[5] Small Business Administration, "Preventing Burglary and Robbery Loss."

Effect-to-Cause Pattern

To use an effect-to-cause pattern, begin the paragraph with the effect—the result or outcome of something—and then identify its causes. This pattern is especially useful when substantiating why something happened. Make sure that you document the relationship between effects and their causes with specific, relevant information. In the following paragraph, the writer links increased tourism (the effect) to its multiple causes.

> Over the last eighteen months tourism has continued to increase in Hillview. A major reason for this increase is the opening of the Rocky Mountain Theme Park. Attendance at this park has grown each year since its opening in 1988. The completion of the Dodge County Metro Center in March of last year also contributed to increased tourism. Residents from nearby states frequently attend rock concerts at the center and often spend an extra day or two in Hillview to shop or to sightsee. Three new hotels have also increased tourism. In the past year five conventions were held in Hillview, two more than last year.

Combination of Patterns

Not all paragraphs will follow one pattern consistently, from beginning to end. Depending on your topic and how you organize it for your readers, an individual paragraph can use more than one pattern. For example, a pamphlet prepared by the American Dental Association on the warning signs of gum disease includes the following paragraph that uses definition and cause-to-effect patterns.

> Gum disease, simply put, is an infection of the gums. It is caused by plaque, a sticky, colorless film of bacteria that constantly forms on the teeth. These bacteria create toxins that irritate the gums, causing them to become inflamed and to bleed easily. Over a period of time, if the irritation persists, the gums pull away from the teeth, forming pockets. Plaque then forms in these pockets. Eventually the infection starts destroying the gum tissue and the underlying bone. The teeth may then become loose and fall out or need to be removed.

Here is a paragraph from a site inspection report (see pages 604–610) that uses description plus comparison and contrast to help readers better understand the relative conditions at two underground storage tank sites.

> We inspected the tanks at Madisonville and Lacombia for suspected leakage and found that both were defective but for different reasons. The petroleum tank located at Madisonville is in an area that has seen less company activity over the last few years. It is an old-fashioned steel tank that has no protective coating. The tank clearly showed signs of seepage in the northeast corner judging by the contamination of the soil around this area. Moisture around the tank has corroded the steel casing. The tank at Lacombia, however, is in an active area. It is a relatively new tank—2 years old—that has a protective coating. While we detected no problems from spills or overfills, there was leakage at the pipe joints because they were not fastened securely. We recommend that the Madisonville tank be retired, but with further repair and maintenance the Lacombia tank can be available again.

The following paragraph combines definition with classification to give readers information about the dangers of a computer virus.

> Like the biological virus for which it was named, a computer virus is a destructive program that invades the host computer, blocking its codes or sending destructive commands. The computer virus, like a virus in the human body, then

reproduces itself on any disk used in the infected computer. Because computers are interconnected across the country, a virus can spread over telephone lines, too. There are three ways in which a virus can appear. Least destructive, it can simply spell out an unexpected but unwelcome message—such as "Merry Christmas"—on the user's screen. Much more dangerous, a virus can destroy data by erasing files or writing over them on hard and floppy disks alike. The virus can wipe out years of research as well as the file necessary to operate the computer. A third way the virus can work is to fill a computer's memory with excessive information, or traffic, blocking out the computer's ability to run. This most pernicious virus infects the computer with something like amnesia.

The Paragraph: An Overview

Paragraphs are essential to the success of your written work. Effective paragraphs result from the process of sorting your thoughts into meaningful groups for your audience. Paragraphs can introduce, support, provide transitions between, and conclude your ideas. A key part of your paragraph is the topic sentence, which should be suitably restricted and placed first in the paragraph to help readers grasp your central idea quickly. One simple model to follow is the T-shape, particularly useful for supporting paragraphs.

In their final form, your paragraphs should be coherent, complete, unified, and the appropriate length for your message. Depending on that message, you may organize your paragraphs according to any of the patterns explained on pages 80–86. A long piece of writing will contain paragraphs following many or all of these patterns.

As this chapter has emphasized, to construct a unified and developed paragraph, you will have to draft and revise your work several times. To make sure that you are on the right track during the revision stage of your work, ask yourself the questions contained in the checklist below for revising paragraphs.

✓ Revision Checklist

To make sure that your paragraphs do the job you intended for them, ask yourself the following questions during the revision stage of your work.

1. Does each of my paragraphs have a clear, restricted topic sentence? Have I made sure that I placed this topic sentence first in the paragraph to help readers grasp the main point of the paragraph quickly? Does each topic sentence forecast and control all the information in this paragraph?

2. Does each paragraph provide my readers with sufficient information about the particular topic I am discussing? Are there enough facts and evidence in this paragraph to satisfy my readers' need for information? Have I anticipated the questions my readers will ask about

this discussion of the topic? If there is not enough information, what kinds of details or interpretations must I add for my readers?

3. Do all the details in this paragraph relate to the idea I am conveying in this paragraph? Have I included only relevant information about the topic covered in this paragraph? Do I need to move information from another paragraph into this paragraph to make it tighter and more relevant? Or do I need to take information out of this paragraph and put it in an earlier or a later paragraph? Or should I remove the information in this paragraph entirely from my memo, letter, or report?

4. Have I organized the information in this paragraph in a clear and logical way? Does the paragraph hold together on its own? Have I selected the most effective pattern(s) of paragraph development? Does my paragraph inform the reader through key signals how the information is ordered? Have I considered using visual clues within my paragraph to help readers process information more easily?

5. Have I signaled to my readers how and why this is a separate paragraph? How have I indicated that my paragraphs are attached—interlocked—to each other? Will my readers know when one paragraph logically begins and another ends? How have I informed my readers that one paragraph is connected to the next? What function does this paragraph serve that others do not? How have I let my readers know this?

6. Have I arranged my paragraphs in the most appropriate order for my readers and the message I want them to receive? Do my paragraphs flow logically and smoothly from each other, or is a paragraph out of logical sequence? Do I need to switch one paragraph with another? Should I move a paragraph to a later place in my report or letter, or bring it forward in my work? Does one point lead to another? What do I need to start off with? What goes in that crucial first paragraph? How should I end—what must be said in my closing remarks to my readers?

Exercises

1. The following sentences would be poor choices for topic sentences because they are too broad. They do not help a reader focus on a single, unified topic. Revise these sentences to make them suitable topic sentences by restricting the topic. The first one has been done for you.
   a. Highway safety saves lives. (Traffic engineers have found that artificial lighting can reduce night accidents.)
   b. Cable stations offer many benefits to subscribers throughout America.
   c. Our company would be interested if conditions were right.
   d. The Social Security System is under attack.

    e.   Accounting (or welding, or any field) is an exciting profession.

    f.   A job applicant's qualifications mean a lot.

    g.   Banks play a significant role in the economy.

    h.   Medical science can perform wonders.

    i.   Knowledge of chemistry will help all students.

    j.   This is a big year for our school.

    k.   Vacations can be taken anywhere and at any time.

2. Write a complete, unified, and coherent paragraph on one of the topic sentences you revised for Exercise 1. Submit at least one draft and one revision (as in Figures 3.1–3.3) with your final copy.

3. The topic sentence is buried in each of the following paragraphs. Find it and rewrite it if necessary and then put it first in the paragraph. If necessary, revise the other sentences in the paragraph to account for the change.

    a.   For a noise barrier to work, it must be high and long enough to block the view of a road. Noise barriers do very little good for homes on a hillside overlooking a road or for buildings that rise above the barrier. Noise barriers can have functional limitations. Openings in the noise barrier for driveway connections or intersecting streets destroy its effectiveness, too. In some areas, homes are scattered too far apart to permit noise barriers to be built at a reasonable cost.

    b.   Sometimes shoplifters have special hooks or belts on the insides of their coats; or they wear tricky aprons and undergarments, which are designed to hold innumerable articles. Some sleight-of-hand thieves slip merchandise into packages or into boxes that have a hinged top, bottom, or end. Salesclerks should know how to spot devices used by shoplifters. Employees should also be suspicious of and watch shoppers who carry bulky packages, knitting bags, shopping bags, and umbrellas. These are handy receptacles for items that a shoplifter purposely knocks off counters.

4. The following paragraphs lack unity. Rewrite them to eliminate unnecessary or irrelevant information.

    a.   The Hanks Company has decided to construct its new lighting store in Burton Hills to attract more customers. This location will serve a busy market of 200,000 customers from Pasco, Downers Grove, and Middletown. Customers in these areas will no longer have to make an hour-long drive to Omaha for special lighting. The new lighting center offers them 23,000 sq. ft. of display space and gives the Hanks Company one of the largest stores in the region. This new location will also attract customers from the Portersville community, who must frequently drive to Omaha. The financing of the lighting center will be done by Perry and Associates of Fort Worth.

    b.   A person does not need extensive training to operate the new Max mainframe computer effectively. In many ways, it is no more difficult to operate than a personal computer. Our employees did object, however, to giving up their PCs; some of these machines have been in the company for 10 years. The Max uses a very simple language called BASIC. This language was developed about 5 years ago and has worked well in other offices like ours. Written in English, BASIC can be taught to our operators in less than a day. Storage capacity and speed will make the Max a valuable addition in the office for our operators.

5. The following paragraphs lack coherence. Rewrite them using the four techniques discussed in this chapter: transitional words and phrases, repetition of key words, the use of personal pronouns and demonstrative adjectives, and grammatical parallelism.

a. High-altitude photography has many uses. Land forms are measured and mapped. Accuracy is important for the measurement of water and other resources. Foresters find out the volume of trees, and foresters will be interested in knowing whether the trees are infested. Wildlife can be measured. Future highways and pipelines are always sketched out on the drawing board. Aerial photography helps city planners and geologists. Applications include shoreline changes. Geologists can measure the damage caused by floods. Changes in the landscape come from storms and hurricanes. Aerial photography records important data.

b. Our company prefers the Lodex word processors. The other models are expensive. About $300 separates the price of a Lodex from the prices charged by other vendors. The service contract provides us with good terms. Repairs are made free of charge for the first 90 days. A discount on parts is available at 30 percent. Flexible software will help our efficiency. Other vendors have limited means. Lodex provides 12 hours of free instruction for our staff.

6. Below is the first draft of a paragraph on foot care. Assume that you have been asked to write a short pamphlet on this topic for a local public health agency. Using the process of revising paragraphs discussed in this chapter, work on this draft until you have developed two complete, unified, and coherent paragraphs from this early draft. Delete or add any details as necessary.

Feet need breathing room. Common foot problems include corns and calluses, athlete's foot, bunions, ingrown toenails, and chronic blistering. Over a lifetime the feet hold up a weight that more than equals several million pounds. We all feel tired at the end of the day at the office or plant. A nurse or a police officer must stand on their feet for at least an 8–12 hour shift. Diseases can be detected from examining the feet. Podiatrists (foot doctors) are called to hospitals to trim the toenails of diabetic patients. Diabetes makes people extra sensitive to foot infections. Standing, stretching, walking, and strenuous exercise are good for the feet. Shoes need to be selected carefully. Skin irritations easily result. Sitting with legs crossed or wearing tight clothing affects the feet. Gym tights can hurt the feet. Wading through cold water or having pressure on the feet from poor-fitting shoes causes poor circulation. Over-the-counter medicines are often advertised as cures for some problems. Foot problems tend to get worse the older we get. But shoes made of leather and low-heeled shoes can help skin and circulation problems. Hot baths work to speed flow to the feet. Improved care helps circulation.

7. Below is an early draft of a letter sent to homeowners to encourage them to conserve water by using less water on their lawns. Revise this letter, paying special attention to the unity, order, development, and coherence of each paragraph.

```
Dear Homeowner:

    Summer is fast approaching. This is the time for
baseball, outdoor barbecues, long lazy days in the
hammock, 4th of July fireworks, vacations, trips to
see friends, etc. It is also the time to take care of
our lawns. We all want to have good-looking lawns.
That takes water and lots of it. We really need to
conserve this precious commodity. Water savings will
justify your investment.
```

You will use more water on your lawn than you will on the rest of your house. Here is a table to measure the ranges

Cooking	Cleaning	Plumbing	Lawn Care
18%	20%	22%	40%

It's impressive. Did you know it takes 10 gallons of water every time you flush your toilet?
You can save money by using inexpensive ground covers.

It has lots of attractive possibilities. Plants will be healthier if you can use mulch and other protective covers. You can use a mixture of 2 to 4 inch layers. This will last for a long time. Decorators use lots of it. Mulch keeps in soil and protects plants in winter and helps them stay cool in the summer. Plants really do not need much to survive, if you are careful. You can purchase mulch at garden centers. You could even prepare your own. You must own a shredder to do this; you cannot do it by hand.

They are like carpets. Plants can spread outwards and look nice. Rosemary, lavender, and other good smelling herbs are nice. They are attractive and will help you to conserve water. Ivy, myture, and dichomdria are good choices for groundcovers. Replace some of your lawn with groundcovers.

You have to prepare your yard before you start anything. Weeds crop up fast. Put some type of protective cover down first. Plants have roots that can seek water through covers.

Check with your extension society, garden shop, or landscaper.

Be careful where you put groundcovers. They are not as hearty as grass. They look good but do have restrictions with them. Irrigation is always a problem. Most water does not reach plant roots. Your sprinkler wastes a lot of your money. Some types of irrigation systems are better than others. Dripping water is better than sprinkling it all over.

Thanks for your cooperation.

8. For each of the following topic sentences, explain which pattern(s) of paragraph organization would be most appropriate and why. Which sentences might benefit from using a combination of patterns? Why?
   a. Computer time-sharing offers the small business many financial advantages over buying its own hardware.
   b. Vandalism is behavior that defaces or destroys property.
   c. Over the last seven years video games have become more sophisticated.
   d. Enzymes in our mouth help us to digest the food we eat.
   e. The living room was redecorated from floor to ceiling.
   f. Computer graphics offers a business many advantages over traditional, manual graphics.
   g. Ergonomics is the applied science of designing equipment to meet the needs of workers.
   h. After inspecting the property on November 30, I found that the major deterioration had begun in the basement and spread upstairs.
   i. For many workers coffee is a necessary evil.
   j. A door lock has a number of important, interconnected parts.
   k. For all practical purposes, ours is a paperless office.
   l. A large oak tree looks like a multicolored umbrella.
   m. The U.S. Postal Service instituted the nine-digit zip code to speed the delivery of mail.
   n. Over-the-counter drugs are packaged to protect consumers from poisoning.
   o. Music videos are mini-musicals.
   p. If not used properly, pesticides are poisonous to people and pets.
   q. Because the park was not carefully kept up, patron use dropped 18 percent in the last six months.
   r. Based on their prices, houses in our town fall into one of four categories.
   s. A roof includes more than just shingles.

9. From the topic sentences in Exercise 8, select three that follow different patterns of organization and write an appropriate paragraph for each.

10. Analyze the paragraphs included in the following article, "Emergency Preparedness via Cable TV." Classify them according to the four types and according to pattern(s) of organization. Discuss the use of transitional words or phrases used to link paragraphs.

Emergency Preparedness via Cable TV
By William Rushton

(1) In any kind of emergency, most Americans turn first to their television sets. Because 98 percent of U.S. homes have TV sets, television is the most immediate and available communications resource we have. Proper understanding of emerging communications technologies and some advance planning on the local level would enable us to enhance significantly the usefulness of this resource for emergency purposes.

(2) Chief among these new technologies is cable television, which currently is capable of bringing 100 or more channels by wire into homes. In the past these American households could at best receive only a dozen or so channels "over the air." Cable has established itself as the highway of the new telecommunications environment. It distributes programs from broadcast stations, satellites, microwave feeds, and local nonbroadcast origination studios ("access centers"). These cable services offer a wide variety of traditional kinds of entertainment and a new world of nonentertainment services. By the end of this decade, virtually all American households will have access to cable services.

(3) Cable's multiplicity of channels gives rise to "narrowcasting," or the targeting of a small segment of an audience and programming its specific needs. Access channels, particularly government access channels, can be used for programs that discuss very narrow and specific issues, with phone-in discussion by the target audience involved. Cable's initial role, therefore, might be in planning for energy emergency preparedness. Phone-in cable shows, for example, offer a mechanism by which the government can *interact* with its citizens.

(4) Another major advantage in using cable in emergency situations is its localism. In most states, cable utilities are franchised by local municipalities, offering access channels (similar to a local community TV "station") to communities that might not have a local broadcast station. During the blizzard of 1978, for example, the town of Danbury, Connecticut (which had no broadcast television station) effectively used its cable system as a 24-hour emergency information center.

(5) Many cable systems have specific emergency facilities built in, such as an emergency command station or a direct feed from such a facility. Moreover, the centralized nature of cable distribution (from a processing center called a "head end") allows a cable operator to run an electronic message (or "crawl") along the bottom of the screen on all channels simultaneously, announcing an emergency and calling public attention to a specific channel for relevant emergency details. In the case of a derailed tank car of hazardous chemicals, for example, or a community downwind from a nuclear power plant accident, it might be easier to reach the affected area by phone calls or electronic messages directly to a cable system or two than to try to reach all the broadcast stations, running the risk of panic in nonaffected areas. Instructions to one zone might be vastly different from instructions to another. Moreover, new devices are on the market now that would allow your cable to signal you even if the television set is off, a service no other broadcast outlet can offer.

(6) Another advantage of cable TV is that in the event of a severe long-term emergency—such as disruptions of imported oil supplies, with resulting restrictions on private auto use—cable television offers what may be our only long-term solution for certain public information-dissemination and service-delivery tasks. "Teleconferences," "telecourses," and "telemedicine" (preventive medical care and social work activities) can be offered over cable without making the viewer travel. Not all information or social service activities can be conveyed on cable, of course, but enough of them can be so that any medium-to-long-range energy crisis could be made more manageable. In the long term, cable might be our only alternative to curtailing or eliminating such services altogether in an emergency.

(7) In conclusion, cable television can provide many emergency services for the public good. The technology is here, and its applications are proven and helpful. Cable television is a major contribution to community emergency preparedness.

U.S. Department of Energy, *The Energy Consumer* Dec. 1980–Jan. 1981:24.

4

Writing: Sentences

A successful paragraph depends on successful sentences. Once you have revised the organization and structure of your paragraphs, you should begin revising your sentences. They must be clear, concise, and coherent as well as error-free. Proofreading for grammatical mistakes alone does not guarantee that your sentences will be effective. As is the case with constructing a successful paragraph, writing effective sentences takes time and work.

Sentences and the Writing Process

In all likelihood you will not find yourself writing logical, polished sentences in your first or even second draft. Do not worry. Generally, writers are not concerned about the final form of their sentences during the drafting or early revising stages. At those points they are occupied with the larger units of their work—the order in which information is best placed for readers and the accuracy and relevance of that information for their audience. In fact, striving for "perfect" sentences early in the writing process will probably interrupt the flow of your ideas and may lead to the paralysis known as writer's block. For this reason, most writers postpone sentence-level revisions until their drafts begin to take final shape. The closer you move toward the final copy of your work, the more you need to be concerned about how your sentences read, that is, how easy they are for readers to understand and how clearly they convey your message.

Like revising your paragraphs, revising your sentences requires a great deal of rewriting. Recall from Chapters 2 and 3 how many times William Tisch and the writers for the Seacoast Lab brochure and the Fenton Industries memo revised their sentences to make their work clear, concise, and easy to read. As you *re*write and *re*vise your sentences for clarity and coherence, you will be discovering for yourself and defining for your readers how your thoughts relate to one another. Of course, heed this word of caution: Allow some time between the drafting and the revising/editing stages. When you return to your work after a day or even a few hours, you will be amazed at how many things you spot to correct.

By developing the skills discussed in this chapter during the revision and editing phases of your work, you will make valuable progress toward writing successfully on the job.

Clear Sentences and Your Career

The way in which you construct and revise your sentences can determine whether you succeed or fail in the world of work. Your sentences reveal a lot about you. They tell readers how well or how poorly you can convey a message and how much you value your reader's time and energy. If your sentences are clear, concise, and varied, readers will find your message easier to understand and to act on. They will thank you for not having to reread your work in order to understand your message. If you write readable sentences, you predispose your reader to respond positively to you and your message. Clear writers earn high marks from employers and customers and are in great demand in the work force.

Readers' Chief Complaints About Bad Sentences

If your sentences are unclear and wordy, your readers will dread receiving memos, letters, and reports from you. Such writing makes your readers' job hard and unpleasant. Here are some complaints readers in the business world have about writers' poor sentences.

1. "This sentence is too long; I have a hard time following the writer's message from one end of the sentence to the other."
2. "What does this sentence say? I must have read it five times, and I still don't know what the writer is trying to communicate."
3. "What's the subject of the sentence—who is doing what?"
4. "To what does the 'it' or 'they' refer?"
5. "The writer puts me to sleep with short and choppy sentences that read like they were written for a grade school primer. I am insulted by the writer's style because it is condescending."
6. "This sentence says the same thing as the writer's previous two sentences. Why does the writer have to repeat? Does the writer think I am dense and cannot understand something without having it repeated?"
7. "This sentence says one thing, and the next sentence—or the sentence later in the paragraph—says just the opposite. Which am I to believe? Is the writer sure of what he or she is doing?"
8. "Is the writer serious? What he or she is describing is logically impossible, an incredible feat."

Because of poor sentences that contain these problems, readers will question a writer's ability to think clearly and logically. Employers certainly do not look favorably on writers who embarrass them or cost the company time and money because of unclear or misleading sentences.

What This Chapter Can Do for You

The goal of Chapter 4 is to help you write clear and readable sentences. It starts out with some basics in sentence structure and punctuation and then turns to ways of helping you revise your sentences until they become clean and lean. By studying this chapter carefully, you will learn to

- construct and punctuate sentences correctly.
- use the appropriate voice (active or passive).
- use parallel constructions.
- write sentences that say what you mean.
- write sentences that are economical and easy to read.

Constructing and Punctuating Sentences

A *sentence* is a complete thought, expressed by a subject and a verb, that can make sense standing alone. The first step toward success in writing sentences is learning to recognize the difference between phrases and clauses.

The Difference Between Phrases and Clauses

A *phrase* is a group of words that does not contain a subject and a verb; phrases cannot make sense standing alone. Phrases cannot be sentences.

in the park	**No subject** Who is in the park?
	No verb What was done in the park?
for every patient in intensive care	**No subject** Who did something for every patient?
	No verb What was done for the patients?

A *clause* does contain a subject and a verb, but *not every clause is a sentence.* Only *independent* (or *main*) *clauses* can stand alone as sentences. Here is an example of an independent clause that is a complete sentence.

subject   verb   object

The president closed the college.

A *dependent* (or *subordinate*) *clause* also contains a subject and a verb, but does not make complete sense and cannot stand alone. Why? A dependent clause contains a subordinating conjunction—*after, although, as, because, before, even though, if, since, unless, when, where, whereas, while*—at the beginning of the clause. Such conjunctions subordinate the clause in which they appear and make the clause dependent for meaning and completion on an independent clause.

After
Before
Because $\Big\}$ the president closed the college
Even though
Unless

"After the president closed the college" is not a complete thought. This dependent clause leaves us in suspense. It needs to be completed with an independent clause telling us what happened "after."

dependent clause	independent clause		
	subject	verb	phrase
After the president closed the college,	we	played	in the snow.

Sentence Fragments

Complete sentences do not leave the reader hanging in midair, wondering who did something, how it was done, or under what conditions it was done. An incomplete sentence is called a *fragment.* Fragments may be phrases or dependent clauses. They either lack a verb or a subject or have broken away from an independent (main) clause. A fragment is isolated; it needs an overhaul to supply missing parts to turn it into an independent clause or to glue it back to the independent clause from which it became separated.

You can avoid writing sentence fragments by following a few rules. In the next few pages, incorrect examples are preceded by a minus sign; corrected versions, by a plus sign.

1. Do not use a subordinate clause as a sentence. Even though it contains a subject and a verb, a subordinate clause standing alone is still a fragment. To avoid this kind of sentence fragment, simply join the two clauses (the independent clause and the dependent clause containing a subordinating conjunction) with a comma—*not* a period or semicolon.

- Unless we agreed to the plan. (What would happen?)
- Unless we agreed to the plan; the project manager would discontinue the operation. (A semicolon cannot set off the subordinate clause.)
+ Unless we agreed to the plan, the project manager would discontinue the operation.

- Because safety precautions were taken. (What happened?)
+ Because safety precautions were taken, ten construction workers escaped injury.

Sometimes subordinate clauses appear at the end of a sentence. They may be introduced by a subordinate conjunction, an adverb, or a relative pronoun (*that, which, who*). Do not separate these clauses from the preceding independent clause with a period, thus turning them into fragments.

- Some of the new employees selected the high-risk option in their policy. While others did not.
+ Some of the new employees selected the high-risk option in their policy, while others did not. (The *while* subordinates the clause, and therefore that clause cannot stand alone.)

   − An all-volunteer fire department posed some problems. Especially for residents in the western part of town.

   + An all-volunteer fire department posed some problems, especially for residents in the western part of town. (The word *especially* qualifies *problems,* referred to in the independent clause.)

2. Every sentence must have a subject telling the reader who does the action.

   − Being extra careful not to spill the water. (Who?)

   + The aide was extra careful not to spill the water.

3. Every sentence must have a complete verb. Watch especially for verbs ending in *-ing*. They need another verb (some form of *to be*) to make them complete.

   − The woman in the blue uniform. (What did she do?)

   + The woman in the blue uniform directed traffic.

   − The machine running in the computer department. (Did what?)

You can change the last fragment into a sentence by supplying the correct form of the verb.

   + The machine *is* running in the computer department.

   + The machine *runs* in the computer department.

Or you can revise the entire sentence, adding a new thought.

   + The machine running in the computer department handles all new accounts.

4. Do not detach prepositional phrases (beginning with *at, by, for, from, in, to, with,* and so forth) **from independent clauses.** Such phrases are not complete thoughts and cannot stand alone. Correct the error by leaving the phrases attached to the sentence to which they belong.

   − By three o'clock the next day. (What was to happen?)

   + The supervisor wanted our reports by three o'clock the next day.

   − For every patient in intensive care. (What was done?)

   + Nurses kept hourly reports for every patient in intensive care.

The Comma Splice

Fragments occur when you use only bits and pieces of complete sentences. Another common error that some writers commit involves just the reverse kind of action. They weakly and wrongly join two complete sentences (independent clauses) with a comma as if those two sentences were really only one sentence. This error is called a *comma splice.* Here is an example.

   − Gasoline prices have risen by 10 percent in the last month, we will drive the car less often.

Two independent clauses (complete sentences) exist:

> Gasoline prices have risen by 10 percent in the last month.
> We will drive the car less often.

A comma alone lacks the power to separate independent clauses. As the preceding example shows, many pronouns—*I, he, she, it, we, they*—are used as the subjects of independent clauses. A comma splice will result if you place a comma instead of a semicolon between two independent clauses where the second clause opens with a pronoun.

> − Rosa approved the plan, she liked its cost-effective approach.
> + Rosa approved the plan; she liked its cost-effective approach.

However, relative pronouns (*who, whom, which, that*) are preceded by a comma, not a period or a semicolon, when they introduce subordinate clauses.

> − She approved the plan. Which had the cost-effective approach.
> + She approved the plan, which had the cost-effective approach.

Four Ways to Correct Comma Splices

1. Remove the comma separating two independent clauses and replace it with a period. Then capitalize the first letter of the first word of the newly reinstated sentence.

> + Gasoline prices have risen by 10 percent in the last month. We will drive the car less often.

2. Insert a coordinating conjunction (*and, but, or, nor, for, yet*) **after the comma.** Together, the conjunction and the comma properly separate the two independent clauses.

> + Gasoline prices have risen by 10 percent in the last month, and we will drive the car less often.

3. Rewrite the sentence (if it makes sense to do so). Turn the first independent clause into a dependent clause by adding a subordinate conjunction; then insert a comma and add the second independent clause.

> + Because gasoline prices have risen by 10 percent in the last month, we will drive the car less often.

4. Delete the comma and insert a semicolon.

> + Gasoline prices have risen by 10 percent in the last month; we will drive the car less often.

(Of the four ways to correct the comma splice, this last example is the most suitable for the sample sentence, because the price of gasoline affects how much a car is driven.)

The semicolon is an effective and forceful punctuation mark when the two independent clauses are closely related, that is, when they announce contrasting or parallel views, as the two following examples reveal.

+ The union favored the new legislation; the company opposed it. (contrasting views)
+ Night classes help the college and the community; more students can take more credit hours. (parallel views)

How *Not* to Correct Comma Splices

Some writers mistakenly try to correct comma splices by inserting a conjunctive adverb (*also, consequently, furthermore, however, moreover, nevertheless, then, therefore*) after the comma.

− Gasoline prices have risen by 10 percent in the last month, consequently we will drive the car less often.

Because the conjunctive adverb (*consequently*) is not as powerful as the coordinating conjunction (*and, but, for*), the error is not eliminated. If you use a conjunctive adverb—*consequently, however, nevertheless*—you still must insert a semicolon or a period before it, as the following examples show.

+ Gasoline prices have risen by 10 percent in the last month; consequently, we will drive the car less often.
+ Gasoline prices have risen by 10 percent in the last month. Consequently, we will drive the car less often.

Using the Appropriate Voice: Active or Passive

"Voice" refers to whether the subject of a sentence performs the action or receives it. In the active voice a subject performs the action and appears in the first (and subject) part of the sentence. In the passive voice the subject becomes the recipient of the action; the performer of the action no longer occupies the first part of the sentence, but now appears in the last part or is even omitted.

Active voice   **1.** The recruiting staff made three visits.
Passive voice   **2.** Three visits were made by the recruiting staff.
Passive voice   **3.** Three visits were made.

Sentence 1 stresses the actions of the staff. In sentence 2 and especially in 3 the writer is more interested in the number of visits than in who made them.

When to Use the Active Voice

The active voice is usually more forceful and direct than is the passive voice. It generally requires fewer words than does the passive voice. Sentence 2 contains two more words than are in sentence 1: *were* and *by*. These extra words show how passives are formed. Verbs in the passive voice are constructed with some form of the verb *to be* followed by a *past participle* (here, *made*); often a prepositional phrase with *by* indicates the presence of a passive verb: *by the recruiting staff*. You can often change the passive into the active voice by making the object of the *by* phrase the subject of the sentence: *The recruiting staff made three visits.*

Advantages of Using the Active Voice

Since both the active and the passive voices have advantages, use both in your work. The active voice, however, offers writers these benefits.

1. **The active voice gives instructions authority and clarity.**

   Active Remove the hex nut.
   Passive The hex nut should be removed.

   Active Wear protective eyeglasses.
   Passive Protective eyeglasses should be worn.

2. **The active voice can eliminate awkwardness.**

   Active I completed two years of technical training.
   Passive Two years of technical training were completed by me.

   Active Ms. Yamoto spoke about the new design.
   Passive The new design was spoken about by Ms. Yamoto.

3. **The active voice lets readers know that another person, not a machine, is writing to them in letters and reports.**

   Active The tour director arranged the plans for your travel.
   Passive Plans have been arranged for your travel.

   Active I can make an appointment for you.
   Passive An appointment can be made for you.

You will find that using sentences in the active voice will make your letters and reports easier to read and to follow. The movement of the action in the active voice propels readers forward; the backward movement of the action in the passive voice, along with the extra words required for its construction, slows readers down. The active voice shows exactly who is in charge and who has accomplished certain tasks. For these reasons, be careful that you do not overuse the passive voice as you revise your work.

Below are two versions of the same paragraph—the first is written in the passive voice and the second in the active voice. Which version do you find more direct and easier to read? Why?

Passive New guidelines for reimbursement for travel expenses have been put into effect by our agency. A copy of these guidelines should be studied by employees before their request for payment is filed. Two important changes have been made from the previous guidelines and need to be called to your attention. First, all requests are to be submitted by the fifth of the month instead of the fifteenth. Second, no action can be taken on any request that has been submitted after that date without further documentation being accounted for.

Active Our agency has established new guidelines for reimbursement for travel expenses. You need to study these guidelines before you make your next request for payment. I would like to call two important changes to your attention. First, you should submit all your requests by the fifth rather than the fifteenth of the month. Second, we cannot file any request made after that date without asking you for further documentation. I appreciate your cooperation.

Note how the first version overuses the passive voice, making the message harder for the reader to follow. The passive voice also makes the writer sound impersonal and unfriendly. After revision, the sentence written in the active voice is more direct, emphatic, and personable.

When to Use the Passive Voice

Scientists often use the passive voice to emphasize the experiment or the procedure rather than the individual performing it. They believe that references to "I" detract from the objectivity of the work. Many scientists would prefer the second of the following two sentences.

> Active The biologist performed the experiment three times in 48 hours.
> Passive The experiment was performed three times in 48 hours.

Clearly, some contexts call for the "I" and the active voice in reporting scientific data. But the passive voice does have its advantages when you are writing about a process—changing hydrogen and oxygen into water, for example—when the emphasis is not on the human actor, but on the changes brought about through scientific law.

The passive voice also serves the following useful functions.

1. **The passive voice can be used when the actor is unknown.**

   The car was stolen at noon. (The thief's identity is not known.)

   The practice was started in 1965. (Who started it is not known.)

   Monthly house payments are scaled down during the first five years of the mortgage. (By whom?)

2. **The passive voice can be used when the object is more important for the reader than is the actor.**

   The injection of insulin was given at 6:30 A.M.

   Pieces of the bullet were found in the dining room wall.

   The generator was periodically inspected.

3. **The passive voice can be used as a business strategy when anonymity is necessary or when emphasis on the subject has unfavorable ethical implications.** Compare these two sentences.

   Mr. Corcoran fired the mechanic.

   The mechanic was fired.

The first sentence emphasizes the fact that it was Mr. Corcoran who dismissed the mechanic; the second sentence does not even mention Mr. Corcoran.

Using Parallelism

Parallelism expresses the similarity of ideas by placing them in the same grammatical form. Parallel forms may use the same part of speech or the same type of phrase or clause. Using parallel grammatical units for parallel ideas enables you to group related points, to clarify relationships, and to emphasize your message for readers. Readers seeing repeated grammatical forms will find it easier to read your work and to understand the comparisons you are making. To use parallelism effectively, make sure that the grammatical forms are the same and that the ideas actually are equal and related. The following examples show parallelism in grammatical forms.

Present participle	listen*ing*	read*ing*	writ*ing*	speak*ing*
Infinitive	*to* listen	*to* read	*to* write	*to* speak
Noun	listen*er*	read*er*	writ*er*	speak*er*
Lack of parallelism	to listen	reading	writing	spoken

Note how parallelism is violated in the following example in which each duty of a proposal writer is expressed in a different grammatical form.

The specific duties of a proposal writer involve

- defining the problem for readers.
- the need to describe the solution.
- establishment of a schedule.
- is responsible for budget plans.
- has assigned personnel.
- writes progress reports.

Suitably revised, the writer's duties in the following list are parallel because they have equal importance and because they are expressed with the same grammatical form (all start with present participles).

The specific duties of a proposal writer involve

- defining the problem for readers.
- describing the solution.
- establishing a schedule.
- planning a budget.
- assigning personnel.
- writing progress reports.

Note how the writer of the following sentence calls attention to the report's characteristics through the series of adjectives.

The report was clear, concise, and informative.

Compare the following faulty sentences (in which words are not parallel) with the corrected versions.

 − The student was enthusiastic, cooperative, and she knew the material very well. (After two parallel adjectives, the writer introduces an independent clause and thus destroys the parallelism.)
 + The student was enthusiastic, cooperative, and knowledgeable. (all adjectives)

When you list a group of parallel words in a series, be sure that you are consistent in using *the, a, in,* or *that* with them. Use the article, preposition, or pronoun either before each element or before only the first element.

- – We have stores in Cleveland, Detroit, Kokomo, and in Chicago.

- + We have stores in Cleveland, in Detroit, in Kokomo, and in Chicago.
- + We have stores in Cleveland, Detroit, Kokomo, and Chicago.

Parallelism is used with prepositional phrases to group related information.

- – The new lights were installed within the hallways, on the roof, and they were included in the parking lot, too.
- + The new lights were installed within the hallways, on the roof, and in the parking lot.

Parallelism of clauses and verbal phrases works well as long as you warn readers by beginning each element in exactly the same way.

- – The management asks that all new employees fill out insurance forms, that they take the required physical examination, they pick up parking passes, and come to the orientation seminar. (Each dependent clause should begin with *that.*)
- + The management asks that all new employees fill out insurance forms, that they take the required physical examination, that they pick up parking passes, and that they come to the orientation seminar.

- – Hiring qualified employees is a matter of screening applicants carefully, interviewing them diplomatically, and then to run a reference check. (Two present participles are followed by an infinitive.)
- + Hiring qualified employees is a matter of screening applicants carefully, interviewing them diplomatically, and running a reference check.

Establishing proper parallelism can be especially tricky in sentences that use the following *correlative conjunctions: either/or, neither/nor,* and *both/and.* Keep in mind that the information on either side of these correlatives has to be grammatically identical. Study the following faulty examples and their revisions.

- – He told the operator to either repair the equipment or to replace it. (*Either* is *in the middle of* one infinitive and its counterpart *or* is *in front of* the other infinitive.)
- + He told the operator either to repair the equipment or to replace it. (Both *either* and *or* have the same position: *before* the infinitive.)

- – All employees are entitled to both fifteen vacation days and to eight holidays. (This is confusing; do the employees receive two fifteen-day vacation periods?)
- + All employees are entitled both to fifteen vacation days and to eight holidays.

Writing Sentences That Say What You Mean

Your sentences should say exactly what you mean, without double talk, misplaced humor, or nonsense. Sentences are composed of words and word groups that influence each other. Like molecules, they bump and rub into each other, exerting a strong reciprocal influence.

It's easy to overlook the kinds of errors discussed below when you first write a sentence or even after you have finished one or more drafts of a letter or memo. But you can eliminate these errors by reminding yourself, as you are revising and editing your work, to read your sentences to see how one group of words fits into and relates to another. If you are composing on a word processor, don't be lazy; scroll the text of your letter or report up and down to see how one sentence connects to another.

Logical Sentences

Sentences should not contradict themselves or make outlandish claims. The following examples contain errors in logic; note how easily the suggested revisions handle the problem.

Illogical The manager's order established a new precedent for our time. (A precedent is something that has already been established; hence it cannot be new.)

Revision The manager's order established a precedent.

Illogical Steel roll-away shutters make it possible for the sun to be shaded in the summer and to have it shine in the winter. (The sun is far too large to shade; the writer meant that a room or a house, much smaller than the sun, could be shaded with the shutters.)

Revision Steel roll-away shutters make it possible for owners to shade their living rooms in the summer and to admit sunshine during the winter.

To recognize and avoid illogical constructions, make sure you

- fully understand the meaning and proper usage of each word you use; consult a dictionary if you are uncertain.
- isolate the basic sentence elements (subject, verb, object) from all descriptive words and phrases to determine if the action of the verb can logically be performed by the subject of the sentence on the direct object.

Sentences Using Contextually Appropriate Words

Sentences should use the combination of words most appropriate for the subject matter you are writing about. Here are some illustrations of sentences containing inappropriate words, together with suggested revisions.

Inappropriate The building materials need to be explained in small, concrete steps. (The writer was thinking of "concrete" in terms of teaching; the context, though, encourages the reader to picture cement stairs.)

Revision The building materials need to be explained separately and carefully.

Inappropriate The members of the Nuclear Regulatory Commission saw fear radiated on the faces of the residents. (The word "radiated" is obviously ill advised; use a neutral term.)

Revision The members of the Nuclear Regulatory Commission saw fear reflected on the faces of the residents.

> **Inappropriate** The game warden is shooting for an increase in the number of non-resident licenses this year.
>
> **Revision** The game warden hopes to increase the number of nonresident licenses this year.

Sentences with Well-Placed Modifiers

A *modifier* is a word, phrase, or clause that describes, limits, or qualifies the meaning of another word or word group. A modifier can consist of one word (a *green* car), a prepositional phrase (the man *in the telephone booth*), a relative clause (the woman *who won the marathon*), or an *-ing* or *-ed* phrase (*walking three miles a day,* the student was in good shape; *seated in the first row,* we saw everything on stage). You will learn more about modifiers and readability on page 111.

A *dangling modifier* is one that cannot logically modify any word in the sentence.

> − When answering the question, his notebook fell off the table.

One way to correct the error is to insert the right subject after the *-ing* phrase.

> + When answering the question, he knocked his notebook off the table.

You can also turn the phrase into a subordinate clause.

> + When he answered the question, his notebook fell off the table.
> + His notebook fell off the table as he answered the question.

A *misplaced modifier* illogically modifies the wrong word or words in the sentence. The result is often comical.

> − Hiding in the corner, growling and snarling, our guide spotted the frightened cub. (Is our guide growling and snarling in the corner?)
> − All travel requests must be submitted by employees in green ink. (Are the employees covered in green ink?)

The problem with both of the examples above is word order. The modifers are misplaced because they are attached to the wrong words in the sentence. Correct the error by moving the modifier where it belongs.

> + Hiding in the corner, growling and snarling, the frightened cub was spotted by our guide.
> + All travel requests by employees must be submitted in green ink.

Misplaced modifiers may also be corrected by recasting the sentence.

> + While the frightened cub was hiding in the corner, growling and snarling, our guide spotted it.
> + Our guide spotted the growling and snarling, frightened cub, which was hiding in the corner.

Note that each "correct" version has a slightly different emphasis; the choice depends on whether you want to stress the guide or the cub.

Misplacing a relative clause (introduced by such relative pronouns as *who, whom, that, which*) can also lead to problems with modification.

- Our firm decided not to move to the office in Salem that needs remodeling. (It is the office, not the town, that needs remodeling.)
- Our firm decided not to move to the office that needs remodeling in Salem. (The prepositional phrase "in Salem" is too far removed from "office," the word it modifies.)

+ Our firm decided not to move to the Salem office that needs remodeling.

- The salesperson recorded the merchandise for the customer that the store had discounted. (The merchandise was discounted, not the customer.)
- The salesperson recorded the merchandise that the store had discounted for the customer. (The salesperson recorded for the customer; the store did not discount for the customer.)

+ The salesperson recorded for the customer the merchandise that the store had discounted.

To avoid problem sentences like those above, always place the relative clause immediately after the word it modifies.

Correct Use of Pronoun References in Sentences

Sentences will be vague if they contain a faulty use of pronouns. When you use a pronoun whose *antecedent* (the person, place, or object the pronoun refers to) is unclear, you risk confusing your reader. At the revision stage, double-check pronouns to make sure they clearly refer to the correct antecedent. Here are some examples of unclear pronoun references, with revisions following.

Unclear   After the plants are clean, we separate the stems from the roots and place them in the sun to dry. (Is it the stems or the roots that lie in the sun?)

Revision   After the plants are clean, we separate the stems from the roots and place the stems in the sun to dry.

Unclear   The park ranger was pleased to see the workers planting new trees and installing new benches. This will attract more tourists. (The trees or the benches?)

Revision   The park ranger was pleased to see the workers planting new trees and installing new benches, for the new trees will attract more tourists.

Unclear   When Bill talked with his boss, he became angry. (Who became angry, Bill or his boss?)

Revision   When he talked with his boss, Bill became angry.

You can correct faulty pronoun references by replacing the unclear pronoun with the noun it stands for as in the last example; the vague *he* in the independent clause is replaced by the clear and specific *Bill.* The reader will know exactly which word is the subject of the sentence. Another way to correct misleading pronouns is to rewrite the sentence as in the second example above.

Seven Guidelines for Writing Readable Sentences

Use of correct grammar and punctuation alone cannot guarantee that your sentences will be easy to read and understand. Wordy, unclear sentences in the passive voice will only frustrate your reader. No one wants to waste time rereading an unclear sentence. Furthermore, your reader will suspect that you cut corners in the writing process. Perhaps you skipped the revising or editing stage. Maybe you did not put your work aside for a while so you could come back to it with "fresh eyes" or have someone else look it over. Remember that writing readable sentences takes time, especially at the beginning of the revision process.

This section will give you seven specific guidelines to follow during revision to help you write easy-to-read—lean and clean—sentences. As you study these guidelines, keep in mind that readability depends on

- the length of your sentences.
- the order in which you list information in your sentences.
- the way in which you signal the relationship among your sentences.

1. Write Sentences That Tell Who Does What to Whom or What

The clearest sentence pattern in English is the subject-verb-object (*s-v-o*) pattern.

    s   v   o

Sue mowed the grass.

            s   v   o

Today's newspaper contains a special supplement on our school.

This pattern tells who does what to whom. Readers find this pattern easiest to read and understand because it provides direct and specific information about the action. Hard-to-read sentences obscure or scramble information about the subject, the verb, or the object. Poor writers, for example, bury the subject in prepositional phrases in the middle or the end of the sentence, smother the verb in phrases, or allow an object to act like a subject.

Not all clear sentences, however, follow the subject-verb-object pattern. You might use a subordinate clause in addition to the subject, verb, and object in the independent clause. Regardless of your sentence pattern, make sure that your sentences give readers clear information about who performs what action to whom.

To write sentences that tell readers clearly what's going on, follow these steps. First, identify the subject: the person, place, or concept that controls the main action. (Avoid using vague words such as *factors, conditions, processes,* or *elements* for subjects; these words will lead to ambiguity; see Chapter 5, pages 123–127.) Next, select an action-packed verb that shows what the subject does. Then specify the object that is acted upon by the real subject through the verb.

In the following unclear sentences, subjects are hidden in the middle of their sentences. You can revise these sentences to tell clearly what has happened.

    Unclear The preparation of the patient for surgery was done correctly by the nurse. (Who did what to whom?)

    Revision The nurse correctly prepared the patient for surgery.

Unclear An assessment of the market helped our company design its new food blender. (The main action is designing. Who did it?)

Revision Our company designed its new food blender by assessing the market.

Unclear The fact that delivery schedules were changed hurt our business. (Who is the subject—*the fact that? delivery schedules?* What actually hurt business?)

Revision Changes in delivery schedules hurt our business.

Unclear The control of the ceiling limits of glycidyl ethers on the part of the employers for the optimum safety of workers in the workplace is necessary. (Who is responsible for taking action? What action did they take? For whom was that action taken?)

Revision For the safety of workers, employers must control the ceiling limits of glycidyl ethers.

Start your sentence with its real subject. Don't delay the subject by putting unimportant or unnecessary words ahead of it. You give readers a false and slow start by beginning with a dummy subject such as *there is/there are, it appears that, it seems that.* These impersonal constructions push the real subject back and make it harder to read the sentence. The result is a wordy and less emphatic sentence, as the following revisions show.

Dummy subject There is only one option that is feasible.

Real subject Only one option is feasible.

Dummy subject There were many times during the trial when the defense attorney asked for a recess.

Real subject The defense attorney asked for a recess many times during the trial.

Dummy subject It is essential to realize that each quarter the manager needs accurate figures to prepare the budget.

Real subject The manager needs accurate figures each quarter to prepare the budget.

2. Arrange Information Logically Within Your Sentences

The order in which you list information within a sentence can help or hinder a reader in understanding your message. You cannot list details in just any order. Draft different versions of your sentences to make sure readers receive information in the most logical, helpful way. The pattern you use will, of course, depend on your topic. The content of the sentence will help you to choose the most logical pattern: chronological, cause to effect, action to reaction, and the like.

Poor They shut off the computer once they finish with their program.

More logical Once they finish their program, they shut off the computer. (Since finishing the program precedes shutting the computer off, give readers the information in this order.)

Poor My strengths are in neurological and geriatric nursing to give you some background about my work experiences. '

More logical To give you some background about my work experiences, my strengths are in neurological and geriatric nursing. (Tell readers why you are giving them the details first, so that they know what the details mean.)

3. Avoid Needlessly Complex or Lengthy Sentences

How long should your sentence be? The answers to this question vary, depending on the educational level of your audience and the subject you are writing about. You can be guided by one safe rule, however: write so that it is easy for your reader to understand you. Generally, the longer the sentence, the more difficult it is to understand; therefore, do not pile one clause on another. Instead, revise one overly long sentence into two or even three more manageable ones.

Most readers have very little trouble with sentences ranging from 8 to 15 words. On the other hand, readers find sentences over 20 to 23 words much more difficult. As a general rule, keep your sentences under 18 words in order to reach most readers. The first sentence below is too long for readers to understand, even the second time through. The revision is much easier to read.

Too long The planning committee decided that the awards banquet should be held on May 15 at 6:30, since the other two dates (May 7 and May 22) suggested by the hospitality committee conflict with local sports events, even though one of those events could be changed to fit our needs.

Easier to read The planning committee has decided to hold the awards banquet on May 15 at 6:30. The other dates suggested by the hospitality committee—May 7 and May 22—conflict with two local sports events. Although the date of one of those sports events could be changed, the planning committee still believes that May 15 is our best choice.

4. Combine a Series of Short, Choppy Sentences

Avoiding long, complex sentences only to write short, simplistic ones will not make your reader's job easier. In fact, a memo, letter, or report written exclusively in short, staccato sentences sounds immature and makes for boring reading. To avoid this error, vary your sentences both in length and structure. The most effective on-the-job writing blends short sentences with longer ones to achieve variety and to reflect different logical relationships. For example, a sentence containing a subordinate clause followed by an independent clause may signal a cause-to-effect relationship to readers. A sentence with a series of parallel independent clauses points to the equality of the ideas spelled out in these clauses. A short sentence at the end of a paragraph can emphatically summarize a main idea. Don't be afraid to trim your sentences as you revise or to split one long sentence into two shorter ones. But when you find yourself writing a series of short, choppy sentences, such as in the following example, combine them where possible and use connective words similar to those italicized in the revision.

Choppy Secretaries have many responsibilities. Their responsibilities are important. They must answer telephones. They must take dictation. Sometimes the speaker talks very fast. Then the secretary must be quick to transcribe

what is heard. Words could be missed. Secretaries must also prepare letters. This will take a great deal of time and concentration. These letters are
copied and stored properly for reference.

Revision Secretaries have many important responsibilities. *These* include answering
the telephones and taking dictation. *When* a speaker talks rapidly, the secretary will have to transcribe quickly *so* that no words are omitted. *Among
the most demanding* of their duties are preparing letters accurately *and
then* making copies of them and storing those copies properly for future
reference.

5. Use Strong, Active Verbs Rather Than Verb Phrases with Verbs Disguised as Nouns

In trying to sound important, many writers avoid using simple, graphic verbs (see
Chapter 5, pages 129–130). Instead, these bureaucratic writers add a suffix
(*-ation, -ance, -ment, -ence*) to a direct verb (*determine*) to make a noun (*determination*) and then couple the new noun with *make, provide,* or *work* to produce
a weak verb phrase (for example, *make a determination of, provide maintenance of, work in cooperation with*). Such a verb phrase imprisons the active
verb inside a noun. The following sentences with weak verb phrases are rewritten
to make them more readable and emphatic.

Weak The officer made an assessment of the damages the storm had caused.
Strong The officer assessed the damage the storm had caused.

Weak The investigators made an entrance into the wilderness site at dusk.
Strong The investigators entered the wilderness site at dusk.

Weak The city provided the employment of two work crews to assist the strengthening of the dam.
Strong The city employed two work crews to strengthen the dam.

6. Avoid Piling Up Modifiers in Front of a Noun

It's hard for readers to grasp your message when you string a series of modifiers in
front of a noun. Modifiers are subordinate units that should clarify and qualify the
noun to which they refer. When you put too many of them in the reader's path to
the noun, you confuse the reader who does not know how one modifier relates to
another modifier or to the noun. To avoid this problem, rephrase the sentence by
placing some of the modifiers in prepositional phrases after or before the nouns
they modify.

Crowded The ordinance contract number vehicle identification plate had to be
checked against inventory numbers.
Spaced The ordinance contract number on the vehicle identification plate had to
be checked against the inventory numbers.

Crowded The vibration noise control heat pump condenser quieter can make your
customer happier.
Spaced The quieter on the condenser for the heat pump will make your customer
happier by controlling noise and vibrations.

7. Avoid Unnecessary *That/Which* Clauses

Wordiness can be the writer's greatest weakness and the reader's most common complaint. (Chapter 5 will help you find the words and phrases you need for a more concise, direct style.) *That/which* clauses using some form of the verb *to be* (*is, are, were, was*) are infamous for adding words but not meaning. They are popular with bureaucratic writers, who like to draw out an idea beyond the number of words needed. The information contained in *that/which* clauses can often be adequately represented by an adjective, as the following wordy sentences and their revisions show.

Wordy The pain medication that was prescribed by the doctor was very helpful to her father.

Concise The pain medication prescribed by the doctor helped her father. (Note how the revision reduces "was helpful to" to "helped" to further save words and time.)

Wordy I think the news magazine, which appears bi-monthly, will be one which keeps employees up to date on current events at Balko Industries.

Concise I think the bi-monthly magazine will inform employees about current events at Balko Industries.

Wordy The organizational plan that was approved last week contains a number of points which are considered to be especially important for new employees.

Concise The organizational plan approved last week contains important points for new employees.

✓ Revision Checklist

Here are some questions to ask yourself as you revise your sentences.

1. Does each of my sentences express a complete thought?
2. If a sentence contains two independent clauses, are the clauses separated by either a coordinating conjunction or a semicolon?
3. Are my sentences written in the active voice to make them easy to read?
4. Where have I used the passive voice?
5. Have I used the passive voice too much? If so, have I suitably revised some of my sentences into the active voice?
6. Are all the elements within a series—words, phrases, clauses—grammatically parallel?
7. Can the action of the verb be logically carried out by the subject of my sentence?
8. When a sentence contains a series of words, phrases, or clauses, are all of my modifiers placed closely to the words they modify?

9. Do all of my pronouns refer clearly to their antecedents?
10. Have I eliminated and revised all vague subjects and weak verbs?
11. Have I used the most direct, accessible sentence patterns for my reader?
12. Are my sentences too long? Will my audience understand them on the first reading?

Exercises

1. Punctuate the following sentences correctly.
   a. Cooking can kill many bacteria in food, it cannot kill them all.
   b. Bass fishing attracts many tourists to the lake. Not just during the summer but also during the fall.
   c. No new accounts will be opened today, therefore the credit office is closed.
   d. The charges for our service are reasonable, they come to barely $35.
   e. Ms. Jones-Fairley likes our contract, she will sign it and mail it tomorrow.
   f. The Land Rover is popular with sports enthusiasts partly because it is economical. And partly because it is so rugged.
   g. The patient received an injection for pain, however, he said that it did not help.
   h. Because real estate values soared; many buyers were unable to own their own homes. Which angered them.
   i. The college is offering five sections of Business English this term, many of them are in the late afternoon and evening.
   j. The sales manager had to prepare her report by that afternoon. Because the buyer wanted to review it before the conference tomorrow.
   k. Buses leave for Dayton punctually. On the hour and on the half.

2. The following sentences contain an awkward use of the passive voice. Rewrite them using the active voice to make them less awkward and easier to read.
   a. Little attention has been paid by your office to our request for additional information.
   b. The enclosed forms should be completed by you no later than August 15.
   c. The dinner was planned by her staff to celebrate her thirtieth birthday.
   d. A comet was seen by those citizens who stayed up late last evening.
   e. Discretion should be exercised by employees when answering complaint letters.
   f. Faster ways of notifying customers have been found by one of our employees.
   g. Appropriate uniforms are to be worn by all police officers attending the ceremony.

    h. The blocking of the canal had been planned by the Corps of Engineers for two years.

    i. It was determined by management not to approve a new employees' health center.

3. The following sentences contain errors in parallelism. Correct these sentences to make the grammatical units in them parallel.

    a. Willard likes swimming, hiking, and to fish.

    b. Silver is used in aerial photography, microfilming, for medical and industrial x-rays, and printers use it, too, to make photographic plates.

    c. Please return overshipments promptly and also I want you to reimburse any amounts paid over charges.

    d. You either must repair the circuit or it has to be replaced.

    e. Use a visual to emphasize key points, as a way of arousing interest, and when you want to summarize a lot of statistical data.

    f. The agency did not know who was responsible, where the individual lived, or the time the individual would return.

    g. In the saddle stitch method, printed material is bound using metal staples or cloth stitches are inserted.

    h. Once a conference is on our schedule, the personnel director is responsible for sending out announcements, the seating arrangements, what type of menu to serve, and also has to provide information on housing.

    i. We received questions from customers on how long it takes to complete the process, the cost required for additional safety features used in the process, and whether marketing advantages associated with the process were present.

    j. The shipment neither was on time nor could it have been accurate.

    k. The local television station either had to change its programming or it would be in trouble with the FCC.

4. The following sentences are contradictory or contain words that are inappropriate for the context. Rewrite these sentences to correct the errors.

    a. In metric terms, our new olympic swimming pool is twenty-five feet long.

    b. His report discusses the differences in jogging between the United States and Great Britain.

    c. The operator fed the load onto the truck using a hydraulic fork.

    d. Sampling all of the residents of Cherry Hill, we found that 25 percent wanted the zoning laws to remain the same, 40 percent wanted them modified to include multiple family housing, and the other 45 percent wanted changes in housing and transportation.

    e. The watch commander was happy to report that convictions exceeded arrests.

    f. The local committee threw its spirited support behind the opposition to the new liquor laws.

    g. The nonsoluble retaining wall will let in only a small amount of water.

    h. New drilling techniques make it possible to create oil faster.

    i. The applicant did not plan ahead and was, therefore, ready for the interviewer's questions.

    j. Health food stores take a great interest in nuts.

5. Rewrite the following sentences to correct dangling and misplaced modifiers.

    a. When preparing school papers, your dictionary will be a great aid.

    b. Using the Heimlich maneuver, a piece of food will be forced out of a person's airway.

    c. We purchased a new model from the salesclerk with adjustable arms.

    d. Topped with a tasty raspberry vinaigrette, the waiter brought us a delicious salad.

    e. Allowing for a 3 percent margin for error, the specifications arrived on the builder's desk this morning.

    f. Before turning the patient, intravenous solutions are given.

    g. The bank almost closed before we got there.

    h. Fastened securely, the officer left the compound.

    i. The teacher gave the test to the new student that covered the first third of the textbook.

    j. The plumber repaired the sink in our office that was stopped up since last week.

    k. The show dog ran away from the trainer with a leash around his neck.

    l. All travel requests must be submitted by employees in triplicate.

    m. The meal is prepared by the chef delicately seasoned with oregano.

    n. Almost maintenance-free, the housekeeper liked the new electric broom.

    o. Before placing the specimen under the microscope, proper care has to be taken.

    p. About the size of a quarter, most Americans did not like the Susan B. Anthony dollar.

    q. My neighbor went to see the dentist with a huge cavity.

    r. Turning the machine counterclockwise, the springs were loosened.

    s. The tax collector sent a bill to every property owner in Madison County that was due by April 1.

6. Rewrite the following sentences to correct faulty pronoun references.

    a. The head nurse ordered the aide and the technician to help the patient in Room 334. She came at once.

    b. The boss sent four different memos to the maintenance department about the problems with refuse on the weekends. They really made an impact on the department.

    c. When Barbara saw Mary, she shouted with joy.

    d. The filter was placed over the vent, but it was too small.

    e. The machine had to be primed and oiled regularly, which ensured a quick start.

    f. An all-purpose battery would be better in this car than an expensive one.

g. The white mice were placed in the new cages, and they were to be cleaned daily.

h. Mr. Martin told Mr. Rodriguez that he had found his glasses.

i. A check-up is important for good health. That is something you want to have.

j. Fourteen recruits joined the force in the months of July, August, and September. They will not be forgotten.

7. Rewrite the following sentences to make them easier to read. They contain one or more of the errors discussed on pages 108–112.

a. There are a number of businesses that have succumbed to failure recently due to the fact of their being mismanaged.

b. The work activities classification internal quarterly notification report is due at the end of this week.

c. Long open conveyor belts, which are used for the transportation of coal particles, can be considered to be a significant source of pollution.

d. It is, therefore, expensive to secure the importation of food from abroad because so much of it is shipped by costly carriers.

e. It seems apparent that there are a number of inconsistencies between the reports from Baxterville and New Platz.

f. The continuation of the fluoridation of the city water supply is advocated strenuously by the residents of West Allentown.

g. Evasive action roadblock techniques diminish the promotion of terrorist activities.

h. Flowing from hot to cold substances, heat is a form of energy.

i. The power is supplied by a six-cylinder, in-line, liquid-cooled, standard-regulation, gasoline-powered engine located in the front of the truck.

j. To rotate the auger at a slower speed with more power, place the transmission in first gear.

k. Relative to emissions from the iron and steel processes, inspection techniques have certain fundamental characteristics regarding costs which are the same for every technique so used.

l. The recent purchase of a Multi-Writer can lead to the improvement of routine office data-processing functions, which will save the company many hours of time and dollars in costs, provided that effective training programs accompany the acquisition of the Multi-Writer and that it does not become dated and that it is compatible with our existing data-processing equipment, which resulted in a large expenditure for the firm last year.

m. If it has the appearance of being spoiled or gives an emission of an odor, the destruction of the food shipment is imperative.

n. There are a number of precautions that it is believed by the Department of Public Safety must be put into effect within the next year.

Writing: Words

Words are the essential building blocks of any piece of writing. They are the nuts and bolts of communication. But you do not start a major building project with handfuls of nuts and bolts. First, you have to develop a larger plan. That plan or design is at the heart of the writing process described in Chapter 2. The writing process (the design) starts with the large decisions writers make about the overall development, organization, and arrangement of information suitable for their audience. When writers establish their audience's needs and the scope of their message, they have a context in which their words will be read. When the design is in place, then it is time to concentrate on the nuts and bolts, the words.

Choosing the right words does not just happen; it does not easily fall into place. You have to work hard at it. Selecting the right words is a vital part of the writing process. Remember, however, that the writing process does not refer to a series of steps that always follow in sequence. Writers can—and usually do—shift back and forth from one element of the process to another. The right word or phrase may occur to you at any point from your first draft through your final copy. And although you may find the right words for part of your message early in the writing process, be aware that you have an obligation to your reader to make sure that all your words are as carefully chosen as the facts you have gathered for your entire message. Hence, it is essential to make several passes through your work during the revision and editing phases to see that your words are accurate and appropriate for the reader. In the process, you will add, delete, and substitute words for clarity, and conciseness, and you should also check for spelling and usage.

Effective writers make sure their words convey the right meaning and tone; they choose words that are lean and clean—concise and precise. Wrong words can ruin the process of communication with your reader. Inappropriate, incorrect, or blustery words can offend and/or confuse your reader. But if you choose your words skillfully to say exactly what you want, your writing will be more effective and better received by readers. They will be more apt to accept your message and agree with your conclusions and recommendations. Precise words give readers the information they need to grasp your message the first time; and concise words ensure that readers will not waste time because of wordiness.

Chapter 5 discusses some common problems you need to be aware of in selecting your words and also offers practical suggestions on how and why to make effective word choices during the revising and editing phases of your work. Specifically, after reading this chapter and applying its principles to the process of your writing, you will learn to

- check the spelling of words carefully.
- match the right word with the right meaning.
- select precise words.
- cut unnecessary words.
- eliminate sexist language.
- avoid jargon and slang.

Spelling Words Correctly

Your written work will be judged in part on how well you spell. A misspelled word may seem like a small matter, but on an employment application, memo, incident report, or letter, it stands out to your discredit. You will look careless, or even worse, uneducated to a client or supervisor. Readers will inevitably wonder about other skills if your spelling is incorrect.

Your professional work places a double duty on you as a speller. You must learn to spell both the technical terms of your field and the common words of the English language. The following suggestions can help you to improve your spelling:

1. Keep a college-level dictionary at your desk (not on a shelf where you have to reach for it) and use it. Better yet, buy a small pocket dictionary and carry it with you.
2. Also keep on your desk a specialized dictionary or manual that lists the technical vocabulary you use on your job.
3. Make a list of the words you have the most trouble spelling as well as any new and difficult words you encounter. Write them down in a small spiral notebook for easy reference.
4. Double-check your spelling before submitting your work.
5. Review the suggestions on proofreading found on pages 149–150. Have someone help you proofread, too.

If you prepare your work on a word processor, you may have the option of using a spell-checking program. Spell checkers are very handy for flagging potential problem words. But beware! Spell checkers only recognize words that have been listed in them. A proper name or infrequently used word may be flagged as an error even though the word is spelled correctly. When you compile a list of technical words you use regularly and words that you find particularly difficult, add them to the spell-check program. Even then the spell checker cannot tell you if a word is the right one for the context. For example, it will not differentiate between *too* and *two* or *there* and *their.* In short, do not rely exclusively on spell checkers. It is your responsibility to make sure your words are spelled correctly. You must be the final judge.

Table 5.1 (pp. 120–121) lists some of the most frequently misspelled words in business and technical writing. Use this table as a handy reference. But also note that the following suggestions can help you become a better speller. The chances are that many of the words that cause you difficulty are the same ones that give others trouble. Attention to these danger areas will pay dividends.

1. **Silent letters.**

ac*q*uaint	fas*c*inate	le*i*sure
ais*l*e	fore*a*rm	maneuver
*a*scend	ga*u*ge	min*i*ature
*c*holesterol	hemmorr*h*age	mor*t*gage
code*i*ne	hyg*i*ene	ne*u*tral
colum*n*	*k*napsack	vacu*u*m
diaphra*gm*	like*l*y	We*d*nesday

2. **Use of *ie* and *ei*. In general, *i* before *e,* except after *c*.**

ie	*ei*	*exceptions*
believe	ceiling	ancient
cashier	weight	conscience
chief	deceive	deficient
experience	perceive	financier
yield	receive	society

3. Double consonants. Many words double a consonant when a verb changes from present to past tense (*prefer / preferred*) or when the root form changes from verb to noun (*occur / occurrence*).

admit / admi*tt*ed / admi*tt*ance
commit / commi*tt*ed/ *but* commitment
omit / omi*tt*ed
plan / plan*n*ing
repel / repe*ll*ing / repe*ll*ent
write / wri*tt*en / *but* writing
profit / *but* profited

4. Prefixes and suffixes. When adding a prefix (*il-, mis-, un-*), do not change the spelling of the word to which it is attached.

*il*logical
*mis*spell
*un*necessary

TABLE 5.1   Frequently Misspelled Words in Business and Technical Writing

absence	changeover	embarrass	maintenance
abundance	chief	eminent	manageable
accept	column	environment	maneuver
acceptable	commercial	equipped	manufacturer
accessible	commitment	exaggerate	marriage
accidentally	committed	exceed	memento
accommodate	comparative	excellence	mischievous
accumulate	competent	exercise	missile
accustomed	conceit	exhaust	misspell
achieve	conceive	existence	moccasin
acknowledge	condemn	expedient	morale
acquaint	conscience	familiar	necessary
acquire	conscientious	favorite	neighbor
across	conscious	February	ninth
address	consistent	fluorescent	noticeable
adolescent	convenience	forcibly	nuisance
affiliate	convenient	fulfill	obstacle
aggravate	courteous	gauge	occasion
aggressive	criticism	government	occasionally
all right	criticize	grammar	occur
a lot	curiosity	guarantee	occurrence
annihilate	deceive	guard	omission
apparatus	decide	harass	opportunity
apparent	definite	humorous	optimistic
apparition	definitely	hypocrisy	paid
appearance	dependent	incidentally	parallel
appropriate	descend	incredible	pasture
arctic	descendant	independence	perceive
argument	desirable	indispensable	permanent
ascend	desperate	inevitably	permissible
ascertain	determine	innocuous	persevere
assemble	develop	inoculate	persistence
assessment	diffident	interest	personnel
auxiliary	disagree	interference	perspiration
beginning	disappear	irrelevant	persuade
belief	disappoint •	irresistible	poison
believe	disastrous	itinerary	pollute
breath	discipline	judgment	possession
breathe	discriminate	knowledge	potato
bureaucracy	dispel	leisure	precede
business	dissatisfied	length	preference
calendar	dominant	lenient	preferred
carriage	duel	license	prevalent
category	dyeing	likelihood	primitive
cemetery	efficient	livelihood	privilege
certain	eighth	luxury	procedure
changeable	eligible	magnificent	proceed

TABLE 5.1 (continued)

prominent	recommend	satellite	tendency
pronunciation	referral	scarcity	transferred
propaganda	referred	seize	twelfth
propellant	relief	separate	tyranny
prophesy	relieve	sergeant	unanimous
publicly	remembrance	sherbet	unnecessary
pursue	reminisce	similar	unveil
quandary	repetition	sponsor	vacuum
quantity	resistance	stationary	vengeance
questionnaire	restaurant	stationery	visible
recede	rhythm	superficial	vitamin
receipt	ridiculous	superintendent	warrant
receive	roommate	supersede	wholly
recognize	sacrilegious	suppress	withholding

Watch out for the following suffixes.

-able	*-iable*	*-ible*
acceptable	appreciable	audible
dependable	justifiable	combustible
noticeable	negotiable	edible
profitable	reliable	eligible
serviceable	variable	visible

5. Plurals.

- When a word ends in *y*, drop the *y* and add *-ies* if the *y* follows a consonant: *apology / apologies; army / armies; history / histories; library / libraries; party / parties.* If the word ends in *y* and the *y* follows a vowel, just add *s: bay / bays; toy / toys; turkey / turkeys.*
- Words that end in *f* or *fe* usually change these letters to *v* before adding *-es: calf / calves; half / halves; knife / knives; life / lives; leaf / leaves; self / selves; shelf / shelves; wife / wives.*
- Nouns ending in *o* after a vowel form their plurals by adding *s: patio / patios; stereo / stereos; studio / studios; zoo / zoos.* When the *o* follows a consonant, add *-es* to form the plural: *echo / echoes; hero / heroes; potato / potatoes; tomato / tomatoes.* Exception: *lasso / lassos; piano / pianos; tobacco / tobaccos.*
- Some nouns do not form their plural by adding *-s* or *-es.* Instead, they use an older kind of plural (*ox / oxen; child / children*), or they indicate a change in number in the middle of a word rather than at the end (*foot / feet; man / men*), or they use a foreign plural (*criterion / criteria; curriculum / curricula; phenomenon / phenomena; syllabus / syllabi*). Some nouns for animals are the same for both singular and plural: *fish, deer, sheep, snipe.* Finally, some words are "false" plurals; they end in *s,* leading you to think that they are plural. These nouns, however, are always singular

in meaning and are never spelled without the final *s: economics, mathematics, measles, pediatrics, scissors.*

6. Apostrophes. Apostrophes can cause some writers a lot of trouble. Basically, apostrophes are used for four reasons: (1) contractions, (2) possessives, (3) plurals, and (4) abbreviations. The guidelines below will help you to sort out these uses of the apostrophe.

1. To form a contraction, the apostrophe takes the place of the missing letter or letters: *I've = I have; doesn't = does not; he's = he is; it's = it is. Its* is a possessive pronoun (the dog and its bone), not a contraction. There is no such form as *its'.*

2. To form a possessive, follow these rules.

   a. If a singular or plural noun does not end in an **-s,** add **'s** to show possession.

Mary's locker	the woman's jacket
the truck's battery	the women's jackets
San Francisco's streets	anybody's time
children's books	the company's policy

   b. If a plural noun ends in **-s,** add just the **'** to indicate possession.

employees' benefits	computers' speed
lawyers' fees	police officers' training
horses' auction	the boss's schedule (singular noun)

   c. If a proper name ends in **-s,** use **'s** to form the possessive.

Jones's account	Keats's poetry
the Williams's house	James's contract

   d. If it is a compound noun, add an **'** or an **'s** to the end of the word.

brother-in-law's business	Ms. Allison Jones-Wyatt's order

   e. If you wish to indicate shared possession, add just **'s** to the last name.

Warner and Kline's Computer Shop	Sue and Anne's major

      If you want to indicate separate possession, add an **'s** to each name.

John's and Mary's transcripts	Shakespeare's and Byron's poetry

3. To form the plural of numbers and capital letters used as nouns, including abbreviations without periods, just add **s.** To avoid misreading some capital letters, however, you may need to add the apostrophe.

during the 1980s	all perfect 10s
his SATs	several local YMCAs
the 3 Rs	straight A's

4. For abbreviations with periods, however, and for lowercase letters used as nouns, form the plural by adding **'s**.

his *p*'s and *q*'s   Ph.D.'s

Matching the Right Word With the Right Meaning

The English language contains many common words that are frequently mistaken (and so confused) for each other because they are pronounced alike but spelled differently. These words are called homonyms. *Meat* (food) and *meet* (to greet) are examples. When a dispatcher orders employees to keep overtime to a "bear minimum," no reference to a grizzly is intended; rather, *bear* has been confused with *bare*. Similarly, the mechanic who writes on a work order to "idol" down a car has confused *idol* (religious image) with *idle* (a verb meaning to slow down). Remember, your word processor's spell checker can never tell you if you have confused *bear* for *bare* or *idol* for *idle*.

The words in the following list frequently are mistaken for one another. Some are true homonyms; others are just similar in spelling, pronunciation, or usage. By studying the correct spelling, part of speech, and meaning of each, you will save yourself time and embarrassment.

accept (v) to receive, to acknowledge: *We accept your proposal.*
except (prep) excluding, but: *Everyone attended the meeting except David.*

access (n) the right to use: *We don't have access to all of their files.*
excess (adj) superfluous: *Please remove all excess materials from this file.*

adapt (v) to adjust to: *We will have to adapt to the new phone system.*
adept (adj) skillful: *Cheryl is very adept at word processing.*
adopt (v) to select by choice: *Let's adopt a new technique.*

advice (n) a recommendation: *I should have taken Leroy's advice.*
advise (v) to counsel: *Our lawyers advised us not to sign the contract.*

affect (v) to change, to influence: *Has the detour on Route 22 affected your travel plans?*
effect (n) a result: *What was the effect of the new procedure?*
effect (v) to bring about: *We will try to effect a change in company policy.*

all ready (adj) two-word phrase *all + ready;* to be finished; to be prepared: *We are all ready for the inspector's visit.*
already (adv) previously, before a given time: *Our supply department already ordered the replacement valve.*

attain (v) to achieve, to reach: *My sister soon attained the position of partner at the accounting firm.*
obtain (v) to get, to receive: *You must obtain a job application from the personnel office.*

beside (prep) next to: *I keep a dictionary beside my word processor.*
besides (prep) in addition to: *Besides Juan and Suzanne, who will attend the seminar?*

brake (v) to stop: *I always wear my seat belt in case I need to brake suddenly.*
brake (n) a mechanism to stop a vehicle: *She hit the brakes just in time.*
break (v) to split, to crack: *He always breaks pencils when he's angry.*
break (n) a split, a separation: *Let's take a short break before Hal's presentation.*

capital (adj) major, chief: *I think that is a capital idea.*
capital (adj) upper-case: *Always begin names of cities and states with a capital letter.*
capital (n) wealth in money or property: *We can't start a new business without some capital.*
capital (n) the governing city of a state or country: *Concord is the capital of New Hampshire.*
capitol (n) the building where a state legislature meets: *My cousin is a guide at the capitol.* (Note: The *C* in *Capitol* is always capitalized when it refers to the Capitol Building in Washington, D.C.)

cent (n) one penny: *My old car isn't worth a cent.*
scent (n) smell: *I detected the scent of ammonia coming from the supply room.*
sent (v) transmitted (past tense of *send*): *I sent the blueprints by overnight express.*

cite (v) to document: *Please cite several examples to support your claim.*
site (n) place, location: *They want to build a parking lot on the site of the old theatre.*
sight (n) vision: *I will never forget the sight of our general manager changing that flat tire on the highway.*

coarse (adj) rough: *This paper is too coarse to use for our new brochure.*
course (n) class: *Kim wants to take a course in computer programming.*
course (n) plan of action: *We must decide immediately what course to take.* (Also, *of course*, meaning certainly: *Of course, I'll take you to the airport.*)

complement (v) to add to, to fill out: *His graphs and charts complemented my proposal.*
compliment (v) to praise: *The customer complimented us on our courteous staff.*

continually (adv) frequently and regularly: *This answering machine continually disconnects the caller in the middle of the message.*
continuously (adv) constantly: *The air conditioning is on continuously during the summer.*

discreet (adj) showing respect, being tactful: *The manager was discreet in answering the complaint letter.*
discrete (adj) separate, distinct: *Put those figures into discrete categories for processing.*

dual (adj) double: *A clock-radio serves a dual purpose.*
duel (n) a fight, a battle: *The argument almost turned into a real duel.*

eminent (adj) prominent, highly esteemed: *Dr. Rollins is the most eminent pediatrician in our community.*
imminent (adj) about to happen: *A hostile takeover of that company is imminent.*

fair (adj) just, legal: *It would be fair to give our employees extra sick leave benefits.*
fare (n) price of travel: *We should try to make early reservations so we can get a discount fare.*

foreword (n) preface, introduction to a book: *The foreword outlined the author's goals and objectives in her research study.*
forward (adv) toward a time or place; in advance: *We moved the time of the visit forward on the calendar so we could meet the overseas manager.*
forward (v) to send ahead: *We forwarded his mail to his new address.*

hear (v) to listen: *The members in the back of the auditorium couldn't hear the speaker.*
here (adv) in this place: *Let's post the bulletin here so everyone can see it.*

imply (v) to suggest: *Mr. Chin implied that the mechanics had taken too long for their lunch break.*
infer (v) to draw a conclusion: *We can infer from these sales figures that the new advertising campaign is working.*

it's (noun + verb) contraction of *it* and *is*: *Do you think it's too early to tell?*
its (adj) possessive form of *it*: *That old typewriter is on its last legs.*

lay/laid/laid (v) to put down: *Lay aside that project for now. He laid aside the project. He had already laid aside the project twice before.*
lie/lay/lain (v) to recline: *I think I'll lie down for a while. He lay there for only ten minutes before the firefighter rescued him. She has lain out in the sun too often.*

lose (v) to misplace, to fail to win: *Be careful not to lose my calculator. I hope I don't lose my seat on the planning board.*
loose (adj) not tight: *The printer ribbon was too loose.*

maybe (adv) perhaps: *Maybe we can sell them our top-of-the-line model.*
may be (v) two-word verbal phrase, *may + be*: *I may be home late tonight if the meeting runs over.*

pair (n) two, a couple: *We could use a pair of new copy machines.*
pare (v) to cut down: *Try to pare that list so it will fit on one page.*
pear (n) a fruit: *Chris has a pear for dessert every day.*

passed (v) went by (past tense of *pass*): *He passed me in the hall without recognizing me.*
past (n) time gone by: *We've never used their services in the past.*

peace (n) calm: *There was peace in the office while the phones were dead.*
piece (n) a portion: *They just ordered a new piece of equipment to make the job go more smoothly.*

personal (adj) private: *The manager closes her door only if she's making a personal phone call.*
personnel (n) staff of employees: *All personnel must take part in tomorrow's fire drill.*

perspective (n) view: *From the customer's perspective, we are a fair and courteous company.*
prospective (adj) expected, likely to happen or become: *Send the new brochure to all prospective customers.*

plain (adj) simple: *The plain truth is that they just don't want to spend the money on repairs.*
plains (n) a flat, open area of land: *Miguel grew up on the plains of Texas.*
plane (n) short for *airplane*: *He took an early plane to Phoenix.*
plane (n) a device used to make a surface smooth and level: *I'll borrow their plane so we can finish sanding this door.*

precede (v) to go before: *A slide show will precede the open discussion.*
proceed (v) to carry on, to go ahead: *Proceed as if we had never received that letter.*

principal (adj) main, chief: *Sales of washers and dryers constitute their principal source of revenue.*
principal (n) the head of a school: *She was a high school principal before she entered the business world.*
principle (n) a policy, a belief: *Salesclerks should operate on the principle that the customer is always right.*

respectfully (adv) with esteem: *One should always treat managers respectfully.*
respectively (adv) in the order mentioned: *Paragraphs and sentences are discussed in Chapters 3 and 4, respectively.*

right (adj) correct: *You're on the right track.*
right (adj) the opposite of left: *His right hand ached from so much writing.*
rite (n) a ceremony or ritual: *The rite of marriage is a sacred one.*
write (v) to form letters: *Tony had to write a summary of his findings.*

stationary (adj) not moving: *Maria rides a stationary bicycle for an hour every morning.*
stationery (n) writing supplies, such as paper and envelopes: *Please stop off at the stationery store and buy some more address labels.*

than (conj) as opposed to (used in comparisons): *He is a faster keyboarder than his predecessor.*
then (adv) at that time: *First she called the client; then she summarized their conversation in a letter.*

their (adj) possessive form of *they*: *All of the lab technicians took their vacations during January.*
there (adv) in that place: *Please put the printer in there.*
they're (noun + verb) contraction of *they* and *are*: *They're our two best customer service representatives.*

two (n) a number: *I sent her only two copies.*
to (prep) toward: *Akiko was already on her way to the bank when we saw her.*
too (adv) also: *You can come along too.*

wear (v) to dress: *All employees must wear the same uniform.*
where (adv) at what place: *Where did I leave my coffee cup?*

weather (n) climate: *The fall weather is beautiful in Boston.*
whether (conj) if: *I don't know whether Ms. Hall plans to attend.*

weak (adj) not strong: *My opening argument was too weak.*
week (n) seven days: *Marco was out sick all week.*

who's (noun + verb) contraction of *who* and *is*: *Who's up next for a promotion?*
whose (adj) possessive form of *who*: *Whose idea was that in the first place?*

you're (noun + verb) contraction of *you* and *are*: *You're going to like their decision.*
your (adj) possessive form of *you*: *They agree with your ideas.*

Selecting Precise Words

Clear writing can save an employer time and money, and it can save you the frustration of additional explanations over the phone or of rewriting your work. Precise writing gets the job done right the first time. You can be precise, though, only if your words are. After all, your words take the place of the references they describe. Your words should answer the questions readers ask themselves as they read.

- How big?
- How expensive?
- How much?

- How quickly?
- What color?
- How many?
- Who?
- Where?
- When?

To write precisely, use concrete, specific words rather than vague, general ones. Choose words that appeal to the reader's five senses—words that help a reader to see, hear, smell, taste, and touch. For example, the phrase "piece of office equipment" is vague. "An IBM microcomputer with a 14-inch VGA color monitor" is precise.

Words such as *aspect, condition, creature, factor, nice, situation, thing,* and *ways* raise more questions than they answer. Is a "nice" house made of brick or covered with aluminum siding? Does it have gas or electric heat? Will you find it in the city, the suburbs, or the country? Here is another example of the advantage of using exact words.

General   With adequate storage fish keeps for some time.
Specific   If refrigerated at 32°F (0°C) and covered with crushed ice, fresh fish may be stored up to three days.

Unlike the first sentence, the second sentence provides the reader with helpful, practical information.

There is a wide range between "general" and "specific." In Table 5.2 note that the general terms in the far left column gradually become more precise as you proceed to the right.

How can you be sure that your words are precise, that they are specific and not vague? Follow these three simple procedures as you revise your work for the reader.

1. Circle all your nouns. Do they point to a specific person, place, or object? Could your reader separate that person, place, or object from all others like it? If

TABLE 5.2   The Range Between General and Specific Terms

General ←			→ *Specific*
vehicle	truck	pickup	Dodge wide cab
medication	injection	barbiturate	Seconal 100 mg.
food	protein	poultry	Chicken Kiev
residence	house	cottage	Tudor cottage
official	federal agent	USDA inspector	Mary Whitton
reasonable	inexpensive	bargain	20 percent off $500 sale price
circumstance	disaster	storm	Hurricane Andrew

so, you have a specific word. If readers or listeners cannot quickly identify an object, person, or place from your description, you have used a general word.

2. Underline all your adjectives. Do they tell readers the exact color, size, texture, quantity, or quality you want to convey? Adjectives like *bad, fantastic, nice, good, great, interesting, numerous, serious,* and *small* will not help your audience see vividly or measure accurately. Next, see if you need every adjective you have underlined. A noun or verb may render some adjectives unnecessary; the adjective or adverb may be repeating what the noun or verb has already said—for example, "shout loudly" (shouts are always loud), "a big Saint Bernard" (such dogs are always big), "a small 3" × 5" card" (is there a large 3" × 5" card?).

3. Star all your verbs. Do they show lively movement, or have they fallen limp on the page? Check your verbs for their activity level; they should be full of information for readers about how and why something happened. Give readers something specific and concrete to watch. Vague verbs such as *appear, concern, consider, evidence, exist, relate, seem,* or any of the forms of *to be* (*is, are, was, were*) lack information about specific action. These verbs are especially sluggish when combined with "there are" and "it is" constructions such as the following: "It appears that there are some troubles with the company truck." This sentence would move any employer to scream, "What happened?" Note the increased action level in the revised sentence: "The company truck ran over a roofing nail, which punctured the right front tire." Choose graphic verbs such as *accelerate, complete, carry out, direct, duplicate, emerge, increase, force, juggle, mount, program, push, scatter, squeeze, support, streamline, test, turn around.* If your starred verbs vibrate with action, you help readers to grasp your meaning precisely. You will also make reading your work easier and more lively.

If you are preparing your work on a word processor, you can use command keys to boldface your nouns, underline adjectives, and italicize your verbs.

Cutting Out Unnecessary Words

Too many people in business and industry think the more words, the better. Nothing could be more self-defeating. Your readers are busy; unnecessary words slow them down. Make every word work. When a word takes up space but gives no meaning, cut it. Cut out any words you can from your sentences. If the sentence still makes sense and reads correctly, you have eliminated wordiness.

The phrases on the left should be replaced with the precise words on the right.

Wordy Draft	**Concise Revision**
at a slow rate	slowly
at an early date	early
at the point where	where
at this point in time	now
be in agreement with	agree

Wordy Draft	Concise Revision
bring to a conclusion	conclude, end
bring together	combine, join
by means of	with
come to terms with	agree, accept
due to the fact that	because
express an opinion that	believe
feel quite certain about	believe
for the length of time that	while
for the period of	for
for the purpose of	to
in an effort to	to
in such a manner that	so
in the area / case / field of	in
in the event that	if
in the neighborhood of	approximately
look something like	resemble
serve the function of	function as
show a tendency to	tend
take into consideration	consider
take under advisement	consider
take place in such a manner	occur
with reference to	regarding, about
with the result that	so

The following tips will help you to eliminate other kinds of wordiness just as easily during the revision and editing stages of your work.

1. Replace a wordy phrase or clause with a one- or two-word synonym.

Wordy The college has parking zones for different areas for people living on campus as well as for those who do not live on campus and who commute to school.

Revision The college has different parking zones for resident and commuter students. (Twenty words of the original sentence—everything after "areas for"—have been reduced to four words: "resident and commuter students.")

Wordy Many banks use a system of tubes to move small items by means of air pressure from one place to another.

Revision Many banks use pneumatic tubes to send small items from one place to another. (Using the phrase "pneumatic tubes" will save many words and identify the system more precisely—provided, of course, that your reader knows what pneumatic tubes are.)

2. Combine sentences beginning with the same subject or ending with an object that becomes the subject of the next sentence.

Wordy I asked the inspector if she were going to visit the plant this afternoon. I also asked her if she would come alone.

Revision I asked the inspector if she were going to visit the plant alone this afternoon.

Wordy Homeowners want to buy low-maintenance plants. These low-maintenance plants include the ever-popular holly and boxwood varieties. These plants are also inexpensive.

Revision Homeowners want to buy such low-maintenance and inexpensive plants as holly and boxwood. (This revision combines three sentences into one, condenses twenty-four words into fourteen, and joins three related thoughts.)

Another kind of wordiness comes from using redundant expressions. Being redundant means that you say the same thing a second time, in different words. "Fellow colleague," "component parts," and "corrosive acid" are phrases that contain this kind of double speech; a fellow *is* a colleague, a component *is* a part, and acid *is* corrosive. Redundant expressions are uneconomical and are often clichés. The suggested revisions on the right are preferable to the redundant phrases on the left.

Redundant	Concise Revision
absolutely essential	essential
advance reservations	reservations
basic necessities	necessities, needs
cease and desist	stop
close proximity	proximity, nearness
each and every	each, every, all
end result	result
eradicate completely	eradicate
exposed opening	opening
fair and just	fair
final conclusions / final outcome	conclusions / outcome
first and foremost	first
full and complete	full, complete
grand total	total
null and void	void
passing fad	fad
personal opinion	opinion
prerecorded	recorded
over and done with	over
tried and true	tried, proven
unexpected surprise	surprise

Watch for repetitious words, phrases, or clauses within a sentence. Sometimes one sentence or one part of a sentence needlessly duplicates another.

Redundant The post office hires part-time help, especially around the holidays, to handle the large amounts of mail at Christmas time.

Revised The post office often hires part-time help to handle the large amounts of mail at Christmas time. ("Especially around the holidays" means the same thing as "at Christmas time.")

Redundant The fermenting activity of yeast is due to an enzyme called zymase. This enzyme produces chemical changes in yeast.

Revised The fermenting activity of yeast is due to an enzyme called zymase. (The second sentence says vaguely what the first sentence says precisely; delete it.)

Redundant To provide more room for employees' cars, the security department is studying ways to expand the employees' parking lot.

Revised The security department is studying ways to expand the employees' parking lot. (Since the first phrase says nothing that the reader does not know from the independent clause, cut it.)

Adding a prepositional phrase can sometimes contribute to redundancy. The italicized words below are redundant because of the unnecessary qualification they impose on the word they modify. Be on the lookout for the italicized phrases and delete them.

audible *to the ear*	hard *to the touch*
bitter *in taste*	honest *in character*
fly *through the air*	light *in weight*
orange *in color*	soft *in texture*
rectangular *in shape*	tall *in height*
second *in sequence*	twenty *in number*
short *in duration*	visible *to the eye*

Certain combinations of verbs and adverbs are also redundant. Again, the italicized words below should be deleted.

advance *forward*	lift *up*
burn *up*	merge *together*
cancel *out*	open *up*
circle *around*	plan *ahead*
close *off*	probed *into*
commute *back and forth*	prove *conclusively*
combine *together*	refer *back*
continue *on*	repeat *again*
drop *down*	reply *back*
funnel *through*	revert *back*
join *together*	write *down*

Figure 5.1 shows a draft of a memo that Trudy Wallace wants to send to her boss about installing cellular phones in the company cars. Like many early drafts, Wallace's represents her attempt to get her ideas down on paper without worrying about finding the most concise and precise words. Her early draft is bloated with unnecessary words, expendable phrases, and repetitious ideas.

After preparing a number of further drafts and revisions, Trudy Wallace was able to streamline her memo to Lee Chadwick and eliminate the wordiness of her earlier draft. Note how, in Figure 5.2, she pruned wordy expressions, combined sentences to cut out duplication, and found a two-word phrase, "telephone tag," to replace the unnecessarily complex description of calling clients back. This revised version is only 102 words, as opposed to 266 words in the draft. Not only has Wallace streamlined her message but she has made it easier to read.

FIGURE 5.1   Wordy draft for a memo.

TO: Lee Chadwick
FROM: Trudy Wallace   *T. W.*
DATE: May 3, 1994
SUBJECT: Installing cellular phones

   Due to the amount of time our sales force spends traveling on the roads each day, it strikes me as beneficial to look into the distinct possibility of installing cellular car phones in our company cars. Such an installation would benefit our sales force in a variety of multiple ways. The sales force could increase their efficiency and morale with the installation of these car phones. With the aid of a cellular phone we could bring together our customers and our sales force a lot easier. Rather than wasting an amount of time in the neighborhood of 40 to 50 minutes each day tracking down phones on the road, our sales people could have a shortened period of time to respond to calls using their cellular phones in their cars. The response rate of returning a call could be markedly reduced and dropped down. Moreover, by having cellular phones in their cars the sales people would minimize the problems of returning calls to people and then finding out they are out and then having to call them back. It is difficult to catch people this way. Cellular phones would increase both the convenience and the ease by which we operate our business. I think it would be absolutely essential to the ongoing operation of our company's business today to respond fully and completely to the possibility such a proposal affords us. It would therefore appear safe to conclude that with reference to the issue of cellular phones that every means at our disposal should be brought to bear on including such phones in our company cars.

FIGURE 5.2   The memo in Figure 5.1 revised for conciseness.

TO: Lee Chadwick
FROM: Trudy Wallace   *T. W.*
DATE: May 3, 1994
SUBJECT: Installing cellular phones

   Because our sales people spend so much time on the road, I think we should install cellular phones to increase employee efficiency and improve morale. Cellular phones would help our sales people get in touch with their clients a lot easier and faster. They would not waste 40 to 50 minutes each day looking for phones to call clients. And they would save even more time by not having to play telephone tag.

   I think installing cellular phones is a wise investment, and so with your approval, I will obtain more information from suppliers to prepare a formal proposal to request bids.

Eliminating Sexist Language

Sexist language unfairly assigns responsibilities, jobs, or titles to individuals on the basis of sex. Such language discriminates in favor of one sex at the expense of the other, usually women. Sexist language is often based on sexist stereotypes that show men as superior to women. For example, calling politicians "city fathers" or "favorite sons" follows the stereotypical picture of politicians as male; such phrases discriminate against women who do or could hold public office. Sexist phrases assume engineers, physicians, or pilots are male (*he, his, him*) and social workers, nurses, and secretaries are female (*she, her*), although members of both sexes belong to these professions. Sexist language offers a distorted view of our society and deprives women of their equal rights.

In business settings, a company that sends invitations to a party to "employees and their wives" or "customers and their wives" is guilty of using sexist language. Revised to eliminate sexism, the invitation should read to "employees and their spouses (or guests)" or "customers and their associates."

Sexist phrases include *gal Friday, little woman, lady of the house, the best man for the job, the weaker sex, woman's work, working wives,* and *young man on the way up.* Using such sexist terms, you will not only offend but exclude many members of the audience you want to reach.

One way to eliminate sexist language from your writing is to replace sexist words with neutral ones. Neutral words do *not* refer to a specific sex; they are genderless. Note how the sexist words on the left can be replaced by neutral, non-sexist ones on the right.

Sexist	Neutral
authoress	writer, author
businessman	businessperson
chairman	chair, chairperson
craftsman	skilled worker
fireman	firefighter
foreman	supervisor
janitress	cleaning person
lady physician	physician
landlord, landlady	owner
mailman/postman	mail carrier
man-hours	work-hours
mankind	humanity
manmade	synthetic, artificial
manpower	strength, effort, power
men	human beings, people
modern man	modern society
policeman	police officer
salesman	salesperson, clerk
stewardess	flight attendant
workman	worker

Using the masculine pronouns (*he, his, him*) when referring to a group that includes both men and women is also sexist.

Every worker must submit his travel expenses by Monday.

Workers may include women as well as men, and to assume all workers are men is misleading and unfair to women. You can avoid such sexist language by doing one of the following.

1. Make the subject of your sentence plural and thus neutral.

   Workers must submit their travel expenses by Monday.

2. Use *his or her* instead of *his.*

   Every worker must submit his or her travel expenses by Monday.

3. Reword the sentence using the passive voice.

   All travel expenses must be submitted by Monday.

Moreover, in some contexts exclusive use of the masculine pronoun might invite a lawsuit. For example, you would be violating federal employment laws prohibiting discrimination on the basis of sex if you wrote the following in a help-wanted advertisement for your company.

   Each applicant must submit his transcript with his application. He must also have 3 letters of recommendation sent to us from individuals familiar with his work.

From the language of this ad, one would assume that only men could be applicants for the position.

There are other sexist uses of language you need to avoid. Eliminate such sexist salutations as *Dear Sir* or *Dear Gentlemen* from your letters (see page 157). Moreover, do not single out a woman's physical appearance (a tall blonde), marital status (a divorcée), or age (middle-aged mother). It is unjust and insulting to introduce sexist distinctions.

Avoiding Jargon and Slang

Jargon

Jargon is shop talk, the specialized vocabulary of a particular occupation. Jargon includes, for example, an *IPPB* (Intermittent Positive Pressure Breathing) *machine* in respiratory therapy, *hard water* (water containing more than 85.5 parts per million of calcium carbonate) in geology, or *pixel* (minimum amount of light on a CRT screen) in computer science. Such technical terms are necessary, but should be used only when the following three conditions are met.

1. The audience understands jargon and expects the writer to use it.
2. A technical term or phrase conveys a precise idea that could not be adequately described with a common word or phrase—for instance, *flange pan* instead of *cake pan.*
3. The kind of form or report you are completing requires jargon—for example, a patient's hospital record, a specification sheet, or a legal description.

The word *jargon* has another meaning besides the legitimate technical language of a profession. More often, it refers to phony, inflated, and uselessly complex language. Jargon is a label attached to pompous words (pseudoscientific jawbreakers) some writers use instead of the much more simple, natural, and direct vocabulary their readers better understand and value. Jargon is language that puts on airs; it reeks of the stuffiness found in some business letters (see pages 171–174). People who favor jargon dislike pleasantly clear and direct verbs. For the unassuming verb *get,* they substitute *procure;* for *simplify* or *ease,* they choose (or *elect,* in jargon) *facilitate;* rather than *join* or *connect,* they prefer to *interface.* They also use trendy, bureaucratic nouns instead of much more clear and direct ones—*parameters* for *limits* or *scope; viability* for *possibility* or *likelihood; domicile* for *residence; ambience* for *atmosphere;* and *input* for *advice, suggestion,* or *contribution.*

Here are three characteristics of jargon, together with suggestions for doing away with it.

1. Pompous words. Use short, serviceable words instead of pompous expressions (*verbiage* in jargon). Your readers will appreciate your clarity and your honesty. Cut a three-word smoke screen (*scholastic achievement profile*) to one word (*transcript*). *Aquatic support system* could be written *life jacket.*

Note how the original, clear first sentences of Herman Melville's *Moby-Dick* lose their clarity and directness in the jargon translation that follows.

The Original:

Call me Ishmael. Some years ago—never mind how long precisely—having little or no money in my purse and nothing in particular to interest me on shore, I thought I would sail about a little and see the watery part of the world.

The Translation:

You may identify me by the nomenclature of Ishmael. At a point in time several years previous to the current temporal zone—the precise number of which is extraneous information—devoid of sufficient monetary resources and lacking physical and/or psychical stimuli within the confines of my sphere of activity on land, I initiated several thought processes and concluded that I would commandeer a vessel of navigation with which to explore the aquatic component of this planet.[1]

2. Use of -ize and -ation words. Avoid words such as *finalize* (for conclude); *hypothesize, energize, personalize, conceptualize* (for think); *optimize* (for improve); *prioritize* (for rank); *visualize* (for see); *utilize* (for use); *verbalization* (for statement); *conflagration* (for fire); *democratization* (for democracy); *socialization* (for acceptance); *precipitation* (for rain, sleet, or snow); *illumination* (for light); *institutionalization* (for company policy).

3. Excessive or unclear abbreviations. Do not use abbreviations that, while they may be understood by professionals in your field, will confuse readers unfamiliar with such shorthand. For example, if a nurse told patients that they would

---

[1] The example originally appeared in the *Brown Alumni Monthly;* by the permission of Debra Shore.

have to be NPO (initials indicating that patients are to have nothing by mouth) for a GB vis. (X-ray of the gallbladder), the patients would certainly be baffled—and perhaps terrified. The writer of the following letter to Ann Landers sums up the situation well.

> **Dear Ann Landers:** The growing tendency to call everything by initials is extremely irritating. I've discussed this with others and find that I am not alone.
>
> It wasn't so bad when there were just a few, such as the CIO, the AFL and the CIA. Now we have the IRS, the ERA, the IUD, the NAACP, HEW, MIT, ORT and DNA.
>
> Where I work, quarterly meetings are mandatory. We must sit and listen for an hour and a half to talk like this: "The IAM met with the TQA and discussed the YTD. We must now check back with the IRA and do something about the LTC." I become thoroughly confused trying to sort out the meaning of the initials.
>
> What's more, I feel like a fool because I don't know what's going on. Will you please tell those double-dome intellectuals to call things by their names and not assume that because THEY know what all the initials mean, everybody else does?—Abbreviated into Oblivion in Kalamazoo
>
> **Dear Kal.:** IOU warm thanks for writing such an OK letter. I am printing it PDQ.[2]

---

[2] Reprinted by permission of Ann Landers and Field Newspaper Syndicate.

For those readers who might be unfamiliar with an abbreviation, the writer should give the full name once, followed by the abbreviation in parentheses: political action committee (PAC); urban transit authority (UTA). From that point on, the writer can use the abbreviation.

Before you use technical terms or inflated words that you think will sound important, consider your reader. That reader will appreciate your choosing words that are easy to understand and that express your ideas clearly and quickly. As you revise your work, make a special effort to keep your words simple, direct, and familiar.

Slang

All of us use slang when we talk to our friends. It is a sign that we are comfortable with the people we know best. Slang, however, is out of place in professional communication, written or oral. Slang is playful, irreverent, and sometimes vulgar—qualities not appreciated in business communication. You need not be a stuffed shirt, but don't be too casual, either. Here are examples of slang terms to avoid in your professional writing; a more formal equivalent is given in parentheses.

airhead (absent-minded person)
awesome (outstanding)
bad (good)

bag (avoid confronting, skip)
blow off (ignore)
bodacious (good; exceptional)
chill [out] (relax)
cool, neat (interesting, exciting)
cop out (take the easy way out, let down)
dude (man; person)
dump on (burden another with one's problems)
geek, nerd (socially inept person)
get on someone's case (check up on someone)
goof off (slack off, be lazy)
peel out (drive off recklessly)
radical (great, special)
rip off (steal)
spaced out, spacy (absent-minded)
stressed out, uptight (tense, nervous)
ticked off (angered)

✓ Revision Checklist

Using the guidelines discussed in this chapter, you will be better able to revise and edit the words in your memos, letters, reports, and other occupational writing. Here are some questions to ask about your words as you revise and edit your memo, letters, and reports.

1. Have I checked the spelling of every word that I may be unsure about, especially those words that have given me trouble in the past?
2. Does each word I have used convey the exact meaning I want? That is, have I made sure I did not confuse one word (*stationary*) for another (*stationery*)?
3. Are all my words precise? Have I replaced vague words (*factor, thing*) with more specific ones so that there is no doubt in my readers' minds about times, quantities, costs, names, or places?
4. Have I trimmed unnecessary words, deleted redundant phrases and clauses, and removed inflated phrases? Is every word in my letter, memo, or report loaded with meaning?
5. Did I eliminate sexist language and revise my pronoun usage so that I have not discriminated against any members of a particular occupation or group?
6. Is my work free from jargon that my readers might not understand? Have I explained any technical material these readers need to know about in clear, easily understandable words?
7. Have I identified and replaced any slang with formal language?

Exercises

1. The following sentences contain misspelled words. Find these words and correct them.

   a. The superviser did not find our performance acceptible on the new equiptment.

   b. Unusual occurance reports help safety commitees make thier decesions.

   c. If the carburator is not adjusted proparly, the timing will be alwrong.

   d. Students must recieve twenty-five hours of instruction to become familar with the trafic control problems.

   e. Only the patience family is admited to the intensive care unit.

   f. To describe the suspect's physical apparance, aquaint your self with the correct descripters.

   g. Eat high nutriant foods containing protiens, carbohidrates, and sufficeint ruffage.

   h. Unflammable liquids could be dangerus.

   i. Some freindly newly weds occupyed the bridel suit.

   j. These archetectural designs are unexpensive.

   k. According to City Ordnance 67, combustables cannot be storred on open shelfs.

   l. I will have a zerox copy of the order preparred for you.

   m. We have printed new calandars with pictures of wild turkies and deers on them.

   n. Gasaline prices will reach a cieling before autum.

2. The following sentences contain mistakes in using apostrophes. Find and correct these mistakes.

   a. We tried to survey everybodies opinion but couldnt include all the member's who work the night shift. Well try tomorrow to find them.

   b. The mens' locker room was painted last March, was'nt it?

   c. Freud and Einstein's theories changed the way we'ved looked at the world.

   d. The Smiths new house is much larger than the Sanders.

   e. He's report had too many words's and contained too many Is.

   f. When the mayors conference was held in Detroit last year, the keynote speakers notes embarrassingly fell to the floor.

   g. Marion and Beatrice's daughters both attended the accelerated math student's seminar in Kalamazoo, which wasnt too far away.

   h. The bolt came off it's shaft during the first cycle. It's too bad we didnt double-check the system.

   i. Because the print was so light, all the xs looked like ys on everyones's copy. The vendors repair crew wasnt able to fix the word processor today.

   j. Adkins's and Kaplan's new restaurant on Broadway Street is a big success.

   k. Margaret Bridges'-Bowers new office is on the second floor. It's walls still need to be painted.

3. Select the appropriate word in the following sentences and briefly explain your choice.

  a. My new listings book is larger (then / than) last year's.

  b. All new (personnel / personal) reported to pick up (there / their) identification cards.

  c. Regardless of (it's / its) price, buy the property so the firm does not (lose / loose) it. We must (attain / obtain) it.

  d. She kept her (stationary / stationery) on the desk (beside / besides) her printer where she could easily reach it.

  e. The fabric was (course / coarse) and cheap, and the buyer refused to (choose / chose) it.

  f. Please (except / accept) this (complementary / complimentary) offer with our best wishes.

  g. The (principle / principal) reason given was that our test scores were (to / too) low and the superintendent was afraid none of us would (pass / past) the test.

  h. Corn grows well on the flat (plains / planes) of Illinois.

  i. Smoking (affects / effects) blood pressure.

  j. Our squad had to (sight / cite) every violation so that it could be reported in the district commander's log.

  k. Unusually hot days in March often cause a lot of bad (weather / whether).

  l. (Its / It's) possible to find a (peace / piece) of metal in the shop.

  m. The applicant (who's / whose) credentials were so suitable for our position took another job working for a (pare / pair) of attorneys.

  n. We had (all ready / already) notified the watch commander about the problem.

  o. She was very (adept / adapt) at (adapting / adopting) the new guidelines to suit our agency.

  p. The customer made the (rite / right) choice in selecting our firm; we have the (capitol / capital) to develop the project correctly.

  q. The new floor manager was on her feet (continually / continuously) during the month of August to assist customers.

  r. Ms. Thompkins asked us to (foreword / forward) her check when it arrived.

4. The following sentences contain vague and abstract words. Replace them with concrete ones. The first sentence has been done for you.

  a. The individual saw the occurrence. (The police officer from the second district saw the young boy steal Ms. Saliba's purse.)

  b. Three factors disturbed the crew when it had to deliberate.

  c. The case she outlined sounded interesting.

  d. Circumstances indicated that we follow another course of action in handling this matter.

  e. The nature of the area is such that alternative measures must be sought.

  f. It happened this week.

  g. The materials were incomplete; we found defects, too.

     h.   The causes of the action seemed to be good.

     i.   The phenomenon she discussed happened occasionally in our area.

     j.   The individual sought an immediate solution to the problem.

5. The following sentences contain limp, sluggish verbs. Revise these sentences replacing vague verbs with active, precise ones. The first one has been done for you.

     a.   Tourists are on the beach each August. (Tourists crowd the beach each August.)

     b.   The writer seemed concerned.

     c.   All the points in the proposal relate to our expansion plans.

     d.   There exist three possible solutions that appear attractive.

     e.   Obtaining appraisals is important.

     f.   There are many problems that appear to be significant.

     g.   Computers are tools that exist in each business office.

     h.   It is apparent that the new equipment has its purpose.

     i.   A computer timesharing program will get work accomplished.

     j.   The new law is harmful to our district.

6. The following sentences contain wordy expressions. Revise them to eliminate these expressions.

     a.   Due to the fact that the bus was late, we did not get home until after midnight.

     b.   In an effort to correct some health violations, we fixed the refrigerator in such a way that it would not cause us any more trouble.

     c.   You will have to connect together the terminals with the assistance of a Phillips screwdriver.

     d.   In terms of our ability to meet the demands of those individuals living in the Thames district, all that we can articulate adequately at this date on the calendar is that every effort will be made to find appropriate work crews to find, gather, and remove the refuse left by the storm.

     e.   Our manager is very supportive of our efforts to expand our line of coats, hats, shirts, pants, blouses, dresses, and socks for young children between the ages of two weeks and one year.

     f.   For the length of time that the powder is left around the edges of the room, you might want to check the walls and doors.

     g.   The patient's arm was soaked in warm water with the result that she felt much better and in such a way that the doctor discharged her.

     h.   I am in agreement with the terms in your letter of July 25 and I feel quite certain the manager will respond favorably in an effort to secure the contract.

7. The following sentences are redundant. Revise these sentences to remove unnecessary repetition.

     a.   It was a foreign import.

     b.   The owner's car was light azure blue in color and a convertible model.

     c.   The president told them to terminate the plan and end it.

     d.   A student delivered an oral talk to fellow classmates.

e. The crew was traveling and in transit; therefore, it could not be reached.

f. The troops advanced forward even when they were confronted face-to-face with hazardous dangers staring them in the eyes.

g. The chemistry major had to reread the chapter on bonding again.

h. The chief canceled our leaves when the major requested additional, further officers.

i. The clamp was connected together with the hose.

j. After explaining the new policy, the office manager centered her discussion around the ways of implementing and carrying out that policy in our routine, daily activities.

k. When the technician walked into the room, the patient was really bleeding profusely.

l. She came to her final conclusion after referring back to the occurrence report.

m. Although the diamond was oval in shape, it still would satisfy the buyer.

n. First and foremost, the guests received a complimentary bottle of wine, which did not cost them a cent.

o. He received personalized and individual care.

p. A knife, tent, and food supplies are basic necessities on an outdoor camping trip in the woods.

q. The report will specifically and exclusively deal with urban problems affecting the city.

r. The local, neighborhood commission gave sufficient and adequate reasons for letting the carpenter work independently and use her own resources.

s. They have legal recourse as promised by law.

8. The following sentences contain sexist language. Revise them to eliminate all sexist words and phrases.

a. The Constitution of the United States promises each man freedom of speech.

b. The city will hire more firemen and policemen at the beginning of the fiscal year.

c. In the last five years, our company has been a leader in developing man-made fibers.

d. Taylor Community College enrolled more than 2,000 coeds last term.

e. Our office advertised for a couple of girls to work part-time as receptionists in a 20-man department.

f. Each pilot is required to have his physical examination this month.

g. All engineers and their wives are invited to attend the reception.

h. Job applicants should always spell the employer's name correctly or he may not respond favorably to their letter.

i. On the medical-surgical floors, every nurse is required to rotate her work shift.

j. Every shopper should realize the value of her coupons.

k. The businessman's lunch offers a variety of specials.

l. The new financial program is designed to help the common man.

    m. The foreman believes that a woman's work is never done.

    n. A new copywriter must learn to take criticism like a man.

9. The following paragraphs are wordy and full of jargon. Revise these paragraphs to make them more readable and concise by replacing the jargon with clear and appropriate words.

    a. It has been verified conclusively by this writer that our institution must of necessity install more bicycle holding racks for the convenience of students, faculty, and staff. These parking modules should be fastened securely to walls outside strategic locations on the campus. They could be positioned there by work crews or even by the security forces who vigilantly patrol the campus grounds. There are many students in particular who would value the installation of these racks. Their bicycles could be stationed there by them, and they would know that safety measures have been taken to ensure that none of their bicycles would be apprehended or confiscated illegally. Besides the precaution factor, these racks would afford users maximized convenience in utilizing their means of transportation when they have academic business to conduct, whether at the learning resource center or in the instructional facilities.

    b. On the basis of preliminary investigations, it would seem reasonable to hypothesize that among the situational factors predisposing the Smith family toward showing pronounced psychological identification with the San Francisco Giants is the fact that the Smiths make their domicile in the San Francisco area. In the absence of contrariwise considerations, the Smiths's attitudinal preferences would in this respect interface with earlier behavioral studies. These studies, within acceptable parameters, correlate the fan's domicile with athletic allegiance. Yet it would be counterproductive to establish domicility as the sole determining factor for the Smiths's preference. Certain sociometric studies of the Smiths disclose a factor of atypicality which enters into an analysis of their determinations. One of these factors is that a younger Smith sibling is a participant in the athletic organization in question.

Correspondence

Letter Writing: Some Basics

Letters are probably the kind of writing you will do most frequently on your job. Because letters are so important, Chapters 6, 7, and 8 are devoted exclusively to ways of writing letters effectively. This chapter introduces the entire process and provides some guidelines, problem-solving techniques, definitions, and revision strategies common to all letter writing.

The Importance of Letters

A letter can be defined as a formal or informal written message that is carefully prepared and addressed to a specific audience and that has a clearly announced function. Letters are more formal than the memos that are written to people who work in your office. They are both a personal and professional means of communication. Effective letters clearly announce their purpose and are written in complete sentences in a style that (1) follows an appropriate format, (2) courteously addresses the reader, and (3) selects the most precise language.

Companies annually spend millions of dollars writing letters. The U.S. Postal Service estimates that it moves more than a billion pieces of mail a day. Much of this mail is taken up by first-class business letters. In terms of materials and time, the average business letter now costs between eight and twelve dollars to compose, dictate, type, proofread, mail, store, and retrieve. Not surprisingly, many companies own fax machines that allow them to send a letter across the country in a few minutes. But even with such machines, businesses need people to research, draft, revise, edit, and proofread the letters. Numerous companies offer their employees seminars on how to write clear and appropriate letters. The skill of clear and diplomatic letter writing can be learned and can lead you to advancement and rewards.

Why are letters so important to the employer and the employee? Letters represent the public image of the company and the professional competence of the writer. They can influence people favorably or unfavorably. Basically, letters serve the following five functions.

1. Letters provide information. They can give instructions and can inform readers about a new policy, a change in time for deliveries, an alteration in procedures, a new product, or a service.

2. Letters prompt action. They can help the writer collect money from overdue accounts, alter a city ordinance, speed the shipment of new parts, initiate a policy, call a meeting, or waive a requirement.

3. Letters establish goodwill. They can thank someone, convey congratulations, respond to a complaint, settle an account satisfactorily, or provide a recommendation.

4. Letters sell. They can sell a product, a service, or the writer's own skills.

5. Letters follow up on telephone calls and other types of conversation. They can also provide documentation and clarification of oral agreements.

Letters accomplish all these goals by following certain conventions (rules or customary practices). These conventions are the ways in which businesses and their readers expect letters to look and to be written. This chapter will show you how to incorporate these conventions into the drafts and revisions of your letters and will also provide numerous examples for you to study.

The Process of Writing a Letter

Even though it is far shorter than a proposal, report, or set of instructions, a one- or two-page business letter still requires planning and research, as longer business documents do. All the techniques of the writing process discussed in Chapter 2 (pages 28–39) apply to letters as well. An effective letter may require several drafts and revisions before you are ready to prepare the final copy. You cannot just sit down and dash off a letter and hope that it will best represent you and your company. Much more work than that is involved.

Before you ever start keyboarding your letter, you need to ask and successfully answer the following three questions.

1. Will my audience be favorably disposed to what I am going to say, or will they be disappointed by my news?
2. What kinds of homework will my audience expect me to have done—what kinds of information do they expect me to include in my letter to them?
3. How will they use that information?

Once you have raised and answered these questions, you will be better able to start the process of writing a successful business letter.

That process, of course, should begin with some preliminary research. Your research could be as simple as refreshing your memory about one of your company's products or services, taking a quick look through your company's files for previous correspondence with the customer or client, or conferring with a coworker about the client's file or special needs. Once you have a strong sense of your audience's needs and the types of information you must have to meet those needs, you will be better able to start outlining and drafting your letter. Get your thoughts down first by drafting, and then be concerned about revising and editing to find the appropriate language and tone. Many letter writers go astray by thinking that the hardest part of writing a letter is putting their ideas into the right language. The hardest part of writing a letter is first knowing what must be said to whom, why, and where in the letter. (Chapter 7, on the various types of business letters, will give you helpful information on organizing and preparing your correspondence.) Once you have successfully resolved these points, you can focus on language during the late drafting and revising stages. Pages 169–172 will give you some specific guidelines on how to make the language of your letter clear, concise, and contemporary.

Typing/Printing and Proofreading Letters

The first thing a reader notices about a letter is how the words and paragraphs are arranged on the page. Your audience is influenced by the way your letter looks even before they read its contents. A neat, clean, and professional looking letter tells the reader that the work, service, or skill the writer promises to deliver will be done in the same way. Strikeovers (crossing out one letter by typing another letter on top of it), messy erasures that leave the paper bare in one spot, blotches of liquid corrector smeared across the page, and handwritten changes inserted to correct errors all look unprofessional and distract the reader from understanding your message quickly and accurately. With word processors in use in most businesses today, you can produce professional-looking letters easily.

The way in which a letter is typed or printed on the page significantly affects the visual impression it makes. If using a typewriter, you can avoid crowded or lopsided letters if you take a few minutes to estimate the length of the message before you type it. You do not want to start a brief letter at the top of the page and leave three-fourths of the page blank. Plan to start near the center of the page. Also avoid cramming a long letter onto one page; sometimes you will have to use a second sheet. A letter that is squeezed onto one page will deprive the reader of necessary and pleasant white space.

Specific typing instructions are included later in the chapter. Here are a few general hints. Leave generous margins of approximately 1 1/2 inches all around your letter. Have more white space at the top than at the bottom, and watch right-hand margins in particular, since it is easy to exceed their limits. Shorter letters may require wider margins than longer letters, but don't exceed a margin of 1 1/2 inches on the right-hand side. If you use a word processor, set 1 1/2 inch margins as the default.

Be especially careful about the typewriter or printer you use. Make sure that all typewriter keys work and that none of them produces a broken or half letter. Clean your keys and buy a new ribbon so that your typed letter will not be fuzzy or messy. If you are using word processing equipment to prepare your letter, use a letter-quality printer. Letters from a dot matrix printer generally do not look as crisp, fresh, or professional. Choose a space density that will be pleasant and inviting to the eye. Crowding too many letters on a line will not inspire your reader's confidence. Your letter will look like it's hard to read.

Proofread everything that has your name on it, even if you did not keyboard it. You cannot blame a keyboarder for spelling mistakes or other errors. As the writer, you are responsible for the final product. When a letter goes out with your signature, you are telling the reader that you are accountable for everything in it. Make sure you proofread your letter for errors of fact, miscalculations, and misrepresentations (contradictions between what you say in your letter and what is stated in a brochure or other company document). Pay close attention to the accuracy of costs, dates, and serial numbers.

Typographical errors can be costly and embarrassing. If you want to tell a steady customer that "the order will be hard to fill" and you keyboard instead that "the order will be hard to bill," confusion will result. Poor keyboarding and proofreading can also lead to omitted letters ("the ill arrived" for "the bill arrived"), transpositions ("hte" for "the," "nad" for "and," "sti" for "its"), or omitted words ("the market value of the was high").

As we saw, you will find a word processor's spell-check program useful. But be careful not to rely on such a program completely. Mistakes can creep in. Moreover, you may have to write a letter someday when a spell-check program is not available. It never hurts to proofread your own letter. Proofreading is reading in slow motion. Here are eight ways to proofread effectively. You may want to combine all of them to ensure accuracy.

1. Read the letter word for word from the bottom to the top.
2. Read the letter from start to finish aloud. Pronounce each word carefully to make yourself more aware of typographical errors or omitted words. Look at every letter of every word. Don't skim.
3. Place your finger under each word as you read the letter silently.
4. Double-check the spelling of all names. Errors here are sure to cause problems. Watch for inconsistencies (e.g., Phillip in one place; Philip in another).
5. Have a friend read the letter. Four eyes are better than two.
6. Have your friend read the original copy of the letter aloud while you follow the typed or printed copy.
7. If you have the time, proofread the letter the following day.
8. Never proofread when you are tired, and avoid reading large amounts of material in one sitting.

Letter Formats

Letter format refers to the way in which you type or print a letter—where you indent and where you place certain kinds of information. A number of letter for-

FIGURE 6.1   Full block letter format.

Nevada Insurance Research Agency /
7500 SOUTH MAPLEWOOD DRIVE, LAS VEGAS, NEVADA 89152-0026 / (702) 555-9876

Bradley Fuller, CPCU	**Carmen Tredeau, CPCU**	**Theodore Kendrick**
Chairperson	**President**	**Vice President, Public Affairs**

Shelly Lampier-Hawn, CPCU	**H.B. Little, CPCU**
Vice President, Research	**Vice President, Actuary**

April 4, 1994

Ms. Molly Georgopolous, C.P.A.
Business Manager
Conyers, Inc.
3400 South Madison
Reno, NV 89554-3212

Dear Ms. Georgopolous:

*All typing/
printing
lined up
against
left-hand
margin*

As I promised in our telephone conversation this afternoon, I am enclosing a study of the Nevada financial responsibility law. I hope that it will help you prepare your report.

I wish to emphasize again that probably 95 percent of all individuals who are involved in an accident do obtain reimbursement for hospital and doctor bills and for damages to their automobiles. If individuals have insurance, they can receive reimbursement from their own carrier. If they do not have insurance and the other driver is uninsured and judged to be at fault, the State Bureau of Motor Vehicles will revoke that party's driver's license and license plates until all costs for injuries and damages are paid.

Please call upon me again if I may be of help to you.

Sincerely yours,

Carmen Tredeau

Carmen Tredeau, President

CT/ lmb

Encl.

mats exist. Two of the most often used in the business world are the full block format (Figure 6.1) and the semiblock format (Figure 6.2 [p. 152]). Gaining popularity is a third format known as the Administrative Management Society (AMS) simplified style, illustrated in Figure 6.3 (p. 153). Before you choose a letter format, find out if your employer has a preference.

FIGURE 6.2 Semiblock letter format.

Writer's address ⎫
and date are ⎬   7239 East Daphne Parkway
indented. ⎭   Mobile, AL 36608-1012

January 31, 1994

Mr. Travis Boykin, Manager
Scandia Gifts
703 Hardy Street
Hattiesburg, MS 39401-4633

Dear Mr. Boykin:

I would appreciate knowing if you currently stock the Crescent pattern of model 5678 and how much you charge per model number. I would also like to know if you have special prices per box order.

The name of your store is listed in the Annual Catalog as the closest distributor of Copenhagen products in my area. Would you please give me directions to your shop from Mobile and the hours you are open.

I look forward to hearing from you.

Complimentary ⎫   Sincerely yours,
close and writer's ⎬   *Arthur T. Mc Cormack*
name are indented. ⎭   Arthur T. McCormack

FIGURE 6.3   AMS simplified letter format.

OFFICE PROPERTY MANAGEMENT ASSOCIATES
2400 SOUTH LINCOLN HIGHWAY
LIVINGSTON, NJ 07040–9990

TELEPHONE (201)-555-3740   FAX (201)-555-6575

April 19, 1994

Mr. W. T. Albritton
Albritton and Sharp Accounting Services
Suite 400
Suburban Office Complex
Livingston, NJ 07038-2389

IMPROVED SERVICES AT SUBURBAN OFFICE COMPLEX

At our April meeting, Office Property Management Associates discussed a
number of requests you and other tenants made at the Suburban Office
Complex. I am happy to inform you that the following improvements in
services will go into effect at the Suburban Office Complex within 45 days.

 1. Effective June 6, you will have an on-site manager, Judy Fiorelli, who will
    be happy to answer any questions you may have about the Complex and
    will help you solve any problems.
 2. The parking lot on the southwest side will be resurfaced during the week
    of June 13–20. During this time, would you and your staff please park
    your vehicles in the north or the east lots.
 3. A new outdoor security lighting system will be installed by June 17. Work
    on this system should not inconvenience you.

I welcome your comments on these changes or suggestions for additional
ones. Please feel free to call or write me.

Gladys T. Mullins-Osborne

GLADYS T. MULLINS-OSBORNE, VICE PRESIDENT

tc

The full block style is the easiest to use because all information in the letter is keyboarded flush against the left-hand margin. You will not have to worry about indenting paragraphs or aligning dates with signatures. Figure 6.1 shows a full block letter keyboarded on letterhead stationery (specially printed stationery giving a company's name, address, telephone number, and sometimes the names of its chief executives or the company logo). The use of letterhead stationery eliminates the need to keyboard a writer's address. On plain stationery, the writer's address is placed flush with the left-hand margin, directly above the date.

In contrast, the semiblock style (Figure 6.2) has the writer's address (if it is not imprinted on a letterhead), date, complimentary close, and the signature at the right-hand side of the letter. You must make a number of adjustments to align the date with the complimentary close and must remember to go back to the left side to note any enclosures with the letter. Paragraphs within a letter in the semiblock style can be flush against the left-hand margin or indented.

The AMS style follows the block format in which every line begins at the left-hand margin, including any numbered items such as those in Figure 6.3. But unlike the block format, the AMS style omits the salutation and complimentary close. In place of the salutation it includes a subject line (without using the word *subject*), typed or printed in all capital letters, three spaces down from the inside address. Three spaces after the subject line comes the first paragraph of the letter. The writer's name and title are typed in capital letters on the same line four lines after the last paragraph of the letter. The keyboarder initials appear two lines beneath the writer's name. Because the AMS style saves keyboarding time (and thus company money), many offices now use it.

If your letter runs to a second page, use a sheet of plain white bond paper rather than company letterhead. About nine lines, or 1 1/2 inches from the top of the page, type the reader's name on the left-hand side, a simple arabic 2 in the center, and the date of the letter on the right-hand side.

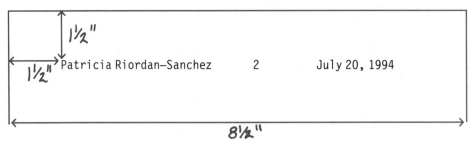

Alternatively, put "Page 2" and the date directly under the recipient's name on the left-hand side. However, never number the first page of a letter, even if your letter is just one page long.

Parts of a Letter

A letter must contain many parts to communicate its message. These parts and their placement in your letter form the basic conventions of effective letter writing. Your reader will be in the habit of looking for certain information in certain places in your letter. It is your responsibility as a letter writer to meet your reader's expectations. By doing so you will create a good impression.

In the following discussion, those parts of a letter marked with an asterisk are found in every letter you will write. Figure 6.4 (p. 156) contains a sample letter displaying all the parts discussed below. Note where each part is placed in the letter.

*Date Line

Where you place the month, day, and year depends on the format you are using. If you are using the full block style or the AMS simplified style, the date line is flush with the left-hand margin. If you are using the semiblock style, the date can be placed at the center point, centered under a company letterhead, or flush with the right-hand margin. The date line appears two lines below the writer's address or letterhead.

Spell out the name of the month in full; type "September" and "March" rather than abbreviating to "Sept." or "Mar." Most frequently the date line is keyboarded this way: November 15, 1994. Yet many international firms prefer to date correspondence with the day followed by month and year (15 November 1994), with no commas separating the day, month, and year.

*Inside Address

The inside address, which is the same address that goes on the envelope, is always placed against the left-hand margin, two lines below the date line. It contains the name, title (if any), company, street address, city, state, and zip code of the person or company to which you are writing. If possible, try to write to a specific individual in a company instead of using "Sales Manager" or "President." Check correspondence, telephone directories, or annual reports. Call the company if you have to. You will get off to a bad start if you do not spell that person's name right; don't put Anderson for Andersen, Kean for Keen, or MacDermott for McDermott.

Single-space the inside address, but do not use any punctuation at the end of the lines. The name of the individual, together with a courtesy title such as Mr., Ms., Dr., Professor, goes on the first line. When writing to a woman, use Ms. unless she expressly asks to be called Mrs. or Miss. A woman's marital status is not an issue. The initials M.D., Ph.D., or D.P.H. should not be added after you use Dr. Use either Janice Howell, M.D., or Dr. Janice Howell, *not* Dr. Janice Howell, M.D. Any military titles (Captain, Corporal), academic ranks (Professor, Assistant Professor), or religious designations (Reverend, Father, Sister) should be written out in full and the first letter capitalized.

If the individual to whom you are writing holds an office or has a title within the company, put a comma after the person's name, followed by the title: Ms. Kathy Buel, President. Use the courtesy title Ms. and capitalize the "P" in President. If the title contains more than one word, put the title on the next line: Mr. Henry Gerald/Director of Computer Services. If you cannot obtain the individual's name or if you are writing to an entire corporation or section of a company, put the department or company name on one line and the street address on the next line: Public Relations Department/The Doulet Brace Company/1343 Jackson Street/Chicago, IL 60624–1205.

FIGURE 6.4   A sample letter, full block format, with all parts labeled.

Letterhead	**MADISON AND MOORE, INC.** Professional Architects 7900 South Manheim Road Crystal Springs, NE 71003-0092
Date line	December 12, 1994
Inside address	Ms. Paula Jordan Systems Consultant Broadacres Development Corp. 12 East River Street Detroit, MI 48001-0422
Salutation	Dear Ms. Jordan:
Subject line	SUBJECT: Request for alternate duplex plans, No. 32134
Body of letter	Thank you for your letter of December 6, 1994. I have discussed your request with the officials in our Planning Department and have learned that the forms we used are no longer available. In searching through my files, however, I have come across the enclosed catalog from a Nevada firm that might be helpful to you. This firm, Nevada Designers, offers plans very similar to the ones you are interested in, as you can tell from the design I checked on page 23 of their catalog. I hope this will help your project and I wish you success in your venture.
Complimentary close	Sincerely yours,
Company name	MADISON AND MOORE, INC.
Signature	*William Newhouse*
Writer's name and title	William Newhouse Office Manager
Keyboarder's identification	WN/kpl
Enclosure	Encl. Catalog
Copy to	cc: Planning Department

The last line of the inside address contains the city, state, and zip code. Table 6.1 (p. 158) lists the official U.S. Postal Service abbreviations—two capital letters without periods—for the states and territories of the United States. Acceptable abbreviations for the provinces of Canada are listed at the bottom of the table. Pay special attention to those abbreviations beginning with the same letter. For example, mail going to Jackson, Mississippi (MS), could go astray if a letter without a zip code used the same abbreviation for Michigan (MI). Also note the difference between AR (Arkansas) and AK (Alaska). If you are writing to someone in a foreign country, type the name of that country in capital letters alone on the last line of the inside address.

Salutation

The greeting part of your letter, or the salutation, is placed flush against the left-hand margin in both the full block and semiblock formats and is omitted in the AMS simplified format. Begin with *Dear,* a convention showing respect for your reader, and then follow with a courtesy title, the reader's last name, and a colon (Dear Mr. Brown:). A comma is used only for an informal letter. The salutation is determined by the first line of the inside address and must be consistent with it. If you are not sure of the sex of the reader, use the reader's full name: "Dear Terry Banks."

If you are writing to a large group of readers, use an individual's relevant designation: "Dear Pilot," "Dear Homeowners." When writing to a company, use the company name—"Dear Macy's," "Dear Saperstein Textiles"—not the sexist "Dear Gentlemen." Similarly, if you are writing to a group that includes both men and women, use Dear Ladies and Gentlemen, but not the sexist "Dear Sirs." (For a discussion of sexist language and how to avoid it, review pages 134–135.)

And finally, if you are on a first-name basis with your reader and using his or her last name would be awkward, simply write "Dear Bill" or "Dear Sue."

Subject Line

The subject line can provide a concise summary of the letter (something like a title) or it can list account numbers, order notations, or referral numbers so that the reader can at once check the files and see what the status of your account or policy is. Your most recent letter can then be placed accurately in your file. In both the full block and semiblock formats, the subject line, preceded by the word SUBJECT in capital letters, is placed two spaces below the salutation, flush with the left-hand margin.

```
Dear Ms. Hogan:

SUBJECT: Repair of model 7342
```

Or it can be moved to the right-hand side of the letter, on the same line with the salutation,

```
Dear Ms. Hogan:              SUBJECT: Repair of model 7342
```

TABLE 6.1   U.S. Postal Service Abbreviations and Canadian Province Abbreviations

U.S. state/ territory	Abbreviation	U.S. state/ territory	Abbreviation
Alabama	AL	Montana	MT
Alaska	AK	Nebraska	NE
Arizona	AZ	Nevada	NV
Arkansas	AR	New Hampshire	NH
American Samoa	AS	New Jersey	NJ
California	CA	New Mexico	NM
Colorado	CO	New York	NY
Connecticut	CT	North Carolina	NC
Delaware	DE	North Dakota	ND
District of Columbia	DC	Ohio	OH
Florida	FL	Oklahoma	OK
Georgia	GA	Oregon	OR
Guam	GU	Pennsylvania	PA
Hawaii	HI	Puerto Rico	PR
Idaho	ID	Rhode Island	RI
Illinois	IL	South Carolina	SC
Indiana	IN	South Dakota	SD
Iowa	IA	Tennessee	TN
Kansas	KS	Trust Territories	TT
Kentucky	KY	Texas	TX
Louisiana	LA	Utah	UT
Maine	ME	Vermont	VT
Maryland	MD	Virginia	VA
Massachusetts	MA	Virgin Islands	VI
Michigan	MI	Washington	WA
Minnesota	MN	West Virginia	WV
Mississippi	MS	Wisconsin	WI
Missouri	MO	Wyoming	WY

Canadian province	Abbreviation	Canadian province	Abbreviation
Alberta	AB	Nova Scotia	NS
British Columbia	BC	Ontario	ON
Labrador	LB	Prince Edward Island	PE
Manitoba	MB	Quebec	PQ
New Brunswick	NB	Saskatchewan	SK
Newfoundland	NF	Yukon Territory	YT
Northwest Territories	NT		

Review page 154 and Figure 6.3 for style and placement of the subject line in an AMS simplified style letter.

*Body of the Letter

The body of a letter contains the message. In the full block format, paragraphs are never indented; in the semiblock and AMS simplified formats, paragraphs may or may not be indented five spaces. Whichever style you choose, single-space within the paragraph, but double-space between paragraphs.

While some of your letters will be only a few lines long, many of them will extend to three or more paragraphs. As a rule, begin your letter with your purpose. Tell readers in the first paragraph why you are writing to them and why your letter is important to them. In a second (or subsequent) paragraph, develop your message with factual support. But don't bury important points within the middle or end of your paragraph. Follow the techniques of paragraph writing discussed in Chapter 3. In your last paragraph, bring readers to a true sense of conclusion. Tell them what you have done for them, what they should do for you, what will happen next, when they will hear from you again, or any combination of these messages. Don't leave readers hanging.

Consider the appearance of your paragraphs, too. Review pages 78–80.

Complimentary Close

Except in an AMS simplified style letter (where the complimentary close is omitted), the complimentary close always appears two spaces below the body of the letter, flush with the left-hand margin in the full block format and at the center point, aligned with the date, for the semiblock format. As the term suggests, the complimentary close ends the letter politely. For most business correspondence, the standard close is *Sincerely yours, Sincerely, Yours sincerely, Best wishes,* or *Respectfully.* Avoid flowery closes such as *Faithfully yours,* or *Forever yours.* Capitalize only the first letter of the complimentary close, and follow the entire close with a comma.

*Signature

The typed name appears four spaces below the complimentary close (or, in an AMS simplified style letter, below the last line of the body), either on the left side (full block or AMS simplified format) or at the center point (semiblock format). You need four spaces so that your name, when you write it out, will not look squeezed in. Always sign your name in ink, just as it is typed. Your name not only indicates who you are, but also verifies that the contents of your letter have your approval. An unsigned letter indicates carelessness or, worse, indifference toward your reader.

Some firms like to have the company name as well as the employee's name in the signature section. If so, type the company name in capital letters two spaces below the complimentary close, and then sign your name. Add your title underneath your typed name. Here is an example:

```
Sincerely yours,

THE FINELLI COMPANY



Robert Stavropoulos
Cover Coordinator
```

Reference Initials

When a letter is keyboarded for you, the keyboarder initials are placed two spaces below your typed name. These initials appear in lower-case letters and follow your initials, which appear in capital letters. The notation WBT/vgh or WBT:vgh, for example, means that Winnie B. Thompson's letter was keyboarded by Victor G. Higgins. The company thus has a record in its files of who dictated the letter and who keyboarded it. Do not list any initials if you keyboard your own letter.

Enclosure(s) Line

The enclosure line is placed two spaces beneath the reference initials (or your keyboarded name if you keyboard your own letter). This line informs the reader that additional materials (brochures, diagrams, forms, job descriptions, a proposal) accompany your letter. You can use the word "Enclosure" in full or abbreviate it to "Encl." Most writers indicate briefly what is being enclosed (Encl. Incident report; Encl. Résumé) or at least give the number of enclosures (Encl. 3). Sometimes the title of an enclosure is given, for example, Encl. "The 1994 Sales Report to the Management of Powers Industries."

Copy or Copies Distributed

The initials "cc" or "xc" (in lower-case letters with no space between them) indicate that a letter has been duplicated and sent to other people or departments. Place these initials, followed by a colon and the appropriate names, two spaces below the enclosure line.

```
cc: Jessica Bandy
    Service Dept.
```

Letters are copied and sent to a third party for a variety of reasons. You may be required to send copies of all your correspondence to your boss. Additionally, you may send copies of certain letters to a specific individual who needs to be kept apprised of an ongoing situation, or another department in your firm may be interested in your letter. When you are sending a copy of your letter to more than one individual, list these individuals in alphabetical order or by corporate rank.

```
cc: Janice Algood          xc: Plant Superintendent Swarr
    Peter Lemon                Comptroller Algood
    Robbie Swarr               Shift 1 Supervisor Lemon
```

Often letters are copied for other readers without the knowledge of the person to whom the letter is addressed. Such copies are called "blind copies." But professional courtesy dictates that you tell the reader that a copy of your letter is being sent to someone else.

Addressing an Envelope

When addressing an envelope, use a standard 9 1/2" × 4 1/8" white envelope or, as most firms do when they mail statements, an envelope measuring 6 1/2" × 3 5/8" with a window (a transparent cellophane opening) showing the customer's address. When you use a window envelope, make sure the complete address is visible in case the letter slides to the right or to the left in the envelope. Because most mail is sorted by high-speed electronic scanning equipment, the U.S. Postal Service has established regulations concerning envelope size. In particular, avoid odd-shaped envelopes and small, invitation-sized ones. Review the regulations listed on page 11 for proper envelope sizes. The U.S. Postal Service also offers discounts to large and small corporate mailers who use the zip+4 barcoding system. Preprinted return envelopes or labels carry *bar codes* that indicate the type of correspondence at the top of the envelope and the address at the bottom.

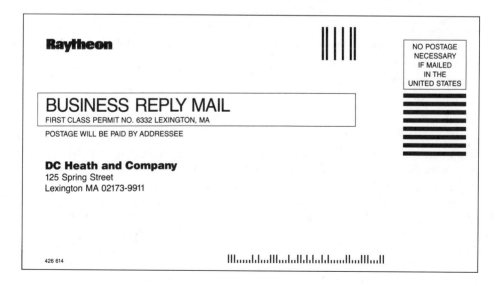

Outside Address

An envelope has two parts: the outside address and the return address, as shown in Figure 6.5 (p. 162). The outside address, the same as the reader's inside address

FIGURE 6.5   **A properly addressed envelope.**

```
Thomas Addington
45 Simmons Road, Apt. 2B  } Return address
Medvale, VT 05402-1521    )



                      ( Ms. Patricia Barnes
                      | General Manager
     Outside address  { Courtesy Motors
                      | 1700 Lakewood Street
                      ( Boston, MA 02127-3160
```

on your letter, should be single-spaced and centered on the envelope. Make sure the print is clear and sharp. Although the Postal Service recommends using all capitals and no punctuation on the envelope, most companies still prefer to use standard capitalization and punctuation on both the inside and outside addresses. Leave at least one-half inch of white space between the last line of the address and the bottom of the envelope. Never exceed five lines for an address, and make sure that all lines of the address are lined up flush left. If an individual's address contains both a street address and a rural route, highway, floor, apartment, room, or suite number, put all this information on the same line: 809 Troup Street, Apt. 7B. If an individual does not live at an address permanently, you will have to send the letter in care of (c/o) the permanent resident.

```
Ms. Mary Jane Truax
c/o Ms. Faye Jelinick
33 West 91st Street
New York, NY 10072-3678
```

Always use a zip code, even if a letter is going to someone in your city, because a letter with a zip code will arrive at its destination sooner. Leave one or two spaces between words and between state abbreviations and zip codes.

Every mail delivery area in the United States now has a nine-digit zip code. The first five digits direct mail to a particular geographic location (a neighborhood or area in New York City or San Francisco, for example) while the last four digits provide a further geographic breakdown (a unit within a company, a floor of a large office building, a college post office box).

Return Address and Special Instructions

You should always use a return address, which is your address. It should appear at the upper left-hand side of the envelope (not on the back flap), single-spaced, and without any courtesy title.

FIGURE 6.6   An envelope with an attention line.

```
Kathy Kooperman
769 East 45th Street
Baltimore, MD 21224-6025




                    Attention: Ms. Faye Gladstone
                    The Placement Office
                    East Central Community College
                    Baltimore, MD 21228-0710
```

Sometimes special mailing directions are also required. In such cases, one of the following designations is added to the envelope.

- **Attention.** This word on the envelope is followed by the name of the individual to whom you are writing. When an attention line is necessary, always put it first. The attention line is particularly helpful when you have been dealing regularly with one section, department, or individual in a large company—such as the credit officer, parts warehouse, or statistics office. An attention line also helps a company sort and route its mail faster.
- **Hold for Arrival.** Individuals may be away on business or on vacation, and you want the letter to reach them on their return. Perhaps, too, you are writing to someone who will arrive at a hotel or firm after your letter does. The notation "Hold for Arrival" ensures that your letter is not returned or thrown away.
- **Personal** or **Confidential.** This designation indicates that only the individual to whom you are writing should open and read your letter.
- **Please Forward.** This designation asks that your letter be sent on to a new address after an individual has moved. Note that the U.S. Postal Service will forward mail for only six months.

All such special instructions, except the attention line, are placed at the top left, two spaces below the return address. The attention line is typed on the first line of the reader's address, as shown in Figure 6.6.

Making a Good Impression on Your Reader

You have just learned about the mechanical requirements your letter must fulfill. Now we will discuss the content of your letter—what you say and how you say it. Writing letters means communicating to influence your readers, not to alienate or antagonize them. Keep in mind that writers of effective letters are like successful diplomats in that they represent both their company and themselves. The image you want readers to have of you and your company is projected through your letter. You want readers to see you as courteous, credible, and professional.

To write an effective letter like that, first put yourself in the reader's position. What kinds of letters do you like to receive? You would at once rule out letters that are vague, impersonal, sarcastic, pushy, or condescending. You want letters addressed to you to be polite, businesslike, and considerate of your needs and requests. If you have questions, you want them answered honestly, courteously, and fully. You do not want someone to waste your time with a long, puffy letter when a few well-chosen sentences would have done the job much better.

What do you as a writer have to do to send such effective letters? Adopt the "you attitude"; in other words, signal to readers that they and their needs are of utmost importance. Incorporating this "you attitude" means that you should be able to answer "Yes" to these two questions: (1) Will my readers receive a positive image of me? (2) Have I chosen words that convey both my respect for the readers and my concern for their questions and comments? The first question deals with your overall view of readers. Do your letters paint them as clever or stupid, practical managers or spendthrifts? The second question deals with specific language and tone conveying your view of the reader. Words can burn or soothe. Choose them carefully. As you revise your letters, you will become more concerned about the ways a reader will respond to you and your message.

Figures 6.7 and 6.8 contain two versions of the same letter. Which one would you rather receive? Why?

The Process of Achieving the "You Attitude": Four Guidelines

As you draft and revise your work, pay special attention to the following four guidelines that will help you make a good impression on your reader.

1. Never forget that your reader is a real person. Avoid writing cold, impersonal letters that sound as if they were form letters or tape-recorded messages on a telephone. Let the readers know that you are writing to them as individuals. Neglecting this rule, a large clinic once sent its customers this statement: "Your bill is overdue. If you pay it by the 15th of this month, no one except the computer will know that it was late." Similarly, the letter below violates every rule of personal and personable communications.

> It has come to our attention that policy number 342q-765r has been delinquent in payment and is in arrears for the sum of $302.35. To keep the policy in force for the duration of its life, a minimum payment of $50.00 must reach this office by the last day of the month. Failure to submit payment will result in the cancellation of the aforementioned policy.

This example displays no sense of one individual writing to another, of a customer with a name, personal history, or specific needs. The letter uses cold and stilted

FIGURE 6.7   A letter lacking the "you attitude."

BROWN COUNTY
Office of the Tax Assessor
County Building, Room 200
Ventura, Missouri 56780-0102

March 4, 1994

Mr. Ted B. Ladner
451 West Hawthorne Lane
Morris, MO 64507-3005

Dear Mr. Ladner:

You have made a mistake by writing to the wrong office here at the
County Building. There is no way we can even attempt to verify the
kinds of details you are demanding from Brown County.

Simply put, by carefully examining the 1993 tax bill you said you
received, you should have realized that it is the Tax Collector's Office,
not the Tax Assessor's, that will have to handle the problem you claim
exists.

In short, call or write the Tax Collector of Brown County.

Thank you!

Tracey Kowalski

Tracey Kowalski

FIGURE 6.8 A you-centered revision of Figure 6.7.

BROWN COUNTY
Office of the Tax Assessor
County Building, Room 200
Ventura, Missouri 56780-0102

March 4, 1994

Mr. Ted B. Ladner
451 West Hawthorne Lane
Morris, MO 64507-3005

Dear Mr. Ladner:

Thank you for writing about the difficulties you encountered with your 1993 tax bill. I wish I could help you, but it is the Tax Collector's Office that issues your annual property tax bill. Our office does not prepare individual homeowners' bills.

If you will kindly direct your questions to Paulette Sutton at the Brown County Tax Collector's Office, Room 100, County Building, Ventura, Missouri 56780-0100, I am sure that she will be able to assist you. Should you wish to call her, the number is 458-3455.

Respectfully,

Tracey Kowalski
Tracey Kowalski

language ("delinquent in payment," "in arrears for," "aforementioned policy"). Revised, this letter contains the necessary personal (and human) touch.

> We have not yet received your payment for your insurance policy (#342q-765r). By sending us your check for $50.00 within the next three weeks, you will keep your policy in force and can continue to enjoy the financial benefits and emotional security it offers you.

The benefits to the particular reader are stressed, and the reader is addressed directly as a valued customer.

Don't be afraid of using "you" in your letters. Readers will feel more friendly toward you and your message. (Of course, no amount of "you's" will help if they appear in a condescending context such as the letter in Figure 6.7.) In fact, you might even use the reader's name or the name of his or her company within your letter to create goodwill and to show your interest.

2. Keep the reader in the forefront of your letter. Make sure that the reader's needs control the tone, message, and organization of your letter. This is the essence of the "you attitude." No one likes people who talk about themselves all the time. What is true about conversation is equally true of letters. Stress the "you," not the "I" or the "we." Again, try to find out about your readers. Here is a paragraph from a letter that forgets about the reader.

> **Draft**
> I think that our rug shampooer is the best on the market. Our firm has invested a lot of time and money to ensure that it is the most economical and efficient shampooer available today. We have found that our customers are very satisfied with the results of our machine. We have sold thousands of these shampooers, and we are proud of our accomplishment. We hope that we can sell you one of our fantastic machines.

The example above talks the reader into boredom by spending all its time on the machine, the company, and the sales success. Readers are interested in how *they* can benefit from the machine, not in how much profit the company makes from selling it. To win the readers' confidence, the writer needs to show how they will find the product useful, economical, and worthwhile at home or at work. Here is a reader-centered revision.

> **Revision**
> Our rug shampooer would make cleaning your Happy Rest Motel rooms easier for you. It is equipped with a heavy-duty motor that will handle your 200 rooms with ease. Moreover, that motor will give frequently used areas, such as the lobby or hallways, a fresh and clean look you can be proud of.

Note how in this revision the writer shifted attention away from bragging about how "we have sold thousands" to the benefits the reader will gain by purchasing the product.

3. Be courteous and tactful. However serious the problem or the degree of your anger at the time, refrain from turning your letter into a punch through the mail. Capture the reader's goodwill, and the rewards will be greater for you. The following words can create a bad taste in the reader's mouth.

it's defective	unprofessional (job, attitude, etc.)
I demand	your failure
I insist	you contend
we reject	you allege
that's no excuse for	you should have known
totally unacceptable	your outlandish claim

Use words that emphasize the "you attitude," and avoid offensive language. Compare the discourteous sentences on the left with the courteous revisions on the right.

Discourteous	Courteous Revision
We must discontinue your service unless payment is received by the date shown.	Please send us your payment by November 4 so that your service will not be interrupted.
You completely misunderstood my letter.	I am sorry that my letter did not explain that more clearly.
Your claim that our product was defective on delivery is outlandish.	We are sorry to learn that you were dissatisfied with the condition of our product when it reached you.
The rotten coil you installed caused all my trouble.	The trouble may be caused by a malfunctioning coil.
You are sorely mistaken about the warranty.	We are sorry to learn about the difficulty you experienced over the service terms in our warranty.
The new printer you sold me is third-rate and you charged first-rate prices.	Since the printer is still under warranty, I hope that you can make the repairs easily and quickly.
Obviously your company is wrong. I wonder if all the people at Acme are as inept as you.	I would appreciate receiving a more detailed explanation from your home office about this matter.
Needless to say, you have misread your warranty agreement.	Clause 17 in your warranty agreement does not cover the problem you have called to our attention.
It goes without saying that your suggestion is not worth considering.	It was thoughtful of you to send me your suggestion, but unfortunately we cannot implement it right now.

The last two discourteous examples above begin with phrases that frequently set readers on edge. It's best to avoid using *needless to say* or *it goes without saying* since they can quickly set up a barrier between a reader and writer.

4. Be neither boastful nor meek. These two strategies—one based on pride and the other on humility—often lead inexperienced letter writers into trouble.

On the one hand, they believe that a forceful statement will make a good impression on the reader. Or perhaps they think that a cautious and humble approach will be the least offensive way to earn the reader's respect. Both paths are wrong.

Aggressive letters, filled with boasts, rarely appeal to readers. Letters should radiate confidence without sounding as if the writer had written a letter of self-recommendation. Letters should let the facts speak directly and pleasantly for themselves. The sentences on the left boast; those on the right capture confidence with grace.

Boastful	Graceful Revision
You will find me the most diplomatic employee you ever hired.	Much of my previous work has been in answering and adjusting customer complaints.
The Sun and Sea unqualifyingly promises the nicest rooms on the Coast.	Each room at the Sun and Sea has its own private bath and bar refrigerator.
I have performed that procedure so many times I can do it in my sleep.	I have performed all kinds of IV therapy as part of standard procedure.
The Check-Pack offers you incomparable customer convenience.	The Check-Pack gives you a free safe-deposit box.

At the other extreme, some writers stress only their own inadequacy. Their attitude as projected in their letters is "I am the most unworthy person who ever lived, and I would be eternally grateful if you even let my letter sit on your desk, let alone open it." Readers will dismiss such writers as pitiful, unqualified weaklings. Note how the meek sentences on the left are rewritten more positively on the right.

Meek	Positive Revision
I know that you have a busy schedule and do not always have time to respond, but I would be appreciative if you could send me your brochure on how to apply Brakelite.	Please send me your brochure on how to apply Brakelite.
I know the season is almost over, but could you possibly let me know something about rates for the rest of the summer.	I am interested in renting a cabin in late August (24–31) and would like to know about your rates for that week.
I will be grateful for whatever employment opportunities you could kindly give me.	I will welcome the opportunity to discuss my qualifications with you.

Using the Most Effective Language in Your Letters

How you say something in a letter can be as crucial to your success as what you say. An effective letter requires you to pay attention, especially during the revision stage, to the words and tone of voice you use. Three simple suggestions can help.

Your letters should be (1) **clear**, (2) **concise**, and (3) **contemporary**. Regard these principles of letter writing as the three Cs.

1. Be clear. Clarity obviously is the most important quality of a business letter. If your message cannot be understood easily, you have wasted your reader's time. Confusion costs time and money. Plan what you are going to say—what your objective is—by taking a few minutes to jot down some questions you want answered or some answers to questions asked of you. Doing this will actually save you time. Review pages 28-29 in Chapter 2.

Choose precise details appropriate for your audience. In choosing exact words, answer the reader's five fundamental questions—*who? what? why? where?* and *how?* Supply concrete words, facts, details, numbers. On the left are some examples of vague sentences that will puzzle a reader because necessary details are missing. These sentences have been revised on the right, with exact words replacing unclear ones.

Vague	Clear Revision
Please send me some copies of your recent brochure I can use at work.	Please send me 4 copies of your brochure on the new salt substitute to share with my fellow dietitians.
You can expect an appraisal in the next few weeks.	You will receive an estimate on the installation of a new 50,000 BTU air-conditioning unit no later than July 12.
One of our New York stores carries that product.	Our store at 856 East Fifth Avenue sells the entire line of Texworld gloves.
I would like some information about your scheduling policies to Rio de Janeiro.	Please let me know if Worldwide Air has a weekday morning flight to Rio de Janeiro and how far in advance reservations would have to be made for that flight.
The fee for that service is nominal.	The fee for caulking the five windows on the first floor will be $45.

2. Be concise. "Get to the point" is one of the most frequent commands in the business world. A concise letter does not ramble; instead, it is easy to read and to act on. As you draft and then revise your letter, ask yourself these two questions: (1) What is the main message I want to tell my reader? (2) Does every sentence and paragraph stick to the main point? The secret to efficient correspondence is to get to the main point at once, as in the following examples.

```
Your order will be delivered by July 26, as you
requested.

I am happy to confirm the figures we discussed in our
telephone conversation last Wednesday.

I request an extension of two weeks in paying my note.

Please accept our apologies for the damaged Movak
shipped to you last week.
```

```
Here is the report you asked our accountant to
prepare. It does contain the new figures on the
Manchester store you wanted.
```

Many letter writers get off to a deadly slow start by repeating, often word for word, the contents of the letter to which they are responding.

First Draft
```
I have your letter of March 23 before me in which you
ask if our office knows of any all-electric duplexes
for rent less than five years old and that would be
appropriate for senior citizens. You also ask if these
duplexes are close to shopping and medical facilities.
```

Revised
```
Thank you for your letter of March 23. Our office
does rent all-electric duplexes suitable for senior
citizens. We have two units, each renting for $375 a
month, that are four blocks from the Mendez Clinic and
two blocks from the Edgewater Mall.
```

Another way to write a concise letter is to include only material that is absolutely relevant. For example, in a letter complaining about inadequate or faulty telephone service, mentioning color preferences for extension telephones would be inappropriate. In a request for information on transferring credits from one college to another, do not ask about intramural sports.

Finally, make sure that your letter is not wordy (review the pertinent sections of Chapters 4 and 5, pages 108–112, 129–133). By taking a few minutes to revise your letters before they are keyboarded, you can write shorter, more useful letters.

3. Be contemporary. Being contemporary does not mean you should use slang expressions ("I had a tire ripped off"; "That rejection was a bummer") or informal language that is inappropriate ("Doing business with Bindex is a hassle"). Nor should you go to the other extreme and become too stiff and formal. Sound friendly and natural. Write to your reader as if you were carrying on a professional conversation with him or her. Business letters today are upbeat, simple, and direct. A business letter is readable and believable; it should not be old-fashioned and flowery.

Often individuals are afraid to write naturally because they fear that they will not sound important. They resort to using phrases that remind them (and the reader) of "legalese"—language that smells of contracts, deeds, and starched collars. The following list of words and phrases on the left contains musty expressions that have crept into letters for years; the list on the right contains modern equivalents.

Musty Expression	**Modern Revision**
aforementioned	previously mentioned
ascertain	find out
at this present writing	now
I am in receipt of	I have

Musty Expression	Modern Revision
attached herewith	enclosed
at your earliest possible date	soon
I beg to differ	I disagree
we beg to advise	we believe, think
I am cognizant of	I know
contents duly noted	we realize
endeavor	try
forthwith	at once
henceforth	after this
hereafter, heretofore, hereby	(drop these three "h's" entirely)
we humbly request	we ask
immediate future	soon
in lieu of	instead of
kindly advise	let us know
optimum	best
pursuant	concerning
please be advised that	I am happy (or sorry) to tell you that
please find enclosed	I'm enclosing
pending your reply	until I hear from you
per our conversation	when we spoke
prior to	before
we regret to inform you that	we are sorry that
remittance	payment
remuneration	cost, salary, pay
rest assured that	you can be sure that
your letter arrived and I have same	I have your letter
take the liberty to inform you	happy to tell you
thanking you in advance	thank you
the undersigned/the writer	I
under separate cover	I'm also sending you
the wherewithal	the way
yours of recent date	your recent letter
your communication	your phone call, your memo, your order

Figure 6.9 contains a letter in stilted language written by Brendan T. Mundell to Patricia Lipinski, an executive whose firm has been overcharged for airplane tickets. Mundell's letter overflows with flowery, old-fashioned expressions. The effect is that Mundell's message—offering an apology, a credit, and a promise to correct the situation—is long-winded and pompous. It even sounds insincere. Note how the revision in Figure 6.10 (p. 174), free of such stilted expressions, is shorter, clearer, and far more personable.

FIGURE 6.9   A letter written in stilted, old-fashioned language.

NORTHERN INTERNATIONAL AIRWAYS
3000 Airline Highway
Tyler, ME 04462-3000
(207) 555-6300
July 15, 1994

Ms. Patricia Lipinski
Vice President
Lindsay Electronics
4500 South Mahoney Drive
Buffalo, NY 14214-4514

Dear Ms. Lipinski:

Please be advised that I am in receipt of yours of July 6th. I would like to take this opportunity to say that we are very cognizant of our commitment to good corporate customers like Lindsay and extend our deepest regret and disappointment for the problems your firm has experienced with Northern. Herewith allow me to explain what we will do by way of restitution.

Remittance is beyond any doubt due your firm, and I hasten to rectify the situation with regard to our error. Forthwith we are adjusting your account #7530, crediting it with the $706.82 you were surcharged erroneously. Moreover, inasmuch as Lindsay is a valuable procurer of our services, I am highly pleased to announce that we are also enchancing your Travel-Pass account with another 3,000 miles.

I would also like to bring to your attention that in an endeavor to correct such billing errors in the immediate future, I have routed copies of your communication with us to the manager of our billing department. I am confident that pursuant to your letter he will take necessary action at his earliest possible convenience to ascertain the entire situation behind this problem and make the necessary adjustments and alterations in our procedures. Your bringing this matter to us will have the positive effect of helping us to process more equitably and expeditiously according to the terms of our contractual understanding.

Once again, I want to take the liberty to assure you that Lindsay Electronics is one of our most valued clients. Rest assured that we will take every step imaginable not to jeopardize our long-standing relationship with you. We are all indebted to you for your faith in us, and I hope that all the aforementioned problems have now been satisfactorily resolved for you. Thanking you, I am

Sincerely yours,

Brendan T. Mundell

Brendan T. Mundell
General Manager

FIGURE 6.10 **A revised copy of the stilted letter in Figure 6.9.**

NORTHERN INTERNATIONAL AIRWAYS
3000 Airline Highway
Tyler, ME 04462-3000
(207) 555-6300
July 15, 1994

Ms. Patricia Lipinski
Vice President
Lindsay Electronics
4500 South Mahoney Drive
Buffalo, NY 14214-4514

Dear Ms. Lipinski:

Thank you for your letter of July 6. I am sorry to learn about the billing problems
your employees encountered while traveling on Northern earlier this month. We
care very much when we have inconvenienced a good customer like Lindsay
Electronics. Please accept my apology.

Lindsay is unquestionably entitled to compensation for our billing error. I am
crediting your account #7530 with $706.82, the amount you were overcharged.
Furthermore, in appreciation of Lindsay's business, I am also crediting your
Travel-Pass account with a bonus 3,000 miles.

To help us avoid similar incidents, I have sent a copy of your letter to the manager
of our billing department. I know that he will want to learn about Lindsay's
experience and will use your comments constructively in an effort to revise our
billing procedures.

As a Frequent Flyer account member, Lindsay is one of our most important
customers, and we will continue to work hard to deserve your support.
Please call me if I can help you in the future.

Sincerely yours,

Brendan T. Mundell

Brendan T. Mundell
General Manager

Writing for International Readers

As part of your job, you will very likely have to write to a reader who is not a native speaker of English, or an English as a Second Language (ESL) audience. Many American businesses are multinational corporations with branches and customers throughout the world. These companies depend on international trade to stay in business; each year a larger share of America's gross national product (GNP) depends on foreign markets. To communicate with ESL customers and coworkers, you will have to write "international English,"[1] a language that is easily understood in a world that has shrunk to the size of a global village (or marketplace) thanks to international trade. Some of your ESL readers will have an excellent command of English; others will have only basic literacy in English. You can expect to write a variety of documents to these readers—letters of inquiry and sales letters, product descriptions, proposals, and even operating instructions. The clearer and easier your written communications are to ESL audiences, the better your chances are of doing business with them. The most important point to keep in mind is that you have to be sensitive to your audience's ability to understand your English while being aware of your obligation to respect your ESL readers' cultural traditions.

Four Guidelines to Communicate with ESL Readers

Here are four guidelines to follow when you write to an ESL audience.

1. Use common, easily understood vocabulary. In your letters and other written communications, use a basic, simplified English. That is, use words that have a high frequency (widely understood) as opposed to words that have a low frequency (not used or understood by many speakers). Consult a helpful dictionary of basic English such as *The New York Times Everyday Dictionary,* edited by Thomas M. Paikeday (New York ·Times Books, 1982). Avoid such low-frequency words as the following by substituting a simpler translation, such as that in parentheses: refrain (stop); forestall (prevent); exude (discharge); exultant (happy).

Be careful, however, that the simple, basic English words you use are not ambiguous. For example, the sentence "We fired the engine" written to an ESL reader could lead to misunderstanding. An ESL reader would not automatically be aware of the multiple meanings of the word *fire.* Unfamiliar with the context in which the word *fire* means "start up," an ESL reader might think the word means only to "set on fire, inflame," which is not what the writer intended. Such interpretation is likely because most bilingual dictionaries that your ESL reader would consult do not offer two meanings of a word.

Be careful about the technical vocabulary you use as well. While an ESL reader may be more familiar with technical terms than with other English words, make

---

[1] I am indebted to Professor George Haber of the New York Institute of Technology for his advice on *international English,* a term he has developed for an area he has been researching for some time.

sure the technical word or phrase you include is widely known and not just a word or meaning used only at your plant or office. Also stay away from technical terms in fields other than the one with which your ESL reader is familiar.

2. Avoid using idiomatic expressions. As with the example of *fire* on p. 175, the following phrases and expressions can confuse and even startle an ESL reader: "I am all ears"; "sleep on it"; "throw cold water on it"; "burn the midnight oil"; "hit the nail on the head"; "he landed in hot water"; "easy come, easy go"; "you bet your life"; "get a handle on it"; "cut off your nose to spite your face." Such figurative (and often colorful) expressions are especially difficult for an ESL reader to understand, and by using them you make the reader ask for clarification and run the risk of offending your audience. The meaning of these and other similar phrases is not literal; it is figurative, a reflection of our culture, *not* your reader's. An ESL reader will approach these phrases as the separate meaning of the individual words, not as a collective unit of meaning.

Imagine the horror an ESL reader—a potential customer in Asia or Africa, for example—might experience if you wrote this about a sale concluded at a branch office: "Last week we made a killing in our office." Revise such a sentence to omit the idiomatic expression and substitute a clear, unambiguous translation easily understood in international English, for example, "We made a large sale last week." Or in place of "You hit the nail on the head," write "You have clearly understood what must be done." For "Sleep on it," you might say, "Please take a week or two to make your decision."

3. Delete any sports (or gambling) metaphors from your communications with ESL readers. These metaphors, which most often reflect American popular culture, do not translate word for word for non-native speakers and so can interfere with your communication with them. In all likelihood, your audience has no equivalent in its culture for American sporting games and events. Here are a few of the sports metaphors to avoid: "you are out in left field," "we are in the ballpark," "we struck out," "we fumbled the ball," "go out for a long pass," "the bases are loaded," "drop the ball," "out of bounds," "down for the count," and "made a pass." With the help of a basic English dictionary, find nonfigurative translations for these expressions that an ESL reader can understand or quickly look up in a bilingual dictionary.

4. Keep your sentences simple and easy to understand. Select grammar and sentence patterns that will cause the least amount of trouble for an ESL reader. World languages, especially Asian languages, divide information in sentence units far differently from the way English does. Keep in mind that the shorter and less complicated your sentences are, the easier they will be for an ESL reader to process. Long (more than fifteen words) and complex (many clauses) sentences can be so difficult for ESL readers to understand that they may skip over them. To minimize misunderstanding, stick to the subject-verb-object pattern as much as possible. Reread pages 108–112 on sentence structure for some further suggestions.

Respecting the Cultural Traditions of Your ESL Readers

Using simple words and concise sentences certainly will help you to write more effectively and clearly to your ESL audience. But to avoid even greater troubles, you also must be concerned with respecting the cultural traditions, values, and preferences of your readers. Cultures differ widely in the way they send and receive information. What is acceptable in one culture may be offensive in another. Respecting the cultural practices of your reader can have far more impact on him or her than the price and quality of your product or service. When you write a letter to an ESL reader, pay special attention to your tone, the way you start and conclude your letter, and the type and amount of information you include.

You also need to be aware of cultural (and communication) taboos when preparing your letter to your ESL reader. As a general rule, steer clear of controversial topics—politics, elections, American troubles with the reader's country in the past, unflattering news stories about the reader's country. Before you dash off a letter to a prospective ESL client, find out as much as you can about his or her country's customs, especially the ways in which business is conducted and what is regarded as courteous and discourteous. You can go to the library for information or ask a person from that country (a foreign student; a coworker raised in that culture) about proper communication protocols. You may even wish to call that country's embassy or consulate to learn about proper communication etiquette, for example, how to address the reader in the salutation of a business letter.

Let's say that you had to write a sales letter (see pages 201–211) to an Asian business executive. You would have to employ two different strategies in writing such a letter for an American reader as opposed to an Asian one. For an American executive, the best strategy would be to take a direct approach—fast, hard-hitting, getting to the point quickly, and bashing the opposition or competition. A sales letter to an American reader would be polite but direct. But such a strategy would be counterproductive in a sales letter to an Asian reader. Business in East Asia is associated with religion, friendship, and a great many social courtesies. The Asian way of doing business, including writing and receiving letters, is far more subtle, indirect, and personal (complimentary) than in America. The American style of directness and insistence would be perceived as rude or unfair in, say, Japan, China, or Korea. A hard-sell letter to an Asian reader would be a sign of arrogance, and arrogance suggests inequality for such a reader. A sales letter to an Asian reader, therefore, should establish a friendship, a relationship in which trust is dealt with first and business details later. It is standard in Japanese companies, for example, to have executives meet three or four times just to socialize before beginning business negotiations.

To better understand the differences between communicating with an American reader as opposed to an Asian one, study the sales letters included in Figures 6.11 and 6.12. These letters, written by Sandra DiFusco for Starbrook Electronics, sell the same product, but Figure 6.11 is addressed to an American executive while Figure 6.12 shows how that same message is adapted for a businessperson in Seoul. Note how the American letter in Figure 6.11 starts off

FIGURE 6.11 Sales letter to an American firm.

STARBROOK ELECTRONICS
Perry, TX 75432-3465
(207) 555-2121
December 2, 1993

Mr. Ellis Fanner
Administrator
Morgan General Hospital
Morgan, OR 97342-0091

Dear Mr. Fanner:

How many times have the physicians who work at Morgan General asked when you would be getting MRI (magnetic resonance imaging) equipment? Having the latest, state-of-the-art imaging equipment is important to maintain your reputation as a leading health care provider in the Morgan River Valley.

As the world leader in designing and manufacturing MRI equipment, Starbrook can offer you the latest technology available. This diagnostic technology will save patients time and improve the care you give them. With the MRI capability of our Imaging 500, Morgan General can deliver more accurate and timely diagnoses. Within two hours you can determine whether a patient has had a stroke rather than having to wait a day or longer with more conventional X-ray or scanner technology. Thanks to our Imaging 500 model, Morgan General can also improve diagnoses for orthopedic and cardiac problems. Our Imaging 500 offers much more extensive internal imaging than any of our competitors' equipment.

By obtaining the Imaging 500, Morgan General will surpass all other health care providers in the Morgan River Valley. No other hospital within a hundred mile radius has one. By acting now, you, too, will receive Starbrook's unsurpassed guarantee of service and clarity. You are guaranteed one year's free maintenance by our team of experts. We will give you free upgrades to make sure your Imaging 500 stays state of the art. Since software updates change so often and so radically, no other MRI dealer dares to make such an offer. We deliver what we promise. Ask any of our recent, satisfied customers—Tennessee General, New York Uptown General, or Nevada Statewide HMO.

We are hosting a demonstration for hospital administrators on the 4th of January in Portland and would like to see you there. Don't hesitate to call me to arrange for your free showing.

Sincerely,

Susan DiFusco

Susan DiFusco
Assistant Manager

FIGURE 6.12   Sales letter to an ESL reader.

STARBROOK ELECTRONICS
Perry, TX 75432-3465
(713) 555-2121
December 2, 1993

Mr. Sun-Lin Kim
Administrator, Tangki Hospital
210-214 Jenji Road
Seoul, Korea

Dear Mr. Kim:

I am happy and honored to have the privilege of introducing myself to you through this letter. In your beautiful language I say "Hang wenur paddamnya nensa trenemyada" on behalf of my firm of Starbrook Electronics.

Please let us know if in some way we might be of assistance to you. One of the ways we may be able to assist you is by informing you about our new Imaging 500, an MRI (magnetic resonance imaging) piece of equipment. This new model can offer you and the patients you serve many advantages over conventional X-ray and even scanner models. Your physicians can offer quicker diagnoses for patients with strokes, heart attacks, or orthopedic injuries. MRI pictures can give you clearer and deeper pictures than any X-ray could.

It would be a great honor to provide Tangki Hospital with one of our Imaging 500s. If you buy the Imaging 500, we will give you all maintenance and software updates free for one year. Such service will provide the best in health care for the many people who look to you for help.

Kindly let me know if I may give you further information about the Imaging 500. It would be a special day to meet you and to give you and your staff a demonstration of our Imaging 500.

Sincerely yours,

Susan DiFusco

Susan DiFusco
Assistant Manager

politely but much more directly, something a Korean reader would regard as blunt or unacceptable. The sales letter written to the Korean audience starts not with business but with a compliment to the reader and his company, praising them for trustworthiness and wishing them much prosperity in the future. The successful writer addressing a Korean administrator would not get to the bottom line right away but use the introductory paragraph to show his or her respect for the company and the reader—the equivalent of the Japanese business executives socializing first before any mention of business is made.

Compare the second and third paragraphs of the letters in Figures 6.11 and 6.12. While the letter to the American reader launches an aggressive campaign to get the reader's business, the letter to the Korean reader avoids the hard sell of American business tactics. Sandra DiFusco knew that she must not advertise too strenuously for her Korean reader. The more she boasted about Starbrook's work, the less likely she would make a sale. She recognized from discussions with other Asian business people over the years that she had to supply key information—such as the application and the advantages of her product—without overwhelming her audience. Note, too, how the letter to the American in Figure 6.11 attacks the competition by stating how much better Starbrook's offer is. For Asian readers, on the other hand, it would be considered impolite to boast that your product is better than another company's or that your firm is currently doing business with other firms in the reader's country. The Asian way is to avoid anything impolite or too direct.

Finally, see how the conclusions of the two letters differ. In the letter in Figure 6.11 to an American audience, DiFusco strongly urges her potential customer to get in touch with her. Such a "call to action" is customary in a sales letter to an American firm. But in her concluding paragraph to Sun-Lin Kim, DiFusco adopts a more reserved and personal tone. Note her use of such appropriate phrases as "kindly let me know" and "it would be a special day" expressing the friendly sentiments of respect and honor that would especially appeal to her reader.

✓ Revision Checklist

Here is a checklist of twenty questions you need to ask yourself as you revise and edit your letter before mailing it. These questions deal with the format, style, and content of your letter. If you answer "no" to any one of the questions, you need to do some more rewriting, remembering all elements of the writing process. If you can answer each question satisfactorily, you will be off to a good start at communicating effectively with your reader.

1. Does my letter look neat and professional?
2. Have I followed one letter format (full block, semiblock, or AMS simplified) consistently?

3. Are my margins wide enough—at least 1 1/2 inches all the way around?
4. Did I spell every word, including the reader's name, correctly?
5. Have I proofread carefully and corrected every typographical error?
6. Are all my facts—costs, policy numbers, model types, dates, addresses—correct?
7. Did I tell the reader exactly why I am writing?
8. Does my letter adopt the "you attitude"?
9. Are my words clear and precise, and have I used basic, unambiguous international English for my ESL reader?
10. Is my letter free from flowery and stuffy language, and have I eliminated figurative expressions which might startle or confuse my ESL readers?
11. Do I get my message across politely and sincerely, and is it culturally appropriate for my ESL audience?
12. Have I answered the reader's questions without including irrelevant material?
13. Have I eliminated unnecessary repetition?
14. Have I included all necessary information—dates, quantities, locations, names, costs, references to previous orders or letters?
15. Does my last paragraph sum up my letter appropriately?
16. Have I chosen an appropriate complimentary close (in the full block or semiblock format)?
17. Have I signed my letter in blue or black ink?
18. Have I indicated an enclosure line if I am sending something with the letter?
19. Is my return address on the upper left front of the envelope?
20. Does the reader's name and address on the envelope match the inside address?

Exercises

1. What kinds of letters do you receive addressed to you at home? At your work? Write a paragraph about one of these kinds of letters, indicating why it was sent to you and what it wanted you to do.

2. Find two business letters and bring them to class. Be prepared to identify the various parts of a letter discussed in this chapter.

3. Bring to class letters following the full block format, the semiblock format, and the AMS style. How do they differ in format?

4. Find a form letter that is addressed to "Dear Customer," "Postal Patron," or "Dear Resident" and rewrite it to make it more personal.

5. Correct the following inside addresses.

a. Dr. Ann Clarke, M.D.
1730 East Jefferson
Jackson, MI. 46759

b. To: Tommy Jones
Secretary to Mrs. Franks
Donlevey labs
Cleveland, O. 45362

c. Debbie Hinkle
432 Parkway
N. Y. C. 10054

d. Mr. Charles Howe, Acme Pro.
P.O. Box 675
1234 S. e. Boulevard
Gainesville, Flor. 32601

e. Alex Goings, man.
Pittfield Industries
Longview, TEXAS 76450

f. ATTENTION: G. Yancy
Police Academy
1329 Tucker
N. O., La. 3410-70122

g. David and Mahenny
Lawyers
Dobbs Build.
L.A. 94756

h. CONFIDENTIAL
Jordon Foods, INC.
Miller Str.
Lincoln, Neb. 2103

6. Write appropriate inside addresses and salutations to (a) a woman who has not specified her marital status; (b) an officer in the armed forces; (c) a professor at your school; (d) an assistant manager at your local bank; (e) a member of the clergy; (f) your congressperson.

7. Which of the following complimentary closes is suitable for a business letter to someone you have never written to before and do not know?

Yours,	Cordially,	Very truly yours,
Gratefully yours,	Blissfully,	Happily yours,
Sincerely,	Thankfully yours,	Patiently yours,
Faithfully,	Yours truly,	Truly,

8. Find and correct the typographical errors in the following letter.

Dear MR. Jones;

I am very much enterested in finding a copy of your most recent brochure on nutrition. I am najoring in in foodscience at Westgatte Community Colledge and would appreciate obtainning some infornation about your polcies and procedurs in the disrtibution of hot lucnchs in teh elemantery grades. Your extenaive operatiom in this area has been priased for its thoroghness nad flexibilty.

If you have any copies of this borchure, or other instructons I mihgt see, I would like to use them in my class repotrs. With yoor permision, I would like to shafe these materials with my homeeconomics calss.

Sincerly yours,

J. P. Allen

9. Rewrite the following sentences to make them more personal.
   a. It becomes incumbent upon this office to cancel order #2394.
   b. Management has suggested the curtailment of parking privileges.
   c. ALL USERS OF HYDROPLEX: Desist from ordering replacement valves during the period of Dec. 19–29.
   d. The request for a new catalog has been honored; it will be shipped to same address soon.
   e. Perseverance and attention to detail have made this writer important to company in-house work.
   f. The Director of Nurses hereby notifies staff that a general meeting will be held Monday afternoon at 3:00 P.M. sharp. Attendance is mandatory.
   g. Reports will be filed by appropriate personnel no later than the scheduled plans allow.

10. The following sentences are discourteous, boastful, excessively humble, vague, or do not reflect the "you attitude." Rewrite them to correct these mistakes.
    a. Something is obviously wrong in your head office. They have once more sent me the wrong model number. Can they ever get things straight?
    b. My instructor wants me to do a term paper on safety regulations at a small factory. Since you are the manager of a small factory, send me all the information I need at once. My grade depends heavily on all this.
    c. It is apparent that you are in business to rip off the public.
    d. I was wondering if you could possibly see your way into sending me the local chapter president's name and address, if you have the time, that is.
    e. I have waited for my confirmation for two weeks now. Do you expect me to wait forever or can I get some action?
    f. Although I have never attempted to catalog books before, and really do not know my way around the library, I would very much like to be considered at some later date convenient to you for a part-time afternoon position.
    g. It goes without saying that we cannot honor your request.
    h. May I take just a moment of your valuable time to point out that our hours for the next three weeks will change and we trust and pray that no one in your agency will be terribly inconvenienced by this.
    i. Your application has been received and will be kept on file for six months. If we are interested in you, we will notify you. If you do not hear from us, please do not write us again. The soaring costs of correspondence and the large number of applicants make the burden of answering pointless letters extremely heavy.
    j. My past performance as a medical technologist has left nothing to be desired.
    k. Credit means a lot to some people. But obviously you do not care about yours. If you did, you would have sent us the $149.95 you rightfully owe us three months ago. What's wrong with you?

11. The following letter is filled with musty expressions, which bury key ideas. Rewrite it to make it shorter, clearer, and more reader-centered.

Dear Ms. Granedi:

This is in response to your firm's letter of recent date inquiring about the types of additional services that may be available to business customers of the First National Bank of Bentonville. The question of a possible time frame for the implementation of said services was also raised in the aforementioned letter. Pursuant to these queries, the following answers, this office trusts, will prove helpful.

Please be advised that the Board of Directors at First National Bank has a continuing reputation for servicing the needs of the Bentonville community, especially the business community. For the last fifty years—half of a century—First National Bank has provided the funds necessary for the growth, success, and expansion of many local firms, yours included. This financial support has bestowed many opportunities on a multitude of business owners, residents of Bentonville, and even residents of surrounding local communities.

The Board is at this present writing currently deliberating, with its characteristic caution, over a variety of options suggested to us by our patrons, including your firm. These options, if the Board decides to act upon them, would enhance the business opportunities for financial transactions at First National Bank. Among the two options receiving attention by the Board at this point in time are the creation of a branch office in the rapidly growing north side of Bentonville. This area has many customers who rely on the services of First National Bank. The Board may also place a business loan department in the new branch.

If this office of the First National Bank of Bentonville might be of further helpful assistance, please advise. Remember banking with First National Bank is a community privilege.

Soundly yours,

M. T. Watkins
Public Relations Director

12. Write a business letter to one of the following individuals and submit an appropriate envelope with your letter.
   a. your mayor, asking for an appointment and explaining why you need one
   b. your college president, stressing the need for more parking spaces or for computer terminals in a library
   c. the local water department, asking for information about fluoride supplements
   d. an editor of a weekly magazine, asking permission to reprint an article in a school newspaper
   e. the author of an article you have read recently, telling why you like or dislike the views presented
   f. a disc jockey at a local radio station, asking for more songs by a certain group
   g. a computer dealer, asking about software packages and explaining your company's special needs

13. Rewrite the following letters making them appropriate for an ESL reader. As you revise these letters, pay attention to both the words you use as well as the sentence constructions you employ. Consider the reader's cultural traditions, too.

   a. Dear Chum,

   Our stateside boss hit the ceiling earlier today when she learned that our sales quota for this quarter fell preciptiously short. Were I in her spot, I would have exploded too. Numerous missives to her underlings warned them to get off the dime and on the stick, but they were oblivious to such. These are the breaks in our business, right?

   Let's hope that next quarter's sales take a turn for the best. If they are as disasterous, we all may be in hot water. Until then, we will have to watch our p's and q's around here.

   Cheers,

   b. Dear Mr. Wong,

   It's not every day that you have the chance to get in on the ground floor of a deal so good you can actually taste it. But Off-Wall Street Mutual can make the difference in your financial future. Give me a moment to convince you.

   By becoming a member of our international investing group you can just about insure your success. We know all the ins and the outs of long-term investing and can save you a bundle. Our analysts are the best in the business and always look long and hard for the most propitious business deals. The stocks we select with your interests in mind are as safe as a bank and not nearly so costly for you. We can save you money by investing your money. We are penny pinchers with our client's initial investments, but we are King Midas when it comes to transforming those investments into pure gold.

I am enclosing a brochure for you to study, and I really hope you will examine it carefully. You would be foolish to let a deal like Off-Wall Street Mutual pass you by. Go for it.

Hurriedly,

c. Dear Mr. Bafaloukos,

My firm is taking a survey of businesses in your part of the world to see if there is any likelihood of getting you on board our international computer network and so I thought I would drop you a line to see if you might like to take the chance. In today's uncertain world business events can change over night and without proper communication you could be left out in the cold. We can help you.

Not only do we interface with major exchanges all around the globe but we make sure that we get the facts to you pronto. We do not sit on our hands here at Intertel. Check out the enclosed data sheet on who and how we serve and I have no doubts that you will give us a call to find out about joining up.

One last point: can you really risk going out on a limb without first knowing that you have all the facts at your fingertips about worldwide business events? Intertel is there to save you.

Fondly,

14. Interview a student at your school or a coworker who was born and raised in a foreign country about the proper etiquette in writing a business letter to someone from his or her country. With that student's assistance, write a letter (a sales letter or a letter asking for information) to an executive from that country.

15. In a letter to your instructor, describe the kinds of adaptations you had to make for the ESL reader you wrote to in Exercise 14.

Types of Business Correspondence

Receiving and answering business correspondence—memos and letters—are vital to the success of a company and its employees. The way you prepare your correspondence will reflect on your professional abilities and your company's reputation. When memos and letters are written clearly, effectively, and promptly, you and your employer profit. When they are done poorly, everyone suffers. For this reason, being an effective writer of memos and letters is a necessary and prized skill. In fact, the higher up the corporate ladder you climb, the more you will be expected to write—and write well.

Chapter 7 discusses six common types of business correspondence that you will be expected to write on the job:

1. memos
2. order letters
3. inquiry letters
4. special request letters
5. sales letters
6. customer relations letters

These six kinds of correspondence will introduce you to a variety of formats and a number of writing strategies and techniques. Generally speaking, memos, the least formal type of correspondence, convey brief notes or instructions; order, inquiry, and special request letters give and request information in differing contexts; sales letters require a description of your product or service and a convincing argument for your reader; and customer relations letters are vital to company image and customer satisfaction. Many of these six types of correspondence can be transmitted through the "electronic office" described below.

Correspondence in the Electronic Office

You can prepare your correspondence in a variety of ways. You may handwrite a memo to a coworker or type a letter to a customer. More than likely, though, you will be sending your messages via computers and fax machines. See pages 417–422 for a description of the types of electronic equipment often found in offices today. Office technology has changed rapidly over the last several years to help business people communicate with each other more quickly and cost-effectively.

One frequently used type of office technology is *E-mail*, or electronic mail. With E-mail you send and receive messages through your personal computer, which is linked via phone lines, or **modems**, to a communication network. Functioning like an electronic mailbox, your computer can receive and store messages when you are out and then inform you that they are waiting. You can then pull these messages up on your screen, make a hard (printed) copy if necessary (see Figure 7.1), and even file the message on disk for future reference. Through your computer you can communicate quickly and efficiently with people in your office, coworkers at branch offices, or employees and customers across the country and around the world. E-mail is delivered in a few minutes or hours at most. There is no waiting for postal delivery, and you don't have to worry about repeatedly exchanging telephone messages. Like a message sent via a fax machine, E-mail messages can speed up domestic and international business. But unlike a fax machine, your computer will allow you to store and later retrieve E-mail messages.

Adapting Your Style for E-Mail and Fax Messages

As with other types of communication, you still have to plan your messages carefully when using a fax machine or E-mail. This technology does not relieve you of the responsibility of preparing and organizing your message with your reader's needs in mind. In fact, this communication technology requires you to adhere to the following guidelines about style, tone and confidentiality:

1. Keep in mind that the receiver of your E-mail will be reading it on a CRT screen that is 60 to 65 percent smaller than a piece of standard business stationery (8 1/2 × 11 inches). This smaller-size screen requires that you keep your message succinct and to the point. Your reader will not appreciate repeatedly scrolling to find out what you have to say. As with written correspondence, you should use margins and lines containing no more than sixty characters to enhance readability.

2. Watch the length of your sentences and paragraphs. It is intimidating for a reader to see his or her screen taken over by one, unbroken paragraph. Keep your paragraphs to three or four sentences, and always double-space between paragraphs.

FIGURE 7.1   A memo sent by E-mail to a coworker.

Note for Allen

_____

Northeast Technologies

FROM: Melinda
DATE: Mon., Jan. 3, 1994 2:34 PM
SUBJECT: Working collaboratively on annual report for Northeast Technologies
TO: Allen

To follow up on our conversation yesterday regarding working together on this
year's annual report, I have talked with Peter and Margaret and found that their
schedules are flexible. They are both free to meet with us next Tuesday the
11th—at 10:30 a.m. in the upstairs conference room.

Like us, Margaret and Peter think we need first to draft a two- to three-page
overview that addresses Northeast's strategic goals and objectives for fiscal year
1995.

It would be a big help if you would bring copies of the last three years' reports. I
will call Ms. Jhandez for a copy of the speech she gave last month to the Powell
Chamber of Commerce. If memory serves me correctly, she did a first-rate job
summarizing Northeast's accomplishments for 1993. We will certainly want to
quote some of her remarks.

I am looking forward to working with you, Margaret, and Peter. See you on Tuesday.

---

3. In your attempt to be concise, do not turn your E-mail into telegrams—short,
clipped commands. Write your messages in full sentences and do not leave out
words. You do not want to appear as if you begrudge the reader your time or consideration. A telegraphic message—"Fax report immediately; need same for meeting"—makes you sound discourteous and hard to get along with.

4. Avoid sending messages in all capital letters. Not only will such a message be
harder to read, but it will not look like a professional piece of correspondence on
the screen or if the receiver decides to make a hard copy. Observe all the rules of
effective correspondence found in Chapter 6. Although E-mail is even more informal than a written memo, you should still be concerned about correct spelling
and proper punctuation. You should also avoid peculiar abbreviations, slang, and
unfamiliar jargon.

5. Avoid humor, sarcasm, and joke-telling. Just as these are out of place in professional correspondence sent through the mail, they are inappropriate in a fax or
a piece of E-mail.

6. Be very careful about sending a confidential message via E-mail or a fax. Unless you know that your receiver's phone lines are strictly private and secured, your message could be read by any individual in the receiver's office. Privacy is a major problem in today's computerized office. Likewise, do not say anything critical about a coworker or boss. Do not spread gossip. You never know who will read (and reveal) your message.

Memos

Memorandum, from which the noun "memo" comes, is a Latin word signifying that something is to be remembered. The Latin meaning points to the memo's chief function: to record information of immediate importance and interest in the busy world of work. Memos are in-house correspondence sent up and down the corporate ladder—from managers to employees and from employees to managers. They are also sent to and from coworkers. Memos allow a business or agency to communicate with itself in its day-to-day operations.

Functions of Memos

Memos have a variety of functions. They are written to

- announce a company policy or plan.
- make a request.
- explain a procedure or give instructions.
- clarify or summarize an issue.
- alert readers to a problem.
- confirm what has been decided in a conversation.
- remind readers about a meeting, policy, or procedure.
- provide documentation necessary for business.
- offer suggestions or recommendations.

Memos are invaluable written records. They are also used for short reports; see Chapter 16 for examples of field, trip, or progress reports in memo format. Many internal proposals (pages 559–560) also are written as memos.

Memo Format

Memos can vary in format. Some companies use standard, printed forms (Figure 7.2), while others have their names (letterhead) printed on their memos, as in Figure 7.3 (p. 192). Memos can be printed on 8 1/2" × 11" sheets of paper or on half sheets. The smaller-size paper is useful for shorter communications and encourages the writer to be concise. You can make your own memos by including the necessary parts discussed on pages 191–195.

As you can see from looking at Figures 7.1 through 7.5, memos look different from letters. They are more streamlined and less formal. Because they are sent to individuals within your company, memos do not need the formalities necessary in

FIGURE 7.2   Standard memo form without letterhead.

                                    MEMO

TO: All RNs

FROM: Margaret Wojak, Director of Nurses *M.W.*

DATE: August 16, 1994

SUBJECT: RN identity patches

Effective September 1, 1994, all RNs will have the choice of wearing caps or an
identity patch. Patches should be sewn on the upper right arm of lab coats or
uniforms so that staff and patients can easily identify you as an RN. Those RNs
wishing to wear identity patches may obtain them for one dollar apiece at the
Health Uniforms Shop directly across from the hospital on Ames Street. Please call
me at Extension 732 if you have any questions.

---

business letters. Memos, therefore, do not contain an inside address, salutation, complimentary close, or signature line.

Basically, the memo consists of two parts: the identifying information at the top and the message following this information. The identifying information includes these easily recognized parts: the *To, From, Date,* and *Subject* lines.

TO: Aileen Kelly   DATE: January 31, 1994
    Data Processing
    Manager

FROM: Stacy Kaufman   SUBJECT: Progress report on
      Operator, Level II   preparing the
                                      fall schedule

On the *To* line write the name and job title of the individual(s) who will receive your memo or a copy of it. If your memo is going to more than one reader, make sure you list your readers in the order of their importance in your company or agency, as Mike Gonzalez does in Figure 7.4 (p. 193). The vice-president's name appears before the public relations director's. If you are on a first-name basis with the reader, just use his or her first name. Otherwise, include the reader's first and last names. In some companies memos are sent to everyone whose name is on a distribution list. If your name is on the list for receiving information on a given project or from one or more departments, you will get every memo from these sources. Your name may appear on a number of lists. Don't send copies of your memos to individuals who don't need them. You will only increase the paper inflation or electronic traffic in an office.

On the *From* line write your name (first name only if your reader refers to you by it) and your job title (unless it is unnecessary for your reader). Some writers put their handwritten initials after their typed name to verify that the message comes from them.

FIGURE 7.3   Memo on letterhead stationery.

BILL'S CATERING SERVICE
56 North Jones
Canton, Ohio 45307-0299
(216) 555-4232

TO: Marge Adcox   DATE: November 23, 1994

FROM: Roger Blackmore *R.B.*   SUBJECT: Review of Management
                                                  Training Seminar

As you requested, I attended the Management Training Seminar (November 19–20). Here is a review of the major points made by the director, Jack Lowery.

1. The individual conducting the training sessions should always talk in a loud voice so that the trainees can hear him or her.

2. The main purpose of the training session should always be announced so that the trainees can focus on a specific set of topics.

3. Instructors should allow at least a ten-minute break for each two-hour session. A brief break will help to increase the trainees' attention spans and allow for better learning.

4. The easiest tasks should be assigned first; more complicated ones should follow.

5. The instructor should provide feedback to the trainees at the end of each major section.

I will be happy to meet with you to discuss these points in detail. These training techniques could be used in our orientation program. Let me know when it would be convenient for you to discuss these points.

FIGURE 7.4   A memo that uses headings.

RAMCO INDUSTRIES
"Where Technology Shapes Tomorrow"

TO: Rachel Mohler   SUBJECT: Ways to Increase
        Vice-President, Corp. Affairs   Ramco's Community
        Harrison Snowden   Involvement
        Public Relations Director

FROM: Mike Gonzalez *M. G.*   DATE: March 3, 1994

At our planning session in early February, our division managers stressed
the need to generate favorable publicity for our new Ramco plant in
Mayfield. Such publicity would help to highlight Ramco's anticipated
community involvement. You asked me to investigate ways in which Ramco's
visibility in the Mayfield community might be enhanced. This memo suggests
three plans we might pursue.

Create a Scholarship Fund
Ramco would receive favorable publicity by creating a scholarship at
Mayfield Community College for any student interested in a career in
industrial technology. A scholarship for one year at Mayfield Community
College would cost Ramco $3,800. The scholarship could be awarded by a
committee composed of Ramco's executives and administrators at Mayfield
Community College. Such a scholarship would emphasize Ramco's support
for industrial education and our interest in a local college.

Offer Factory Tours
Short guided tours of the Mayfield factory would introduce the Mayfield
community to Ramco's products and innovative technology. The tours might
be organized for community and civic groups—the members of the YMCA
and YWCA, senior citizens' clubs, schools. On these tours, individuals would
see the care we take in our production, our equipment, and the speed with
which we ship our products. Of special interest to visitors would be Ramco's
use of industrial robots. These tours must be scheduled well in advance so
they do not conflict with our production schedules. A question-and-answer
period could follow each tour.

Provide Guest Speakers
A number of our employees would be excellent guest speakers at social
and educational meetings in Mayfield. Possible topics would include the
technological advances Ramco has made in manufacturing and engineering
and how these advances help consumers. It would be relatively easy to
compile a list of interesting speakers from our engineering, safety, and
transportation departments.

Please give me your comments as soon as possible. If we are going to put
one or more of the suggestions into practice before the plant opens, we'll
need to act by the end of this month.

FIGURE 7.5   Memo with a clear introduction, discussion, and conclusion.

MEMORANDUM

Dearborne Equipment Company
204 South Mill St.
South Orange, NJ 02341-3420
(609) 555-9848

TO: Machine Shop Employees   DATE: September 27, 1994

FROM: Janet Hempstead   SUBJECT: Keeping Brake Machines Clean
Shop Supervisor

During the past two weeks I have received a number of reports that the brake machines are not being cleaned properly after each use. Through this memo I want to emphasize and explain the importance of keeping these machines clean for the safety of all employees.

When the brake machines are used, the cutter chops off small particles of metal from the brake drums. These particles settle on the machines and create a potentially hazardous situation for anyone working on or near the machines. If the machines are not cleaned routinely before being used again, these metal particles could fly into an individual's face when the brake drum is spinning.

To prevent accidents like this from happening, please make sure you vacuum the brake machines after each use. You will find two vacuum cleaners for this purpose in the shop--one of them is located in work area 1-A and the other, a reserve model, is in the storage area. Vacuuming brake machines is quick and easy; it should take no more than a few seconds. I am sure you will agree that this is a small amount of time to make the shop safer for all of us.

Thanks for your cooperation. If you have any questions, please call me at Extension 123 or come by my office.

On the *Subject* line write the purpose of your memo. The subject line serves as the title of your memo. Be precise so that readers can file your memo correctly. Vague subject lines such as "New Policy," "Operating Difficulties," or "Shared Computer Time" do not identify your message accurately and may suggest that your message is not carefully restricted or developed. "Shared Computer Time," for example, does not tell readers if your memo will discuss new equipment, corporate arrangements, or vendors; offer additional or fewer hours; or warn employees about abusing the system.

On the *Date* line do not simply list the day of the week. Give the calendar date and year—June 8, 1994.

Memo Protocol and Company Politics

Memos are important tools for any company or agency. They reflect its politics, policies, and organization. Memos are sent down the administrative ladder from presidents, vice-presidents, managers, and so on to employees, and memos are sent up the ladder, too, from employees to their bosses. Workers also send memos to each other. Figures 7.2 and 7.5 illustrate memos sent from the top down, while Figures 7.3 and 7.4 are memos sent from employees to their supervisors. Figure 7.1 shows a memo from one worker to another.

Companies have their own memo protocol, or accepted ways in which memos are formatted, organized, written, and routed. In fact, some companies offer protocol seminars on how employees are to prepare memos. In the corporate world, protocol determines where your memo will go. For example, it would be presumptuous of you to send copies of all your memos to the vice-president. You would offend your immediate supervisor, who would think that you are trying to avoid going through proper company channels. Conversely, a vice-president may want a memo from him or her to be distributed to the staff by another, lower administrator, to ensure that the staff is being informed and that responses are not sent back up to the vice-president but instead go through a lower administrative channel. You need to familiarize yourself early in your employment with how your company wants memos to be directed.

You may be asked to write a memo for the vice-president or supervisor to sign. Your writing skills may, therefore, need to include the ability to write in another person's voice to some degree. Moreover, as we have seen in Chapter 2 (pages 39–40), it is very common in offices for two or more people to collaborate as a team in preparing memoranda, as they do in preparing reports and proposals.

Memo Style and Tone

The style and tone of your memos will be controlled by your audience within (or sometimes outside) your company or agency. Writing to a coworker whom you know well, you can adopt a casual, conversational tone. You want to come across as friendly and cooperative to a coworker. In fact, to do otherwise would make you look self-important, stuffy, or hard to work with. When writing a memo to a manager or customer, though, you want to have a more formal tone than when

writing to a coworker or peer. Your boss will expect you to show a more respect-
ful, even official, posture. Here are two ways of expressing the same message,
with the first more suitable for a coworker and the second more appropriate
for a boss.

> **Coworker** I think we should go ahead with Alison's plan for reorganization. It seems
> like a safe option to me, and I don't think we can lose.

> **Boss** I propose that we adopt the organizational plan developed by Alison
> Pierson. Her recommendations are carefully researched and satisfactorily
> answer all the questions our office has about the plan.

Finally, just because a memo is usually an in-house communication, do not
think that the quality of your writing is unimportant. Your employer and coworkers deserve the same clear and concise writing and attention to the "you attitude"
that your customers do. In fact, your job may depend on preparing correct, persuasive, and readable memos. Keep in mind that memos require the same care
and follow the same rules of effective writing as letters do. You might want to
review the guidelines on persuasive writing on pages 18-20.

Strategies for Organizing a Memo

Your memos need to be drafted and organized so that readers can find information quickly and act on it promptly. For longer, more complex communications,
such as the memos in Figures 7.3-7.5, the message of your memo might be
divided into three parts: (1) introduction, (2) discussion, (3) conclusion.

In the introductory section of your memo, tell readers clearly about the problem, procedure, question, or policy that prompted your writing to them. Link the
first sentence of your memo to the subject line. Explain briefly any background
information the reader needs to know. Be specific about what you are going to
accomplish in your memo. Note, for example, the ways in which the writers in
Figures 7.3 and 7.4 tell the readers why a list of items is provided and why recommendations are included. Do not be afraid to come right out and say, "This memo
explains new parking procedures" or "This memo summarizes the action taken at
the industrial site near Evansville to reduce air pollution."

In the discussion section, explain with relevant detail the procedures, policies, or problems you are calling to the readers' attention. Tell them why a problem or procedure is important, who will be affected by it and why, what caused it,
why changes are necessary, and what those changes are. Give precise dates,
times, and locations. For example, note how carefully the writer of the memo in
Figure 7.5 explains the problem and procedure in cleaning the brake machine.

Provide a conclusion that states specifically how you want the reader to
respond to your memo. To get readers to act appropriately, you can do one or
more of the following in your conclusion.

1. Ask the readers to call you if they have any questions.
2. Request a reply—in writing, over the telephone, or in person—by a specific
   date.
3. Provide a list of recommendations that the readers are to accept, revise, or
   reject.

Throughout your memo use organizational markers (see pages 16-17) to make information easy for readers to follow. When you have a large number of related points, as the writer of the memo in Figure 7.3 does, number them so that the reader can comprehend them more easily. Bulleted items and numbers help you organize information and also assist your readers in following your work. Lists in a memo point out comparisons and contrasts easily. Underlining or using bold-face type for key sentences will also help readers by emphasizing important points. But do not abuse this technique by underlining or boldfacing too much. Only underline or boldface points that contain summaries or draw conclusions. Memo reports, such as in Figure 7.4, use headings to separate information for readers so that they can find it more quickly. Headings (often discovered from brainstorming and polished and refined through revision) will also help you organize information as you write.

Order Letters

Order letters are straightforward notices informing a seller that you want to purchase a product or service. To make sure that you receive exactly what you want, your letter must be clear, precise, and accurate. Double-check the seller's brochure, catalog, or agency manual before you write your order letter.

Order letters address the following five points.

1. Description of the product or service. Specify the name, model or stock number, quantity, color, weight, height, width, size, or any special features that separate one model from another (e.g., chrome as opposed to copper handles). Make your letter easy to read by itemizing when you order more than one product. Listing the products or materials in tabular form will set them apart and allow the seller an opportunity to check off each item as it is being prepared for shipment.

2. Price of the product or service. Indicate precisely the price per unit, per carload, or per carton, and then multiply that price by the number you are ordering. For example, ask for "twelve units @ $5 a unit." Do not put down the cost of one item ($5) for the dozen you are requesting. You will receive only one.

3. Shipping instructions. Do you want the product sent by first-class or fourth-class mail, an express mail carrier or priority mail? Specify any special handling instructions—Do not fold; Use hand stamp; Refrigerate or Pack in Dry Ice; Ship to the Production Department.

4. Date needed. Is there a rush date? Is there a date after which you do not want the order filled at all?

5. Method of payment. Businesses with good credit standing are sent a bill. Individuals, however, may be required to pay beforehand. If so, are you enclosing a check or money order? Is the product to arrive COD (cash on delivery)? If you use a charge card, specify which card, and include your account number. Will you be paying in installments? State how much you are including and when and how the balance is to be paid.

Orders can be considered external or internal. An external order is sent to an individual or company you do not work for or with. You will refer to the five points just discussed and use a letter or sometimes a form provided by the company from which you are ordering the product. Figure 7.6 shows a sample order letter written in the AMS format for letters discussed on page 154.

FIGURE 7.6   An order letter.

DAVIS CONSTRUCTION COMPANY
1200 South Devon
Millersville, Pennsylvania 17321

712-555-1000   **FAX 712-555-4221**

April 4, 1994

E. F. Johnson and Associates
820 Frontage Road
P.O. Box 1007
St. Louis, MO 64211-1007

ORDERING MATERIALS

Please send us by first-class mail the following materials listed in your 1994 catalog entitled *Personnel Forms for Monitoring Selection, Administration, and Evaluation:*

Catalog Number	Title	Number of Copies	Total Cost
P-4	Personnel Interviewer's Survey	25	$20.00
P-5	Health Information Questionnaire	100	48.00
EA-4	Personnel Application Forms	25	24.00
ATS-6	Health History	1	3.00
			$95.00

Mail these forms, send them to the Personnel Department in care of my attention. Please send them within the next ten days and telephone me collect if there will be any delay.

A check for one half the amount ($47.50) is enclosed, and the balance will be paid upon receipt of the materials.

Roberta Youngblood

ROBERTA YOUNGBLOOD, PERSONNEL OFFICER

Encl.: Check 3467 for $47.50

An internal order, often called a *requisition,* asks one individual or department or section of your company to supply another with necessary materials, equipment, service, or publications. A letter is not necessary for an internal order; instead, use a memo or a specially provided form.

Inquiry Letters

An inquiry letter asks for information about a product, service, publication, or procedure. Businesses frequently exchange such letters. As a customer, you too have occasion to ask for catalogs, names of stores in your town selling a special line of products, and the price, size, and color of a particular object. Businesses are eager to receive such inquiries and will answer them swiftly because they promise a future sale.

Figure 7.7 (p. 200) illustrates a letter of inquiry. Addressed to a real estate office managing a large number of apartment complexes, Michael Ortega's letter follows the three basic rules for an effective inquiry letter:

1. It states exactly what information the writer wants.
2. It indicates clearly why the writer must have this information.
3. It specifies when the writer must have the information.

Whenever you request information, be sure to supply appropriate stock and model numbers, pertinent page numbers, or exact descriptions. You might even clip and mail the advertisement describing the product you want. Vague or general letters delay a response to you. Had Michael Ortega written the following letter to Acme, he would not have helped his family move: "Please send me some information on housing in Roanoke. My family and I plan to move there soon." Such a letter does not indicate whether he wants to rent or buy, whether he is interested in a large or small apartment, furnished or unfurnished, where he would like to be located, or the rent he is willing to pay. Similarly, a letter asking a firm to "send me all the information you have on microwave ovens" might bring back a detailed service manual when the writer wanted only prices of the top-selling models.

Special Request Letters

Special request letters make a special demand, not a routine inquiry. Among other things, these letters can ask a company for information that you as a student will use in a paper, an individual for a copy of an article or a speech, or an agency for facts that your company needs to prepare a proposal or sell a product. The person or company being asked for help stands to gain no financial reward for supplying this information; the only reward is the goodwill such a response creates.

Make your request clear and easy to answer. Supply readers with addressed, postage-paid envelopes and a telephone number for any questions.

FIGURE 7.7   A letter of inquiry.

---

403 South Main Street
Kingsport, TN 37721-0217
March 2, 1994

Mr. Fred Stonehill
Property Manager
Acme Property Corporation
Main and Broadway
Roanoke, VA 24015-1100

Dear Mr. Stonehill:

Please let me know if you will have any two-bedroom
furnished apartments available for rent during the
months of June, July, and August. I am willing to pay
up to $425 a month plus utilities. My wife, one-year-
old son, and I will be moving to Roanoke for the summer
so that I can take classes at Virginia Western
Community College. If possible, we would like to have
an apartment that is within two or three miles of the
college. We do not have any pets.

I would appreciate hearing from you within the next two
weeks. My phone number is (606) 555-8957. The best time
to reach me is between 6:00 p.m. and 9:00 p.m.

If you have any suitable vacancies, we would be happy
to drive to Roanoke to look at them and give you a
deposit to hold an apartment for us. Thank you for your
help.

Sincerely yours,

Michael Ortega

Michael Ortega

Saying "please" and "thank you" will help you get the information you want. Also, do not expect your reader to write the paper or proposal for you. Asking for information is quite different from asking readers to organize and write it for you. Follow these seven points when asking for information in a special request letter.

1. State who you are and why you are writing.
2. Indicate clearly your reason for requesting the information.
3. Give the reader precisely and succinctly the questions you want answered. List, number, and separate the questions.
4. Specify exactly when you need the information. Allow sufficient time—at least three weeks.
5. Offer to forward a copy of your report, paper, or survey in gratitude for the help you were given.
6. If you want to reprint or publish the materials you ask for, indicate that you will secure whatever permissions are necessary. State that you will keep the information confidential if that is appropriate.
7. Thank the reader for helping.

Figure 7.8 (p. 202) gives an example of a letter that follows these guidelines.

Sales Letters

A sales letter is written to persuade the reader to buy a product, try a service, support some cause, or participate in some activity. A sales letter can also serve as a method of introducing yourself to potential customers. No matter what profession you have chosen, knowing how to write a sales letter is an invaluable skill. There will always be times when you have to sell a product, a service, an idea, a point of view, or yourself!

You have undoubtedly received numerous sales letters from military recruiters, local merchants, charitable organizations, and campus groups. Sales letters face a lot of competition that you will have to overcome.

To write an effective sales letter, you have to do three things:

1. Identify and limit your audience.
2. Find out exactly what the needs of this group are.
3. Determine precisely what you want your readers to do after reading your sales letter.

These three points require that you do adequate homework about both your audience and the product or service you are selling.

In deciding whom you want to reach, you will also be investigating the needs of your audience. Do you want to write a letter to all the nurses in your state district nurses' association or only the pediatric nurses at a particular hospital? Are you writing to all homeowners who purchased aluminum siding from your company in the last three years or just in the last three months? Sometimes a sales letter will be duplicated and sent to hundreds of readers, as in Figure 7.9 (p. 203);

FIGURE 7.8   A special request letter.

234 Springdale Street
Rochester, NY 14618-0422
February 3, 1994

Ms. Victoria Lohrbach-Vitelli
Research Director
Creative Marketing Association
198 Madison Avenue
New York, NY 10016-0092

Dear Ms. Lohrbach-Vitelli:

I am a sophomore student at Monroe College in Rochester,
and I am preparing a term paper on the topic "Current
Marketing Practices." As part of my research for this
paper, I am writing an overview of marketing practices
for the past twenty-five years. Two of your publications would be of great help to me. Would you please
send me the following pamphlets:

1. A History of Marketing in the United States (CMA 15)
2. Creative Marketing Comes of Age (CMA 27)

I would appreciate receiving these materials by February 28 and will be pleased to send you a copy of
my paper in late May. Creative Marketing Association
will, of course, be fully cited in my bibliography.

Thank you for your assistance. I look forward to
hearing from you. My phone number is (717) 555-4329.

Sincerely yours,

Julie Kawatsu

Julie Kawatsu

FIGURE 7.9   A sales letter sent to a selected group of readers.

TIMES MIRROR

THE C. V. MOSBY COMPANY · 11830 WESTLINE INDUSTRIAL DRIVE, ST. LOUIS, MISSOURI 63141
314-872-8370 · CABLE ADDRESS "MOSBYCO"

Dear Doctor:

After you look it up, do you really know which drug is best for YOUR patient . . . and Why?

It all depends on where you look . If you consult standard "cookbook" guides to current drug therapy, you'll have only the personal opinions of one or two physicians on which drug they prefer to treat a specific disease.

However, if you consult the new **DRUGS OF CHOICE**, you'll have an authoritative, critical, unbiased appraisal of all drugs in current use, written specifically to support and verify your selection of the optimum drug for a specific patient in a particular clinical situation.

DRUGS OF CHOICE is the only drug therapy book that recognizes that you alone can fit drug and patient together, and thus gives you all the facts necessary to assist you in that "fitting." Dr. Modell and his 45 eminent contributors discuss all drugs available for a particular condition, based on their specialized knowledge and experience, substantiated by selected references. You will note updating in every chapter, particularly those on diuretics and drugs for cardiac arrhythmias.

You'll find a more complete description of the new **DRUGS OF CHOICE** on the specially prepared brochure enclosed, including table of contents, distinguished contributors, and 54 timesaving tables. Take a moment now to examine it; then examine the book itself for 30 days at our expense . Just complete the examination certificate and return it to us in the postage–paid envelope provided.

Each time you sign a prescription, you, and you alone, endorse the safety and quality of the drug prescribed. If you're going to look it up, you want the whole story. And only one book offers you that . . . **DRUGS OF CHOICE**. Can you afford to be without it?

Sincerely,

William J. DeRoze

William J. DeRoze
for The C. V. Mosby Company

WJD: ne

Letter adapted courtesy of the C. V. Mosby Company.

sometimes you may write to only one reader, as in Figures 7.10 and 7.11. Some helpful considerations in audience analysis are occupation, age, consumer needs or habits, geographic location, and memberships. Your employer may have a mailing list that you should consult. Once you have selected those who should receive your letter, you have made a great deal of headway in knowing what you will say to that audience and how.

FIGURE 7.10   A sales letter addressed to an individual.

Faithful Answering Service
4300 South Wabash
Lincoln, Oregon 97407-6028

September 27, 1994

Ms. Katherine Eubanks
Eubanks Pest Control
18 West Gannon Drive
Lincoln, OR 97411-4219

Dear Ms. Eubanks:

Gets reader's attention

How much business do you lose when your telephone rings and you are not there to answer it? A prospective client or steady customer might call one of the other 22 exterminators listed in the **Lincoln Yellow Pages**.

Highlights service's appeal

You will never miss a call if you use the Faithful Answering Service. Our courteous and experienced operators are on duty twenty-four hours a day, every day of the year. They are prompt, too. Your telephone will be answered before the caller hears the third ring.

Shows application to customer

You tell us when we are needed by simply calling and giving us your identifying code number. We will then be ready to take your messages or to transfer calls to any number you give us. When you are out of the office, a quick call to us can save you extra trips, time, and gas. Your customers will also be happier, knowing that you can be reached whenever they need you to solve their pest problems.

Calls for action

All this convenience and peace of mind can be yours, Ms. Eubanks, for less than 90 cents a day. And if you act by October 4, you can have your Faithful service installed **free of charge** and save the $25 installation fee. We promise to have your phone connected within three days after we hear from you.

I urge you to call us at **555-3434** by October 4. You can call us at any time, day or night. Don't forget we are here twenty-four hours a day.

Sincerely yours,

Samuel Heywood

Samuel Heywood, Owner

FIGURE 7.11 A sales letter soliciting a financial contribution.

ELMWOOD VOLUNTEER FIRE DEPARTMENT
Elmwood, Idaho 87549

To report a fire 911   **To volunteer 555-7878**

January 31, 1994

Mr. Alex B. Sutton
1453 North Prentiss Drive
Elmwood, ID 87549

Dear Mr. Sutton:

You can protect your home and your loved ones from life-threatening fire by supporting the Elmwood Volunteer Fire Department. The safety and security of our homes depend on the proven ability of our Volunteer Fire Department.

Thanks to your support in the past, the Elmwood VFD was able to purchase a new Powers V-10 pumping engine last year. This vehicle offers state-of-the-art capabilities in firefighting. Most large city fire departments own this engine to protect their citizens. All of our volunteers have been trained to operate the Powers and have proven themselves many times this past year. These volunteers work to guard you, and their invaluable service costs you, the taxpayer, nothing.

In 1993 alone the Elmwood volunteer firefighters logged over **1,000** hours in responding to 36 emergency calls, three of them within a few blocks of your home on Prentiss Drive. Insurance adjusters have estimated that without the Elmwood VFD more than 100 lives and more than $5 million in property might have been lost. One of your neighbors, Ms. Sarah Capsky, told the <u>Elmwood News</u>: "Our volunteer fire department saved my house, my three kids, and our two dogs. They deserve everyone's respect and gratitude."

To continue to protect you and your home, the Elmwood VFD needs your support. We cannot make it on our tax allocation from the county alone. In fact, tax dollars covered only the downpayment for the Powers V-10. The balance of the $145,000—nearly $110,000—must come from all of us in Elmwood.

Won't you take a minute to fill out the enclosed, postage-paid pledge card and return it by **February 28**? You can even authorize a monthly contribution from your checking account. At the end of our pledge drive I will send you a full financial report. Please help us protect Ms. Capsky's neighbors as if your life depended on it.

Respectfully,

Alice Sano
Alice Sano
Captain, Elmwood VFD

The "you attitude" is crucial. A sales letter is not written to provide elaborate explanations about a product. That kind of information comes after the sale. Nor is a sales letter written to proclaim the merits of your company. Here is a safe rule to follow: Don't boast or be a bore. The sales letter is written to persuade readers to buy, support, or join. Everything in the letter should be directed toward that goal. Appeal to readers' emotions, pocketbooks, health, or self-images. Where appropriate, focus on animal rights issues (for instance, many companies inform buyers that they do not use animals to test their products on). Entertain, amuse, coax, inform, or flatter the reader. The central question is: What are we trying to do for you, our customer? Ask yourself that question before you begin writing and you will be using effective reader psychology.

To succeed, your sales letters must employ the most effective language possible. Use concrete, specific words (see Chapter 5, page 128) instead of abstract ones. Select words that appeal to the reader's senses. You will have a greater chance of selling the reader if he or she can hear, see, taste, or touch your product. Find verbs, as you draft and revise, that are colorful, that put the reader in the picture, so to speak. Try to make the reader the subject of most of your sentences. That way he or she can visualize himself or herself buying or using your product or service.

Be as objective with your evidence as with your language. Do everything you can to gain your reader's confidence. Avoid untruths, exaggerations, false comparisons, and unsupported generalizations. Honesty is the best way to make a sale. If readers suspect you are playing false with them, they lose confidence in you and your company. If you do your homework about your product or your service, you will be able to give readers the honest, necessary evidence they deserve and demand. Remember that your key selling strategy is winning the reader over to your point of view.

Sales letters follow a time-honored and workable plan; that is, each sales letter follows what can be called the "*four A's*":

1. gets the reader's *attention*
2. highlights the product's *appeal*
3. shows the customer the product's *application*
4. ends with a specific request for *action*

These four parts may be handled in less than four paragraphs. Note how, in Figures 7.10 and 7.11, these four parts are labeled for you. Holding a sales letter down to one page or less will keep the reader's attention. Television commercials and ads in magazines provide useful models of this fourfold approach to the customer. The next time you see one of these ads, try to identify the "four A's."

Getting the Reader's Attention

Your opening sentence is crucial. If you lose readers here, you will have lost them forever. A typical television commercial has thirty to sixty seconds to sell viewers; your first sentence has about two to five seconds to catch the readers' attention and prompt them to read on. That first sentence is bait on a hook. It must show readers how their problems could be solved, their profits increased, or their pleasures enriched. The reader's attitude will be, "What's in this for me?"

Avoid an opening that is flat, vague, or lengthy. Beginning with a statement such as "I have great news for you" tells the readers nothing. They are more likely to toss your letter away if it does not contain something personally relevant in the first sentence. Tell them what the news is by selecting something that will appeal to their wallets, their emotions, or their chances to look better in the eyes of others. A letter for a pesticide that begins, "The cockroach could become the next endangered species if a California manufacturer has its way" offers some interesting, specific news. Keep your opening short, one or two sentences at most.

The following six techniques are a few of the many ways to begin a sales letter. Each technique requires you to adapt it to your product or service.

1. Asking a question. Mention something that readers are vitally concerned about that is also relevant to your product or service. Look, for example, at the opening question in Figure 7.9. Avoid such general questions as, "Are you happy?" or "Would you like to make money?" Use more specific questions with concrete language. For example, an ad for a home-study training course in crime investigation and identification asked readers, "Are you promotable? Are you ready to step into a bigger job?" And an ad for Air Force Reserve Nursing asked nurses, "Are you looking for something 30,000 feet out of the ordinary?" These are precise questions relevant to the offers they introduce. Similarly, a sales letter beginning with, "Could you use $100?" zeroes in on one particular desire of the reader. Since your main goal is to persuade readers to continue reading your letter, choose a question that they will want to see answered.

2. Employing a "how to" statement. This is one of the most frequently used openers in a sales letter, as in Figures 7.10 and 7.11. The reason for its success is simple—the letter promises to tell readers something practical and profitable. Here are some effective "how to" statements: "We can show you how to increase your plant growth up to 91%." "Here is how to save $500 on your next vacation." "This is how to provide nourishing lunches for less than eighty cents a person." These "how to" statements attract the readers' attention by introducing a subject that promises rewards and then shows how to gain those rewards.

3. Using flattery. Appeal to the reader's ego. But remember that readers are not naive; they will be suspicious of false praise. Compliment the reader professionally or praise the reader for some specific actions. An effective sales letter for a school supply shop was sent to every new member of a campus sorority announcing, "You've made the right choice in joining Delta Zeta. Now, let us make the right choice in helping you select your supplies this term."

4. Offering a free gift. Everyone likes to receive something for nothing or to boast about a bargain. Often you can lure readers further into your letter by telling them that there is a sale going on and that they can save a lot of money or that they can get the second product free or at half price if they purchase the first one at full price. One book club promises prospective customers, "We'll give you three books for $1 and a free tote bag to put them in with your membership." An automobile dealer promises $50 to every customer who test-drives a new car. A local realtor tempts customers to see lots for sale with, "Enclosed is a coupon worth $25 in gas for seeing Deer Run Trails Estates."

5. Introducing a comparison. Compare your product or service with conventional or standard products or procedures. For instance, a jacket firm told police officers that if they purchased a particular jacket, they were really getting three in one, because this product had a lining for winter and a covering used for greater visibility at night.

6. Announcing a change. Link your sales offer to a current event that will directly affect your prospective customer. When the sales tax on cars was about to be increased by 3 percent in one state, an automobile dealer sent sales letters to potential buyers, alerting them to the implications of delaying their purchase: "The sales tax on new cars will jump a WHOPPING 3 percent effective the first of next month. You may not think that 3 percent will mean that much money, but on a new 1994 model that increase could cost you an extra $700." The sales letter continued: "Couldn't you use that money for something else, say, those extras you've always wanted, like a CD player or an extended warranty?"

Calling Attention to the Product's Appeal

Once you have aroused the reader's attention, introduce the product or service. Make it so attractive, so necessary, and so profitable that the reader will want to buy or use the product or service. Don't lose the momentum you have gained with your introduction by boring the reader with petty details, flat descriptions, elaborate inventories, or trivial boasts. Appeal to the reader's intellect, emotions, or both, while introducing the product. In Figure 7.9 Mosby Company's mass-mailing letter appeals to the physician's professional requirements for an up-to-date book. In Figure 7.11 the captain of a volunteer fire department urges citizens to help pay for a piece of fire equipment that might save their lives and property. Here is an emotional appeal by the Gulf Stream Fruit Company:

> Can you, when you bite into an orange, tell where it was grown? If it tastes better than any you have ever eaten . . . full of rich, golden flavor, brimming with juice, sparkling with sunshine . . . then you know it was grown here in our famous Indian River Valley where we have handpicked it, at the very peak of its flavor, just for your order.[1]

From a leading question, the sales letter moves to a vivid description of the product, the name of the supplier, and the customer's ability to recognize how special both the product and he or she is to the Gulf Stream Fruit Company. Using another kind of appeal, the manufacturers of Tree Saw show how their product can decrease customers' fears and increase their safety:

> The greatest invention since the ladder, and a lot safer. With the Tree Saw, you can cut branches thirty feet above the ground. No need to call in a tree surgeon. And you don't have to risk your life on a shaky ladder. Just toss the beanbag weight of the flexible Tree Saw over a branch. Pull on each end of the control rope to make a clean cut. Spring pruning is quick and safe with this perfect tool.[2]

---

[1] "Gifts from Gulf Stream," Gulf Stream Fruit Company, Ft. Lauderdale, Fla. Reprinted by permission.

[2] Reprinted courtesy Green Mountain Products, Inc., Norwalk, Conn.

Showing the Customer the Product's Application

The third part of your sales letter lets readers know how and why the product is worthwhile for them. Here is the place where you give evidence of the value of what you are selling. You have to be careful, though, that you do not overwhelm readers with facts, statistics, detailed mechanical descriptions, or elaborate arguments. The emphasis is still on the use of the product and not on the company that manufactures or sells it. The shift from your company to your prospective customer is essential to any sale. The sales letter in Figure 7.9 emphasizes the importance of the physician's role in prescribing drugs: "You alone can fit drug and patient together." The Omnifax sales message on page 210 is addressed to busy office workers who are concerned about the increasing number of incoming and outgoing messages they deal with each day. Note how the details about this fax equipment are all related to those reader-centered issues.

What evidence should you use to convince the reader? Concentrate on descriptions of the product or service that emphasize state-of-the-art design and construction, efficiency, convenience, usefulness, and economy. Any special features or changes in the product or service that make it more attractive for the customer should be mentioned. For example, an ad for a greenhouse manufacturer stressed that in addition to using its structure just for a place to grow plants, customers would also find it a "perfect sun room enclosure for year-round 'outdoor' activities, gardening or leisure health spa." One plumbing contractor emphasized that she had been in business for more than fifteen successful years.

Testimonials—endorsements from previous customers as well as from specialists—may also convince readers to respond favorably to your letter. Rather than saying that hundreds of customers are satisfied with your product, get two or three of those happy customers to allow you to quote them in your letter. A large nursing home published residents' compliments about the food and care to show that it was a good place to live. A private boarding school printed a brief biography (with now and then pictures) of a successful graduate to prove that the school inspires students to leadership. A roach powder firm tells customers that its product is used at the White House. Note how Captain Sano persuasively uses Ms. Capsky's endorsement in the third and fourth paragraphs of her sales letter in Figure 7.11. You might also cite awards, honors, or accreditations that your product or service has won.

Worth mentioning also are warranties, guarantees, services, or special considerations that will make the customer's life easier or happier. One store advises readers: "As usual, there is no charge for local deliveries when purchases are over $100." Tell the reader that labor and parts are good for a year, two years, or however long they last. Emphasize that you will refund the price if the customer is not completely satisfied. Tell customers that they do not have to wait for parts or that you will loan them a replacement if they do.

You may be obligated to mention costs in your letter. Postpone discussion of them until the reader has been shown how appealing and valuable the product is. Of course, if price is a key selling point, mention it early in the letter. Readers will react more favorably to costs after they have seen the reasons why the product or

A sales message emphasizing the "you" attitude.

Buy one, get yourself free.

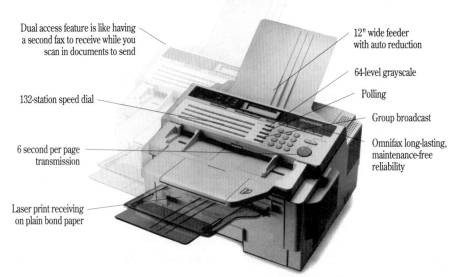

Dual access feature is like having a second fax to receive while you scan in documents to send

132-station speed dial

6 second per page transmission

Laser print receiving on plain bond paper

12" wide feeder with auto reduction

64-level grayscale

Polling

Group broadcast

Omnifax long-lasting, maintenance-free reliability

If you're tired of wasting time at the fax machine, you need an Omnifax L40. A full-featured plain paper fax machine with full dual access operation. Which simply means that, unlike most of us, it can efficiently do two things at once.

It can scan in documents for sending while it's receiving or sending. This is a tremendous time saver.

Consecutive transmissions can be prioritized and sent later. And its handy priority-interrupt feature can override long transmissions to send critical messages, then resume the previous operation without skipping a beat.

Plus, the L40 is packed with all the other time and money

saving features you'd expect from Omnifax. Like 132-station speed dial, group broadcast, 64-level grayscale, and 6 second per page laser printing, just to name a few.

If you need an expanded memory, greater security, or more paper capacity, consider our Omnifax L41 model.

Either way, it's like getting two fax machines for the price of one. On just one telephone line. Leaving you free to handle more important business.

You won't have to think twice to conclude that the Omnifax L40 could be the most valuable office machine you ever owned. So call us now for all the details at **800-221-8330**.

OMNIFAX®

Depend on it.

service is useful. Do not bluntly state the cost. Relate prices, charges, or fees to the benefits provided by the services or products to which they apply. Customers then see how much they are getting for their money. An electric blanket ad tells customers that it costs only four cents a night to be warm and comfortable. That sounds more inviting than just listing the cost of the blanket as $40. A dealer who installs steel shutters does not tell readers the exact price of the product, but does indicate that they will save money by buying it: "Virtually maintenance free, your Reel Shutters also offer substantial savings in energy costs by reducing your loss through radiation by as much as 65% . . . and that lowers your utility bills by 35%." Relate costs to the reader's profit or convenience. One charitable organization asks readers to contribute $200 a year, which amounted to less than sixty cents a day, or the price of a cup of coffee.

Ending with a Specific Request for Action

This last section of your letter is vital. If the reader ignores your request for action, your letter has been written in vain. Tell readers exactly what you want them to do and make it easy and pleasurable to do it. Do you want them to fill out a post-card ordering your product, send for a brochure, come into your store, take a test drive, participate in a meeting, or fill out a pledge card, as in Figure 7.11? Tell them if they have to sign an order blank or merely initial it. Is there an enclosed stamped envelope for their convenience? Is there a deadline for taking advantage of a sale price or bonus? "Come to our store tomorrow between 10 A.M. and 10 P.M. to get your free lounge chair with the purchase of any bedroom suite." As with price, link the benefits the customers will receive to their responses. "Respond and be rewarded" is the basic message of the last section of your letter. Note that in Figure 7.9 the call to action is made in the next-to-last paragraph, but is followed by a brief reminder of the significance of the action. Figure 7.10 shows a call-to-action statement in the last paragraph. The letter urges the reader to act immediately in order to take advantage of the free installation.

Customer Relations Letters

Much business correspondence deals explicitly with establishing and maintaining friendly working relations. Such correspondence, known as customer relations letters, sends readers good news or bad news, acceptances or refusals. Good news tells customers that you have the product or service they want at a reasonable price, that you agree with them about a problem they brought to your attention and that you are solving it exactly the way they want, that you are approving their loan, or that you are grateful to them for their business. Thank you letters, congratulations letters, or adjustment letters saying "Yes" are examples of good news messages.

Bad news messages inform readers that you do not like the work or equipment they have sold you, that you do not have the equipment or service they want or you cannot provide it at the price they want to pay, that you cannot refund their purchase price or perform a service again as they requested, that you are raising their rent or not renewing their lease, or that you want them to pay what they owe you now. Bad news messages can come to readers through complaint letters, adjustment letters that say "No," or collection letters.

Regardless of the type of news—good or bad—you have to convey to readers, you need to be a diplomatic and persuasive writer. Customer relations letters show how you and your company regard the people with whom you do business. These letters should reveal your sensitivity to their needs. After all, you want to keep them as customers and you never know when you may work with them again. Writing effective customer relations letters requires skill in human relations and reader psychology. The first lesson to learn is that you cannot look at your letter only from your (the writer's) perspective. You have to see the letter from the reader's perspective and anticipate the reader's needs and reactions. Ask yourself how you would feel if you received the same letter. What would be your view of the writer and the writer's company?

As you read this section, keep in mind the two basic principles captured in the words "the customers always write."

1. Customers will write about how they would like to be or have been treated—to thank, to complain, to request an explanation.
2. Customers have certain rights that you must respect in your correspondence with them. They deserve a prompt and courteous reply, whether or not they are correct. If you refuse their request, they deserve to know why; if they owe you money, you should give them an opportunity to explain and a chance, up to a point, to set up a payment schedule.

Planning Your Customer Relations Letters

Whether you are sending good news or bad, you have to determine what to say and how to say it. As with your other written work, do some preliminary planning. Outline for a few minutes to find your ideas. Your outline does not have to be formal or even neatly written—a few scribbles sometimes will be enough to get you started. By outlining, you will save (not lose) time, for you can identify your main points, exclude unnecessary or unimportant ones, and avoid the risk of forgetting something essential. Fortified by your outline, you will feel more confident as you draft your letter. In the process of drafting and revising that letter, consider whether your reader will bristle at or accept the words you use. Your choice of words will determine the success or failure of your letter. You might want to review the appropriate discussions on tone (pages 12; 38) and the "you attitude" (pages 164–169).

Being Direct or Indirect

Your message, tone, and knowledge of your reader are essential ingredients in a successful customer relations letter. But success involves something more than knowing how to use the right words to get across your main ideas. It is also crucial to know where and how to start, and especially, where to present your main point. Not every customer relations letter starts by giving the reader the writer's main point, judgment, conclusion, or reaction. *Where you place your main idea is determined by the type of letter you are writing.* Good news messages require one tactic; bad news, another.

If you are writing a good news letter, use the direct approach. Start your letter with the welcome, pleasant news that the reader wants to hear. Don't postpone this opportunity to put your reader in the right frame of mind. Then provide any relevant supporting details, explanations, or commentary. Being direct is advantageous when you have good news to convey.

But if you have bad news to report, do not open your letter with it. Be indirect. Prepare your reader for the bad news. Do everything you can to keep the tension level down. If you throw the bad news at your reader right away, you run the risk of jeopardizing the goodwill you want to create and sustain. Again, put yourself in the reader's place. Consider how you would react to a letter that began, "We regret to inform you that . . . ," "Your order cannot be filled," or "Your application for a loan has been denied." Having been denied, disappointed, or even offended in a first sentence or paragraph, the reader is not likely to give you his or her attentive cooperation thereafter.

Notice how A. J. Griffin's bad news letter in Figure 7.12 curtly starts off with the bad news of a rent increase. Receiving such a letter, the owner of Flowers by Dan could certainly not be blamed for looking for a new place of business. Or if he did pay the increase, Griffin's letter would hardly ensure that Mr. Sobol

FIGURE 7.12   An ineffective bad news letter.

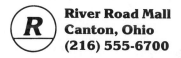

River Road Mall
Canton, Ohio
(216) 555-6700

December 1, 1993

Mr. Daniel Sobol
Flowers by Dan
Lower Level
River Road Mall

Dear Mr. Sobol:

This is to inform you of a rent increase. Starting next month your new rent will be $950, resulting in a 15 percent increase.

Please make sure your January rent check includes this increase.

Sincerely yours,

A. J. Griffin

A. J. Griffin
Manager

FIGURE 7.13 A diplomatic bad news letter.

**River Road Mall
Canton, Ohio
(216) 555-6700**

December 1, 1993

Mr. Daniel Sobol
Flowers by Dan
Lower Level
River Road Mall

Dear Mr. Sobol:

It's been a pleasure to have you as a tenant at the Mall for the past two years, and we look forward to serving you in the future.

Over the last two years we have experienced a dramatic increase here at River Road Mall in the costs of security, maintenance, pest control, utilities, insurance premiums, and taxes. Last year we tried to absorb these increases and so did not have to raise your rent. Unfortunately, we find that we cannot do it again for 1994 and so regretfully we must increase your rent by 15%, to $950 a month, effective January 1, 1994.

We do not like to raise rents, and we know that you do not like it either. But we also know that you do not want us to compromise on the quality of service that you and your customers expect and deserve from River Road Mall.

Please let us know how we can assist you in the future. We wish you a very successful and profitable 1994.

Cordially,

A. J. Griffin

A. J. Griffin
Manager

would remain a happy tenant at River Road. Griffin was too direct when he should have been diplomatically indirect. He did not consider his reader's reaction; all he was concerned about was delivering his message.

Compare the revised version of Griffin's letter in Figure 7.13 with his curt message in Figure 7.12. In the revised version, Griffin begins tactfully with a few pleasant, positive words designed to put his reader in a good frame of mind about the management of River Road Mall. Then Griffin gives some background information that the owner of Flowers by Dan can relate to. A businessperson himself, Mr. Sobol doubtless has experienced some recent increases in his own costs. Griffin makes one more attempt to encourage Sobol to recall his good feelings about the Mall—last year they did not raise rents—before introducing the bad news of a rent increase. And even after giving the bad news, Griffin softens the blow by saying that the Mall knows it is bad news. Griffin's tactic here is to defuse some of the anger that Sobol will inevitably feel. Griffin then ends on a positive, upbeat note: a prosperous future for Flowers by Dan.

Types of Customer Relations Letters

Thank-You Letters

A thank-you letter tells how much a person's acts or words have meant to you. In the business world thank-you letters show that the writer is a responsible individual who values human relations. Even if you have already expressed your gratitude in person or over the telephone, a letter further emphasizes your thoughtfulness and courtesy.

Thank-you letters are routinely sent to customers after a major purchase.

Car Salesperson I enjoyed helping you select your new Buick. Your satisfaction with your car, me, and our dealership is my first concern. Please let me know if I may help you in the future. I wish you many happy miles in your Buick.

Bank Thank you for opening a checking account with First Federal. We are honored to serve you in all your banking needs. The staff of First Federal promises to give you fast, courteous service whenever you come in. You, our customer, are our most valued asset.

Electronics Store Just a short note to say that we are proud to have you as one of our customers. We hope your new Widevision television set brings you many hours of fun-filled entertainment. We welcome the chance to serve you again with any of your home entertainment needs.

You should also write a thank-you letter for special occasions when an individual or company does something extra—something that did not have to be done or that was especially helpful. Thank-you letters also figure significantly in a job search, which will be covered in Chapter 8. The individuals who write your letters of recommendation, as well as the prospective employers who interview you, deserve thank-you letters. Figure 7.14 (p. 216) contains a thank-you letter to Mr. Butler, to whom Robert Jackson wrote (see Figure 8.1 [p. 254]) for a reference. Also see the letter in Figure 8.17 to a prospective employer after the candidate has been interviewed.

Thank-you letters are easy to write. Your main concerns are being specific about what you liked and explaining why you are grateful. Begin with a simple, direct statement of gratitude identifying what has pleased you. Indicate how and when this service was provided. Mention the names of individuals responsible for

FIGURE 7.14   A thank-you letter.

```
5432 South Kenneth Avenue
Chicago, IL 60651-0396
April 29, 1994


Mr. Sonny Butler, Manager
Empire Supermarket
4000 West 79th Street
Chicago, IL 60652-4300


Dear Mr. Butler:

Thank you very much for writing a letter of recommendation to
be included in my dossier at the Placement Office at Moraine
Valley Community College. I appreciate your taking the time to
do this, and I am especially grateful for the many kind things
you said you had included in your letter. Your praise of my
work for Empire will certainly help me in finding a job in
retail sales.

Once again, thank you for your recommendation. I will let you
know how my job search goes.

Sincerely yours,

Robert B. Jackson

Robert B. Jackson
```

the work and why their work was so helpful. Also indicate why this service deserves special thanks—that is, how the action helped you or your company.

The letter in Figure 7.15 illustrates an apt thank-you letter. A local merchant thanks a glass company for the exceptional service she received. When the Dole Glass Company has any need of hardware parts, it will certainly be favorably disposed to order from Granger Hardware because of Ms. Stovall-Granger's kind and welcome thank-you letter.

Congratulation Letters

When you put your praise into a letter, you show considerable thoughtfulness. You could call the individual on the telephone or speak to him or her in person to extend your congratulations. But a letter shows that you have made an extra

FIGURE 7.15   A thank-you letter.

 **Granger Hardware Store**

Serving Fair View Since 1945

20 N.E. Hasse Road
Fair View, NJ 02386-0691
(201) 555-2895

February 23, 1994

Mr. Randolph Della Sinta, Manager
Dole Glass Company
Managers Highway
Kensington, NJ 02384-8205

Dear Mr. Della Sinta:

I am grateful to the Dole Glass Company for giving me outstanding
service last Sunday night, February 20. My store's front plate-glass
window (21 feet by 12 feet) was smashed by flying debris. Your crew,
Paula Romero and Tim Tulley, were at my store thirty minutes after I
phoned them late Sunday night. They quickly cleared away the glass
and measured my window. Realizing that the plates they had on their
truck would not fit my window, they drove all the way back to your
Devonshire warehouse to locate a suitable piece. They could have
waited until the next day to do this, but they returned and
installed the new glass window in record time.

Their service was exceptional. It allowed me to open my store on
Monday morning for business as usual. If your crew had not worked so
quickly and made that extra trip, I would have been forced to board
up my store and close on Monday to have the repairs made.

I have the highest opinion of Dole Glass and your two employees who
came to my store two days ago.

Cordially,

Barbara Stovall-Granger

Barbara Stovall-Granger
Owner

effort. This personal touch also says far more than a greeting card with a pre-printed message.

The occasions for such letters are many. In the business world you might congratulate someone for being promoted, opening a new business or expanding an existing one, or being honored for an accomplishment (for example, having the highest sales record of the month or year). When you honor someone for a distinction, you also honor his or her company. In your own community you create goodwill by congratulating someone for being elected to public office, serving on a civic committee, or receiving an award. In addition to complimenting people for professional or civic achievements, you may congratulate them for engagements, marriages, births, graduations, and anniversaries.

Congratulatory letters must arrive at the right time. Write as soon after the accomplishment as you can. Good news travels fast; acknowledging the individual's honor quickly shows that you are keeping track of events and are eager to express your congratulations. A late letter will say that you did not have the time to write, that the news was not very important to you, or that you belatedly joined everyone else in sending your good wishes.

Keep your letters short and sincere. But a one-sentence letter—"Congratulations on your promotion"—is inappropriate. A letter this short looks as if you sent it not because you were sincerely interested in the individual, but because you felt obligated to write something.

You need not write four or five long paragraphs. A long congratulatory letter with flowery language and backslapping suggests insincerity. Excessive praise is doubtful praise.

A sincere yet brief letter of congratulation praises one or two significant points of the individual's accomplishment. The following two paragraphs provide a suitable congratulatory letter.

Dear Ms. Bozanich:

Congratulations on being promoted to branch manager of the Powersville store. Your work in the field for the Jordan Company will profit you and us in your new position.

I wish you great success as branch manager. Please call me if I can help you in any way.

Sincerely,

Casey Meyer

Casey Meyer

This next congratulatory letter selects a few details, including the place where the writer learned of the reader's achievement, to show the writer's sincere interest.

Dear Mr. Goshin:

Congratulations on your new title of Certified Insurance Counselor just announced in the <u>Midtown Financial Record</u>. It certainly is an honor to be among only two thousand agents in the country who can sign C.I.C. after their name.

You have my best wishes for continuing success in your insurance business.

Sincerely yours,

Jennifer Rodriguez

Jennifer Rodriguez

One last point about congratulatory letters: Do not use them to sell a product or service. By calling attention to your company's services, you reveal your congratulations are only a gimmick, not a sincere expression of goodwill.

Follow-Up Letters

A follow-up letter is sent by a company after a sale to thank the customer for buying a product or using a service and to encourage the customer to buy more products and use more services in the future. A follow-up letter is, therefore, a combination thank-you note and sales letter. The letter in Figure 7.16 (p. 220) is sent to customers soon after they have purchased an appliance and offers them the option of a continued maintenance policy. The letter in Figure 7.17 (p. 221) shows how an income tax preparation service attempts to obtain repeat business. Both of these letters follow helpful guidelines.

1. They begin with a brief and sincere expression of gratitude for having served the customer.
2. They discuss the benefits (advantages) already known to the customer. Then, they transfer the company's dedication to the customer from the product or service already sold to a new or continuing sales area.
3. They end with a specific request for future business.

Occasionally, a follow-up letter is sent to a good customer who, for some reason, has stopped doing business with the company. Perhaps the customer has closed an account of long standing, no longer comes to the store, discontinued a subscription, or fails to send in an order for a product or service. Such a follow-up letter should try to find out why the customer has stopped doing business and to persuade that customer to resume business dealings. Study the letter in Figure 7.18 (p. 222), in which Jim Margolis first politely inquires whether Mr. Janeck has experienced a problem and then urges him to come back to the store.

FIGURE 7.16   A follow-up letter to sell a maintenance agreement.

 Dynamic Appliance Company
100 Walden Parkway
Denver, Colorado 80203-4296
(303) 555-9681

August 9, 1994

Mr. John H. Abbott
3715 Mayview Drive
Cottage Grove, MN 53261-1852

Dear Mr. Abbott:

We are delighted that you have purchased a Dynamic appliance. To
help ensure your satisfaction, this appliance is backed by a Dynamic
warranty. At the same time, we realize that you bought the appliance to serve
you not just for the period covered by the warranty but for many years to
come. That's why the purchase of a Dynamic Maintenance Agreement at this
time is one of the wisest investments you can make.

A Dynamic Maintenance Agreement provides savings benefits many
cost-conscious customers want and look for today. It helps extend the life of
the appliance through an annual, on-request maintenance checkup. And if
you need service, **it provides for as many service calls as necessary for
repairs due to normal use—at no extra charge to you.**

All this coverage is now available to you at a special introductory price
of $55 a year. This price takes into consideration the warranty coverage you
have remaining. Act now, by filling out and returning the enclosed form.

Sincerely

Carole Morrow

Carole Morrow
Sales Representative
Extension 285

Encl.

FIGURE 7.17   **A follow-up letter to encourage repeat business.**

TAYLOR TAX SERVICE
HIGHWAY 10 NORTH
JENNINGS, TX 78326

December 1, 1994

Ms. Laurie Pavlovich
345 Jefferson St.
Jennings, TX 78326

Dear Ms. Pavlovich:

Thank you for using our services in February of this year. We were pleased
to help you prepare your 1993 federal and state income tax returns. Our
goal is to save you every tax dollar to which you are entitled. If you ever
have any questions about your return, we are open all year long to help you.

We are looking forward to serving you again next year. Some new federal
tax laws, which go into effect January 1, will change the kind of deductions
you can declare. These changes might appreciably increase the size of your
refund. Our consultants have studied these new laws and are ready to
explain them to you and apply them to your return.

Another important tax matter influencing your 1993 returns will be any
losses you may have suffered because of the hailstorms and tornadoes that
hit our area three months ago. Our consultants are specially trained to assist
you in filing proper damage claims with your federal and state returns.

To make using our services even easier, we can help you file your tax
return electronically, which will speed up any refund you are entitled to.
Please call us at **555-3457** or **555-7853** as soon as you have received all your
forms in order to set up an appointment. We are waiting to serve you any
day of the week from 9:00 A.M. to 9:00 P.M.

Sincerely yours,

TAYLOR TAX SERVICE

J. P. Sanchez

J. P. Sanchez
Manager

FIGURE 7.18   **A follow-up letter to maintain customer goodwill.**

BROADWAY CLEANERS
Broadway at Davis Drive
Baltimore, Maryland 21228-6210
555-1962

April 6, 1994

Mr. Edward Janeck
34 Brompton Lane
Apartment 143
Baltimore, MD 21227-0102

Dear Mr. Janeck:

Thank you for allowing us to take care of your cleaning needs for more than
three years now. It has been our pleasure to see you in the store each week
and to clean your shirts, slacks, and coats to your satisfaction. Since you
have not come in during the last month, we are concerned that we may have in
some way disappointed you. We hope not, because you are a valuable customer
whose goodwill we do not want to lose.

If there is something wrong, please tell us about it. We welcome any
suggestions on how we can serve you better. Our goal is to have a spotless
reputation in the eyes of our customers.

The next time you need some garments cleaned, won't you please bring them to
us, along with the enclosed coupon worth $10 on your next bill? We look
forward to seeing you again--soon.

Sincerely yours,

Jim Margolis

Jim Margolis, Manager

Encl.

Complaint Letters

Each of us at some time has been frustrated by a defective product, inadequate service, or incorrect billing. Usually our first response is to write a letter dripping with juicy insults. But a hate letter rarely gets results and can in fact hurt the writer and create an unfavorable image of the company being represented. A complaint letter is a delicate one to write.

A complaint letter is written for more reasons than just blowing off steam. You want some specific action taken. By adopting the right tone, you increase your chances of getting what you want. Do not call the reader names, hurl insults, or refuse to do business with the company again. Register your complaint courteously and tolerantly. Companies want to be fair to you in order to keep you as a satisfied customer and correct defective products so that other customers will not be inconvenienced. The "you attitude" is especially important here to maintain the reader's goodwill.

An effective complaint letter can be written by an individual consumer or by a company. Figure 7.19 (p. 224) shows Michael Trigg's complaint about a defective fishing reel; Figure 7.20 (p. 225) expresses a restaurant's dissatisfaction with an industrial dishwasher. Present your case logically, and provide enough detail to obtain a speedy settlement. To accomplish this objective, follow these five steps.

1. Begin with a detailed description of the product or service. Give the appropriate model numbers, size(s), quantity, color. Indicate when and where (specific address) you purchased it, and also how much warranty time remains. Indicate if you are returning the product to the company and how you are sending it—U.S. mail, UPS, or the like. If you are complaining about a service, give the name of the company, the date of the service, the personnel providing it, and their exact duties.

2. State exactly what is wrong with the product or service. Precise information will enable the reader to understand and act on your complaint. How many times did the machine work before it stopped, what parts were malfunctioning, what parts of a job were not done or were done poorly, and when did all this happen? Stating that "the brake shoes were defective" tells very little about how long they were on your car, how effectively they may have been installed, or what condition they were in when they ceased functioning safely. Reach some conclusion, even if you qualify your remarks with words like "apparently," "possibly," or "seemingly" when you describe the difficulty.

3. Briefly describe the inconvenience you have experienced. In this section of the complaint letter, show that your problems were directly caused by the defective product or service. To build your case, give precise details about the time and money you lost. Don't just say you had "numerous difficulties." If you purchased a calculator and it broke down during a mathematics examination, say so (but do not blame the calculator company if you failed the course). Did you have to pay a mechanic to fix your car when it was stalled on the road, did you have to take time away from your other chores to clean up a mess made by a leaky new washing machine, did you have to buy a new telephone answering machine?

FIGURE 7.19   A complaint letter from a consumer.

```
17 Westwood
Magnolia, MA 02171
September 15, 1994



Mr. Ralph Montoya, Manager
Customer Relations Department
Smith Sports Equipment Company
P.O. Box 287
Tulsa, OK 74109-1014

Dear Mr. Montoya:

On August 31, 1994, I purchased a Smith reel, model 191, at
the Uni-Mart Store on Marsh Avenue in Magnolia. The reel sold
for $54.95 plus tax. Since the reel is not working effectively,
I am returning it to you under separate cover by first-class
mail.

I had made no more than five casts with the reel when it
began to malfunction. The button that releases the spool and
allows the line to cast will not spring back into position
after casting. In addition, the gears make a grinding noise
when I try to retrieve the line. Because of these problems, I
was unable to continue my participation in the Gloucester
Fishing Tournament.

I am requesting that a new reel be sent to me free of charge
in place of the defective one I returned. I would also like
to know what was wrong with this defective reel.

I would appreciate your handling my claim within the next two
weeks, if at all possible.

Sincerely yours,

Michael Trigg

Michael Trigg
```

FIGURE 7.20   A complaint letter faxed from a business.

The Loft
Cameron and Dale
Sunnyside, California 91793-4116
213-555-7500
FAX 213-555-7523

June 17, 1994

Priscilla Dubrow
Customer Relations Department
Superflex Products
San Diego, CA 93141-0808

Dear Ms. Dubrow:

On September 15, 1993, we purchased a Superflex industrial
dishwasher, model 3203876, at the Hillcrest Store at 3400 Broadway
Drive in Sunnyside, for $2,000. In the last three weeks, our
restaurant has had repeated problems with this machine. Three more
months of warranty remain on this dishwasher.

The machine does not complete a full cycle; it stops before the
final rinsing and thus leaves the dishes still dirty. It appears
that the cycle regulators are not working properly because they
refuse to shift into the next necessary gear. Attempts to repair the
machine by the Hillcrest crew on June 3, 10, and 16 have been
unsuccessful.

Our restaurant has been greatly inconvenienced. The kitchen team has
been forced to sort, clean, and sanitize utensils, dishes, pans, and
pots by hand. Moreover, our expenses for proper detergents have
increased.

We want your main office to send another repair crew at once to fix
this machine. If your crew is unable to do this, we want a discount
worth the amount of warranty life on this model to be applied to the
purchase of a new Superflex dishwasher. This amount would come to
$400, or 20 percent of the original purchase price.

So that our business is not further disrupted, we would appreciate
your resolving this problem within the next week.

Sincerely yours,

Emily Rashon

Emily Rashon
Manager

4. Indicate precisely what you want done. Do not simply write that you "want something done," that "adequate measures must be taken," or that "the situation should be corrected." State that you want your purchase price refunded, your model repaired or replaced, or a completely new repair crew provided. Maybe you want only an apology from the company for some discourteous treatment. If you are asking for damages, state your request in dollars and cents, and include a copy of any bills resulting from the problem. Perhaps you had to rent a car, were forced to pay a janitorial service to clean up, or had to rent equipment at a higher rate because the company did not make its deliveries as promised.

5. Ask for prompt handling of your claim. Ask that an answer be provided to any question you may have (such as finding out where calls came from that you were billed for but did not make). And ask that your claim be handled as quickly as possible. You might even specify a reasonable time by which you want to hear from the writer or need the problem fixed.

Adjustment Letters

Adjustment letters tell customers dissatisfied with a product or service how their claim will be settled. Adjustment letters should reconcile the differences that exist between a customer and a firm and restore the customer's confidence in that firm.

Rather than ignoring or quarreling with complaint letters, most companies view answering them as good for business. Many large firms maintain separate claims and adjustment departments just to respond to disappointed customers. By writing to complain about a product or service, the customer alerts your company to a problem that can be remedied to avoid similar complaints in the future. Customers who have taken the time to put complaints in writing obviously want and deserve a reply. If you do not answer the customer's letter politely, you may lose a lot of business—not just the customer's business, but also that of his or her friends, family, and associates, who will all have been told about your discourtesy.

An effective adjustment letter requires diplomacy; be prompt, courteous, and decisive. Do not brush the complaint aside in hopes that it will be forgotten. Investigate the complaint quickly and determine its validity by checking previous correspondence, warranty statements, guarantees, and your firm's policies on merchandise and service. In some cases you may even have to send returned damaged merchandise to your firm's laboratory to determine who is at fault.

A noncommittal letter signals to the customer that you have failed to investigate the claim or are stalling for time. Do not resort to vague statements like the following:

- We will do what we can to solve your problems as soon as possible.
- A company policy prohibits our returning your purchase price in full.
- Your request, while legitimate, will take time to process.
- We will act on your request with your best interest in mind.
- While we cannot now determine the extent of an adjustment, we will be back in touch with you.

Customers want to be told that they are right; or if they cannot get what they request, they will demand to know why, in the most explicit terms. At the other extreme, do not overdo an apology by agreeing that the company is "completely at fault," that "such shoddy merchandise is inexcusable," or that "it was a careless mistake on our part." An expression of regret need not jeopardize all future business dealings. If you make your company look too bad, you risk losing the customer permanently. When you comply with a request, a begrudging tone will destroy the goodwill created by your refund or replacement.

Adjustment Letters That Tell the Customer "Yes"

If investigation reveals the customer's complaint to be valid, you must write a letter saying "Yes, you are right; we will give you what you asked for." Such a letter is easy to write if you remember a few useful suggestions. As with a good news message, start with the favorable news the customer wants to hear and that will put him or her in a positive frame of mind to read the rest of your letter. Also, make the customers realize that you sincerely agree with them—not to feel as if you are reluctantly honoring their request. For example, if your airline lost or misplaced luggage, apologize to the customer before you offer a settlement. The two examples of adjustment letters saying "Yes" show you how to write this kind of correspondence. The first example, Figure 7.21 (p. 228), says "Yes" to Michael Trigg's letter in Figure 7.19. You might want to reread the Trigg complaint letter to see what problems Ralph Montoya faced when he had to write to Mr. Trigg. The second example of an adjustment letter that says "Yes" is in Figure 7.22 (p. 229). It responds to a customer who has complained about an incorrect billing. The following four steps will help you write a "Yes" adjustment letter.

1. Admit immediately that the customer's complaint is justified and apologize. Briefly state that you are sorry and thank the customer for writing to inform you.

2. State precisely what you are going to do to correct the problem. Are you going to cancel a bill, return a damaged camera in good working order, repaint a room, enclose a free pass, provide a complimentary dinner, or give the customer credit toward another purchase? Do not postpone the good news the customer wants to hear. The rest of your letter will be much more appreciated and convincing. In Figure 7.21 Michael Trigg is told that he will receive a new reel; in Figure 7.22 Kathryn Brumfield is informed that she will not be charged for parts or service.

3. Tell customers exactly what happened. They deserve an explanation for the inconvenience they suffered. Note how the explanations in Figures 7.21 and 7.22 give only the essential details; they do not bother the reader with side issues or petty remarks about who was to blame. Don't threaten to fire one of your employees because of a customer's problem. Assure customers that the mishap is not typical of your company's operations. While your comments should not shift the blame, your letter should center on the unusual reason or circumstance for the difficulty. Avoid promising, however, that the problem will never recur. Not only is such a guarantee unnecessary, but also keeping it may be beyond your control.

FIGURE 7.21   An adjustment letter saying "Yes."

Smith Sports Equipment
P.O. Box 287
Tulsa, Oklahoma 74109-1014
(918) 555-0164

September 21, 1994

Mr. Michael Trigg
17 Westwood
Magnolia, MA 02171

Dear Mr. Trigg:

Thank you for alerting us in your letter of September 15 to the problems you had with one of our model 191 spincast reels. I am sorry for the inconvenience the reel has caused you. A new Smith reel is on its way to you.

We have examined your reel and found the problem. It seems that a retaining pin on the button spring was improperly installed by one of our new soldering machines on the assembly line. We have thoroughly inspected, repaired, and cleaned this soldering machine to eliminate the problem. Our company has been making quality reels since 1955. We hope that your new Smith reel brings you years of pleasure and many good catches, especially next year at the Gloucester Fishing Tournament.

We appreciate your business and look forward to serving you again.

Respectfully,

SMITH SPORTS EQUIPMENT

Ralph Montoya

Ralph Montoya, Manager
Customer Relations Department

FIGURE 7.22   An adjustment letter saying "Yes."

Brunelli Motors

Route 3A   Giddings, Kansas 62034-8100   (913) 555-1521

October 6, 1994

Ms. Kathryn Brumfield
34 East Main
Giddings, KS 62034-1123

Dear Ms. Brumfield:

We appreciate your notifying us, in your letter of September 30, about the
problem you have experienced regarding warranty coverage on your new
Phantom Hawk GT. The bills sent to you were incorrect, and I have already
canceled them. Please accept my apologies. You should not have been
charged for a new shroud or for repairs to the damaged fan and hose, since
all these parts, and labor on them, are covered by warranty.

The problem was the result of an error in the way charges were listed. Our
firm has just begun using a new billing system to give customers better
service, and the mechanic apparently punched the wrong code number on
your account. I have instructed our mechanics to double-check their code
numbers before submitting them to the Billing Department. We hope that
this policy will help us to serve you and our other customers more efficiently.

We value you as a customer of Brunelli Motors. When you are ready for
another Phantom, I hope that you will once again visit our dealership.

Sincerely yours,

a. y. O'Donnel

A. Y. O'Donnel
Service Manager

4. End on a friendly, and positive, note. Do not remind customers of the trouble they have gone through. Leave them with a good feeling about your company. Say that you are looking forward to seeing them again, that you will gladly work with them on any future orders, or that you can always be reached for questions.

Adjustment Letters That Tell the Customer "No"

Writing to tell customers "No" is obviously more difficult than agreeing with them. You are faced with the sensitive task of conveying bad news, while at the same time convincing the reader that your position is fair, logical, and consistent. Do not accuse or argue. Avoid remarks such as the following that blame, scold, or remind customers of a wrongdoing and hence may cost you their business.

- You obviously did not read the instruction manual.
- Our records show that you purchased the set after the policy went into effect.
- The company policy plainly states that such refunds are unallowable.
- You were negligent in running the machine.
- You claim that our word processor was poorly constructed.
- Your error, not our merchandise, is to blame.
- You must be mistaken about the merchandise.
- As any intelligent person could tell, the switch had to be "off."
- Your complaint is unjustified.

The following five suggestions will help you say "No" diplomatically. Practical applications of these suggestions can be found in Figures 7.23 and 7.24 (p. 232). Contrast the rejection of Michael Trigg's complaint in Figure 7.23 with the favorable response to it in Figure 7.21.

1. Thank customers for writing. Make a friendly start by putting them in a good frame of mind. The letter writers in Figures 7.23 and 7.24 say that they are thankful that the customers brought the matter to their attention. As with other bad news letters, never begin with a refusal. You need time to calm and convince customers. Telling them "No" ("We regret to inform you") in the first sentence or two will negatively color their reactions to the rest of the letter. Also, never begin letters with "I was surprised to learn that you found our product defective (*or* our service inefficient)" or "We cannot understand how such a problem occurred. We have been in business for years, and nothing like this has ever happened." Such openings put customers on the defensive. Use the indirect approach discussed on pages 213-214.

2. State the problem so that customers realize that you understand their complaint. You thereby prove that you are not trying to misrepresent what they have told you.

3. Explain what happened with the product or service before you give customers a decision. Provide a factual explanation to show customers that they are being treated fairly. Convince them of the logic and consistency of your point of view. Rather than focusing on the customer's mishandling of merchandise or failure to observe details of a service contract, state the proper ways of

FIGURE 7.23   An adjustment letter saying "No."

Smith Sports Equipment
P.O. Box 287
Tulsa, Oklahoma 74109-1014
(918) 555-0164

September 21, 1994

Mr. Michael Trigg
17 Westwood
Magnolia, MA 02171

Dear Mr. Trigg:

Thank you for writing to us on September 15 about the trouble you experienced with our model 191 spincast reel. We were sorry to hear about the difficulties you had with the release button and gears.

We have examined your reel and have found the trouble. It seems that a retaining pin on the button spring was pushed into the side of the reel casing, thereby making the gears inoperable. The retaining pin is a vital yet delicate part of your reel. In order to function properly, it has to be pushed gently. Since the pin was not used in this way, we are not able to refund your purchase price.

We will be pleased, however, to repair your reel for $9.98 and return it to you for hours of fishing pleasure. Please let us know your decision.

I look forward to hearing from you.

Respectfully,

SMITH SPORTS EQUIPMENT

Ralph Montoya

Ralph Montoya, Manager
Customer Relations Department

FIGURE 7.24   An adjustment letter saying "No."

HEALTH AIR, INC.
4300 Marshall Drive
Salt Lake City, Utah 84113-1521
(801) 555-6028

August 19, 1994

Ms. Denise Southby, Director
Bradley General Hospital
Bradley, IL 60610-4615

Dear Ms. Southby:

Thank you for your letter of August 10 explaining the problems you have encountered with our Puritan Bennett MAII ventilator. We were sorry to learn that you could not get the high-volume PAO_2 alarm circuit to work.

Our ventilator is a high-volume, low-frequency machine that is capable of delivering up to 40 ml. of water pressure. The ventilator runs with a center of gravity attachment that is on the right side of the diode. The trouble you are having with the high oxygen alarm system is due to an overload on your piped-in oxygen. Our laboratory inspection of the ventilator you returned indicates that the high-pressure system had blown a vital adaptor in the machine. Our company cannot be responsible for any type of overload caused by an oxygen system of which we are unaware. We cannot, therefore, send you a replacement ventilator free of charge. Your ventilator is being returned to you.

We would, however, be very glad to send you another model of the adaptor, which would be more compatible with your system, as soon as we receive your order. The price of the adaptor is $600, and our factory representative will be happy to install it for you at no charge. Please let me know your decision.

We welcome the opportunity to assist you in providing quality health care at Bradley General.

Sincerely yours,

R. P. Gilford

R. P. Gilford
Customer Service Department

handling a piece of equipment or the terms outlined in an agreement. For instance, instead of writing "By reading the instructions on the side of the paint can, you would have avoided the streaking condition that you claim resulted," tell the customer that "Hi-Gloss Paint requires two applications, four hours apart, for a clear and smooth finish." In this way you remind customers of the right way of applying the paint without pointing an accusing finger at them. Note how the explanations in Figures 7.23 and 7.24 emphasize the right way of using the product.

4. Give your decision without hedging. Do not say that perhaps some type of restitution could be made later or that further proof would have been helpful. Indecision will infuriate customers who believe that they have already presented a sound, convincing case. Never apologize for your decision. Avoid using the words *reject, claim,* or *grant. Reject* is too harsh and impersonal. *Complaint* implies your distrust of the customer's complaint and suggests that questionable differences of opinion remain. *Grant* signals that you have it in your power to respond favorably but decline to do so; a grant is the kind of favor a ruler might give a subject. Instead, use words that reconcile.

5. Leave the door open for better and continued business. Whenever possible, help customers solve their problem by offering to send them a new product or part, and quote the full sales price. Note how the second-to-last paragraphs of the letters in Figures 7.23 and 7.24 do this diplomatically.

Refusal of Credit Letters

A special set of bad news letters deals with a company refusing credit to an individual or another company. Writing such a letter requires a great deal of sensitivity. You want to be clear and firm about your decision; at the same time, you do not want to alienate the reader and risk losing his or her business in the future.

When you refuse someone credit, begin on a positive—not a negative—note. Find something to thank the reader about; starting with something positive will make the bad news easier to take. Compliment the reader's company or previous good credit achievements (if known); certainly express gratitude to the individual for wanting to do business with your company.

In a second paragraph provide a clear-cut explanation of why you must refuse the request for credit, but base your explanation on facts, not personal shortcomings or liabilities. Appropriate reasons to cite for a refusal of credit include (a) reminding the reader of a lack of business experience or prior credit, (b) pointing out that the individual or company is "overextended" and needs more time to pay off existing obligations, (c) calling attention to current unfavorable or unstable financial conditions, (d) indicating that an order is too large to process without some prepayment, or (e) noting that a company lacks the equipment or personnel to do the business for which they are seeking credit.

Conclude your letter refusing credit with something positive again. Encourage the reader to reapply when business conditions have improved or when the reader's firm is in a better financial position. Make an attempt to keep the reader

FIGURE 7.25 An effective letter refusing credit.

WEST COAST CREDIT, INC.
4800 Ridge Road
Los Angeles, CA 91666

Phone (914) 555-3500   FAX (914) 555-4323

October 19, 1994

Mr. Otto L. King
Sunshine Interiors
8235 Mimosa Highway
Vinedale, CA 92004

Dear Mr. King:

Begins on a positive note

We appreciate your interest in wanting to do business with West Coast Credit. It is always gratifying to our institution to see a store like yours open in an expanding community like Vinedale.

Denies credit but explains why

In reviewing your credit application, we checked into the business history and credit references you supplied. We also called your local credit bureau. While we found nothing negative in your credit history, we did determine that for a business of your size you have reached a maximum level of indebtedness. For that reason, we believe that it would not be the best time to extend your credit line.

Encourages reader to reapply

We would, however, encourage you to resubmit your application in six to eight months. By that time we hope that the growing market in your area will profitably allow you to take on additional credit lines. In the meantime, we wish you every success.

Cordially,

B. Rimes-Assante

B. Rimes-Assante
Manager

---

as a potential customer, eager to try you again. Figure 7.25 illustrates an effective letter that denies credit, following the organizational plan just discussed.

Writing a letter denying credit to an ESL reader requires double tact. As you saw on pages 177–178, you have to consider the cultural expectations of such an audience and use easily understood "international English." Compare the inappro-

FIGURE 7.26   An inappropriate letter refusing credit to an ESL reader.

CONSOLIDATED PLASTICS
999 Industrial Blvd.
Bambrake, NH 01243

Phone (603) 555-7000
FAX (603) 555-4321

May 25, 1994

Mr. Jan Buwalda
Mendson SA, Inc.
Hoofdstraat 23
Dokkum, The Netherlands 1234 XK

Mr. Jan Buwalda:

I have received herewith your request and news about your company. Thanks.

Regarding that request to open a credit account with us, it just cannot be done. I don't know how things are expedited in your country, but in America giving credit to a first-time foreign customer is just not standard business practice. As you will understand, your credit rating is unacceptable as far as we are concerned. You will be expected to pay in cash for your first transaction with us. We'll evaluate the situation thereafter.

Let me know how you anticipate proceeding.

Sincerely,

Emma Corson

Emma Corson
Accounts Executive

priate refusal letter contained in Figure 7.26 with the far more diplomatic, and more acceptably worded, letter in Figure 7.27 (p. 236). The letter in Figure 7.26 is rude, uses words an ESL reader may not understand ("expedited," "herewith"), and does not encourage future business dealings with Consolidated Plastics. The more diplomatic letter in Figure 7.27 follows the guidelines for effective communication with ESL readers and adheres to the suggestions for denying credit. In Figure 7.27, Emma Corson compliments her reader and his firm, expresses an interest in doing business with Mendson SA, and helps her reader to understand how Consolidated's credit policy can even help Mendson in the future.

FIGURE 7.27   A diplomatic letter refusing credit to an ESL reader.

CONSOLIDATED PLASTICS
999 Industrial Blvd.
Bambrake, NH 01243

Phone (603) 555-7000
FAX (603) 555-4321

May 25, 1994

Mr. Jan Buwalda
Mendson SA, Inc.
Hoofdstraat 23
Dokkum, The Netherlands 1234 XK

Dear Mr. Buwalda:

Thank you very much for your letter inquiring about opening a credit account with our firm. It is always a pleasure to hear from potential customers in Holland. I was most interested to learn about Mendson's diverse activities.

We understand and share your company's wish to have an American supplier to work with you. Having Mendson as a customer would be beneficial for Consolidated Plastics, too. Working with you would allow us to enter a new market. However, I am afraid that we cannot open new accounts on credit. If you would kindly send us your check for the first month's supplies you need, we would rush your shipment to you. This will establish an account with us, and you can charge your second month's supplies on that account.

Please write or fax me if you have any questions. My fax number is at the top of the letter. I look forward to serving you and Mendson in any way I can.

Cordially,

Emma Corson

Emma Corson
Accounts Executive

Collection Letters

Collection letters are, unfortunately, a part of every business's concern. They require the same tact and fairness as do complaint, adjustment, and refusal of credit letters. While the majority of your customers will pay their bills promptly, some will not pay on time, and a few others may not pay until they are threatened with legal action or harassment from a collection agency.

Each nonpayment case should be evaluated separately. A nasty collection letter sent after only one month's nonpayment to an otherwise good customer can damage your relationship and send that customer elsewhere. One credit company sends this gentle reminder to a customer who is late a first time.

Have You Forgotten "Our Date"?

The one on which you promised to make regular payments on your account?

Of course, if you have put your payment in the mail, please accept our thanks and disregard this reminder. But, if the date merely slipped your mind, won't you send us a check today? Payments made on time help you avoid additional charges and maintain a good credit record.

If there is some reason you cannot make this payment now, please come into our office or call us.

On the other hand, three overly cordial, easygoing letters sent over three or four months to a customer who is a poor credit risk may encourage that individual to postpone payment, perhaps indefinitely.

Many businesses send four letters to customers before turning matters over to an attorney or a collection agency. Letters to poor credit risks are sent at shorter intervals than letters to good credit risks. Each letter in the series employs a different technique, ranging from giving compliments and offering flexible credit terms to issuing demands for immediate payment or threats of legal consequences. One small hospital uses four collection letters, illustrated in Figures 7.28 through 7.31 (pages 238–241), to encourage ex-patients to pay their bills.

The letter in Figure 7.28 (p. 238) typifies the function of a first collection letter. It is a friendly reminder that an account is due. The tone of the letter is cordial and sincere—now is *not* the time to say "Pay up or else!" A first collection letter should stress how valuable the customer is, as does the first paragraph in Figure 7.28. Note also that the first paragraph underscores how pleased the hospital is to have provided the care the patient needed. The last sentence of that paragraph unobtrusively introduces the word "finances" in the context of service. The second paragraph, after allowing for possible questions concerning the bill, makes a request for payment. Inducements to make that payment are offered: (1) a flexible payment schedule and (2) an escape from the inconvenience (or embarrassment)

FIGURE 7.28   A first collection letter.

 **Baldwin County Hospital** P.O. Box 222   Notown, MA 02138-1098   (617) 555-3000

May 16, 1994

Mr. Howard Peterson
318 Brook Avenue #8A
Notown, MA 02146-1074

Re: Inpatient Services
Date of Hospitalization: April 1–3, 1994
Balance Due: $3725.48

Dear Mr. Peterson:

We are grateful that we were able to serve your health needs during your recent stay at the Baldwin County Hospital. It is our continuing goal to provide the best possible hospital care for residents of Baldwin County and its vicinity. You will readily understand that to do so we must keep our finances up to date.

Our records show that the above balance remains due on your account. Unless you have a question concerning the figure, we would appreciate receiving your prompt payment. If you are unable to pay the full amount at this time, we will be happy to set up a schedule of partial payments. Just fill in the appropriate blanks below, and return this letter to me. That will enable us to avoid billing you on a "Past Due" basis. Thank you for your cooperation.

Sincerely,

Morris T. Jukes

Morris T. Jukes
Accounts Receivable Department

( ) I will pay $_____ ( ) weekly; ( ) monthly, on my account.

( ) Enclosed is a check for full payment in the amount of $_____.

_____
Signature

of receiving past-due notices. The bottom of the letter conveniently lists payment-schedule options available to the patient.

If, after a month to six weeks, the customer still does not make a payment, send a second letter, such as the one illustrated in Figure 7.29. This letter begins with a gentle reminder that the balance due has not yet been paid. The second

FIGURE 7.29   A second collection letter.

**Baldwin
County
Hospital**   P.O. Box 222   Notown, MA 02138-1098   (617) 555-3000

June 20, 1994

Mr. Howard Peterson
318 Brook Avenue #8A
Notown, MA 02146-1074

Re: Inpatient Services
Date of Hospitalization: April 1–3, 1994
Balance Due: $3725.48

Dear Mr. Peterson:

Since we have not received a reply to our letter of May 16, we want to remind
you of the balance that remains on your account.

If there is some difficulty, drop by and see us today; we will do our best to help.
Otherwise. we would appreciate receiving your payment in full by return mail.

Our ability to provide health services to others depends to a great extent upon
your cooperation. Please do not let us down.

Sincerely,

Morris T. Jukes

Morris T. Jukes
Accounts Receivable Department

paragraph politely inquires if something is wrong, thus acknowledging that not all
nonpayments stem from willful neglect. While this second collection letter
acknowledges that there might be some "difficulty," it firmly reminds the patient
to pay if there is no financial trouble. The last sentence makes another strong
appeal to the patient's community obligation. Note that unlike the first letter, no

FIGURE 7.30   A third collection letter.

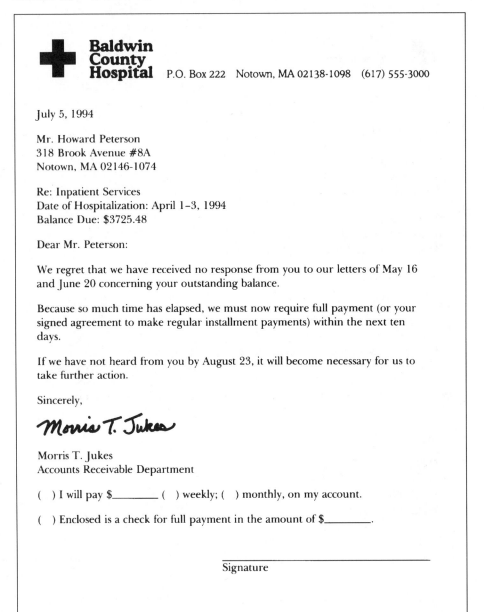

**Baldwin
County
Hospital**   P.O. Box 222   Notown, MA 02138-1098   (617) 555-3000

July 5, 1994

Mr. Howard Peterson
318 Brook Avenue #8A
Notown, MA 02146-1074

Re: Inpatient Services
Date of Hospitalization: April 1–3, 1994
Balance Due: $3725.48

Dear Mr. Peterson:

We regret that we have received no response from you to our letters of May 16
and June 20 concerning your outstanding balance.

Because so much time has elapsed, we must now require full payment (or your
signed agreement to make regular installment payments) within the next ten
days.

If we have not heard from you by August 23, it will become necessary for us to
take further action.

Sincerely,

Morris T. Jukes

Morris T. Jukes
Accounts Receivable Department

(   ) I will pay $_____ (   ) weekly; (   ) monthly, on my account.

(   ) Enclosed is a check for full payment in the amount of $_____.

_____
Signature

payment schedule appears at the bottom of the letter, thus giving the reader a
chance to explain any delay.

When still more time elapses and no payment is made, creditors send a third
letter, an example of which appears in Figure 7.30. The creditor's tone and tactics
have changed. From the cooperative tone of "What's wrong; can we help?" in the

FIGURE 7.31   A fourth and final collection letter.

Baldwin County Hospital   P.O. Box 222   Notown, MA 02138-1098   (617) 555-3000

August 26, 1994

Mr. Howard Peterson
318 Brook Avenue #8A
Notown, MA 02146-1074

Re: Inpatient Services
Date of Hospitalization: April 1–3, 1994
Balance Due: $3725.48

Dear Mr. Peterson:

During the past few months we have written to you several times concerning your outstanding balance.

As you may recall, we offered to arrange for installment payments or to help you in any way that we could. Since you have not responded, we must demand your payment in full at this time.

If we do not hear from you within ten days, we will have no alternative but to turn your account over to our collection agency.

Sincerely,

Morris T. Jukes

Morris T. Jukes
Accounts Receivable Department

second collection letter, the third letter switches to the much more direct "We have waited a long time. Pay, or at least begin to pay, your bill now." The third collection letter, which must be more forceful than the second, announces that serious consequences will result if the creditor does not receive a payment from the customer. The vague threat, "further action," wisely does not commit the hospital to take legal action or to speak to a collection agency, its last resort. The third letter should still give the delinquent customer a way out, and so this one contains some useful, face-saving options listed at the bottom of the letter.

If after receiving these three letters, the customer still does not respond, the creditor sends a fourth letter containing a specific threat that will be carried out. Note, though, how the letter in Figure 7.31 does not begin with that bad news. Instead, it reminds the patient of all the efforts the hospital has expended to collect its bills. The letter clearly points out that the time for concessions is over. Then it announces what consequences will result if the patient still does not pay. The letter gives proper legal notification that the patient has ten days to respond. This fourth collection letter attempts to frighten the customer into payment and does not have to seek or give any explanations. If the hospital, or any company, fails to carry its threat to turn delinquent accounts over to a collection agency or attorney, however, it will quickly get a reputation for having all bark but no bite— a reputation that would make it difficult to collect its debts in the future.

✓ Revision Checklist

This chapter has shown you how to prepare some common types of business correspondence. Regardless of the kind of letter or memo you have to write, you will increase your chances for success if you can during revision successfully answer the following questions:

1. Have I planned what I am going to say to my readers? Did I do the necessary homework and doublechecking to answer any questions about my message? Have I proved to my readers that I am knowledgeable about the topic I am addressing?
2. Did I use an appropriate (and consistent) format for my memos and letters?
3. Do the organization, style, tone, and routing order of my memos follow acceptable company protocol?
4. Have I satisfactorily adapted the style and length of my fax and/or E-mail message for my readers?
5. Have I organized and, if necessary, labeled the information in my memos and letters in the most effective way for my message and for my readers?

6. Did I emphasize the "you attitude" with my readers—whether employer, customer/client, or coworker? Will my reader see me as courteous, professional, and easy to work with?

7. Have I used clear and concise language that is appropriate for my reader?

8. Did I begin my correspondence with reader-effective strategies? If I am reporting good news, have I told the reader right away? If I must convey bad news, have I been diplomatically indirect?

9. Does my sales letter follow the four A's? Have I identified and convinced my target audience?

10. Are my complaint letters written in a calm and courteous tone? Do they clearly inform the reader what is wrong, why it is wrong, and how I would like the problem resolved?

11. Are my adjustment letters that say "Yes" sincere and to the point? Are those that say "No" fair? Do they acknowledge the reader's point of view and provide a clear explanation for my refusal?

12. Is my correspondence timely? Have I been prompt and reasonable in answering all my correspondence—both from people in my company as well as from my customers?

Exercises

1. Write a memo to your employer saying that you will be out of town two days next week and three the following week for **one** of the following reasons: (a) to inspect some land your firm is thinking of buying, (b) to investigate some claims, (c) to look at some new office space for a branch your firm is thinking of opening in a city five hundred miles away, (d) to attend a conference sponsored by a professional society, or (e) to pay calls on customers. In your memo, be very specific about dates, places, times, and reasons.

2. Write a memo to two or three of your coworkers on the same subject you chose for Exercise 1 above.

3. Send a memo to your public relations department informing it that you are completing a degree or work for a certificate, and indicate how the information could be useful for its publicity campaign.

4. Write a memo to the payroll department notifying it that there is a mistake in your last paycheck. Explain exactly what the error is and give precise figures.

5. You are a manager of a local art museum. Write a memo to the Chamber of Commerce in which you put the following information into proper memo format.

   Old hours: Mon.–Fri. 9–5; closed Sat. except during July and August when you are open 9–12
   New hours: Mon.–Th. 8:30–4:30; Fri.–Sat. 9–9
   Old rates: Adults $3.00; senior citizens $1.00; children under 12 free
   New rates: Adults $4.50; senior citizens $1.00; children under 12 free but must be accompanied by an adult
   Added features: Paintings by Thora Horne, local artist; sculpture from West Indies in display area all summer; guided tours available with a party of six or more; lounge areas will offer patrons sandwiches and soft drinks during May, June, July, and August

6. Select some change (in policy, schedule, or personnel assignment) you encountered in a job you held in the last two or three years and write an appropriate memo describing that change. Assume you are your former employer explaining the change to employees.

7. Write a letter in which you order merchandise from a vendor's or wholesaler's catalog. Specify the quantity, size, stock number, and cost. Also include delivery instructions, the date by which you must receive the merchandise, and the way in which you will pay for it.

8. Write a letter of inquiry to a utility company, a safety or health care agency, or a company in your town, asking for a brochure describing its services to the community. Be specific about your reasons for requesting this information.

9. In which course(s) are you or will you be writing a paper or report? Write to an agency or company that could supply you with helpful information for the paper and request its aid. Indicate why you are writing, precisely what information you need, and why you need it, and offer to share your paper or report with the company.

10. Examine an ad in a magazine or a TV commercial, and then write a one-page assessment in which you identify the four parts of its sales message.

11. Choose one of the following and write a sales letter addressed to an appropriate audience on why they should
    a. major in the same subject you did.
    b. live in your neighborhood.
    c. be happy taking a vacation where you did last year.
    d. dine at a particular restaurant.
    e. shop at a store you have worked for or will work for.
    f. have their cars repaired at a specific garage.
    g. give their real estate business to a particular agency.

12. Find at least two sales letters you, your family, or your firm has received, and in a memo to your instructor or employer, evaluate them according to how

well they follow the four parts of a sales letter discussed in this chapter. Attach these sales letters to your evaluation. If your memo is addressed to your boss, indicate how you can improve on your competition's sales letters.

13. Write a sales letter about the effectiveness of sales letters to an individual who has told you that almost everyone throws them away as soon as he or she gets them.

14. Rewrite the following sales letter to make it more effective. Add any details you think are relevant.

```
Dear Pizza Lovers:

Allow me to introduce myself. My name is Rudy Moore
and I am the new manager of Tasty Pizza Parlor in
town. The Parlor is located at the intersection of
North Miller Parkway and 95th Street. We are open from
10 a.m. to 11 p.m., except on the weekends, when we
are open later.

I think you will be as happy as I am to learn that
Tasty's will now offer free delivery to an extended
service area. As a result, you can get your Tasty
Pizza hot when you want it.

Please see your weekly newspapers for our ad. We also
are offering customers a coupon. It is a real deal for
you.

I know you will enjoy Tasty's and I hope to see you.
I am always interested in hearing from you about our
service and our fine product. We want to take your
order soon. Please come in.
```

15. Write a thank-you letter in response to one of the following:
 a. a gift you have received from a coworker
 b. a letter of recommendation someone wrote for you
 c. some business that was directed to you or your employer
 d. a dinner or other social occasion to which you were invited by a customer or your employer or agency

16. Write a congratulation letter to someone for one of the following:
 a. being promoted
 b. winning an award at school
 c. being named salesperson of the month
 d. completing a special course or degree
 e. being elected to public office
 f. concluding a business deal (selling a product, renegotiating a contract)
 g. opening a new store or branch
 h. joining your firm or agency

17. Send a follow-up letter to one of the individuals below:
    a. a customer who informs you that he or she will no longer do business with your firm because your prices are too high
    b. a family of four who stayed at your motel for two weeks last summer
    c. a church group that used your catering services last month
    d. a customer who exchanged a dress or coat for the purchase price
    e. a customer who bought a new car from you one year ago
    f. a company that bought some software from you nine months ago but now you must say that software has been improved

18. Write a bad news letter to an appropriate reader about one of the following:
    a. Your company has to discontinue Saturday deliveries because of rising labor and fuel costs.
    b. You are the manager of an insurance company writing to tell one of your customers that because of reckless driving, his or her rates are going to increase.
    c. You have to refuse to send a bonus gift to a customer because that customer sent in an order after the expiration date for providing that bonus gift.
    d. You have to discontinue a model that a business customer wants to reorder.
    e. You have to notify residents of a community that a bus route is being discontinued.
    f. You represent the water department and have to tell residents of a community that they cannot water their lawns for the next month because of a serious water shortage in your town.
    g. You cannot send customers a catalog—which your company used to send free of charge—unless they first send $5 for the cost of that catalog.
    h. You cannot repair a particular piece of equipment because the customer still owes your company for three previous service visits.

19. Write a good news letter about the opposite of one of the situations listed in Exercise 18 above.

20. You just found out that a business that applied for credit has missed its last mortgage payment. You have to refuse credit to this local firm that has been in business successfully for eight years. Write a refusal letter without jeopardizing future business dealings.

21. Write a complaint letter about one of the following:
    a. an error in your utility, telephone, or credit card bill
    b. discourteous service you received on an airplane or bus
    c. a frozen food product of poor quality
    d. a shipment that arrives late and damaged
    e. an insurance payment to you that is $50 less than it should be
    f. a public television station's policy of not showing a particular series
    g. junk mail that you are receiving

22. Write the complaint letter to which the adjustment letter in Figure 7.22 responds.

23. Write the complaint letter to which the adjustment letter in Figure 7.24 responds.

24. Rewrite the following complaint letter to make it more precise and less emotional.

    Dear Sir:

    We recently purchased a machine from your Albany
    store and paid a great deal of money for it. This
    machine, supposedly the best model in your line, has
    caused us nothing but trouble each time we use it.
    Really, can't you do any better with your technology?

    We expect you to stand by your products. The
    warranties you give with them should make you
    accountable for shoddy workmanship. Let us know at
    once what you intend to do about our problem. If you
    cannot or are unwilling to correct the situation, we
    will take our business elsewhere, and then you will
    be sorry.

    Sincerely yours,

25. Write an adjustment letter saying "Yes" to the manager of The Loft whose letter is included in Figure 7.20.

26. Write an adjustment letter saying "No" to the customer who received the "Yes" adjustment letter included in Figure 7.22.

27. Rewrite the following ineffective adjustment letter saying "Yes."

    Dear Mr. Smith:

    We are extremely sorry to learn that you found the
    suit you purchased from us unsatisfactory. The
    problem obviously stems from the fact that you
    selected it from the rack marked "Factory Seconds."
    In all honesty, we have had a lot of problems because
    of this rack. I guess we should know better than to
    try to feature inferior merchandise along with the
    name-brand clothing that we sell. But we originally
    thought that our customers would accept poorer
    quality merchandise if it saved them some money. That
    was our mistake.

    Please accept our apologies. If you will bring your
    "Factory Second" suit to us, we will see what we can
    do about honoring your request.

    Sincerely yours,

28. Rewrite the following ineffective adjustment letter saying "No."

Dear Customer:

Our company is unwilling to give you a new toaster or
to refund your purchase price. After examining the
toaster you sent to us, we found that the fault was
not ours, as you insist, but yours.

Let me explain. Our toaster is made to take a lot of
punishment. But being dropped on the floor or poked
inside with a knife, as you probably did, exceeds all
decent treatment. You must be careful if you expect
your appliances to last. Your negligence in this case
is so bad that the toaster could not be repaired.

In the future, consider using your appliances
according to the guidelines set down in warranty
books. That's why they are written.

Since you are now in the market for a new toaster,
let me suggest that you purchase our new heavy-duty
model, number 67342, called the Counter-Whiz. I am
taking the liberty of sending you some information
about this model. I do hope you at least go to see
one at your local appliance center.

Sincerely,

29. Assume that you work in the student services department at a local college
and that you have been asked to write collection letters to those graduates
who are not paying off their student loans on time. Write a series of four collection letters to be sent at appropriate times. The first letter is sent after the
student misses only one payment, the second letter after two nonpayments,
the third letter after three nonpayments, and the fourth letter after four nonpayments.

30. Rewrite the following collection letter *twice*, the first time making it appropriate for a first notice and the second time making it suitable for a second
notice.

Dear Customer:

You may recall that you owe us the slight sum of
$89.56 for the plumbing work we did for you in
January. To you such bills may appear trivial, but
in order to stay in business we have to collect from
everyone, from the little guy like you to the big
companies we help.

Do not be a problem for us. Pay what you owe. If you
do not send us a check for the above amount in the
next few days, we will somehow get the money out of
you. Whether you pay the easy way by sending us a
check now or whether we put a hard-nosed collection
agency on your case is entirely up to you.

Sincerely yours,

31. Assume that you are a sales representative for the publisher of this textbook. The chairperson of the Springfield College Business Department calls you to ask for information about *Successful Writing at Work,* because the department is meeting tomorrow to choose a textbook for the next school year. Write a sales letter to fax to this department chairperson.

32. Working with two classmates, collaboratively write a memo to your instructor in which you explain what you have found most helpful in this chapter and how it has helped you as a writer. Include any on-the-job writing assignments you may have had.

How to Get a Job: Résumés, Letters, Applications, Interviews, and Evaluations

Obtaining a job today involves a lot of hard work. Before your name is added to the payroll, you will have to do more than simply walk into a personnel office and fill out an application form. Furthermore, finding the *right* job takes time. And finding the right person to fill that job also takes time for the employer. From the employer's viewpoint, the stages in the search for a valuable employee include the following:

1. deciding on what duties and responsibilities go with the job and determining the qualifications the future employee should possess
2. advertising the job
3. reading and evaluating résumés and letters of application
4. having candidates complete application forms
5. requesting further proof of the candidates' skills—letters of recommendation, transcripts
6. interviewing selected candidates
7. offering the job to the best-qualified individual

Sometimes these steps are interchangeable, especially steps 4 and 5, but generally speaking, employers go through a long and detailed process to select employees. Step 3, for example, is among the most important for employers (and the most crucial for job candidates). At this stage employers often classify job seekers into one of three groups: those they definitely want to interview; those they may want to interview; and those they have no interest in.

As a job seeker you will have to know how and when to give the employer all the kinds of information the seven steps require. You will also have to follow a certain schedule in your search for a job. The following eight procedures will be required of you:

1. analyzing your strengths and restricting your job search
2. preparing a dossier (placement file)
3. looking in the right places for a job
4. constructing a résumé
5. writing a letter of application
6. filling out a job application
7. going to an interview
8. accepting or declining a job

Your timetable should match that of your prospective employer.

Chapter 8 shows you how to begin your job search and how to prepare appropriate letters that are a part of the job-search process. You will need to write a letter of application, letters requesting others to write recommendations for you, letters thanking employers for interviews, and letters accepting or declining a position. In addition to discussing each of these kinds of letters, this chapter shows you how to assemble the supporting data—dossiers, résumés—that employers request. You will also find some practical advice on how to handle yourself at an interview. The chapter concludes with the kinds of evaluations—of yourself and of others—that you can expect to write once you have worked on your job.

The eight steps of your job search are arranged in this chapter in the order in which you are most likely to proceed when you start looking for a job. By reading about these stages in sequence, you will have the benefit of going through a dry run of the employment process itself.

Analyzing Your Strengths and Restricting Your Job Search

Individuals who advise students about how to get a job have isolated two "fatal assumptions" that many job seekers hold. If you assume the following two points, chances are that you will *not* be very successful in your job search.[1]

1. I should remain loose (vague) about what I want so I'm free to respond to any opportunity.
2. The employer has the upper hand in the whole process.

The first "fatal assumption" will disqualify you for any position for which your major has prepared you. Your first responsibility is to identify your professional qualifications. Employers want to hire individuals with highly developed technical skills and training. Your education and experience should help you to identify and emphasize your marketable skills. Make an inventory of your accomplishments in your major or job and then decide which specialty within your chosen career appeals to you most. If you are enrolled in a criminal justice program, do you want

---

[1] Lewis E. Patterson and Ernest M. Schuttenberg, *College Board Review* (Fall 1979): 15.

a position as a corrections officer, a security official, or a member of the local police force? If you are in a nursing program, do you want to work in a large hospital, a nursing home, or a state health agency? What kinds of patients do you want to care for—geriatric, pediatric, psychiatric? If your major is food science, do you want to be a caterer or a restaurant owner, or would you rather work for an industrial or hospitality employer? If you already hold a position and want to advance yourself professionally, ask yourself where you would like to relocate and what type of additional responsibilities you want to assume. In short, ask yourself: Where do I want to work and why?

Avoid applying for positions for which you are either overqualified or underqualified. If a position requires ten years of on-the-job experience and you are just starting out, you will only waste the employer's time, and your own, by applying. On the other hand, if you have two or three years of experience in the food industry, for example, you would not apply for a position that calls for someone who has no training.

The second "fatal assumption"—assuming that the employer controls the entire job-search process—is equally misleading. To a large extent, you can determine whether you are a serious contender for a job by the letters and résumés you write and the self-image you present. Even in today's highly competitive job market, you can secure a suitable job if you keep in mind that the basic purpose of all job correspondence is to sell yourself. Letters and résumés are sales tools to earn you an interview and eventually the job. Be confident and convincing. Believe in yourself and your abilities. Employers almost always have a shortage of good, qualified employees.

Preparing a Dossier

The job placement office or career center at your school will assist you by providing counseling; notifying you of available, relevant jobs; and arranging on-campus interviews. The job placement office may also help you establish your *dossier*, sometimes referred to as your placement file.

The dossier, a French word for a bundle of documents, is your own personal file that is stored at the placement office. This file contains information about you that substantiates and supplements the facts you will list in your résumé and letter of application. Your dossier should contain your letters of recommendation; copies of these letters are made and sent out to prospective employers, thus relieving those who have recommended you of writing an original letter each time you apply for a job. You may also want to include unsolicited letters—those awarding you a scholarship, praising you as the employee of the month, or honoring you for some community service. Be very selective about these kinds of letters; you do not want to crowd your dossier with less important items that will compete for attention with your academic recommendations. The dossier also contains biographical information, a listing of your job experiences, and your academic transcript(s). You may ask that your dossier be sent to an employer, or employers may request it themselves if you have listed the placement office address on your résumé.

The most important part of your dossier is the letter-of-recommendation section. Whom should you ask to recommend you? Your present or previous employer (even for a summer job) is a logical choice, but be cautious here. If your current employer knows that your education is preparing you for another profession, or if you are working at a part-time job while you are in school, you should obtain a letter of recommendation to be included in your dossier. If you are happily and successfully employed and are looking for a new position only for professional advancement or a better salary, you may not want your present employer to know that you are searching for a new job. You have the right to request a prospective employer to respect your confidence (for instance, not to call you at work) until you become a leading candidate. At that point you may be happy to have your current employer consulted for a reference. On the other hand, if you are on bad terms with your current employer and want to find a new, more suitable position, you need to inform the prospective employer as honestly and professionally as you can with the least damage to yourself. No sure solution exists.

Be sure to ask two or three of your professors to be references. Choose teachers who know and like your work, have graded your papers, and have supervised you in fieldwork or laboratory activities. Superiors who knew your work in the military are also likely candidates. Recommendations from these individuals will be regarded as more objective than a letter from a member of the clergy or from a neighbor. Of course, if you are asked specifically for a character reference, by all means ask a member of the clergy.

Make sure that you ask permission of these individuals before you list them as references. This is a courtesy, and it will also give them time to write an appropriate letter for you. Imagine how damaging it would be for you if a prospective employer called one of your teachers whom you had not yet asked to serve as a reference. What if the teacher responded that he or she did not even know you were looking for a job or, worse yet, said you had not had the courtesy to ask to use his or her name as a reference? When you ask for permission in a letter or in person, stress how much a strong letter of support means to you and find out if the individual is willing to write such a letter. It is important to emphasize that you need a strong letter of recommendation; a general or weak one will hurt your chances in your job search. As a help to your references, tell them what kind of jobs you are applying for and keep them up-to-date about your educational and occupational achievements. Figure 8.1 (p. 254) shows a sample letter requesting an individual to serve as a reference.

You have a legal right to determine whether you want to see your letters or not. If you have read your recommendations, that fact is noted on the dossier. Some employers feel that if the candidates see what is written about them, the writers of the letters of recommendation will be less frank and even unwilling to volunteer critical information. If you waive your right to see the letters written about you, you must sign an appropriate form, a copy of which is then given to the individual recommending you. Keep in mind, too, that some individuals may refuse to write a letter that they know you will see; they may prefer absolute confidentiality. Figure 8.2 (p. 255) shows a confidential evaluation form. Before you make any decision about seeing your letters, get the advice of your instructors and your placement counselor.

FIGURE 8.1   Request for a letter of recommendation.

```
5432 South Kenneth Avenue
Chicago, IL 60651
March 30, 1994

Mr. Sonny Butler, Manager
Empire Supermarket
4000 West 79th Street
Chicago, IL 60652-4300

Dear Mr. Butler:

I was employed at your store from September 1992 through
August 1993.  During my employment, I worked part time as
a stock clerk and relief cashier, and during the summer
months I was a full-time employee in the produce
department, helping to fill in while Bill Dirksen and
Vivian Rogers were away on their vacations.

I enjoyed my work at Empire, and I learned a great deal
about ordering stock, arranging merchandise, and
assisting customers.

This May I will receive my A.A. degree from Moraine Valley
Community College in retail merchandising.  I have already
begun preparing for my job search for a position in retail
sales.  Would you be willing to write a letter of
recommendation for me in which you mention what you regard
as my greatest strengths as one of your employees?  To
assist you, I can send you a letter of recommendation form
from the Placement Office at Moraine Valley.  Your letter
would become a part of my permanent placement file.

I look forward to hearing from you.  I thought you might
like to see the enclosed résumé, which shows what I have
been doing since I left Empire.

Sincerely yours,

Robert B. Jackson

Robert B. Jackson

Encl. Résumé
```

FIGURE 8.2   A confidential evaluation form.

Return this form to:

OFFICE OF CAREER DEVELOPMENT & PLACEMENT
VALDOSTA STATE COLLEGE
Valdosta, Georgia 31601

CONFIDENTIAL EVALUATION

TO THE CANDIDATE: (type in)

Candidate's   Name of
Full Name _____   Reference _____
        first   middle   last

Courses under this instructor (title, quarter, year) or Period of employment _____

_____

Today's date _____Your (anticipated) date of graduation _____Degree program _____

TO THE TEACHER OR EMPLOYER:

Please note that this is a confidential evaluation. The candidate has waived his or her right of access to this evaluation. We shall appreciate both a rating and a statement regarding the candidate's suitability for employment. Your evaluation will become a permanent part of his or her placement record which is made available to employers and graduate schools. *Do not show it to the candidate.* Also, *please type* this form if possible. Blue ink does not duplicate clearly. Once this form is on file you may refer future requests concerning this candidate to the Career Development & Placement Office for a reply.

Indicate degree of acquaintance with candidate:

Length of acquaintance: _____

☐ Know personally

☐ Know as a student

☐ Know only as a member of a large class

☐ Know as an employee

	Unable to Observe	Excellent	Above Average	Average	Below Average	Poor
Appearance						
Academic Performance (within subject (s) under your supervision)						
Promptness in assignments; regularity of attendance						
Ability to communicate: Orally						
In Writing						
Initiative						
Leadership						
Social qualities (congeniality, interest in others)						
Promise in _____ (specify field)						
Suitability for graduate school						

STATEMENT: (Please elaborate on the above and comment on any other appropriate points. This statement is considered an <u>important</u> part of the total evaluation.)

Signature _____

Title & Dept. _____

Institution or Organization _____

Date: _____   Address _____

Do not wait until you begin applying for jobs to establish your dossier. Most placement offices recommend that candidates set up their dossiers at least three to six months before they begin looking for jobs. You will thus ensure that your letters of recommendation are on file and that you have benefited from the placement office's services. In advising you, the placement counselor will ask that you complete a confidential questionnaire about your geographic preferences, salary expectations, and the types of positions for which you are qualified. With this information on hand, the placement office will be better prepared to advise you and to notify you of appropriate openings.

Some placement offices charge a small fee for their services, while others provide their services free of charge.

Looking in the Right Places for a Job

One way to search for a job is simply to send out a batch of letters to companies you want to work for. But how do you know what jobs, if any, these companies have available, what qualifications they are looking for, and what application procedures and deadlines they want you to follow? You can avoid these uncertainties by knowing where to look for a job and knowing what a specific job requires. Such information will make your search easier and, in all likelihood, more successful. Here are a number of sources to consult.

1. Do not overlook the obvious: the newspaper. Look at local newspapers as well as large city papers with a wide circulation: the *New York Times,* the *Chicago Tribune,* the *Los Angeles Times,* the *New Orleans Times-Picayune,* the *Cleveland Plain Dealer.* The Sunday editions usually advertise positions available all over the country. Check the classified section under a number of possibly relevant categories (e.g., "Computer Programmers" as well as "Programmers"). The *National Business Employment Weekly,* published by the *Wall Street Journal,* lists jobs in many different areas, including technical and managerial. The ads you find may list the name, address, and phone number of the company seeking employees or may be "blind," that is, listing only a post office box to conceal the employer's identity.

2. Investigate openings listed in professional and trade journals in your major. The *American Journal of Nursing,* for example, carries notices of openings arranged by geographic location in each of its monthly issues; and *Food Technology* prints in each issue a section called "Professional Placement," which lists jobs from all over the country. Consult the *Encyclopedia of Associations* for a list of journals and newsletters in your profession.

3. Visit your college's placement office. Counselors keep an up-to-date file of available positions and can also tell you when a firm's recruiter will be on campus to conduct interviews. They can also help you locate summer and part-time work, both on and off campus.

When you visit the placement office, also examine a current issue of the *College Placement Annual,* a useful catalog that lists the addresses of more than one thousand employers in business, industry, and government. The *CPA* also gives information on the kinds of requirements job candidates are expected to have for these positions.

4. Check with your state and local employment offices. They also have a current file of positions and offer some counseling (free of charge). Some educational television stations even broadcast information (qualifications, salary) about positions on file at a state employment office. If you are interested in working for the U.S. government, visit a Civil Service Commission Office, a Federal Job Information Center, or any government agency. Get the addresses from the white pages of your phone book.

5. Visit the personnel department of a company or agency to see if there are any current openings or if any vacancies are anticipated. Often you will be given an application to fill out even if there is not a current opening, or your name will be placed on a list. But do not call employers asking about openings. A visit shows a more serious interest. Also, they are more likely to remember you if a job does develop. New openings often arise unexpectedly in business and industry.

6. Let your relatives, friends, neighbors, members of the clergy, and professors know that you are looking for a job. They may hear of something and can notify you. Better yet, they may recommend you for the position—with a phone call, a trip to the personnel department (if they work for the company), or a letter. A respected employee can open the door for you. John D. Erdlen and Donald H. Sweet, experts on the job search, cite the following as a primary rule of job hunting: "Don't do anything yourself you can get someone with influence to do for you."

7. Write to your local Chamber of Commerce. Although not a placement center, the Chamber of Commerce can give you the names and addresses of employers likely to hire individuals with your qualifications, as well as information about these companies to use in a letter of application or at an interview. Many companies planning to relocate or expand first notify a chamber of commerce to identify a potential labor force. Should a company decide to move to your area, your chamber of commerce would know about it and would be a good place to acquire such information.

8. Use a résumé database service. For a fee (usually between $40 and $80), you can have a résumé of your qualifications (see pages 258–280) placed in a database made available to prospective employers who pay an access fee to scan the database looking for suitable job candidates. The résumés have been classified according to a job candidate's area(s) of expertise, making it easy for employers to find job seekers whom they want to interview. These résumé databases are available at job fairs, career centers, and personnel offices, for both private and government employers.

9. Use a video résumé. In some parts of the country, job hunters have made twenty-second "video résumés" that are aired on local television stations. In a video résumé, the job seeker must make his or her sales pitch quickly and effectively, emphasizing the one or two strengths that will encourage a potential employer to call the station and get the job seeker's phone number. The job seeker has to sell features such as his or her work accomplishments, the amount of sales dollars he or she brought into a company, or the years of experience he or she brings to a new employer. You can inquire at the local office of your state employment service about whether any local television stations offer this public service to job seekers.

10. Check the *Federal Register.* The U.S. government is one of the biggest employers in the country. The *Federal Register,* a privately published sourcebook, lists more than twenty thousand civil service jobs each month. It is available in many libraries.

11. Register with a professional employment agency. Some agencies list two kinds of jobs—those that are found for the applicant free of charge (because the employer pays the fee) and those for which the applicant pays a fee. Sometimes that fee can be stiff—for example, a percentage of your first year's salary. Employment agencies often find out about jobs through channels already available to you. Before turning your search over to a professional employment agency, however, make sure that you have exhausted all the previously mentioned services and be sure to ask who pays the fee for the service.

Preparing a Résumé

The résumé, sometimes called a *data sheet* or *curriculum vitae,* is a factual and concise summary of your qualifications for the job. It is not your life's history or an emotional autobiography, nor is it a transcript of your college work.

A résumé highlights your proven accomplishments and abilities. It is a record of results—showing a prospective employer that you have what it takes (in education and experience) to do the job. The résumé is a one-page (no more than two-page) outline accompanying your letter of application for a job. Résumés are never sent alone and should never be faxed unless an employer asks you to. You may, however, bring one with you to an interview. Certainly you should have copies available for recruiters if you schedule campus interviews. The main function of the résumé is to present information about your education, experience, and other achievements accurately and quickly so that a busy personnel manager or department head will want to interview you. Your résumé should make a good first impression.

The Process of Writing Your Résumé

As with other types of writing, preparing your résumé requires that you work through a process. You cannot produce a polished résumé in an hour. But having a clear idea about the type of job you want and your qualifications for it should get you off to a good start.

Getting Started—Ask Key Questions

Begin with the prewriting strategies discussed in Chapter 2 (pages 29–32) to identify your strengths and achievements. Ask yourself important questions about your school and job work. What classes did you excel in? Did you write a paper or report or conduct an experiment that received a highly favorable response from your instructor? Did you win an award or a scholarship? On the job, did you improve a procedure, receive a raise or merit pay, or earn a promotion? Write down everything you think is a skill or achievement—from jobs (full- or part-time, summer), school (course work, workshops, labs, extracurricular activities, sports), the military, or community work. Do not overlook skills you have in operating equipment (particularly computers). Circle or underline any awards or honors as well as responsibilities you have had. Don't be worried if you produce a rather lengthy list of seemingly unrelated activities. From this brainstormed list (or clustered grouping) you will have a working inventory of accomplishments from which you can begin to restrict and organize material for the final copy of your résumé.

Scrutinize Your Accomplishments

The next step is to be highly critical of your working inventory. Cross off any repetitions, eliminate unimportant or irrelevant items, try to sort items into related categories, and add whatever information you think is valuable.

As you criticize and supplement your list, examine your accomplishments the way a prospective employer might. The chief question an employer will ask about you (and all other applicants) is: "What can this person do for our company?" Employers are results-oriented; they read résumés looking for clear proof of your marketable skills. You have to convince your reader (or group of readers, since résumés often circulate among a hiring committee) that you have succeeded in the past and will do so in the future. Pay special attention to your four or five most significant, job-worthy strengths and work especially hard on them. While not everything you have done might relate directly to a particular job, indicate how your own achievements might be relevant to the employer's specific needs. For example, responsibility in handling money or supervising others in a grocery store establishes your ability to do the same things in another business context. Don't make the mistake of saying your employer trusted you "with small or modest amounts of money." Such a statement only calls your trustworthiness and judgment into question.

Résumé-Writing Techniques—Using "Selling Clauses"

The next step in preparing a winning résumé is to translate the items in your list of accomplishments into appropriate résumé entries. There is a big difference between résumés and other types of work-related documents. Résumés generally are written in short sentences (clauses really) that omit the subject "I." Instead of complete sentences, résumés use action-packed *selling clauses* that convince prospective employers that you are the right person for the job. Look at the résumés in this chapter (Figures 8.3–8.7 [pp. 262–275]) for examples of these sell-ing clauses, or résumé entries.

How can you effectively convert the information in your restricted brain-stormed list into these selling clauses? Select the most appropriate language and describe your school and work experiences using the following pattern:

show what you did	about what	for/to whom
completed	monthly reports	for production department
classified	plant specimens	in college herbarium
tested	experimental surface coatings	in polymer labs
collected	delinquent accounts	for credit bureau
tutored	college athletes	in algebra course

To demonstrate your skills and accomplishments, use strong action verbs that leave no doubt about your achievements in your reader's mind. Table 8.1 lists some action verbs that can help you to showcase your strengths. You may even find it useful to use two verbs to describe your work: *built and maintained auto-matic feeder for conveyor belt; monitored and updated state membership data-bases for New Hampshire Chiropractic Association; calculated and disbursed wages for ten Mayco employees.* When you are preparing your list of résumé entries, be careful that you do not overuse the same verb—for example, *devel-oped a program, developed a policy, developed new techniques.* Also avoid vague, limp verbs such as *know about, am involved in, am experienced in.* These weak verbs do not broadcast your specific duties or accomplishments. Also stay clear of such vague words as *factors, duties,* and so on. They do not show or tell exactly what you did.

Revising Your Résumé

The revision stage of the résumé-writing process helps you to address your audi-ence effectively. When you have what seems like a final draft, show your résumé to two or three people whose opinion you value, individuals who may have what is called "business sense." Ask a teacher, a placement counselor, or someone who has worked in the profession for a number of years to criticize your résumé the way a prospective employer would. You might also ask someone you know who is already employed by the company you are interested in to read your résumé and point out things you need to add, delete, emphasize, or rearrange. Revise your résumé in light of these readers' comments.

Keep in mind that all employers are looking for employees who are intelli-gent, cooperative, and responsible. Employers want to hire people who can com-municate well, organize effectively, learn material quickly, and be team players. Your résumé (like your letter of application) needs to demonstrate that you have done these things in a previous job, in school, or in another organization. Again, by revising your résumé with the employer's needs in mind, you can be appropri-ately selective and persuasive.

Finally, double-check your dates, titles, company and school names, and make sure there are no inconsistencies that could confuse a reader.

TABLE 8.1   Action Verbs to Use in Your Résumé

accommodated	conducted	headed	prepared
administered	coordinated	implemented	reconciled
analyzed	dealt in	improved	researched
arranged	determined	increased	scheduled
assembled	developed	informed	selected
attended	directed	initiated	served
built	drafted	instituted	settled
calculated	established	instructed	supervised
coached	estimated	maintained	taught
collected	evaluated	managed	tracked
communicated	expedited	managed	trained
compiled	figured	operated	tutored
composed	guided	organized	weighed
computed	handled	oversaw	wrote
		performed	

How Much Should You Include on a Résumé?

How much should you include on your résumé? Both experienced candidates and recent graduates with limited experience ask this question. The dangers involve including too much or putting in too little. If you have years of experience and have recently returned to school, you may risk flooding your prospective employer with too many details. You cannot possibly include every detail of your job(s) for the last ten or twenty years. Therefore, you must be selective and emphasize only those skills and positions most likely to earn you the job. You may have to eliminate the earliest jobs you had and those that do not relate to your present employment search. You also may have to combine and condense the skills you acquired over many years and through many jobs. Figure 8.3 (p. 262) shows a résumé from Anna Cassetti, an individual who had years of job experience before she returned to school. Take a look, too, at Patrice Cooper Bolger's résumé (Figure 8.7 [p. 275]) and Donald Kitto-Klein's (Figure 8.8 [p. 276]). These individuals also have a great deal of experience to offer prospective employers.

Many job candidates who have spent most of their lives in school are faced with the other extreme: not having much job experience to put down. The worst thing to do is to write "None" for experience. Any part-time or summer job, as well as volunteer work done at school for a library or science laboratory, shows a prospective employer that you are responsible and knowledgeable about the obligations of being an employee. So, too, do any internships you may have had or community work you may have done. Figure 8.4 (p. 264) shows a résumé from Anthony Jones, a student with very little job experience; Figure 8.5 (p. 267) shows one from Maria Lopez, a student with just a few years of experience.

Some employment counselors advise candidates to prepare no more than a one-page résumé. However, depending on your education and job experience, you may want to include a second page. A good rule of thumb is that if you have more than one degree beyond high school and if you have had more than two full-

FIGURE 8.3   Résumé from an individual with ten years' job experience.

RÉSUMÉ
ANNA C. CASSETTI

6457 Blackstone Avenue
Fort Worth, TX 76321-6733
(817) 555-5657

MacMurray Real Estate
1700 Ross Boulevard
Haltom City, TX 77320-1700
(817) 555-7211

CAREER OBJECTIVE

Full-time sales position with large real estate office in the Phoenix or Tucson area with specific opportunities in real estate appraisal and tax counseling.

EXPERIENCE

1992–present *MacMurray Real Estate, Haltom City, Texas*
Real estate agent. Worked in small office (two salespersons plus broker) with limited listings; sold individually $850,000 in residential property; appraised both residential and commercial listings.

1986–1991 *Dallman Federal Savings and Loan, Inc., Fort Worth, Texas*
Chief Teller. Responsible for supervising, training, and coordinating activities of six full-time and two part-time tellers. Promoted to Chief Teller, March 1988.

1986 (Sept.–Dec.) *H&R Block, Westover Hills, Texas*
Tax consultant; ordered stock.

1983–1985 *Cruckshank's Hardware Store, Fort Worth, Texas*
Salesperson.

1979–1983 *U.S. Navy*
Honorably discharged with rank of Petty Officer, Third Class. Served as stores manager.

EDUCATION

1985–1991 *Texas Christian University, Fort Worth, Texas*
Awarded B.S. degree in Real Estate Management. Completed thirty-three hours in business and real estate courses with a concentration in real estate finance, appraising, and property management. Also completed nine hours in computer science and data processing. Wrote reports on appraisal procedures as part of supervised training program during my last term.

FIGURE 8.3   (Continued)

Cassetti 2

1984   *H&R Block, Westover Hills, Texas*
(Sept.–Dec.)   Earned diploma in Basic Income Tax Preparation after
                     completing intensive ten-week course.

1979–1980   *U.S. Naval Base, San Diego, California*
                     Attended U.S. Navy's Supply Management School.
                     Applied principles of stores management at Newport
                     Naval Base.

PERSONAL

Texas Realtor's License: 756a2737

HOBBIES AND INTERESTS

Chair, Financial Committee, Grace Presbyterian Church,
Fort Worth. Have also worked with Junior Achievement
advising teenagers in business management. Enjoy
golfing and hiking.

REFERENCES

My complete dossier is available from the Placement
Office, Texas Christian University, Fort Worth, TX
76119-6811.

time professional jobs, you will probably need a two-page résumé to present your experience adequately. You might want to experiment with preparing a two-page chronological résumé, as Anna Cassetti has done (Figure 8.3) and a one-page bullet résumé (explained on page 271), as Donald Kitto-Klein has done in the letter in Figure 8.8.

What Should You Exclude from a Résumé?

Knowing what to exclude from a résumé is as important as knowing what to include. Here are some details to exclude from your résumé:

- salary demands or expectations
- preferences for work schedules, days off, or overtime
- comments about fringe benefits
- travel restrictions
- reasons for leaving your last job
- your photograph (unless you are applying for a modeling or acting job)
- comments about your family, spouse, or children
- height, weight, hair or eye color
- any handicaps

Save any questions or preferences you have for the interview. The résumé should be written appropriately to get you that interview.

FIGURE 8.4   Résumé from a student with little job experience.

RÉSUMÉ

ANTHONY H. JONES
73 Allenwood Boulevard
Santa Rosa, California 95401-1074
(707) 555-6390

CAREER OBJECTIVE

Full-time position as a layout artist with a commercial publishing house.

EDUCATION

1992-1994   **SANTA ROSA JUNIOR COLLEGE**, A.S. degree to be awarded in May 1994
Dean's list in 1993, GPA 3.4
Major: Industrial Graphics Illustration, with specialty in design layout
Related course included:

Design Principles	Desktop Publishing
Photography	Graphic Communication

APPRENTICESHIP, McAdam Publishers

Major projects included:
Assisting layout editors.
Writing detailed reports on the kinds of designs, photographs,
and artwork used in <u>Living in Sonoma County</u>
and <u>Real Estate in Sonoma County</u> magazines.

1989-1992   **SANTA ROSA HIGH SCHOOL**
Electives included drawing, photography, and industrial arts.
Provided major artwork for student magazine, <u>Thunder</u>.

EXPERIENCE

1992-1994   **SALESPERSON**, Buchman's Department Store
(part-time)   Duties included:
Assisting customers in sporting goods and appliance departments.
Coordinated sport shop by displaying merchandise.

PERSONAL

VOLUNTEER, Santa Rosa Humane Society. Designed posters for 1993 fund drive.

REFERENCES

Mr. Albert Fong	Ms. Margaret Feinstein	Dr. Gloria Cernek-Willis
Art Department	Layout Editor	Art Department
Santa Rosa Junior College	McAdam Publishers	Santa Rosa Junior College
Santa Rosa, CA 95401-1099	Santa Rosa, CA 95401-1079	Santa Rosa, CA 95401-1099
(707) 555-6300	(707) 555-8699	(707) 555-6300

Parts of a Résumé

Name, Address, Phone

Center this information at the top of the page under the word RÉSUMÉ. (Capitalize the word RÉSUMÉ and be sure to add the two accent marks by hand if your typewriter or printer cannot.) Capitalize all the letters of your name (do not use a nickname) to make it stand out, but do not capitalize every letter of your address. Include the zip code and telephone number with the correct area code so a prospective employer can call you for an interview. If you have two addresses, it is wise to list them both. Many job seekers list a permanent (home) and a school address. It is also perfectly acceptable to list two phone numbers if one of them is where you receive messages during the day and the other in the evening, or if one is a home and the other a work number.

Career Objective Statement

One of the first things a prospective employer reads is your career objective statement, also called an employment objective. It tells your prospective employer what kind of job you are looking for and are qualified to take. Such a statement involves self-evaluation and will influence everything else you list. To write an effective one, ask yourself four basic questions: (1) What kind of job do I want? (2) What kind of job am I qualified for? (3) What kinds of skills do I possess? (4) What kinds of skills do I want to learn? Do not apply for a position that requires experience you lack or demands skills you do not possess. On the other hand, do not give the impression that you will take anything.

Define your job goal precisely so that prospective employers can measure your experience and education against their needs. You may even want to tailor your career objective statement to correspond more closely to the description of each specific job you are applying for. Be careful not to be too broad or too restricted. If your focus is too broad, you could shut yourself out of the job you are seeking. If your focus is too restricted, you might not be considered for any other related openings offered by a company. Rather than simply saying "sales work" or "law enforcement," concentrate on specific immediate and long-range goals within your chosen career, for example: "Full-time position with urban police force, eventually allowing me to gain experience in correctional counseling"; "Management trainee in personnel department, providing opportunity for professional growth and advancement in insurance counseling"; "Full-time position as staff nurse on medical-surgical unit with opportunity for primary care nursing." Demonstrate to your prospective employer your current level of competence, and, through a career objective statement, show your willingness to advance in the organization.

Depending on your background and the types of jobs you are qualified for, you might formulate two or three different career or employment objectives. Again, keep in mind that it might be to your advantage to prepare several versions of your résumé if you have access to a word processor, adapting your objective depending on the job skills a prospective employer is looking for. If you are using only one résumé, which you intend to photocopy, you might even consider omitting a career objective because the jobs you could apply for may change. If there's the slightest possibility that your career objective statement is irrelevant or wrong for an employer, you could be excluded from the competition.

Your Credentials

The order of the next two categories—Education and Experience—can vary. Generally, if you have lots of experience before or after your college work, list experiences first. Years of experience will impress a prospective employer. Note that for Anna Cassetti (Figure 8.3), Patrice Cooper Bolger (Figure 8.7), and Donald Kitto-Klein (Figure 8.8), experience is their best selling point and so they placed this category ahead of education. However, if you are still in school or a recent graduate short on job experience, list education first, as Anthony Jones (Figure 8.4) did. Maria Lopez (Figure 8.5) also decided to place her education before her job experience, because the job she was applying for required the formal training she received at Miami-Dade Community College.

Education

In listing your educational experiences, begin with your most recent education first, and then list everything significant since high school. Make sure you give the names of the schools and the dates you attended. Don't overlook any military schools you attended. Indicate when you received your latest degree, diploma, or certificate or when you expect to receive it. You need not list every school if you have transferred frequently. Do indicate your major and minor in college work and emphasize written and oral communications courses you have completed. Employers are impressed by students who can write and speak well. But remember, a résumé is not a transcript. Do not simply list a series of courses. Your goal is to convince your prospective employer that you have special abilities. Simply listing standard courses will not set you apart from hundreds of other applicants taking similar courses across the country. Moreover, an employer may not know exactly what might be covered in your college's advanced accounting course. Mention the number of credit hours you have completed and then indicate by subject area the courses in your major most relevant for the position for which you are applying.

Try to avoid vague titles such as Science 103 or Nursing IV. Instead, concentrate on the kinds of skills you learned. For example, "30 hours in planning and development courses specializing in transportation, land use, and community facilities and 12 hours in field methods of gathering, interpreting, and writing a description of survey data were required." Or state that "24 hours in my major included courses in business marketing, management, and materials in addition to 12 hours in computer science." Any computer skills you have are especially important to employers because computers are used in all areas of business and industry. You might list the computer languages you are competent in, as Donald Kitto-Klein does (Figure 8.8). Also note any laboratory work, fieldwork, internship, or cooperative educational work. It is important to an employer looking for someone with previous practical experience. List your GPA (grade point average)

FIGURE 8.5   Résumé from a student with some job experience.

RÉSUMÉ

MARIA H. LOPEZ
1725 Brooke Street
Miami, Florida 32701-2121
(305) 555-3429

Career Objective	Full-time position assisting dentist in providing dental health care and counseling and performing preventive dental treatments; especially interested in learning more about pedodontics.
Education August 1991– May 1993	**Miami-Dade Community College, Miami, Florida** Will receive A.S. degree in dental hygiene in May. Have completed nine courses in oral pathology, dental materials and specialties, periodontics, and community dental health. Currently enrolled in clinical dental hygiene program. Experienced with procedures and instruments used with oral prophylaxis techniques. Subject of major project was proper nutrition for preschoolers. Minor area of interest is psychology (twelve hours completed). Received excellent evaluations in business writing course. GPA is 3.3. Plan to take American Dental Assistants' Examination on June 2.
1984–1988	**Miami North High School, Miami, Florida** Took electives in electronics and secretarial science.
Work Experience April 1989– July 1991	**St. Francis Hospital, Miami Beach, Florida** Full-time unit clerk on the pediatric floor. Duties included ordering supplies, maintaining records, transcribing orders, and greeting and assisting visitors.
June 1988– April 1989	**Murphy Construction Company, Miami, Florida** Secretary-receptionist. Did keyboarding, filing, and mailing in small office (four employees).
Summers 1986–1987	**City of Hialeah, Florida** Water meter reader.
Personal	Health: Excellent; Bilingual: Spanish/English.

FIGURE 8.5   (Continued)

Lopez 2

Hobbies and Interests	Swimming, reading (especially applied psychology), and tennis. Have done volunteer work for church day-care center.
References	The following individuals have written letters of recommendation for my placement file, available from the Placement Center, Miami-Dade Community College, Medical Center Campus, Miami, FL 33127-2225.

Sister Mary James
Head Nurse
Pediatric Unit
St. Francis Hospital
10003 Collins Avenue
Miami Beach, FL 33141-4041
(305) 555-5113

Professor Mitchell Pellborne
Department of Dental Hygiene
Miami-Dade Community College
Medical Center Campus
Miami, FL 33127-2223
(305) 555-3872

Mildred Pecos, D.D.S.
9800 Exchange Avenue
Miami, FL 33167-6028
(305) 555-1039

Mr. Jack Murphy
1203 Francis Street
Miami, FL 33157-6819
(305) 555-6767

---

only if it is 3.0 or above and your rank in class only if you are in the top 35 percent. Otherwise, indicate your GPA in just your major or during your last term, if it is above 3.0.

Also list any academic honors you have won (dean's list, department awards, school honors, scholarships, grants, or honorable mentions). Point out if you were a finalist for an award or other honor. Similarly, if you wrote a major paper or report or did a technical project that was nominated for an award or cited by a professor for merit, record that fact, too. Indicate membership in any honor societies in your major because such participation will show that you are professionally active. You also should mention training programs (EMT, secretarial), institutes or special workshops, company-sponsored seminars you have attended, or any apprenticeships you have completed. If you have attended many of these learning programs, do not list your high school. Applicants with limited educational experience may include their high school, the date of graduation, and, if helpful, any special training related to their current work (shops, labs, trips) and any honors. As a rule, though, high school activities should be deemphasized.

Experience

This is the most important category for many employers. It shows them that you have held jobs before and that you are responsible. Beginning with your most recent position, include both full- and part-time work, and list the dates, company name, titles you held, and major responsibilities. Do not mention why you left a job. Give the most attention to your latest, most relevant position. If it happens to be your second most recent position, keep the correct order, but spend more time on it. Discuss jobs that you held eight or nine years ago only if your experiences then are relevant to the position you are looking for now. If these jobs were not relevant, just list the places of employment or do not mention them at all.

In describing your position, emphasize any responsibility you had that involved handling money, other employees, customer accounts, services, programs, or writing letters and reports. Prospective employers are interested in your leadership abilities, financial shrewdness, tact in dealing with the public, and communication skills. They are also favorably impressed by promotions you may have earned.

Provide a short description of your duties and achievements. This is the place to use your "selling clauses" (pages 259–260). Don't just say you "worked for a newspaper"—your prospective employer won't know if you wrote editorials, sold advertising space, or delivered papers. Perhaps you were an assistant to the ads editor and were responsible for arranging and verifying copy. Say so. That is impressive and informative. Rather than saying that you were a secretary, indicate that you wrote business letters, organized files, prepared schedules for part-time help in an office of twenty-five people, or assisted the manager in preparing accounts. If you were an assistant manager of a restaurant or fast-food establishment, you might say you wrote daily reports on the status of perishable goods, communicated with distributors, and so forth.

Do not exaggerate or lie about your job duties. It will catch up with you. Don't call yourself an assistant buyer when you were a sales clerk. If you were a clerical assistant to an attorney, don't sell yourself as a paralegal. Do not inflate your role to the point of calling a receptionist a "communications consultant" or a waiter a "food services manager." But don't assume that your work experience was so routine, so ordinary, that it was unimportant and could not help you in your job search. You need to show your prospective employer that no matter what you did, you did it well, exceptionally well in fact. For example, rather than just saying you were a nurse's aide, include some selling clauses about working with patients and assisting the nursing staff. Emphasize your responsibilities and how you carried them out professionally as part of a health care team. Look at Donald Kitto-Klein's résumé (Figure 8.8) to see how he uses effective selling clauses to describe the skills that he acquired through several positions.

If you have held many jobs, which ones should you list, and which ones should you omit? As a general rule, highlight whatever positions are most relevant for the job you are seeking now. Your summer job as a lifeguard who knew life-saving techniques may help you in finding a position as a respiratory therapist. Waiting on tables is good experience for candidates who want to obtain a position with a hospitality chain or a food-service organization. Do not forget jobs you may have had at school—stacking books in the library, typing for a teacher, cleaning buildings, tutoring. Employers are not impressed by baby-sitting or lawn-mowing jobs, however, unless you can relate those duties to the position you are seeking. Certainly, if you were looking for a job in horticulture, any experience you had with lawns, plants, or trees would be of interest to an employer.

If you have had several jobs in the last ten or twenty years, list only those in which your responsibilities were significant and relevant to your present search for a job. Avoid stringing out five or six temporary jobs (each under three months). Combine all of them into one brief statement or omit them. Remember, space is at a premium on your résumé. If you have been a full-time mother for ten years before returning to school or the job market, indicate the management skills you developed in running a household and any community or civic service, as Patrice Cooper Bolger does in her résumé in Figure 8.7. Note how she relates her family and community accomplishments to the specific job she seeks.

Personal (*Optional*)

Federal employment laws prohibit discrimination on the basis of sex, race, national origin, religion, or marital status. But if you think that any of this personal information might help land you the job, then you are free to include it. For example, if you are applying for a sales position requiring extensive travel, mentioning that you are single would inform the employer that you do not have family obligations to restrict you. Moreover, if you are applying for a position in a child day-care center or one as a teacher's aide, the fact that you have children may be important to your employer. Other pertinent personal details include any foreign languages you speak or any special licenses and certificates you hold. For example, if you are bilingual in Spanish, Vietnamese, or Chinese and are applying for a position in customer relations work in a bank or hospital, list that fact. It will be a drawing card with your employer. If you have already passed nursing state boards or earned a pilot's license, state that by indicating your appropriate license numbers. Ultimately, common sense dictates that you reveal only personal information that is required or that underscores your qualifications for the job.

Hobbies or Interests (*Optional*)

This category is of least value to a prospective employer, *if there is no connection between it and the rest of your résumé*. Of course, if a pastime, sport, or hobby has a direct bearing on the kind of job you are applying for or the kinds of subjects you studied in school, then by all means list and briefly describe it. For example, the following activities may be appropriate for careers listed after them: weight lifting for construction work; photography for advertising; volunteer work for nursing or social work; gardening for a horticultural position; civic work for law enforcement. Include extracurricular activities or community service, especially if you held some office (treasurer of the local Lions Club, manager of a college basketball team). Exclude such obvious interests as reading, meeting new people, or listening to music.

References

You can inform readers of your résumé that you will provide references on request or that they can obtain a copy of your dossier from your placement center; or you can list the names, titles, addresses, and telephone numbers of three or four individuals directly on your résumé. Prospective employers can then write to you, ask for your dossier, or directly write or call the individuals whose names have been given. Listing the names of your references is useful only when they are well known in a community or belong to the same profession in which you are seeking employment. In these cases you profit from the magic a recognizable name or title gives you. If you list your references on your résumé, include no more than three or four names.

In this section of your résumé, you may also want to indicate that you have a portfolio of your work that can be sent to a prospective employer.

Organizing Your Résumé by Function or Skill Areas

The résumés in Figures 8.3–8.5 are organized chronologically. Information about the job applicants is listed year by year under two main categories—Education and Experience. This is the traditional way to organize a résumé. It is straightforward and easy to read, and employers find it acceptable. The chronological sequence works especially well when you can show a clear continuity toward progress in your career through your job(s) and in schoolwork or when you want to apply for a similar job with another company. A chronological résumé is appropriate for students with limited experience who want to emphasize recent educational achievements.

There are other ways to organize a résumé as well. Depending on your experiences and accomplishments, you might organize your résumé according to *function* or *skill areas*. According to this plan, you would *not* list your information chronologically within categories labeled "Experience" and "Education." Instead, you would sort your achievements and abilities—whether from coursework, jobs, extracurricular activities, or technical skills—into two to four key skill areas. Some of these areas might be labeled "Sales," "Public Relations," "Training," "Management," "Research," "Technical Capabilities," "Counseling," "Group Leadership," "Communications," "Working with People," "Computer Skills," "Problem-Solving Skills," and so forth. Under each area you would list three to five points illustrating your achievements in that area. Skills or functional résumés are often called *bullet résumés* because they offer a list of the candidate's main strengths, each introduced by a bullet. Some employers prefer the bullet résumé because they can skim the candidate's list of qualifications in a few seconds.

The important feature of a functional résumé is that you try to discover and emphasize those major strengths or skills in which you believe a prospective employer is most interested. To draft a functional résumé successfully, you must first have a clear idea about the type of job you are seeking.

Figure 8.6 (p. 272) shows what Anna Cassetti's chronological résumé (Figure 8.3) might look like if she had organized it according to function. Note how the three functional areas she selected ("Sales/Financial Management," "Public Relations," and "Business Communication") effectively allowed her to capitalize on her diverse experiences.

Advantages of a Functional / Skills Résumé

A functional résumé has a number of advantages for some job seekers. Since it does not tie a job candidate to a strict chronological account, a functional résumé

FIGURE 8.6   Anna Cassetti's résumé organized by function, or skill areas.

RÉSUMÉ
ANNA C. CASSETTI

Home
6457 South Blackstone Avenue
Fort Worth, Texas 76321-6733
(817) 555-5657

Office
MacMurray Real Estate
1700 Ross Boulevard
Haltom City, TX 77320-1700
(817) 555-7211

CAREER OBJECTIVE

Full-time sales position with large real estate office in the Phoenix or Tucson area with specific opportunities in real estate appraisals and tax consulting.

SALES/ FINANCIAL MANAGEMENT SKILLS

- Licensed (Texas) real estate appraiser with extensive knowledge of real estate codes, appraisal procedures, and market conditions
- Achieved notable success in selling residential property in Fort Worth
- Served as a tax consultant with special interest and competence in real estate sales
- Performed general banking procedures as chief teller
- Responsible for maintaining, purchasing, and ordering supplies for ship's stores in U.S. Navy

PUBLIC RELATIONS SKILLS

- Have developed positive, professional image in helping clients select appropriate property for their needs and income
- Counseled commercial and individual clients about taxes
- Supervised, trained, and coordinated the activities of six bank tellers
- Established rapport in assisting customers with their banking needs
- Chaired a financial committee at Grace Presbyterian Church, Fort Worth, Texas

FIGURE 8.6   (Continued)

Cassetti 2

<table>
<tr>
<td>BUSINESS COMMUNICATION SKILLS</td>
<td>

• Prepared standard real estate appraisals
• Wrote in-depth business reports on appraisal procedures, property management problems, and banking policies affecting real estate transactions
• Proficient in Corpsheet and other spreadsheet programs
• Conducted small group training and sales sessions

</td>
</tr>
<tr>
<td>EDUCATION</td>
<td>

B.S. in real estate management, 1991
Texas Christian University, Fort Worth.
Advanced course work taken in business, finance, and real estate; minor in data processing

Diploma, Basic Income Tax Preparation, 1984
H&R Block, Westover Hills, Texas

</td>
</tr>
<tr>
<td>EMPLOYMENT HISTORY</td>
<td>

MacMurray Real Estate, Haltom City, Texas: 1992–present; sales agent

Dallman Federal Savings and Loan, Inc., Fort Worth 1986–1991; Chief Teller

H&R Block, Westover Hills, Texas: Sept.–Dec. 1986; consultant, tax preparer

Cruckshank's Hardware Store, Fort Worth, Texas: 1983–1985; salesperson

U.S. Navy, San Diego, California (last duty station): 1979–1983; stores manager; honorably discharged with rank of Petty Officer, Third Class

</td>
</tr>
<tr>
<td>HOBBIES AND INTERESTS</td>
<td>

Golfing; hiking; worked with Junior Achievement advising teenagers about business management

</td>
</tr>
<tr>
<td>REFERENCES</td>
<td>

Complete dossier is available from the Placement Office, Texas Christian University, Fort Worth, TX 76119-6811.

</td>
</tr>
</table>

can offer a useful, productive way to fill in gaps in education or employment. If you were laid off, left school for several years, or moved around, you do not have to worry about accounting for the gaps in time. Note how Patrice Cooper Bolger profitably uses a functional résumé format in Figure 8.7. She was out of school for more than ten years because of family commitments, yet she uses the experiences she acquired during those years to her advantage in her résumé organized by "Skills, Responsibilities, Experiences." She successfully translated her many accomplishments in managing a home and working on charitable and community projects into marketable skills of great interest to a prospective employer. A functional résumé also clearly emphasizes general skills acquired over a long period of time, so individuals who have had many different types of jobs in diverse fields may prefer to write a functional rather than a chronological résumé, as Donald Kitto-Klein does in Figure 8.8. Finally, unlike a chronological résumé, a functional résumé does not force the job seeker to emphasize his or her most recent experience or educational achievement at the expense of an earlier accomplishment.

Although functional résumés have many advantages, we need to point out a warning in using them. Some employment counselors advise job seekers to prepare a chronological and a functional skills résumé, because employers may want to have a chronology of the candidate's experience as well. You should have both types of résumé on hand.

Preparing a Skills Résumé

When you prepare a functional or skills résumé, start with your name, address, telephone number, and career objective, just as in a chronological résumé. To find the best two or three functional areas to include, use the prewriting strategies (especially clustering and brainstorming) discussed in Chapter 2 (pages 29-31). Think of your skills areas as the common denominators that cross job and educational boundaries—the common threads that link and highlight your diverse experiences. Note how Donald Kitto-Klein (Figure 8.8) was able to pull together a series of related, marketable skills from the many different jobs he held over the last several years. After you discover and suitably revise the information to be included in your categories, only briefly list your educational and work experiences, as Anna Cassetti in Figure 8.6, Patrice Cooper Bolger in Figure 8.7, and Donald Kitto-Klein in Figure 8.8 do.

You might want to prepare two different versions of your résumé—a chronological as well as a functional one—to see which sells your talents best. Again, get the advice of your instructor or placement counselor about which one works best for you.

The Appearance of Your Résumé

The appearance of your résumé is as important as its content. It should be inviting and pleasing to the eye. Employers may receive as many as two hundred résumés for one position and spend as little as sixty to ninety seconds on each. Preparing a résumé involves skills highly valued on the job—neatness, the ability to organize and summarize, and most important, a sense of proportion. If your résumé is professional looking, employers will predict that the work you do for them will be

FIGURE 8.7   Patrice Cooper Bolger's résumé organized by skill areas.

RÉSUMÉ
PATRICE COOPER BOLGER
1215 Lakeview
Westhampton, Michigan 46532
616-555-4772

EMPLOYMENT OBJECTIVE   Seek full-time position as public affairs officer in health care, educational, or charitable facility

SKILLS, RESPONSIBILITIES, EXPERIENCES

Organizational Communication

- **Delivered** 20 presentations to neighborhood and civic groups on educational and civic issues
- **Transcribed** minutes and helped formulate agenda as president for large, local PTA for last 6 1/2 years
- **Possess** excellent keyboard skills and knowledge of Wordmatch 5.4
- **Updated** and **maintained** computerized mailing lists for Teens in Trouble and Foster Parents' Association

Money Management

- **Spearheaded** 3 major fundraising drives (total of $120,000 collected)
- **Prepared** and **implemented** large family budget (3 children; 8 foster children) for 15 years
- **Served as financial secretary**, Broad Street United Methodist Church for 4 years
- **Awarded** "Volunteer of the Year" (1991) by Michigan Foster Child Placement Agency for Budget Planning

Administration

- **Organized** volunteers for American Kidney Fund (last 5 years)
- **Established** and **oversaw** neighborhood carpool (17 drivers; more than 50 children) for 7 years
- **Coordinated** after-school tutoring program for Teens in Trouble; president since 1990

EDUCATION   A.A. Metropolitan Community College, 1985

B.S. Mid-Michigan College, expected 1995; major: public administration; minor: psychology. GPA 3.35

WORK EXPERIENCE   Secretary, 1978–1987 (full and part-time): Merrymount Plastics; Foley and Wasson; Westhampton Health Dept.; G & K Electric

Assembly Line Worker, 1975–1977, Universal Motors

REFERENCES   Available on request.

FIGURE 8.8   Donald Kitto-Klein's résumé organized by skill areas.

RÉSUMÉ

DONALD KITTO-KLEIN

56 South Ardmore Way	Tazewell Industries
Petersburg, NY 15438	Grand Banks, NY 15532
(716) 555-9032	(716) 555-4800, Ext. 5398

EMPLOYMENT OBJECTIVE   Supervisory position in Computer Maintenance and Repair Department

COMPUTER LANGUAGES   Pascal, Basic, Fortran

SYSTEMS EXPERIENCE   IBM PC, IBM 370, Macintosh

COMPUTER MAINTENANCE / REPAIR SKILLS
- Serviced PCs on regular basis for 3 1/2 years
- Worked extensively on IBM and Macintosh spreadsheet / database software
- Modified software billing program
- Coordinated maintenance / repair activities

PEOPLE SKILLS
- Assisted customers in selecting hardware and software
- Supervised three computer repair technicians
- Worked closely with computer manufacturers and suppliers to minimize hardware down time
- Elected to employee benefits committee
- Promoted to first-shift repair team leader

COMMUNICATION SKILLS
- Collaboratively wrote safety manual for power company road crews
- Taught in-house training sessions on computer maintenance, protection, and viruses
- Devised routing systems to expedite work orders and follow-up procedures
- Coordinated small groups meeting in systems analysis

EMPLOYMENT   Tazewell Industries, Team Leader, Maintenance, 1991–present
Business Graphics and Computers Store, Salesperson, 1987–1991
U.S. Army, Specialist, 4/E, 1981–1987
Grand Valley Power Company, Repairperson, 1979–1980

EDUCATION   A.S., Grand Valley Technical Institute, 1991
U.S. Army schools in computer programs, 1982–1986

REFERENCES   Available on request.

done the same way. A résumé can make that good first impression for you; a poorly prepared one assures that you will not get a second chance.

Given the short time employers spend scanning each résumé, you cannot expect them to hunt for information about you. Help potential employers spot your achievements by making your résumé easy to read with wide margins, dark type, and clearly divided sections with headings. Employers will also be looking for accuracy (a spelling mistake can be fatal) and consistency.

There are a variety of ways you can prepare your résumé. You can take it to a printer, who for a relatively modest fee will phototypeset your résumé, giving it a highly professional look. This is what Anna Cassetti did (Figures 8.3 and 8.6). You will reap many advantages this way—your résumé will look neat, professional, crisp—but you will have to buy at least twenty-five to fifty copies of the same one. There is no way to tailor your résumé if the need arises; you cannot add, delete, or emphasize information as your job search progresses.

Another option is to have your résumé produced on a word processor, as did María H. Lopez, Patrice Cooper Bolger, and Donald Kitto-Klein (Figures 8.5, 8.7, 8.8). You can take advantage of different sizes of type and use boldface or italics to separate and highlight information. But do not make the size of print so small that it is difficult for a prospective employer to read. Stay as close to 10-point type as possible. Be careful that you do not overuse visual effects. You can also justify your margins (that is, make the right side of your résumé line up just as the left-hand side does). Perhaps the greatest advantage of putting your résumé on a disk is that you can easily add or delete information without having to type the entire résumé over again. Some software programs can even make your word-processed résumé look like it was typeset by a printer.

Still another option is to hire a professional typist to do your résumé. Be sure to explain in detail how you want it to look.

Whatever method you choose, keep in mind these important rules. Avoid the twin dangers of crowding too much information on the page or of leaving huge, highly conspicuous chunks of white space at the bottom and sides. A crowded résumé suggests that you cannot summarize, whereas too much blank space points to a lack of achievements. You should, of course, leave white space between categories to emphasize certain points and to make reading your résumé easier. Study Figures 8.3–8.8 again. Type or print a number of versions to experiment with spacing.

Print or type your résumé on good quality 8 1/2" × 11" white or off-white bond paper (at least 20 lb. stock). In fact, recruiters in one study preferred white to colored paper.[2] Never use flimsy computer paper with perforated strips. If you use a word processor, avoid running your résumé off on a dot matrix printer. Use a letter-quality or laser printer.

Your prospective employer will expect a professional-looking copy, so never send a carbon, mimeographed, or thermofaxed copy of your résumé. And avoid

---

[2] John Penrose, "A Discrepancy Analysis of the Job-Getting Process and a Study of Résumé Techniques," *Journal of Business Communication* 21 (Summer 1984): 3–15.

FIGURE 8.9   A poor résumé.

RÉSUMÉ

JAMES L. McPHERSON
33 North Platte Road   *Poor alignment*
Noland, New Mexico   *No zip code*
                         No telephone number

                    Spelling
PERSONNEL:

            ⌐Age: 22yrs. 6 mos.   *Spelling*   Wieght: 156 lbs
            │Marital Status: Engaged   Height: 5'10"   *Abbreviation*
Not needed│Religion: Presbyterian   Health: O.K.   *Slang*

CAREER OBJECTIVE: I like to work outdoors and want
Poor typing   to get any suitable job *Too broad*
                           in the forrestry industry.

EDUCATION: *Spelling*
1989–1994   Attended Noland Junior College,
                           Noland, N.M. 84546. I took courses
                           in English, Outdoor Recreation,
Listing courses at random Forrest Surveying, Forrest *Spelling*
says nothing about specific Management, Forest Economics,
skills   Park Administration, Human
          Spelling   Rolations, Recreation
          Margin   Maintenance, Communications
                           and Mathematics, and Science. I
          Why   did better my secondyear   *Typing*
          mention?   than my first. In my English and
                           Communications courses I wrote
          Spelling   papers and delivered sppeeches
                           about the forrest. Also, I went on
                           two or three lengthy field trips /
                           in the north.   *Margin*

                           What skills did he learn?
Wrong   1889   I attended Noland Junior College
century   part-time. *Why a separate entry?*

                                   Hyphen missing
             1988   I graduated from Noland High
                           School, where I played basket-
                           ball my third year and fourth year.
                           I also was the team co-captain.
                           Helped out with The Torch.
        Vague phrase
                                        What is it?

FIGURE 8.9 (Continued)

Underscore	EXPERIENCE:	Worked for Walgreen's. Address:
	1988—1989 *Doing what?*	754 South Loma Blvd. Also I joined
	Abbreviation	the (N. Mexico) National Guard. We
		were sent to Ft. Carson for our
		basic training. *Why mention Ft. Carson?*
		What does he do in the Guard?
Capitalize	Hobbies:	I like swimming, jogging, and water
		polo. *So what?*
	REFERENCES:	

No telephone numbers or zip codes

Mr. Henry R. Pepeer	Dr. John Lyons	Alice McPherson
P.O. Box 768	Noland Junior College	33 N. Platte
Noland, N.M.	Noland, N.M.	Noland, N.M.
Who is he?	*What department?*	*Relative is not an impartial reference*

rushing to the nearest photocopy machine in the library or student union to make a copy. It may come out with black dots or streaks on it. Try to locate the best-working photocopier you can. And try to have your résumé duplicated on bond paper, too. It will be worth the extra pennies.

Proofread your résumé to make sure that it is letter perfect. Ask two or three people to check it for you, too. Because you will be supplying many prospective employers with a copy of your résumé, a single error in it would appear each time you sent it out. Check and double-check the spelling of any words or names about which you may be unsure. Avoid strikeovers, crossed-out letters, or crookedly printed lines. Figure 8.9 contains a poorly prepared résumé and the reasons why it is bad. Figure 8.10 (p. 280) shows an evaluation form used by six experts from business, industry, and education who judged student résumés prepared for a workshop at the University of Colorado, Boulder. After you complete a final draft of your résumé, evaluate it according to the ten criteria on the form. Then revise and edit until it satisfies these criteria and is ready for final typing or printing.

FIGURE 8.10   A résumé evaluation form.

1. Clarity of job objective	not on résumé ☐	very unclear				extremely clear	
		1	2	3	4	5	

2. Essence of educational informa-tion	not on résumé ☐	too much or too little information				extremely concise and informative	
		1	2	3	4	5	

3. Description of job experience with skills emphasis	not on résumé ☐	poor description of skills				excellent description of skills	
		1	2	3	4	5	

4. Additional positive information that supports job objective	not on résumé ☐	irrelevant additional information				very supportive additional information	
		1	2	3	4	5	

5. Correctness of usage, spelling, and grammer	poorly written and typed				well written and typed	
	1	2	3	4	5	

6. Organization	poorly organized				extremely well organized	
	1	2	3	4	5	

7. Ease of reading (layout)	very difficult to read				very easy to read	
	1	2	3	4	5	

8. Quality of reproduction (paper, print)	poor quality				excellent quality	
	1	2	3	4	5	

9. Attractiveness	not attractive				very attractive	
	1	2	3	4	5	

10. Overall rating	poor résumé				excellent résumé	
	1	2	3	4	5	

Writing a Letter of Application

Along with your résumé, you must send your prospective employer a letter of application, one of the most important pieces of correspondence you may ever write. Its goal is to get you an interview and ultimately the job. Letters you write in applying for jobs should be personable, professional, and persuasive—the three Ps. Knowing how the letter of application and résumé work together and how they differ can give you a better idea of how to begin your letter.

How the Letter and Résumé Differ

The résumé is a compilation of facts—a record of dates, your important achievements, names, places, addresses, and jobs. You will have your résumé duplicated, and you will send a copy to each prospective employer. Your letter of application, however, is much more personal. You must write a new, original letter to each prospective employer. Photocopied letters of application say that you did not care enough, that you did not want to spend the time and energy to answer the employer's ad personally. Each letter of application should be tailored to a specific job. It should respond precisely to the kinds of qualifications the employer seeks. The letter of application is a sales letter emphasizing and applying the most relevant details (of education, experience, and talents) on your résumé. In short, the résumé contains the raw material that the letter of application transforms into a finished and highly marketable product—you!

Résumé Facts You Exclude from a Letter of Application

The letter of application should not simply repeat the details listed in your résumé. In fact, the following details belong only on your résumé and should not be restated in the letter: (1) personal data including license or certificate numbers, (2) the specific names of courses in your major, (3) your hobbies, and (4) the names and addresses of all your references. Duplicating these details in your letter gives no new information to help persuade prospective employers that you are the individual they are seeking.

Finding Information About Your Prospective Employer

One of the best ways to sell yourself to future employers is to demonstrate that you have some knowledge of their company. A number of years ago, a college was looking for an instructor and was pleased with one candidate who referred to the college's specific courses by their numbers in her letter of application. This individual went to the profitable trouble of reading the college's catalog before applying.

Do a little similar homework; investigate the job and the company. It is to your advantage to find out as much as possible about a prospective employer. Some things you need to find out include whether the company is privately or publicly owned; what its chief products and/or services are; whether it has subsidiaries or is a subsidiary of a larger company in the United States or overseas.

The following directories will give you much useful information about businesses and industries you are thinking of applying to.

- *Million Dollar Directory.* Parsippany, NJ: Dun's Marketing Services, 1959–present.

  Published annually, this multivolume directory records alphabetically all U.S. companies and U.S. subsidiaries of foreign companies with a net worth of $500,000. It will give you such vital information as company addresses and telephone numbers, the names of major executives, the chief divisions of the company, the types of products and/or services the company supplies, the annual sales figures, and the number of individuals employed by the company.

- *Directory of Corporate Affiliations: Who Owns Whom.* Wilmette, IL: National Register Publishing, 1967–present.

  This directory, published annually, is divided into a number of sections offering an alphabetical listing of subsidiaries with the names of their parent companies; the names and addresses of these parent companies together with the names of the company executives; and the same information for the parent company's subsidiaries.

- *Standard and Poor's Register of Corporations, Directors and Executives.* New York: Standard and Poor's, 1928–present.

  This volume of a three-volume reference work lists mostly U.S. companies, their addresses, executives, annual sales, and number of employees. It also provides biographical information about the company's executives, the location of the company, and any subsidiaries.

- *Principal International Businesses.* London: Dun and Bradstreet International, Ltd., 1974–present.

  This annual directory lists companies by country and then alphabetically within each country. As with the other directories above, it supplies the company address as well as the location of any subsidiaries, chief executives, sales volume, and number of employees.

Figure 8.11 reprints part of a page from *Standard and Poor's Register.* You can also find information about prospective employers in the *Thomas Register of American Manufacturers, Forbes* magazine (especially the "Annual Directory" issue published in May), and the issue of *Fortune* magazine listing the "Fortune 500" companies. The *Business Periodicals Index* (see pages 324–326) is also a helpful guide to stories written about different companies in various business publications (e.g., the *Wall Street Journal* or *Money* magazine). You can also obtain information from the company itself by writing an inquiry letter (see pages 199–201) for brochures, descriptions, company magazines, and annual reports a number of months before you actually apply. Check with the Chamber of Commerce. Ask people who work in the company.

FIGURE 8.11   Portion of a company description from *Standard and Poor's Register of Corporations*.

Digi International Inc.

CAPITALIZATION (Sept. 30 '91)

LONG TERM DEBT—None.
STOCK—   Auth. Shs. Outstg. Shs.
Pfd. $0.01 par............   2,000,000
None
Common $0.05 par.....   *15,000,000
†13,487,106
  *Incl. 656,250 optioned to employees and others, with 688,350 for future grants— all adjtd. for 3-for-2 split Mar. 16, 1992.
  †Adjtd. for 3-for-2 split Mar. 16, 1992.

CORPORATE BACKGROUND

Company is a leading producer of data communications hardware and software products that permit microcomputers to function as the central processing unit of a multi-user computer systems, allowing one or more persons to share the computing power, as well as the programs and data, of one microcomputer. Principal products control input and output (I/O) of data between a microcomputer's central processing unit (CPU) and terminals and other serial devices. Products allow up to 128 terminals to connect with a single microcomputer by means of a single expansion slot and incorporating on-board microprocessors that relieve the microcomputer's CPU from handling a substantial number of I/O functions, thereby preserving power of the host microcomputer.

Company's product line has been broadened to include a wide array of connectivity solutions that enhance the operations of multi-user computer systems in a variety of operation system environments.

SUBSIDIARIES—wholly owned—
DigiBoard, Inc. F.S.C.
DigiBoard GmbH
Arnet Corp.

PROPERTY—Plants are leased in St. Louis Park, Minn., and Nashville, Tenn.

EMPLOYEES— Sept. 30, 1991, 166.

INCORPORATED in Del. in July, 1989, to merge Digiboard, Inc., a Minn. company incorporated in July, 1985.

Mar. 1, 1991, acquired Arnet Corp., Nashville, Tenn., a producer of data communications hardware and software products that permit microcomputers to function as multiuser systems, for $5,500,000 and the assumption of certain liabilities.

CHAIRMAN & CHIEF EXEC OFFICER, J. P. Schinas; PRES & CHIEF OPER OFFICER, Mykola Moroz; V-P, CHIEF FIN OFFICER & TREAS, G. A. Wall; SECY, J. E. Nicholson; V-Ps, G. L. Deaner, D. D. Henry.

DIRECTORS—W. K. Drake, R. E. Eichhorn, R. E. Offerdahl, J. P. Schinas, David Stanley, Mykola Moroz.

OFFICE—6400 Flying Cloud Drive, Eden Prairie, MN 55344 (Tel.: 612-943-9020). ANNUAL MEETING—In Jan.

STOCK DATA

COMMON OFFERED—

Date	Shares	Price	Comm.
10-5-89..............	*1,300,000	$10.00	*$0.73
9-19-91..............	†1,500,000	23.75	†1.37

  *William Blair & Co., et al., incl. 300,000 for stockholders. An additional 195,000 shs. (100,000 by Co.; 95,000 by selling stockholders) were available to cover over-allotments— 105,000 taken (51,795 from Co.; 53,205 from selling stockholders).
  †William Blair & Co., Piper, Jaffray & Hopwood Inc.; incl. 500,000 for stockholders.

STOCKHOLDERS— Nov. 30, 1990, 128 (of record). After sale of Com. Sept. 19, 1991, J. P. Schinas owned or controlled 16.3% of the Com. and R. E. Offerdahl 6.6%.

TRANSFER AGENT & REGISTRAR— Norwest Bank Minn., N.A., South St. Paul.

Reprinted from Standard and Poor's "Corporation Records," vol. 53, No. 2, Sect. 2 (April 1992), by permission.

Except in response to a blind ad, write directly to the individual responsible for hiring—the personnel officer, the supervisor, the director of nurses, the district manager. You can call the company and ask the switchboard operator to give you the name of this individual. Ask for the correct spelling of the name, too.

Drafting the Letter of Application

The letter of application should follow the standard conventions discussed in Chapter 6. It should be typed neatly or printed on a plain white sheet of good bond paper, 8 1/2" × 11". Make sure that your typewriter or printer works perfectly and that the type does not appear faded. Proofread meticulously; a spelling error here will harm your chances. Double-check the spelling of your prospective employer's name and the company name. Call the company switchboard, if necessary, to make sure you have the right person and the right spelling. Never send your letter to "To Whom It May Concern" or "Personnel Director." Try to get an individual's name, except in the case of a blind ad. Avoid abbreviations ("thru" for "through," "nite" for "night"), slang expressions, or unnecessary jargon. Don't forget the "you attitude." Employers are not impressed by boastful proclamations ("I am the most efficient and effective safety engineer," "I am a natural-born nurse"). Trying to appeal to an employer's sympathies will not work either. One student wrote that he needed the job to pay tuition and a car loan. The employer was not impressed. Another applicant spent so much time on advantages to her that she forgot the employer entirely: "I have worked with this kind of equipment before, and this experience will give me the edge in running it. Moreover, I can adjust more quickly to my working environment."

The best letters of application are to the point and are readable. Your letter will be seen as an example of your writing skills. Keep in mind that employers will receive many letters and that yours will have to compete for their time. You want your letter to be placed in the "definitely interview" category discussed on page 000. A letter of application should not exceed one page; it is to your advantage to keep it short. However, you should not write a telegraphic message of only two or three sentences. Strive for brevity and clarity. Emphasize your qualifications with specific evidence; don't let them get lost in a sea of words. A three-paragraph letter will be sufficient for most candidates. Figures 8.12-8.15 (pp. 285-289) contain model letters. Anthony Jones (Figure 8.12) and Maria Lopez (Figure 8.13 [p. 286]) have less job experience and rely mostly on their educational training. Compare their letters with those written by Patrice Cooper Bolger (Figure 8.14 [p. 288]) and Donald Kitto-Klein (Figure 8.15 [p. 289]).

Above all, remind yourself to take advantage of the techniques involved in the process of writing. In your eagerness to get your letter of application in the mail, don't be tempted to send a prospective employer your first draft. A first or even second draft can rarely sell your abilities as well as a third, fourth, or even fifth revision can. Write and rewrite your application letter until you are convinced it presents you in the best light possible.

The discussion that follows will give you some suggestions on how to do just that.

The First Paragraph

The first paragraph of your application letter is your introduction. It should answer three questions: (1) why you are writing (by mentioning the specific position you are applying for), (2) where or how you learned of the job, and (3) what your most important qualification is for the job. Begin your letter by stating directly that you are writing to apply for a job. Don't say that you "want to apply for the job," for such an opening raises the question "Why don't you then?" And avoid starting off in an unconventional or boastful way: "Are you looking for a dynamic, young, and talented photographer?" Do not begin with a question; be more positive and professional. If you learned of the job through a newspaper or journal, make sure that you underscore its title.

> I am applying for the food-service manager position
> you advertised in the May 10 edition of the <u>Los
> Angeles Times</u>.

FIGURE 8.12   Letter of application from Anthony Jones, a recent graduate with little job experience.

73 Allenwood Boulevard
Santa Rosa, CA 95401-1074

May 23, 1994

Ms. Jocelyn Nogasaki
Personnel Manager
Megalith Publishing Company
1001 Heathcliff Row
San Francisco, CA 94123-7707

Dear. Ms. Nogasaki:

I am applying for the layout editor position advertised on
May 22 in the San Francisco Chronicle. Early next month, I
will receive an A.S. degree in industrial graphics
illustration from Santa Rosa Junior College.

With a special interest in the publishing industry, I have
successfully completed more than forty credit hours in
courses directly related to layout design, where I acquired
skills in drafting, reproduction processes, and production
techniques. You might like to know that many of the design
patterns of Megalith publications were used as models in my
graphic communications and photographic technology classes.
My studies have also led to practical experience at McAdam
Publishers, as part of my Santa Rosa apprenticeship program.
Working at McAdam's, I was responsible for assisting the
design department in photo research and in the preparation of
mockups. Other related experience I have had includes artwork
and proofreading for the student magazine, Thunder. As you
will note on the enclosed résumé, I have also had experience
in displaying merchandise at Buchman's Department Store.

I would appreciate the opportunity to discuss with you my
qualifications in industrial graphics. After June 12, I will
be available for an interview at any time that is convenient
for you.

Sincerely yours,

Anthony H Jones

Anthony H. Jones

Encl. Résumé

FIGURE 8.13   **Letter of application from Maria Lopez, a recent graduate with some job experience.**

1725 Brooke Street
Miami, FL 32701-2121

May 14, 1993

Dr. Marvin Hendrady
Suite 34
Medical/Dental Plaza
839 Causeway Drive
Miami, FL 32706-2468

Dear Dr. Hendrady:

Mr. Mitchell Pellborne, my clinical instructor at Miami-Dade Community College, informs me that you are looking for a dental hygienist to work in your northside office. I am writing to apply for that position. This month I will graduate with an A.S. degree in the dental hygienist program at Miami-Dade Community College, and I will take the American Dental Assistants Examination in early June.

I have successfully completed all course work and clinical programs in oral hygiene, anatomy, and prophylaxis techniques. During my clinical training, I received intensive practical instruction from a number of local dentists, including Dr. Mildred Pecos. Since your northside office specializes in pedodental care, you might find the subject of my major project--proper nutrition for preschoolers--especially relevant. I have also had some related job experience in working with children in a health care setting. For a year and a half, I was employed as a ward clerk on the pediatric unit at St. Francis Hospital, and my experience in greeting patients, filling out forms, and assisting the nursing staff would be valuable to you in running your office. You will find more detailed information about me and my experience in the enclosed résumé.

I would welcome the opportunity to talk with you about the position and my interest in pedodontics. I am available for an interview any time after 2:30 until June 11. After that date, I could come to your office any time at your convenience.

Sincerely yours,

Maria H. Lopez

Maria H. Lopez

Encl. Résumé

Do not waste the employer's time and your space on the page by repeating verbatim the words of the advertisement. If you learned of the job from a professor, friend, or employee at the firm, state that fact also. Next, indicate your chief qualification—you will soon graduate with an A.A. in food service, you have worked in the large restaurant of a major hotel chain, or you have ten years' experience managing a cafeteria. Select one fact that justifies your suitability for the job.

The Second Paragraph

To show why and how you are qualified for the job, the second paragraph of your application letter emphasizes your education and work background. Recent graduates with little work experience will, of course, spend more time on their education, but even if you have much experience, don't forget your education. Stress your most important educational accomplishments. Employers want to know what skills and expertise your education has given you and how those skills apply to their particular job. Simply saying that you will graduate with a degree in criminal justice does not explain how you, unlike all the other graduates of a criminal justice program, are best qualified for the job. Indicate that in thirty-six hours of course work you have specialized in industrial security and that you have twelve hours in business and communications. That says something specific. Rather than boasting that you are qualified, give the facts to prove it. If your GPA is relatively high or if you have won an award, mention that. Do not worry about repeating important information in both your letter and résumé.

After you discuss your educational qualifications, turn to your job experience. The best letters show how the two are related. Employers like to see continuity between a candidate's school and job experience. Provide that link by showing how the jobs you have held have something in common with your major—in terms of responsibility, research, customer relations, community service. Say that your course work in data processing helped you to be a better programmer for your previous employer, that your summer jobs for the local park district reinforced your studies in human services. However, do not dwell on being a nurse's aide three years ago when you have nearly completed a degree program to be an R.N. Busing tables in a restaurant is good experience, but do not let that job overshadow your current work as a management trainee for a large hotel chain.

Above all, the second paragraph of your application letter must relate your education and experience directly to the employer's job. Tell exactly how your school work and job experience qualify you to function and advance in the job advertised. Here, your homework on what the company is like should pay off. In her letter of application in Figure 8.14, Patrice Cooper Bolger demonstrates how the wealth of her previous experiences relates specifically to Tanselle Mental Health's outreach programs. Note in Figure 8.13 how Maria Lopez uses her knowledge of Dr. Hendrady's specialty in pedodontics to her advantage; in Figure 8.12 Anthony Jones profitably emphasizes how he gained his knowledge of and respect for Megalith publications.

Your second paragraph may run to six or seven sentences. You might want to spend three sentences on your educational qualifications and three on your job experience; or perhaps your work or civic and community experiences are so rich

FIGURE 8.14   Letter of application from Patrice Cooper Bolger, a recent graduate
with community and civic experience.

PATRICE COOPER BOLGER

1215 Lakeview Avenue
Westhampton, MI 46532
616-555-4772

February 10, 1994

Dr. Lindsay Bafaloukos
Tanselle Mental Health Agency
4400 West Gallagher Drive
Tanselle, MI 46392

Dear Dr. Bafaloukos:

At a recent meeting of the County Services Council, a member of your staff,
Homer Strickland, informed me that you will be hiring a public affairs
coordinator. Because of my extensive experience and commitment to
community affairs, I would appreciate your considering me for this opening.
I expect to receive my B.S. in public administration from Mid-Michigan College
next year.

For the last ten years, I have organized several community groups with
outreach programs similar to Tanselle's. I have held administrative positions in
the PTA and the Foster Parents' Association, and have been president of Teens in
Trouble, a volunteer group providing academic assistance to dysfunctional teens.
My responsibilities with Teens have included coordinating our activities with
various school programs, scheduling tutorials, and representing the organization
before community and state agencies. I have been commended, in the
community and at Mid-Michigan College, for my organizational, budgeting, and
communication skills. My twenty presentations on foster home care and Teens in
Trouble demonstrate that I am an effective speaker, a skill your agency would
find valuable. Through my course work at Mid-Michigan and my participation in
Teens and Foster Parents, I can bring the practical experience and formal
education in communication and behavioral psychology necessary to promote
Tanselle's goals. The enclosed résumé provides the details of my experience and
education.

I would enjoy discussing my work with Teens and the other organizations
with you. I am available for an interview any day after 11:00 a.m. Please reach
me at the phone number at the top of this letter.

Sincerely yours,

Patrice Cooper Bolger

Patrice Cooper Bolger

Encl. Résumé

FIGURE 8.15 **Letter of application from Donald Kitto-Klein, who has strong work experience.**

Donald Kitto-Klein

56 South Ardmore Way
Petersburg, NY 15438

(716) 555-9032

November 4, 1994

Ms. Akki Shibuto
Vice President, Operations
Patterson Corporation
Sun Valley, CA 94356

Dear Ms. Shibuto:

I am writing to apply for the position of Director of Computer Services advertised in the November issue of *Computer Marketing News*. My technical knowledge of computers and my proven ability to work with people in a large organization such as Patterson's qualify me to be a productive member of your management team.

For the last three and one-half years, I have been responsible for all phases of computer maintenance and repair at Tazewell Industries. As a regular part of my duties I have serviced and repaired 15 to 20 PCs a month as well as supervised the operation of a mainframe. I have successfully coordinated the activities of my department with Tazewell's other offices and worked closely with vendors and manufacturers. I have also prepared several training programs and regularly offer highly praised in-house training seminars. Because I have worked so effectively with Tazewell management officers in maintenance and repair, and with other Tazewell offices, I was promoted to repair team leader last year. I would like to put my ability to motivate personnel and to manage computer services to work for you and the Patterson Corporation. My educational achievements include a degree in computer technology from Grand Valley and certificates from U.S. Army schools in computers. The enclosed résumé will give you information about these and my other accomplishments.

I am eager to talk with you about what you expect from your next director and how my experience and technical skills will help you in reaching your goals. I am available for an interview at your convenience. I look forward to hearing from you.

Sincerely yours,

Donald Kitto-Klein

Donald Kitto-Klein

that you will spend four or more sentences on them, as Patrice Cooper Bolger does. At any rate, do not neglect education for experience or vice versa. Refer to your résumé, and do not forget to say that you are including it with your letter.

The Third Paragraph

The third paragraph has three functions: (1) to emphasize once again your major qualification, (2) to ask for an interview, and (3) to indicate when you are available for that interview. Paragraph three is short—about two or three sentences. End gracefully and professionally. Don't leave the reader with just one weak sentence: "I would like to have an interview at your convenience." Such a sentence does nothing to sell you. Say that you would appreciate talking with the employer further to discuss your qualifications. Then mention your chief talent. Indicate your interest in the job and give the times you are available for an interview. If you are going to a professional meeting where the employer might be present, or if you are visiting the employer's city, say so. Following are some poor ways to close the letter and reasons to avoid them.

Pushy	I would like to set up an interview with you. Please phone me to arrange a convenient time. (That's the employer's prerogative, not yours.)
Too Informal	I do not live too far from your office. Let's meet for coffee sometime next week. (Say that since you live nearby, you will be available for an interview.)
Too Humble	I know that you are busy, but I would really like to have an interview. (Say you would like to discuss your qualifications further.)
Introduces New Subject	I would like to discuss other qualifications you have in mind for the job. (How do you know what the interviewer might have in mind?)

Note how the closing paragraphs in Figures 8.12–8.15 avoid these errors.

Filling Out a Job Application

At some point in your job search, you will be asked to complete a prospective employer's application form. A recruiter may hand you a job application form at a campus interview, or you may be mailed a form in response to your letter of application. Most often, though, you will be given an application to complete when you are at the employer's office. The job application form, your letter of application, and your résumé are the three key written documents employers use to screen applicants.

Application forms can vary tremendously. But they all ask you to give information about your education, any military service, present and previous employment, references, general state of health, and reasons for wanting to work for the company or agency. Since these topics overlap with those on your résumé, bring the résumé with you to the employer's office to make sure you don't omit something important. Some forms even require you to attach your résumé. But *under no circumstances* should you attach a résumé to a blank form instead of filling the form out. Employers want their own forms completed by job seekers.

The following general guidelines can help you to complete an application form.

1. Read the instructions before you begin. Then quickly scan all the questions so you won't supply information in one spot only to find that it's asked for specifically later in the job application.
2. Answer all the questions. Some forms instruct you to put N/A (not applicable) rather than leave a space blank.
3. Print neatly, using a black or blue ball-point pen. Do not use a felt-tip pen or a pencil.
4. Double-check numbers—Social Security, driver's license, area and zip codes, registration numbers, union certificates.
5. Do not write in spaces marked "For Office Use Only."
6. Check spelling and punctuation.
7. Be as neat as you can. Do not write over the lines or in the margins or insert asterisks indicating further clarification. If you need more room to answer a question, attach a separate sheet of paper. Make sure that your name and the specific question number appear on the attached sheet.
8. Be truthful. Don't say you can type seventy words a minute when you have trouble with thirty.
9. Be as precise as possible. For "previous experience," do not just say "construction worker"; indicate "building inspector," "mason," "carpenter."
10. When asked about salary expectations, avoid extremes. If you have done your homework, you will have a sense of the established range. Do not put "minimum wage"; an employer has to give you that anyway.
11. Many applications ask you to comment on your experience and education, giving you one or two inches of space for your answer. Fill the blank space with facts, not padding. Giving just one or two small details will not sell your talents and will only point to your lack of self-expression and confidence. Many employers, including the federal government, rank prospective employees on the basis of their answers to such a question. So, as a rule of thumb, provide as much relevant information as space allows, and make sure that you are positive, not negative, about your previous position and employer.
12. Sign the application, verifying that what you have written is true and complete. Your signature is essential if you must have a security clearance or if the company has to release any of the information you have provided or obtain your permission to find out more about you.

Individuals desiring to work for one of the many branches of the U.S. government complete a "Personal Qualifications Statement." That form contains many of the kinds of questions you can expect future employers to ask you. The government, like so many employers, expects job candidates to have done their homework. The first question asks the applicant to identify the desired job by title and number—information readily available from a civil service or governmental agency. Since the federal government is the largest employer in the nation, many users of this book will complete this form. You can obtain a copy of the form from a Federal Job Information Center.

Figure 8.16 contains an application form similar to ones used by private companies. This form asks applicants to give reasons for leaving previous jobs and also requires them to write a "personal essay" stating why the company should hire them. Both of these requirements will require tact and thought. If you were fired from a past job, it is not to your advantage to simply state that fact. Indicate further relevant information, such as that the industry suffered a recession, and you were laid off or that your company merged and your office or department was eliminated. More frequently, though, your reasons for leaving a job will be financial, educational, or geographic. You may have received a better offer, decided to return to school, or planned to move to another town.

Writing the personal essay will require that you convince the employer of your sincerity and qualifications. In doing so, do not dwell on what the company can do for you. Concentrate on how your previous experience and education will help your employer; emphasize, too, your willingness to learn new techniques and skills on the job. Do not be afraid to cite specific accomplishments; your success will depend on it.

Going to an Interview

An interview can be challenging, threatening, friendly, or chatty; sometimes it is all of these. By the time you arrive at the interview stage, you are far along in your job search. Basically, there are two kinds of interviews. One is a *screening interview,* to which numerous applicants have been invited so that a company can narrow down the candidates. Campus interviews are an example of screening interviews. The other kind of interview is known as a *line interview;* the employer invites only a few select applicants to the company's office for a tour and detailed conversation.

Preparing for an Interview

An interview gives the employer a chance to see how you look, act, and react. Once in a while interviewers intentionally create stressful situations for you, such as inviting you to smoke and not providing an ashtray. But most employers do not want to trick you. They want to see how well you can talk about yourself and your work; they also want to see how well you listen and respond to their questions. At some interviews job candidates are shown a film about the company and are then given a quiz about that film. Interviewers expect applicants to be nervous, but you can free yourself of some anxiety if you know what to expect.

Interviews can last half an hour or extend to two or three days. Most often, though, an interview will last approximately one hour. It has been estimated that

FIGURE 8.16   Sample job application form.

Miller Electric Supply Company

APPLICATION FOR EMPLOYMENT

Date _____

SS# _____

PERSONAL INFORMATION

Name _____
              Last   First   Middle

Present address _____

Phone no. _____

Height _____ Weight _____

If related to anyone in our company,
state name, relationship, and position _____

EMPLOYMENT DESIRED

Position applying for _____ or _____

Health Status   Excellent _____ Good _____ Fair _____ Poor _____

EDUCATIONAL BACKGROUND

Name and location of school	Years attended	Date graduated	Subjects majored in
High school			
College			
Other			

Military service _____ Duties _____

_____

Dates _____

In case of emergency, notify:

Name _____

Address _____

Phone number _____

FIGURE 8.16 (Continued)

EMPLOYMENT RECORD

Former employer	Address	Salary & position	Reason for leaving	Dates employed

REFERENCES

Give the names of three persons not related to you whom you have known for at least one year:

Name	Address	Business	Years acquainted

Why did you leave your last job? Explain your answer in detail.

_____

_____

_____

PERSONAL ESSAY

Please state why you feel we should hire you for the position desired, including any qualifications not mentioned above. Attach another sheet if necessary.

_____

_____

_____

_____

_____

_____

_____

DO NOT WRITE BELOW THIS LINE—FOR OFFICE USE ONLY

Date interviewed _____ By _____

General appearance _____

Attitude _____

Date hired (if any) _____

Salary _____

Position _____

the applicant will do about 80 to 90 percent of the talking. Since you will be asked to speak at length, make the following preparations before your interview.

1. Do your homework about the employer—history, types of products or services provided, number of employees, location of main, branch, and overseas offices, contributions to industry or the community. Consult such relevant sources as those listed on pages 281–283.
2. Review the technical skills most relevant for the job. You might want to reread sections of a textbook, study some recent journal articles, or talk to a professor or an employee you know from the company.
3. Prepare a brief (one- or two-minute) review of your qualifications to deliver orally should you be asked about yourself. For some hints on oral presentations, see pages 676–678.
4. Bring your résumé with you. Your interviewer will have a copy on the desk, so you can be sure that its contents will be the subject of many questions. Be able to elaborate on and supplement what is on your résumé. Any extra details or information that bring your résumé up to date ("I received my degree last week"; "I'll get the results of my state board examinations in one week") will be appreciated.

Questions to Expect at an Interview

You can expect questions about your education, job experience, and ambitions. An interviewer will ask you questions about courses, schools, technical skills, and job goals. Through these questions an interviewer attempts to discover your good points as well as your bad ones. A common interviewer strategy is to postpone questions about your bad points until near the end of the interview. Once a relaxed atmosphere has been established, the interviewer thinks that you may be less reluctant to talk about your weaknesses. The following fifteen questions are typical of those you can expect from interviewers.

1. Tell us something about yourself. (Here's where the prepared one-minute oral presentation of yourself comes in handy.)
2. Why do you want to work for us? (Recall any job goals you have and apply them specifically to the job under discussion.)
3. What qualifications do you have for the job? (Mention educational achievements in addition to any relevant work experience.)
4. What could you possibly offer us that other candidates do not have? (Say "enthusiasm," being a team player, and problem-solving abilities in addition to educational achievements.)
5. Why did you attend this school? (Be honest—location, costs, programs.)
6. Why did you major in "X"? (Do not simply say financial benefits; concentrate on both practical and professional benefits. Be able to state career objectives.)
7. Why did you get a grade of "C" in a course? (Do not hurt your chances of being hired by saying that you could have done better if you tried; that response shows a lack of motivation most employers find unacceptable.

Explain what the trouble was and mention that you corrected it in a course in which you made a B or an A.)

8. What extracurricular activities did you participate in while in high school or college? (Indicate any duties or responsibilities you had—handling money, writing memos, coordinating events; if you were not able to participate in such activities, tell the interviewer that a part-time job, community or church activities, or commuting a long way to school each day prevented your participating. Such answers sound better than saying that you did not like sports or fraternities or clubs in school.)

9. Did you learn as much as you wanted from your course work? (This is a loaded question. Indicate that you learned a great deal but now look forward to the opportunity to gain more practical skill, to put into practice the principles you have learned; say that you will never be through learning about your major.)

10. Why was your summer job important? (Highlight skills you learned, people you helped, employers you pleased.)

11. What is your greatest strength? (Being a team player, cooperation, willingness to learn, ability to grasp difficult concepts easily, managing time or money, taking criticism easily, and profiting from criticism are all appropriate answers.)

12. What is your greatest shortcoming? (Be honest here and mention it, but then turn to ways in which you are improving. You obviously don't want to say something deadly like, "I can never seem to finish what I start" or "I hate being criticized." You should neither dwell on your weaknesses nor keep silent about them. Saying "None" to this kind of question is as inadvisable as rattling off a list of wrongdoings.)

13. How much did you earn at your last job and what salary would you expect from us? (Some job counselors wrongly advise interviewees to lie about their past salaries in order to get a larger one from the future employer. But if the prospective employer checks your last salary and finds that you have lied, you lose. It is better to round off your last salary to the nearest thousand. As far as present salary is concerned, if you did your homework, you should have a sense of the salary range.)

14. Why did you leave your last job? (Usually you will have educational reasons: "I returned to school full-time" or geographical reasons: "I moved from Jackson to Springfield." *Never attack your previous employer.* This only makes you look bad.)

15. Is there anything else you want to discuss? (Here is your opportunity to end the interview with more information about yourself. You might take time to reiterate your strengths, to correct an earlier answer, or to indicate your desire to work for the company.)

Of course, you will have a chance throughout the interview to ask questions, too. Do not forget important points about the job: responsibilities, opportunities for further training, security, and chances for promotion. You will also want to ask about salary (but do not dwell on it), fringe benefits, schedules, vacations, and bonuses. If you spend time on these subjects, especially during the first part of the interview, you tell the interviewer that you are more interested in the rewards of the job than in the duties and challenges it offers. Do not go to the interview with dollar signs flashing in your eyes.

Some questions an interviewer may not legally ask you. Questions about your age, marital status, ethnic background, race, or any physical handicaps violate equal opportunity employment laws. Even so, some employers may disguise their interest in these subjects by asking you indirect questions about them. A question such as "Will your husband care if you have to work overtime?" or "How many children do you have?" could probe into your personal life. Confronted with such questions, it is best to answer them positively ("My home life will not interfere with my job," "My family understands that overtime may be required") rather than bristling defensively, "It's none of your business if I have a husband."

Interview Do's and Don'ts

Keep in mind some other interview "do's" and "don'ts."

1. Be on time. If you are unavoidably delayed, telephone to apologize and set up another interview. Go to the interview alone.
2. Dress appropriately for the occasion.
3. Speak slowly and distinctly; do not nervously hurry to finish your sentences, and never interrupt or finish an interviewer's sentences.
4. Do not smoke, even if the interviewer offers you a cigarette. Also refrain from chewing gum, fidgeting, or tapping your foot against the floor or a chair.
5. Maintain eye contact with the interviewer; do not sheepishly stare at the floor or the desk. Body language is equally important. For instance, don't fold your arms—that's a signal indicating you are closed to the interviewer's suggestions and comments.
6. And one last point: When the interview is over, thank the interviewer for considering you for the job.

The Follow-up Letter

Within a week after the interview, it is a good strategy to send a follow-up letter thanking the interviewer for his or her time and interest in you. The letter will keep your name fresh in the interviewer's mind. Do not forget that this individual interviewed other candidates, too—some of them probably on the same day as you. In your follow-up letter, you can reemphasize your qualifications for the job by showing how they apply to conditions described by the interviewer; you might also ask for some further information to show your interest in the job and the employer. You could even refer to a detail, such as a tour or film that was part of the interview. A sample follow-up letter appears in Figure 8.17 (p. 298).

FIGURE 8.17   A follow-up letter.

2739 East Street
Latrobe, PA 17042-0312
September 20, 1994

Mr. Jack Fukurai
Personnel Manager
Transatlantic Steel Company
1334 Ridge Road N.E.
Pittsburgh, PA 17122-3107

Dear Mr. Fukurai:

I enjoyed talking with you last Wednesday and learning more about the
security officer position available at Transatlantic Steel. It was
especially helpful to take a tour of the plant's north gate section to see
the types of challenges it presents for the security officer stationed
there.

As you noted at my interview, my training in surveillance electronics has
prepared me to operate the sophisticated equipment Transatlantic has
installed at the north gate. I was grateful to Ms. Turner for taking time
to show me this equipment.

I am looking forward to receiving the brochure about Transatlantic's
employees services. Would it also be possible for you to include a copy of
the newsletter introducing the new security equipment to the employees?

Thank you for considering me for the position and for the hospitality you
showed me. I look forward to hearing from you. After my visit last week, I
know that Transatlantic Steel would be an excellent place to work.

Sincerely yours,

Marcia Le Borde

Marcia Le Borde

Accepting or Declining a Job

Even if you have verbally agreed to take a job, you still have to respond formally in writing. Your letter will make your acceptance official and will probably be included in your permanent personnel file. Accepting a job is easy. Make this communication with your new employer a model of clarity and diplomacy. Respond to the offer as soon as possible (certainly within two weeks). Often a time limit is specified. A sample acceptance letter appears in Figure 8.18. In the first sentence tell the employer that you are accepting the job, and refer to the date of the letter offering you the position. Indicate when you can begin the job. Then mention any pleasant associations from your interview or any specific challenges you are anticipating. That should take no more than a paragraph. Do not douse your letter with praise for the employer or the job.

In a second paragraph express your plans to fulfill any further requirements for the job—going to the personnel office, taking a physical examination, having a

FIGURE 8.18   Letter accepting a job.

73 Park Street
Evansville, WI 53536-1016
June 29, 1994

Ms. Melinda A. Haas, Manager
Weise's Department Store
Janesville Mall
Janesville, WI 53545-1014

Dear Ms. Haas:

I am pleased to accept the position of assistant controller that you offered me in your letter of June 22. Starting on July 18 will be no problem for me. I look forward to helping Ms. Meyers in the business office. In the next few months I know that I will learn a great deal about Weise's.

As you requested, I will make an appointment for early next week with the Personnel Department to discuss travel policies, salary payment schedules, and insurance coverage.

I am eager to start working for Weise's.

Cordially,

Kevin Dubinski

Kevin Dubinski

copy of a certificate or license forwarded, sending a final transcript of your college work. A final one-sentence paragraph might state that you are looking forward to starting your new job.

Refusing a job requires tact. You are obligated to inform an employer why you are not taking the job. Since the employer has spent time interviewing you, respond with courtesy and candor. For an example of a refusal letter, see Figure 8.19.

Do not bluntly begin with the refusal. Instead, prepare the reader for bad news by starting with a complimentary remark about the job, the interview, or the company. Then move to your refusal and supply an honest but not elaborate explanation of why you are not taking the job. Many students cite educational opportunities, work schedules, geographic preference, health reasons, or better,

FIGURE 8.19   Letter refusing a job.

345 Melba Lane
Bellingham, WA 98225-4912
March 8, 1994

Ms. Gail Buckholtz
Assistant Editor
The Everett News
Everett, WA 98421-1016

Dear Ms. Buckholtz:

I enjoyed meeting you and the staff photographers at my recent interview for the photography position at the News. Your plans for the special weekend supplements are exciting, and I know that I would have enjoyed my assignments greatly. But because I have decided to continue my education part time at Western Washington University in Bellingham, I have accepted a position with the Bellingham American. Not having to commute to Everett every day will give me more time for my studies and also for my free-lance work.

Thank you for your generous offer and for the time you and the staff spent explaining your plans to me. I wish you much success with the supplements.

Sincerely yours,

George Alexander

George Alexander

more relevant professional opportunities. End on a friendly note, because you may be interested in working for the company in the future and do not want to cause any bad feelings.

Employment Evaluations

Even after you have been hired and have been working at your job for a while, you may be expected to write convincingly about your qualifications for that job. In the past, employee evaluations for promotions and salary increases were handled by supervisors and administrative personnel. Today, many companies annually ask employees to grade themselves in addition to having supervisors do an assessment. The two evaluations are then compared, and employees are given the opportunity to see and respond to what their supervisors have written about them. Employees may also be asked to evaluate their supervisors. Thus employees must know how to evaluate themselves and others effectively. For this reason it is a good idea to keep a record of your achievements and commendations on the job.

What kinds of questions can you expect your employer to ask? Here are a few of the most common.

1. What are your current duties?
2. How well do you perform them?
3. What improvements can you make?
4. What would you like to accomplish in the next year?
5. Where would you rank yourself in comparison with others in your department?
6. What special contributions have you made to the company (or agency) in the last year?
7. Why do you deserve a raise or a promotion?

Before you answer such questions, keep in mind that your readers know you are automatically prejudiced in your behalf; objectivity, therefore, will be deemed a virtue. Rather than saying only that you are invaluable or that you are a hard worker, tell your employer why you hold this view of your work. Giving relevant facts—cite how many customers you visited and sold products to, mention any exceptional services you performed for clients, or any ways you saved the company money or improved communication. Indicate how your work benefited the company and your fellow employees. Did you make any suggestions that improved services or schedules? If your supervisor praised your work, cite his or her comments and give dates.

Keep your assessment short and to the point. Also make sure that your comments about your accomplishments directly pertain to your assigned duties. At the other extreme, do not sell yourself short by saying that you did what was expected of you or that you accomplished what you were told. Tell your reader how you performed routine tasks with skill and to the benefit of the company. A credible answer to question 3 would indicate that you have made a mistake, but would also indicate what you have done to correct it and to ensure that it will not occur again.

When asked to evaluate your supervisor, be objective. Avoid cheap shots or any attempts to get even for grievances. Questions of leadership, honesty, respect, and clarity in explaining job goals are usually found on evaluations of one's supervisors. Respond according to these criteria with facts and with honesty.

Your employer may supply you with a form (or checklist) for your evaluation of yourself, your supervisor, or for both. Or you may be instructed to write a formal letter of assessment. In either case, proofread carefully what you write for spelling and punctuation. You should also make a copy for your own records.

✓ Revision Checklist

As we have seen in this chapter, applying for a job is not done in one simple step. It requires that you go through a carefully organized process, with each step asking you to prepare certain types of written documents. The list of questions below covers the various stages you will have to go through until you are hired and ready to start work. By answering them affirmatively, you will increase your chances of getting the job you want.

1. Have I restricted the types of job(s) for which I am qualified?
2. Did I prepare a dossier at my school placement office with letters from professors, employers, and community officials who can recommend me and my work very highly?
3. Have I identified the places where jobs in my field are advertised?
4. Did I notify friends, relatives, clergy, and individuals who are employed by the companies I want to work for that I am on the job market? Did I check with the Chamber of Commerce, state employment office, any government agencies that I may like to work for?
5. Have I made a careful inventory of my strengths in order to prepare my résumé?
6. Did I eliminate all the weak, irrelevant, repetitious, and dated material from my inventory?
7. Have I translated the accomplishments from my inventory into "selling clauses," each introduced by a strong verb that demonstrates to a prospective employer that I am an accomplished individual who can get positive results on the job?
8. Did I write a restricted career/employment objective?
9. Have I determined the most beneficial résumé format for me to use—chronological or skills? Or both?

10. Is my résumé attractive and easy to read? Are the headings logical, and do they follow the most persuasive order for me?
11. If I am using a chronological format, have I determined whether it is better to list my education before or after my experience? Why?
12. Have I made sure that I did not include too much or too little on my résumé?
13. Did I have someone—a professor, someone in my field of work—critique my résumé?
14. Have I proofread my résumé to make sure everything on it is accurate and spelled correctly?
15. Does my letter of application show how my specific skills and background apply to and meet an employer's exact needs? Have I demonstrated that I am the right person for the job?
16. Did I make sure I included my résumé with my letter of application?
17. If invited for an interview, have I prepared a short oral report about myself and my accomplishments?
18. Have I sent my prospective employer a follow-up letter within a few days after the interview to show my interest in the position?
19. Depending on my situation, have I sent the prospective employer a polite acceptance or rejection letter?
20. Have I been objective, yet persuasive, on any job evaluations I have to complete?

Exercises

1. Make a brainstormed list of your marketable job skills. To do this, first concentrate on the specialized kinds of skills you learned in your major or on your job (for example, giving injections, fingerprinting, preparing specialized menus, keeping a ledger book, operating a computer, learning a computer language). List as many of these skills as you can think of; then organize them into three or four separate categories that reflect your major abilities.

2. Translate the list of skills from Exercise 1 into a number of "selling clauses" (see pages 259–260), each introduced with a strong action verb.

3. Using at least three different sources, compile a list of ten employers for whom you would like to work. Get their names, addresses, phone numbers, and the names of the managers or personnel officers. Then select one company and write a profile about it—location, services, kinds of products or services offered, number of employees working for it, clients served, types of schedules used.

4. Tell your college placement office when you will begin your job search. The office will almost certainly give you some forms to complete. Bring these forms to class and discuss the kinds of questions they contain and the most effective ways to answer them.

5. Obtain some personal evaluation forms from your placement office. Write a sample letter to a former or current teacher and employer, asking for a recommendation. Tell these individuals what kinds of jobs you will be looking for and politely mention how a strong letter would help you in your job search. Make sure that you bring them up-to-date about your educational progress and any employment you have had since you worked for them.

6. Request an application form for employment from a local store, hospital, government agency, or company. Bring the form to class and be prepared to discuss the best ways of completing it.

7. Which of the following would belong on your résumé? Which ones would not belong? Why?
   a. student I.D. number
   b. Social Security number
   c. the zip codes of your references' addresses
   d. a list of all your English courses in college
   e. section numbers of the courses in your major
   f. statement that you are recently divorced
   g. subscriptions to journals in your field
   h. the titles of any stories or poems you published in a high school literary magazine or newspaper
   i. your GPA
   j. foreign languages you studied
   k. years you attended college
   l. the date you were discharged from the service
   m. names of the neighbors you are using as references
   n. your religion
   o. job titles you held
   p. your summer job washing dishes
   q. your telephone number
   r. the reason you changed schools
   s. your current status with the National Guard
   t. the name of your favorite professor in college
   u. your work for the Red Cross
   v. hours a week you spend reading science fiction
   w. the title of your last term paper in your major
   x. the name of the agency or business where you worked last

8. Indicate what is wrong with the following career objective statements and rewrite them to make them more precise and professional.
   a. Job in a dentist's office.
   b. Position with a safety emphasis.
   c. Desire growth position in a large department store.
   d. Am looking for entry position in health sciences with an emphasis on caring for older people.
   e. Position in sales with fast promotion rate.
   f. Want a job working with semiconductor circuits.

g. I would like a position in fashion, especially one working with modern fashion.

h. Desire a good-paying job, hours: 8–4:30, with double pay for overtime. Would like to stay in the Omaha area.

i. Insurance work.

j. Computer operator in large office.

k. Personal secretary.

l. Job with preschoolers.

m. Full-time position with hospitality chain.

n. I want a career in nursing.

o. Police work, particularly in suburb of large city.

p. A job that lets me be me.

q. Desire fun job selling cosmetics.

r. Any position for a qualified dietitian.

s. Although I have not made up my mind about which area of forestry I shall go into, I am looking for a job that offers me training and rewards based upon my potential.

9. Rewrite the following bad résumé to make it more precise and persuasive. Include additional details where necessary and exclude any details that you think would hurt the job seeker's chances. Also correct any inconsistencies.

RÉSUMÉ OF

Powell T. Harrison
8604 So. Kirkpatrick St.
Ardville, Ohio
345 37 8760
614 234 4587

PERSONAL	Confidential
CAREER OBJECTIVE	Seek good paying position with progressive Sunbelt company.
EDUCATION 1991–1994	Will receive degree from Central Tech. Institute in Arch. St. Earned high average last semester. Took necessary courses for major; interested in systems, plans, and design development.
1987–1991	Attended Ardville High School, Ardville, OH; took all courses required. Served on several student committees.
EXPERIENCE	None, except for numerous part-time jobs and student apprenticeship in the Ardville area. As part of student app. worked with local firm for two months.

| HOBBIES | Watching MTV, playing Nintendo video games. Member of Junior Achievement. |
| REFERENCES | Please write for names and addresses. |

---

10. Determine what is wrong with the following sentences in a letter of application. Rewrite them to eliminate any mistakes, to focus on the "you attitude," or to make them more precise.

a. Even though I have very little actual job experience, I can make up for it in enthusiasm.

b. My qualifications will prove that I am the best person for your job.

c. I would enjoy working with your other employees.

d. This letter is my application for any job you now have open or expect to fill in the near future.

e. Next month, my family and I will be moving to Detroit, and I must get a job in the area. Will you have anything open?

f. If you are interested in me, then I hope that we make some type of arrangements to interview each other soon.

g. I have not included a résumé since all pertinent information about me is in this letter.

h. My GPA is only 2.5, but I did make two Bs in my last term.

i. I hope to take state boards soon.

j. Your company, or so I have heard through the grapevine, has excellent fringe benefits. That is what I care about most, so I am applying for any position which you may advertise.

k. I am writing to ask you to kindly consider whether I would be a qualified person for the position you announced in the newspaper.

l. I have made plans to further my education.

m. My résumé speaks for itself.

n. I could not possibly accept a position which required weekend work, and night work is out, too.

o. In my own estimation, I am a go-getter—an eager beaver, so to speak.

p. My last employer was dead wrong when he let me go. I think he regrets it now.

q. When you want to arrange an interview time, give me a call. I am home every afternoon after four.

11. Why is the following letter of application ineffective? Rewrite it to make it more precise and appropriate.

Apartment 32
Jeggler Drive
Talcott, Arizona

Monday

Grandt Corporation
Production Supervisor
Capital City, Arizona

Dear Sir:

I am writing to ask you if your company will consider me for the position you announced in the newspaper yesterday. I believe that with my education (I have an associate degree) and experience (I have worked four years as a freight supervisor), I could fill your job.

My school work was done at two junior colleges, and I took more than enough courses in business management and modern packaging. In fact, here is a list of some of my courses: Supervision, Materials Management, Work Experience in Management, Business Machines, Loading and Landing Tactics, Introduction to Packaging, Art Design, Modern Business Principles, and Small Business Management. In addition, I have worked as a loading dock supervisor for the last two years, and before that I worked in the military in the Quartermaster Corps.

Please let me know if you are interested in me. I would like to have an interview with you at the earliest possible date, since there are some other firms also interested in me, too.

Eagerly yours,

George D. Milhous

---

12. From the Sunday edition of your local newspaper, clip ads for two or three jobs you are qualified to fill and then write a letter of application for one of them.

13. Write a chronologically organized résumé to go along with the letter you wrote for Exercise 12 above.

14. Write a functional résumé for your application letter in Exercise 12.

15. Write an appropriate job application letter to accompany Anna Cassetti's résumés in Figures 8.3 and 8.6.

16. Write a letter to a local business inquiring about summer employment. Indicate that you can work only for one summer and that you will be going back to school by September 1.

17. Rewrite this follow-up letter to make it more professional.

```
Dear Mr. Gage:

It was good talking to you yesterday. The job is even
more attractive than I thought. I had no idea that the
salary was in the $21,000 to $22,000 range. That is
excellent money for someone starting out.

I am sorry that I did not know the answers to your
questions on the use of the new laser printers. After
checking with my instructor, Dr. Patricia Holmes, I
can give you a full and complete answer now. If you
would like me to put it in writing, please let me
know, and I shall be happy to oblige you. I do not
want you to think that I am not properly trained.

I am really excited about working for your company.
And I am staying glued to the phone in the hopes that
you will give me that call that will start me on a
great career.

Absolutely yours,


C. K. Randolph
```

Gathering and
Summarizing Information

III

9

Finding and Using Library Materials

A personnel director asked an applicant during a job interview to name the titles of two or three major journals in the applicant's field. When the applicant could not come up with any titles, the applicant's chances for employment at the company became slim. The question was typical, fair, and relevant. The interviewer knew that an applicant's success in the job depends on the quality of information supplied to the employer. Employers expect carefully researched answers; they will not be satisfied with guesses.

Research, or the careful investigation of material found in books, magazines, pamphlets, films, and other sources (including resource people), is a vital part of every occupation. Companies expect their employees to be able to research a problem, find information, and prepare bibliographies for any number of reasons, such as writing proposals and long reports. You might conduct research by telephoning someone in the next department for information or by thumbing through a company catalog. Or you might engage in research by studying reference works in a library or by preparing statistical or analytical surveys. You must be informed about the latest developments in your field, and you must be able to communicate your findings accurately and concisely. Doing research is a practical skill like swimming, running, or keyboarding. Once learned, it is easy to perform. Knowing how to do research in your field offers lifelong benefits.

The information in Chapter 9 can save you from suffering the embarrassment experienced by the job applicant described above. Specifically, Chapter 9 discusses major reference works in print and on-line—where to find them and how to use them. The appendix to this chapter (pages 346-352) contains information about specific reference works (indexes, encyclopedias, dictionaries, and abstracts) that will be extremely valuable to you in your research.

The Process of Doing Research

Just as there is a process for writing—brainstorming, drafting, revising, editing—there is a process involved in doing research. In research, you go through the steps of finding, assessing, and incorporating information into your written work. Basically, that process includes following these strategies:

1. Identify and limit your topic. Check with your instructor or boss to make sure that you understand the assignment—its scope and purpose. For example, you would have trouble writing a restricted and focused paper or report about lasers. That subject is too broad and too complex. You cannot just march into the library with some vague idea about writing on lasers and hope to produce a successful paper or report. Thousands of articles and books have been written about lasers. Instead, you need to narrow the subject in one of several ways: through time (for example, the history of lasers—when and where they were first used); through space or environment (for example, lasers for security purposes in automotive plants); through reference to key personnel or users (for example, physicians using lasers in gallbladder surgery); or some restricted combination of time, space, and personnel.

2. Once you have limited your subject, you are in a better position to limit your research successfully. A narrowed topic actually assists you in identifying appropriate research materials and what you need to gather from them. With a focused subject—for example, lasers used in automatic teller machines—your research will have profitable parameters. With that topic, you know that you'll have to find articles, books, and other reference materials relating to the technology of banking, not those on medical or security topics.

3. The next step is to locate these materials—learn where they are found in your school, company, or public library, or whether you must borrow these materials from another library. Also find out if important information on your restricted topic is located in print sources—books, encyclopedias, statistical guides, journal articles—or in electronic ones, or in a combination of them.

4. Once you find the appropriate sources, the next step is knowing how to use them. Determine if there are any special preparations. For example, if you are having a computer search done, you will have to work closely with a librarian who will ask you for key terms to conduct the search. You may also have to know how to use special equipment (e.g., audiovisual) or software.

5. The next step is to familiarize yourself with these library materials. The quickest way is to look at the parts of a work that most easily alert readers to the topics covered. Prefaces and introductions typically spell out an author's or reference work's purpose and scope. Also examine indexes to find significant terms, ideas, places, or people that might be relevant to your research. If you are looking at articles in journals, carefully examine abstracts or summaries and any list of key terms included with them. Pay special attention to footnotes, bibliographies, or lists of works cited to see if they refer you to other relevant sources.

6. Turn to appropriate sections of a book or journal article you identify as important for your work, and skim them. You are on a search mission at this point, trying to find out how much (if any) of the work you need to digest.

7. If a source seems to offer a great deal of information on your topic, do not spend hours in the library reading it word for word. Photocopy relevant pages, but always include the author's name, title, and the source on your copy so that you will have pertinent publication information if you decide to quote or paraphrase this source in your paper or report.

8. Write down the author, title, and date (include volume numbers for journal articles and publisher's name for books) of the work on notecards.

Once you have chosen a limited topic to research, you can continue the process at the library.

The Library and Its Sections

You may think of your library as a single building, but that building is divided into many sections. When you walk into a library, probably the first section you see is the circulation desk—in many ways, the business center of the library. You go to the circulation desk to borrow or return books, to pick up materials you may have ordered from another library, or to find out if a book has been checked out. From the circulation desk you can move to any one of the following parts of the library to use materials. (The page numbers after each area refer to the page numbers of this chapter where you will find a description of the particular unit and the materials in it.)

- the library catalog (pages 313–319)
- the stacks (pages 319–321)
- periodical holdings and indexes (pages 321–326)
- computer resources (pages 326–330)
- reference books (pages 331–333)
- government documents (pages 333–335)
- the popular press (pages 335–337)
- audiovisual materials (pages 337–339)

Books

The Library Catalog

The library catalog is your guide to the library; it will tell you what books your library owns and where you can find them. The card catalog is often located in a prominent place, usually near the entrance to your library. Traditionally housed in cabinets with numerous drawers, the card catalog contains 3" × 5" cards for each book, filmstrip, tape recording, or microfilm in the library. Although the card catalog may list the specific journals and magazines the library subscribes to, it will not contain information about the contents of individual articles in these publications. For that kind of information you will have to consult your library's periodical holding list and the periodical indexes discussed later in this chapter.

The cabinets of the card catalog are rapidly being replaced by computer terminals at company, school, and public libraries. The computer links users to the *on-line catalog*, or database, containing information about the books and other materials in the library. With access to this database, you can find information about titles, authors, subject areas, and location of materials as well as learn whether a book has been checked out, is placed on reserve, is noncirculating (as most reference books are), or is available to be checked out. Also, if a book is checked out, the due date will be given.

Because the computerized catalog offers library users better and more extensive access to the library's holdings, it is often called the *on-line catalog*. A computerized library catalog can make your library research easier. You can search this computerized catalog by a variety of methods. By simply pressing the corresponding keys for subject, author, title, or a combination of these computer files, you can search the library's entire book holdings at once. For example, a subject search will display on the computer screen all the books that contain the key subject term or terms you are investigating. Suppose you are searching lasers in printing; the subject search will display on the screen all the titles of the books that combine lasers and printing. It will also retrieve all those items that deal with this topic, even if the book titles do not include the words *laser* and *printing*.

The on-line catalog is a valuable tool for expanding searches (as seen in *lasers and printing*), but it is an equally valuable tool for narrowing your searches. For example, you could ask the computer to search for *lasers not military*. This would allow you to narrow a broad topic (such as lasers), focusing on only those nonmilitary aspects you are interested in.

A further advantage of an on-line catalog is that you will find a printer beside some of the computer terminals that will allow you to obtain a hard copy of the titles your search has displayed on the screen. After printing the titles, you can start your *working bibliography*, complete with publishing information and the location of these sources in your library, to begin your preliminary research.

How Material in the Library Catalog Is Alphabetized

You can use three methods to find a book in the catalog—whether housed in cabinets or computerized on-line. You can look for it under the author's name, under the title, or under the subject it discusses. Some libraries may have separate cabinets for each of these three designations (author, title, subject); all three are, as we saw, combined in an on-line catalog. Information in all three categories is listed alphabetically, either letter by letter or word by word. These two ways of alphabetizing entries can make a big difference, as the following examples show:

Letter by Letter		Word by Word	
fire	fire escape	fire	firearm
firearm	firefly	fire drill	firefly
fire drill	firetrap	fire escape	firetrap
	fire wall	fire wall	

The letter-by-letter method is based on the sequence of individual letters regardless of whether an entry contains one word or two. Hence, *firearm* comes before *fire drill.* Under the word-by-word method, each entry is alphabetized according to the letters in the first word, whether that entry is made up of one word or two. *Fire wall* comes ahead of *firearm* and *firefly* because the word *fire* is a part of both of these words and alphabetically precedes them. Find out which method your library uses so you can look up entries more quickly and more accurately. The following alphabetical rules apply to both methods and will help you search for an entry in the library catalog.

1. An author's last name beginning with *Mc* is listed as if the *Mc* were spelled *Mac;* so *McDonald* will be listed in the catalog as if it were *MacDonald.* Hyphenated last names are found at the end of the alphabetical letter beginning the first of two hyphenated names. A book by Alan Jones-Davies, for example, would be listed at the end of the Js, not under the Ds.
2. Disregard definite and indefinite articles—*the, a,* or *an*—at the beginning of a title. A book with the title *A New Fashion Guide* will be found in the Ns.
3. Abbreviations, acronyms (NATO, VISTA, and other words formed from the first letters of several words), and numbers can be alphabetized in one of two ways. They can be alphabetized as if they were spelled out in full, so a book entitled *Mr. and Ms. Average American* would be found in the title section of the catalog under *Mister* and *22 Ways to Better Health* would be listed under *Twenty-Two.* A book written by IBM would be listed under *International Business Machines.* And a study put out by the ANA would be found in the author section under *American Nurses Association.* But some libraries file acronyms alphabetically at the beginning of the letter (*NASA, NATO, native*).

Author Card

One way to find a book is to locate the *author card* in a catalog. Spell the author's name correctly and record first names or initials accurately. If you know only the last name, and if it is a common one, your search may take a great deal of extra time. An *author card* for a book by Martin Meyerson can be seen in Figure 9.1 (p. 316). To find Meyerson's book, you would look under the M's until you come to Meyerson and then find Martin. The author card(s) tells you what titles by that author are in your library. Each card will tell you where to find the book, when it was written, who published it, and where. Figure 9.1 is coded to show you what each number, abbreviation, and symbol means.

Title Card

Figure 9.2 (p. 317) shows a *title card.* It is identical to an author card except that the title of the book is listed twice—once as a heading on top of the card and again as part of the entry itself. It is easy to find this card when you know the first word of the title. Keep in mind that the articles *a, an,* or *the* at the beginning of the title are omitted in alphabetizing. With the Meyerson book you do not have an

FIGURE 9.1   Author information in the library catalog.

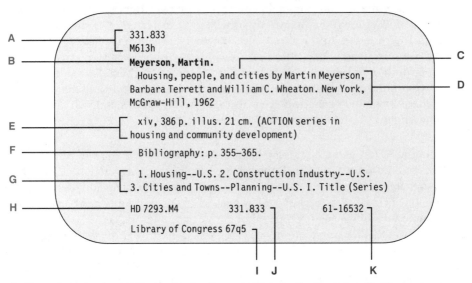

A   The *call number* locates the book in the library. In this case the library has filed the book according to the Dewey decimal system.

B   The *author's name* is always listed with the last name (surname) first. Sometimes a card also gives the author's date of birth and, if the author is deceased, the date of death. If a book has more than one author or editor, only the author whose name appears first in the book is listed in the upper-left-hand corner.

C   The *title* of the book.

D   The names of any *coauthors or coeditors and pertinent publication information*—city, publisher, and date of publication.

E   A *physical description of the book*—number of pages from the preface (usually numbered in lower-case roman numerals) through the index, whether the book is illustrated (illus.) and the height (in centimeters) of the book. Also noted is whether the book is part of a special series or is issued under a special imprint (or publishing arrangement).

F   This book contains a *bibliography* on pages 355 to 365.

G   List of the *other headings in the subject catalog under which the book is listed*.

H   The *Library of Congress designation* for this book would be in the A position if the library followed the Library of Congress system of classification rather than the Dewey decimal one.

I   "Library of Congress" means that a copy of the book is in the national library.

J   The *Dewey decimal number.*

K   *Identification numbers used by librarians.* You need not be concerned with this designation.

FIGURE 9.2   Title information in the library catalog.

```
331.833
M613h      Housing, people, and cities.
Meyerson, Martin.
   Housing, people, and cities by Martin Meyerson,
Barbara Terrett and William C. Wheaton. New York,
McGraw-Hill, 1962

      xiv, 386 p. illus. 21 cm. (ACTION series in
   housing and community development)

      Bibliography: p. 355–365.

      1. Housing--U.S. 2. Construction Industry--U.S.
   3. Cities and Towns--Planning--U.S. I. Title (Series)

   HD 7293.M4        331.833        61-16532

   Library of Congress 67q5
```

article for the first word of the title; just search for the book under the Hs in the title section of the library catalog.

Subject Card

Figure 9.3 shows the *subject card* for the Meyerson book. Again, the subject card is identical to the author card except that a subject heading—marked with distinctive red or black ink—is located at the top of the card. Many times students start with the subject section of the library catalog since they do not have titles or authors in mind early in their search. The subject catalog also lists reference works (abstracts, bibliographies, dictionaries, handbooks, and indexes) that will guide you to specific titles.

The subject section divides a topic into subheadings or groups and alerts readers to other, related topics. Looking under the subject section for "construction,"

FIGURE 9.3   Subject information in the library catalog.

```
331.833
M613h    CONSTRUCTION INDUSTRY—UNITED STATES
Meyerson, Martin.
   Housing, people, and cities by Martin Meyerson,
Barbara Terrett and William C. Wheaton. New York,
McGraw-Hill, 1962.

      xiv, 386 p. illus. 21 cm. (ACTION series in
   housing and community development)

      Bibliography: p. 355–365.

      1. Housing--U.S. 2. Construction Industry--U.S.
   3. Cities and Towns--Planning--U.S. I. Title (Series)

   HD 7293.M4        331.833        61-16532

   Library of Congress 67q5
```

you would first find a cross-reference, or "see also," card, illustrated in Figure 9.4. This card refers you to other subject categories (references) you should check for information in addition to the cards gathered under the "construction" heading. Next, you would find the following breakdown of the topic with appropriate books listed for each:

- construction dictionary
- construction equipment
- construction handbook
- construction, housing
- construction industry

Stopping at the last subheading, "construction industry," you could find even more subclassifications:

- accounting
- automation
- contracts
- costs
- data processing
- law and legislation
- management
- personnel
- subcontracting
- United States

Meyerson's book would be found under this last subheading, "United States."

Subject cards break down topics into subcategories and list appropriate titles under each subcategory or refer readers to other parts of the subject catalog. They also list on the entry card beneath the title of the book other relevant topics to consult directly. Examine the Meyerson card in Figure 9.3. Following the biblio-

FIGURE 9.4 **"See also" information in the library catalog.**

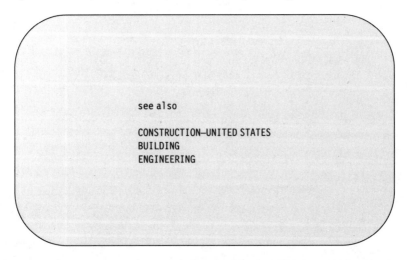

```
see also

CONSTRUCTION–UNITED STATES
BUILDING
ENGINEERING
```

graphic information, the card lists three other subject areas that will help readers find additional information: (1) housing, (2) construction, and (3) cities and towns.

The Stacks

The majority of space in a library is taken up by the rows of bookshelves, called *stacks*. Your library may have open or closed stacks. If the stacks are open, you are free to walk along the rows to find the books you need. If they are closed, a member of the library staff will find a book for you after you present a call slip identifying—by author, title, and number—the book you want.

Call Numbers

Regardless of which system your library uses, you will have to know the call number of the book you want. Call numbers or letters are found in the upper left-hand side of the card in the catalog. Your library may use either the Library of Congress (abbreviated LC) or the Dewey decimal system. Table 9.1 shows a section of the

TABLE 9.1   A Sample of Headings from Call-Number Sections

Library of Congress		*Dewey Decimal*	
Q	Science	500	Pure Sciences
	Q Science (General)	510	Mathematics
	QA Mathematics	520	Astronomy and allied sciences
	QB Astronomy	530	Physics
	QC Physics	540	Chemistry and allied sciences
	QD Chemistry	550	Sciences of earth and other worlds
	QE Geology	560	Paleontology
	QH Natural History	570	Life sciences
	QK Botany	580	Botanical sciences
	QL Zoology	590	Zoological sciences
	QM Human anatomy	600	Technology (Applied sciences)
	QP Physiology	610	Medical sciences
	QR Microbiology	620	Engineering and allied operations
R	Medicine	630	Agriculture
	R Medicine (General)	640	Domestic arts and sciences
	RB Pathology	650	Managerial services
	RK Dentistry	660	Chemical and related technologies
	RT Nursing	670	Manufactures
S	Agriculture	680	Miscellaneous manufacturing
	S Agriculture (General)	690	Buildings
	SB Plant culture		
	SD Forestry		
	SF Animal culture		

Library of Congress, Subject Cataloging Division. *LC Classification Outline*, 3rd ed. (Washington, D.C.: U.S. Government Printing Office, 1975); Melvil Dewey, *Decimal Classification and Relative Index: The Second Summary* (New York, 1971), 450.

LC system and some of the divisions in the Dewey decimal system. The LC system divides all areas of knowledge into twenty-one categories that are differentiated by capital letters of the alphabet. Subdivisions are labeled with a combination of letters and numbers. As its name implies, the Dewey decimal system divides knowledge into ten large categories indicated by numerical groups ranging from 000 to the 900s. Each large division is divided into groups of ten subdivisions. The first number in a Dewey classification indicates the large category of knowledge in which a book is found, and the second and third numbers specify exact areas of that large group.

Meyerson's book, *Housing, People, and Cities,* is classified in the LC system by the letters HD. The letter H indicates that the book falls into the large category marked "Social Sciences," and D signifies that the book belongs in the subcategory "Economics," as opposed to "Statistics" (HA) or "Sociology" (HM–HX). The Dewey number for Meyerson's book is 331.833—that is, it falls into the 300s, "Social Sciences"; the 30s of the 300s is the subdivision "Economics."

Shelves

Once you know the call number, you should check where the book is shelved if your library has open stacks. Your library may post maps that show the location of books by their call numbers. When you know the approximate location of a book, go to that section of the library and look at the markers posted at the end of each row of stacks. Then walk down the appropriate row to find your book. Most books will have their call numbers on the *spine,* or the place where the book is bound, as illustrated in Figure 9.5. Some especially thin books have their call numbers on the outside front cover.

If the book you are looking for is not on the shelf, go to the circulation desk to see if it has been checked out. If so, you can ask the librarian to hold it for you when it comes back. Perhaps the book can be used only in the library (then it is

FIGURE 9.5   Spine of a book with call number.

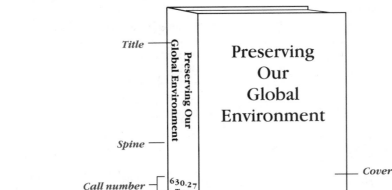

said to be "on reserve"), in which case you will have to sign it out from the circulation desk. If the librarian discovers that the book has not been checked out or is not on reserve, it may be misshelved. Check with the library in the next few days to see if it has been found.

Periodical Holdings and Indexes

Your research will not be confined exclusively to books. Some of it will lead you to the wealth of information contained in periodicals. A *periodical* is a magazine or journal that is published at established, frequent intervals—weekly, bimonthly (once every two months), quarterly. The word *magazine* refers to periodicals—*Gentleman's Quarterly, Redbook,* or *TIME*—that appeal to a diverse audience and that treat popular themes. The word *journal* characterizes technical or scholarly periodicals, such as the *American Journal of Nursing* or the *American Waterworks Journal,* whose audiences read them for professional or scientific information in special fields.

Periodicals have certain advantages over books when it comes to research. Because they take less time to produce than books, periodicals can give you more recent information on a topic. Further, periodicals are not as restricted as books. A book usually discusses one subject from one point of view, but a periodical can contain ten different articles, each covering a separate topic and each offering a different perspective. This is not to imply that you should ignore books and focus solely on magazines or journals. Use both, but be aware of the differences.

To find appropriate articles in magazines and journals, you need to use indexes. An *index* is a listing by subject, and sometimes also by author, of articles that have appeared within a specified period of time. An index tells you what articles have appeared on your subject, where they were published, who wrote them, and whether they contain any special information, such as bibliographies, illustrations, diagrams and maps, or portraits. You would be lost without indexes. You could never successfully thumb through all the periodicals in the library to determine which ones contain an article you could use. Furthermore, your library might not subscribe to all the journals and magazines that contain articles related to your subject. The indexes let you know what is available beyond your own library's holdings.

The *Readers' Guide to Periodical Literature*

One basic index is the *Readers' Guide to Periodical Literature,* which has been listing information on periodicals since 1900. The *Readers' Guide* indexes information from more than two hundred periodicals, mostly popular magazines and a few scientific journals. The *Guide*'s main purpose is to list periodicals of interest to the general, not technical, reader. Therefore, you will find articles from *Good Housekeeping, Parents' Magazine,* and *Reader's Digest* indexed, but not articles from *Hospitals, Journal of Petroleum Technology,* or *Professional Safety.* For journal articles, you will have to consult the more specialized indexes discussed later in this chapter.

The *Readers' Guide* is published every month. Every three months the *Guide* combines issues to form a cumulative index for that period. Every year these three-month indexes are collected and bound into one large yearly index that can weigh as much as a large dictionary.

The *Readers' Guide* allows you to search for an article by topic, subtopic, author's name, and, whenever appropriate, title. At the beginning of every issue you will find two important keys. One key tells you which periodicals were surveyed for that particular issue of the *Readers' Guide*. Along with this information is a list of abbreviations that will be used for those periodicals throughout the issue. For example, *Saturday Review* will be listed as *Sat R* and *Working Woman* will be found as *Work Wom*. The other key lists abbreviations for months, bibliographic facts, and titles. Refer to both keys as you "decode" the entries in an issue.

Figure 9.6 contains an excerpt from the *Readers' Guide* for April–July 1991. This excerpt will show you how the *Readers' Guide* is organized and how abbreviations are used. Like the subject designations in the library catalog, the *Readers' Guide* refers users to other, related topics in the issue. The reader is told to "see also" entries under related headings. The articles are then divided into appropriate categories.

FIGURE 9.6   **An excerpt from the *Readers' Guide*.**

EXTREMITIES *See* Limbs (Anatomy)
EXXON CORPORATION
   See also
   Exxon Valdez (Ship) oil spill, 1989
EXXON VALDEZ (SHIP) OIL SPILL, 1989
   Exxon case ends, but not effects of spill. il *National Parks*
   65:16 My/Je '91   *Author of article here, (J. Wheelwright)*
   Muzzling science [Exxon Valdez oil spill] J. Wheelwright.
   por *Newsweek* 117:10 Ap 22 '91   *"il" means the article has illustrations*
   One deal that was too good for Exxon. S. Begley. il
   Newsweek 117:54 My 6 '91
   Turn Exxon into a model environmental citizen. M. Galen.
   il *Business Week* p44 My 20 '91
        Cleanup
   A lesson learned, again, at Valdez [overly ambitious
   cleanup] R. A. Kerr. *Science* 252:371 Ap 19 '91
   Oil spill leaves crude mark on Alaska. *National Parks*   *Magazine citation includes name of magazine, volume, page numbers, and date*
   65:13-14 Mr/Ap '91

*Subject heading
Cross-reference*   **EYE**
        See also
        Cornea
        Retina
        Vision

*Article title
"por" means article
includes portrait*   **Care and hygiene**
   Therapy for your eyes, dimestore reading glasses, and
   other farsighted matters. S. Seligson. *In Health* 5:86
   Mr/Ap '91
        Diseases and defects
        See also
        Blindness
        Cataracts (Eye defect)
        Glaucoma
        Onchocerciasis
        Retinitis pigmentosa
        Xerophthalmia
   Eyes on the blink [problems associated with aging] S.
   Seligson. il *In Health* 5:80-6 Mr/Ap '91

FIGURE 9.6 (Continued)

Examination
See also
Eye charts
Vision should be tested early [children] il *USA Today
(Periodical)* 119:7 F '91
Movements
Eye movements can help us see trouble ahead [AIDS
attacking brain; research by Steven Feldon] il *USA
Today (Periodical)* 119:1-2 F '91
Movement of neural activity on the superior colliculus
motor map during gaze shifts [cats] D. P. Munoz and
others. bibl f il *Science* 251:1358-60 Mr 15 '91
Surgery
See also
Cataracts (Eye defect)—Surgery
Cornea—Surgery
EYE, ARTIFICIAL
Eye for an eye [use of tiny video cameras and brain
electrodes; work of Richard Normann and Terry
Hambrecht] L. Kaufman. il *American Health* 10:9-10
My '91
EYE CHARTS
Test your vision. J. Hastings. il In *Health* 5:83 Mr/Ap '91
EYE DROPS, WASHES, ETC.
Keep your peepers shut! It may enhance eye medica-
tions. il *Prevention (Emmaus, Pa.)* 43:14+ Ap '91
Contamination
Eye drop danger. L. Kaufman. il *American Health* 10:8
Ap '91
EYE MAKEUP *See* Makeup
EYE MOVEMENTS *See* Eye—Movements
EYEGLASSES
See also
Sunglasses

*An explanatory
note to clarify
article*

*"See" reference;
the subject heading on
this topic is* Makeup

In addition to listing articles under the subjects they discuss, the *Readers' Guide* indexes articles according to author. Some authors also have articles written about them. In this case the *Readers' Guide* first lists the works *by* the author and immediately following those articles lists works *about* the author. Look at Figure 9.7. The excerpt from Bill Cosby's book (a work *by* him) comes first, followed by three articles *about* him. Note that portraits and/or photographs ("pors") accompany each article about him.

FIGURE 9.7 Entries from *Readers' Guide* for articles about one person.

---

*Author and name
heading (Cosby
wrote the first two
articles)*

COSBY, BILL, 1937-
"Give from the heart" [cover story] il pors *Redbook* 176:91
D '90
What's ahead for blacks and whites? il por *Ebony* 46:61 N
'90
about
Bill Cosby tells the daring move he made to make 'The
Cosby show' sparkle [cover story] il pors *Jet* 79:56-60 N
12 '90
Cosby axes kids' mural from TV show's opening and gives
explanation. il *Jet* 79:58-9 N 5 '90

Specialized Indexes

While the *Readers' Guide* is a good source to consult, remember that the *Guide* is limited to "periodicals of general interest published in the United States." Your research may require you to read professional journals in your field—journals that the *Readers' Guide* does not index. To find information published in professional journals, you will need to consult a specialized index. These indexes are guides to the literature in particular subject areas—business, farming, food service, nursing, public safety, respiratory therapy, and many others. Some indexes (print versions as opposed to on-line versions discussed below) cover sixty or more years of work (*Applied Science & Technology Index* or *Index Medicus*); other indexes were established within the past five to ten years (*Criminal Justice Periodical Index* or *Environmental Index*). You will find a list of some important specialized indexes in the appendix to this chapter. But perhaps the two most important specialized indexes are the *Applied Science & Technology Index* and the *Business Periodicals Index*.

Applied Science & Technology Index

If you need to locate information about a technical subject, you would be wise to start with the *Applied Science & Technology Index*. The *Index* is a guide to more than three hundred specialized journals in a wide range of scientific and technical fields. The prefatory note to each issue of the *Index* reminds readers of this breadth of coverage.

> Subject fields indexed include aeronautics and space science, atmospheric sciences, chemistry, computer technology and applications, construction industry, energy resources and research, engineering, fire and fire prevention, food and food industry, geology, machinery, mathematics, metallurgy, mineralogy, oceanography, petroleum and gas, physics, plastics, textile industry and fabrics, transportation and other industrial and mechanical arts.

Like the *Readers' Guide,* the *Index* is organized alphabetically by subject. Many of these subjects are subdivided to assist users further. Take a look at Figure 9.8, which reprints a section of the *Index,* to see how useful these subclassifications can be. Information published about concrete is categorized according to aggregate, air entrainment, durability, failure, specifications, and so forth. The subclassifications in the *Applied Science & Technology Index* might give you an idea for a research paper and then assist you in gathering relevant and thorough information on that topic.

Business Periodicals Index

Published since 1958, the *Business Periodicals Index* is invaluable when you are researching a topic in or about business and industry. The *Business Periodicals Index* surveys more than three hundred business publications published in English. Subjects that are indexed include accounting, advertising, communications, computer technology and applications, finance, industrial relations, management, occupational health and safety, office automation, personnel, real estate,

FIGURE 9.8   An excerpt from the *Applied Science & Technology Index.*

Computers—Traffic control use—*cont.*
Technology tackles traffic woes. S. Machlis. il diags
  Des News 47:148-50+ O 7 '91
                Traffic engineering use
                See also
            Traffic engineering software
Concentrating collectors
                Computer simulation
Analysis of a two-stage linear Fresnel reflector solar
  concentrator. D. Feuermann and J. M. Gordon.
  bibl diags *J Sol Energy Eng* 113:272-9 N '91
                Mathematical models
CPCs with segmented absorbers. M Kéita and H. S.
  Robertson. bibl diags *Sol Energy* 47 no4:269-77
  '91
Optical properties of V-trough concentrators. N.
  Fraiden- raich and G. J. Almeida. bibl diags *Sol
  Energy* 47 no3:147-55 '91
Concentrators
                See also
            Evaporators
Concert halls *See* Music halls
Concrete
                See also
            Cement
            Concrete construction
            Concrete slabs
            Prestressed concrete
            Reinforced concrete
                Aggregate
                See also
            Concrete waste
                Air entrainment
Fiber-optic refractive-index sensor for use in fresh
  concrete. F. Ansari and Q.-Y. Chen. diags *Appl
  Opt* 30:4056-9 O 1 '91
                Durability
Design considerations for service life. E. Hognestad.
  bibl il *Concr Int* 13:57-60 Mr '91; Discussion.
  13:8-11 O '91
Durability of post-tensioned prestressed concrete
  structures. C. L. Freyermuth. bibl il diags *Concr
  Int* 13: 58-65 O '91
                Failure
Constitutive equations for concrete in failure state.
  R. de Boer and H. T. Dresenkamp. bibl diags *J
  Eng Mech* 115:1591-608 Ag '89; Discussion.
  117:2450-1 O '91

---

telecommunications, and transportation. Like the *Applied Science & Technology Index,* the *Business Periodicals Index* is organized alphabetically by subject and offers many useful subheadings. Note how the excerpt from the *Business Periodicals Index* contained in Figure 9.9 (p. 326) arranges and classifies information about credit cards and how it helps users to find information about companies and individuals.

FIGURE 9.9 An excerpt from the *Business Periodicals Index.*

Credit analysis—Data processing—Programs—*cont.*
Mastering the numbers game [Ratio Master: a compiled Lotus 1-2-3 spread sheet] J. J. Parisi. *Bus Credit* 93:32-3 N-D '91

Credit applications
Binding arbitration language for credit application. *Bus Credit* 93:29 N-D '91

Credit associations
See also
FCIB-NACM Corporation
National Association of Credit Management

Credit authorization *See* Credit card authorization

Credit card authorization
See also
Credit card authorization services

Communication systems
Bankcard authorization: what the retail executive needs to know [supplement] diag il *Chain Store Age Exec* 67 sec3:2B-20B N '91
Voice technology sets new service standards in bank card processing [Southwestern States Bankcard Association; credit card authorizations by phone] C. Ring. *Telemarketing* 10:38-9 N '91

Terminology
The ABC's of bankcard authorization. *Chain Store Age Exec* 67 sec3:20B N '91

Credit card authorization services
See also
Southwestern States Bankcard Association
What to look for in a vendor. *Chain Store Age Exec* 67 sec3:16B N '91

Credit cards
See also
Affinity credit cards
Credit card authorization
Gasoline credit cards
Point-of-sale systems
See also the following corporate names
American Express Travel Related Services Company
Credit card scoring: profits by the numbers [computer credit-scoring models] K. Morrall. *Bankers Mon* 108:25+ N '91

Advertising
Amex $60M media may split O&M for Chiat/Day in review [agency showdown over media buying and planning responsibilities] R. Joseph. *Mediaweek* 1:3 N 25 '91
Core Amex business on the line: Green Card creative being tested in Canada after U.S. agency shift. R. Scotland. il *Marketing* 96:1 N 18 '91

Fees
Don't wait for them—cut your own credit-card fees. *Money* 20:15-16+ '91 Year-end issue

Fraudulent use
The bottom line: maximizing sales and profits [retailers and bankcard fraud] *Chain Store Age Exec* 67 sec3:14B-15B N '91

Interest
Statements to the Congress [comments on credit and charge card legislation] J. P. LaWare. *Fed Reserve Bull* 77:983-7 D '91
When credit-card issuers say relax, don't! [hidden cost of charging] D. Dunn. tab *Bus Week* p146 Ja 13 '92

Laws and regulations
Statements to the Congress [comments on credit and charge card legislation] J. P. LaWare. *Fed Reserve Bull* 77:983-7 D '91

Marketing
Amex reveals rewards program [Canadian ad campaign introduces point system] il *Marketing* 96:16 N 18 '91
Can affinity cards work for publishers? [Sports Illustrated's SportsPass Visa Card] L. I. Fried. il *Folio* 19:30+ Ag '90

Security measures
The bottom line: maximizing sales and profits [retailers and bankcard fraud] *Chain Store Age Exec* 67 sec3:14B-15B N '91

Selection
Helping consumers choose a credit card [Canada] A. D'Astous and D. Miquelon. bibl diags graphs tabs *J Consum Aff* 25:278-94 Wint '91

Business Periodicals Index, Vol. 34, No. 7, March 1992, p. 97. Copyright © 1992 by the H. W. Wilson Company.

Using the Computer in Your Library Research

A computer can make your library research easier, more accurate, and far more comprehensive. Computers are essential guides to the ever-expanding number of publications available today. More than forty thousand books are published in America each year, and the number of articles and reports in technical journals published in just one month alone is staggering. Thanks to computer technology, it is possible to search through this mountain of information and locate the materials you need on your topic. As we have already seen, many libraries have switched to a computerized catalog to help patrons find out a variety of things about a given book. Furthermore, many businesses regularly conduct computer searches to find the most current information on a topic before preparing a proposal or a report.

A computerized search offers many advantages. It is a fast alternative to a manual search through an index or abstract, because you can go through ten to fifteen years of an index in just a few minutes. A computer search can also help you locate items that you may otherwise miss and can give you access to materials your library does not have.

Conducting a computer search usually begins by consulting a trained librarian who will either perform the search for you or assist you in doing your own search. Basically, the procedure is simple. Information found in various indexes and abstracts is stored in on-line databases. (A *database* is an electronic index service that contains a file of information from which the computer then retrieves the key citations you need.) Several hundred databases exist. In fact, almost every professional discipline has its own database—aerospace (*Aerospace Database*), criminal justice (*Criminal Justice Periodical Index*), nursing (*Cumulative Index to Nursing & Allied Health Literature*), chemistry (*Chemistry Abstracts*), business (*Business Periodicals Index; Trade and Industry Index;* etc.), psychology (*Psychological Abstracts*), engineering (*COMPENDEX*), and so forth.

To search an appropriate database you must first narrow your topic and then give the librarian a key word or phrase (as well as some alternates) that summarizes your topic. For example, to find out specific information about such broad topics as child abuse, artificial intelligence, or laser printers, you would need to restrict your focus more. Also, you may want to put chronological limits on your search, say, to articles published after 1990. Or perhaps you are interested in finding films, reports, or conference proceedings as well as articles. The librarian will then enter this key phrase or word, along with any restrictions you have indicated, into the computer to search the database(s) for materials about your topic. Having completed its search, the computer will list on the display screen the number of entries (articles, books, reports, etc.) that are filed under this key word or phrase. With another command, the computer will then print out a list of bibliographic citations, thus saving you the trouble of having to write them out by hand.

Now we will take a look at the two ways you can search databases using a computer. One of these uses a compact disk and the other employs an on-line search.

Compact Disks

This type of computerized reference work is known as a *CD-ROM* ("compact disk, read-only memory"), meaning that information about the periodicals, encyclopedias, books, and other reference works is stored on a self-contained disk. A disk can store an incredible amount of information. Updata, a CD-ROM distributor, states in a recent catalog that "a CD-ROM can hold up to 600 megabytes (mb) of data, the equivalent of about 1600 floppy disks or a quarter of a million single-space typewritten pages. What a space saver!" It is also a closed system; that is, you are restricted to information placed on the disk. In many instances, this information is updated each month or two and a new disk is then made available for library patrons.

One of the most frequently used compact disk retrieval systems is InfoTrac, available from the Information Access Company. This electronic periodical index far surpasses any printed index in coverage. A single InfoTrac disk, for example, stores bibliographical information about more than one million articles published in more than two thousand periodicals in a variety of databases in business, law, health technology, psychology, and education. If your library subscribes to the General BusinessFile of InfoTrac, you gain access to more than bibliographic information. All of the information contained in the *Business Index, Company ProFile*, and *Investext* databases is integrated. Article citations from business and management publications are linked with company directory information, the full text of newswire reports, and company and industry investment reports. General BusinessFile is the most comprehensive single source database for research on all aspects of business, management, industries, and companies. Like printed indexes, InfoTrac is organized into subject categories with subheadings in each main subject category. InfoTrac begins coverage with articles published in 1980 and supplies two disks to cover the ten-year period from 1980 to 1990. Updated disks are sent to libraries each month. To use InfoTrac you may not need the help of a librarian, but you still must enter a key phrase or word into the computer for it to search the database file and to identify all the appropriate citations to the articles listed on the compact disk. It does this in less than a minute. With another simple command, InfoTrac prints a list of complete bibliographic citations of these articles. In some instances, full texts of selected articles can also be printed.

On-line Searches

On-line searches are available at many libraries. An on-line search works like this. A library subscribes to a particular computerized information retrieval service that has numerous databases stored in its host, mainframe computer. Via its computer terminal, your library is able to dial into these databases. There are more than three thousand different databases, and while no one retrieval service offers access to all of them, these services do supply their customers with vast amounts of information. Many of the databases correspond to printed indexes (e.g., *Business Periodicals Index*), while others are available only through on-line searches—that is, there is no print equivalent for them. An on-line search can offer you bibliographic information (a list of articles and other references for a preliminary working bibliography), copies of abstracts of articles included in certain databases, and in some cases, even copies of the publications themselves. An on-line search can save you time. You can retrieve in a few minutes bibliographic information that would take you hours if you did it manually.

On-line searching differs from compact disks by giving you access to more current material, since information can be continuously fed into the mainframe computer. Furthermore, an on-line search will give you more search options (ways of pulling information out of a database) than you would have using a disk. You can combine terms and even create ones that are not found in printed subject indexes. Finally, some on-line searches offer more specialized (and technical) databases than disks do. Keep in mind, though, that many on-line search services are now making their databases available on disks as well. You might want to consult K. Y. Marcaccio's *Computer-Readable Databases: A Directory and Data Sourcebook,* 8th ed. (Detroit: Gale, 1992).

Below are five on-line searches that you might be likely to use; note that there is some overlap among these different services.

1. DIALOG gives you access to more than 380 bibliographic databases (with more than 260 million entries) in a wide range of fields: agriculture and food sciences (*AGRICOLA*), chemistry (*Chemical Industry Notes*), medicine (*MEDLINE*), oceanography (*Oceanic Abstracts*), business (ABI/INFORM), and social sciences (SOCIAL SCISEARCH). Using DIALOG you can quickly (within a microsecond) search five or six years' worth of *Financial Times, Business Week, Fortune, Forbes,* or *Chemical Week,* and many other publications for information relating directly to your topic. DIALOG also gives users access to information from federal agencies (e.g., *IRS Taxinfo*), professional societies, commercial organizations, and a variety of products and services (especially through the *Electronic Yellow Pages*).

2. WILSONLINE offers subscribers computerized access to the bibliographic information contained in many of the indexes published by the H. W. Wilson Company. Some of these indexes are *Applied Science & Technology Index, Book Review Digest, General Science Index, Readers' Guide to Periodical Literature, Index to Legal Periodicals,* and the *Social Science Index.* WILSONLINE, like most databases, is not cumulative—it does not go back forty or fifty years. Coverage on WILSONLINE varies and will probably change continuously as more information (and years) are added to the individual databases.

3. Bibliographic Retrieval Service (BRS) provides patrons with access to more than 160 different databases from government agencies, professional organizations, and publishers. Among the databases available through BRS are *AIDS Articles, Books in Print, Computer & Mathematics Search, Family Resources, Magazine Index, MEDLINE, National Technical Information Service, RIVE (Resources in Vocational Education), Sports Database,* and *Robotics Information Database.*

4. Dow Jones News/Retrieval supplies access to articles and other information found in the *Wall Street Journal* and *Barron's.*

5. ERIC (Educational Resources Information Center) is a database published by the U.S. Department of Education that indexes more than 700 journals and magazines in education and related areas. The subject index directs users to a variety of educational topics related to both school and on-the-job sites.

Suggestions on Using Computerized Searches

Here is some practical advice on running a computer literature search.

1. Prepare for your search. Do not just walk into the library and tell the librarian you are interested in taxes, credit cards, drug enforcement, or another large topic. Rather than asking for all the information on acid rain, first decide on what restricted area of acid rain you need to research in detail—its effect on crops, its prevention, its danger to the ozone layer, its political effects on neighboring countries, and so on.

2. Conduct a preliminary manual search first to find out approximately how much is written on the topic. Thus you will have some idea whether you will be asking for ten entries or one hundred. Take a look at relevant subject headings in a print index for the last two or three years to get a rough estimate.

3. Be prepared to work with the librarian to refine your search even further. Often the librarian can use two or three different key phrases or words, or a combination or modification of them. Keep in mind that you are not limited to subject terms found in print indexes.

4. Realize that there are limits to the periods of time that databases scan. In some cases, databases will not cover more than the last few years.

5. Understand that libraries often will charge for a computer search. Patrons are usually charged per citation retrieval and per minute for each minute spent connected (via telephone lines) to the database. It is not uncommon to spend $30-$40 for a search on *DIALOG,* for example. You can set a limit on how much you are willing to spend before the search starts.

6. Recognize that your library may have limited access to databases in your field. You may need to use another library that subscribes to additional databases.

Finding a Periodical in Your Library

Once you find an article in an index or through a computer search, your next job is to locate and read it. Libraries list their periodical holdings in different ways. Some libraries list them in a separate catalog; others maintain a holdings list in the form of a computer printout; and still others list them in the general (or library) catalog. The holdings list will tell you to which journals and magazines your library subscribes and how far back the subscription goes. If the journal you are looking for is not on your library's periodical holdings list, you will have to go to another library or seek assistance through interlibrary loan.

If the library has the periodical you are looking for, it may be in a number of places, depending on the date of the issue. Recent periodicals are often housed in a periodicals reading room. Older back issues may be bound with other issues for that year and gathered together in a hard, permanent cover and shelved like a book. Many libraries shelve bound periodicals according to subject matter or alphabetically by title in an area of the library separate from the stacks. Another method of storing back issues is to put them on microfilm or microfiche, which stores information concisely and economically. (Microfilm and microfiche are discussed on pages 338-339.)

Reference Books

The works discussed in this section are kept in the reference room in the library. Reference books usually may not be checked out of the library. More detailed information on specific reference works is given in the appendix to this chapter.

Encyclopedias

The word *encyclopedia* comes from a Greek phrase meaning "general education." Some encyclopedias provide information on an incredibly broad range of subjects. These comprehensive encyclopedias take years to produce and are written by a staff of experts from every major field of knowledge. The information in an encyclopedia is arranged alphabetically, with some subjects receiving as much as twenty pages of coverage. A general encyclopedia can get you started in your research by explaining some key terms, offering a quick summary, and supplying you with a list of further readings. Another advantage of encyclopedias is the colorful and varied illustrations they offer. Three useful general encyclopedias are *Collier's Encyclopedia,* 24 volumes; *Encyclopedia Americana,* 30 volumes; and *New Encyclopaedia Britannica,* 30 volumes.

Do not attempt to do all your research using only encyclopedias, however. They have their limitations. For one thing, the information in them is designed for the general reader, not the specialist. For another reason, general encyclopedias, however good, do not contain the most current information on a subject, especially on technical matters. For that kind of up-to-date material, you must consult periodicals and specialized reference books. Finally, relying on encyclopedias alone reveals your lack of ability to find and use more specialized and restricted sources.

Dictionaries

Dictionaries are perhaps the most important reference tool, because they help you to understand the information gathered from the other works (books, periodicals, pamphlets) that make up the bulk of your research. In addition to giving the meaning of words, dictionaries indicate spelling, pronunciation, etymology (word history), and usage. Generally speaking, dictionaries fall into two categories: general English-language dictionaries and more specialized dictionaries used by a specific profession.

English-language dictionaries are either unabridged or abridged. An unabridged dictionary is a large, comprehensive guide to all the words of the language. The following unabridged dictionaries are excellent references: *Funk & Wagnalls New Standard Dictionary of the English Language,* the *Oxford English Dictionary,* the *Random House Dictionary of the English Language* (2d ed.), and *Webster's Third New International Dictionary of the English Language.* The *Oxford English Dictionary* is a historical dictionary; that is, it lists the dates when a word was first used and how it was used and supplies illustrative quotations.

Abridged dictionaries are much smaller. They can range from a pocket dictionary to a large compilation with photographs and other illustrations. The following abridged dictionaries are useful: the *American Heritage Dictionary,* the

Random House College Dictionary, Webster's New Collegiate Dictionary, and *Webster's New World Dictionary.*

You will frequently use dictionaries, such as those described in the appendix, that contain the specialized vocabulary of your profession. These specialized, or field, dictionaries not only define the words used in the literature of a profession but also help to characterize that profession's scope and importance.

Abstracts

An *abstract* is a short summary. In addition to listing the author's name, title, and publication data, an abstract will give a short summary of the content and scope of the book, article, or pamphlet. By condensing this information, an abstract can save users hours of time by letting them know if the work is relevant to their topic. Figure 9.10 contains an abstract that appeared in *Women's Studies Abstracts* of an article about the increasing numbers of women joining municipal police departments.

Use abstracts with caution, however, for they are not a substitute for the article or book they summarize. A few sentences highlighting the content of a book or article obviously omit much. When in doubt about what is omitted, read the original work to uncover the details, the rationale, and the dimensions of the whole problem. Never quote from an abstract; always cite material from the original work.

Not every field has an abstracting service, nor is every article or book always abstracted. The titles of abstracts found in the appendix to this chapter will give

FIGURE 9.10   An example from *Women's Studies Abstracts.*

1221A. Martin, Susan E. "Women on the move?--A report on the status of women in policing." Women and Criminal Justice 1 (1989): 21-40.

Since the passage of the 1972 Amendments to the Civil Rights Act, many police departments have eliminated discriminatory personal policies, but the impact of these changes is largely unexplored. This article examines evidence of change in the status of women in municiple police agencies in the past decade, based on the response of 319 agencies serving populations over 50,000 to a mail survey. The data indicate that the population of women in large and medium-sized police departments has increased from 4.2 percent of sworn personal in 1978 to 8.8 percent in 1986. The proportion of women supervisors also has increased during the same period. Currently women are accepted as recruits in proportion to their representation among the applicants, but they still constitute a small portion (20 percent) of the applicant pool. Women now are assigned to field operations units (principally patrol) in proportion to their representation in policing. Affirmative action policies have had a major impact on the current entry rate and overall representation of women in policing, although some changes have occurred across the board. The paper concludes with some policy recommendations for accelerating the slow pace of change in the status of women in policing.

Source: *Women's Studies Abstracts.* Vol. 19, no. 3 (1990): 13.

you a clear idea of the range of fields that do offer this valuable service. Chapter 11 (pages 413–415) will give you guidelines on how to write your own abstracts.

Handbooks, Manuals, and Almanacs

Handbooks, manuals, and almanacs supply you with definitions of terms in your field, statistical facts, explanations of procedures, and authoritative reviews of the kinds of practical and professional problems and solutions you will encounter on the job. In the library catalog these works will be marked *Ref.* or *R.*, indicating that they are shelved in the reference section of your library.

When you look for the reference books in your field, make sure that you use the most up-to-date ones. Also, consult more than one manual or handbook in your field. Compare their discussions of the same topic; different approaches or emphases will help you to research a given procedure more accurately.

Government Documents

The U.S. government, through its diverse agencies and departments, engages vigorously in conducting research and in publishing its findings. This published material, collectively referred to as *government documents,* can be in the form of journal articles, pamphlets, research reports, transcripts of government hearings, speeches, or books. These materials have immense practical value for the research you do in your field. Government reports, for example, will discuss care of the aged, flood insurance, farming techniques, fire precautions, housing costs, outdoor recreation, and urban development.

Three indexes to government documents are especially helpful in guiding you through this vast store of information.

1. The *Monthly Catalog of U.S. Government Publications.* Published since 1895 by the GPO (Government Printing Office), this index lists government documents published during that month. The catalog is arranged by agencies that publish or sponsor works (e.g., the departments of Agriculture, Commerce, Interior, State, and so forth). At the back of each issue there is also an index to subjects, authors, titles, key words in titles, reports, and contract numbers. Each entry provides the author's or agency's name, the title, the date, a brief description of the contents of the document (including whether it contains a bibliography, maps, or index), when and where the research was conducted, who sponsored it (including a contract number), the price, and how to order a copy. Figure 9.11 (p. 334) shows you how to interpret a sample entry.

2. The *Index to Government Periodicals.* Published since 1970, this subject and author guide to more than two hundred periodicals published by the federal government is issued quarterly and cumulated annually. The titles of some of these periodicals suggest their research value: *American Rehabilitation, Fire Management Notes, Highway and Urban Mass Transportation, Marine*

FIGURE 9.11 Sample entry with explanation of codes from the *Monthly Catalog* of *U.S. Government Publications*.

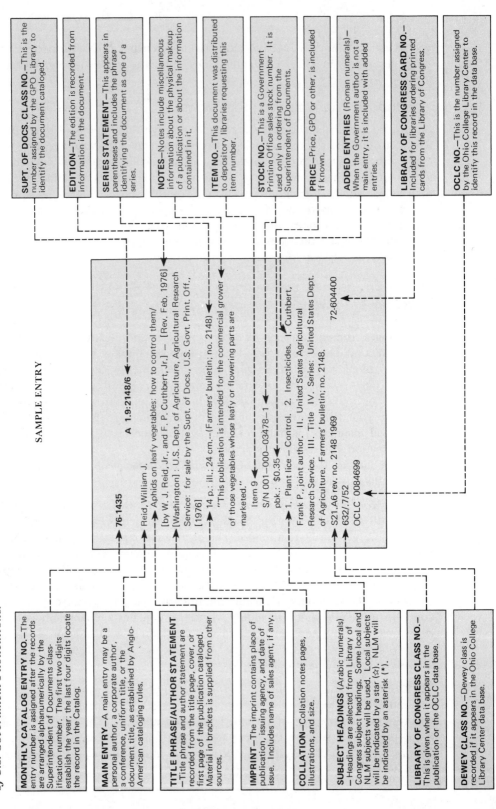

FIGURE 9.12   Some entries from *Index to Government Periodicals*.

GRAHAM, Thomas K.
How do you fit? il Approach 32 7 13 My **87-013**
GRAHAM, Vickie M.
Getting S. A. savvy. il Airman 31 6 17-22 Je **87-009**
Mountain medics. il Airman 31 3 36-39 Mr **87-009**
Testing our high-tech future—now! il Airman 31 1 29-33 Ja **87-009**
GRAIN
Look ahead byproducts and markets. Farmline 8 4 5 Ap **87-253**
Measuring government's role in agriculture around the world. Doug Martinez, il, ref, tab Farmline 8 5 3-5+ My **87-253**
                    Byproducts
Despite obstacles, potential exists for sorghum sales. For Agric 25 5 9-11 My **87-052**
Feed grains project a success in Middle East. For Agric 25 5 2 My **87-052**
                    Consumption
Biggest potential grain markets are middle-income countries. Mervin Yetley and Suzanne Marks, il, ch For Agric 25 4 1£ Ap **87-052**
Rising incomes encourage coarse grain use in developing world. Gary Vocke, For Agric 25 4 20 Ap **87-052**
                    Diseases
Preserving the stuff of life. Stephen Berberich, ch Agric Res 35 4 6-9 Ap **87-004**
                    Drying
Plans afoot to expand grain storage capacity. For Agric 25 4 22 Ap **87-052**
                    Exports
Export growth markets for U.S. grain

GRAMM-RUDMAN-HOLLINGS Act See
Balanced Budget and Emergency Deficit Reduction Act
GRANADE, H. Ray
Gambierdiscus toxicus from the Caribbean: a source of toxins involved in ciguatera. Joseph P. McMillan and others, ref, tab Marine Fish Rev 48 4 48-52 **86-065**
GRAND Duchy of Luxembourg See
Luxembourg
GRANITE
Radon vs. lung cancer: new study weighs the risks. Richard E. Toohey, il, gr Logos 5 1 7-11 Spr **87-340**
GRANT, Cheryl E.
Hickman catheter clots: a common occurrence despite daily heparin flushing. Anita Johnson Anderson and others, ref, tab Cancer Treat Rep 71 6 651-653 Je **87-176**
GRANT, Don
Great Lakes forest fire compact. Don Grant and Art Sutton, mp Fire Man Notes 48 1 21 **87-184**
GRANT, Ulysses S.
Dismantling the myth. Harry J. Maihafer, il, por Mil Rev 67 6 58-62 Je **87-283**
GRANTS See
Federal aid
Foundations
Scholarships and fellowships
GRANULOCYTES   urogenital tumor cells.
                                         J Nat

Index to Government Periodicals (April–June 1987): 153. © Infordata International. Chicago, 1987.

Fisheries Review, Occupational Outlook Quarterly, Pesticides Monitoring Journal, and *Tree Planters' Notes.* Figure 9.12 shows some entries from this index.

3. *CIS/Index to Publications of the United States Congress.* Published monthly since 1970 by the Congressional Information Service (CIS), this reference work indexes and abstracts House and Senate documents, reports, hearings, investigations, and other publications. It is a particularly valuable guide to legislative investigations and decisions. Annual cumulative volumes are published.

States and counties also engage in research and publish their findings. The Library of Congress publishes the *Monthly Checklist of State Publications,* which lists, according to the individual states, such materials as pamphlets, statistical studies, yearbooks, and histories. At the county level, practical advice and publications are available on a wide range of topics in agriculture, education, food science, housing, and water resources. You may want to check with your county agent for copies of relevant publications.

The Popular Press

The "popular press" includes reading material written in nontechnical language for the general public. Pamphlets, brochures, consumer manuals, and newspapers constitute the popular press. This section will show you where to find them indexed and how to obtain copies of specific articles.

Vertical File Materials

Every library receives, as part of its collection of popular press, materials that are best classified as temporary, or "ephemeral," documents. These materials—pamphlets, catalogs, promotional materials, posters, charts, and maps—are stored in the library's *vertical files,* often one or a series of file cabinets, or in a library's special collections department. Although these materials may not be listed in the library catalog, the titles (and sources) may suggest the kinds of topics they cover: "A Guide to the New Jelico Drill" (from a manufacturer), "High Blood Pressure" (from the American Heart Association), "Highway Safety" (from a state highway department), "So You Want to Be a Geologist" (from a professional society), "A Map of the Olympic Sites" (from the Olympic committee). In addition, you will find clippings from newspapers and magazines on topics that the librarian believes are of interest to patrons.

You may also want to consult the *Vertical File Index* (1936–), which lists these pamphlets, posters, maps, charts, brochures, and so forth under subject headings, along with a title index. Another especially helpful feature of the *Vertical File Index* is that it lists the addresses of the companies and associations from whom you may obtain a copy of the publication, sometimes free of charge. It is therefore a good reference to use when you are job hunting.

Indexes to Newspapers

In many ways newspapers provide a valuable source of information relevant to the research you do in school or on the job. Newspapers provide information about community projects, financial changes, or recreational facilities that might be useful. Newspapers can also help you to locate new markets or sites or expand those your company or agency already has.

A thorough guide to the newspapers published in the United States and Canada is the *Gale Directory of Publications,* formerly known as the *Ayer Directory of Periodicals.* This work, issued annually, lists the date a paper began publication; its current address, rates, and circulation; and its religious or political preference. The directory also includes a capsule history of the community served by the paper. Unfortunately, it will not refer you to specific stories. For that information you need to consult an index. The best one is the *New York Times Index,* which indexes by subject and author stories that have appeared in its paper since 1851. This index also summarizes stories and reprints the photographs, maps, and other illustrations that accompanied some of the stories. Still another advantage this comprehensive index offers is that you can find the date of an event in it and then use that date to see how a local newspaper covered the story. Many libraries have the back issues of the *New York Times* on microfilm.

In addition to the *New York Times Index,* you should also look at the indexes to the stories published in four newspapers representing four main areas of the country: the East Coast (*Washington Post*), the Midwest (*Chicago Tribune*), the South (*New Orleans Times-Picayune*), and the West Coast (*Los Angeles Times*). You might also consult the very valuable *Wall Street Journal* and *Christian Science Monitor,* which publish their own indexes.

Almost every newspaper is indexed. Often you can find the index to your local newspaper in that section of a newspaper office called the "morgue," where all the back issues of a paper are stored. To use the index, all you need is the date of the story you are interested in. Newspapers gladly allow readers access to back issues, often help by conducting computerized searches of topics, and may even photocopy a story for you.

NewsBank

Begun in 1982, NewsBank is an extremely useful newspaper reference service that offers both a collection of newspaper stories and indexes to the topics in them. NewsBank supplies the full text of selected articles and reviews found in newspapers from more than five hundred cities across the United States. It reprints stories on microfiche (transparent four-by-six-inch cards on which the pages of the newspaper are greatly reduced; see page 339). While you will not find stories from the readily available *New York Times, Wall Street Journal,* or *Christian Science Monitor* in NewsBank, you will be able to locate articles that have appeared in major newspapers in cities such as Atlanta, Cincinnati, Houston, Kansas City, Las Vegas, Oakland (CA), Providence (RI), and many others. The articles that NewsBank selects for inclusion deal with a wide range of topics including business and economic development, consumer affairs, employment, the environment, films and television, health, housing and land development, the performing arts, social relations, and transportation. NewsBank makes stories from across the country easy to obtain and to read and allows the researcher to see how a story may be reported differently from one section of the country to another.

The *NewsBank Index,* which is issued monthly, offers a multilevel index system to allow researchers to scan the material for different aspects of a subject. The *Index* is organized by subject headings and by geographic regions. But it is important to keep in mind that the particular citations from NewsBank in the *Index* refer to the NewsBank microfiche card numbers and not to the page numbers or sections from the original newspapers from which they are taken. Since NewsBank makes materials from these five hundred newspapers easily available to library users, it may not be too long before documenting by NewsBank microfiche numbers is widely accepted. In addition to the *Index,* NewsBank's *Reviews in the Arts* and *Names in the News* (both for individuals and groups) are essential guides to the collection.

Audiovisual Materials

Audiovisual materials include records, cassettes, tape recordings, audio compact disks, photographs, films, and microforms. These materials are shelved in a separate part of the library that contains the proper equipment to use them conveniently and properly. Audiovisual titles are listed in the library catalog and perhaps also in a separate audiovisual catalog. One particular type of audiovisual material, microforms, deserves special attention.

The name *microforms* refers to a number of research tools—microfilm, microfiche, microcards—that all make use of microphotography. Each of these library tools presents a great deal of information reduced from its original size and stored compactly on film or tape. The microform process saves the library space, increases the durability of the documents, and offers libraries a wider range of titles for far less money. Microforms are used frequently in business and industry as well. Hospitals can store patients' records much more economically and banks can put canceled checks on microforms for safe storage and easy reference.

Microfilm

A microfilm is a strip of black-and-white film on which reduced images are found. Microfilm is stored on reels, cartridges, or cassettes, as shown in Figure 9.13. These reduced images are microscopic pictures of the pages of books, articles, newspapers, court proceedings, and so forth. The size of these pages has been reduced by microphotography to a fraction of their original size. Believe it or not, "a 1,245-page Bible can be reproduced on a one-inch square piece of microfilm. If the Library of Congress chose, it could store its 270 miles of books and other reference material in six standard filing cabinets."[1] A library could save 95 percent of its space if it converted all its holdings to microfilm.

The advantages microfilm offers are many. Without it, no library could possibly save all the back issues of a local newspaper, let alone a large, nationally famous paper such as the *New York Times.* Moreover, newspapers tear, yellow, and crumble after being used by readers for a few weeks. Using microfilm, a library can store a newspaper's daily issues from an entire month on one reel. A special machine called a *microfilm reader* enlarges the images for reading. Your library has at least one or two of these machines and possibly more. Your librarian will be pleased to show you how to operate one.

FIGURE 9.13   Examples of microfilm stored on (a) reels, (b) cartridges, and (c) cassettes.

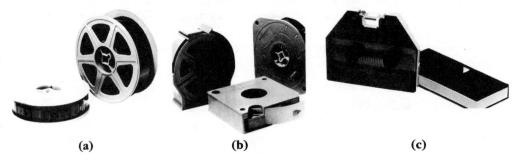

(a)   (b)   (c)

---

[1] *Nation's Business* (Mar. 1971): 20.

FIGURE 9.14   **A sample microfiche.**

E. Stevens Rice, *Fiche and Reel* (Ann Arbor, MI.: Xerox, n.d.): 13. Used by permission.

Microfiche

Microfiche (pronounced "micro feesh") is a close cousin to microfilm. The microfiche process, as described in our discussion of NewsBank, reduces the pages of books, articles, or any other printed materials and puts them on film. Each fiche (or film card) may hold as many as ninety to one hundred pages. Superfiche, an even more compact method of reproduction, can put 300 to 400 pages on a single four-by-six-inch card. A common reduction rate is 24:1. Figure 9.14 shows a sample microfiche. More than fifty-five pages of a periodical are placed on this single card. As with microfilm, you need a special machine to see the material condensed onto microfiche. Using a *microfiche reader*, you slide the four-by-six-inch card onto a tray, push the tray underneath a magnifying lens, and see the material projected and enlarged on a lighted screen. To find the page you want, you simply slide the tray up or down or from right to left.

A *microcard* is identical to a microfiche except that the film is printed on an opaque, not transparent, card.

Note-Taking

Once you have consulted the appropriate sources, you need some systematic way to record relevant information from them in preparing your paper or report. Before you can begin drafting your work, you must be able to organize and classify data from your research efficiently. (Even after you start to draft your report, you will probably need to continue your research and take additional notes.)

Note-taking is the crucial link between finding sources and writing a report. Never trust your memory to keep all your research facts straight. Taking notes is time well spent. Do not be too quick in getting it done or too eager to begin writing your paper. Careless note-taking may cause you to forget page numbers, publishers, dates, or even titles; you might need this information at 2:00 A.M. when the library is closed and your paper is due at 8:00 A.M. Not copying accurately from a source could lead you to omit key words in a quotation or even worse, misrepresent or contradict what the author has said. Carelessness could result in crediting one author with another's work.

Basically, you will be preparing two kinds of notes. One type, on the sources you read, will become your working bibliography. The other type will be reserved for the specific information you take from these sources in the form of direct quotations, paraphrases, or summaries.

Traditionally, researchers have used three-by-five-inch and four-by-six-inch index cards for their note-taking. Some researchers prefer spiral-bound notebooks. A laptop computer or computerized notebook, which you can easily take with you to the library, can greatly help you store and retrieve your notes.

How to Prepare Bibliography Notes

Look at the sample card shown in Figure 9.15. To record accurate and meaningful information on cards, follow these practical guidelines:

1. Use only three-by-five-inch index cards. Do not be tempted to use slips of paper or looseleaf notebook paper; cards are less likely to get lost, and they will help you to organize, alphabetize, and label material.
2. Write on only one side of the card. It is easier to copy and check information when you list it all on one side.
3. Use a ballpoint pen to write your notes. Felt-tip pens or pencils may smudge. Write legibly; print if necessary.
4. Put only one title (article or book or film) on each card. These cards will later have to be arranged in alphabetical order for your Works Cited page (see pages 360–366); if you place two titles on one card, you could end up retyping your entire Works Cited page (to put these "missing" entries in), or you could run the risk of omitting one of the titles.

Whether you use cards or a portable computer, follow these guidelines:

1. Include full bibliographic information for each source. For books, list author, title, chapter titles, edition, date, city of publication, publisher, and page numbers; for articles, supply author, title, journal, volume number, date, and page numbers.
2. Decode and spell out any periodical index or journal abbreviations. Record periodical entries with their full and accurate bibliographic information. (See Chapter 10 on documentation.) The abbreviated entries in indexes such as the *Readers' Guide* or the *Applied Science & Technology Index* are not in

FIGURE 9.15   Card containing bibliographic information on a source.

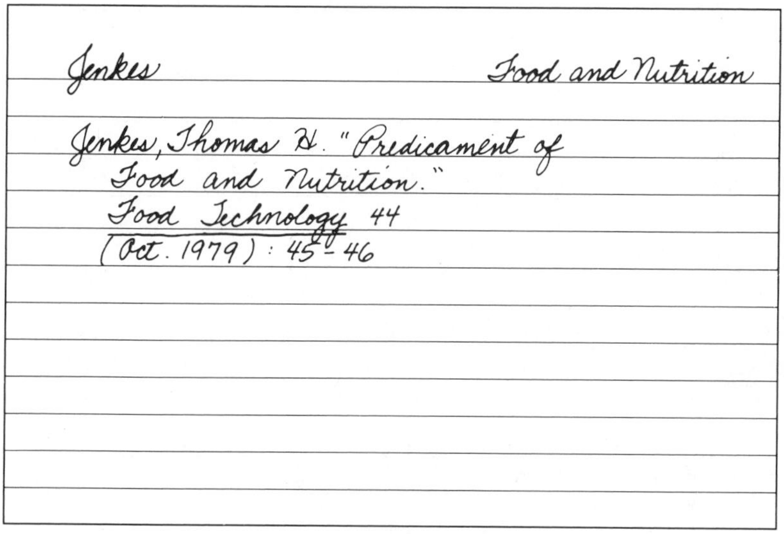

acceptable format for parenthetical documentation or Works Cited page entries in your paper or report.

3. Record the call numbers of the book or periodical (in the upper left-hand corner, if you use cards) so you will know where to find the source again if you need it. If you are using more than one library, also indicate at which library you found the source.

How to Prepare Information Notes

While your bibliography notes will give you important facts about authors, titles, and publication data, your information notes will give you the specific details from these sources that you need to write your paper. Your notes will contain direct quotations from, or paraphrases of, your sources. Quotations and paraphrases are discussed on pages 342–344. Here are some guidelines to follow when preparing note cards like those shown in Figures 9.16 (p. 342) and 9.17. (p. 343):

1. Use four-by-six-inch cards to keep them separate from the three-by-five bibliography cards.
2. Write on only one side of the card. It will be easier for you to arrange the cards in the order you may need them for your paper.
3. Don't include notes from two different sources on one card.

Again, whether you use cards or a laptop computer, follow these guidelines.

1. Copy names, facts, dates, statistics accurately from the source. Be sure, too, that you record the author's words correctly; you may want to quote these words verbatim in your paper. Always compare what you have written with the original.

FIGURE 9.16   Note card containing a direct quotation.

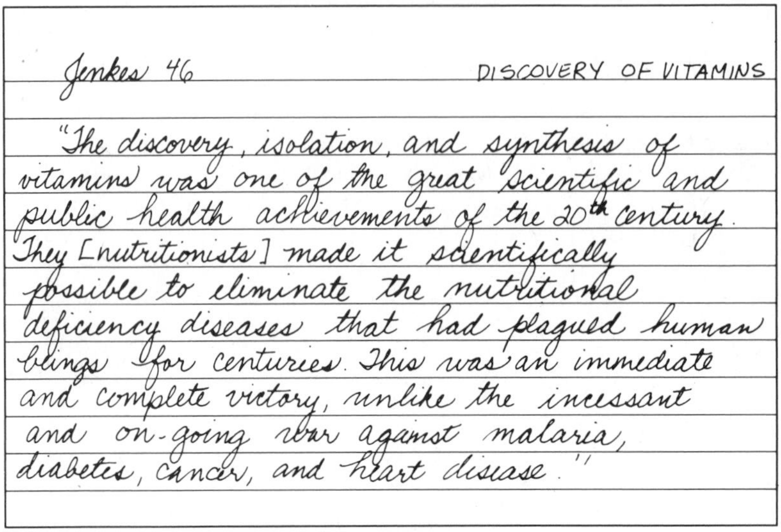

Jenkes 46   DISCOVERY OF VITAMINS

"The discovery, isolation, and synthesis of vitamins was one of the great scientific and public health achievements of the 20th century. They [nutritionists] made it scientifically possible to eliminate the nutritional deficiency diseases that had plagued human beings for centuries. This was an immediate and complete victory, unlike the incessant and on-going war against malaria, diabetes, cancer, and heart disease."

2. Make sure that you distinguish quotations from your own paraphrase by placing quotation marks around any words and sentences you record directly from a source.
3. Write a code word or phrase (in the upper right-hand corner, if you use cards) to identify the topic treated by the source or the information written on the card from that source. Using code words such as "characteristics," "function of," "history of," or "location of" will help you to organize when you write your paper. Figure 9.16 shows how one writer used these code words.
4. You might indicate in the note why the material is significant to your argument or where you might include such information in your report or paper. In Figure 9.17 the writer has identified a possible use for the Dampier paraphrase. You might also write your response to a quotation to help you later organize your paper. But be careful not to include any of your comments within a quotation or paraphrase.
5. Write a short title of the book or journal article (in the upper left-hand corner, if you use cards) or include the author's last name so that the information note is coded to your bibliography note. If your notes extend to a second card, make sure you include the source, with appropriate page number(s) on this second card.

To Quote or Not to Quote

Before recording information from sources, ask yourself these three questions: (1) How much should I take down? (2) How often should I copy the author's words verbatim to use direct quotations? (3) When should I paraphrase or summarize? A safe rule to follow is: Do not be a human photocopying machine. If you write down too many of the author's own words, you will simply be transferring the author's words from the book or article to your paper. That will show that you

FIGURE 9.17 Note card containing a paraphrase.

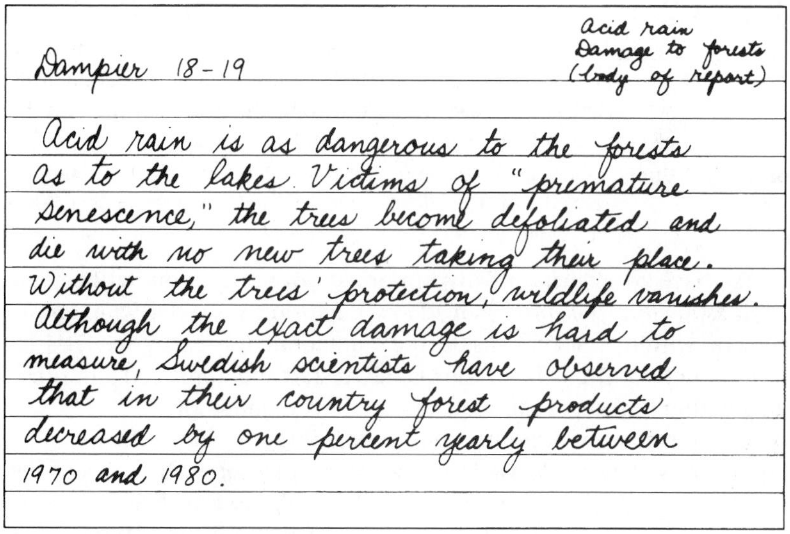

Dampier 18–19

Acid rain
Damage to forests
(body of report)

Acid rain is as dangerous to the forests as to the lakes. Victims of "premature senescence," the trees become defoliated and die with no new trees taking their place. Without the trees' protection, wildlife vanishes. Although the exact damage is hard to measure, Swedish scientists have observed that in their country forest products decreased by one percent yearly between 1970 and 1980.

have read the work but have not evaluated its findings. Do not use direct quotations simply as a filler.

Direct quotations should be used sparingly and saved for when they count most. When an author has summarized a great deal of significant information concisely into a few well-chosen sentences, you may want to quote this summary verbatim. Or if a writer has clarified a difficult concept exceedingly well, you may want to include this clarification exactly as it is listed. And certainly the author's chief statement or thesis may deserve to be quoted directly. Figure 9.16 contains such an important statement. Just be careful that you do not quote verbatim all of the evidence leading to that conclusion. The conclusion may be pointedly expressed in two or three sentences; the evidence could cover many pages. If you are worried about exactly how much to quote verbatim, keep in mind that no more than 10 to 15 percent of your paper should be made up of direct quotations. Remember that when you quote someone directly, you are telling your readers that these words are the most important part of the author's work as far as you are concerned. Be a selective filter, not a large funnel.

There will be times when a sentence or passage is particularly useful, but you may not want to quote it in its entirety. You may want to delete some words that are not really necessary for your purpose. These omissions are indicated by using *ellipsis* (three spaced dots within the sentence to indicate where the words are omitted). Here are some examples.

Full Quotation: "Diet and nutrition, which researchers have studied extensively, significantly affect oral health."

Quotation with Ellipsis: "Diet and nutrition . . . significantly affect oral health."

When the omission occurs at the end of the sentence, you must include the end-of-sentence punctuation after the ellipsis. In the following example, note how the shortened sentence ends with four spaced dots: a period and the three dots for the ellipsis.

Full Quotation: "Decisions on how to operate the company should be based on the most accurate and relevant information available from both within the company and from the specific community that the establishment serves."

Quotation with Ellipsis: "Decisions on how to operate the company should be based on the most accurate and relevant information available. . . ."

At times you may have to insert your own information within a quotation. This addition, known as an *interpolation,* is made by enclosing your clarifying identification or remark within brackets inside the quotation; for example, "It [the new transportation network] has been thoroughly tested and approved." In other words, anything within brackets is not part of the original quotation.

Most of your note-taking will be devoted to paraphrasing rather than writing down direct quotations. A *paraphrase* is a restatement in your own words of the author's ideas. Even though you are using your own words to translate or restate, you still must document the paraphrase because you are using the author's facts and interpretations. You do not use quotation marks, though. When you include a paraphrase in your paper, you should be careful to do four things:

1. Be faithful to the author's meaning. Do not alter facts or introduce new ideas.
2. Follow the order in which the author presents the information.
3. Include in your paraphrase only what is relevant for your paper. Delete any details not essential for your work.
4. Use paraphrases in your report selectively. You do not want your work to be merely a restatement of someone else's.

Paraphrased material can be introduced in your paper with an appropriate identifying phrase, such as "According to Dampier's study," "To paraphrase Dampier," or "As Dampier observes." Figure 9.17 shows a note card containing a paraphrase of the following quotation.

> While the effects of acid rain are felt first in lakes, which act as natural collection points, some scientists fear there may be extensive damage to forests as well. In the process described by one researcher as "premature senescence," trees exposed to acid sprays lose their leaves, wilt, and finally die. New trees may not grow to replace them. Deprived of natural cover, wildlife may flee or die. The extent of the damage to forest lands is extremely difficult to determine, but scientists find the trend worrisome. In Sweden, for example, one estimate calculates that the yield in forest products decreased by about one percent each year during the 1970s.[2]

---

[2] Bill Dampier, "Now Even the Rain Is Dangerous," *International Wildlife* 10 (Mar.–Apr. 1980): 18–19.

✓ Revision Checklist

Like the writing process itself, doing research means going through a number of steps. In order to make sure your research is complete and accurate, you need to be able to answer the following questions successfully.

1. Is my topic significant and relevant for my audience?
2. Have I limited the scope of my topic before I began my research?
3. After narrowing my topic, did I make a list of key terms to aid me in my research?
4. Have I consulted books and periodicals in my research?
5. Did I check specialized indexes as well as general indexes? Have I also consulted indexes and guides to government documents?
6. Did I check library catalogs for records, tape recordings, films, or other nonprint sources?
7. On my bibliography cards, did I correctly copy all the publication information that I will need? Do my notecards have page numbers where I paraphrased or quoted material?
8. On my notecards have I clearly indicated which material is quoted and which is paraphrased?
9. Did I accurately copy quoted material onto my notecards? Have I double-checked my sources carefully?
10. Am I making sure that I am not quoting excessively?
11. Do all my paraphrases fairly and accurately represent the original material?
12. Have I clearly distinguished my comments and responses from the source material I have used?
13. Did I use correct punctuation with my direct quotations—especially ellipses and brackets?
14. Have I kept careful records about precise bibliographic information on all the sources that I consulted, especially those from which I am quoting or paraphrasing?

APPENDIX: Some Helpful Reference Works

After the title of each of the following reference works is a brief annotation indicating, sometimes with a direct quotation taken from the particular work, its audience, organization, and coverage. The dates in parentheses after indexes and abstracts refer to the year in which they began publication.

Indexes

Bibliographic Index: A Cumulative Bibliography of Bibliographies (1937). Issued three times a year, this index lists bibliographies on people, technical and popular subjects, and organizations that have appeared in journal or magazine articles, books, or separately.

Bibliography and Index of Geology (1969). Published monthly, this international index to earth sciences literature covers such sources as serials, government reports, proceedings and papers presented at scientific meetings, books, maps, and other monographs. This title supersedes both *Bibliography and Index of North American Geology* and *Bibliography and Index Exclusive of North America*.

Biological and Agricultural Index (1945). This index is published monthly with quarterly and yearly cumulative issues. Formerly called *Agricultural Index,* this work indexes about 200 periodicals in such fields as agricultural economics, animal husbandry, ecology, food science, forestry, horticulture, marine biology, nutrition, soil science, and veterinary medicine.

Criminal Justice Periodical Index (1975). Published yearly, this index contains both an author and subject list. It is a guide to articles in more than 100 journals in law enforcement, corrections, paralegal work, security, and traffic enforcement.

Cumulative Index to Nursing & Allied Health Literature (1955). Published bimonthly, this index surveys over 250 journals and magazines and English-language books in the nursing and allied health fields. Nurses, respiratory and physical therapists, social workers, radiological and medical technicians will find this index a convenient guide to literature in their fields.

Education Index (1929). This index is published every month except July and August. It lists periodicals that deal with all aspects of education from driver training to adult and continuing education.

Engineering Index (1937). This index, issued monthly, includes subject, author, and translation lists directing users to a variety of materials in engineering developments. It is also available in a machine-readable version under the title of *COMPENDEX.*

Hospital Literature Index (1945). Published quarterly, this "is a subject-author index of literature about the administration, planning, financing of medical care facilities and about administrative aspects of medical, paramedical, and prepayment fields." While it does not survey nursing literature, it does cover administrative and educational issues in allied health fields.

Index to Legal Periodicals (1926). This index is published monthly, except September, and contains a subject and author index to more than 350 law journals published worldwide. "Case notes or discussions of recent cases are listed by the name of the case discussed at the end of the subheading 'Cases.'" It also includes a book review index.

Index Medicus (1879). Published monthly by the National Library of Medicine in Washington, D.C., this index surveys more than 2,500 journals published worldwide in medicine and ancillary fields (for example, medical technology, medical records, respiratory therapy, etc.). It contains subject and author sections and translates titles of articles not written in English.

Monthly Index Listings (1971–1976), formerly *Index of Supermarket Articles* (1935). Published by the Supermarket Institute in Chicago, this index surveys articles on supermarkets and food suppliers published in such journals as *Chain Store Age, Grocery Editions, Progressive Grocer, Supermarket Merchandising*, and *Supermarket Manager*.

Science Citation Index (1961). Published bimonthly by the Institute for Scientific Information, this index covers more than 2,000 journals in a wide range of fields, including agriculture, computer science and cybernetics, engineering technology, forestry, medicine, metallurgy and mining, oceanography, polymer science, substance abuse, and water resources. It provides access to all articles written by researchers as well as all citations to an author's work in the literature by means of five related sections—citation index, patent citation index, corporate index, source index, and permuterm (word associations) index.

Social Sciences Index and *Humanities Index* (1907). Known as the *International Index* from 1907 to 1965 and the *Social Sciences and Humanities Index* from 1965 to 1974, these two works now list articles in many of the social sciences (e.g., sociology, political science) and the humanities.

Encyclopedias

The Arnold Encyclopedia of Real Estate, edited by Alvin Arnold and Jack Kusnet. Boston: Warren, Gorham & Lamont, 1978. A topical "Entry Finder" at the back "classifies selected entries into twelve major subjects"; contains annual yearbook updates.

Encyclopedia of Animal Care, edited by Geoffrey P. West. 15th ed. London: A. & C. Black, 1985. This work gives information on "the diseases, breeding, and health of domesticated animals and is intended for farmers, public health officials and breeders who do not need a veterinary reference work or who need more detail than a popular magazine provides."

Encyclopedia of Architectural Technology, edited by Pedro Guedes. New York: McGraw-Hill, 1979. "Architect, art historian, and engineer" as well as the "concerned" layperson should profit from this book. It is divided into six sections: stylistic periods; building forms and building types; structures; structural, mechanical and environmental systems; building materials; and tools, techniques, and fixings. The encyclopedia offers 800 illustrations.

Encyclopedia of Banking and Finance, edited by Glenn G. Munn. 8th ed. Revised and expanded by F. L. Garcia. Boston: Bankers Publishing Company, 1983. Written for the general public, this encyclopedia includes more than 4,000 entries dealing with banking terminology. A "Quick Index" and extensive cross-references make this work easy to use.

Encyclopedia of Careers and Vocational Guidance. 6th ed. Chicago: J. G. Ferguson, 1984. 3 vols. Provides useful overviews of the kinds of requirements and responsibilities necessary for numerous technical and managerial positions.

Encyclopedia of Computer Science and Engineering, edited by Anthony Ralston. 2nd ed. New York: Van Nostrand Reinhold, 1983. This work has a helpful list of titles on related subjects at the beginning of each section. It also has appendixes on abbreviations, acronyms, mathematical notations, numerical tables, and key high-level languages.

Encyclopedia of Food Technology and Food Science Series. Westport, Connecticut: Avi Publishing. Vol. 1 *The Encyclopedia of Food Engineering,* edited by C. W. Hall, A. W. Farrall, and A. L. Rippen, 1971. Vol. 2 *The Encyclopedia of Food Technology,* edited by Arnold H. Johnson and Martin S. Peterson, 1974. Vol. 3 *The Encyclopedia of Food Science,* edited by Arnold H. Johnson and Martin S. Peterson, 1978.

Encyclopedia of Marine Resources, edited by Frank E. Firth. New York: Van Nostrand Reinhold, 1979. Information on the "most significant aspects of the ocean's resources" will be of interest to biologists, food technologists, fishery management specialists, and others.

Encyclopedia of Materials Handling, edited by Douglas Woodley. New York: Pergamon, 1964. 2 vols. It contains valuable chapters on machines (conveyors, elevators, cranes, hoists, trucks, etc.), unitization, and loading and transportation.

Encyclopedia of Practical Photography, edited by Eastman Kodak Company. Garden City, New York: Amphoto, 1979. 14 vols. In this work the "emphasis . . . is on practical advice and instruction in using light, film, and chemicals to get the most of your equipment. Here you will find the how-to information necessary for actual production of photographic images."

Encyclopedia of Textiles, edited by the editors of *American Fabrics Magazine.* 3rd ed. Englewood Cliffs, New Jersey: Prentice-Hall, 1980. This is a "reference guide for every person concerned with the producing and marketing of fibers and fabrics, and for the professions of designing and advertising which service the textile industry." A lavishly illustrated work, this encyclopedia contains information on the history, production, and manufacturing of natural and synthetic fibers, colors and dyes, and textile printing.

Encyclopedia of Urban Planning, edited by Arnold Whittick. New York: McGraw-Hill, 1974. Reprint: Huntington, New York: R. E. Krieger, 1980. A preface describes and defines urban planning. Numerous pictures, maps, and drawings and a bibliography at the end of each section are included in this encyclopedia, which provides information on international projects, urban renewal, legislation, and other topics.

Food & Nutrition Encyclopedia, edited by A. H. Ensminger et al. Clovis, California: Pegus Press, 1983. 2 vols; 1,600 illustrations. The goal of this work is "to produce the most complete and in-depth foods and nutrition source ever." Containing more than 2,800 entries, it "covers all aspects of food-nutrition-health with adequate historical and interpretive context. Each article includes all relevant aspects of the topic."

Goodheart-Wilcox Automotive Encyclopedia, edited by William K. Toboldt, Larry Johnson, and Steven W. Olive. South Holland, Illinois: Goodheart-Wilcox, 1989. Detailed guide to auto repair and maintenance.

McGraw-Hill Encyclopedia of Energy, edited by Sybil P. Parker. 2nd ed. New York: McGraw-Hill, 1981. This encyclopedia is divided into two sections: "Energy Perspectives" and "Energy Technology." The encyclopedia "with its more than 300 articles written by specialists is designed to aid the student, librarian, scientist, engineer, teacher, and lay reader with any information on any aspect of energy from the economic and political to the environmental and technological."

McGraw-Hill Encyclopedia of Environmental Science, edited by Sybil P. Parker. 2nd ed. New York: McGraw-Hill, 1980. This work contains 300 alphabetically arranged articles, most of which include a bibliography. There is also an analytical index.

McGraw-Hill Encyclopedia of Food, Agriculture & Nutrition, edited by Daniel N. Lapedes. New York: McGraw-Hill, 1977. Following five feature articles are 400 alphabetically arranged articles on subjects dealing with "the cultivation, harvesting, and processing of food crops; food manufacturing; and health and nutrition—from the economic and political to the technological."

McGraw-Hill Encyclopedia of Science and Technology, edited by Sybil P. Parker. 7th ed. New York: McGraw-Hill, 1992. 20 vols. Extremely wide-ranging, this is the most comprehensive encyclopedia you can consult for scientific and technological subjects.

The New Encyclopedia of Furniture, edited by Joseph Aronson. New York: Crown, 1967. This work contains numerous drawings and designs of period pieces. A bibliography and a glossary of designers is found at the end of the work.

The New York Botanical Garden Illustrated Encyclopedia of Horticulture, edited by Thomas H. Everett. New York: Garland Publishing, 1984. 10 vols. This work provides a "comprehensive description and evaluation of horticulture as it is known and practiced in the United States and Canada by amateurs and by professionals, including those responsible for botanical gardens, public parks, and industrial landscapes."

Dictionaries

Dictionary of Architecture and Construction, edited by Cyril M. Harris. New York: McGraw-Hill, 1975. This dictionary provides definitions of terms "encountered in the everyday practice of architecture and construction and in their associated fields." It emphasizes terms from the building trades and includes information on "building products and materials, and related terms dealing with their design, appearance, performance, installation, and testing"; it also covers construction equipment.

Dictionary of Computers, Data Processing, and Telecommunications, edited by Jerry M. Rosenberg. 2nd ed. New York: Wiley, 1987. Offering more than 10,000 entries, "this work contains terms that relate directly or indirectly to usage of hardware and software, including the broad categories of computers, data processing, distributed data processing, home computers, information transmission, microprocessors, minicomputers, personal computers, programming languages, telecommunications, and word processing."

Dictionary of Computing, edited by Valerie Illingworth. 3rd ed. New York: Oxford, 1990. Written for both the professional and layperson, this dictionary includes more than 4,000 terms used in computer science and related fields such as electronics, logic, and mathematics. It offers a number of useful supplements containing diagrams.

Dictionary of Nutrition and Food Technology, edited by Arnold E. Bender. 6th ed. Boston: Butterworths, 1990. This dictionary is for students in agriculture, commerce, food science, dietetics, home economics, sociology, and medicine. "The purpose of this dictionary is to assist the specialist from one field to understand the technical terms used by the variety of specialists in the food fields."

Dictionary of Practical Law, edited by Charles F. Hemphill, Jr. and Phyllis D. Hemphill. Englewood Cliffs, New Jersey: Prentice-Hall, 1979. "This dictionary was prepared for the needs of law students, paralegal courses, legal secretaries, and students in the administration of justice, corrections, and rehabilitation. It was also written for the needs of working police officers, and for those who simply want a definition of legal terms in everyday language."

Fairchild's Dictionary of Textiles, edited by Isabel B. Wingate. 5th ed. New York: Fairchild, 1979. It includes "terms, often of several words used or once used in the textile industry, to identify the thousands of fiber-based products employed for either the consumer or industrial purposes, along with the fibers and production processes and major equipment." It is useful to "people in all branches of industry: manufacturing, sales, producers, designers."

McGraw-Hill Dictionary of Scientific and Technical Terms, edited by Sybil P. Parker. 4th ed. New York: McGraw-Hill, 1989. It includes terms used by professionals in agriculture, ecology, data processing, food engineering, graphic arts, medicine, microbiology, navigation, oceanography, petrology, and veterinary medicine; it supplies "also known as" terms and emphasizes definitions rather than pronunciation.

Means Illustrated Construction Dictionary, edited by Kornelis Smit. Kingston, Massachusetts: R. S. Means Co., 1985. Written in simple, straightforward language, this dictionary offers definitions of conventional as well as regional and colloquial terms used in all phases of the construction industry. It includes the most recent technology and provides a contemporary rather than a historical perspective.

Modern Dictionary of Electronics, edited by Rudolf F. Graf. 6th ed. Indianapolis: Howard W. Sams, 1984. This work supplies detailed definitions of words, concepts, and abbreviations used by many professionals in electronics and electrical engineering.

Mosby's Medical Nursing and Allied Health Dictionary, 3rd ed. St. Louis: Mosby Year Book, 1990. According to the preface, this is "a reference book of consummate usefulness to nurses and other health professionals." Contains full-sentence definitions, includes information about etymology and pronunciation, and provides extensive cross-references and illustrations.

Office Automation: A Glossary and Guide, edited by Nancy MacLellan Edwards. White Plains, New York: Van Nostrand Reinhold, 1983. Intended for office service managers, operations managers, purchasing agents, or "anyone who is not a professional in any of the technical areas, but who must understand their applications, their abbreviations, their symbols, and their jargon when undertaking needs analyses, evaluating equipment, talking with vendors, implementing systems, and training personnel."

Prentice-Hall Dictionary of Business, Finance, and Law, edited by Michael Downey Rice. Englewood Cliffs, New Jersey: Prentice-Hall, 1983. Intended "for business people who deal with the law, and for lawyers who deal with business," this work is also useful for students of business and law, engineering, economics, and public administration.

Professional Secretary's Encyclopedic Dictionary, edited by the Prentice-Hall Editorial Staff; revised by Mary A. DeVries. 4th ed. Englewood Cliffs, New Jersey: Prentice-Hall, 1989. This work contains information on all aspects of secretarial practice, covering everything from "color coding" to "records management" to word processing.

Stedman's Medical Dictionary. 25th ed. Baltimore, Maryland: Williams and Wilkins, 1990. Illustrated. This is a highly technical work that contains terms from all medical specialties. Heavily illustrated, it provides information on pronunciations, etymologies, spellings, and word groups.

Abstracts

Acid Rain Abstracts (1990). This work provides a comprehensive 100-word summary of each entry, plus all bibliographic information.

Air Pollution Abstracts (1970–1976). Compiled by the Air Pollution Technical Information Center of the Environmental Protection Agency, this work contains a subject and author index and surveys periodicals, books, hearings, investigations, and other legislative actions.

Biological Abstracts (1926). This work surveys more than 5,000 journals in every biological field; it also lists new books.

CAD/CAM Abstracts (1988). This work provides a comprehensive 100-word summary of each entry, plus all bibliographic information. Topics concern computer-aided design and manufacturing.

Chemical Abstracts (1907). This work, the most comprehensive source for international chemical literature, is issued weekly with semiannual cumulative indexing. Materials indexed include journal articles, patents, reviews, technical reports, monographs, conference proceedings, symposia, dissertations, and books. Weekly issues provide keyword, author, and patent indexes.

Communication Abstracts (1977). Issued four times a year, this work provides a "comprehensive source of information about communication-related publications worldwide," including articles, reports, and books. Subject categories include advertising, broadcasting, communication theory and practice, journalism, public relations, and radio and television (for example, audiences, effects, programming). It excludes "general film-related topics."

Computer & Control Abstracts (1969). Issued monthly, this work "forms the world's major English-language abstracting service covering the fields of computer and control engineering." It includes more than 40,000 items per year and contains subject, author, and subsidiary indexes.

Criminal Justice Abstracts (1968). Issued quarterly by the National Council on Crime and Delinquency, this reference contains an author and subject index.

Criminology and Penology Abstracts (1980), formerly *Abstracts on Criminology and Penology and Excerpta Criminologica* (1961). This is "an international abstracting service covering the etiology of crime and juvenile delinquency, and control and treatment of offenders, criminal procedure, and the administration of justice."

Ecology Abstracts (1980), formerly *Applied Ecology Abstracts* (1974). Compiled monthly by Information Retrieval Limited, this abstract reviews 5,000 journals for appropriate articles. Subject categories include terrestrial and aquatic resources, control, agrochemicals, grasslands, wetlands, and pollution and pollutants.

EMBASE (1974). An on-line database that offers both abstracts and citations on research literature on drugs; of interest to health care and health science professionals.

Environmental Abstracts (1987). Published annually, this abstract service "offers *keyword direct access* to more than 55,000 citations appearing in 2,000 of the world's most significant environmental publications. The abstract compiles and cross-references environmental material from major scientific, technical, professional, trade, and general periodicals, government documents, proceedings, research reports, newspapers, books and speeches."

Health and Safety Sciences Abstracts (1985). Issued quarterly, this work abstracts articles on industrial safety, environmental conditions affecting the work site and workers, transportation, and occupational risks.

Metals Abstracts (1968). Previously known as *Metallurgical Abstracts* (1934–1967), this abstract covers more than 1,000 journals.

Nursing Abstracts (1979). Formerly relevant abstracts were published in the journal *Nursing Research*. Published bimonthly, this work offers abstracts on nursing from almost 80 journals; of interest to a variety of health care professionals.

Oceanic Abstracts (1984). This work surveys information on oceans (pollution, food source, oil exploration, geology) found in periodicals, books, and reports from government and private agencies. It was known as *Oceanic Journal* (1964–1967) and *Oceanic Citation Journal* (1968–1971).

Physics Abstracts (1922). This bimonthly reference covers all aspects of physics literature. Each issue contains the following indexes: author, bibliography, book, conference, and corporate author.

Psychological Abstracts (1927). Abstracts appear in two bound volumes a year and offer "nonevaluative summaries of the world's literature in psychology and related disciplines"; this reference work includes a subject and author index. Some of the topics are nervous disorders, motor performance, sex differences, and sleep disorders.

Robotics Abstracts (1983). This work provides a comprehensive 100-word summary of each entry, plus all bibliographic information.

Social Work Research & Abstracts (1977), formerly *Abstracts for Social Workers* (1965). Published quarterly by the National Association of Social Workers, this abstract contains a subject and author index. Topics are divided into six categories, of which "Fields of Service" is the largest.

Sociological Abstracts (1952). Issued five times a year, this work divides sociological literature into thirty-one categories (for example, poverty, violence, women's studies). Issues are bound every three months; it contains a subject and author index.

Solar Energy Update (1976–1986). Published monthly by the Technical Information Center of the Department of Energy (Oak Ridge, Tennessee), these abstracts cover current scientific and technical reports, journal articles, conference papers and proceedings, books, patents, theses, and monographs.

Work Related Abstracts (1990), formerly *Employment Relations Abstracts* (1950). Published monthly, this abstract covers a wide variety of work-based issues in areas such as management, labor and union relations, and the like.

Exercises

1. Find out if your library gives patrons a map or description of its holdings. If it does, bring a copy of the map or description to class. If the library does not offer such a map or description, draw one indicating the location of the circulation desk, the library catalog, the reference room, the stacks, the periodicals room or section, vertical files, government documents, and audiovisuals.

2. Find any book in the library and write a brief description of the steps you took to locate that book—from your search in the library catalog to your actu-

ally checking the book out of the library. Refer to your map you used in Exercise 1.

3. If your library has an on-line public access catalog, compare its listing of the book you found in Exercise 2 to the book's listing in the library's card catalog.

4. Using the materials discussed in this chapter, locate the following works in your major. If your library does not have them, select titles that are most closely related to your major and explain how they would be useful to you. Prepare a separate bibliography card for each title.
   a. an index to periodicals
   b. titles of three important journals
   c. an abstract of an article appearing in one of these journals
   d. a term in a specialized dictionary
   e. a description or illustration in a specialized encyclopedia
   f. a film or tape recording
   g. two government documents
   h. a story in the *New York Times* or one of the newspapers covered by NewsBank which, in the last year, discussed a topic of interest to students in your major

5. In the subject section of the library catalog, find a topic that is subdivided in the way books on construction are listed in Figure 9.3. After you do this, divide these subdivisions even further until you have a restricted topic for a research report. Bring your topic to class.

6. Using the subject, author, and title catalogs, find four or five books on the topic you selected for Exercise 5. Write a bibliography card for each book.

7. Prepare a list (providing full bibliographic information) of 15 articles for the restricted topic you selected for Exercise 5. At least five of these articles should come from periodicals *not* listed in the *Readers' Guide.*

8. Write a short memo (two to three paragraphs) to your instructor describing the types of computer searches your library offers and how such a search would assist you in researching the topic you selected in Exercise 5.

9. Identify three computerized databases that would help you run an on-line search in your research at school or on the job. Prepare a list of five journals/periodicals that you would be able to find indexed on each of these databases. Do not include the same journals/periodicals more than once, even though they may appear in more than one database. Be sure to consult a librarian if you need help; he or she may be able to direct you to lists of journals/periodicals indexed on each database.

10. Choose a term that is frequently used in your profession—a technical, scientific, or occupational word or phrase. Then look up its meaning in a (a) specialized dictionary or encyclopedia and (b) general dictionary or encyclopedia. You might also check the *Oxford English Dictionary.* Write a brief

report (one or two paragraphs) on how these definitions are alike and how they differ—that is, what's left out in the general dictionary and why?

11. Using appropriate reference works discussed in this chapter, answer any five of the following questions. After your answer, list the specific works you used. Supply complete bibliographic information. For books, indicate author or editor, title, edition, place of publication and publisher, date, and volume and page number. For journals and magazines, include volume and page number; for newspapers, precise date and page number.

    a. Who invented the digital computer?

    b. What is biomass?

    c. How many calories are there in an orange?

    d. List three interviews that Ronald Reagan granted between 1988 and 1991.

    e. Whom did *TIME* magazine select as "Man of the Year" for 1992?

    f. What is the boiling point of coal tar?

    g. What was the headline in the *New York Times* the day you were born?

    h. List three publications issued by the U.S. Department of the Interior from 1985 to the present on outdoor recreation.

    i. What was the population of Spokane, Washington, in 1990?

    j. List three articles published between 1988 and 1992 on the advantages of teleconferencing.

    k. Who discovered the neutrino?

    l. What is the first recorded (printed) use of the word *ozone?*

    m. List three articles giving job applicants information on the effective use of body language during an interview.

    n. Who wrote *The Advance of American Nursing* in 1978?

    o. Give the title, date, and page number and author (if listed) of a story in your local newspaper that focused on child abuse in the last year.

    p. When was Sandra Day O'Connor appointed to the Supreme Court? Give the exact date.

    q. List the titles of three articles on the abuse of credit cards that have appeared in professional journals within the past two or three years.

    r. What is a high key photograph?

    s. Name five plants that have the word *fly* as part of their common name.

12. Write a paraphrase of two of the following paragraphs.

    a. Deep-fat frying is a mainstay of any successful fast-food operation and is one of the most commonly used procedures for the preparation and production of foods in the world. During the deep-frying process, oxidation and hydrolysis take place in the shortening and eventually change its functional, sensory, and nutritional quality. Current fat tests available to food operation managers for determining when used shortening should be discarded typically require identification of a change in some physical attribute of the shortening, such as color, smoke, foam development, etc. However, by the time these changes become evident, a considerable amount of degradation has usually already taken place.[3]

b. Ponds excavated in areas of flat terrain usually require prepared spillways. If surface runoff must enter an excavated pond through a channel or ditch, rather than through a broad shallow drainageway, the overfall from the ditch bottom to the bottom of the pond can create a serious erosion problem unless the ditch is protected. Scouring can take place in the side slope of the pond and for a considerable distance upstream in the ditch. The resulting sediment tends to reduce the depth and capacity of the pond. Protect by placing one or more lengths of rigid pipe in the ditch and extend them over the side slope of the excavation. The extended portion of the pipe or pipes may be either cantilevered or supported with timbers. The diameter of the pipe or pipes depends on the peak rate of runoff that can be expected from a 10-year frequency storm. If you need more than one pipe inlet, the combined capacity should equal or exceed the estimated peak rate of runoff.[4]

c. Police administrators have long recognized the value of computers for records management, crime analysis, personnel deployment, and other vital areas. The ability to manage information over short and long terms is directly proportional to the success of an individual or an agency. Until recently, however, computers have not been financially feasible for most police agencies. The National Crime Information Center (NCIC), established by the FBI in 1967, provided the only computerized resource for many departments. Other police agencies were able to use their state government's computer, but they were required to share it with other agencies. Consequently, only a few programs for law enforcement could be developed.[5]

---

[3] Vincent J. Graziano, "Portable Instrument Rapidly Measures Quality of Frying Fat in Food Service Operations," *Food Technology* 33 (Sept. 1979): 50. Copyright © by Institute of Food Technologists. Reprinted by permission.

[4] U.S. Department of Agriculture, Soil Conservation Service. *Ponds for Water Supply and Recreation* (Washington, D.C.: U.S. Department of Agriculture Handbook No. 387, 1971): 48.

[5] Lee McGhee and Glenn Whiteacre, "Microcomputers for Law Enforcement," *FBI Law Enforcement Bulletin* (Mar. 1983): 24.

Documenting Sources

Documentation is at the heart of all the research you will do at school or on the job. To document means to furnish readers with information about the materials (books, articles, pamphlets, films, interviews, questionnaires) you have used for the factual support of your statements. Without proper documentation, you will not be able to persuade a customer to buy your company's product or service and you will not convince your boss that you are doing your best work.

This chapter will give you practical and precise directions on what to document and how to do it efficiently and consistently. Of the various systems (or formats) of documentation, perhaps footnoting is the one most familiar to you. In this chapter you will learn about other methods of documenting your sources. The major emphasis, however, will be on the *parenthetical documentation* system advocated by the Modern Language Association. You will find a sample research paper using parenthetical documentation at the end of this chapter.

The Whys and Hows of Documentation

Before looking at the specific techniques you need to use when you document, it's necessary to understand why documentation is so important and the major role it plays in your writing strategies.

Why Is Documentation Important?

Documentation is important for at least three reasons:

1. Documentation informs your readers that you have done your homework. It proves that you have consulted experts on the subject and have relied on the most current and authoritative sources to build your case.
2. Documentation gives proper credit to these sources. Citing works by name is not a simple act of courtesy; it is an ethical requirement and, because so much of this material is protected by copyright, a point of law. By documenting your sources, you will avoid being accused of *plagiarism*—that is, stealing someone else's ideas and listing them as your own. If you are found guilty of plagiarism, you could be expelled from school or fired from your job.
3. Documentation informs readers about a specific book or article you used. They may want to read it themselves for additional information or to verify the facts you have listed from that source.

What Must Be Documented?

This question often puzzles writers. If you document the following materials, you will be sure to avoid plagiarism and to assist the reader of your research paper or report:

- any direct quotation(s), even a single phrase or key word. Quotations from the Bible, from Shakespeare, or from any literary text should be identified according to the specific work (*Exodus, Merchant of Venice*) and the place in that work (for example, act 3, scene 4, line 23, listed as 3.4.23).
- any paraphrase or summary of another individual's written work or from an oral report or presentation.
- any opinions—expressed verbally or in writing—that are not your own or any views that you could not have reached without the help of another source.
- any statistical data that you have not compiled yourself.
- any visuals that you have not prepared yourself—photographs, tables, charts. If you construct a visual based on someone else's data, you must acknowledge that source.
- any software programs that you did not develop yourself.

Of course, do not document obvious facts, such as normal body temperature, well-known dates (the first moon landing in 1969); historical information (Ronald Reagan was the fortieth president of the U.S.); formulas (H_2O; the quadratic formula); or proverbs from folklore ("The hand is quicker than the eye").

Documentation in the Writing Process

Documentation is a vital activity in the process of writing a research paper or report. Documentation begins as you start researching your topic and continues during the course of organizing, drafting, revising, and even editing your work. You need to keep a careful record of the sources you use and the exact material you take from them. By listing this information on note and bibliography cards (see pages 340–342), you are able to create such a record. Then as you begin organizing and drafting your paper, selecting appropriate details and ideas from your sources, you transfer information from your note and bibliography cards to the text of your paper. Throughout various drafts you need to be sure you document precisely what you are using and then add every source you refer to in the text of your paper on the Works Cited page (discussed below). During revision (and editing) be careful to check and double-check the accuracy of your documentation. This means making sure names, page numbers, dates, and quotations are correct and that bibliographic information mentioned in the text of your paper matches that on your Works Cited page(s) precisely.

Parenthetical and Footnote Documentation

Numerous formats exist for documenting sources. Two of these formats are *parenthetical documentation* and *footnote documentation.* The following section will introduce you to parenthetical documentation by contrasting it with the footnote method.

A widely used system of parenthetical documentation is found in the *MLA Handbook for Writers of Research Papers,* Third Edition, edited by Joseph Gibaldi and Walter S. Achtert (New York: Modern Language Association, 1988). Although used primarily by individuals in the humanities, the MLA system is in many ways very similar to the methods of documenting sources in the sciences, technological fields, and business. For that reason this method will be emphasized in this chapter. The MLA system does not recommend footnotes or endnotes to document sources, nor does it contain a bibliography of works the writer may have consulted but has not cited directly in the paper.

Instead, the MLA uses parenthetical, or in-text, documentation. According to this method, the writer tells readers directly in the text of the paper, at the moment the acknowledgment is necessary, what reference is being cited—by including the author's last name in parentheses together with the appropriate page number(s) from which the information is borrowed. Seeing the citation (Morgan 205), for example, the reader knows that the writer has borrowed information from a work by Morgan, specifically from page 205 of that work. Such sources (authors' names with page numbers) refer to an alphabetical list of works that the writer has cited in the text of the paper. This list—called "Works Cited" or "References Cited"—is placed at the end of your report or paper.

As you may recall from other writing courses, when you document using footnotes or endnotes, you insert a slightly raised numeral immediately after the information you wish to document, like this: [1]. In many books, the source of the information is provided in a footnote at the bottom (or "foot") of the page, pre-

FIGURE 10.1   A paragraph using endnotes to document sources.

> Technical writing has expanded rapidly since World War II. The newest market seeking technical writers is data processing. In fact, it is "one of the fastest growing fields for technical writers."[1] Technical writers are especially in demand to prepare the documentation necessary for computer software systems manufactured by many different companies.[2] In preparing this documentation, the technical writer often has to explain complex information to audiences totally unfamiliar with computers. This obstacle is increasingly difficult to overcome because of the growing complexity of computers. To solve this problem, "the technical writer must function like a computer specialist while thinking like a layperson."[3]

> Endnotes
>
> [1]Julie Teunissen, "Opportunities for Technical Writers," Computer Outlook 10 (1991): 98.
>
> [2]George Tullos, "Technical Writers and the Needs of the Computer Industry," Journal of Computer Operations 17 (1990): 13.
>
> [3]Mary Bronstein, The New Generation of Technical Writers (San Francisco: Harbor House, 1993) 45.

ceded by the same raised numeral [1]. In other books and in most papers and reports, all of the sources are listed together on an endnotes page at the end of the entire paper. The order in which the endnotes are listed must correspond exactly to the order in which the information is cited within the paper. When readers see a [7], for instance, they expect to find information about the particular source for that information at [7] on the endnotes page. Footnotes and endnotes provide the same details: author's name, title of the work, place of publication, publisher, date of publication, and page numbers.

Figure 10.1 shows a paragraph that uses endnote documentation and a section of the endnotes page containing information about the sources. Figure 10.2 (p. 360) shows how the same paragraph is prepared using parenthetical documentation and reprints the relevant section of the Works Cited page.

To provide accurate parenthetical documentation for your readers, you must first prepare a careful Works Cited page and then include the documentation in the right form and place in your text. Preparing the Works Cited page and documenting within the text of a paper are discussed in the next two sections.

FIGURE 10.2   The same paragraph as in Figure 10.1 using parenthetical documentation of sources.

Technical writing has expanded rapidly since World War II. The newest market seeking technical writers is data processing. In fact, it is "one of the fastest growing fields for technical writers" (Teunissen 98). Technical writers are especially in demand to prepare the documentation necessary for computer software systems manufactured by many different companies (Tullos 13). In preparing this documentation, the technical writer often has to explain complex information to audiences totally unfamiliar with computers. This obstacle is increasingly difficult to overcome because of the growing complexity of computers. To solve this problem, "the technical writer must function like a computer specialist while thinking like a layperson" (Bronstein 45).

Works Cited

Bronstein, Mary.   The New Generation of Technical Writers. San Francisco: Harbor House, 1993.

Teunissen, Julie.   "Opportunities for Technical Writers." Computer Outlook 10 (1991): 98–99.

Tullos, George.   "Technical Writers and the Needs of the Computer Industry."   Journal of Computer Operations 17 (1990): 13.

Preparing the Works Cited Page

Before you can document your sources parenthetically you must first establish what those sources are. Even though the list of references cited comes at the end of your paper, it is important that you prepare this list *before* you start to document. By preparing the list first, you will know what sources you must cite and what page numbers you must list. You will also avoid accidentally omitting a source. And you can use your Works Cited page to verify information listed in the text of your paper.

When you prepare your list of references, you must include the information in the following order:

Books	**Articles**
author(s) or editor(s)	author(s)
title (underscored or in italics)	title of article (put in quotation marks)
edition (if second or subsequent)	name of journal (underscored or in italics)
place of publication	volume number (in arabic numerals)
publisher's name	date of publication
date of publication	page number(s)

The examples below show you how to list different types of books and articles.

■ *Book by one author*

Enockson, Paul G. A Guide for Selecting Computers and

Software for Small Businesses. Reston, VA:

Reston Books, 1983.

Note that no page numbers are listed in this citation because the appropriate page numbers to Enockson's book would be included parenthetically in the paper.

■ *Two or more books by the same author*

Flesch, Rudolf. Art of Readable Writing. New York:

Harper, 1974.

---. Say What You Mean. New York: Harper, 1972.

When you cite two or more works by the same author, do not repeat the author's name in subsequent references. Type three hyphens in place of the name and then a period. (List the works in alphabetical order.)

■ *Book by two or three authors*

Muggins, Carolyn, and Keith Applebauer. The Art of

Interviewing. Chicago: General Books, 1989.

Both authors' names are listed in the order they appear on the title page; do not worry about alphabetical order. But make sure that the first author's name is listed in reverse order.

■ *Book by more than three authors*

Dossey, Barbara Montgomery, et al. Critical Care

Nursing: Body, Mind, Spirit. 3rd ed.

Philadelphia: Lippincott, 1992.

When there are more than three authors, list only the first author's name in reverse order and add "et al." ("and others") after the comma following the first author's name. Note that when a book has a subtitle, you must include it. Separate the title and subtitle by a colon, as in the Dossey entry on p. 361. When a book goes into a second or subsequent edition, list that fact after the title, as in the Dossey book.

▪ *Corporate author*

Educational Foundation of the National Restaurant

    Association. <u>Applied Foodservice Sanitation</u>.

    3rd ed. New York: Wiley, 1987.

A corporate author refers to an organization, society, association, institution, or government agency that publishes a work under its own name, for example, the Federal Aviation Administration. In the example above, the Foundation (often cited as EFNRA) wrote the book. The name of the state is not used after well-known cities such as New York, Boston, Chicago, or San Francisco. The state is given after a smaller city to tell readers that the book was published, for instance, in Lexington, Massachusetts, as opposed to Lexington, Kentucky, or Lexington, Virginia. For this reason the writer using the Enockson book—see the example under *Book by one author*—cites the state, Virginia.

▪ *An edited collection of essays*

Tyson-Jones, Sandra, ed. <u>The Ten Best Ways to Invest</u>

    <u>in Stocks and Bonds</u>. New York: Merrimack, 1994.

The abbreviation "ed." for *editor* follows the editor's name listed in reverse order.

▪ *An essay included within a collection*

Holcomb, Barry T. "Municipal Bonds: A Good Investment

    Opportunity." <u>The Ten Best Ways to Invest in</u>

    <u>Stocks and Bonds</u>. Ed. Sandra Tyson-Jones. New

    York: Merrimack, 1994. 321-29.

The name of the author of the article in this collection comes first—in reverse order—and then the title of the article in quotation marks. Next comes the title of the collection underscored. The editor's name is listed after the title, with "Ed." before her name to indicate that she is the editor. Do not list the editor's name in reverse order. Note that page numbers for the essay within the collection conclude the entry.

▪ *An article in a professional journal*

Hedges, Robert. "Banking in the Year 2015." <u>Bank</u>

    <u>Marketing</u> 23 (1991): 29-33.

Note how a reference to a journal article differs from one citing a book. The title of the article is in quotation marks, not underscored; no place of publication is listed. The volume number immediately follows the title of the journal with no intervening punctuation. And the page number(s) on which the article is found follow the colon placed after the publication date within parentheses.

■ *A signed magazine article*

```
Woolley, Suzanne.  "Gold Still Isn't Much of a

    Prospect."  Business Week 6 Apr. 1992: 79.
```

Unlike the more scholarly journal articles, popular and frequently issued magazines (such as *Business Week, TIME, U.S. News & World Report*) are listed by date and not volume number. Note again, the page number(s) following the date; no "p." or "pp." should be used with them.

■ *An unsigned magazine article*

```
"How to Respond to Tax Planks."  U.S. News & World

    Report 10 Feb. 1992: 28.
```

Many magazine articles do not carry an author's name (or by-line) because they are written by one of the staff members of the magazine. If this is the case, begin with the title of the article. Unsigned works are always listed according to the first word of their title (excluding *a, an,* or *the*).

■ *An article in a newspaper*

```
Wittington, Delores.   "The Dollar Buys More Vacation

    Overseas This Year."  Springfield Herald 30 Mar.

    1989, late ed., sec. 2: 10.
```

Give the title of the newspaper as it appears at the top of the first page of the newspaper, including the name of the city if it is part of that title. If the name of the city does not appear in the title, place it in square brackets immediately following the title, for example, *Reporter* [Allendale]. List the article by day, month, and year, *not* according to the cumbersome volume and issue numbers. Identify section, page, and edition information for readers. In the example above, readers know that the story appeared in the late edition on page 10 in section 2. Sometimes the story you cite will not require these details. The example below cites an article found on page B4 of a paper that issues only one edition per day.

```
Carroll, Paul B.   "New Computers, Led by IBM, Help

    Scientists See." Wall Street Journal 25 July

    1991: B4.
```

■ *An article in an encyclopedia*

```
Truxal, John G.  "Telemetering."  McGraw-Hill

    Encyclopedia of Science and Technology.  7th ed.

    1992.
```

Because it is a multivolume, alphabetical work, only the particular edition and year of an encyclopedia have to be listed on the Works Cited page. If you cite the name of the author of an article in an encyclopedia, begin your reference with his or her last name. Some encyclopedia articles are not signed.

■ *A pamphlet*

```
National Institute on Aging.  Bound for Good Health: A

    Collection of Age Papers.  Bethesda, MD: National

    Institute on Aging, 1991.
```

Document a pamphlet the same way you would a book. Note here that the corporate author is also the publisher of the book.

■ *A film*

```
Understanding Asthma.  Sound filmstrip.  Philadelphia:

    Health Care Media, 1988.  37 min.
```

Underscore the title of a film and include the medium, distributor, and date. Other information, such as individual contributors to the film, may be added after the title, if significant, to your in-text use of the source. If you indicate the length of the film, include this information last.

■ *Radio or television program*

```
60 Minutes.  CBS News.  16 Oct. 1988.

"The Dilemma."  Rich Man, Poor Man.  PBS.  WTQA,

    Lincoln.  13 Sept. 1993.
```

Underscore the title of a program but put an individual episode in a series within quotation marks, as in the title from *Rich Man, Poor Man* above. (In your Works Cited page, *60 Minutes* would be listed under "S" for "Sixty.")

■ *Computer program*

```
WordPerfect.  Vers. 5.1 for Windows.  Computer

    software.  WordPerfect Corp., Orem, UT, 1989.

Microsoft Excel.  Vers. 2.2.  Computer software.

    Microsoft Corp., 1989.  Apple Macintosh SE, 1024

    KB, disk.
```

Software information may also include the operating system for which the software is designed (Apple Macintosh SE), the system's amount of memory in kilobytes (1024 KB), and the form of the program (disk).

■ *Cartoon or advertisement*

Lees, Charlotta. Cartoon. <u>Miami Magazine</u>. Aug.

1990: 36.

American Resort Council. "Leisure Life Pays Off."

Advertisement. <u>Vacation Life</u> Feb. 1993: 71.

■ *A published interview*

Zeluto, Thomas. "Interview with Former Budget

Director." <u>Findlay Magazine</u> Oct. 1988: 2-4.

Begin with the name of the individual being interviewed. Then indicate the title of the interview.

■ *An unpublished interview*

Cilwik, Martin. CEO, Emerson Plastics. Personal

Interview. 7 Aug. 1993.

Jensen, Barbara. Professor of Physics, Berry College.

Telephone interview. 15 May 1992.

Begin with the name of the individual—in reverse order—and then indicate how and when the interview was conducted.

■ *A questionnaire*

Questionnaire for Secretaries. Distributed between

16-20 Nov. 1991. Seager Construction Company.

How to Alphabetize the Works in Your Reference List

Your list of references must be in alphabetical order to enable readers to find them quickly. Here are some guidelines to follow when you alphabetize your list.

1. Make sure that each author's name is in correct alphabetical sequence with the author's (or the first of multiple authors') names in reverse order. Thus, you would have Jones, Sally T., not Sally T. Jones.

2. Hyphenated last names should be alphabetized according to the first of the hyphenated names.

Grundy, Alex H.
Mendez-Greene, A. Y.
Mundt, Jill

3. List corporate authors as you would names of individuals, but do not invert the corporate name.

Marine Fisheries Association
Nally, Mark
National Bureau of Standards
Nuttal, Marion

4. List names beginning with the same letters according to the number of letters in each name—the shorter names precede the longer ones.

Lund, Michael
Lundford, Sarah
Lundforth, Jeffrey

5. Disregard the article (*a, an, the*) when you list an unsigned article or a film.

The Cable Television Guidebook (an unsigned pamphlet, listed under C on the Works Cited page)
The Godfather, Part III (film, listed under G)
"An Improved Means of Detecting Computer Crime" (unsigned article, listed under I)

Documenting Within the Text

The Works Cited list does not, of course, tell readers what you actually borrowed from your sources or where that information is located within a source. To give readers that information you must include documentation within the text of your paper or report. As you write and revise your rough draft(s), make sure that you insert the author's name and appropriate page number(s) for each one of the sources that you use. Be sure also that the information you include parenthetically within the text—names, page numbers, short titles—precisely matches the information you supplied under Works Cited at the end of your paper or report. Short titles within parenthetical citations should begin with the first key word used in the title. Double-check the spelling of names, page numbers, and publication data against the titles on your Works Cited page. Remember, if you fail to document within your text, you are guilty of plagiarism; and if your documentation is incorrect or incomplete, readers will have trouble finding the source and may doubt the reliability of your work.

Parenthetical, or in-text, documentation is relatively simple. Keep your documentation brief and to the point so you do not interrupt the reader's train of thought. In most cases, all you will need to include is the author's last name and appropriate page number(s) in parentheses, usually at the end of the sentence. For unsigned articles or radio and television programs, you would use a shortened title in place of an author's name. Note in the following example that no mark of punctuation appears before the parentheses and that a period follows them. Also, no "page" or "p." or comma comes between the author's name and the page number within the parentheses.

> About 5 percent of the world's population has diabetes mellitus, and 25 percent of the world's population acts as carriers of the disease (Walton 56).

Seeing this parenthetical documentation, the reader will expect to find the title and publication information about Walton's study correctly listed after Walton's name on your Works Cited page.

> Walton, J. H. <u>Common Diseases of the World</u>. New
>
> York: Medical Books, 1988.

The number after Walton's name in the parenthetical documentation refers to the page number where the information you cite can be found.

You may refer to the same work more than once in your paper or report. For second or subsequent references you will use the same method of documentation. As in the Walton example above, you will place Walton's name and the appropriate page number—even if it is the same as in the previous reference(s)—within parentheses following the borrowed information. Of course, if you include Walton's name within the sentence, there is no need to repeat it in the parentheses; all you need do is give the page number. The exact placement of the author's name within the sentence will be discussed later.

If you are using a work that has two authors, list both their last names parenthetically.

> Tourism has increased by 21 percent this last quarter, thanks to individuals passing through our state on their way to the World's Fair (Muscovi and Klein 2-3).

If one of the works you use has three or more authors, list just the first author's last name in parentheses followed by et al. and the page number(s).

> The principles of ergonomics have revolutionized the design of office furniture (Brodsky et al. 345-47).

If the work you are borrowing from has a corporate author, use a shortened version of the name within the parentheses as in the following example where "Commission" replaces "Commission on Wage and Price Control":

> Salaries for local electricians were at or above the national average (Commission 145).

In all of the preceding examples, the names of the authors have appeared in parentheses. However, you may cite the author's name within your text. If so, there is no need to repeat it parenthetically. Include only the appropriate page number(s) within parentheses. The following examples show three different, acceptable ways of citing an author's name in the text and indicate how writers can document page references.

```
Clausen sees the renovation of downtown areas as one of
the most challenging issues facing city governments
today (29).

As Clausen notes, the renovation of downtown areas is
one of the most challenging issues facing city
governments today (29).

The renovation of downtown areas, according to Clausen,
is one of the most challenging issues facing city
governments today (29).
```

Similarly, if you list the title of a reference or anonymous work within the text of your paper, you need not repeat it for your parenthetical documentation.

```
According to the Encyclopaedia Britannica, Cecil B.
deMille's King of Kings was seen by nearly 800,000,000
individuals (3:458).
```

The first number in parentheses refers to the volume number of the *Encyclopaedia Britannica;* the second points to the page number of that volume. In this case, the writer wisely gives both volume and page numbers to indicate that the information is listed under deMille and not the title of the film.

If you are citing information from two or more works by the same author, you will have to inform readers clearly from which work a particular fact or opinion comes. Let's say that you used information from the following works:

```
Howe, Grace.  The Management of an Office.  New York:

     Business Publications, 1992.

---.  "Systems Control for Small Businesses."  The

     Modern Office 15 (1994): 67-81.
```

You have a number of ways to tell readers from which specific work by Grace Howe you are borrowing material.

1. Cite the author's name, short title, and page number parenthetically.

```
Communication stations are necessary in an office to
provide a maximum flow of information (Howe,
Management 132).
```

Include a comma after the author's name.

2. Mention the author's name in your sentence and a short title and page number within parentheses.

```
Howe thinks communication stations in an office are
necessary to provide a maximum flow of information
(Management 132).
```

3. Give the author's name and a shortened title in the text with only the page number included parenthetically.

> According to Howe's article, "Systems Control," productivity increases by at least 20 percent after each training session involving data processing techniques (71).

Occasionally you will have to cite two sources at the same time to document a point. Include the names of the authors of both sources just as if you were listing them individually but separate each source with a semicolon.

> The use of salt domes to store radioactive wastes has come under severe attack (Jelinek 56-57; McPherson and Chin 23-26).

Be careful, though, that you do not overload readers by including a long string of references in your parenthetical documentation as the following example does.

> Wind energy has been successfully used in both rural and urban settings (Bailey 34; Henderson 9; Kreuse 78; Mankowitz 98-99; Olsen 456-58; Vincenti 23; Walker and Smith 43).

Rather than interrupting the reader and crowding references together, consider revising your sentence to make the subject more precise and the references more restricted.

> Wind energy has long benefited the farm community (Kreuse 78; Walker and Smith 43). But recent experiments in New York City have shown the effectiveness of this form of energy for apartment dwellers, too (Bailey 34; Henderson 9). Similar experiments in San Francisco also show how wind power helps urban residents (Mankowitz 98-99; Olsen 456-58; Vincenti 23).

If you include a quotation, place the parenthetical documentation at the end of the sentence containing the quotation.

> Pilmer has observed that coffee "is only mildly addictive in the sense that withdrawal will not harm you or produce violent symptoms" (16).

Note that the period follows the parentheses, not the quotation marks. Even if the quotation is short and appears in the middle of the sentence, place the documentation at the end of the sentence.

> Alvin Toffler uses the phrase "third wave" to characterize the scientific and computer revolution (34).

If the material you quote runs to more than four typed lines, set the quotation apart from the text by indenting it *ten spaces* on the left-hand side and by

eliminating the quotation marks. Double-space the quotation. Place the parenthetical documentation after the quotation as in the following example:

```
L. J. Ronsivalli offers this interesting analogy of how
radiation can penetrate solid objects:
                One might wonder how an x-ray, a gamma ray,
                or a cosmic ray can penetrate something as
                solid as a brick or a piece of wood. We can't
                see that within the atomic structures of the
                brick and the wood there are spaces for the
                radiation to enter. If we look at a cloud, we
                can see its shape, but because distance has
                made them too small, we can't see the
                droplets of moisture of which the cloud is
                made. Much too small for the eyes to see,
                even with the help of a microscope, the
                atomic structure of solid materials is made
                of very small particles with a lot of space
                between them. In fact, solids are mostly
                empty spaces. (20-21)
```

If you omit anything from a quotation, follow the rules governing ellipses on
pages 343-344.

If you take a quotation from any place but the original source (if, for example,
the quotation you want to use is included in the book you are citing but originally
came from another book or article), you should document that fact by including
"qtd. in" in your parenthetical documentation.

```
The monthly business meeting serves a number of
valuable functions. In fact, perhaps the most
important one is that "chain-of-command meetings
provide the opportunity to pass information up as well
as down the administrative ladder" (qtd. in Munroe 87).
```

This documentation lets readers know that you found the quotation in Munroe,
not in the original work from which these words come.

Documentation in Scientific and Technical Writing

Numerous other formats exist for documenting sources. Many professions publish
their own style sheet or book to provide such instruction (e.g., the *Publication*

Manual of the American Psychological Association, the *Council of Biology Editors' Style Manual,* the American Institute of Physics's *Style Manual for Guidance in the Preparation of Papers*) or recommend that writers follow the format used in a specific technical or scholarly journal. Every professional group, however, would advise writers *against* using the formats and abbreviations found in periodical indexes such as the *Readers' Guide* or the *Applied Science & Technology Index.* The way information is listed in these sources is not offered as a model of documentation. Before you write a paper or report, ask your instructor or employer about the format he or she prefers.

Many professions use the *author-date method of documentation* or the *ordered references method.* Like the MLA style just discussed, both methods rely on parenthetical documentation; that is, rather than using footnotes or endnotes with raised arabic numerals, the particular information about the source is placed directly in the text within parentheses. A brief overview of these two methods will show you how this is done.

The Author-Date Method

With this method, the writer does not use notes or note numbers at all. Instead, information about a reference or quotation is placed in the text of the paper or report.

> The theory that new housing becomes increasingly
> expensive as buyers move farther north has been
> recently advanced (Jones, 1993, p. 13).

The reader sees that Jones developed this theory on page 13 of a work written in 1993. If Jones's name were mentioned in the text, "Jones advances the theory that new housing . . . ," only (1993, p. 13) would be listed. To find Jones's work, readers turn to an alphabetical list of references at the end of the paper, report, or article where, under Jones, they find a bibliographic entry for the work. As in the MLA system, only works actually cited in a paper are listed in the reference list. If two works by Jones were cited, the references for both of them are given. If they were done in the same year, they are differentiated in the text *and* in the list of references by a lower-case letter *a* and *b.* For example:

> Housing is increasingly more expensive on the north
> side than on the south (Jones, 1993a, p. 22).
>
> A recent study has established a demographic pattern
> for small cities in the Midwest (Jones, 1993b, p. 73).

In the accompanying list of references, the two works by Jones might be listed as follows:

> Jones, T. 1993a. The cost of housing on Lincoln's
> northside. Urban Studies, <u>72</u>: 10-24.
>
> Jones, T. 1993b. Demographic density in three
> Midwestern small cities. Cincinnati: Western
> University Press.

According to this method of documentation, only the first word of the title (even if it is *a, an,* or *the*) and proper nouns are capitalized in the reference list. Titles are neither underscored nor put into quotation marks. The volume number of a journal is often underscored or italicized and followed by a colon to distinguish it from the page numbers that are listed immediately thereafter.

The Ordered References Method

Like the author-date method, the ordered references method uses parenthetical documentation, but relies on numbers rather than authors' names to identify a source. The references in a paper are numbered in the order in which they appear. For example,

> `Three new products help reduce bacterial infection in`
> `restaurant kitchens (7:47).`

The "7" indicates that this is the seventh source found in the reference list; "47" refers to the page number of that source. Sources, therefore, are not listed in alphabetical order, as they are in the author-date method. Each time a source is mentioned, the same number is used. If your first cited source is listed again near the middle or end of your paper, or if it is cited three times in a row, it is still listed parenthetically as (1:). The page numbers after the colon may or may not change.

1 inch

Janet Hempstead
Professor Smith
Business Writing 112
December 7, 1992

*Type the body of the
report double-space
throughout*

Stress and the Computer Programmer

1 inch

1 inch

Since computers were born in the middle of the 1940s,
they have increasingly become a part of everyone's life. Once
computers were used "primarily to construct and control our
nation's missiles and spaceships" (Fisher, Origins 6). But
now they have made their way into corporations, classrooms,
and homes. It is a rare business that does not own at least
one microcomputer.

The computer's enormous capacity for processing
information offers us more control over our lives, greater
freedom of choice, and the opportunity for richer
interactions with one another and the world around us
(Fisher, "Computers" 11). But computers could not perform
the numerous tasks they do without human management.
Without being programmed to do a specific job, the computer
would be worthless. In the world of business and industry,
the importance of such programming functions makes the job
of the computer programmer essential. According to the
U.S. Bureau of Labor Statistics, there were more than
519,000 jobs for computer programmers in the late 1980's and

2

the opportunities for future positions continue to be
excellent (217).

The computer programmer's job, however, is neither easy
nor calm. It is misleading to view the programmer as a cold,
robot-like creature who acts more like a machine than a
human being. The programmer is often wrongly seen as an
individual unthreatened by emotions or untouched by the
conflicts and demands that affect other workers. On the
contrary, programmers are under considerable stress on
their highly technical jobs. This paper will study the
problems of job-related stress that affect computer
programmers by discussing (1) the symptoms that can result
from stress involved in programming a computer, (2) the
causes of that stress, (3) the effects of that stress for
programmers and their employers, and (4) the specific
techniques programmers can use to reduce or control their
stress levels on the job.

Symptoms of Stress Related to Computer Programming

Stress is any disturbance or reaction that alters the
body's normal functions. Katherine Lodjac, a noted
researcher on stress management, has said that "everyone
needs some stress to function, but the major question is how
we handle that stress" (qtd. in Holden 182). Some people

3

are naturally stress prone; others are not. Recent research

has shown that individuals' reactions to potentially

stressful situations vary greatly, depending on their

personalities (Rice 84–85). What is true for the general

population is equally true for programmers. Computer work

demands absolute--and exhausting--attention to detail.

Those workers who bury themselves in programs,

instructions, and codes will be more likely to exhibit the

symptoms of stress than those who do not. Programmers who

allow separate time for work and relaxation will be less

prone to experience stress than their colleagues who do

not. Yet regardless of how it is handled, stress is an

inescapable part of every computer programmer's life.

Because of their particular work, programmers are

especially susceptible to symptoms linked to stress. They

have to spend long hours at their work stations, often

straining their eyes to focus on images on a moving VDT

screen. This eye movement can trigger tension around the

eyes, headaches, blurred vision, nausea, and fatigue,

many of the symptoms of stress identified in a study by

Wong and Johnson (108–10). Programmers often complain of

severe lower backaches from having to sit for hours in

poorly designed chairs and having to slouch into

uncomfortable positions to read VDT screens clearly.

Ergonomically designed office furniture will relieve some

4

of this stress for the programmer (Overton 89-90). The American National Standards Institute has prepared useful guidelines, <u>American National Standards for Human Factors Engineering of Visual Display Terminal Workstations</u>, on the ergonomics of VDT workstations that should be of great interest to programmers.

If the programmer does not identify and treat stress-related symptoms, even more serious ones may develop. Many symptoms of prolonged or severe stress include carpal tunnel syndrome, spastic colitis, gastritis, migraine headaches, urinary problems, and rashes (Danner and Dworkin 66). For the programmer under constant stress, the risk of hypertension, or high blood pressure, is especially great (Danner and Dworkin 68). If the programmer has a family history of blood pressure problems, of course, the danger is greater. But even if the computer programmer does not have such a history, a few years immersed in the pressures of the job may cause a dangerously elevated blood pressure (Wong and Johnson 109). Recent research affecting programmers also indicates that there is "a link between job strain and increased heart mass--another risk factor in heart disease" ("Heartbreaking Work" 14). Besides these physical problems, the programmer under prolonged stress can develop emotional problems that adversely affect job performance, lifestyle, and family life (Rice 81).

5

Causes of Stress on Computer Programmers

Computer programmers are under almost constant stress.
As we have seen, part of that stress may come from the kinds
of hardware programmers use. But the full cause of the
programmer's stress goes far beyond hardware. Stress is
built into the programmer's very occupation. According to a
recent computer science graduate from Northeast Community
College, now a computer programmer at Denver Industries,
"The stress starts from the day you accept the position"
(Ricks, interview).

Companies have high expectations for their programmers.
They demand perfect work and may not always allow the
programmer sufficient time to debug a program. The
importance a company assigns to programming is, of course,
justified. A company depends on the programmer to develop
and test programs and to prepare manuals for computer users.
The following job description for a computer programmer
issued by the U.S. Bureau of Labor Statistics points to the
stress-producing responsibilities placed on an individual
choosing programming as a career:

> In hiring programmers, employers look for people
> who can think logically and are capable of exacting
> analytical work. The ability to work with abstract
> concepts and to do technique analysis is especially

6

important for systems programmers because they
work with the software that controls the computers's operation. The job calls for patience,
persistence, and the ability to work with extreme
accuracy even under pressure. Ingenuity and
imagination are particularly important when programmers must find new ways to solve a problem. (217)

One of the most significant causes of stress for
programmers is working under a deadline to produce a highly
technical document, often on very short notice. The
programmer knows that a delay can seriously affect his or
her work--creating a terrifying backlog--or the work of
another individual or department in the company. As Bob
Turnbull, the chief programmer at Data Processing
Corporation, aptly observed, "I once was given an hour to
write a program for an important set of instructions when I
could have used at least five hours to get the job finished"
(Turnbull, interview).

The way in which programmers work with others can also
elevate their stress level. In some companies, programmers
work in groups or in teams for large, highly technical
projects. This working arrangement may be easy and pleasant
for the programmer who enjoys interacting with others, thus
lessening an individual programmer's tension and stress.

But not every programmer prefers to work as part of a team. As Lee A. Norris pointed out, the team approach may be more frustrating for the programmer than the deadline (32). Disagreements and potential delays may result from such team interaction. And when two or more programmers disagree, because of either egos or errors, they may not be able to meet deadlines, and so their stress levels may increase. "The Group Stress Syndrome is . . . a frequent and disturbing occurrence at many large plants" (Norris 33).

Effects of Stress for Programmers and Their Employers

Stress on the job can have many serious side effects for both programmer and employer. On-the-job stress can force employees to adopt potentially unhealthy ways of handling stress. In a survey published in Industrial Psychology Review, the most frequently reported harmful methods for coping with stress were overeating, overdrinking, smoking, drug use, and "perpetual anger to thwart what the individual perceives as a growing number of personal attacks" (Danner 73). These unhealthy reactions can seriously hurt programmers and their work.

When stress attacks the programmer, the employer also suffers. A weakened or rushed programmer is more likely to make mistakes. Brown and Rosenbaum argue that repeated

8

exposure to highly stressful situations--like

programming--can temporarily lower an individual's IQ (112).

This may be the reason why more mistakes are made by

employees under stress. Even a slight error by a programmer

can cost the company time and money: "Last year a single

programming error resulted in our having to redo the payroll

for the first week of March--a six-hour job" (Ricks,

interview). Because of a mistake made by a Pacific Bell

programmer, the phone lines, including the 911 emergency

number, were out of commission for 30 minutes in San Luis

Obispo, California, in late 1990 ("Programmer Error").

If only 1 percent of the more than 519,000 U.S. computer

programmers--5,190--made one error each week, companies

could stand to lose millions of dollars each year.

    Illnesses caused by stress can also significantly

increase absenteeism. The physical ravages of

stress--ulcers, fatigue, hypertension--are responsible

for many lost workdays. An employee suffering from stress-

induced illness may lose as many as 10 to 30 working days

each year ("High Cost of Stress" 29). This lost time

spells trouble for the employer worried about decreased

productivity. When the programmer is ill, work in a number

of departments may fall behind or an additional burden is

placed on other employees. Moreover, employers must pay

higher health care costs when programmers are stricken with

9

job-related stress. As Alan Farnham reports, "In medical

treatment and time lost, stress cases cost, on the average,

twice as much as other workplace injuries: more than

$15,000 each" (72).

How the Computer Programmer Can Control Stress

Stress has been correctly called a disease (Danner 73;

Rice 78; Wong and Johnson 106). As we have seen, it is a

disease to which programmers may be particularly vulnerable.

In order to control this disease successfully, programmers

must acknowledge that their symptoms are stress-related and

then take steps to control these symptoms. To do this,

programmers must be prepared to make changes in their work

habits and in their attitudes toward work.

On the job, the programmer should, in Fisher's words,

be aware of "working for long periods of time without a single

restful break" ("Computers" 12). A few rest periods

throughout the day will help to relieve the programmer's

tension and reduce the level of stress. These rest periods

do not have to be long or costly for the company. Some might

be taken right where the programmer works--"minute

vacations," as Ricks calls them (Interview). One computer

program, LifeGuard by Visionary Software, actually tells users

when to take a break by counting keystrokes and mouse

10

clicks and then suggests eye, wrist, and arm exercises to do
at the keyboard (Bulkeley).

On a larger scale, stress counselors recommend
biofeedback, meditation, and breathing techniques to
relieve stress ("Overdosing"). In fact, the progressive
muscle relaxation techniques advocated by Jablonski take
only a few minutes and can quickly refresh and relax the
programmer (8–10). A brief change of scenery--a short walk
to the water cooler or around a desk--will also relieve
eyestrain: "Escape from the computer or the desk even for a
few seconds heightens the worker's spirits" (Jablonski 9).

Vigorous physical activity in the middle of the day can
reduce stress, which, without release, can build up to
monstrous proportions by the end of the day. During lunch
breaks many executives are beginning to jog, play a quick
game of handball, or do calisthenics. Some companies like
Southwest Industries have built gyms on their plant site to
help employees work off stress before and after work
("Killer Stress"). Programmers need to exercise often to
reduce their stress levels.

Many companies now also have stress-reduction programs
or psychological counseling sessions for employees
(Rice 84). Appropriately enough, some corporations refer
to these as "wellness promotion programs" (Farnham 76–7).
If these services are available, the programmer should take

advantage of them. They benefit both the employee and the company by defusing the worker's tension and thereby increasing productivity. As Fisher points out in his influential study The Origins and Development of the Computer in the Modern World, "Sophisticated hardware can solve many of our technological problems, but the ultimate success of this hardware depends upon the mental health of human beings who use it" (169).

The programmer also needs to have a healthy attitude about work. Perhaps one of the greatest causes of stress in the lives of technical workers is "their desire for per-fection" (Danner and Dworkin 65). Some programmers believe that they will be regarded as failures if they write just one bad program. This "Win-or-Lose-Everything Syndrome," as Danner calls it (75), can be devastating. Programmers should not judge their future careers on the outcome of a single program. If a program fails, the programmer should adopt an optimistic attitude that the next one will be better (Norris 34). Equally important, programmers need to adopt a more positive attitude about the parts of their jobs they like most, for example, helping others. They should not feel as though they have no control over their jobs or that they are trapped, two of the leading causes of stress (Farnham 78; "Overdosing"; Wong and Johnson 109—110).

12

Conclusion

     Because of their highly technical and demanding

positions, computer programmers are frequent victims of

stress. The symptoms of stress may be eyestrain, fatigue,

backaches, ulcers, or, even more serious, hypertension.

Stress may be caused by computer hardware, by unrealistic

expectations of employers, and by the programmers' own

desire for job perfection. The effects of stress in the

workplace are serious for programmers and employers.

Confronted with stress, the programmer may develop

unhealthy coping mechanisms. Moreover, stress-related

diseases can lead to employee absenteeism, costing an

employer time and money. While programmers cannot

eliminate stress from their lives, they can alleviate it

by taking "minute vacations" (Ricks, interview) devoted

to relaxation and exercise techniques. Perhaps, though,

the most effective antidote for the problems of stress on

the job is for programmers to put a healthy distance

between their job and their home life.

13

Works Cited

American National Standards Institute. <u>American National</u>

   <u>Standards for Human Factors Engineering of Visual</u>

   <u>Display Terminal Workstations</u>. Santa Monica, CA:

   Human Factors Society, 1988.

Brown, Bernard, and Lillian Rosenbaum. "How Stress Lowers

   IQ Scores." <u>Science Digest</u> Oct. 1983: 112–14.

Bulkeley, William M. "Computer Users' Ills Attract More

   Attention." <u>Wall Street Journal</u> 1 May 1991: B1.

Danner, G. T. "Wrong Ways of Coping with Stress: A Survey."

   <u>Industrial Psychology Review</u> 32 (1992): 73–89.

Danner, G. T., and Martin Dworkin. "A Correlation of

   Physical Diseases with Stress Factors." <u>Journal of</u>

   <u>Health and Society</u> 11 (1991): 63–70.

Farnham, Alan. "Who Beats Stress--and How." <u>Fortune</u>

   7 Oct. 1991: 71+.

Fisher, Harold. "Computers and Personal Freedom."

   <u>Computer World</u> 31 Jan. 1990: 11–12.

---. <u>The Origins and Development of the Computer in the</u>

   <u>Modern World</u>. San Francisco: Data-Master, 1991.

"Heartbreaking Work." <u>Prevention</u> Nov. 1990: 14–15.

"The High Cost of Stress." <u>U.S. News & World Report</u> 10 May

   1983: 29.

Holden, W. A. "When Stress Can Hurt Your Health." <u>McCalls</u>

   Apr. 1981: 182–84.

14

Jablonski, Margaret. "Exercise Your Stress Away."

    Healthy Executive May 1991: 8–10.

"Killer Stress: How Business Deals with It." Inside

    Business Today. CBS. WBCK, Middletown, TX. 5 Nov.

    1992.

Norris, Lee A. "Together or Apart?: Group Dynamics and

    Deficiencies in the Computer Center." Computer

    Science 7 (1992): 31–35.

"Overdosing on Stress, and the 101 Ways to Relieve It." U.S.

    News & World Report 23 Sept. 1991: 74.

Overton, James P., Jr. "Ergonomics, Office Design, and

    Stress." Today's Office Feb. 1983: 89+.

"Programmer Error Kills Phones for 30 Minutes." San Luis

    Obispo Telegram Tribune 10 Oct. 1990: A5.

Rice, Berkeley. "Can Companies Kill?" Psychology Today

    June 1989: 78–85.

Ricks, Larrisa. Personal interview. 2 Nov. 1992.

Turnbull, Bob. Personal Interview. 10 Nov. 1992.

U.S. Bureau of Labor Statistics. "Computer Programmers."

    Occupational Outlook Handbook. 1990–1991 ed. 215–17.

Wong, Carl, and Janis Johnson. "Stress and Health in Silicon

    Valley." Industrial Management 14 (1989): 106–11.

Sample Research Paper Using MLA In-Text Documentation

Study the sample research paper (pages 373–386) on stress and computer programmers to see how the student author has successfully used the MLA system of documentation. Compare the references mentioned in the text with the Works Cited page to see how the writer has handled documentation appropriately. The sample long report in Chapter 17 (pages 638–657) also uses the MLA system of parenthetical documentation.

✓ Revision Checklist

Here are some useful questions to ask yourself about the documentation of your research as you revise and edit. Asking yourself these questions will help you to spot any trouble areas in documenting your work. When you have answered each question satisfactorily, you will know that you are giving your readers the documentation they need to verify your work and to accept it.

1. Have I given full and proper credit to sources I consulted and to whom I am indebted for the preparation of my work?
2. Did I record all direct quotations precisely and accurately?
3. Have I paraphrased information correctly, and have I acknowledged the rightful sources?
4. Have I consistently followed the MLA (or other) method of documentation?
5. Are all the in-text (parenthetical) references in my report fully included in my Works Cited page(s)? Have I caught and corrected any inconsistencies in names, titles, or page references?
6. Have I made sure that I do not string a long list of parenthetical references to make the reader's job harder? Have I focused and restricted my references?
7. If I used more than one work by the same author, have I clearly indicated which work I am referring to in the text of my paper?
8. Have I made sure that *only* the works referred to in my paper are included in the listing in my Works Cited page(s)?
9. Have I correctly alphabetized the entries in my Works Cited pages(s)?
10. Have I double-checked the spelling of authors' and publishers' names and the accuracy of all publication information in the Works Cited page(s)?

Exercises

1. Ask a professor in your major what he or she regards as the most widely respected periodical in your field. Find a copy of this periodical and explain its method of documentation (providing examples). How does it differ from the MLA method?

2. Put the following pieces of bibliographic information in proper form according to the MLA method of documentation for Works Cited:
   a. New York, Hawthorn Publishing Company, John Anderson, 1993, pages 95–97, second edition, *A New Way to Process Film.*
   b. *American Journal of Nursing,* Karen E. Forbes and Shirlee A. Stokes, July 1984, pages 884–88, "Saving the Diabetic Foot." vol. 84.
   c. *Air Quality Management,* the Environmental Protection Agency, Office of Air and Radiation, the Government Printing Office, available after November 1991, free of charge, page 8.
   d. *Southern Living,* Steve Bender, page 72, "Native Magnolias," June 1988.
   e. an interview with your local police chief that took place in the college auditorium after she delivered a talk on crime prevention on Wednesday, January 10, 1990. Her name is Tina B. Holmes.
   f. today's editorial in your local newspaper.
   g. Pyramid Films, Inc., *Pulse of Life,* 1986, Santa Monica, California, order number 342br.
   h. *Essays on Food Sanitation,* John Smith (editor), Framingham, Massachusetts, 3rd edition, pages 345–356, Mary Grossart (author), Albion Publishing Company, "Selection of Effective Chemical Agents," 1988.
   i. March 16, 1992, page 46, Judith H. Dobrzynski, "The Art Market May Be on Its Way Back," *Business Week.*
   j. January to February of 1989, pages 43–53, "Smoke Detectors and Alarms," Bertschinger, Susan, *Fire Journal.*
   k. 7th ed. of *McGraw-Hill Encyclopedia of Science & Technology,* "Lasers."
   l. "Fax Boxes Keep Your Laser Printer Busy," page 127, Stan Miastkowski, vol. 16, *Byte,* Feb. 1991.
   m. *Pro-Cite* (Personal Bibliographic Software), version 3.4, by Victor Rosenberg et al. Copyright 1992. For IBM-AT with DOS 2.0 or higher. Disk format.

3. Put the bibliographic references you listed in MLA format in Exercise 2 into the format that one of the periodicals in your major uses.

4. Convert the bibliographic information given for one article in the periodical you chose for Exercise 1 to the MLA parenthetical style.

5. The following passage contains mistakes in the MLA method of documentation. Find these mistakes and explain how they can be corrected.

    More and more companies are allowing employees to
    "telecommute" (see Smith; Dawson; Brown; Gura and

Keith; and Allen). One expert defines telecommuting as
"home-based work" (13). Having terminals in their
homes "allows employees to work at a variety of jobs"
("New Employment Opportunities"). It has been
estimated that currently 700,000 employees work out of
their homes (Pennington, p. 56). That number is sure
to increase as computer-based businesses multiply in
the 1990s (Brown). In one of her recent articles on
telecommuting, Holcomb found that "in the last year
alone 43 companies in the metropolitan Phoenix area
made this option available to their employees" (167).

Employees who telecommute cite a variety of
benefits for such an arrangement (see in particular
articles by Gura, Smith, and Kaplan). One employee of
a mail order company whose opinion was quoted observed
that "I can save about 15-17 hours a week in driving
time" (from Allen). Working at home allows the telecommuting employee to work at his or her optimum times
("The Day Does Not Have to Start at 9:00 A.M."). Also,
in articles by Kaplan and Keith the benefits of not
having to leave home are emphasized: "A telecommuting
parent does not have to worry about child care" (39).
Telecommuting may "be here to stay" (quoted in a
number of different sources).

6. Submit your preliminary list of references (your tentative Works Cited
page[s]) for a research paper or long report to your instructor.

11

Summarizing Material

A summary is a brief restatement of the main points in a book, report, article, laboratory test, meeting, or convention. A summary saves readers hours of time, because they do not have to study the original or attend a conference. A summary can reduce a report or article by 85 to 95 percent (or even more) or capture the essential points of a three-day convention in a one-page memo. Moreover, a summary can tell readers if they should even be concerned about the original; it may be irrelevant for their purposes. Finally, since only the most important points of a work are included in a summary, readers will know they are given the crucial information they need.

The Importance of Summaries

Summaries can be found all around you. Television and radio stations regularly air two-minute news broadcasts—sometimes called "newsbreaks"—to summarize in a few sentences the major stories covered in more detail on the evening news. Popular news magazines such as *TIME, Newsweek,* and *U.S. News & World Report* have a large readership because of their ability to condense seven days of news into short, readable articles highlighting key personalities, events, and issues.

Newspapers also employ summaries for their readers' convenience. Daily newspapers such as the *Wall Street Journal* or weekly papers such as *Barron's: A Business and Financial Weekly* or the *National Law Journal* print on the first page brief summaries of news stories that are discussed in detail later in the paper. Some newspapers simply print a column entitled "News Summary" on the

FIGURE 11.1   A summary of the copyright status of colorized films.

> ### Copyrights Approved for "Colorization."
>
> Computer-colored films would be granted copyright status if those tinted versions revealed a certain degree of human creativity and were produced by existing computer-coloring technology, the U.S. Copyright Office of the Library of Congress ruled June 19.
>
> The ruling came after months of debate surrounding the "colorization" process, a debate that had reached all the way to the U.S. Senate.
>
> The copyright office ruled that computer-colored versions of black-and-white films were entitled to copyright protection as "derivative works." Such protection gave a studio the right, generally for 75 years, to distribute a colored version of a movie through broadcast and cable-TV outlets and to sell videotape copies. The studio could also collect damages from companies that copied the colored films.
>
> Films would not be eligible for copyright protection if the tinting "consists of the addition of only a relatively few number of colors to an existing black-and-white motion picture."

The Facts On File Weekly World News Digest. © 1987 by Facts On File, Inc. Reprinted with permission of Facts On File, Inc., New York.

first or second page of an issue to condense major news stories. *Facts On File's News Digest* comprehensively summarizes world news every week. Figure 11.1 illustrates a summary that appeared in *Facts On File* about copyright status for computer-colored films. Note how a few paragraphs capture and emphasize the most significant data that may have taken weeks and numerous reports or stories to record. The *Reader's Digest,* one of the most widely read publications in America, is devoted largely to condensing articles, stories, and even books while still preserving the essential message, flavor, and wording of the original.

As a student, you probably will find it is critical to know how to write summaries when you gather and record research. Summaries are crucial in highlighting key ideas from material that students have to include, and frequently evaluate, in research papers. See Chapters 9 and 10 for more information on using summaries in your library research and documentation.

On the job, writing summaries for employers or coworkers is a regular and important responsibility. Each profession has its own special needs for summaries. Chapter 16 discusses a variety of reports—progress, sales, periodic, trip, test, and incident—whose effectiveness depends on a faithful summary of events. You may be asked to summarize a business trip lasting one week into one or two pages for your company or agency. A busy manager may ask you to read and condense a ninety-page report so that she will have a knowledgeable overview of its contents. To cite another example of using summaries on the job, acute-care nurses must write a one- or two-page discharge summary for patients who are being referred to another agency (home health, nursing home, rehabilitation center). These nurses must read the patient's record carefully and summarize what has happened to the patient since admission to the hospital. They must note any surgeries, treatments, diagnoses, and prognoses and indicate necessary follow-up treatments (medications, office visits, outpatient care, x-rays).

You may have to write summaries for individuals outside your company or agency to inform them about the work your employer is doing. Public relations news releases or updates are written for the news media to give them the most up-to-date information about important events at the writer's company or agency. Figure 11.2 contains a summary of ongoing research being done at the National Institute of Standards and Technology, an agency of the U.S. Commerce Department's Technology Administration. This summary, written for editors and others outside the agency, presents basic information on the objectives, methods, findings, and funding of important research on refrigerants that can help save our environment.

FIGURE 11.2   A news release summarizing a research investigation written for individuals outside the company/agency.

NEWS RELEASE

Media Contact: Jan Kosko, 301 / 975-2767

Two Mixtures Could Replace Banned Refrigerant
NIST researchers say two refrigerant mixtures appear promising as environmentally safe replacements for R22, a refrigerant widely used in residential heat pumps. The Clean Air Act of 1990 calls for hydrochlorofluorocarbons (HCFCs), such as R22, to be phased out starting in 2015. HCFCs belong to a family of chemicals believed to be damaging to the Earth's atmosphere. The two mixtures, named R32/R134a and R32/R152a, *do not contain chlorine or bromine,* the two main catalysts some believe are destroying the Earth's ozone layer. The researchers used a NIST-developed computer simulation program, called CYCLE11, and a laboratory version of a heat pump to examine how the mixtures would perform in the machine. The NIST study showed that the two mixtures could perform up to 15 percent better than R22. NIST is currently conducting flammability testing to evaluate the one possible drawback, the fact that both mixtures contain at least one flammable component. This research is being funded primarily by the Electric Power Research Institute with some additional support from the U.S. Environmental Protection Agency.

NIST Update May 11, 1992: 1-2.

Contents of a Summary

The chief problem in writing a summary is deciding what to include and what to omit. As we have just seen, a summary, after all, is a much abbreviated version of the original; it is a streamlined review of *only* the most significant points. You will not help your readers save time by simply rephrasing large sections of the original and calling the new version a summary. That will only supply readers with another report, not a summary. You need to make your summary lean and useful by briefly telling readers about the main points: the purpose, scope, conclusions, and recommendations. A summary should concisely answer the readers' two most important questions: (1) What findings does the report or meeting offer? and (2) How do these findings apply to my business, research, or job? Note how the summary in Figure 11.2 successfully answers these questions by indicating why R32/R134a and R32/R152a are safer, how they can be used, and who has funded the research.

How long should a summary be? While it is hard to set down precise limits about length, effective summaries are generally 5 to 15 percent of the length of the original. The complexity of the material being summarized and your audience's exact needs can help you to determine an appropriate length. To help you know what is most important for your summary, the following suggestions will guide you on what to include and what to omit.

What to Include in a Summary

1. Purpose. A summary should indicate why the article or report was written or why a convention or meeting was held. (Often a report is written or a meeting is called to solve a problem or to explore new areas of interest.) Your summary should give the reader a brief introduction (even one sentence will do) indicating the main purpose of the report or conference.

2. Essential specifics. Include only the names, costs, codes, places, or dates essential to understanding the original. To summarize a public law, for example, you need to include the law number, the date it was signed into law, and the name(s) of litigants.

3. Conclusions or results. Emphasize what was the final vote, the result of the tests, the proposed solution to the problem.

4. Recommendations or implications. Readers will be concerned especially with important recommendations—what they are, when they can be carried out, why they are necessary.

What to Omit in a Summary

1. Opinion. Avoid injecting opinions—your own, the author's, or a speaker's. You distract readers from grasping main points by saying that the report was too long or that it missed the main point, or that a salesperson from Detroit monopolized the meetings, or that the author in a digression took the Land Commission to task for failing to act properly. A later section of this chapter (pages 405–408) will deal with evaluative summaries.

2. New data. Stick to the original article, report, book, or meeting. Avoid introducing comparisons with other works or conferences, because readers will expect a digest of only the material being summarized.

3. Irrelevant specifics. Do not include any biographical details about the author of an article. Although many journals contain a section entitled "notes on contributors," this information plays no role in the reader's understanding of your summary.

4. Examples. Illustrations, explanations, and descriptions are unnecessary in a summary. Readers must know outcomes, results, and recommendations, not the specific details leading up to those results.

5. Background. Material in introductions to articles, reports, and conferences can often be excluded from a summary. These "lead-ins" prepare the reader for a discussion of the subject by presenting background information, anecdotes, and details that will be of little interest to readers who want a summary to give them the big picture.

6. Reference data. Exclude information found in footnotes, bibliographies, appendixes, tables, or graphs. All such information supports rather than expresses conclusions and recommendations.

7. Jargon. Technical definitions or jargon in the original may confuse rather than clarify the essential information the general reader is seeking.

The Process of Preparing a Summary

To write an effective summary, you need to proceed through a series of steps. Basically, you will have to read the material very carefully, making sure that you understand it thoroughly. Then you will have to identify the major points and exclude everything else. Finally, you will have to put the essence of the material into your own words. You may find using a word processor helpful at this final stage. The process of writing a summary demands an organized plan. Follow these steps to prepare your summary effectively.

1. Read the material once in its entirety to get an overall impression of what it is about. Become familiar with large issues, such as the purpose and organization of the work, and the audience for whom it was written. Look at visual cues—headings, subheadings, words in italic or boldface type, notes in the margin—that will later help you to classify main ideas and summarize the work. Also see if the author has included any mini-summaries within the article or report or if there is a concluding summary after an article or a chapter of a book.

2. Reread the material. Read it a second time or more often if necessary. To locate all and only the main points, underline them in the work; or, if the work is a book or an article in a journal that belongs to the library, take notes on a separate sheet of paper. (You may find it easier to photocopy articles so that you can underline.) To spot the main points, pay attention to the key transitional words (see page 74). Such words often fall into the following categories.

- *Words that enumerate:* first, second, third, initially, subsequently, finally, next, another
- *Words that express causation:* accordingly, as a result, because, consequently, therefore, thus
- *Words that express contrasts and comparisons:* although, by the same token, despite, different from, furthermore, however, in contrast, in comparison, in addition, less than, likewise, more than, more readily, not only . . . but also, on the other hand, the same is true for, similar, unlike
- *Words that signal essentials:* basically, best, central, crucial, foremost, fundamental, indispensable, in general, important, leading, major, obviously, principal, significant

Also pay special attention to the first and last sentences of each paragraph. Often the first sentence of a paragraph contains the topic sentence, and the last sentence summarizes the paragraph or provides some type of transition to the next paragraph.

You also have to be alert for words signaling information you do *not* want to include in your summary, such as the following:

- *Words announcing opinion or inconclusive findings:* from my personal experience, I feel, I admit, in my opinion, might possibly show, perhaps, personally, may sometimes result in, has little idea about, questionable, presumably, subject to change, open to interpretation
- *Words pointing out examples or explanations:* as noted in, as shown by, circumstances include, explained by, for example, for instance, illustrated by, in terms of, learned through, represented by, such as, specifically in, stated in

3. Collect your underlined material or notes and organize the information into a rough-draft summary. At this stage do not be concerned about how your sentences read. Use the language of the original, together with any necessary connective words or phrases of your own. Keyboard the rough draft into your word processor, if you are using one. You will more than likely have more material here than will appear in the final version. Do not worry; you are engaged in a process of selection and elimination. Your purpose at this stage is to extract the principal ideas from the examples, explanations, and opinions surrounding them.

4. Read through and revise your rough draft(s) and delete whatever information you can. As you revise, see how many of your underlined points can be condensed, combined, or eliminated. You may find that you have repeated a point. Check your draft against the original for accuracy and importance. Make sure that you are faithful to the original by preserving its emphases and sequence. Using a word processor will make it easy for you to make changes and deletions without rekeying the entire summary.

5. Now put the revised version into your own words. Again, make sure that your reworded summary has eliminated nonessential words. Connect your sentences with conjunctive adverbs (*also, although, because, consequently, however, nevertheless, since*) to show relationships between ideas in the original. Compare this version of your summary with the original material to double-check your facts.

6. Do not include remarks that repeatedly call attention to the fact that you are writing a summary. You may want to indicate initially that you are providing a summary, but avoid such remarks as "The author of this article states that water pollution is a major problem in Baytown"; "On page 13 of the article three examples, not discussed here, are found."

7. Edit your summary to make sure it reads clearly and concisely. Check to be certain it is coherent, too. Tell the reader how one point flows into another. Also proofread your summary carefully.

8. Identify the source you have just summarized. Do this by including pertinent bibliographic information in the title of your summary or in a footnote or endnote. This gives proper credit to the original source and informs your readers where they can find the complete text if they want more details.

Figure 11.3, a 1,500-word article entitled "Counting on the Census," appeared in the *Journal of American Insurance* and hence would be of primary interest to individuals in the insurance field. Assume that you are asked to write a summary of this article for your boss, a busy insurance executive. By following the steps outlined previously, you would first read the article carefully two or three times and then underscore the most important points, signaled by key words. Note what has been underscored in the article. Also study the comments in the margins; these explain why certain information is to be included or excluded from the summary.

FIGURE 11.3   The original article with important points underscored for use in a summary.

Counting on the Census

Delete introductory material, here used to provide a background

Probably no other people but Americans have such as obsession with constantly counting and cataloguing themselves. With help from computers, we've now got more information about ourselves than ever before: an awe-inspiring amount of information, highly sophisticated and often very specific in nature

With so much data-mania around, it's no wonder that the most well-known survey, that just-completed once-a-decade population count conducted by the Census Bureau, is generating more interest than ever. Aside from the controversies—questions about its accuracy and

Delete details of lesser importance

debate over the problem of illegal aliens—Americans are paying attention to the 1980 Census because not only will it confirm our own notions of what we as a nation have become, but also because there's a lot of cold hard cash riding on the results.

Important conclusion

This massive survey will document, on both a large and local scale, the far-reaching social changes of the 1970s. It will chronicle what has happened to each of us over the past ten years: if, like other Americans, we've moved often, and ever south and westward; if we've had smaller families, and bought larger homes. The population count will lend a certain sense of continuity or historical perspective to these changes measuring them against nearly 200 years of American demographic history. The fact that the twentieth census will find a majority of one- and two-person households (they numbered nearly half in 1970 and have been on the rise ever since) is all the more remarkable in light of the 1790 count, in which half of all those fledgling American households consisted of six or more people, and only a tenth had one or two persons living alone.

Include significant point

Delete explanations and examples

Important finding

Results from the head count will add depth and specificity to what we already know, filling in the outlines of our broadbrush figures. "Surveys may tell you what's happened," says Roger Herriot of the Census Bureau, "the census tells you to whom and where."

Delete explanation and following quotation

The final tally will reveal both small group and small area data—important, useful information that is available nowhere else. A housewife's decision to return to work is significant as part of a national trend (since 1978, half of all American women age 16 and older—42 million of them—were in the labor force); yet it's even more meaningful when also placed in the context of how many other women of the same age, living in the same state, town, or even neighborhood, are also working.

Include important information

Delete statistics

Significant conclusion

On the more pragmatic side, the census appeals to our more avid interests, as we are urged to stand up and be counted to get our fair share—of political representation, and federal money. The constitutionally mandated count is no longer just a means of changing the boundaries of congressional districts to reflect

Key words signaling important application

Delete facts indicating former use

Include financial use

Combine types of programs

Delete examples

Key words "also much" introducing
important idea

Include reason why census is so
important to insurers

Include relevant change affecting
insurers; delete statistics

Include these "two areas" significantly
highlighted by key words "vital role"

Another important point, but delete the
statistics

Emphasize insurance needs

population shifts; since 1970, it also has been used to determine where and how more than $50 billion in public welfare and federal revenue-sharing money will be spent. Of special interest to insurers are federal programs on vocational rehabilitation, highway safety, law enforcement assistance, energy research and development, and alcohol and drug abuse, which are among the more than 100 programs using census statistics to guide the allocation of funds to states and local communities. Funding for the Cooperative Extension Service, for example, hinges upon a state's rural and farm population; while spending for the Headstart program relies on the number of children of poverty-level families in a particular community.

There is also much that the insurance industry, the property/casualty side of the business included, can cull from the reams of data generated by the census. The count will be industry's first opportunity for a look at the demographic trends of the next decade, trends which will play a major role in shaping business in the years just ahead. This glimpse into the future will allow insurers, known for their sophisticated application of data, to evaluate—and anticipate—these changes on a local level, where business is actually conducted.

One change in store for this country is that, in the 1980s, the elderly as a group will be getting larger. Between 1950 and 1978, that part of our population age 65 and older doubled in size, and it is expected to increase even further in the coming years. This means a growing need for more resources to meet the financial and medical requirements of the elderly—two areas where the insurance industry will play a vital role.

Also getting its first few gray hairs will be the "baby boom" generation, whose members now fall into the 25 to 34 age group. The fastest-growing segment of the population, its ranks swelled by 35 percent between 1970 and 1978, according to census figures. Members of this group, who have dominated the social changes of the past 20 years, will again set the pace in the next decade. They'll enter their prime years in terms of earning and buying power, pumping up demand for both durable goods and housing, as well as property insurance to cover their investments.

Include main point here	Indeed, property/casualty insurers will be able to glean some valuable information from the questions asked on this year's census. Although only two relate directly to property insurance (one asks homeowners the annual premium for fire and hazard insurance on their property; another inquires whether the regular monthly mortgage payment includes these payments or not), more than half of all the questions are concerned with housing. Some are general, requesting information on owning or renting, the number of rooms in living quarters, and the type of building; while others are quite specific, asking how you heat your home, which fuel you use for cooking, house and water heating, and how much you pay each month for electricity, water, gas, oil or coal (interestingly, census tests have shown that people tend to overestimate their utility costs).
"Although" points to subordinate idea; delete it and examples	
Include major observation	
Delete examples of types of questions	
Restatement of main point	Compiling housing data has been a census assignment since 1850, yet the emphasis placed on the topic on this year's questionnaire is unprecedented. This is due, in part, to the growing number of requests the Census Bureau has received about housing in general, and shelter costs in particular, according to Census housing expert Bill Downs, who says that federal agencies, as well as state and local governments, are among the big users of this type of information.
Delete explanation	
Delete example	A 1976 bureau survey found, for example, that the average owner of a mortgaged home was paying 18 percent of his/her annual income in that year for the mortgage, real estate taxes, property insurance, utilities, fuel, and trash collection. How much that figure will change in 1980, in light of soaring fuel costs, and other factors such as the 45 percent jump in the average price of a new, one-family home, should be of wide interest to property insurers, among others.
Include main point relevant to insurance agents/executives	
Of less significance, but still include	Also of interest but of somewhat more limited use, will be both the number and size of America's homes. Analysts predict that the 1980 count will find that the number of housing units in this country has increased 20 percent since the last census was taken in 1970: twice the rate of the population growth. Along with an increase in the number of households (at a rate three times as fast as that of the rise in population between the years 1970 and 1978 alone),
Delete statistics	

Include main points	these figures reflect a continuing decline in the average size of households.
Delete statistics following this point	At the same time people are choosing to live with fewer other people, they are also living in larger houses. Between 1970 and 1976, the number of five-room housing units (homes, mobile homes and trailers, apartments, and condominiums) rose from 16.9 to 19.2 million; while homes with seven or more rooms grew in number from 11.9 to 15.9 million.
	Unless a change is imminent, this trend,
Delete opinion and qualification	which reflects to a degree the self-indulgent and free-spending lifestyle cultivated by many during the 1970s, has dire implications for our energy needs in the future. Fewer people in bigger living areas means energy inefficiency, wasting the energy and resources needed to construct and heat these homes—a loss that increased conservation can only partly remedy.
Parallel point	Equally ominous in view of the energy
Key phrase for audience	crunch, and of interest to automobile insurers, is the fact that the 1980 census should show no
Include essential point	let-up in America's dependence on the car as a means of transportation. In 1975, of the 73 million households in the U.S., nearly 63 million
Delete statistics	had at least one automobile, according to census bureau figures. Further, owning a home
Key word indicating another conclusion	seems to go hand in hand with owning a car: nearly all homeowners have at least one car, while renters are considerably less likely to purchase a vehicle. Moreover, the number of two-car households more than doubled between
Delete clarifying statistics	1960 and 1975, and is expected to have jumped even higher in the years since.
Key word emphasizing results	The final report, however, may shed light on one transportation alternative. Questions on the number of one-ton trucks and vans, and on whether people who use cars, trucks, or vans
Key reference to audience's use of information	to get to work ride with other people (and if so, how many) will give transportation planners as well as auto insurers some insight into the extent of car and van pooling. This information is the first step in learning how to encourage more people to try this energy-efficient way for commuting.
Not an essential point	Of course, insurance companies use many sources of information other than the once-a-decade census to keep themselves abreast of important demographic changes. Yet insurers,
Brief restatement of article thesis	like many other businesses, still count on the census and the more than 300,000 pages of resulting statistics to tell them where we've been and where we as a nation are going.

Delete information
in tables; used only
for support

	1970	1980	% Change
Population of the U.S.	207,976,452	222,000,000 (est.)	9%
No. of Housing Units in the U.S.	69,000,000	86,000,000 (est.)	23%
No. of House- holds in the U.S.	64,000,000	79,000,000 (est.)	26%

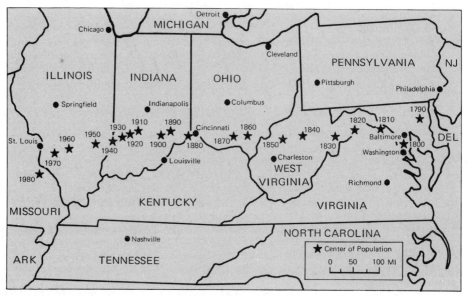

Source: U.S. Bureau of the Census

Delete this caption explaining map—note essential for grasping main points of the article.

Westward Ho!

If the United States were a gigantic table, and everybody stood up right now where they lived, where would the table balance? This may seem like a question of demographic trivia, but in 1980 it will take on historical importance as the nation's center of population moves, for the first time, west of the Mississippi River.

After the first census in 1790, the center of population was just east of Balti-more. It has moved slowly westward ever since, reflecting the general migration of the population. After the 1970 census, it was just south of Mascoutah, Illinois, about 30 miles east of the Mississippi. After the 1980 head count, the center of population will move across the river and slightly to the south, reflecting the recent population shift to the sunbelt states.

Journal of American Insurance (Winter 1979/80). Reprinted by permission

After you have identified the main points, extract them from the article and, still using the language of the article, join them into a coherent working draft summary as in Figure 11.4. The necessary connective words added to the language of the original article are underscored. This working draft then has to be

FIGURE 11.4   A working draft summary of Figure 11.3.

Aside from the controversies about its accuracy, Americans are paying attention to the 1980 Census because there's a lot of cold, hard cash riding on the results. This massive survey will document far-reaching social changes. The twentieth census will find a majority of one- and two-person households, all the more remarkable in light of the 1790 count. The final tally will reveal important useful information available nowhere else. A housewife's decision to return to work is significant as part of a national trend, and even more meaningful in context. On the more pragmatic side, the census count is no longer just a means of changing boundaries but it also affects where $50 billion in public welfare and federal revenue-sharing will be spent. Of special interest to insurers are federal programs on vocational rehabilitation, highway safety, law enforcement assistance, and energy research. There is also much the property/casualty side of the business can gain from the census, which will play a major role in business—evaluating and anticipating changes. One change is that the elderly population will be increasing. This means more resources—financial and medical—in two areas where the insurance industry will play a vital role. Also, the 25 to 34 age group, which is the fastest-growing part of the population, will demand property insurance. Indeed, property/casualty insurers will glean valuable information from the questions asked on the census, more than half of all the questions are concerned with housing. This is an emphasis on the topic of this year's questionnaire that is unprecedented. How much costs for houses will change should be of wide interest to property insurers among others. Also of interest but of somewhat more limited use, the number and size of American houses have increased. Along with an increase in the number of households, there is a continuing decline in the average size of households. At the same time people are choosing to live with fewer other people, they are also living in larger houses. This trend has dire implications for our energy needs in the future. Fewer people in bigger living areas mean energy inefficiency. Equally ominous and of interest to automobile insurers, the 1980 census should show no let-up in America's dependence on the car as a means of transportation. Further, owning a home seems to go hand in hand with owning a car; renters are less likely to purchase a vehicle. The final report, however, may shed light on one transportation alternative. Questions on the number of trucks and vans and on whether people who use cars, trucks, or vans to go to work will ride with other people will give transportation planners as well as auto insurers some insights into the extent of car and van pooling. This information will be the first step in learning how to encourage this energy-efficient way for commuting. Insurance companies use many sources of information, yet insurers still count on the census.

shortened and rewritten in your own words to produce the compact final version of your summary, as in Figure 11.5. Only 152 words long, this summary is 12 percent of the length of the original article and records only major conclusions relevant to the audience for the article.

FIGURE 11.5   A final, effective summary of Figure 11.3.

"Counting on the Census," Journal of American Insurance (1979/80): 13–15.

A lot of money rides on the result of the census. Information on where we live, our household size, and women in the work force affects the funding of federal programs. Because many of these programs concern public safety, health, and energy, they are of crucial importance to insurers. Census figures will also help insurers evaluate the needs of future policyholders. A larger elderly population will require more medical and financial assistance; the fast-growing adult population (ages 25–34) will need more property insurance. Since a majority of census questions deal with housing, property/casualty insurers will learn more about increasingly expensive home ownership. The census will also tell insurers that Americans will waste energy by occupying larger homes with fewer people per household. Moreover, homeowners (as opposed to renters) will buy more cars for transportation. However, information on vehicle pooling may give auto insurers encouraging news about energy conservation.

To further understand the effectiveness of the summary in Figure 11.5, review the wordy and misleading summary of the same article in Figure 11.6 (p. 404). The latter not only is too long but also dwells on minor details at the expense of major points. It includes unnecessary examples, statistics, and names; it even adds new information while ignoring crucial points about the function of the census to insurers. But even more serious, this summary distorts the meaning and the intention of the original article. The reader concludes that the article says the census is not very valuable for insurance agents and executives—just the opposite of the point the article makes. You can avoid such mistakes by de-emphasizing minor points, by making sure that all parts of your summary agree with the original, and by not letting your own opinions cloud issues that the author of the article stresses.

FIGURE 11.6   A misleading summary of Figure 11.3.

Nonessential introductory material

Possible flaw in census not important to article's thesis

Delete historical background and official's name

Minor point in article given major attention; new information and opinion also added

Examples not necessary; do not call attention to summary

Omit opinion

Ambiguous statement; misses main point that elderly population is increasing

Distorts article, which deals with value of census for insurers

Statistics not related to audience

How is all this relevant to insurers?

Distorts article, which emphasizes usefulness of census for insurers; this statement makes census sound unimportant for insurers and overemphasizes a minor point

Americans like to keep track of themselves with very advanced computers. People wonder, though, about the accuracy of the census as a counting tool since it sometimes includes information about illegal aliens. But the census, a part of America's demographic history since 1790, does serve many important functions, says Roger Herriot of the Census Bureau in Washington, D.C. The census tells us that half of all American women over the age of 16 work full-time. Also, the census establishes our congressional districts, and this is very important for our representatives, especially if they find themselves in a new district because of changes in the population. The census also helps allocate federal funds for such programs as the Cooperative Extension Service and Headstart, which are important programs to list in this summary. Furthermore, the census helps predict future insurance business, always a laudable goal. Old people and the young, too, will increase our population. But as far as property insurance is concerned, only two questions appear on this topic on the census, which is almost exclusively concerned with what home fuels, mortgages, and building materials we have. Bill Downs says the government needs this kind of information. It is no wonder since in 1976 people paid 18 percent of their income for housing and will pay 45 percent in 1980. Extravagant Americans want big houses, big cars, and will waste energy using them. Americans should use car pools. But the insurance companies, as the last crucial paragraph of the article states, will not be at too bad a disadvantage since they can rely on other sources of information than what is provided in the census.

Evaluative Summaries

To write an evaluative summary, also called a *critique,* follow all the guidelines previously discussed in this chapter except one. The one major exception is that an evaluative summary includes your *opinion,* or view, of the material.

Your instructors and employers may often ask you to summarize and assess what you have read. In school you may have to write a book report or compile a critical, annotated bibliography commenting on the usefulness of the material you found in those sources. On the job your employer may ask you to condense a report and judge the merits of that report, paying special attention to whether the report's recommendations should be followed, modified, or ignored. Your company or agency may also ask you to write short evaluative summaries of job applications (see pages 281–292) or sales proposals (see pages 568–576) it has received or perhaps of conferences you might have attended, as Roger Blackmore does in Figure 7.3 (p. 192).

An evaluative summary is usually short—not more than 5 to 10 percent of the length of the original. Your evaluation should blend in with your summary of the material. Rather than save all your assessments until the end of your summary, place them directly next to the summary of the points to which they apply so that your reader sees them in context. You may also want to include an especially helpful quotation from the original to emphasize the kind of recommendation you are making. In evaluating the material, include information on both the content and style of the original. Here are some questions on content and style that you should answer for readers of your evaluative summary.

Evaluating the Content

1. How carefully is the subject researched? Is the material accurate and up-to-date? Are important details missing? Exactly what has the author left out? Where could the reader find the missing information? If the material is inaccurate, will the whole work be affected or just a part of it?

2. Is the writer or speaker objective? Are conclusions supported by evidence? Is the writer or speaker following a particular theory, program, or school of thought? Is this fact made clear in the source? Has the author or speaker emphasized one point at the expense of others? What are the writer's qualifications and background?

3. Does the work achieve the goal? Is the topic too large to be adequately discussed in a single talk, article, or book? Is the work sketchy? Are there digressions, tangents, or irrelevant materials? Do the recommendations make sense?

4. Is the material relevant to the audience for whom you are writing your evaluative summary? How would that audience use it? Is the entire work relevant or just part of it? Why? Would this work be useful for all members of your agency (or community) or only for those working in certain areas? Why? What answers offered by the work would help to solve a specific problem you or others have encountered on the job?

Evaluating the Style

1. Is the material readable? Is it well written and easy to follow? Does it contain helpful headings, careful summaries, and appropriate examples?

2. What kind of vocabulary does the writer or speaker use? Are there many technical terms or jargon? Is it written for the layperson? Is the language precise or vague? Would your audience have to skip certain sections that are too complicated?

3. What visuals are included? Charts? Graphs? Photographs? How are they used? Are they used effectively? Are there too many or too few of these visuals?

Figures 11.7, 11.8, and 11.9 (p. 408) contain evaluative summaries. Note how the writer's assessments are woven into the condensed version of the original. Figure 11.7 contains a student's opinions of an article summarized for a class in office management procedures. Figure 11.8 shows an evaluative summary in memo format collaboratively written by two employees who have just returned from a seminar. They have divided their labor, one writing the opening paragraph and the summary of "Techniques of Health Assessment" and the other writing summaries of "Assessment of the Heart and Lungs" and "Assessment of the Abdomen." Together they drafted and revised the "Recommendations" and prepared the final copy of the memo. Another kind of evaluative summary—a book review—is shown in Figure 11.9. Many journals print book reviews to inform their professional audiences about the most recent studies in their field. Reviews condense and assess books, reports, government studies, tape cassettes, films, and other materials. The short review in Figure 11.9 comments briefly on usefulness to

FIGURE 11.7   An evaluative summary of an article.

Pastor, Joan and Risa Gechtman, "Delegate to Get Ahead," The Secretary (Jan. 1992): 15-16.

According to this helpful article, office personnel can keep ahead of their workload by delegating responsibilities to subordinates, to peers, and to supervisors. Traditional delegation—to a subordinate—is most effective if the superior selects a staffer capable of performing the task and monitors progress with reasonable deadlines in mind. The authors list several other useful guidelines for successful "downward" delegation. Delegating to peers, a more complicated process, succeeds only if coworkers can see the benefits, to themselves and to the company, of sharing the workload. Workers can also encourage "sideways" delegation by showing appreciation to coworkers and offering them assistance in return. When supervisors overload assignments, subordinates may need to delegate "upwards." A worker can shift responsibility back to supervisors by diplomatically asking them to set priorities for the projects they have assigned. This readable and innovative article can help prevent workers from falling behind in their projects and, consequently, move their company forward.

FIGURE 11.8   A collaboratively written evaluative summary of a seminar.

SABINE COUNTY HOSPITAL
Sabine, TX 77231
512-555-6734
FAX 555-6789

TO: Marge Geberheart, M.S.N.   SUBJECT: Evaluation of Physical
        Director of Nurses   Assessment Seminar

FROM: Wayne Kim, R.N. *W.K.*   DATE: September 14, 1994
        Lee Schoppe, R.N. *L.S.*

On September 7, Doris Gandy, R.N., and Rick Vargass, R.N., both on the staff of
Houston Presbyterian Hospital, conducted a practical and worthwhile seminar on
physical assessment. The one-day seminar was divided into three units: (1) **Techniques
of Health Assessment**, (2) **Assessment of the Heart and Lungs**, and (3) **Assessment
of the Abdomen**.

Techniques of Health Assessment

Four procedures used in physical assessment—inspection, percussion, palpation,
auscultation—were defined and demonstrated. Such return demonstration, used
throughout the seminar, meant we did not have to wait until we went back to work to
practice our skills. The instructors also stressed the proper use of the stethoscope and
the ways of taking a patient's medical history. We were also asked to take the medical
history of the person next to us.

Assessment of the Heart and Lungs

After we inspected the chest externally, we discussed the proper placement of hands for
percussion and palpation and the significance of various breath sounds. Using
stethoscopes, our instructors helped us identify areas of the lung. We listened to and
identified heart sounds. The film on examining the heart and lungs was ineffective since
it included too much detailed information for seminar participants.

Assessment of the Abdomen

The instructors warned that the order of examination of the abdomen differs from that
of the chest cavity. Auscultation, not percussion, follows inspection so that bowel
sounds are not activated. The instructors then clearly identified how to detect bowel
sounds and how to locate the the abdominal and palpate organs.

Recommendations

We strongly recommend a seminar like this for all nurses whose expanding role in the
health care system requires more physical assessments. Although the seminar covered a
wealth of information, the instructors admitted that they discussed only basics. In the
future, however, it would be better to offer separate seminars on the chest cavity and on
the abdomen instead of combining the two topics because of the amount of information
involved and the time required for demonstrations.

FIGURE 11.9   A book review.

Too Close for Complacency. *By Julio Santiago and Darrell Mulroy. JAS, Inc., P.O. Box O, Rosemount, MN 55068. $10.95 plus $2 shipping and handling.*

Glamorized and sensationalized by television, movies, and books, the average citizen's theories and notions of law enforcement survival skills are riddled with half-truths, and are a far cry from the reality of street survival. This is a no-nonsense combat survival skills book written in layperson's language that dispels the myths of what it takes for an officer to survive on the street.

This book is co-authored by two police veterans who have lived to share their experiences and expertise. Julio Santiago, who spent 25 years in law enforcement, is a writer, firearms trainer and instructor, and inventor of the Nite-Site and Fire-Fly. Co-author Darrell Mulroy, besides having served as chief of police on a South Dakota Indian reservation, is also a journalist and speaker.

Much more than a training manual for law enforcement officials, this book, through graphic pictures, tells stories of real-life incidents, and presents a common sense analysis of the problems plaguing all aspects of law enforcement.

Law and Order, Vol. 39, No. 3 (March 1991), p. 107.

the intended audience and on style, provides clarifying information, and explains how the book is developed. For further examples, you may want to look at *Book Review Digest*, which lists excerpts from reviews in many areas.

A book review, or evaluative summary, includes the most important and useful—to a key audience—information about a book or report. Reviews are also important for the kinds of information that they *do not* include—details and irrelevant (for the audience) information that would only clog a summary. For example, the review in Figure 11.9 indicates that the book includes instruction in survival skills needed by police officers in real-life emergencies, but it does not go into details describing these incidents.

Minutes

Minutes of a meeting are a special type of summary. If you are appointed secretary at an office meeting or for an organization to which you belong, you will be required to submit to members of that group an official record of the actions taken. That record, known as the minutes of a meeting, is distributed usually within twenty-four or forty-eight hours after the meeting has adjourned.

The way in which a meeting is conducted may be governed by highly formal parliamentary procedures known as *Robert's Rules of Order.* Usually, though, business and community meetings are less formal. Still, certain matters of protocol generally are observed at meetings. For example, a chairperson usually brings a list of topics to be discussed; this list is known as the *agenda.* Participants then make *motions* (proposals) about these and other topics and then approve, modify, or vote against them. "I move that we accept the Acme Corporation's bid on the two new heating units"; "I would like to change the wording of the original motion to read 'All employees on the night shift will receive a $3.75 per hour differential.' Each motion is then *seconded* (endorsed) by another member of the group. A motion may be *carried* (passed), defeated, withdrawn, or *tabled* (postponed).

To be effective, minutes should be short. Obviously, you cannot repeat what everyone has said. Emphasize the decisions made or the conclusions reached. For example, do not mention any motions (or discussions of them) that have been withdrawn. Nor should you spend a great deal of time on discussions of other motions. Save your readers' time by condensing, in your own words, lengthy discussions and debates (pro and con) as well as reports presented at meetings. List each motion exactly as it is worded in its *final* form and spell accurately and consistently the names of those proposing and seconding the motion. Finally, record precisely the vote for each motion (e.g., "carried 11 to 2").

Be careful not to inject your opinions into the minutes. Avoid any words that interpret (positively or negatively) rather than impartially record. "The motion was offered just in time" or "The motion was poorly stated" violates the rules of impartiality. When you cite individuals by name, do not qualify their actions, saying that "Mr. Sanders pushed the point for the third time." And resist any urge to summarize the usefulness of a discussion or the meeting itself: "The proceedings cleared up a lot of doubts the subcommittee had expressed"; "The meeting was productively short and simple."

What to Include in Minutes

1. The subject and type of meeting—regular monthly meeting, special sales meeting, rules committee meeting.
2. The date, time, and place of the meeting.
3. The names of those present and those absent (if your list does not exceed twenty or twenty-five individuals).
4. The approval or amendment of the minutes of the previous meeting, or that their reading is waived by a majority of those present.
5. Any old business: further discussion and votes on motions tabled at previous meetings.
6. The new business of the meeting: motions proposed, seconded, and voted on. Indicate briefly the discussion preceding the motion and then the names of those making and seconding the motion. Indicate how the vote is taken—

FIGURE 11.10   Minutes of a meeting.

The City of Hampton

Minutes of the Hampton City Council Open Meeting
February 2, 1994

PRESENT: Thomas Baldanza, Grace Corlee (President),
Virginia Downey, Victor Johnson, Roberta Koos,
Kent Leviche (Secretary), Ralph Nowicki,
Barbara Poe, Willard Ralston, Daniel Sullivan,
Morgan Tachiashi, Ruth Vanessa, Wanda Wagner,
and Carlos Zandrillia

ABSENT: Millard Holmes, Wendy O'Gorman

The meeting was held in Room 102 of City Hall and began
at 7:04 P.M. with Grace Corlee presiding.

OLD BUSINESS

The minutes of the previous meeting (January 5, 1994)
were approved as read. The Council returned to a
discussion of a motion tabled at the last meeting about
holding open meetings twice a month rather than once a
month. The motion, which was made by Barbara Poe and
seconded by Willard Ralston, was voted on and defeated
9 to 5.

REPORTS

Two reports were given.

Victor Johnson noted that the Downtown Beautification
Committee had conferred with both the State Office of
Historical Landmarks and the U.S. Department of Housing
and Urban Development about helping Hampton (in terms
of finance and architectural planning) to restore the
Brandon Building. Johnson said he expected to hear from
both departments before next month's meeting.

by secret ballot, by a show of hands, by voice—and its results, including the
number of *abstentions* (decisions not to vote on a motion), if any.

7. The business to be continued at the next meeting: reports to be made, motions to be voted on.

FIGURE 11.10   (Continued)

```
Minutes                    2              February 2, 1994
```

Giving a report on the Zoning Committee, Wanda Wagner observed that fourteen requests for changes had been submitted in January. The Zoning Board has already approved ten of them, including rezoning South Evans Street from residential to medical.

NEW BUSINESS

1. The problems with the downtown parking meters were discussed. Besides the city's difficulties with maintaining them, local merchants have complained that the meters are bad for business. Roberta Koos supplied documentation that removing them would decrease city revenue and increase parking violations. But Morgan Tachiashi identified greater losses to the city from decreased business in the downtown section because of the meters. He therefore moved, and Virginia Downey seconded, that the parking meters should be removed from the downtown section of the city. The motion carried 10 to 4 by secret ballot. Grace Corlee said she would forward an official order to Police Chief Dunn for the removal of the meters effective March 14, 1994.

2. Mary Ricks, President of the Park Ridge Citizens Group, appeared before the Council requesting that automatic traffic lights be installed at the intersection of Brown and Crawford Avenues. After listening to her comments about the dangers to pupils at the Epstein School from speeding cars and the increased flow of traffic from the Granger Furniture Plant, the Council voted unanimously to install automatic signals at the intersection of Brown and Crawford Avenues. A directive was sent to J. T. Adams, Head of the Traffic Department.

---

8. The time the next meeting is to be held, and where.
9. The time the meeting is officially concluded.

Figure 11.10 shows the minutes of a meeting incorporating each of these nine parts. Not every meeting, of course, will require all of them.

FIGURE 11.10   (Continued)

Minutes   3   February 2, 1994

3. Congratulations were extended to Carlos Zandrillia
   for being honored as an Outstanding Citizen by the
   Hampton Chamber of Commerce.

4. A committee to study ways to increase tourism to
   Hampton was formed. The committee members appointed
   were Ruth Vanessa (Chairperson), Ralph Nowicki, and
   Victor Johnson. President Corlee, speaking for the
   Council, requested that the committee pay special
   attention to the use of Lake Hughes in tourism
   advertisements and asked for a preliminary report in
   two months.

5. Thomas Baldanza moved, and Virginia Downey seconded,
   a motion to set aside $9,700.00 from the Recreation
   Department budget for the improvement of equipment
   at Alice V. Davis Park. The motion carried by a vote
   of 12 to 1, with 1 abstention.

There being no further business, the meeting was
adjourned at 9:37. The next open meeting of the Hampton
City Council was set for March 2 at 7:00 P.M. in Room
102 of City Hall.

                        Respectfully submitted,

                        Kent Leviche

                        Kent Leviche, Secretary

                        Minutes approved,

                        Grace Corlee

                        Grace Corlee, President

Abstracts

The Differences Between a Summary and an Abstract

The terms *summary* and *abstract* are often used interchangeably, resulting in some confusion. This problem arises because there are two distinct types of abstracts: *descriptive abstracts* and *informative abstracts*. The informative abstract is another name for a summary; the descriptive abstract is not. Why? An informative abstract (or summary) gives readers conclusions and indicates the results or causes. Look at the summary in Figure 11.5. It explains why the census is important for insurers: the census helps insurers provide better coverage to specific groups. Informative abstracts are found before long reports, such as the report on robots in industry found on pages 638-657. Descriptive abstracts do not give conclusions.

All abstracts share two characteristics: the writer never uses "I" and does not use footnotes.

Writing the Informative Abstract

As a part of your course work or on your job you will have to write an informative abstract for a long report (see Chapter 17, page 632). One way to approach writing the abstract of a report is to think of it as a table of contents in sentence form. The table of contents is, in effect, the final outline; it is easily fleshed out into an abstract, as the following example shows. On the left is the table of contents, and on the right is the abstract written from that outline.

Table of Contents	*Abstract*

Need for Genetic Counseling
  Definition of Genetic Counseling
  Statistics on Genetic Counseling
	Genetic counseling is a service for people with a history of hereditary disease. One in 17 births contains some defect; one-fourth of the patients in hospitals are victims of genetic diseases (including diabetes, mental retardation, and anemia). One of every 200 children born has chromosome abnormalities.

Purpose of Genetic Counseling	Genetic counseling offers parents an alternative to giving birth to children with genetic diseases and assistance for those with children already afflicted. The first

The Counseling Process
  Evaluating the Needs of the Counselees
  Taking a Family History
  Estimating the Risks
  Counseling the Family
	step in counseling is to evaluate the needs of the parents. A family history is prepared and risks of future children being afflicted are evaluated. The life expectancy and possible methods of treatment of any afflicted child also can be determined. Alternatives are presented.

Table of Contents	Abstract

Determination of a Genetic Disorder
  Amniocentesis
  Karyotyping
  Fluorescent Banding
  Staining
	Four prenatal tests are used to determine if a genetic disorder is present: amniocentesis, karyotyping, fluorescent banding, and staining.

Advantages of Genetic Screening
  Lower Cost
  Increased Availability
	The development of these four relatively simple methods has lowered the cost of genetic counseling and increased its availability.

By permission of Professor Mary Scotto.

The system cited above works only if your table of contents is neither too detailed nor too skimpy. Starting off with a good outline of an article or a report provides the best beginning for your abstract. Make sure your sentences are complete and grammatical. Do not omit verbs, conjunctions, and articles. Proper subordination is essential. You should expect to condense whole paragraphs of the original to a sentence, and individual sentences to a phrase, phrases to a single word.

Writing the Descriptive Abstract

A descriptive abstract is short, usually only one or two sentences; it does not go into detail or give conclusions. Hence it is not a summary. A descriptive abstract provides information on what topics a work discusses, but not how or why they are discussed. Relying on a descriptive abstract, busy readers can decide whether they want or need to consult the work itself. Here is a descriptive abstract of the article summarized in Figure 11.5 (page 403).

> **The census will provide information about changes in America's housing preferences, transportation, and energy needs. These data will be valuable to insurers.**

Figure 11.11 contains a group of descriptive abstracts about books of interest to professionals in public welfare. In a few words each abstract tells what kinds of information the books contain, but does not reveal the solutions, plans, views, or recommendations that the authors of these books advance. A descriptive abstract is never a substitute for the report itself.

Where Abstracts Are Found

1. At the beginning of an article, company report, or conference proceedings; on a separate page; or on the title page of the report.
2. On the table-of-contents page of a magazine, briefly highlighting the features of the individual articles in that issue, or at the beginning of the chapter in a book or in advertisements.

FIGURE 11.11   Some descriptive abstracts of books.

Adolescents in Foster Families
Edited by Jane Aldgate, Anthony Maluccio, and Christine Reeves. Chicago: Lyceum Books, 1989. 192 pp. $25.95; $14.95 paper.
Explores British and American perspectives on foster care, including foster parent assessment and training, strategies for successful placement, and preparation for independent living.

Children of Color: Psychological Interventions with Minority Youth
By Jewelle Taylor Gibbs, Larke Nahme Huang and Associates. San Francisco: Jossey-Bass, 1989. 423 pp. $27.95.
Presents comprehensive guidelines for the treatment of minority children and adolescents.

Housing Issues of the 1990s
Edited by Sara Rosenberry and Chester Hartman. New York: Praeger Publishers, 1989. 395 pp. $55.
Discusses national housing goals, populations with special housing needs, and public policies that would provide housing for those unable to acquire it on their own.

Lifestyles of the Elderly: Diversity in Relationships, Health, and Caregiving
Edited by Linda Ade-Ridder and Charles B. Hemon. New York: Plenum Publishing, 1989. 262 pp. $34.50.
Examines older people's diverse approaches to long-term marriage, family and friends, health maintenance, and caregiving.

Understanding Race, Ethnicity, and Power
By Elaine Pinderhughes. New York: Free Press, 1989. 269 pp. $24.95.
Examines the influence of racial and ethnic identity on the psychological and social dynamics of interactions between individuals with diverse backgrounds.

Public Welfare Vol. 4, no. 4 (Fall 1989).

3. In reference works devoted exclusively to publishing collections of abstracts of recent and relevant works in a particular field (e.g., *Abstracts of Hospital Management Studies, Science Abstracts, Sociological Abstracts*). See Chapter 9 (pages 332–333) for a discussion of the usefulness and limitations of these types of abstracts.

The Usefulness of Summaries

By following the process of writing a summary presented in this chapter you will acquire an invaluable skill. If done concisely and accurately, your summary will save readers a great deal of time and demonstrate your ability to provide the big picture. This skill will help you in preparing the types of documents stressed in subsequent chapters: questionnaire reports, proposals, and short, long, and oral reports.

✓ Revision Checklist

If you break your writing process into a series of steps, you will simplify the task of preparing summaries and abstracts. This chapter has outlined steps designed to guide you through each phase of this task. Use the questions below to help you write summaries and abstracts that are both concise and faithful to the original material.

1. Have I read the original thoroughly to gain a clear understanding of the purpose of the work? If necessary, have I reread the original?
2. As I read the original, have I underlined all key transitional words? Main points? Significant findings? Applications? Solutions? Conclusions? Recommendations?
3. Have I clearly separated main points from (a) minor ones, (b) background information, and (c) inconclusive findings?
4. Have I excluded examples, explanations, and statistics from my summary or abstract?
5. Have I deleted information that is not useful to my audience—information that may be too technical or unrelated to their reason for reading my work?
6. Have I changed the language of the original to my own words so that I am not guilty of plagiarism?
7. Does the emphasis of my summary match the emphasis in the original?
8. Does the sequence of information in my summary follow the sequence of the original?
9. Have I added necessary connective words that accurately convey the relationship of the main points in the original?
10. Have I deleted all wordiness and repetitiveness from my summary?
11. Have I correctly and completely cited the source of the original?
12. Have I avoided phrases that draw attention to the fact that I am writing a summary or abstract?
13. For an informative summary, have I summarized the material objectively without adding unnecessary information or commentary?
14. For an evaluative summary, have I been specific in my critique, commenting on both content and style?
15. Have I interspersed my evaluative commentary throughout the summary so that my assessments appear next to the relevant points?
16. For my evaluative summary, have I included a direct quotation to help illustrate or reinforce my recommendation?
17. Is my descriptive abstract short and to the point, and have I made sure it does not express my conclusion?

Exercises

1. Summarize a chapter of a textbook you are now using for a course in your major field. Provide an accurate bibliographic reference for this chapter (author of the textbook, title of the chapter, title of the book, place of publication, publisher's name, date of publication, and page numbers of the chapter).

2. Summarize a lecture you heard recently. Limit your summary to one page. Identify in a bibliographic citation the speaker's name, date, and place of delivery.

3. Listen to a television network evening newscast and also to a later news update on the same station. Select one major story covered on the evening news and indicate which details from it were omitted in the news update.

4. Write a summary of the research paper on stress and computer programmers (pages 373–386) or on robots in the workplace (pages 638–657).

5. Bring to class an article from the *Reader's Digest* and the original material it condensed, usually an article in a journal or magazine published six months to a year earlier. In a paragraph or two indicate what the *Digest* article omits from the original. Also point out how the condensed version is written so that the omitted material is not missed and does not interfere with the reader's understanding of the main points of the article.

6. Assume that you are applying for a job and that the personnel manager asks you to summarize your qualifications for the job in two or three paragraphs. Write those paragraphs and indicate how your background and interests are suited for the specific job. Mention the job by title at the outset of your first paragraph.

7. Write a summary of one of the following articles:
   a. "Microwaves," in Chapter 1, pages 25–26.
   b. "How to Outfit the High-Tech Office," pages 417–422.
   c. "Electronic Publishing: The Next Great Office Revolution," pages 422–425.

8. Write a descriptive abstract of the article you selected in Exercise 7.

How to Outfit the High-Tech Office
by Stanley Zarowin

To qualify for a high-tech label in the 1990s, an office needs most of the following: computers, printers and color plotters, a copier, a facsimile (fax) machine, modems, an electronic library, an optical storage system, and audiovisual and bar-code equipment. An accountant's office, to operate at peak efficiency, is likely to be equipped with most of these items. . . .

While outfitting a high-tech office is a challenge, in many ways designing the office to accommodate all this equipment creates even more of a challenge. Also challenging is the choice of furniture. . . .

Decor is important, too, for aesthetics and to convey the right image to clients. A CPA's office shouldn't look too opulent or the firm may appear extravagant; yet it shouldn't be so austere as to give a firm the appearance it's not successful.

The Design

Whether a CPA firm is building its office from scratch or renovating an existing space, the design should be done by an architect with high-tech office experience. CPA firms that try the do-it-yourself approach or let a contractor handle the design, in an effort to save money, usually regret the decision.

Designing the office should be a two-step process. First, an architect should be hired, on an hourly basis with a preset upper limit, to assess the site suitability. Then, after the site is selected, it's wise to contract with the architect, for a fixed fee, to design and oversee the work. Under a fixed-fee contract, the architect assumes full responsibility and spends whatever time is necessary to do the job. It's best to avoid contracts that tie the architect's fee to total construction costs; such arrangements provide little incentive to keep costs down.

Once the work is under way, it's wise to try to keep alterations to a minimum. Changes incur extra charges and can add up to a significant amount. However, the architect should act as the firm's representative with the contractor, ensuring the work proceeds according to specifications.

Keeping It Light

Lighting deserves special attention because poor illumination contributes to office discomfort and low efficiency. A firm should insist the architect pay special attention to lighting needs early in the design phase.

Unfortunately, many clients instruct designers to save money by using the least-expensive fluorescent lamps. Although such fixtures provide ample general illumination, they are not good for task lighting. Unless lamp louvers are added in the ceiling to disperse the light, such lighting is glaring and makes computer-screen viewing especially uncomfortable. Also, the "cold" color of fluorescent bulbs is distasteful to many.

As a cost compromise, the architect should be asked to consider a dual lighting system—fluorescent for general illumination and incandescent for task lighting. Some of the new fluorescent bulbs produce a "warmer" ambience.

In addition, the designer should be asked to add rheostats to the lighting controls so each user can adjust illumination intensity in a room or over a task. Rheostats cost only a few dollars each and provide a convenient personal touch to a work space.

Counting on Computers

Computers are the heart of the high-tech office. The well-equipped office should have an assortment of them: a small mainframe or a powerful personal computer (PC) to operate a network of computers; PCs or workstations at the desks of most staffers; laptops or notebook PCs for those who travel; and portables for accountants who visit clients and need a computer with more capacity and screen clarity than their smaller cousins. The newest laptops offer power and screen clarity comparable to both lugables and desktop models.

While many older desktop computers—the 8088, XT, and AT models—still work well for most limited applications, clearly the high-tech office should be buying either 386s or even the newer and more powerful 486s for speed and to run advanced application software.

Portable computers should be equipped with built-in or portable modems (and optional fax circuit boards). In that way a traveling accountant can dial the office and tap into its memory bank for files, updates, or even a special software program.

Printers
A high-tech office should have at least four types of printers:

- *A laser printer* for generating tax returns, graphics (for reports and presentations), and extra-sharp images.
- *A high-speed pin (impact) printer* for speed. Such machines are so inexpensive (about $250), it's almost worth linking one to nearly every computer. Most produce good-quality letters, general ledgers, and graphs.
- *An inexpensive ink-jet or bubble-jet printer* for high-quality and graphics printing. Some bubble jets are portable.
- *Color plotters* for graphics, spreadsheets, cash-flow analysis, and overhead displays for presentations.

Backup Provisions
For safety's sake, an accountant's office should provide for data backup in case of a fire or a power failure. The following should be available:

- *Software and hardware to ensure fast and accurate backups of all data.* Magnetic tape, not disks, provides the best choice for large amounts of backup data.
- *An outside facility, in a building other than the CPA's office, in which to store computer data.* In the event of a fire or other disaster at the accountant's office, the backup data will be safe.
- *A "hot site"—an off-premises office.* In the event of a disaster, the staff can be up and running on borrowed computers. The firm should check with computer consultants for such services, or it should consider making an arrangement to use a client's facilities in the event of an emergency.
- *Uninterruptible power supplies (UPS).* The simplest and cheapest UPS kick in automatically the instant the power goes off—giving the computers just enough time to shut down without damage or loss of data.

Office Copiers
In selecting an office copier the real choices are performance, price, and optional features. Today's technology is so advanced that few machines suffer frequent or long downtimes.

Before selecting a copier, the first step is to determine the office's peak volume (in many cases, it's from January to April) and then to compare that figure with the capacity ratings provided by vendors. Buyers should rely on those guides.

If a low-level machine (capable of generating fewer than 30 copies per minute) meets a firm's need, big bargains are available. Sales of such machines have been so slow that manufacturers are offering deep discounts to stimulate business. A typical machine is selling for $2,000 less today than it did five years ago.

Options to consider on all machines are

- *Sorting and collating for multipage documents.* Machines come with 5 to 40 holding bins.
- *Image reduction.* This is necessary so spreadsheets and other large documents can be shrunk to convenient sizes (most fax machines can't handle documents larger than 8 1/2 by 11 inches). Some copiers have only a handful of preset reduction steps; others have a zoom feature that allows reduction in 1 percent steps.
- *Document feeds.* They automatically handle multiple pages.
- *Reverse auto document feed (RADF).* RADFs automatically handle the paper for duplex (double-sided) copying.
- *Sheet bypass.* This allows report covers, separators, address labels, or photos to be inserted during a multipage run.
- *Liquid toner.* Problems with old-style liquid toner machines ("bleeding" ink on copies) have been solved. In fact, today's liquid toner copiers are slightly more reliable than dry toner models because they have fewer moving parts.

Other considerations are as follows:

- *Service contracts.* Copier companies make unusually large profits from service contracts. Because the average copier has an "uptime" of 99.5 percent, such contracts usually are not worth it.
- *Buying supplies.* Despite the claims of copier vendors, the paper they sell is not any better than the paper from any supply house. Any brand is acceptable as long as it passes through the feeder. However, it's advisable to buy toner only from the manufacturer; there can be problems with cheaper, generic formulas.

Library on a Laser Disk

Preprogrammed laser disks literally squeeze an entire accounting library onto a few feet of shelf space and make all the information available at the touch of a button. No high-tech office should be without such an electronic library.

Accessing the data on the disks, which are the computer equivalent of music and video compact disks (CDs), requires a special drive for the computer, called a CD-ROM (read-only memory).

The data can be researched very easily with the help of indexing software. In fact, since the entire operation takes place on a computer, edited text from the electronic library can be copied into the computer's word processor.

Presentations

Accounting firms that do effective marketing know the most powerful sales tools are multimedia and graphic presentations prepared by computer. Such presentations include overhead visual projections, 35mm slides, newsletters with graphics, and promotional pamphlets.

In addition to a 386 computer, here's the equipment needed to handle those projects:

- *Presentation software.* There are several popular programs specifically designed to do desktop publishing and to prepare presentation material.

- *Scanners.* These devices "photograph" images (pictures and text) and convert the images into computer data. The data can be edited, reshaped, and stored by a computer. Scanners come in two basic models: desktop and hand-held. It's best to have both, one to do big jobs and the other to scan a few pages of text from a book.
  Bonus. Scanned text also can be converted into a word processing format by using optical character-reading software, which means long printed reports can be scanned and automatically formatted into documents rather than retyped.
- *Desktop slide recorder.* Another optional purchase, this instrument prepares 35mm slides from material stored in the computer. If a firm does not make many slides, it may be more economical to have a photo service process the conversion.
- *Data displays.* These devices instantly display the color image that shows on a computer screen and project it, via an overhead display, onto a large wall screen.

Optical Image Storage

Accountants are just beginning to make use of optical image storage equipment, which converts images—photos and entire documents—into computer data. The equipment stores the information and indexes it for easy retrieval. Such data also can be transmitted by modem to other computers.

The equipment is similar to the scanning equipment described above; however, in this process the data are stored on laser disks and the equipment is specially designed to handle huge numbers of images.

Prices of the systems range widely. Simple ones cost as little as several thousand dollars, but some of the more sophisticated designs can cost millions.

Accountants who do a lot of litigation work, in which many documents must be stored and quickly retrieved, find optical image storage equipment valuable.

Bar Coding*

During the hectic tax season the comment most often heard in the office is, "Where is the ABC Co. file?" What frequently has happened is the harried accountant who took the file into his/her office forgot to sign out for it. In an office with many workers, such an oversight can cause frayed nerves.

A technology originally designed to read identifying codes on retail products offers a simple solution to the problem. In bar coding, little stripes are printed on a label. When a special computerized light pen is passed over the code, the identity of the item is placed in memory.

In a typical office application, each file is labeled with a bar code, and anyone who takes a file is required to sign out by waving the pen over the label, recording the identity of the file and the person.

The bar-code software and hardware can be added easily to any PC.

Obsolescence

The issue that disturbs most accountants in planning the high-tech office is obsolescence. To be sure, every few years—and sometimes even sooner—new hard-

---

For more information about bar codes in today's office, look at p. 161.

ware or an updated version of software hits the market, making the current technology seem antiquated. Fear of obsolescence is so pervasive that the *Wall Street Journal* recently published a cartoon in which a psychiatrist tells his patient, "But everyone has obsolete computers they bought last year."

One response to this concern is that every year a firm puts off investing in high-tech equipment puts it one year further behind the times, making it even more difficult to get on track. However, a firm does not always have to be at the leading edge of office technology. Equipping an accounting office with the hardware and software that best meets the firm's needs should be the primary goal, not equipping it with the latest or most expensive.

The payoff—in work efficiency and effectiveness—is worth the effort.

Electronic Publishing: The Next Great Office Revolution
By William M. Winsor

Desktop publishing may be the greatest productivity tool in a modern office environment since the introduction of spreadsheet software in the 1970s. Spreadsheet software was the catalyst that brought the microcomputer into the office environment because office workers embraced it with such enthusiasm.

Desktop publishing hasn't quite reached that plateau, but the writing is on the wall. The total desktop publishing market was approximately $453 million in 1986. Not bad, considering desktop publishing really didn't exist until late 1984. By 1990, the total market should reach $4.9 billion, an increase of more than 1,000 percent in just four years! Clearly, desktop publishing has a bright future for a number of reasons:

- Desktop publishing enables people and businesses to develop their own brochures, newsletters, and other documents at a fraction of the cost and time expended sending the work out to a professional graphics studio.
- Desktop publishing doesn't require a great deal of artistic skill, although the ability to conceptualize is helpful.
- Desktop publishing is opening doors to people who never had the ability to produce documents before.

People who had no interest in publishing suddenly discovered they could produce documents after spending a short time learning the technology. For instance, a church secretary can develop the Sunday bulletin in an afternoon, business executives can quickly generate product documentation at the office and marketing specialists can produce a product brochure in a fraction of the time previously required.

There also has been an emergence of new customer and trade publications that use desktop publishing technology. A publisher can now put together an entire magazine at a personal computer without incurring the cost of hiring production artists or designers. All the publisher has to do is print out the pages, leave empty "knockout windows" for the printer to insert photos, and take the pages to the printer. The printer then adds the photos and prints the pages. Instant magazine!

Logical Evolution

Desktop publishing is the result of a logical evolution in publishing. It started with ancient scribes laboriously copying books by hand and evolved into the printing press revolution. Things heated up with computer-generated "cold" type which debuted in the 1950s.

With this process, type was set by computer, pasted on an art board by a layout person, photographed by a printer and transferred to a sheet on the printing press. That concept is moved forward several generations by desktop publishing.

Now an individual can assemble an entire page on a personal computer and produce a finished document. Text is first developed on a word processor and transferred to the screen, then graphics, photos and other art can either be added or developed through several graphics-generating peripherals, such as light pens.

Dot-matrix and laser printers produce a sharp document that is easily reproduced through a photocopy machine. If a large press run is needed, the print-out can be taken to a commercial printer who reproduces the document in quantity. The latter technique is also useful when photographs are used in the document.

Standards Needed

From a base of virtually zero just three years ago, nearly every major hardware and software developer is now involved with desktop publishing. As a result, the same controversy over computer industry standards that has been discussed for years, is now associated with desktop publishing.

The main alternatives are the Apple Macintosh and MS/DOS machines, which include IBM personal computers and a host of clones. Apple pioneered desktop publishing and currently enjoys an edge, but the corporate world is populated by MS/DOS.

Manufacturers recognize the standards issue and are making efforts to overcome compatibility problems so that different machines can "talk" with one another. This is challenging, however, since most MS/DOS machines were not designed to handle the high-resolution graphics and page descriptor languages necessary to utilize desktop publishing technology.

Setting Up

No matter which system is selected, the basics are the same. Hardware requirements should include a personal computer with at least 512K of RAM (random access memory), a high resolution monitor, a "mouse," and a dot-matrix or laser printer. The printer is especially important because it determines the final product's quality.

A dot-matrix printer has a 100 dpi (dots-per-inch) resolution, which is adequate for simple projects, such as newsletters. More sophisticated projects, such as brochures, magazines and documentation require a laser printer that produces 300 dpi text, which is still less than the 1000 dpi-and-up resolution provided by professional printers.

As you would expect, there's a price for performance. Dot-matrix printers can be purchased for about $500, while laser printers go for at least four times that much. In either case, the long-term savings are significant compared with outside typesetting charges of $50 to $100 per page.

Virtually every desktop publishing system relies on a hand-held "mouse" as the principal tool for developing a layout. The mouse is a movable device which is connected to the computer by a small cable. It can be pointed in different directions to select menus and options on the computer screen and build a document.

A mouse is especially helpful when selecting "clip" art and electronically assembling a page. (The term "clip" art originates from the newspaper practice of keeping clip sheets containing drawings that were clipped with scissors and pasted on the page.) The clip art can be selected from a software program and electronically "pasted" onto a page. Because the range of clip art is somewhat limited, an optical scanner enables more complex art to be used.

An optical scanner is a necessary option if photos or other previously produced art is used in the final product. The scanner reads the image and transfers it on to the page. Many scanners are able to read various tones which provide texture to the art. Scanners don't come cheap, however, costing $3,000 to $5,000, which is still considerably less than their $30,000 price tag three years ago.

A light-emitting pen is another option that enables graphics to be hand-drawn on the screen. This art can be original and crisp and works best if the user is an accomplished graphic artist or has access to one. Drawing on a computer requires some of the same skills as drawing on paper, so artistic talent is a definite plus.

Choosing Software

As with any computer system, the software determines how desktop publishing can be used. A basic piece of desktop publishing software will enable a person to lay out the text and art on the page but requires the manual reformatting of text to accommodate graphics. A second generation desktop publishing software program will automatically reformat the text to accommodate graphics.

The availability of font designs in software is another factor. Fonts are the type styles available for printing, such as Gothic, Courier, Helvetica, or Old English. Each style has a certain look and it is up to the individual taste of the person designing the document to determine which font is appropriate. Obviously, the more fonts available, the more flexibility the user has.

Perhaps the most important software element is its capacity. First generation software can create documents up to 32 pages in length, while second generations handle up to 96 pages. Other features to look for in software are

- Kerning, or the ability to automatically adjust the amount of space between letters
- Automatic page numbering
- Ability to change type styles within a line
- Ability to change graphic size without distortion

If a simple newsletter is all that will be produced, a first generation software program in the $100–$200 range will be adequate. However, if reports, documentation, and brochures will be the main focus of the system, then a sophisticated program costing $500 or more may be necessary.

Avoiding Pitfalls

Although desktop publishing opens the world of publishing to everyone, not everyone has the innate conceptual ability to use desktop publishing. A major complaint many layout specialists have is the overuse of graphics. Fortunately, most software programs come with a tips section that outlines how to develop publications. More sophisticated programs may require seminars and professional instruction. See the figure below for typical business uses of desktop publishing.

10 Typical Business Uses for Desktop Publishing

- Internal employee newsletter.
- External customer newsletter.
- Business forms, such as invoices, purchase orders, etc.
- Product documentation, such as owner manuals and instructions.
- Company capability brochures.
- Product sales brochures.
- Product price lists.
- Magazines.
- Meeting information packets.
- Sales kits.

William M. Winsor, "Electronic Publishing: The Next Great Office Revolution." *CPA Journal* Feb. 1988: 90-91. *NIST Update* Mar. 11, 1992: 1-2.

Preparing a Questionnaire and Reporting the Results

A questionnaire asks carefully selected respondents to supply answers to a list of questions. Properly designed, questionnaires can be valuable reference tools that measure the changing winds of opinion, help to forecast trends, and record a wide range of statistical data. Opinion sampling can be a very elaborate operation requiring collaborative expertise in psychology, statistics, and computer science. Some questionnaires, therefore, are costly, sophisticated measuring devices prepared by firms that specialize in gathering information. Other questionnaires, including the ones described in this chapter, are shorter, less formal ones for use on the job or in school. Chapter 12 shows you how to design this type of questionnaire, distribute it, summarize the results, and prepare a report based on those results.

The Usefulness of Questionnaires

Questionnaires play a particularly practical role in schools, business and industry, and government. As a student, you may have recently completed a questionnaire asking you to evaluate a course or a program. You can find questionnaires on campus about extracurricular activities, the hours a pool or tennis court is open, the quality of food at a cafeteria. These questionnaires seek to measure student opinion to improve campus life—both academic and social. In addition to answering a questionnaire, you may at some point in your college career have to design one to gather information for a report or paper.

Questionnaires in business can increase a company's or agency's sales and profits by determining the consumer's needs. A customer's likes and dislikes readily translate into buying power. To determine what consumers say they want, a

FIGURE 12.1   **A short questionnaire.**

We hope that you enjoyed your stay at the Happiness Hotel. In order to make your return visit even more pleasurable, we would appreciate your taking a few minutes to fill out this questionnaire. Thank you. We hope to see you again—soon.

1. How did you find out about the Happiness Hotel?
   □ friends   □ travel agent   □ magazine ads   □ billboard   □ telephone directory
   □ other (please indicate)

2. What condition was your room in when you checked in?
   □ spotless   □ satisfactory   □ unsatisfactory

3. How would you describe your maid service?
   □ excellent   □ good   □ fair   □ poor

4. How was the food in our dining room?
   □ superior   □ good   □ satisfactory   □ needs improvement (please specify)

5. Please rank in order of preference the recreational facilities you used at Happiness Hotel.
   □ pool   □ tennis courts   □ golf course   □ horseback riding

Name _____   Room number _____
(optional)

store can distribute a questionnaire asking for specific comments on store hours, a particular line or brand of merchandise, credit policies, effectiveness of sales-clerks, services after the sale, and the like. A brief questionnaire left in hotel guest rooms is found in Figure 12.1. By analyzing the answers to the short questions, the hotel will know better where to advertise, what to emphasize in those advertisements, and what to correct or expand in its dining room and recreational facilities.

The government is actively engaged in gathering facts and opinions from its citizens. Every ten years a long questionnaire from the Bureau of the Census asks all Americans detailed questions about occupation, income, health, language, and household size. The answers to this lengthy questionnaire help determine how many representatives are sent to Congress and how much of every tax dollar returns to local communities. At the local level, elected officials may distribute questionnaires asking whether a street should be converted into a four-lane highway, a residential area rezoned for shopping facilities, or a new water treatment plant constructed.

Mail Questionnaire Versus Personal Interview Questionnaires

There are some important practical differences between gathering information by mailing a questionnaire and by conducting an interview. Questionnaires have the following advantages over interviews:

1. A mail questionnaire can save time and money; it will reach individuals whether they live in your town or across the country. On a small scale, it can

be done by one person. Contrast this method of collecting information with personal interviews, which require appointments, travel, and time.

2. Mail questionnaires can be completed in the privacy of the home or office by respondents who will not be embarrassed by an interviewer's eye-to-eye questions about age, income, grievances, or preferences. A questionnaire can assure respondents of anonymity and give them more time to answer. Interviews require immediate responses.

3. Properly worded, mail questionnaires can elicit honest, unthreatened responses. An interviewer, however, might unintentionally sway a respondent by gesture, tone of voice, or facial expression.

Mail questionnaires do have drawbacks. The response rate can be very low, because people may think that filling out the questionnaire is a waste of time. Even if they do fill it out, you never know when respondents plan to return the questionnaire. Generally, though, a mail questionnaire is a much more efficient method of gathering information than a personal interview is. You can reach more people in less time with less expense. Reserve interviews for times when you have a very small number of people to reach (not more than ten or fifteen) and when those individuals are authorities in the field rather than a cross section of a population.

Another "personal" type of interview can be conducted over the telephone. Telephone interviews are used when an individual or a company wants to sample a large segment of an audience. Polls about preferences for a candidate or a product are examples. Telephone interviews can be expensive and have drawbacks similar to face-to-face interviews. They are labor intensive because they require a group of trained callers who must be skilled in asking questions especially suited to the ear rather than the eye. Finally, households today receive so many telephone sales solicitations that they tend to be suspicious of legitimate survey calls and hence are less cooperative.

A Questionnaire's Two Audiences

You have two primary audiences to keep in mind when you prepare a questionnaire: (1) the respondents who will fill out your questionnaire and (2) the individuals who will read your report based on responses to the questionnaire. You may later share the results (or, occasionally, even the report itself) with respondents, but they are not the primary audience for whom you write your report. The primary audience is the person or people who will read your report and make decisions based on it. Respondents usually do not make decisions on how to translate opinions into action. The questionnaire links both groups. For example, students, employees, patients, or customers complete a questionnaire to give facts, express opinions, or emphasize the need for change. Using their responses, you write a report for an employer or elected official who can decide what changes, if any, need to be made.

How carefully you poll your questionnaire audience will determine how successful you are with your report audience. You will not meet the needs of either group if your questionnaire contains gaps. Questionnaires that are vague or confusing will produce a report containing these same weaknesses. When questions are clear, concise, and relevant, respondents have a better opportunity to voice their opinions. Your report readers will not have the time or the inclination to read every questionnaire; they will depend on you to summarize the results accurately, arrange them into neat categories, and provide pertinent recommendations.

Chapter 12 emphasizes the needs of both audiences. It first discusses choosing a restricted topic, writing effective questions, and preparing a successful, attractive questionnaire. It then outlines how to select respondents, distribute the questionnaire, and tabulate the results. How to meet report readers' specific expectations constitutes the second part of the chapter and includes guidelines on how to condense information, record numbers properly, incorporate direct quotations, and make recommendations.

Choosing a Restricted Topic

Before constructing your questionnaire, settle on a restricted topic. The key to finding such a topic is remembering that successful questionnaires solicit answers to help solve a particular problem or initiate a specific change. Responses to precise questionnaires can help you to formulate a knowledgeable recommendation to your employer or teacher. The more precise and carefully defined your topic, the more accurate your recommendation will be. A school, business, or agency would soon go bankrupt if it were concerned only with the vague or the general. The topic of your questionnaire should lead to specific action.

If you decided to write a questionnaire on working conditions in your place of employment, you might have found a practical subject but not a precise one. What, specifically, are you interested in learning? You certainly could not write a report on every aspect of your working conditions. Too much is involved. You would spread yourself, your recommendations, and your respondents' answers too thin if you tried to tackle this vast subject. Using the prewriting strategies discussed in Chapter 2 (pages 29–32), you might want to begin by asking yourself what is included in the topic. What smaller, more precise topics can you find in the large issue "working conditions"? Here are some that might be found on a brainstormed list.

supervisors	salaries	temperature
coworkers' responsibilities	parking	profit sharing
schedules	eating facilities	machinery
grievance committees	lighting	coffee/rest breaks
union involvement	safety measures	promotions
fringe benefits		

You would then choose a restricted topic from these subjects and build your questionnaire around it. You will more easily determine respondents' opinions when you ask them about fringe benefits or safety measures than when you ask a series of general questions. The results from your questionnaire, consequently, will be more precise, easier to organize, and more understandable and useful to readers.

Another example might be helpful. Perhaps you want to question respondents about television. That is a roomy topic, so you will have to narrow the range.

For example, are you interested in the following different kinds of television stations?

Public Broadcasting System affiliates
stations owned by the four major networks (ABC, CBS, NBC, Fox)
independent television stations
low-power television stations
superstations (WTBS, WGN, WWOR)
local television stations
foreign language stations

Each of these types of television stations is also a broad subject. You will have to ask yourself exactly what you want the respondents to say about one aspect of television. Again, brainstorm to narrow your focus and restrict your topic.

children's programs	personalities
schedules	news broadcasts
advertising rates	community service messages
reception in your area	sporting events
late night programming	movie offerings

By developing a questionnaire on one of these much more limited subjects, you will achieve useful results.

Writing the Questions

Relevant Questions

Once you have a topic, ask this question: "Exactly what kinds of information about this topic am I looking for?" Determine the types of information you need and then include only relevant questions. A useful technique for evaluating the relevance of a question is to make a short list of possible answers to the question. Do the answers provide useful information? If not, the question is probably irrelevant. Since many of the questionnaires you will have to write are brief (ten to twenty questions), make every question count. However interesting a side issue may be, keep it off your questionnaire. Why ask respondents to write more than is necessary? And why risk distracting them with irrelevant issues?

To illustrate the process of selecting only relevant questions, let's assume that you work for Speedee Tax Consultants and that your manager wants you to write a questionnaire to determine whether first-time customers approve of what Speedee is doing. You are to ask them questions about your service, the time and money they invested, and their suggestions for improving your service. Anything else is unnecessary. The questions on the left side below would be relevant for your questionnaire; those on the right would not.

Relevant questions	Irrelevant questions
Did anyone help you fill out your return last year?	Were you good in high school mathematics?
Did you earn any income outside this state?	Do you consider yourself a blue- or white-collar worker?

Relevant questions	**Irrelevant questions**
Did you have to file a state form this year?	Do you find the state or federal form more confusing?
How did you hear about Speedee?	Have you ever been audited by the IRS?
Did you make an appointment to speak to a Speedee consultant?	Should the IRS extend the filing deadline to June 1?
Was there ample parking room?	What make of car do you drive?
How long did you have to wait if you did not have an appointment?	Did you think the Speedee office was tastefully decorated?
Was the Speedee consultant courteous?	Do you know how much training our employees receive?
Were the consultant's explanations clear or were they given in terms you did not understand?	What kind of computer did the Speedee consultant use?
Did the consultant explain how your return can be filed electronically?	Do you use fax machines often on your job?
On the federal return, were you told whether a short or long form was better for you?	Are there too many tax loopholes for the rich to escape paying their fair share?
Which form (long or short) did you file?	Are you currently employed?
Did the consultant show you how you could lawfully reduce the amount you owed? Increase your refund?	What will you do with your refund, if you receive one?
Were the costs for Speedee's services clearly explained?	Will you have to live on a tighter budget next year?
Did you find those costs fair?	Do you know the name of the owner of Speedee's or how many people we helped last year?
Would you come to Speedee next year?	Would you write your representative in Congress if you had to pay back more than $500?

The relevant questions stick to the issue of most concern to the Speedee Tax Consultants—transforming first-time customers into repeat business. The irrelevant questions stray from the issues of service and costs.

You can use the same brainstorming techniques to generate relevant questions that you used to arrive at a restricted topic. Write down a series of questions—in any order—that you think might pertain to your topic. Then scrutinize each question in light of your topic, purpose, and audience's needs, as in the Speedee example above. Finally, revise and edit your questions to make each exactly on target.

Two Basic Types of Questions

In preparing a questionnaire you can write two kinds of questions: **open-ended (or essay) questions** and **closed (or fixed alternative) questions**. The following sections define each type of question, provide examples, and point out their benefits and drawbacks.

Open-Ended Questions

An open-ended question asks respondents to formulate their answers without being given certain answers to choose among, thus allowing considerable freedom of expression. Open-ended questions use verbs that elicit amplified, extensive responses: *appraise, comment on, compare, describe, discuss, estimate, evaluate, explain, judge.* Here are some sample open-ended questions.

Describe the changes you would make in the registration process at Mesa College.

Explain which part of your job is the hardest to perform and why.

Discuss your reasons for attending Monmouth College.

Judge the effectiveness of a family health practice in which a registered nurse screens patients and decides which ones will see a doctor.

Comment on how you would correct abuses in the food stamp program in Taylorsville.

Open-ended questions are useful for a variety of purposes. They provide a practical means of soliciting information on subjects that would otherwise require options too numerous (or impossible) to list one by one. For example, the question on why students attend a particular college might bring back ten or twelve different and valid answers, some of which might never have occurred to you. Open-ended questions may also be helpful in gathering information on sensitive professional issues. Furthermore, respondents will reveal how knowledgeable they are, thus allowing you to gauge the value of their opinions.

Open-ended questions can be useful to you even before you write the final version of your questionnaire. You can send a few open-ended questions to a small sample of your respondents who, in their answers, can suggest the topics and options to include on the final questionnaire. And on the final copy of your questionnaire, the last question can be an open-ended one asking respondents to comment in detail on any topic covered in the questionnaire or on any topic you may have overlooked.

Finally, open-ended questions are valuable for lengthy studies searching for in-depth responses. If you have much time and relatively few (under fifteen or twenty) respondents, a questionnaire composed mainly of open-ended questions can be rewarding.

But open-ended questions can also pose problems for you and your respondents. This type of question requires a great deal of effort from respondents, who will have to organize, compose, and write their answers. If your question is not direct and sufficiently focused, you could easily get many irrelevant answers from respondents. Moreover, valuable answers might be mixed with these irrelevant comments. Finally, responses to open-ended questions are challenging to summarize (especially when large groups are surveyed), and these responses must be properly coded. (Later sections of this chapter, pages 450–453, discuss some ways to code, record, and tabulate responses.)

Closed Questions

Closed questions offer respondents a limited number of choices. Because closed questions are easier to answer, code, and tabulate, they are used more often than open-ended questions. Closed questions fall into the five categories discussed on the next few pages.

1. Questions that offer only two choices. These are sometimes called *dichotomous questions* because they present the respondent with a dichotomy, a division of the subject into two mutually exclusive parts. The respondent's choice is limited to one of these two parts. Use this type of question only when the topic can be reasonably understood and explained in either/or terms.

a. Yes/no questions

Should women be required to register for the draft?   yes _____   no _____

Is there a history of breast cancer in your family?   yes _____   no _____

Have you already taken Banking 117—Principles of Banking Operations?   yes _____   no _____

b. True/false questions

People who smoke in public places should be fined.   true _____   false _____

Licensed Practical Nurses should, after special training, be allowed to start IV's.   true _____   false _____

Lanse Street must be changed into a one-way street.   true _____   false _____

c. Two specific objects or types identified

Which kind of radio station to you prefer?   AM _____   FM _____

What kind of coffee do you drink most often?   regular_____   decaffeinated _____

What kind of stove does your apartment have?   gas _____   electric _____

2. Multiple-choice questions. These questions usually offer respondents three to five answers from which to choose. One of those answers can be marked "other," "option not given," "do not know," "undecided," or "none."

What type of domesticated animal would you choose for a pet?
dog _____   cat _____   bird _____   fish _____   other (please specify) _____

Which kind of music do you like to listen to most often?
rock 'n' roll _____   country/western _____   jazz _____   classical _____   blues _____
New Age _____

Which agent called on you last month?
Ms. Kelly _____   Mr. Tumbrel _____   Ms. Chin _____   Mr. Lopez _____
No one called _____

How many times a day do you use E-mail?
1 _____   2 _____   3 _____   4 _____   more than 4 (please specify) _____

3. Rating-scale questions. These questions ask readers to rate (or evaluate) an individual, program, policy, or option according to a carefully graduated scale. The respondent indicates the degree or extent of his or her opinion by marking an appropriate number on the scale. Always make sure that you specify precisely what the numbers on a scale mean. Usually this involves defining the items at either end of the scale. If the scale has an odd number of gradations, the middle position is considered a "neutral" opinion, as the following examples illustrate.

> What is your overall view of Mayor Santori's administration?
>
> Excellent   Poor
>   1   2   3   4   5
>
> Central College should change from a semester to a quarter calendar.
>
> Strongly   Strongly
>   agree   disagree
>   1   2   3   4   5

Figure 12.4 (page 445) includes a questionnaire that uses rating-scale questions exclusively.

4. Ranking questions. With these questions a respondent is asked to assess the relative significance of a series of options and to assign each a value, often by labeling them 1, 2, 3, 4.

> Indicate your order of preference for the kind of nursing you would like to do after graduation.
>
> acute care _____   industrial _____   home health _____   school _____
>
> Please rank in order of importance the following reasons for your decision to do your banking at First National.
>
> Superteller _____   Saturday hours _____   Free checking _____   Location _____
> Investment counseling _____
>
> Rank the following types of cuisine in terms of their appeal to you.
>
> Chinese _____   Mexican _____   Italian _____   French _____   German _____

5. Short-answer questions. These questions require respondents to fill in the blank or write a brief answer.

> Give your date of birth (day, month, year): _____
>
> How long have you lived at your current address? _____
>
> Give the names of any community groups to which you belong: _____
> _____
>
> What was your chief reason for accepting a job at Peterson's? _____
> _____
>
> Which types of power tools do you use most often in your job? _____
>
> What magazine do you read most often? _____

Reliable and Valid Questions

Writing questions that work requires much thought and testing. Questions must be reliable *and* valid. A reliable question has the same meaning each time it is asked. It stands the test of time and is precisely and objectively worded so that respondents do not answer it one way on Monday and another way on Wednesday, depending on their mood. Reliable questions are not tricky or filled with loaded words; they are firm and constant. Valid questions do the job the writer intended; that is, they elicit the desired information. An invalid question contains ambiguous, vague words, thus calling into doubt any response made to it. Valid questions are worded so that respondents can understand exactly what the questioner wants to find out. To write reliable and valid questions, follow these suggestions.

1. Phrase your questions precisely. Specify exact quantities, times, or money. The following questions are vague:

Is there enough free swim time at the pool?   yes ____   no ____

If you were offered a good salary, would
you work inside a nuclear power plant?   yes ____   no ____

Is industry responsible for pollution?   yes ____   no ____

Words such as *enough, good, industry,* and *pollution* are vague. Someone trying out for the swim team will interpret "enough" to mean far more hours than does the respondent who goes to the pool two times a week for relaxation. A "good" salary is equally imprecise. The final question does not identify the industry (plastics, textile, oil refinery, paint, rubber), the type of responsibility (through releasing waste into the water or into the air, burying contaminants), and the kind of pollution (air, water, food, soil) involved. To correct vague questions, replace imprecise words with exact ones, as the following revised examples show:

How many hours of free swim time
would you use at the pool each day?   1 ____   2 ____   3 ____   4 ____

Would you work inside a nuclear power
plant for a salary of $50,000 a year?   yes ____   no ____

Has All-Fix, Inc., dumped any oil in the
marsh near your home within the last
six weeks?   yes ____   no ____

2. Ask manageable questions. Broad questions, such as those below, ask respondents to write ten pages just to begin answering them. As a result, respondents will either leave them unanswered or write brief, often vague answers.

What do you think of our government?

What is your view of the economy?

What insurance does a homeowner need?

Like a vague question, a broad question offers the respondent no direction. The words *government, the economy,* and *insurance* cover a multitude of issues.

Wide open, general questions like these really list the whole subject of the questionnaire rather than having each question cover one restricted part of the topic. That one large question needs to be cut into many smaller, more manageable queries. For example, by "government" does the writer mean federal, state, county, or local? And which governmental function, agency, or service (or lack of service) is involved? "The economy" also covers a lot of territory—should the respondent comment on the rate of inflation last month, current interest rates for new home loans, the percentage of unemployment in one city or in one profession, the national trade deficit, or what? When you ask about insurance for a home buyer, do you expect your respondents to discuss all kinds of insurance—life (term and whole life), medical, personal property, and even burial? A request for such an extensive amount of information in a single essay answer would overwhelm even an actuary (an expert in computing statistics on insurance risks and premiums). Replace a broad question with a more manageable one, such as the following examples show:

Would you agree or disagree with a Congressional plan to replace an income tax with a flat-rate tax?　　agree _____　disagree _____

Should the United States government store nuclear wastes in salt domes in Blanton County?　　yes _____　no _____

What percentage of your monthly house payment goes for mortgage insurance?　　_____ %

3. Write questions that let respondents decide for themselves. Avoid using loaded words, such as those in the following questions.

Should we continue to waste taxpayers' money on the construction of the George Street Bridge?

Do you believe we have elected too many weirdos to City Council?

Isn't it useless to keep making agriculture majors submit daily reports?

Should the government reinstate the draft to make sure we have quality and quantity in America's armed services?

You reveal an emotional bias and thereby prejudice respondents with words such as *waste, weirdos, useless,* or *quality and quantity.* The last example is particularly unfair because it suggests that those who answer "no" are against a strong America. Keep the language of your questions impartial, as in these revised examples.

Would you vote for continuing work on the George Street Bridge?　　yes _____　no _____

Do you believe your neighborhood is adequately represented on the City Council?　　yes _____　no _____

Do you want agriculture majors to submit daily reports?　　yes _____　no _____

Do you believe that there should be a draft?　　yes _____　no _____

A question like the following one demands a "yes" response.

> Residents of Lake Mills need better sewerage facilities, don't they?

Rephrase the question to eliminate bias:

> Do Lake Mills residents need a new sewerage facility?   yes _____   no _____

4. Your questions should not insult or indict the respondent. No matter how a question such as "Have you stopped picking fights with your spouse?" is answered, it accuses the respondent of the deed. The following two questions are worded improperly.

> Are you still getting speeding tickets?
>
> Have you missed any more payments lately?

Do not assume that respondents have ever received speeding tickets or missed payments. Instead, ask if they ever did get a ticket or miss a payment.

> Did you ever receive a ticket for
> speeding?   yes _____   no _____
>
> Have you ever missed a payment?   yes _____   no _____

If the answer is yes, you can ask about the number of tickets or missed payments in a following question.

5. Do not write a question that requires the respondents to do your research. Courtesy requires that you not ask them to go to any more trouble than it takes to fill out the questionnaire. Avoid questions such as the following:

> Ask your immediate superior to supply you with the number of models sold last month and please list that number.
>
> After checking your files and last year's manual, indicate the differences between this year's engine specifications and last year's.

You are imposing on respondents when you require them to speak to other people or when you make them search their records to answer your question. Your respondents will probably end up throwing away the entire questionnaire. If you want information from a supervisor, send the supervisor a questionnaire also. If the information you seek is already available to you from other sources (your company's records for last month, for example), do not ask others for it.

6. Limit your questions to recent events. Do not ask respondents to search their memories to recall opinions that they held years ago or to discuss details of an event that they may not now clearly remember. These questions are inappropriate.

> Was your apartment building constructed with energy conservation in mind?
>
> What was your exact gas mileage for city driving when you purchased your brand-new Cougar in 1990?
>
> What kinds of meals did you eat on your vacation two years ago?

7. Write questions in language appropriate for your audience. A questionnaire directed to specialists may well include a few technical terms, but if respondents are not familiar with your jargon, avoid it. Patients asked about hospital service would have difficulty understanding this question.

> Did you receive p.r.n. meds stat?   yes _____   no _____

Reworded as follows, the question is easier to answer.

> Were you given medication when you
> asked for it?   yes _____   no _____

Avoid pretentious vocabulary as well.

> Did the policy of merit raises exacerbate
> the crew's feelings?   yes _____   no _____

Translated into understandable terms, this question reads easily:

> Did the policy of merit raises anger the
> crew?   yes _____   no _____

8. Each question should cover only one item. Do not confront respondents with a question that may demand an unnecessary, misleading, or contradictory choice. For example, "Do you prefer the Beatles or the Rolling Stones?" asks respondents to choose between the two. But respondents may like both groups and could not register their preference as the question is worded. Make two separate questions to be sure of obtaining a reliable response. The following question also is poor, because it assumes that respondents will automatically agree with both adjectives.

> Are the new models more streamlined
> and economical than last year's?   yes _____   no _____

Some may think that the new models are more streamlined but less economical than last year's, while others think just the reverse. Again, ask two separate questions, and do not use more than one adjective per question.

Overloading a question with a series of short interrogative words (*why? how? where? when? what?*) at its close should also be avoided.

> Approximately how many times have you visited Baltimore in the last year? Why?
> When? For how long? How did you travel?

If you need the additional information, ask a series of related questions.

9. Do not ask the same question twice. A question writer may think that there is a fine, subtle difference between two questions, but respondents may be unable to detect any difference. Check one question against another. Make sure, for example, that a question 2 does not duplicate a question 7.

> 2. What is your favorite television program?
> 7. Which program do you like to watch most on television?

2. State your opinion about when placebos should be used.
7. What are the values of placebos?

The writer of the first set of redundant questions failed to see that a favorite program means the one you like to watch. In the second pair the writer wrongly saw a difference between the use of placebos and their value. If they are prescribed for specific patients or used in different kinds of tests, these uses automatically characterize the placebos' value.

10. In multiple-choice questions, supply your respondents with clearly differentiated options. The following question confuses your respondents with overlapping choices.

What kind of car do you think gets the best mileage in the city?
a. a compact _____
b. a subcompact _____
c. a foreign-made car _____
d. an American car _____
e. a diesel _____

These choices are not distinct. A compact or subcompact may also be either a foreign or an American car. The same is true of the diesel. Confronted with these options, respondents are asked two or three questions at the same time. Any answer they would give will be invalid and incomplete. Turn such a question into three separate questions.

1. Do you think that a compact or a subcompact gets better mileage in the city? compact _____ subcompact _____
2. Name any American-made car that equals or surpasses the most economical import in city mileage. _____
3. Would a diesel or a gasoline engine be more economical in city driving? diesel _____ gasoline _____

Be especially careful that questions containing an age category do not overlap as the following example does:

In which age group do you belong?
18–25 _____
25–37 _____
37–45 _____
45–59 _____
59 and over _____

Revised, the question will elicit clear and distinct responses:

In which age group do you belong?
18–25 _____
26–37 _____
38–45 _____
46–59 _____
over 59 _____

Figure 12.2 (p. 440) contains a good example of nonoverlapping categories for age.

FIGURE 12.2   A clearly arranged questionnaire.

AUBURN UNIVERSITY TRAVEL SURVEY
In Cooperation With
Alabama Bureau of Publicity and Information

Dear Traveler: Thank you for traveling in Alabama. We would like to make Alabama a more enjoyable travel destination or vacation state.   Please help us by completing this form **if you have not already done so on this trip.** There is no need to sign your name.

1 Season of travel: 1 ☐ Dec.-Feb.   2 ☐ Mar-May   3 ☐ June-Aug   4 ☐ Sep.-Nov.

2 Home: City _____ State/Country _____

4 Major point *away from home* you are now traveling to/returning from:

6 City/Place _____ State _____

8 Principal mode of travel: 1 ☐ Highway   2 ☐ Air   3 ☐ Bus   4 ☐ Rail

Number and age of persons in party:

Males	Females
9 ____ Under 14	15 ____ Under 14
10 ____ 14-17	16 ____ 14-17
11 ____ 18-29	17 ____ 18-29
12 ____ 30-49	18 ____ 30-49
13 ____ 50-64	19 ____ 50-64
14 ____ 65 or over	20 ____ 65 or over

Activities engaged in while in **Alabama only**—check as many as apply:

21 ☐ Passing thru only	27 ☐ Business
22 ☐ Passing thru, but engaging in the following activities checked	28 ☐ Golfing
	29 ☐ Camping
23 ☐ Visiting friends/relatives	30 ☐ Boating/fishing
24 ☐ Visiting historical sites/places	31 ☐ Watching sports
25 ☐ Beaches/swimming	32 ☐ Personal affairs
26 ☐ Commercial attractions (gardens, amusement parks/centers, etc.)	33 ☐ Attending show or event
	34 ☐ Attending convention/meeting

35 ____ How many days spent in Alabama on this trip?

37 ____ How many nights spent in Alabama on this trip?

39 ____ How many days spent on entire trip?

Nights in **Alabama** were (or will be) at:

41 ☐ Home of friend or relative	45 ☐ Cabin/cottage
42 ☐ Motel	46 ☐ Tent
43 ☐ Hotel	47 ☐ Recreational Vehicle
44 ☐ Rented house/apartment	48 ☐ Travel Trailer

While in **Alabama only**, how much will your party spend on this trip for:

49 _____ Lodging	58 _____ Entertainment/sightseeing
52 _____ Food and beverages	61 _____ Recreation/sports
55 _____ Auto expenses (gas, oil, etc.)	64 _____ Other purchases

67 Annual family income (for statistical purposes only):

1 ☐ Under $5,000	4 ☐ $15,000-20,000	7 ☐ $30,000-40,000
2 ☐ $5,000-10,000	5 ☐ $20,000-25,000	8 ☐ $40,000-50,000
3 ☐ $10,000-15,000	6 ☐ $25,000-30,000	9 ☐ $50,000 or over

We welcome your comments. Please write them on the back side.

THANK YOU FOR YOUR HELP

Reprinted by permission from Dr. James W. Adams, Department of Marketing and Transportation, Auburn University.

11. Include all necessary options in multiple-choice questions and those that ask respondents to rank items. Omissions are especially dangerous when respondents are forced to choose between two extremes and are not given enough options for qualified agreement or disagreement. Give respondents the option of saying that they have no opinion or that they see no change. Here are some ineffective questions because they have limited (omitted) options.

Do you favor the death
penalty?   yes _____   no _____

How do you feel about the new
uniforms we are required to wear?   I like them _____   I do not like them _____

When is the busiest time at
your factory?   morning _____   afternoon _____

Respondents might favor the death penalty only in certain cases; they may approve of one part of a uniform code and not another; and workers may find a night shift the busiest or want to say that the workload varies from one week to another. As these questions are worded, valid responses are impossible. Make the first question, for example, valid by including differentiated options, as follows.

never _____   only for murder of a police officer _____   for any murder _____
other _____   undecided_____

Two Sample Questionnaires

To review the material discussed so far in this chapter, study the questionnaires found in Figures 12.2 and 12.3 (p. 442). The questionnaire in Figure 12.2 asks travelers to complete it while resting at an Alabama hospitality center, and so it does not contain instructions on where and when it should be returned. The other questionnaire in Figure 12.3, a patient satisfaction survey, is mailed to patients after they have been discharged from a major hospital and asks them to fold the questionnaire into a postage-paid envelope and return it. Both questionnaires ask valid, reliable, and relevant questions of their respondents. The choices that respondents are given are also carefully differentiated and nonoverlapping. The Methodist Hospital questionnaire in Figure 12.3 gives respondents "forced choices"—that is, specific responses—but it also allows them to elaborate on their answers by saying "Yes, but . . ." or "No, but . . ." Both questionnaires are easy to complete because they are visually attractive and offer clearly differentiated parts. Note the way the questionnaire in Figure 12.3 uses dark thick and thin lines.

FIGURE 12.3   A carefully worded and formatted questionnaire.

METHODIST HOSPITAL
OF HATTIESBURG, INC.

Dear Patient,

Now that you or your family member has been discharged from Methodist Hospital of Hattiesburg, we would like to ask you some questions about your experience while in our hospital.

You can help us to provide the finest care possible by taking a few minutes to complete and return this questionnaire (no postage is required).

Your comments will be carefully reviewed and will be held in strict confidence by our staff. We welcome your suggestions and thank you for your time in helping us provide quality health care services for you and your family.

Sincerely,

W.K. Ray

WILLIAM K. RAY
President

Please tear off at perforation, fold postage paid side out and mail.

WE WELCOME YOUR EVALUATION AND SUGGESTIONS   Please check your response

YOUR ADMISSION

Were you greeted promptly and courteously
upon entering the registration area? . . . . . . ☐ Yes   ☐ No
Were you registered within 15 minutes
of your arrival? . . . . ☐ Yes   ☐ No
If not, did the hostess explain
the delay? . . . . ☐ Yes   ☐ No
Comments: _____

YOUR ROOM

Were you satisfied with the
appearance of your room? . . . . ☐ Yes   ☐ No
Were you satisfied with the
cleanliness of your room? . . . . ☐ Yes   ☐ No
Were the housekeeping personnel
pleasant and courteous? . . . . ☐ Yes   ☐ No
Comments: _____
_____

YOUR FOOD

Were you generally satisfied with the food? . . . . ☐ Yes   ☐ No
Were you seen by someone from Nutrition and Food Services? . . . . ☐ Yes   ☐ No
If you selected a menu, did you receive what you ordered? . . . . ☐ Yes   ☐ No
How would you rate the following?
  Temperature of food . . . . ☐ Excellent   ☐ Good   ☐ Fair   ☐ Poor
  Quality of food . . . . ☐ Excellent   ☐ Good   ☐ Fair   ☐ Poor
  Variety of food choices . . . . ☐ Excellent   ☐ Good   ☐ Fair   ☐ Poor
Comments: _____

YOUR NURSING CARE

Please rate the quality of your nursing care. . . . . ☐ Excellent   ☐ Good   ☐ Fair   ☐ Poor
Comments: _____

FIGURE 12.3   (Continued)

YOUR DISCHARGE

1. Were you satisfied with the amount of time it took for your discharge? ....□ Yes   □ No
2. Were you given discharge instructions regarding care at home?................................□ Yes   □ No

Comments: _____

OTHER

Were you satisfied with the care and service given by the following?

1. Lab Technicians ....□ Yes	□ No	□ N/A	6. Volunteers ....□ Yes	□ No	□ N/A
2. Physical Therapists ....□ Yes	□ No	□ N/A	7. Social Services ....□ Yes	□ No	□ N/A
3. Respiratory Therapists.......□ Yes	□ No	□ N/A	8. Telephone Operators ....□ Yes	□ No	□ N/A
4. Emergency Room ....□ Yes	□ No	□ N/A	9. X-Ray ....□ Yes	□ No	□ N/A
5. Surgery/Recovery Room .....□ Yes	□ No	□ N/A	10. Other_____□ Yes	□ No	□ N/A

If any member of the staff was especially helpful, let us know. We would like to show our appreciation. _____

_____

How would you rate our hospital overall? ....□ Excellent   □ Good   □ Fair   □ Poor
Would you recommend Methodist Hospital to others?...□ Yes   □ No
Would you return to Methodist Hospital? ....□ Yes   □ No
Was this your first visit to this hospital? ....□ Yes   □ No
Who referred you to Methodist Hospital? ....□ Doctor   □ Family   □ Friend   □ WorkWell   □ Other

Comments: _____

OPTIONAL

Your Name_____

Your Address_____

Your Room/Floor Number _____ Your Phone Number _____ Date _____

WE APPRECIATE YOUR HELP IN EVALUATING OUR CARE!

Writing Effective Instructions

A clear and brief set of instructions should appear at the top of the first page of your questionnaire. To emphasize instructions, you might want to use boldface type or capital letters for certain points. Most word processing software packages include these features. In addition to showing respondents how to fill in their answers, instructions can summarize the topic of the questionnaire. A clear set of instructions will emphasize how easy a questionnaire is to answer and will increase your chances of respondents completing it.

Specifically, what should you tell respondents in your instructions? Indicate the kinds of questions they will be answering: multiple-choice, ranking, fill-in-the-blank, essay. Clearly specify how respondents are to indicate their choices—are they to put a check (✓) or an X, circle a response, or underscore their answers? Look at the questionnaire in Figure 12.4 (p. 445) for an example of helpful instructions. Also, be consistent in the kinds of questions you use and the method respondents are to employ to answer them. For example, do not force respondents to jump from a group of multiple-choice questions to a set of ranking ones and then back to multiple-choice. Do not have respondents circle some answers and check others. As was noted earlier, many questionnaires composed of one type of closed question do conclude with an open-ended question. However, this shift in question type is so commonly used that it is not disturbing to respondents.

Indicate whether respondents are to sign their names or remain anonymous. If their signatures are optional, say so. Tell respondents the date by which you would like them to return the questionnaire, and include a postage-paid envelope. Give your name, address, and telephone number and offer any assistance. Even though this information may duplicate what you have written in a cover letter (discussed on pages 448–450 of this chapter), give it anyway. It is safer to repeat the information than to risk having the respondent not know when and where to return the questionnaire.

Make your instructions as clear as possible. Respondents will be annoyed if they are frequently interrupted by new instructions. If you use a term or concept that must be defined or explained, do it in the question itself.

> Is there any encumbrance (lien, mortgage, judgment, or
> easement) on your property?   yes _____   no _____

A question may require some kind of clarification for a respondent to answer it properly.

> Which three-hour session is best for you to attend?
> *[To clarify this question, give your respondents a choice:]*
> 10:00 A.M. _____   2:00 P.M. _____   8:00 P.M. _____)

Presenting an Attractive Questionnaire

The visual impression your questionnaire makes may determine whether or not respondents complete it. If your questionnaire looks sloppy and is difficult to read and follow, respondents will not bother with it. Therefore, strive to make your questionnaire neat, clear, and easy to read and answer. Note the clarity of the questionnaires in Figures 12.2, 12.3, and 12.4.

One of the best routes to take is to have your questionnaire done using desktop publishing software. It will look like it was typeset by a professional printer. The result may so impress your readers that it could improve your chances of having them respond. Also consider having the questionnaire copied on attractive paper. Undoubtedly, a questionnaire printed on a faded mimeo sheet or on a copying machine that leaves smudges will not invite quick replies, if any. Avoid reducing the size of your questionnaire on a copying machine in an attempt to save space; the small print will be hard to read and also intimidating. Use plenty of white space, which will be pleasing to the respondents' eyes. Proofread meticulously. Also make sure that your questionnaire contains a title, a place for the respondent's name, if desired, and instructions.

FIGURE 12.4   A portion of a questionnaire with explicit instructions.

National Restaurant Association
Travel Study

Date _____   Code _____

Name _____

City _____

Directions: Listed below are a number of statements, some of which deal with eating out and restaurants and some of which deal with general life-style factors. For each statement listed, we would like to know whether you personally agree or disagree with the statement.

After each statement, there are five numbers from one to five. The higher the number, the more you tend to disagree with the statement. The lower the number, the more you tend to agree with the statement. The numbers 1–5 can be described as follows:

1. I strongly agree with the statement.
2. I generally agree with the statement.
3. I neither agree nor disagree.
4. I generally disagree with the statement.
5. I strongly disagree with the statement.

For each statement, please circle the number that best describes your feelings about that statement.

(After you complete the questionnaire, please place this form into the attached stamped, self-addressed envelope and mail. Thanks.)

Statement	Strongly Agree				Strongly Disagree
1 I prefer to order a la carte rather than order a dinner.	1	2	3	4	5
2 I prefer a service charge be automatically added to my bill rather than having to tip.	1	2	3	4	5
3 I like to try new and different menu items.	1	2	3	4	5
4 I prefer a self-service salad bar to being served a salad at the table.	1	2	3	4	5
5 I usually tip a fixed percentage of the bill regardless of the service I get.	1	2	3	4	5
6 Atmosphere is just as important as the quality of the food in selecting a restaurant.	1	2	3	4	5
7 I love to eat.	1	2	3	4	5
8 I usually look for the lowest possible prices when I shop.	1	2	3	4	5
9 Information I get about a product from a friend is usually better than what I get from advertising.	1	2	3	4	5
10 I have annual physical check-ups.	1	2	3	4	5
11 If a new restaurant opened in town, I would probably be among the first to try it out.	1	2	3	4	5
12 My days tend to follow a definite routine, such as eating meals at a regular time, etc.	1	2	3	4	5

The Restaurant Habits of the Business Traveler, prepared by Edward J. Mayo for National Restaurant Association Consumer Attitudes Survey Series, June 1976. Reprinted with permission of the National Restaurant Association.

Selecting Respondents

Once you have restricted your topic and have determined who will read the results of your questionnaire and why, you will have a better idea about the kinds of individuals you need to question. To receive useful answers, you have to exercise great care in selecting your respondents; you cannot do it haphazardly. Finding appropriate respondents for extremely technical questionnaires involves sophisticated sampling strategies far beyond the scope of this book. Texts on statistics and audience surveys contain detailed instructions explaining the specialized methods used by pollsters such as George Gallup or Lou Harris; such pollsters can survey small sections of the population and predict outcomes with less than a 2 percent margin of error. Although not offering this kind of statistical information on sampling techniques, the following discussion does suggest guidelines you can follow when selecting respondents.

To how many people must you send a questionnaire in order to obtain reliable results? The answer depends on your statistics. If you are interested in finding out how technicians in a particular hospital feel about rotating shifts, then your respondents would be all the technicians in that one hospital. Similarly, if you want to determine whether your sorority chapter should have a barbeque or dance at the end of the spring term, you would question every member of your chapter. But your respondents may not always belong to such a limited and easily accessible group. Many times you will have to consider a larger audience whose members could not all be reached and questioned individually. You might want to find out how customers at a certain store feel about a warehouse branch that would sell merchandise at a reduced rate. Certainly you could not question everyone who shops at this store. Or you might be interested in surveying how a certain profession (dairy farmers, dietitians, medical secretaries) would react to a piece of impending legislation. Being unable to question everyone in a particular profession, you would use some form of sampling.

Systematic Random Sampling

The most respected, and valid, way of finding respondents is to follow a *systematic random sampling* technique. Much marketing research is done this way. According to this technique, you choose your target audience or population (all the nurses in your hometown, all students attending your college, all holders of credit cards from a department store), and from this large target population you obtain a cross section by selecting names at random from the group. A random sampling is not like picking names out of a hat. It is far more systematic and fair. For example, from a college directory listing the names of all students enrolled at your school you can choose by random selection every tenth name or, for a smaller margin of error, every fifth name. Thus all respondents (all students listed in the school directory) have an equal chance of being selected for your sample. This equal chance is the heart of the random sampling technique. Figure 12.8 (to be discussed in detail later in this chapter [pp. 455–458]) contains a collaboratively written report on student opinions of a campus newspaper. Because the editors of the paper could not question the entire student body, they sent a questionnaire to every sixth name in the directory and had a 66.66 percent response rate.

Citing another example, let's say that you wanted to find out the customers' preferences for shopping hours at your store. You could stand outside the store and ask everyone who happens to walk by. However, you might talk to people who are visitors to your town and who never have or never will shop at the store, or you could select residents of the town who just stopped to avoid the rain and who never have shopped at the store. To obtain a cross section of those who in fact are customers of the store, you must select as your target population those who are on record as having purchased goods from the store. Perhaps their names are on record as credit card holders. You could then go through the store's list of credit card holders and by random selection pick out names of individuals to whom you will send your questionnaire.

Another way to get a statistically valid sample is to pick names randomly out of the residential listings of your town's telephone book. This selection technique would be a good one if you wanted to find out how a relatively small town or suburb (under 30,000 people) felt about a bond proposal or welfare services. The important point to remember is that the selection process must be systematic and allow each member of the population (in this case, all those individuals listed in the telephone book) an equal chance of being selected.

Stratified Random Sampling

Another valid sampling technique is known as *stratified random sampling*. This approach is used when you have a number of different groups or subgroups to question; it means that you survey each group proportionately. For example, say you want to determine opinion about facilities at a college that was formerly for women only. Today the student body is composed of 70 percent women and 30 percent men. To obtain a fair cross section of these two groups, you need to question each group according to the same percentage it occupies in the college population. Accordingly, if you sent questionnaires to 100 students, you would make sure that 70 questionnaires went to women and 30 to men to reflect the enrollment percentages at the college.

Quota Sampling

Still another type of sampling technique is known as *quota sampling*. Use this technique with great care. Here you choose an audience almost as one would select a quota. You might question the first twenty-five males and first twenty-five females you meet. Such a sampling might be helpful if, for example, it consisted of customers in a store who all saw a demonstration of a dishwasher, and you wanted to get their opinions of that dishwasher. The population is chosen arbitrarily and not selected as carefully as it would be with random sampling, but such a group can help answer your questions, since everyone has seen the product. The problem with quota sampling is that it can lead to a distorted sample in many circumstances. If you wanted to poll student opinion about a campus radio station and all you did was ask for the opinion of ten of your friends who you knew did not like the station, your sample would be biased. These ten friends are a homo-geneous (presorted) group that may not truly represent the view of the student body.

Distributing a Questionnaire

Before submitting your questionnaire to respondents, have someone evaluate it. Ask a student in your major, a teacher, or a coworker to read your questionnaire and tell you whether any of your questions are vague, misleading, or irrelevant. You should pretest your questionnaire on a small representative sample of the larger group you want to survey. Have these individuals pay particular attention to the options you list for multiple-choice questions; make sure that the options are reasonable and sufficient. Such screening may take a few days, but in the long run you will save time and energy. If you send out a questionnaire flawed by poorly worded or irrelevant questions, the answers you receive will be of dubious value. You will have to redo the questionnaire, or you may find yourself busy explaining the questions verbally to respondents who call you for help.

Once you are sure that the questionnaire is right, deliver or mail it to your respondents. Decide which approach is more feasible. Delivering the question-naire in person may create goodwill and may increase your chances of receiving a completed questionnaire back from these individuals. However, when you think a personal visit might influence the content of a reader's response, mail your ques-tionnaire. In any case, make sure your questionnaire reaches respondents at times convenient for them, not just for you. Do not give questionnaires to respondents when other commitments prevent their answering you. For example, students preparing for final or state board examinations will not postpone their studies to fill out your questionnaire. Some large companies close for two weeks in the sum-mer and give all employees and supervisors a vacation. Sending a questionnaire to anyone just before or during that shutdown would be pointless. Asking for com-pleted questionnaires around the Christmas holidays is equally ill advised. If you are aware that respondents will be on vacation, busy, or out of town on business, send your questionnaire at another time.

If you mail your questionnaire, send it by first-class mail and include a stamped, self-addressed envelope. Respondents are far more likely to answer when you make it as easy as possible for them. Make certain that the respondents' names and addresses are correct. People will not be inclined to respond if you spell their names incorrectly or if you address someone with a Mr. when that person is a Ms., or vice versa. Some given names (Pat, Leslie, Terry) apply to both men and women. If you are uncertain, omit the courtesy title and write "Dear Pat Hayes" or "Dear Terry Bronti."

When you mail the questionnaire, enclose a cover letter similar to the one shown in Figure 12.5, and follow these procedures.

1. Introduce yourself and tell why you are writing.
2. Explain the significance of the topic of your questionnaire.
3. Emphasize how important the respondent's answers are.

FIGURE 12.5   A cover letter sent with a questionnaire.

CASSON'S DEPARTMENT STORES
1800 South Paulina
Topeka, KS 66620
913-555-1400

June 3, 1994

Mr. Lonnie Cordova
73 Crestway Park Drive
Topeka, KS 66621

Dear Mr. Cordova:

Thank you for purchasing your new Clearview television set from Casson's. Your opinions about our store and its service policies are important to us.

For this reason, I hope you will complete the enclosed questionnaire. It should not take more than ten minutes, and your answers will help us provide you with even better service in the future. You will find twelve multiple-choice questions; but please feel free to elaborate on any of your answers, if you wish, on the back of the questionnaire.

The questionnaire is easy to return. Just put it in the enclosed postage-paid envelope and drop it in the mail. Please return the questionnaire by June 29, if at all possible. If you have any questions, please call me at extension 412.

Once again, thanks for shopping at Casson's. We will let you know how the results of our questionnaire survey will improve our service to you.

Sincerely yours,

Susan Shapiro

Susan Shapiro
Customer Services

Encl. Questionnaire

4. Tell what benefits the respondent can gain by answering your questionnaire—the most important function of the letter.
5. Discuss the kind of questionnaire you have devised.
6. Ask that the questionnaire be returned by a specified date.
7. Perhaps promise a gift for returning the questionnaire or even send a gift along with the questionnaire. A coupon, a crisp dollar bill, or a donation to the respondent's favorite charity can improve your rate of return.
8. Thank the respondent and promise, if practical to do so, to inform him or her of the outcome.

Depending on your topic and the questionnaire you have constructed, you may also want to assure respondents that their answers will remain confidential. Or you might want to promise them anonymity. Not being required to sign their names, respondents will not worry that anyone, including you, knows what they have answered.

Tabulating Responses

A new phase of your research begins with the return of your questionnaire. You will have to count the completed questionnaires and keep a record of specific responses. Tallying is an important link between the questionnaire and the report; a mistake here can distort (or defeat) all your other efforts.

Tallying by Hand

If you are using a small number of respondents for a school or a civic project, or if you lack access to a computer, you will have to tabulate by hand. Your record keeping will be relatively easy if you follow a consistent and orderly system for listing and categorizing information. One good method is to buy a yellow, legal-size note pad and use a separate tally sheet for each question on your questionnaire. Write the question and its number at the top of the sheet; directly beneath the question, list horizontally the options (the range of choices) that the question offers. For dichotomous questions you will have two columns; for multiple-choice, as many columns as there are choices. Be sure to include the category "no response" in a separate column. If respondents give two contradictory answers to one question, indicate "no response" (N. R.) in your tally since you do not know which answer was intended.

The use of separate tally sheets for each question offers these advantages.

1. You are better able to tabulate, organize, and summarize responses for each question, since all answers to that question are on one sheet.
2. You can more easily check responses against individual questionnaires, since each response is coded by identification and question number.
3. You have the flexibility of comparing responses to various questions by simply pulling tally sheets for these questions and laying the sheets side by side.

4. You have a record of the number of questionnaires returned by any specific date.
5. You can conveniently keep a running tally and will not have to wait until all questionnaires are in to begin counting.

With a separate tally sheet for each question, you will be ready to tabulate responses. When a questionnaire comes in, assign it a code number. The first questionnaire to be returned could be labeled 01, the second 02, the third 03, and so forth. List the identifying numbers (and the names of respondents, if requested, after the numbers) vertically on the left-hand side of each tally sheet. Then, as you check each questionnaire in, you can record a respondent's answer to an individual question in the correct column on the appropriate tally sheet. Figure 12.6 (p. 452) illustrates a sample master tally sheet for a first question.

Coding and tabulating open-ended questions may present problems. You will have to make option columns as you go along, but still impose some type of manageable limits on these options. When you read essay answers, use a highlighter pen to mark the exact comments that most relevantly answer the question. Those comments may be buried in useless remarks; the highlighter pen will make the most relevant remarks stand out. A different color highlighter pen can be used to identify statements you foresee quoting directly in your report, thus making them easier to find later.

Look for patterns of similar responses so you can count the number of times similar comments are made. An open-ended question completed by all of your respondents might elicit several clusters of closely related responses.

Tallying by Computer

If the number of your respondents is large and your employer has decided to tabulate their answers by computer, consult someone in the computer department during the design stage of your questionnaire and before you start to categorize responses. A computer consultant can suggest different ways of coding options to your questionnaire so that the computer will help you to assess the responses properly and quickly. Responses may be translated into numerical or alphabetical symbols to represent various responses.

For smaller projects, if you have basic keyboarding skills, access to a personal computer, and even a modest knowledge of computer applications, you can use valuable software technology to your advantage.

Two common types of software you can use are *spreadsheets* and *database systems.* A spreadsheet allows you to arrange data in rows and columns much like the tally sheet used for manual tabulations in Figure 12.6. Spreadsheets also enable you to make basic arithmetic calculations from data. These calculations might include totals for such questionnaire items as the number of male and female respondents or the number (and percentage) of respondents who answered "yes" or "no" to a dichotomous question. Figure 12.7 (p. 453) illustrates a spreadsheet page. Where averages are important in your research, spreadsheets can help you to calculate them, too. Spreadsheets do not, however, allow for sophisticated

FIGURE 12.6   A tally sheet created by hand.

		YES	NO	N.R.
	Question 1: Have you ever served in the Armed Forces ?			
01	John Malone		X	
02	S. T. Brownly	X		
03	Kathy Ruiz	X		
04	Ruth Tapes		X	
05	Henry Stuart		X	
06	Tim Gordon	X		
07	Shirley McManus		X	
08	Debbie Buzak	X		
09	Donald Shatz		X	
10	Willa Jackson		X	
11	Bruce Page	X		
12	Mary Holka		X	
13	Frances Watts		X	
14	Richard Saperstein	X		
15	Terry Myers		X	
16	Roberta Zimmerman		X	
17	Paula Huppard		X	
18	Chris Sholds	X		
19	John Tzarki	X		
20	Billy Kim	X		
21	Lucy Bennini		X	
22	Marge Appleby	X		
TOTALS		10	12	

FIGURE 12.7   A computer-generated tally sheet.

No.	Last Name	First Name	Q#1	Q#2	Q#3	Q#4	Q#5
1	APPLEBY	MARGE	GOOD	FALSE	TRUE	NO	A
2	BENNINI	LUCY	POOR	FALSE	FALSE	YES	C
3	BROWNLY	S.T.	FAIR	TRUE	TRUE	NO	A
4	BUZAK	DEBBIE	GOOD	TRUE	TRUE	YES	B
5	GORDON	TIM	V.GOOD	FALSE	FALSE	YES	A
6	HOLKA	MARY	GOOD	TRUE	FALSE	NO	A
7	HUPPARD	PAULA	V.GOOD	FALSE	FALSE	YES	B
8	JACKSON	WILLA	FAIR	TRUE	FALSE	NO	C
9	KIM	BILLY	GOOD	FALSE	FALSE	NO	C
10	MALONE	JOHN	POOR	FALSE	TRUE	YES	A
11	MCMANUS	SHIRLEY	GOOD	TRUE	TRUE	YES	A
12	MYERS	TERRY	POOR	TRUE	FALSE	YES	B
13	PAGE	BRUCE	GOOD	TRUE	TRUE	NO	C
14	RUIZ	KATHY	POOR	TRUE	FALSE	YES	A
15	SAPERSTEIN	RICHARD	POOR	FALSE	FALSE	NO	A
16	SHATZ	DONALD	GOOD	TRUE	TRUE	YES	B
17	SHOLDS	CHRIS	POOR	FALSE	FALSE	NO	C
18	STUART	HENRY	FAIR	FALSE	TRUE	YES	A
19	TAPES	RUTH	POOR	TRUE	FALSE	NO	B
20	TZARKI	JOHN	V.GOOD	TRUE	TRUE	YES	A
21	WATTS	FRANCES	POOR	FALSE	FALSE	NO	C
22	ZIMMERMAN	ROBERTA	FAIR	TRUE	TRUE	YES	B

statistical analyses. Yet their "number crunching" capabilities will help you to tabulate even large data sets with ease.

Database programs are computerized filing systems in which you can record separate pieces of information about the individuals who respond to your questionnaire. For example, for each respondent a database could record such characteristics as sex, age, education, as well as responses to specific questions. The database can be useful when your questionnaire relies on open-ended questions. In those cases, each respondent's verbatim response can be stored in his or her own database entry. Database software also allows you to sort through entries. For example, if you wish to examine open-ended responses by males to a particular question, the database application could give you a printout of all the answers by male respondents.

Some software publishers offer integrated applications that include word processor, spreadsheet, and database systems. These integrated packages enable you to move information from one type of application to another. In the case of the database example above, suppose that you wanted to reproduce all of the open-ended responses given by men and women as separate appendices in your report. An integrated software package would allow you to copy information from the database to the word processor.

The software described here is relatively easy to use and can save you much time and effort. It comes in a wide range of prices as well. Some applications are even available free as *shareware,* or public domain software.

Writing Effective Questionnaire Reports

After tabulating the responses, you will have to write a report on your findings. The report should accomplish three functions: (1) summarize the range of responses, (2) draw conclusions, and (3) make recommendations. The report may be brief; a one-page memo or a two-page letter will suffice. At first you may wonder if such a memo or letter is long enough, considering the time and effort you have devoted to the project. But the chief function of the report is to consolidate responses and comment on them. The report should give readers the big picture, of which individual questionnaires are only a part. Providing generalizations based on individual responses, the report does not duplicate every response you have obtained or identify every individual who made a response. If you repeated every scrap of information you obtained, it would be like giving readers the complete set of questionnaires without any necessary summary or commentary.

Writing a report means being selective. Selectivity is not a problem with responses to closed questions. Unless a respondent provides two choices for a dichotomous or multiple-choice question, you will simply tabulate his or her response with all the others you receive. Open-ended questions are more challenging to summarize. Some respondents will include more information than you can use; while part of an answer may be extremely interesting, it may also be irrelevant. Remember, the report is not a catchall for every comment written in response to an open-ended question. It should reflect only those answers that will help readers reach a decision.

Figure 12.8 contains a sample questionnaire survey report and the questionnaire on which it is based. This report is an excellent example of collaborative writing (see pages 455–458). The four student authors shared responsibility based on their background and interests. They all participated in brainstorming and restricting the topic and then met to design the questionnaire. Joe Moore, a computer science major with some marketing experience, tabulated and helped interpret the results. Alice Wong, an allied health major, and Bob Banks, majoring in photojournalism, wrote some early drafts of the report. Deborah Hinkel, a communications major, served as the group coordinator. She was also responsible for revising and editing the final copy. Study this report to see how information is selected and condensed. You might want to refer to it throughout the following discussion.

Rules for Writing Numbers

Your report will rely heavily on numbers, especially percentages. Spell out the word *percent* in a report; do not use the symbol (%). When listing responses in terms of percentages, express the specific percentage in numbers, not words.

Incorrect: Because of inflation, fifty-eight percent of the workers will not buy a new car this year.

Correct: Because of inflation, 58 percent of the workers will not buy a new car this year.

FIGURE 12.8 **A collaboratively written report and the questionnaire on which it is based.**

TO: Professor Marion Andretti
             Faculty Adviser, the Campus Informer

FROM: Deborah H. Hinkel, Bob Banks, Joe Moore, Alice Wong

SUBJECT: Student Opinion of the Campus Informer

DATE: October 5, 1994

PURPOSE AND SCOPE OF THIS SURVEY

Since a number of us have recently joined the staff of the Informer, we
wanted to assess student opinion of the campus newspaper in order to
guide our future editorial decisions. To obtain a clearer sense of
students' needs, we distributed the enclosed questionnaire to a
random sample of 300 of the 1,800 students at Detroit Community College
(DCC) during the week of September 12—16.

Two hundred students replied, giving us a fair cross section. Respondents came from every major in occupational education, with a slight
majority (42 percent) representing three areas—nursing, automotive
mechanics, and retail merchandising. Since many of our respondents
(53 percent) have spent at least two semesters at DCC, they are
familiar with the campus.

RESULTS OF SURVEY

For the most part, these respondents are loyal readers of the Informer.
Fifty-four percent read each issue of the paper, while 31 percent noted
they look at the paper at least once a week. Only 7 percent said they
rarely read the Informer. Of most interest to our readers are articles
on campus events and sporting activities, the two areas ranked first
and second by 76 percent of the students. Sixty-nine percent of the
students stated that the ads were the third most significant reason for
reading the paper. News of academic programs and school clubs ranked
fourth and fifth in student interest, according to 71 percent of the
respondents.

Most students (68 percent) think the Informer should continue to be
published twice a week, although a small percentage of these students
(21 percent, or 27 students) want to see the Informer come out on Monday
and Friday rather than on Tuesday and Friday. Little support exists
for a daily paper (20 percent) and even less for a weekly or bimonthly
one (12 percent). Students may think that there is not enough news for
a daily paper, and that news would be too old if it appeared a week or
two late.

FIGURE 12.8   (Continued)

-2-

The Informer did not receive high marks on its appearance. Forty-six percent of the students thought the layout was only average, while 23 percent of the students believe that the size of our type is too small, that the blue color of our paper is too dark, and the placement of articles is inconsistent. Mildred Cusak, a sophomore welding major, offered this representative comment: "It's hard to follow a story when it is continued on one or two other pages, because the subsequent headlines aren't always clear." A related complaint deals with our photographs. Although 27 percent of the students thought we use enough pictures, 42 percent would like to see us include more." Stories are more enjoyable when an accompanying picture clarifies or highlights the action,"stated a business student who has been at DCC for three semesters. Students were much more satisfied with the way articles are written. Seventy-two percent thought that our language was easy to understand.

Students reached a consensus about retaining our "Faculty Profile" feature. Eighty-two percent indicated they like to know more about the faculty. As one electronics major put it:" I find it interesting to learn about a teacher's family, hobbies, and professional accomplishments."

RECOMMENDATIONS

Based upon the responses to our questionnaire, and especially to the last question on proposed major changes in the paper, we offer the following recommendations:

1. Increase the point size of type and change the color of the Informer from blue to white or cream for easier reading.
2. Use more photographs, especially in covering sports events.
3. Expand our ads section and group similar types of ads--e.g., jobs, items for sale, housing, entertainment--and supply a heading for each group.
4. Run our "Faculty Profile" in each issue, rather than printing it only once or twice a month.

Thank you for considering these recommendations. We would like to meet with you early next week to get your opinion about these changes. If you approve them, we can incorporate these changes in the Informer as early as next semester.

FIGURE 12.8   (Continued)

What's Your Opinion of the Informer?

Please take a few minutes to fill out the following questionnaire
about the Campus Informer, our student newspaper. We on the newspaper
staff are eager to know what you think about the paper so that we can
make sure that it serves your needs. Please return your questionnaire
to Deborah H. Hinkel, the editor, at Scott Hall 107 by Tuesday, September 20. If you have any questions, drop by the newspaper office in
Scott Hall or call 264-3450 between noon and 6:00 p.m. Your views are
important to us and will count. Thanks. Please feel free to sign or not
sign your name.

Name _____

1. How many semesters have you attended Detroit Community College?
   __ 1
   __ 2
   __ 3
   __ 4
   __ more than 4

2. What is your major? _____

3. How often do you read the Informer?
   __ twice a week, or every time it comes out
   __ once a week
   __ once every two weeks
   __ I rarely look at it

4. Rank your reasons for reading the Informer (first =1, second =2,
   etc.)
   __ find out about sports events
   __ learn more about academic programs
   __ look at the ads
   __ follow campus events
   __ learn more about campus clubs

5. How often would you like to see the Informer published?
   __ daily
   __ twice a week (as it is now)
   __ once a week
   __ once every two weeks

FIGURE 12.8   (Continued)

-2-

6. How would you evaluate the _Informer_'s layout (its physical
   appearance)?
   __ outstanding
   __ very good
   __ average
   __ poor

7. Is the _Informer_ written in easy-to-understand language?
   __ yes
   __ no

8. What do you think of the number of pictures used in the _Informer_?
   __ not enough
   __ just right
   __ too many

9. Should the _Informer_ continue to run its "Faculty Profile"
   feature?
   __ run as is (once or twice a month)
   __ run more often (every issue)
   __ run less often (once every two months)
   __ delete it

10. What one major change would you like to make in the _Informer_?
    Why? Use the back of this sheet for your answers, if you need to.

Thank you for your help!

Remember one exception to listing percentages as figures. If a percentage begins a sentence, write the percentage as a *word:*

Incorrect: 55 percent of the sales force thought that the new lights were easy on their eyes.

Correct: Fifty-five percent of the sales force thought that the new lights were easy on their eyes.

You can also list a percentage parenthetically.

Correct: A majority of students (75 percent) prefer the quarter to the semester system.

The word *percentage* should not be used for *percent. Percentage* is used without numbers to indicate a range or a size.

Incorrect: A large percent of the residents favored the new health care policies.

Incorrect: A thirty-five percentage of the residents favored the new health care policies.

Correct: A large percentage of the residents favored the new health care policies.

Correct: Thirty-five percent of the residents favored the new health care policies.

Explaining What the Numbers Mean

Numbers in your report will make it effective and impressive. However, beware of letting figures speak for themselves. Your report is not a statistical table. Organize and assess the numbers you include by telling readers what those numbers mean, why they are significant, and how they characterize various opinions. Numbers are most meaningful when they are placed in a context readers will understand and welcome. Avoid writing a wooden opening that provides no background information.

Poor: A fifteen-question questionnaire was distributed to forty students at Coe Community College between February 14 and February 28, 1994.

Provide a brief explanation of the reasons why you constructed and distributed the questionnaire. Supply information that will help readers connect your topic to the need you saw to question people about it. The lifeless opening just cited could be transformed for the reader's benefit into this kind of introduction.

Effective: For the last two semesters, students at Coe Community College have complained about the textbook rental service. In order to determine what types of changes students wanted, we constructed a questionnaire and sent it to forty students from seven different majors.

In discussing responses to specific questions, use numbers selectively. Prepare readers for the numbers you cite. Do not overwhelm readers with a series of unorganized and uninterpreted figures. If you simply list every response to every question, you will confuse readers. It is your job to impose some order by briefly and simply summarizing the responses.

Poor: Question 2 asked respondents: "How long have you lived in the Hillcrest subdivision?" Twenty-seven percent said they lived in Hillcrest for more than five years; 17 percent indicated they were residents there for at least three years; 34 percent said they lived in Hillcrest for more than one year; and 22 percent said they lived in Hillcrest for less than one year.

Revised: A clear majority of the respondents (78 percent) have lived in the Hillcrest subdivision for more than one year.

Here is another example in which unorganized responses are thrown at the reader.

Poor: For question 3 ("How would you evaluate the service you received after the sale?"), respondents answered as follows: 35 percent said it was all right but a little slow; 25 percent thought it was not adequate; and 40 percent said they had no complaints.

To eliminate confusion, divide the responses into two manageable groups. Readers will profit from a conclusion such as the following.

> **Revised:**   Customers were generally satisfied with the service after the sale; only 25 percent answered that it was inadequate.

The revision above shows the writer's desire to present only essential facts. For example, in reporting responses to yes/no questions, there is no need to give percentages for both the yes answers and the no answers: "75 percent liked the new office hours; 25 percent did not." When you write that 75 percent liked the new office hours, you do not have to tell the reader that 25 percent did not. Of course, if a number of respondents left the question blank, you will have to state that fact.

Using Direct Quotations

In addition to recording percentages, you may want to include a few direct quotations for emphasis. A direct quotation, if it is carefully worded, can serve three useful functions: (1) it can precisely capture the views of an entire group; (2) it might contain a colorful expression that can enliven your report; and (3) it can lend support to your recommendation, especially if it comes from a recognized authority. Because of their summary power, direct quotations will make your report more compact, relevant, and credible.

Choose direct quotations carefully and use them sparingly. Figure 12.8, for example, contains only three quotations. To avoid bias, try not to use the same person for each quotation you include; your report will appear prejudiced if you do not give equal time to both sides. For example, if you are distributing a questionnaire on grading procedures, you might ask whether students prefer one comprehensive final examination to a number of tests. By recording only the following quotation, you would present an unfair picture of students as lazy.

> Students in favor of a single comprehensive final examination liked the freedom from daily preparation and weekly quizzes. As a sophomore majoring in environmental resources noted, "You're playing Russian roulette, but it's worth it for the extra time you have during the semester."

By adding the following observation, you will be giving a more balanced view.

> Those opposed to a single comprehensive examination, however, worried that they could have a bad day or not know what the instructor was looking for. A junior plant science major summarized much of this group's thinking when she wrote, "I want to have more than one chance to make a good grade."

Before using a direct quotation, always obtain permission. If permission is given, put the exact words of the person you are quoting in quotation marks. And, whenever possible, identify the respondent by name, status, position, or major.

Writing a Recommendation

A recommendation should show readers how to transform respondents' answers into action. You can recommend that readers perform certain actions (often by a set time), refrain from performing actions, or choose between alternatives.

Make your recommendations specific and clear-cut. Readers will not benefit from general or indecisive comments. Since profits, customer satisfaction, and improved service may depend on your recommendations, be precise. If you hedge, you betray both respondents and readers. To say that you are not sure what should be done reveals shortcomings in your work. The following recommendations leave no doubt concerning a definite course of action.

Based on the respondents' answers, I recommend that we do three things:

- Expand the employee parking lot to include space for one hundred more cars by August 1, 1994.
- Install a fence around the parking lot.
- Station a security guard on Norris Street between shifts to direct traffic.

Keep your recommendation section short. A single concluding paragraph should be enough. You might want to list recommendations as separate items, each preceded by a raised bullet, as the example above shows, or by numbers, as in Figure 12.8. Or you may want to give your recommendations without itemizing them, as in Figure 12.9 (pp. 462–466). Do not repeat unnecessary percentages and comments you have already listed in your report. Focus instead on the way readers can accomplish what respondents do or do not want. Usually your recommendation will be easy to formulate. It will entail implementing what the majority of respondents want done. Your hardest job will be finding a practical solution to the problem as the respondents define it. It would be foolish to express the opposite of what respondents want without hard facts to back up your opposition. By so doing, you invalidate your questionnaire and discredit yourself. Your recommendation should help readers who are looking for facts to support the right decision.

In some instances, however, you will find that opinions on a crucial issue are almost equally divided. With no majority opinion to guide you (and your readers), your recommendation will take on added significance. Make a recommendation, but admit that opinion is divided. Mary Snyder in Figure 12.9, for instance, endorses the city of Madison as the convention site but includes a necessary warning. There may be times, too, when a majority opinion still calls for qualification. In recommending that a chartered bus be ordered, Ms. Synder at once acknowledges the majority's wishes, but still allows for the most flexible interpretation of the responses. No one loses by the recommendation that she submits.

At the end of your report, tell readers exactly what you would like them to do next—approve your recommendations, meet with you (specify a date) to discuss the recommendations, and the like. See page 196 of Chapter 7 for some other ways to conclude your report.

FIGURE 12.9 A report, the questionnaire on which it is based, and a cover letter.

Mary's Realty
742 Kane Avenue
Superior, WI 54880-2607
(715) 555-5030

Mary's

TO: Gerald Morgan, President,
           Northern Chapter WREA

FROM: Mary Snyder   M. S.

SUBJECT: Report on Convention Preference Questionnaire

DATE: February 9, 1994

PURPOSE OF CONVENTION QUESTIONNAIRE

Four weeks ago, when the state office asked us to poll our chapter
members about their preferences for this year's Wisconsin Real Estate
Association convention, I volunteered to prepare, distribute, and
summarize the results of a questionnaire. Judging from the responses to
that questionnaire (a copy of which is attached), distributed over the
last three weeks, next year's convention will be well attended and
productive. One hundred of our 136 members returned the questionnaire:
22 secretaries/receptionists, 57 salespersons, 12 brokers, and 9
builders. Eighty-five percent of these individuals attended last
year's convention in Green Bay.

RESULTS OF QUESTIONNAIRE

Opinion was sharply divided between Madison (38 percent) and Milwaukee
(35 percent) for the site of the convention. Respondents were more in
agreement when it came to the length of the convention; 69 percent want
it to last $2^{1}/_{2}$ days during the week, not the weekend. Pat Laskey, a
salesperson from Door County, added later in his questionnaire that
"if the convention were any shorter, we could not get our business
completed; if it were any longer, we would be away from the office too
long." Many members want to get back home the third day.

To get to the convention, 64 percent of our members will come by car.
Actually, the total number of cars will be less, since twenty respondents expressed interest in forming a car pool when asked for further
suggestions in question 13. Sixty-one percent of our members will bring
spouses with them. This preference, plus the fact that some of our
members will be sharing rooms, may account for the large request for
single rooms with two double beds (41 percent) and twin beds
(33 percent).

FIGURE 12.9 (Continued)

-2-

An impressive majority (88 percent) wants the annual presidential address scheduled during the banquet. This may be one of the few times our chapter members see each other at meals. Sixty-seven percent disliked the idea of having meals included in the price of the convention. A representative comment comes from Marsha Jabolowicz, a receptionist from Rhinelander, "I want to be able to go to different places suited to my schedule; I do not want to be tied to a rigid itinerary." If they miss each other at meals, members may likely see each other at night spots. Forty percent prefer going to a nightclub for convention entertainment; and 32 percent voted for dancing ("a swinging disco") to be included.

Our members will represent our chapter in force on state committees. Seventy-two percent have agreed to serve on a committee; the committee on marketing captured the attention of 59 members.

RECOMMENDATIONS

On the basis of these responses, I think we should tell the state office that our members prefer a 2 1/2 day convention in Madison, although Milwaukee is a strong alternate location. We will need a large block of double-occupancy rooms; and meals should not be part of the convention package, but dancing or a nightclub should. Further, our members want the presidential address delivered at the banquet.

Our members' preferences are clear in most instances. In forwarding their responses to the state office, I would recommend that we try to charter a bus for those individuals (36 percent) who wanted group transportation provided.

Please let me have your comments on these recommendations by February 21 so that we can start making plans for this year's convention.

FIGURE 12.9   **(Continued)**

A Questionnaire on
Preferences for the 1994 Convention of
the Wisconsin Real Estate Association

Dear Members of the Northern Chapter of the WREA:

Please complete the following questionnaire so that our state office
will be better able to plan for this year's convention. Your comments
will help make this year's gathering even more productive than last
year's.

Thank you for returning your questionnaire to me by January 31. A
stamped, addressed envelope is included for your convenience. If you
have any questions, please write or call me.

Cordially,

Mary Snyder

Mary Snyder
Mary's Realty
742 Kane Avenue
Superior, WI 54880-2607
(715) 555-5030
FAX (715) 555-9270

Name _____

Business address _____

Business telephone _____

Home address _____

Home telephone _____

1. What kind of membership do you hold in the WREA?
   __ secretary/receptionist
   __ salesperson
   __ broker
   __ builder

FIGURE 12.9   (Continued)

-2-

2. Did you attend last year's WREA convention in Green Bay?
   __ yes
   __ no

3. Where would you like the 1994 WREA convention to be held?
   __ Milwaukee
   __ Madison
   __ Eau Claire
   __ La Crosse
   __ other (please specify) ———————————————————

4. How long would you like the convention to last?
   __ 1 day
   __ 1 1/2 days
   __ 2 days
   __ 2 1/2 days
   __ 3 days

5. When would you like the convention to be held?
   __ during the week
   __ on the weekend

6. How would you like to travel to the convention?
   __ by car
   __ by bus
   __ fly
   __ have group transportation provided

7. Will a spouse accompany you?
   __ yes
   __ no

8. What kinds of accommodations will you need?
   __ single room (one double bed)
   __ single room (two twin beds)
   __ single room (two double beds)
   __ two rooms

9. When should the presidential address be given?
   __ at a breakfast meeting
   __ at a luncheon meeting
   __ at a banquet
   __ alone, at a separate meeting

FIGURE 12.9 **(Continued)**

-3-

10. Would you prefer to see meals included in the cost of the convention fees?
    __ yes
    __ no

11. What type of entertainment do you think the WREA should provide at the convention?
    __ dancing
    __ theater
    __ nightclub
    __ other (please specify)

12. Which state committee(s) would you be willing to serve on?
    __ finance
    __ marketing
    __ appraisal
    __ planning
    __ I do not wish to serve on a committee

13. Please feel free to add further comments about any of the previous questions or any other relevant topic you think the WREA should consider in planning this year's convention.

    _____

    _____

    _____

    _____

    _____

    _____

    _____

    Thank you for your cooperation.

✓ Revision Checklist

Questionnaires are valuable research tools that can help you in school and on the job. As this chapter has emphasized, you need to follow a careful process to prepare an effective questionnaire and summarize the results. Here are questions to ask as you revise and test your questionnaire and the report based on it.

1. Have I clearly defined and restricted the topic of my questionnaire?
2. Are all my questions relevant to the topic?
3. Are all my questions valid?
4. Are all my questions reliable?
5. Have I made sure that all options for closed questions do not duplicate or overlap each other?
6. Have I tested my questionnaire on a sample audience to make sure my questions are appropriate and focused?
7. Is my questionnaire clear and easy to follow? Have I made sure that it is attractively formatted with ample space between questions, and have I left enough space for respondents to answer open-ended questions?
8. Have I sent my questionnaire to the most appropriate respondents? Have I reached the respondent audience most informed or concerned about this topic?
9. Have I provided clear instructions to respondents about completing my questionnaire?
10. If necessary, have I included a courteous cover letter thanking respondents for their cooperation?
11. Have I received enough questionnaires from respondents in order to write a reliable report?
12. Have I tabulated the responses carefully and correctly? Did I investigate the possibility of using a computer to tabulate and categorize these responses?
13. Does my report based on my questionnaire accurately reflect the views of my respondents?
14. Have I concisely summarized the respondents' major views without burdening my report audience with unnecessary detail or injecting my own prejudice?
15. Have I accurately explained what the numbers of responses mean to my report audience?
16. Have I quoted my respondents correctly and in context?
17. Have I used the information gathered from the questionnaire to assist my two audiences—my report audience and my questionnaire audience?

18. Does my report consistently address the central concerns of my two audiences?

19. Are my recommendations based on a fair assessment of the opinions of my respondents?

Exercises

1. Write a memo (see pages 190–197 for format and organization) to an employer—previous or current—about a specific problem that needs investigation. Indicate why a questionnaire would be the best means of gathering information and stress how the results would lead to increased sales, better service, or greater productivity. In your memo specify whom you will question, how you will get their names and addresses, and the timetable you will follow in constructing the questionnaire, distributing it, tallying the results, and writing the report.

2. Select some area of interest to a civic organization, club, fraternity or sorority, union, or church group to which you belong. In a letter to the president of this organization, explain how a questionnaire on this specific area would help the group—in membership, long-range planning, meetings, dues, and so on. Volunteer to construct a questionnaire and to distribute it to members of that organization.

3. Write an appropriate closed question (dichotomous, multiple-choice, rating-scale, ranking, or fill-in-the-blank) for each one of the following topics. Where necessary, supply appropriate options.

a. marital status	**j.** local liquor laws
b. general health	**k.** medical costs
c. income	**l.** security on campus
d. religion	**m.** airplanes vs. buses for travel
e. credit rating	**n.** writing a résumé
f. expectation for promotion	**o.** senior citizen discounts
g. vacation preferences	**p.** garbage pickup
h. a household product	**q.** a local television station
i. college tuition	**r.** telephone service

4. The following closed questions (and some of their options) are incorrectly worded. Rewrite the questions and the options to eliminate vague terms, loaded words, jargon, overlapping responses, redundancy, an insufficient range of responses, and the other kinds of errors discussed in this chapter.

a. Should our city risk legalizing gambling?   yes ___   no ___

b. Are people upset with the new leash laws?   yes ___   no ___   maybe ___

c. I find everything I need at one store.   agree ___ disagree ___

d. What kind of classes do you like?
morning ___
afternoon ___
evening ___
fifty-minute ___
seventy-minute ___

e. Do you regularly read a newspaper or current events magazine?   yes ___   no ___

f. Would you characterize yourself as being carpophagous?   yes ___   no ___

g. Do you agree that teaching sex education in our schools has led to more teenage pregnancies and abortions and to looser morals in our already too permissive society?   agree ___ disagree ___

h. Are you married or divorced?   yes ___   no ___

i. What kind of beverage do you like?
coffee ___
tea ___
milk ___
soft drinks ___
carbonated drinks ___

j. Do you vote in all elections as a patriotic citizen?   yes ___   no ___

k. Have you purchased any articles of clothing recently?   yes ___   no ___

l. Into which group would you place yourself?
full-time employee ___
part-time employee ___
work weekends only ___
work nights ___

m. Don't you think our government has spent too much money on relocating refugees?   yes ___   no ___

n. Did you see the recession coming six years ago?   yes ___   no ___

o. Give the name of the person who, in your opinion, cheats most on the time card:
_____

p. How often do you ride your bicycle?
not very often ___
a few times ___
several times ___
as much as I can ___

q. Rank the following in their order of importance to you.
fringe benefits ___
health insurance policy ___
two weeks paid vacation ___
company car ___

r. Is your education meaningful to you now?   yes ___   no ___

s. Where do you live?
with my parents ___
in a trailer court ___
in a condo ___
by myself ___
in an apartment building ___
in a house ___

t. All housing loans should be guaranteed by the federal government, shouldn't they? yes ____ no ____

u. Do you like to swim and to fish?   yes ____ no ____

v. Did the RPT come in the morning or the afternoon?   A.M. ____ P.M. ____

w. Do you understand enough mathematics to be able to complete this simple form by yourself?   yes ____ no ____

5. Rewrite the following open-ended questions to make them more precise and answerable.
   a. What kinds of experiences have you had in the hospital?
   b. What improvements in city services are necessary in the future?
   c. Describe your philosophy of life.
   d. What kinds of entertainment do you like?
   e. Compare and contrast the kinds of housing opportunities in your town.
   f. What appeals to you about your career?
   g. Comment on any changes you have seen in the last year.
   h. Describe in detail all the lectures you have attended this term.
   i. What kinds of investments should a family make today?
   j. Comment on the state of the environment.
   k. Tell me all you know about horse husbandry.
   l. What aspects of transportation in our town should be changed?
   m. What kinds of regulations does the government impose on senior citizens?
   n. What are some problems in higher education today?
   o. What agencies are most successful today?

6. The following questionnaire contains unclear instructions, an inconsistent format, poorly worded and irrelevant questions, and inappropriate options. Rewrite the instructions and the questionnaire.

Hi, how are you today? We think that it would be a good idea for everyone to participate in a coffee fund soon. Complete the enclosed questionnaire soon and return it to me. You will have to circle some of the responses, check others, and write in still some other answers. Answer all the questions you feel confident about. If you check "I do not drink coffee" for any of the responses, use a red pencil; this will help flag your answer. If you do not check this as a response, use a blue or black pen. When you see questions asking for opinions you would rather not give, answer them anyway.

   1. Do you like working here?   yes ____ it's all right ____ no ____

   2. How long have you worked in this office?   0–1 month ____

   3–12 months ____ 1–3 years ____ 3–8 years ____ more than 8 years but less than 12 years ____ more than 12 years ____

   3. What is your current salary? _____ Is it fair? ____

   4. Do you have a cup of coffee before work?   yes ____

   I do not drink coffee ____ sometimes ____ no ____ it varies ____

   5. When do you drink most of your coffee?   A.M. ____ P.M. ____ nights ____

   6. Where do you get your coffee while at work?
      ____ I bring a thermos bottle from home.
      ____ I purchase it before coming to work.
      ____ I stop off at a restaurant and have it.
      ____ I borrow some.
      ____ I do not drink coffee.

7. How much coffee do you drink at work?
___ 0-2 cups a day   ___ 1-2 cups   ___ 3-5 cups   ___ more than 4 cups a day
___ I do not drink coffee   ___ I seldom drink coffee at work

8. How do you like your coffee? Circle one of the following:
a. black
b. black with sugar
c. freshly perked
d. decaffeinated
e. cream
f. instant's OK
g. milk
h. dry roasted
i. freeze-dried
j. decaffeinated freeze-dried
k. mellow roast blend

9. Would you like to have a coffee fund in our office?
a. Yes, right now.
b. Yes, not right now.
If you circled (b), answer one of the following:
___ within the next month
___ within the next six months
___ within the next year
c. No, but I would not oppose a coffee fund.
d. No, I think it is a bad idea.

10. Do you think a coffee fund would be a good idea?   yes ___   no ___

11. Would a coffee fund bring people together?   yes ___   no ___   I do not know right now ___

12. Should we let people buy coffee by the single cup? If so, how much should we charge per cup?
___ we should charge 15¢ a cup
___ twenty cents a cup
___ thirty-five cents
___ whatever they want to contribute

13. Should we allow people outside our office to participate in the coffee fund?
yes ___   no ___   on a limited basis ___   it depends ___

14. How much should we charge people outside the office for a cup of coffee?
___ ten cents
___ fifteen cents
___ twenty cents
___ twenty-five cents
___ thirty cents
___ thirty-five cents
___ the same as we pay
___ twenty to thirty cents a cup
___ I do not want them to buy our coffee

15. Who should prepare the coffee and collect for it?
___ Let's hire a caterer.
___ Everyone in the coffee fund should take a turn.
___ We should appoint two people.
___ We should draw lots.
___ Each of us should share the responsibility by drawing lots.

16. Please add any other comments. You might want to state again whether you are in favor of the fund, how much coffee you drink, and whether the office manager should provide the funds or the time to prepare the coffee.

7. Construct a questionnaire for the topic you selected in either Exercise 1 or Exercise 2. Distribute it to an appropriately focused audience, and then, after tabulating the responses, prepare a report about your findings for your employer or the president of the organization to which you belong. Also supply your employer or president with a blank copy of the questionnaire and a sample cover letter you have sent with your questionnaire.

8. Do Exercise 7 as a collaborative writing group.

9. With two or three of your classmates, write a questionnaire dealing with a current campus issue, such as parking, athletics, library hours, or security, and distribute it to a random sample of students. Tally the results, and write a report with recommendations.

Designing Visuals

Experts estimate that as much as 80 percent of our learning comes through the sense of sight. The written word, of course, forms a large part of our visual information. In conjunction with words, visual aids (hereafter shortened to *visuals*) convey a giant share of the facts we receive. Visuals are especially useful on the job because they help readers to see what you are discussing. Chapter 13 surveys the kinds of visuals you will encounter most frequently and shows you how to read, construct, and use them. It describes visuals you might prepare by hand as well as those you can generate with computers through graphics software packages. A discussion of visuals, however, is not confined to just this chapter. They are important in preparing successful instructions, proposals, and written and oral reports.

The visuals we will deal with can be divided into two categories—*tables* and *figures*. A table lists information in parallel columns or rows for easy comparison of data. Anything that is not a table is considered a figure, including graphs, circle charts, bar charts, pictograms, organizational charts, flow charts, maps, photographs, and drawings. Before looking at the various kinds of visuals, you may find it helpful to know more about the benefits they offer and the caution you must exercise in using them.

The Usefulness of Visuals

How can visuals improve your written work? Here are four reasons why you should use them. Each of the four points is graphically reinforced in Figure 13.1. (p. 474)

FIGURE 13.1   A visual showing the ten most populous countries in the world in 1994.

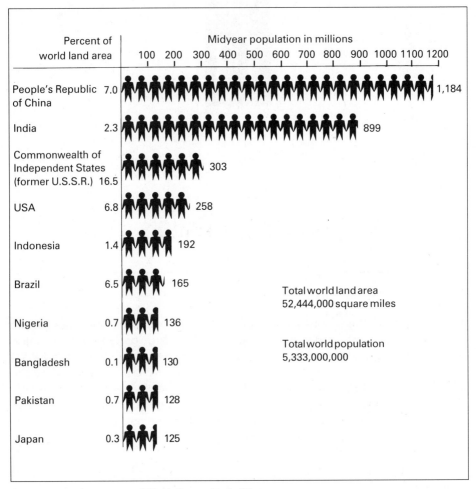

U.S. Department of Commerce and *World Almanac Book of Facts.*

1. Visuals arouse immediate interest. Their size, shape, color, and arrangement are dramatic. They also offer readers relief from looking at sentences and paragraphs. Note how eye-catching (in both number and shape) the symbols are for the world's ten most populous countries represented in Figure 13.1. A visual captures readers' attention by setting important information apart.

2. Visuals simplify concepts. Because many readers are visually oriented, graphics unlock doors of meaning. A visual shows ideas in action when a verbal description may be less forceful or more difficult to understand. Visuals are especially important and helpful when you have to explain something technical in your profession to a nonspecialist group of readers; a visual can make technical information easier to comprehend. Moreover, visuals can simplify densely packed statistical data. The vastness of a country's population and how that population compares with other nations' is much easier to grasp and to remember because of the *pictogram* (picture symbols) in Figure 13.1. Other kinds of visuals also make learning easier. For example, a visual could show the interior parts of a machine or enlarge one element of a piece of equipment to clarify its function or relationship to another part. Readers would therefore feel more confident about operating the machine or performing a procedure.

3. Visuals condense a large quantity of information into a relatively small space. Figure 13.1 collects twenty different pieces of information—the population and amount of land occupied by ten countries—and records the data in far less space than it would take to describe these facts in words. In a discussion of the populations of these countries, how many times would a writer have to repeat the words *population, land area, percent, more, less, greater, lower, in comparison,* or *in contrast?* And even if the writer transcribed all the facts in Figure 13.1 into words, readers would not be able to understand the percentages as easily as they can the rows of symbols. Moreover, readers could understand each country's population, only one country at a time, if it were provided in words. With a visual, readers can grasp the significance and relationship of all ten countries' populations in a single glance.

4. Visuals emphasize relationships. Through the use of arrangement and form, visuals quickly show contrasts, similarities, growth rates, downward and upward movements, fluctuations in price and time, and the influence of one variable on another. Figure 13.1 shows not only how countries compare in population, but also how population compares with land area. India, for example, has about three times more people than the former Soviet Union does, but occupies about one-eighth the space. Other kinds of visuals (pie and bar charts, discussed on pages 489–494) show the relationship of parts to the whole. And the curve of a graph can indicate the sequence of various events, such as average annual snowfall.

Choosing Effective Visuals

You will have to select visuals very carefully. You can prepare them by hand or you may have access to a computer software program that will allow you to create and introduce visuals in your work. Pages 510–512 discuss two graphics software programs you may choose. But whether you create visuals by hand or on the computer, the following suggestions will help you to answer two important questions: (1) When should I use a visual? and (2) How many of them will I need?

1. Use visuals only when they are strictly relevant for your purpose and audience. Visuals should not be included simply as decoration for impressing readers. A short report on fire drills does not need a picture of a fire station to enhance it; a list of instructions on how to prepare a company report does not require a picture of an individual writing at a desk.

FIGURE 13.2   A visual that helps an audience to distinguish similar objects.

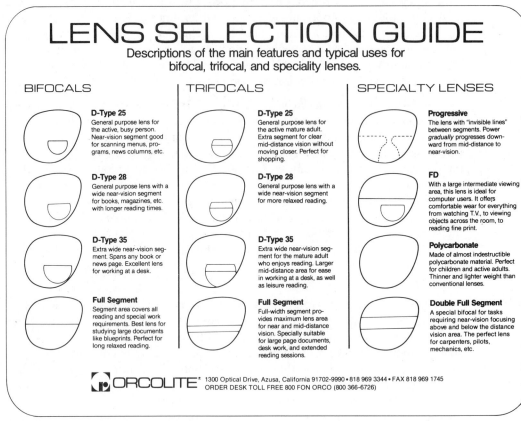

Reprinted by permission of Orcolite–A division of Optical Radiation Corporation.

2. Use visuals when it would be difficult to rely on words alone. As pointed out in a discussion of Figure 13.1, a verbal description is sometimes more difficult to follow and grasp than a visual presentation. Use visuals when you have to describe a piece of equipment with many (or concealed) parts, to explain a difficult concept, or to account for a process. Visuals also are invaluable when you must distinguish among similar-looking places or objects, as the lens selection guide in Figure 13.2 does. This guide is given to customers when they select eyeglass lenses at an optician's office. Note how difficult it would be to explain and describe these various lens to the layperson by using words alone.

3. Use visuals in conjunction with, not as a substitute for, written work. Visuals do not always take the place of words. You may need to explain information contained in a visual. A set of illustrations or a group of tables alone will not satisfy readers looking for summaries or evaluations. Note how the visual accompanying the description of a magnetic resonance imager in Figure 13.3 makes the procedure easier to understand than if the writer used only words or only the

FIGURE 13.3   A visual used in conjunction with written work.

A PICTURE FROM THE INSIDE OUT
At the heart of the magnetic resonance imager is a large magnet that is big enough for you to lie inside. Look at the picture below. The **magnet** directs radio signals to surround sections of your body. When the signals pass through your body, they **resonate** (release a signal). Then your body's response is picked up by a receiver and sent to a computer. The computer analyzes the signal and converts it into a visual **image** of your tissues on a video screen.

1. **The MR Imager**
surrounds your body with a harmless **magnetic** *field and radio signals that safely pass through your body.*

2. **A receiver** *picks up and measures the radio signals that leave, or* **resonate** *from, your body.*

3. **The radio signals** *are turned into a computerized picture—or* **image**—*of your body's tissues.*

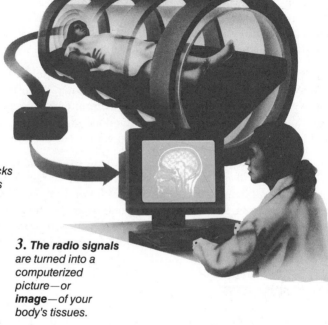

Reprinted by permission of Krames Communications.

visual. The visual and description are appropriately included in a pamphlet intended for teaching patients.

4. Make sure that visuals do not interfere with your message. Too many visuals (some of them duplicating information in your text) will distract readers. If something is self-explanatory, do not include a visual. Avoid visuals that include many more details than you discuss or, worse yet, that present information that contradicts your work.

5. Consider carefully how a specific visual will help your readers. Elaborate graphs are unnecessarily complex for a community group interested only in a clear representation of the rise in food prices over a three-month period. If you must include a detailed, complex visual to make an important point, be prepared to explain it to your readers, especially if they are not familiar with your

work or the technical discipline you are writing about. Generally, the less technical your audience, the more helpful a simple visual is.

**6. Never include a visual of poor quality; each should be clear and easy
to read.** Do not assume that readers will have magnifying glasses on their desks
or that they will tolerate a messy drawing or a faded blueprint. Be especially careful when you reproduce an existing visual. If you photocopy a visual, make sure
that the copy is clear and readable and does not cut off any part of the original.

If you have a computer equipped with a *digitizer* (sometimes called a *flatbed
scanner*), you can copy any type of visual (graphs, photographs, pictograms, diagrams). Simply place the visual face down on the flatbed scanner glass, scan it,
and save the digitized copy as a file on your computer. Later, you can recall the
file of the scanned image, clean it up with a computer application designed for
that purpose, and use it along with a software graphics application to prepare a
complete page layout, including visuals.

7. If you construct your own visual, do a model or sample first. It is hard
to make a perfect visual on the first try. You may have to make several drafts of
your visual to get it right. If you have a computer with graphics software, you can
experiment more easily. But whether done by hand or on a computer, visuals
should be checked against the data you want to display through them.

8. Consider how your visuals will look on the page layout. Visuals should
add to the overall appearance of your work, not detract from it. Observe generous
margins. Don't cram visuals onto a page. If you type your paper and intend to add
visuals later, make sure you leave enough room for them. Many computer systems
will let you move your visuals directly into your word processor document so that
you do not have to worry about their placement on the page.

The Graphic Artist's Desk

To prepare your own effective visuals, you will need the right tools. Most businesses and schools have computers to help you. If yours does not, you don't have
to purchase elaborate equipment to produce clear and professional-looking visuals to accompany your assignments. The materials to do the job can easily be
obtained at your college bookstore or your local office supply store. If you are
preparing your visuals by hand, you may want to purchase the tools and materials
discussed in this section.

The basic tools of the illustrator's trade include a straightedge (or twelve-inch
ruler), a plastic triangle to measure and make angles, a protractor, and a compass
to make arcs. Also it is a good idea to have scissors, glue, and transparent tape on
hand.

You may also need some high-quality writing instruments. You might want to
invest in an artist's pen set containing various points for lettering, sketching, and
making elegant designs in a variety of colors. (If you do not anticipate using the
pen set often, buy a fine felt-tipped pen, or perhaps a few of them in different

FIGURE 13.4   Templates for office planning, for traffic control, and for chemistry.

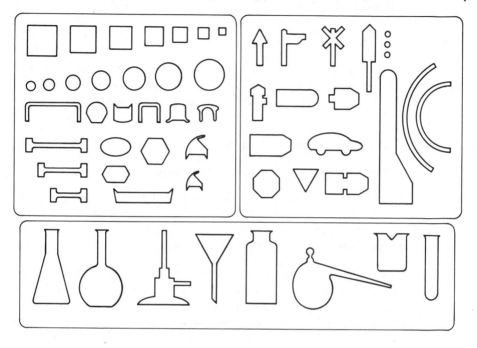

colors.) Use the artist's pens for your final copy, but for rough sketches have a supply of pencils in hard and soft leads. If you make a mistake, soft lead erases easily.

Not only must visuals be designed effectively, they should appear on suitable paper. Depending on your needs, you might want to purchase a drawing pad, some graph paper, maybe a pasteboard, and even some tracing paper.

One of the most serviceable materials you can buy for any graphic work will be *templates.* These are clear plastic sheets that contain a variety of cutout designs that can be traced onto a sheet of paper. Templates offer such basic shapes as circles, triangles, rectangles, trapezoids, dollar signs, and crosses. Other templates offer chemical and mathematical symbols. Depending on your technical needs and interests, you can find a template to suit any purpose. Figure 13.4 shows some sample templates.

If you are using a computer to prepare your visuals, the chances are that a particular graphics software package will make various shapes available to you. See pages 508–513.

Writing About Visuals

Never include a visual without mentioning it in your paper or report. Readers should be told *where* the visual is located and *why* it is there. The following guidelines on identifying, inserting, introducing, and interpreting visuals will help you use them more efficiently.

1. Identifying visuals. Each visual must have a number, a title, or both, that indicate the subject and the way in which it is discussed. A title helps your audience to read your visual and to see it with your purpose in mind. Thus they will not miss the point of view you want them to adopt. An unidentified visual is meaningless. Tables and figures should be numbered separately throughout the text.

Table 1: Paul Jordan's Work Schedule, January 15–23.
Figure 2: The Proper Way to Apply for a Small Business Loan.
Figure 5: Income Estimation Figures for North Point Shopping Center.

If you use a visual that is not your own work, you must identify your source (a specific newspaper, magazine, textbook, federal agency, or individual). If your paper or report is intended for publication, you are required by law to obtain permission to reproduce copyrighted material from the copyright holder.

2. Inserting visuals in the text. Place visuals as close as possible to the discussion of them. Never introduce a visual before a discussion of it; readers will wonder why it is there. By placing an appropriate visual near the beginning of your discussion, you will help your readers understand the discussion better than if you place it near the end. Be sure to tell readers where the visual is found—"below," "on the following page," "to the right," "at the bottom of page 3." If the visual is small enough, insert it directly in the text rather than on a separate page. If your visual occupies an entire page, place that page containing your visual immediately after the page that makes the first reference to it.

3. Introducing visuals. Refer to the visual by its number and, if necessary, mention the title as well. In introducing the visual, though, do not just insert a reference to it; relate the visual to the context of your discussion. Here are three ways of writing a lead-in sentence for visuals.

Poor: Our store saw a dramatic rise in the shipment of electric ranges over the five-year period as opposed to the less impressive increase in washing machines. (See Figure 3.)

This sentence does not tie the visual (Figure 3) into the sentence where it belongs. The visual just trails insignificantly behind.

Better: As Figure 3 shows, our store saw a dramatic rise in the shipment of electric ranges over the five-year period as opposed to the less impressive increase in washing machines.

Mentioning the visual in Figure 3 at the beginning is distracting. Readers will want to stop and look at the visual immediately before they know what it is or how you are using it.

Best: Over the last five-year period, our store realized a dramatic rise in the shipment of electric ranges as opposed to the less impressive increase in the shipment of washing machines, as shown in Figure 3 below.

This sentence is the best of the three because the figure reference and the explanation are in the same sentence, but the reference is not a distraction.

4. Interpreting visuals. Sometimes the figures in a visual tell an incomplete or misleading story, and you will need to interpret them in context. In a study on the benefits of vanpooling, one writer supplied the following visual:

Travel Time (in minutes): Automobile versus Vanpool

Private automobile	*Vanpool*
25	32.5
30	39.0
35	45.5
40	52.0
45	58.5
50	65.0
55	71.5
60	78.0

Source: U.S. Department of Transportation, *Increased Transportation Efficiency Through Ridesharing: The Brokerage Approach* (Washington, D.C., DOT-OS-40096): 45.

The writer then called attention to what the visual did not say.

Although it is estimated that the travel time in a vanpool may be as much as 30% longer than in a private automobile (to allow for pickups), the total trip time for the vanpool user can be about the same as with a private automobile because vanpools eliminate the need to search for parking spaces and to walk to the employment site entrance.[1]

In addition to mentioning a visual by number and title, it may also be necessary to tell readers why it is there and what specifically to look for. Of course, you should not spend time repeating information that is obvious from looking at the visual. But occasionally you will want to interpret the visual for an audience. A director of an alumni association, eager to sell alumni life insurance, used the table that appears on page 482 and then supplied a "sales" conclusion for it.

---

[1] James A. Devine, "Vanpooling: A New Economic Tool," *AIDC Journal* 15 (Oct. 1980): 13. Reprinted by permission.

Consider this table based on the U.S. Department of Labor Consumer Price Index for the past ten years. The value of insurance-benefit dollars decreases right along with dollars used in everyday expenses.

Average Annual Inflation Rates

Year	Inflation rate	Relative dollar value
1982	6.2	$1.00
1983	3.2	.97
1984	4.3	.92
1985	3.6	.88
1986	1.9	.86
1987	3.6	.82
1988	4.1	.77
1989	5.1	.70
1990	4.7	.67
1991	4.7	.64
1992	2.7	.62

If you haven't looked at your life insurance coverage recently, you may be surprised. Benefit levels thought sufficient just a few years ago may be inadequate for current and future needs. For example, a $10,000 benefit from 1982 would have to be increased to $13,844 in 1992 to provide the same level of protection.[2]

[2]Adapted courtesy of Northwestern University Alumni Affairs Office.

Tables

Tables are parallel columns or rows of information that present statistical data. The figures are organized and arranged into categories to show changes in time, distance, cost, employment, or some other quantifiable variable.

But the tabular form can present more than numerical information. Lists of words can also be put into tables. Tables in textbooks summarize material for easy recall—causes of wars, symptoms of diseases, provisions of a law. Various forms of business organizations are compared in Table 13.1. Observe how the table easily summarizes much information and arranges it in quickly identifiable categories.

To prepare a table properly, you must know how to construct and label it. Refer to Table 13.2 (p. 484) as you read the following instructions.

Preparing a Table

First determine the size of the table. If it is small (two or three columns) and you include it within the text, center the table on the page. Leave at least one inch of

TABLE 13.1   Comparison of Forms of Business Organization

	Single proprietorship	Partnership	Corporation
Ease of organization	Easiest	Moderately difficult	Most difficult
Availability of capital	Least	Intermediate	Most (best able to raise capital)
Responsibility	Centered in one person	Spread among partners	Policy set by directors; president supervises day-to-day operation
Incentive to succeed	Centered in one person	Spread among partners	Spread among many
Flexibility	Greatest	Intermediate	Least
Ability to perform varied functions	Dependent on one individual's versatility	Dependent on capabilities of two or more	Best able to employ versatile individuals
Possibility of conflict in management	None	Most prone to conflict	Chain of command reduces internal conflict; wide ownership minimizes disagreement
Taxation	No corporate income tax	No corporate income tax	Corporate income tax
Distribution of profits or losses	All to proprietor	Distributed to partners in accordance with partnership agreement	Profits retained or distributed to stockholders as dividends; losses reduce price of stock
Liability for debts in event of failure	Unlimited	Unlimited, but spread among partners	Limited to each stockholder's investment
Length of life	Limited by one individual's life span (or until he or she goes out of business)	Limited (partnership is reorganized upon death or withdrawal of any partner)	Unlimited (with ownership of shares readily transferable)

Source: Reprinted by permission from Sanford D. Gordon and George G. Dawson, *Introductory Economics*, 6th ed. Lexington, MA: D.C. Heath, 1987: 83.

Table number ⌐   *Column heading* ⌐   *Subcolumn heading*

TABLE 13.2   Veterans Attending Lincoln-Area VFW Posts[a]

Period of service	Years Attending			
	1975	*1980*	*1985*	*1990*
World War I	59	55	22	8
World War II	1330	1309	1100	963
Korean Conflict	240	230	205	186
Vietnam[b]	423	570	598	614

Source: Lincoln VFW Association ◄──── *Origin of data*
[a] Does not include Bayside, Morton, or Westover   } *Footnotes*
[b] August 1964–May 1975

Stub

white space above and below the table. If the table has a title, place it at the top (figure titles go above or below the visual), and triple space before and after the table. You might first want to determine a border and then very neatly put in the columns. Then you will have the right spaces and slots in which to insert your numbers or words. Leave adequate space between columns so that the table will not look crowded or be difficult to decipher.

If the table is large (running to five or six columns), place it on a separate sheet of paper. Again, depending on the size of the table, list the columns at the top of the page or turn the piece of paper broadside and then do the table that way. If possible, use the same margins as with the text of your paper. Make sure that the reader can easily see the numbers and letters of your table.

Some word processing programs include a function to help you create and position a table within your text. Using the table command, specify the number of rows and columns the table will contain, and the word processing software will create an empty table for you to fill in with data or will convert your running text into a table. You can also edit such tables and insert or remove lines separating rows and columns.

Labeling a Table

Provide headings for both the column and subcolumns; in Table 13.2 the column is entitled "Years Attending," and the subcolumns are the years (1975, 1980, 1985, 1990) about which the table gives data. Also provide a title for the *stub,* the first vertical column on the left-hand side. The stub heading is "Period of service" in Table 13.2. The stub lists the items (the wars and conflicts in which the Lincoln-area veterans participated) that are broken down under the subheadings. To separate the stub title and column/subcolumn headings from the body of the table, place a line across the table as in Table 13.2.

Label the categories appropriately and consistently. If some form of measurement is consistently involved, include the unit of measurement as part of the column heading—weight (in pounds), distance (in miles), time (per hour), quantity (per dozen). The unit of measurement should not be repeated for each entry in a column. Also, units should be consistent; do not jump from miles to meters, pounds to ounces.

Wrong:	Weight	Height
	120 lbs	165 cm
	132 lbs	5'9"
	122 lbs	5' 7"
	58.5 kg	172 cm
Correct:	**Weight** **(in kilograms)**	**Height** **(in centimeters)**
	54.0	165
	55.2	176
	54.9	166
	58.5	172

If something in the table needs to be explained or qualified, put in a footnote (often signaled by a small raised letter: [a] or [b]) in the table where the information is to be further identified or qualified. The letter will then refer readers to an explanation directly below the table. In Table 13.2 the [a] after the title points to the qualification that three communities were not considered in the Lincoln area when data for the table were gathered. The [b] after the Vietnam entry in the stub clarifies the official dates for that conflict.

Figures

As we pointed out at the beginning of this chapter, any visual that is not a table is classified as a *figure*. We will now look at nine types of useful figures, starting with *graphs*. If you have a computer, presentation graphics software (discussed on pages 510–512) can make the production of the visuals in this section of Chapter 13 very easy.

Graphs

Graphs transform numbers into pictures. They take statistical data presented in tables and put them into rising and falling lines, steep or gentle curves. Graphs vividly portray changes, fluctuations, trends, increases and decreases in profits, employment, energy, temperatures, or any other statistics that change frequently. The way the lines rise and fall in the graph depicts the kinds of changes and sometimes helps readers forecast trends. The resulting pictures are more dramatic than tables and are easier to read and interpret. Many issues of the *Wall Street Journal,* for example, contain a graph on the first page for the benefit of busy readers who want a great deal of financial information summarized quickly.

Basically, a graph consists of two lines—a *vertical axis* and a *horizontal axis*—that intersect to form a right angle as in Figure 13.5. The space between the two lines contains the picture made by the graph (in Figure 13.5 the amount of snowfall in Springfield between November 1993 and April 1994). The vertical line represents the dependent variable; the horizontal line, the independent variable. The

FIGURE 13.5   A graph of the amount of snowfall in Springfield in Winter, 1994.

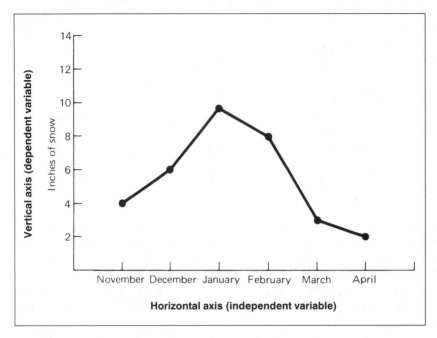

dependent variable is influenced most directly by the independent variable, which is almost always expressed in terms of time or distance. Hence, in Figure 13.5 the given month affects the amount of snow Springfield received. The vertical axis is read from bottom to top; the horizontal axis is read from left to right. When the dependent variable occurs at a particular time on the independent variable (horizontal line), the place where the two points intersect is marked, or plotted, on the graph. After the points are plotted, a line is drawn to connect them; the resulting curve gives a picture of which months had the greatest snow and which the least and what the overall pattern of snowfall was in Springfield.

The way in which scales are set up is crucial to the success of a graph. Many graphs may not have ranges indicated by equally spaced lines (tick marks):

But on most of the graphs you construct, use tick marks as a scale to show values, distances, or time, as in Figure 13.5. The topic will dictate the intervals to use. The time scale (independent variable) can be calculated in minutes, hours, days, or years.

A temperature-pulse-respiration graph is illustrated in Figure 13.6. The day is divided into six four-hour periods, and seven days are represented on one sheet. The temperature axis is divided into degrees (with .2° differences), and a heavy black line shows the *normal line,* making it easier to spot dangerous elevations. The pulse measurements are registered in two-beat differences (each dot repre-

FIGURE 13.6 A temperature-pulse-respiration graph showing the breakdown within ranges.

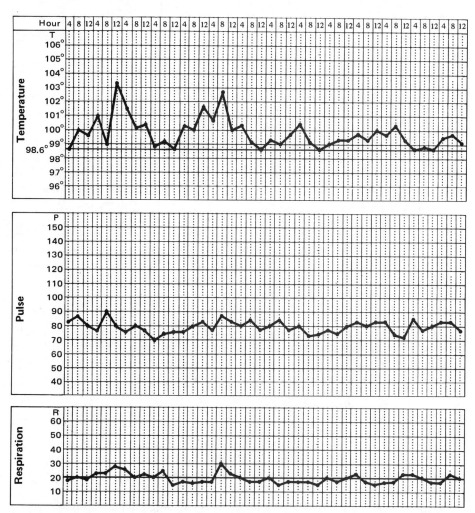

sents two beats within the larger grouping of tens). And the respirations are also measured in twos, each dot there representing every time a patient takes two breaths. Note that the temperature and pulse scales have a *suppressed zero line;* they begin with 95° and thirty beats, not with zero. It would be impossible to have lower numbers for pulse and temperature and expect a patient to live. But the respiration scale begins with zero because it has a lower range (0–60). If these recordings were expressed in tabular form, they would be hard to follow because they would deprive the reader of a curve depicting much information quickly and impressively.

The graphs in Figures 13.5 and 13.6 contain only one line per category. But a graph can have multiple lines to show how a number of *dependent variables* (conditions, products) compare with each other. The six-month sales figures for three

FIGURE 13.7   A multiple-line graph showing sales figures for the first six months of 1994 for three salespeople.

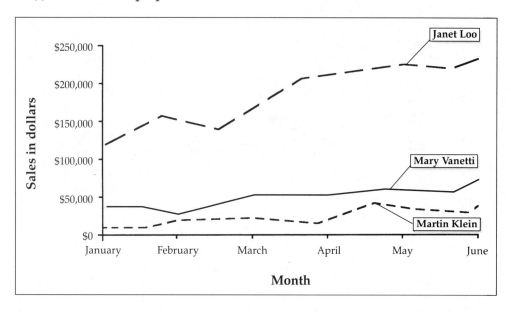

salespeople can be seen in the graph in Figure 13.7. The graph contains a separate line for each of these three salespeople. At a glance readers can see how the three compare and also how many dollars each one generated per month. Note how each person is clearly differentiated from the others by means of dots, dashes, or an unbroken line. Color, if available, can also help distinguish lines. Also, note how each line is clearly labeled so that the label does not cover up other lines or their points of intersection. If the lines do run close together, a *legend,* or explanatory note, underneath or above the graph identifies individual lines. Although some graphs may contain as many as five or six lines, it is better to limit multiple-line graphs to two or three lines (or dependent variables) so that readers can interpret the graph more easily.

Keep in mind the following guidelines when you construct a graph:

1. Inform readers what your scale is: how many dots, boxes, or spaces equal what amounts or times. If you are drawing your own graph, you may want to use graph paper that has tick marks or carefully divided lines.
2. Keep the scale consistent and realistic. If you start with hours, do not switch to days or vice versa. If you are recording annual rates or accounts, do not skip a year or two in the hope that you will save time or be more concise. Do not jump from 1982, 1983, 1984–1986, 1991, 1993. Include all the years you are surveying.
3. For some graphs there is no need to begin with a zero, as was seen in Figure 13.6. For others, you may not have to include numbers beyond seven or eight.
4. Do not draw a line or plot a curve that goes outside the limits of the graph and extends beyond the margin of the page.

Circle Charts

Circle charts are also known as *pie charts,* a name that descriptively points to their construction and interpretation. Figure 13.8 shows an example of a circle chart. The full circle, or pie, represents the whole amount (100 percent) of an industry, profession, or population group. The full circle can stand for the entire budget of a company or family, or it can represent just a single dollar of that budget and show how it is broken down for various expenses. Each slice of the pie, then, stands for a part of the whole. A circle chart effectively allows readers to see two things at once—the relationship of the parts to one another and the relationship of the parts to the whole. If you are using a computer, a 3-D pie chart can emphasize a slice by showing it slightly separated from the rest of the pie as in Figure 13.30.

The circle chart is one of the most easily understood illustrations. For that reason, it is popular in government documents (the Bureau of the Census relies heavily on it), financial reports, and advertising messages. Although many circle charts are based on tables, tables can be very complex and dry and also more detailed than circle charts. The circle gives percentage totals; the table shows how those percentage groups are broken down.

To construct a successful pie chart by hand, you will need a compass to make your circle and a protractor to measure sections of it. The mathematical principle underlying the construction of the circle chart is simple. A circle contains 360°. Translated into percentages, 100% = 360°, 10% = 36°, and 1% = 3.6°. To determine how much space you need for each of your slices, or wedges, figure out the percentage of the whole it expresses and then multiply that number by 3.6. For example, if you are constructing a circle chart to represent a family's budget, the percentage/degree breakdown might be as follows:

Housing	25%	90.0°
Food	22%	79.2°
Energy	20%	72.0°
Clothes	13%	46.8°
Health Care	12%	43.2°
Miscellaneous	8%	28.8°

Don't forget that all the individual slices of the pie must total 100 percent. Now follow these four rules to construct your circle chart.

1. Do not divide a circle, or pie, into too few or too many slices. If you have only three wedges, consider using another type of visual to display them (a bar chart, for example, which will be discussed later). If you have more than seven or eight wedges, you will divide the pie too narrowly, and the overcrowding will destroy the dramatic effect of the illustration. Instead, combine several slices of small percentages (2 percent, 3 percent, 4 percent) into one slice labeled "Other," "Miscellaneous," or "Related Items."

2. Put the largest slice of the pie first, at the 12 o'clock position, and then move clockwise with proportionately smaller slices. Beginning with the biggest slice, you call attention to its importance. The one exception is that the

FIGURE 13.8   A circle chart reflecting the proposed Midtown city budget for 1995.

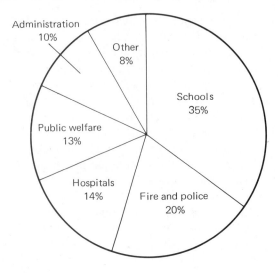

"Other" category (see above) should be placed last, as in Figure 13.8, even when it is largest.

3. Label each slice of the pie. If the slice is large enough, write the identifying term or quantity inside, but make sure that it is horizontal and big enough to read. Do not put in a label upside down or slide it in vertically. If the individual slice of the pie is small, do not try to squeeze in a label. Connect a line to the outside of the pie nearest the slice and insert the appropriate label there, as for Administration in Figure 13.8.

4. You can shade or color alternating slices of the pie to further separate the parts. If you do, be careful not to obscure labels and percentages; also make certain that adjacent slices can be distinguished readily from each other.

Bar Charts

A bar chart shows a series of vertical or horizontal bars to indicate comparisons of statistical data. For instance, vertical bars are used to show increases in quantities (students using a library) in Figure 13.9; horizontal bars depict increases in distance (the number of feet the shotput is thrown by a women's track and field team) in Figure 13.10. Bar charts make a dramatic visual impression on the audience. They are valuable tools in sales meetings to demonstrate how well (or poorly) a product, a service, a particular section of the company has done. You often see bar charts at an office recording the financial goals for the United Way or other charitable drives.

Bar charts are less exact than tables, as Figures 13.9 and 13.10 show. Note that the number of students using the library or the number of feet the shotput is thrown are not expressed in precise figures, as they would be in a table, but are approximated by the length of the bar. Do not assume, however, that the bar chart

FIGURE 13.9 A vertical bar chart showing the number of students using the Adams Memorial Library.

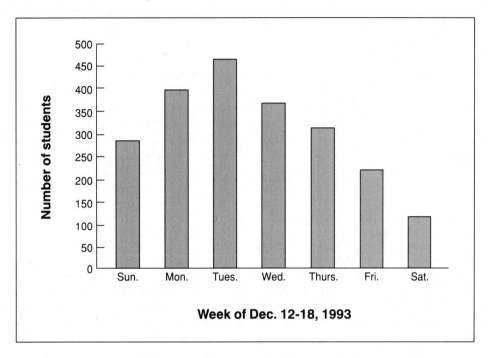

FIGURE 13.10 A horizontal bar chart showing length of shotput throws by a women's track and field team.

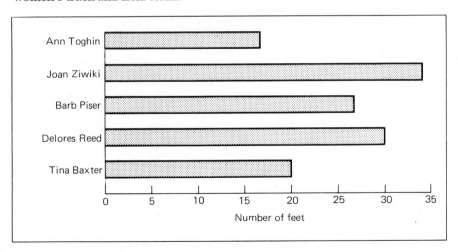

is inaccurate; many bar charts are based on tables. What you lose in precision with a bar chart, you gain in visual flair. Another advantage of a bar chart is that it is easier to construct than a line graph. Finally, a bar chart is much more fluid and dynamic than a circle. The circle is static; the bar chart (like the graph) presents a moving view.

When should you use a bar chart rather than a table or graph? Your audience will help you decide. If you are asked to present statistics on costs for the company accountant, use a table. In that situation the reader demands a precise listing; an accountant does not judge a visual by its eye appeal. However, if you are presenting the same information to a group of stockholders or to a diverse group of employees, a bar chart may be more relevant; such readers are interested in seeing the statistics in action. They are more concerned with the effects of change than with underlying causes and precise statistical details. Since it is limited to a few columns, however, a bar chart cannot convey as much information as a table or graph.

Types of Bar Charts

One of the most common types of bar charts is the one shown in Figure 13.9. Each bar represents one day of the week, and the height of the bar corresponds to the number of students using the library on that day. To read the chart effectively, simply note where the top of the bar is in relation to the vertical scale on the left. The chart compares one type of data (the number of students using the library) over a period of time (one week in the school year).

Another type of chart—a *multiple-bar chart*—is represented in Figure 13.11. Four differently shaded bars are used for each year to represent the amount of money spent on different types of advertising in America. A legend at the top of the chart explains what each bar stands for. This chart measures the amount of

FIGURE 13.11   A multiple-bar chart showing advertising expenditures by selected media: 1980–1995.

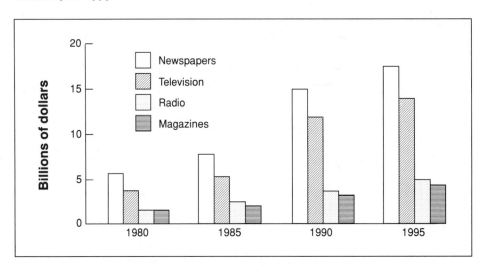

FIGURE 13.12   A segmented bar chart representing total travel expenditures for Weemco Industries in 1994.

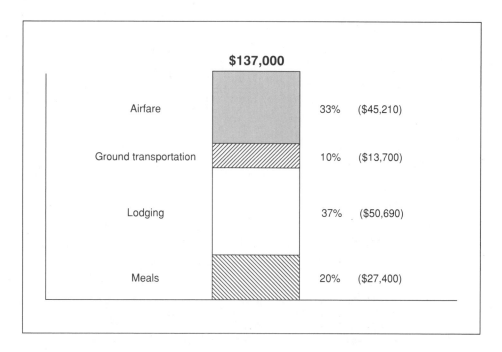

money spent over a period of time (fifteen years) on different media. A word of caution is in order about multiple-bar charts: never use more than four bars in a group for any one year. Otherwise, your chart will become crowded and difficult to read.

Still another kind of bar chart is the *segmented*, or *cross-hatched* (divided), bar, used to show differences within a given category for each comparison. The differences are the components, percentages, or subgroups that make up the whole. A single segmented bar representing the travel expenses Weemco, a small firm, had in 1994 is shown in Figure 13.12. The entire bar totals the cost of $137,000, which came from four different types of expenses (airfare, ground transportation, lodging, and meals). Each of these expenses is represented by a different type of shading on the one column. Combined, the multiple sources account for all travel expenses Weemco had in one year. A group of segmented bars can be used to show multiple comparisons among many categories, as in Figure 13.13 (p. 494), which depicts energy consumption levels and types in five states.

Making a Bar Chart

To construct an accurate bar chart, follow these instructions.

1. Make all the bars the same width; vary only the height (or length) to show differences.

FIGURE 13.13   A multiple-bar, segmented bar chart showing energy consumption by sector in five states that consumed the most energy in a given year.

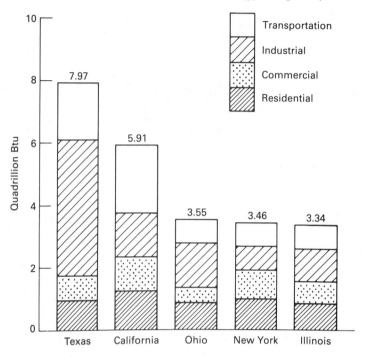

U.S. Energy Information Administration, *Monthly Energy Review,* Mar. 1984.

2. Select an appropriate scale and inform the readers about proportions. Be realistic. Do not construct a bar chart in which columns go off the page or are so small that readers cannot easily note differences. Look at the scale in Figure 13.9, where each division of the vertical column represents fifty students. Keep such divisions consistent; do not make one ten students and another twenty. Also, begin with zero so that the reader can correctly chart fluctuations. Use appropriate proportions on the horizontal scale as well.

3. Identify and use distinctive markings, shadings, or colors on divided bars. Supply a clarifying legend for readers or otherwise indicate the meaning of different portions of a single cross-hatched bar, as in Figure 13.12. But do not introduce unnecessary marks or decorations.

Pictograms

Similar to a bar chart, a pictogram uses pictures instead of bars to represent differences in statistical data, as in Figure 13.1. The pictures or symbols appropriately represent the item(s) being compared. Sometimes the number of pictures indicates change, as in Figure 13.14, where the people figures show Social Security recipients and workers. By increasing the size of the picture or symbol for each unit, a pictogram can also show quantities. Two ways to do this are illustrated in Figures 13.15 and 13.16 (p. 496). In Figure 13.15, a pictogram of increasingly

FIGURE 13.14   A pictogram indicating change in the relationship between Social Security recipients and workers.

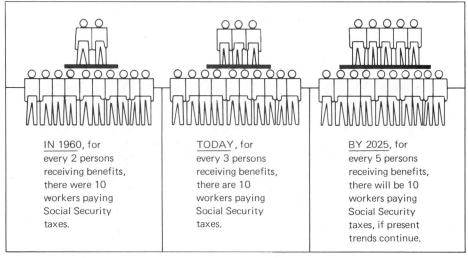

IN 1960, for
every 2 persons
receiving benefits,
there were 10
workers paying
Social Security
taxes.

TODAY, for
every 3 persons
receiving benefits,
there are 10
workers paying
Social Security
taxes.

BY 2025, for
every 5 persons
receiving benefits,
there will be 10
workers paying
Social Security
taxes, if present
trends continue.

Reprinted from *U.S. News & World Report,* 12 Jan. 1981: 65. Copyright, 1981 U.S. News & World Report, Inc. Reprinted by permission.

larger personal computer screens represents the tremendous growth of fax machines used with computers. In Figure 13.16, the cost of marketing farm foods is represented in a pictogram where a dollar bill is divided into slices, the sizes of which symbolize the relative costs for labor, packaging, and so on.

Unless you are preparing your pictogram on a computer, it is usually better to increase the number of symbols rather than their size because differences in sizes are often difficult to construct accurately and hard for the reader to interpret.

FIGURE 13.15   A pictogram indicating the growing use of fax modems with personal computers (units in millions).

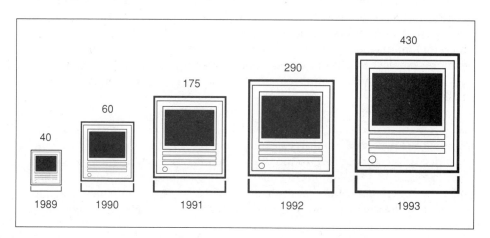

FIGURE 13.16   A pictogram showing the cost of marketing farm foods.

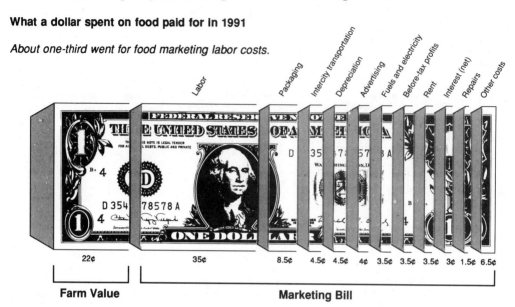

What a dollar spent on food paid for in 1991

About one-third went for food marketing labor costs.

Labor	Packaging	Intercity transportation	Depreciation	Advertising	Fuels and electricity	Before-tax profits	Rent	Interest (net)	Repairs	Other costs

| 22¢ | 35¢ | 8.5¢ | 4.5¢ | 4.5¢ | 4¢ | 3.5¢ | 3.5¢ | 3.5¢ | 3¢ | 1.5¢ | 6.5¢ |

Farm Value   **Marketing Bill**

Includes food eaten at home and away from home. Other costs include property taxes and insurance, accounting and professional services, promotion, bad debts, and many miscellaneous items.

U.S. Department of Agriculture, Office of Public Affairs, *1990 Fact Book of Agriculture* (Washington, D.C.: USDA, 1991). Pub. no. 1063.

Whatever type of pictogram you use, though, always indicate the precise quantities involved by placing numbers after the pictures so that the reader knows exactly how much the pictures represent.

Organizational Charts

Unlike the charts discussed so far, the *organizational chart* does not contain statistical data, nor does it record movements in space or time. Rather, it pictures the chain of command in a company or agency, with the lines of authority stretching down from the chief executive, manager, or administrator to assistant manager, department heads, or supervisors to the work force of employees. The organizational chart also shows the various offices, departments, and units through which orders and information flow in the company or agency. Organizational charts help to inform employees and customers about the composition of the company and also help to coordinate employee efforts in routing information to appropriate departments.

   An organizational chart shows relationship by using lines to connect rectangles or circles to each other, starting at the top with the chief executive and moving down to lower-level employees. (Sometimes the name of the individual holding the office is listed in addition to the title of the office.) Examine the organizational chart in Figure 13.17. Positions of equal authority are on parallel lines, and all jobs under the supervision of one individual are joined by bracketing lines. Individuals who serve in advisory capacities or who are directly responsible to a higher admin-

FIGURE 13.17   An organizational chart representing critical care nursing services at Union General Hospital.

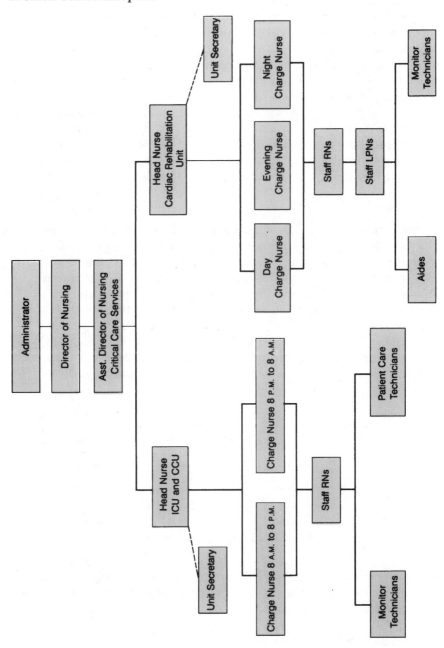

istrator are listed with broken or dotted lines, as depicted in the unit secretary positions in Figure 13.17.

When you prepare an organizational chart, first determine how much of the company or agency you want to depict. Just one branch of nursing services at a large metropolitan hospital—the division of critical care nursing—is presented in Figure 13.17. Note that the intensive and cardiac care units work two shifts a day (8 A.M. to 8 P.M.; 8 P.M. to 8 A.M.), while the cardiac rehabilitation unit works three shifts in a twenty-four-hour period.

Select the extent to which you want to visualize the organization. Then select appropriate circles or boxes to represent units. The shapes should be large enough to contain the titles of the offices they represent. Make sure you label each shape; otherwise, the reader will not know which unit is being depicted. If you represent just a portion of your organization, say so in your text.

Flow Charts

Like the organizational chart, a *flow chart* does not present statistical information. But as its name implies, a flow chart does show movement. It displays the stages in which something is manufactured, accomplished, or produced from beginning to end. Flow charts can also be used to plan the day's or week's activities or, for accounting purposes, to show how income data go into a balance sheet.

A flow chart tells a story with arrows, boxes, and sometimes pictures. Boxes are connected by arrows to visualize the stages of a process. The presence and direction of the arrows tell the reader the order and movement of events involved in the process. Flow charts often proceed from left to right and back again, as in the flow chart below, showing the steps to be taken before graduation.

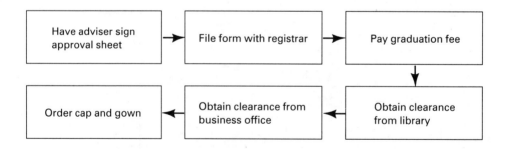

Flow charts can also be constructed to read from top to bottom. Computer programming instructions frequently are written in this way. See, for example, Figure 13.18, which uses a computer programming flow chart to show the steps a student must follow in writing a research paper. The flow chart in Figure 13.19 (p. 500) depicts a more complex procedure—the stages in the operation of a nuclear power plant; readers are asked to follow arrows in several directions. The jagged lines show the contents of the cooling coil and reactor. The cooling water enters from and returns to sources (a pond, a pool, the ocean) not shown at the right-hand side of the chart.

FIGURE 13.18   A computer programming flow chart showing steps in writing a research paper.

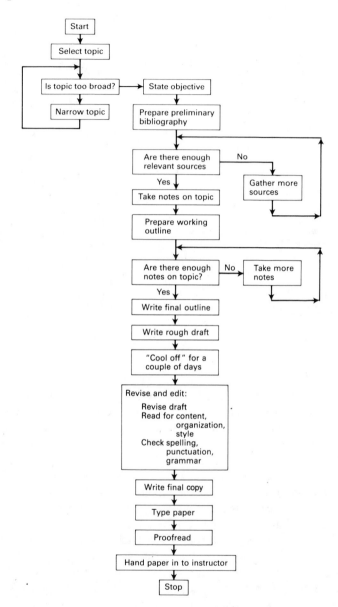

A flow chart should clarify, not complicate, a process. Do not omit any important stages, but at the same time do not introduce unnecessary or unduly detailed information. Do show at least three or four stages, however, and make sure the various stages appear in the correct sequence.

FIGURE 13.19   A complex flow chart showing the operation of a nuclear power plant.

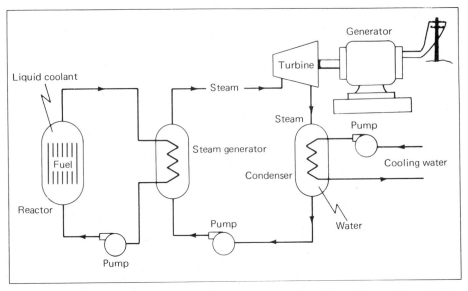

Reprinted by permission of the publisher from *An Environmental Approach to Physical Science*, by Jerry D. Wilson (Lexington, Mass.: D.C. Heath, 1974): 363.

Maps

The maps you use on the job may range from highly sophisticated and detailed geographic tools to simple, hand-drawn sketches. You may use a *small-scale map* that shows large areas (a continent, a state, a county) in rough outline without great detail, such as the map in Figure 13.20. Or you may need a *large-scale map* that displays a good deal of social, economic, or physical data (such as population density, location of retail businesses, hills, expressways, or rivers). That kind of detail is given in the map used by the Smithville Water Department in Figure 13.21 (p. 502). Look at the campus map included in your college catalog. How much detail does it supply, and what kind?

Your job requirements will dictate how detailed your map should be. Architects and builders need extremely detailed maps showing the location of pipes, telephone cables, and easement lines. An urban planner involved in developing a new community or an employee submitting site plans for a company's new location will use less detailed maps. For example, see Figure 16.9 on page 607. Between these two extremes, the individual working for a government agency investigating fire or flood damage to a neighborhood may require a map that indicates individual houses without presenting detailed features of those dwellings.

You may have to construct your own map or find one in a published source (a government document, an atlas, or a publication of an auto club). If you take a map from a source, you must acknowledge that source to avoid plagiarism. If you photocopy it, remember that you may not be able to reproduce colors or fine shading. When preparing a map to include in a report, follow these steps:

FIGURE 13.20   A small-scale map showing location of the world's record water depth for petroleum exploration.

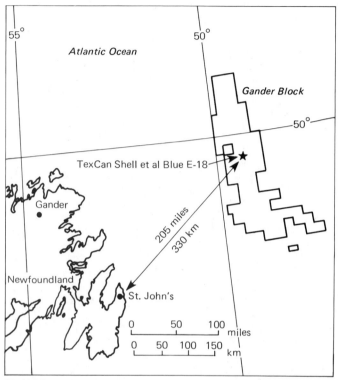

World Oil Dec. 1979: 87. Reprinted by permission.

1. Provide a distance scale that identifies the proportion of inches to miles or inches to feet (e.g., 1" = 10 miles).

2. Use dots, lines, colors, symbols ($\triangle$, $\times$, $\bigcirc$, $\square$), or shading to indicate features. Markings should be clear and distinct.

3. If necessary, include a legend providing an explanation to dotted lines, colors, shadings, or symbols. Note the legend for water filter plants and pumping stations in Figure 13.21.

4. Eliminate any features (rivers, elevations, county seats) that do not directly depict the subject you are discussing. For example, a map showing the crops grown in two adjacent counties need not show all the roads and highways in those counties. A map showing the presence of strip mining needs to indicate elevation, but a map depicting population or religious affiliation need not include topographical (physical) detail. Reservoirs, lakes, and highways are essential in a map locating fire-damaged zones, details easily omitted in a map depicting strip mines.

5. Indicate direction by including an arrow and then citing the direction to which it points, for example, N↑.

FIGURE 13.21 A large-scale map showing location of Smithville Water Department's filter plants and pumping stations.

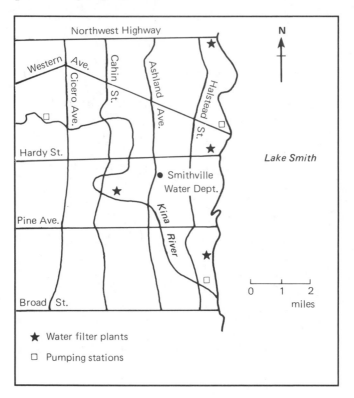

Photographs

Correctly prepared, photographs are an extremely helpful addition to job-related writing. The photograph's chief virtues are realism and clarity. To a reader unfamiliar with an object or a landscape, a photograph may provide a much more convincing view than a simple drawing. Photographs of "before and after" scenes are especially effective.

The company you work for may have a photography or art department to assist you with your picture taking and preparation. A photograph can be touched up by enlarging crucial sections, deleting unnecessary parts (called *cropping*), or inserting white arrows on a black-and-white glossy to draw attention to relevant details. Photographs can be expensive to prepare; so ask your supervisor if you have a sufficient budget before you start ordering them.

If photographic cosmetics are unavailable, however, you will have to use special care when you take a picture. The most important point to remember is that what you see and what the camera records might be two different sights. Before you take a picture, decide how much foreground and background information you need. Include only the details that are *necessary* and *relevant* for your purpose. Inexperienced photographers need to remember the following four points:

1. **Keep the camera in focus.** Make sure that the lighting is proper.

2. **Select the correct angle.** Choose a vantage point that will enable you to record essential information as graphically as possible.

3. **Give the right amount of detail.** Pictures that include too much clutter compete for the reader's attention and detract from the subject. A realtor wanting to show that a house has an attractive front does not need to include sidewalks or streets. At the other extreme, do not cut out a necessary part of a landscape or object. Avoid putting people in a photograph when their presence is not required to show the relative size or operation of an object.

4. **Take the picture from the right distance.** The farther back you stand, the wider your angle will be, and the more the camera will capture with less detail. If you need a shot of a three-story office building, your picture may show only one or two stories if you are standing too close to the building when you photograph it. Standing too far away from an object, however, means that the photograph will reduce the object's importance and record unnecessary details.

To get a graphic sense of the effects of taking a picture the right and the wrong way, study the photographs found in Figures 13.22–13.25 (pp. 503–504). A clear and useful picture of a hydraulic truck (often called a "cherry picker") used to cut

FIGURE 13.22 An effective photograph—truck in foreground, enough background information, and a worker to show size and function of truck.

FIGURE 13.23 A poor photograph—taken from the wrong angle so that everything merges and becomes confusing.

Photograph by David Longmire.

Photograph by David Longmire.

FIGURE 13.24 A poor photograph—focus is on worker, but
there is nothing else to identify
person or work going on.

FIGURE 13.25 A poor photograph—focus is on work
going on, but there is nothing to indicate that worker
is operating from a hydraulic truck.

Photograph by David Longmire.

Photograph by David Longmire.

branches can be seen in Figure 13.22. The photographer rightly placed the truck
in the foreground, but included enough background information to indicate the
truck's function. The worker in the gondola helps to show the size of the parts of
the truck and also enables the reader to visualize the truck in operation.

In Figure 13.23 everything merges because the shot was taken from the wrong
angle. The reader has no sense of the parts of the truck, their size, or their function. Another kind of error can be seen in Figure 13.24. Here the photographer
was more interested in the person than in a piece of equipment. But looking at
this picture, the reader has no idea where the worker came from or what he is
doing up there. Finally, the reader looking at Figure 13.25 has a view of work
going on, but no idea of the truck from which the worker is performing the job.

Drawings

A drawing serves many functions. For example, it can show where an object is
located, how a tool or machine is put together, or what signals are given or steps
taken in a particular situation. A drawing can explain the appearance of an object
to individuals who may never have seen it. A drawing is also helpful to individuals
who may have seen the object but do not have it in front of them as they read your
work. By studying your drawing and following your discussion, readers will be better able to operate, adjust, repair, or order parts for equipment. As you will see,
drawings are essential in giving instructions (pages 530–533).

Drawings generally have two advantages over ordinary photographs:

1. You can include as much or as little detail as necessary in a drawing. The eye of the camera is not usually so selective; it tends to record everything in its path, including details that may be irrelevant for your purpose.
2. A drawing can show interior as well as exterior views, a feature that is particularly useful when the reader must understand what is going on under the case, housing, or hood.

A drawing can be simple, such as the one in Figure 13.26 showing readers exactly where to place smoke detectors in a house. A photograph could not give such an uncluttered picture. Stick figures may also be a useful part of a drawing, as in Figure 13.27 (p. 506), which shows correct landing and take-off signals for pilots.

FIGURE 13.26   A drawing showing where to place smoke detectors in a house.

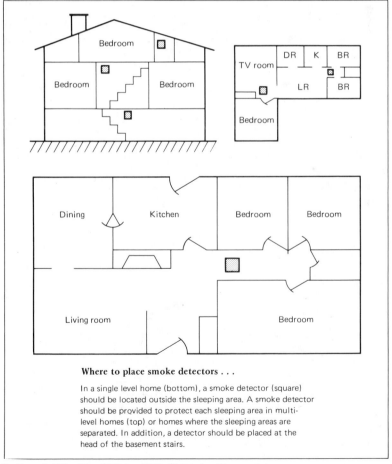

Where to place smoke detectors . . .

In a single level home (bottom), a smoke detector (square) should be located outside the sleeping area. A smoke detector should be provided to protect each sleeping area in multi-level homes (top) or homes where the sleeping areas are separated. In addition, a detector should be placed at the head of the basement stairs.

Southern Building (Dec. 1978–Jan. 1979): 10. Reprinted by permission.

FIGURE 13.27   A drawing using cartoon figures to show correct landing and take-off signals.

U.S. Department of Transportation, *Flight Training Handbook,* AC 61–21A: 54.

FIGURE 13.28   A cutaway drawing showing construction of sanitary sewers with a steel trenching box.

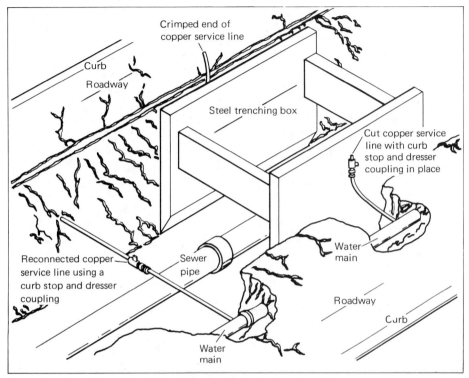

Crimped end of
copper service line

Curb

Roadway

Steel trenching box

Cut copper service
line with curb
stop and dresser
coupling in place

Reconnected copper
service line using a
curb stop and dresser
coupling

Sewer
pipe

Water
main

Roadway

Curb

Water
main

August A. Guerrera, "Grounding of Electric Circuits to Water Services: One Utility's Experience." Reprinted from *Journal of the American Water Works Association* 72 (Feb. 1980): 86. Reprinted by permission. Copyright 1980, the American Water Works Association.

A more detailed drawing can reveal the interior of an object. Such sketches are called *cutaway drawings* because they show internal parts concealed from view. The underground pipes and service lines in a sanitary sewer are shown in Figure 13.28. The earth banking left in the foreground of the sketch shows where these pipes are buried.

Another kind of sketch is known as an *exploded drawing*. This drawing blows the entire object up and apart to show how the individual parts, each kept in order, are arranged. An exploded drawing of a chair is seen in Figure 13.29 (p. 508). The owner can better see how the chair is assembled and can more easily determine how to repair it. Figure 13.29 also uses *callouts,* or labels identifying the components of whatever is being depicted. These labels are often attached to the parts with arrows or lines. As the name suggests, the labels "call out" the parts so readers can identify them quickly. See Figure 14.4 on page 527 for an additional example of an exploded drawing.

FIGURE 13.29 **An exploded drawing of a chair.**

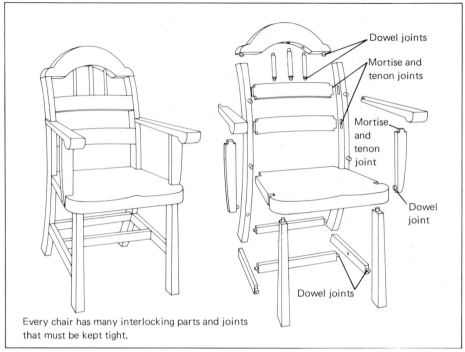

Every chair has many interlocking parts and joints that must be kept tight.

From Reader's Digest *Fix-It Yourself Manual*: 67. Courtesy of Reader's Digest Association, Inc.

When you prepare your own drawings, follow these rules:

1. Whenever necessary, indicate which view of the object you are presenting (for example, aerial, frontal, lateral, reverse, exterior, or interior).

2. Keep the parts of the drawing proportionate unless you are purposely enlarging one section. Then provide readers with a scale.

3. Do not include any extra details. Even the addition of a line or two might distort the reader's view. Do not add decorations to make a drawing look fancy.

Computer Graphics

Computers are being used to produce visuals of all kinds. If you have a computer available, it is a good idea to use it to prepare your visuals. This can involve some time learning how to use the software program you need, but the advantages are well worth it. Numerous computer software packages offer graphic capabilities, and there are also special graphics software packages. (Be cautioned, though, that some of these software packages are quite expensive.) Advances in computer hardware technology have made creating computer graphics relatively easy. With a *mouse* (a hand-held cursor) or a *stylus* (electronic pen) you can create all kinds of visuals. If you have a color printer, your computer can produce visuals in high resolution colors. And you can even make colored transparencies that can be used with an overhead projector. *Scanners,* discussed on page 478, are another piece of computer hardware used to prepare visuals.

Thanks to such technology you can create sophisticated visuals that once had to be done by an artist or a printer. Sitting in front of your own personal computer (provided you have the right software and hardware), you can produce in a few minutes professional-looking graphics in a striking array of colors, shapes, sizes, and dimensions. One software manufacturer advertises that users can select more than five hundred different visual configurations and that they can make numerous changes in these visuals.

Figures 13.30 and 13.31 (p. 510) illustrate two types of graphics you can easily create with a personal computer and a graphics software package. The charting capabilities on a computer are almost endless. All you have to do is plug in the raw numerical data into your computer's database and then, with a few simple keyboard commands, select the most appropriate visual shape (bar or pie chart, pictogram, graph) to display this statistical data. Following your commands, the computer will analyze and plot the data into a proportionately accurate chart or graph from the data you keyed in. The particular visual will then appear on the computer's VDT screen, and with the assistance of a printer it can be produced on

FIGURE 13.30   A computer-generated circle chart showing the proposed Midtown city budget for 1995, using the same data as in Figure 13.8.

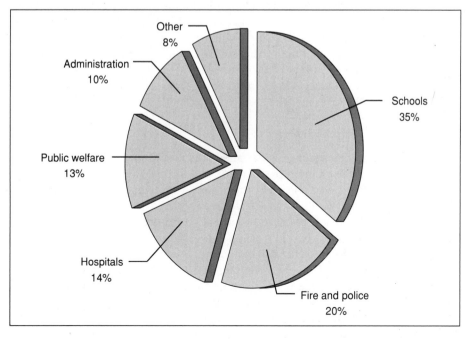

FIGURE 13.31   A computer-generated multiple-bar chart showing advertising expend-itures by selected media: 1980–1995.

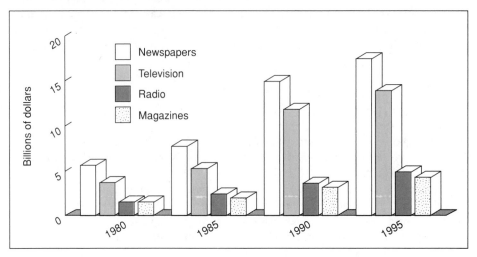

hard copy (paper) in black and white or in color. You do not have to be an experienced artist or mathematician to achieve high-quality results.

Two Types of Graphics Software Packages

There are two types of software packages that can be used in the preparation of visuals. One is a presentation graphics package, such as Harvard Graphics, and the other is a drawing package, such as Adobe Illustrator. Each type of software also includes a collection of pictures and images (such as arrows, boxes, and phones) called a *library,* or *computer clip art.* Figure 13.32 contains some examples of these ready-made images. Computer libraries can include up to two hundred or more different shapes, pictures, and images. From the large assortment of computer clip art, you can select what is most appropriate for your audience's needs and your message to them.

Presentation Graphics Packages

A presentation graphics package is designed specifically to produce the kinds of visuals discussed in this chapter. It will guide you through inputting your data and then let you select the way you want them displayed. Simply plug your raw data into the computer software, or use data already stored in a database or from a spreadsheet program. The presentation graphics software will store this information so you do not have to reenter it when you want to change or update a visual. Your computer then will plot the data you entered into a proportionately accurate chart, graph, or table. In fact, the computer can suggest the most relevant visual representation (graph, pie chart, bar chart, or table) to display your data. This software also lets you tailor-make every other aspect of your visual—what title to use, what scale to follow, what annotations to include, and even what colors to use. The computer gives you more choices than you would ever imagine possible.

FIGURE 13.32   Examples of computer clip art.

Graphics created using The New Print Shop © Broderbund Software, Inc. 1989.

Another benefit of a presentation graphics package is its flexibility and speed. You do not have to decide beforehand such things as the size and proportion of your visual based on the data you need it to represent. The computer does that for you in creating the visual. It also will let you experiment with a number of color combinations so that you can see and judge which one best makes your point.

Drawing Software Packages

A drawing software package serves a more general purpose than a presentation one. It will help you draw any picture you want, but unlike a presentation package, it will not create a graph or chart from data entered into the computer. To make a particular visual with a drawing package, you must instruct the computer to "draw a line from this point to that point, now draw a line from . . ." and so on; you put together visuals from the lines, boxes, arcs, and configurations that *you* draw. You do this just as you would with any normal drawing, one line at a time. A drawing package is very useful for constructing line drawings, graphs, flow charts, and organizational charts. You may need more time to produce a visual with this software than with a presentation package, but you will have greater freedom.

The Capabilities of Computer Graphics

Computers give you enormous graphic capabilities. Using a computer you can create any of the visuals in this chapter plus numerous others. Here is a brief overview of the kinds of visuals you can produce with a computer and the types of alterations you can make in them.

- You can produce black-and-white visuals as well as multicolored graphs, charts, drawings, and so on. Software packages have what is called a "paintspray" feature that allows you to shade in different parts of a visual (or the entire visual) with small, densely placed dots. Such a feature helps you to distinguish one bar or bar segment from another in a bar chart.
- You can create three-dimensional drawings and designs to show different angles, shapes, and even aerial views; this visual capability clearly helps to distinguish exterior from interior views, front views, side views, and overhead views.
- You can move, delete, switch, or explode a part of a visual to make it more effective for the audience and to emphasize an idea in your text.
- You can rotate a part of a visual to see if a different point of view might be more effective.
- You can zoom in on a visual to enlarge it or scale it down to make it appear smaller. With scaling you can vividly and accurately represent topographical features or even the same visual in two different scales.
- You can crop a photograph, reproduce part of it for an insert at the bottom of the visual, or even eliminate something in the middle of a photograph.
- You can join two objects from two separate visuals to show a side-by-side view that otherwise would not be possible.

- You can call up numerous geometric shapes and symbols to clarify, emphasize, or enhance a visual.
- You can display on your screen both the visual (say, a graph or table) and the statistical data on which it is based in two or more *windows* (divisions or files) represented on the screen.
- You can select from among many different *fonts* (typeface designs) and sizes for legends, callouts, and captions.
- You can simulate what something might look like. For example, through computer-simulated projections you can see what a house may look like with a different-shaped roof or how someone might look with a new hairstyle or wearing a particular piece of clothing.

Advantages of Using Computer Graphics in Your Research and Writing

Computer graphics offer more advantages than just striking visual effects. They can also significantly help you in your research and written work. In the process of preparing your work, you can experiment with a variety of visuals to see which one most accurately represents your ideas and which most convincingly displays the data for your audience. After you key in the numerical data, you can, for example, easily switch from a bar chart to a pie chart to a graph. Computer graphics increase your editing capabilities, too. You can delete irrelevant items in a visual or add features of your own. You might update a chart or graph, move information around, or add new headings.

Three-dimensional computer graphics are visually pleasing, and they can also simplify as well as enhance a technical presentation. For example, a computer-generated three-dimensional visual can show the size and shape of an oil spill on the ground or on an ocean, or it can dramatically reveal the electromagnetic field generated in a kitchen by a microwave oven, refrigerator, or other appliances.

With the variety of computer graphics available you do not have to worry about whether you will ever find the exact visual you need or whether you will have to wait for someone to prepare it. Thanks to the computer, you will be able to design and produce the exact kinds of visuals your report calls for. Finally, using graphics software can lessen your anxiety about where and how you will place your visuals in your text. Creating your own visuals, which are stored on the computer's disk and are thus ready to be used at any time, you can easily merge a visual anywhere in your document and not have to worry about whether you have left too much room or not enough.

While there is no doubt that computer graphics will help you on the job, you still need to rely on the basic information on visuals—their kinds and their usefulness—presented in this chapter. These fundamental principles will always apply, no matter how your visuals are created.

✓ Revision Checklist

Your visuals deserve the same careful attention that you give to your written work. As you do with your letters, memos, and reports, you should follow a process of discovering what information can be expressed best through visuals and then designing and incorporating them into your written work. Follow the guidelines listed in this chapter for the specific kinds of visuals you decide to use. But regardless of the types you select, ask yourself the following questions before you include the final version of your visuals in your written work.

1. Have I located all the places in my written work where a visual would help my readers better understand my message? Do I have a valid reason for using each visual that I included?

2. Have I chosen the most effective type of visual (table, chart, graph, pictogram, or photograph) to represent the information my audience needs to understand?

3. Does the information contained in my visuals complement and clarify, not merely repeat, the information in my written work?

4. Are the technical detail and difficulty of my visuals appropriate for my audience and message? Have I included too much or too little information in my visuals?

5. Is each of my visuals attractive, legible, and complete? Are all relevant parts and sections represented?

6. Have I given each visual a title and a number?

7. Where necessary, have I provided a legend, an annotation, or call-outs in appropriate places in my visuals to help my audience understand them more easily?

8. Have I introduced and interpreted each visual in the written text of my work?

9. Have I told my audience where they can find the visual that will help them understand my written work?

10. Have I placed each visual near the written description or commentary to which it pertains?

11. Have I acknowledged the source for any visual that I have taken from copyrighted material? Where necessary, have I given credit to individuals (coworkers, fellow students) who may have prepared a visual I am using or who may have assisted me in preparing it?

GLOSSARY

By way of review, the following is a glossary of terms used in this chapter:

bar chart   a visual using vertical or horizontal bars to measure different data in space and time; bars can also be segmented to show multiple percentages within one bar. Bar charts are used to show a variety of facts for easy comparison.

callouts   labels that identify the parts of an object in a visual.

captions   titles or headings for visuals.

circle chart   a visual shaped in a circle, or pie, whose slices represent the parts of the whole. Circle charts portray budgets, expenditures, shares, and time allotments.

computer clip art   ready-made electronic images, symbols, and pictures available in a computer library.

computer graphics   a variety of visuals generated by a computer; software (programs) and hardware (computer screens, scanners) create these visuals.

cropping   the process of eliminating unnecessary, unwanted details of a photograph by reproducing only the desired portion.

cross-hatching   the process of marking parts of a visual with parallel lines that cross each other obliquely; used to differentiate one bar or slice of a circle chart from another.

cutaway drawing   a sketch in which the exterior covering of an object has been removed to show an interior view.

dependent variable   the element (cost, employment, energy) plotted along the vertical axis of a line graph and most directly influenced by the independent variable.

drawing software packages   computer graphics software that allows users to create visual representations of data either plotted for accuracy or drawn freehand (charts, graphs, general illustrations).

exploded drawing   a sketch of an entire object that has been blown up and apart to show the relationship of parts to one another.

figures   any visuals that are not tables—charts, drawings, graphs, pictograms, photographs, maps.

flow chart   a sketch with boxes and arrows revealing the stages in an activity or process.

graph   a picture that represents the relationship of an independent variable to one or more dependent variables; produces a line or curve to show their movement in time or space. Graphs are used to depict figures that change often—temperatures, rainfall, prices, employment, productions, and so forth.

independent variable   the element, plotted along the horizontal axis of a graph, which most directly and importantly affects the dependent variable; most often, the independent variable is time or distance.

large-scale map   a map that shows a great deal of detail, whether physical (elevations, rivers), economic (income levels), or social (population, religious affiliation).

legend   the explanation, or key, indicating what different colors, shadings, or symbols represent in a visual.

organizational chart   a visual showing the structure of an organization from the chief executive to the work force of employees. An organizational chart reveals the chain of command with areas of authority and responsibility.

pictogram   a visual showing differences in statistical data by means of pictures varying in size, number, or color.

pie chart   see **circle chart**.

presentation graphics software   computer graphics software that allows its users to assemble visual images in digital form for presentation purposes (e.g., audiovisual presentation at a sales conference).

small-scale map   a map that depicts large areas without detail (a town with no streets or subdivisions represented or a state with no cities shown).

stub   the first column on the left-hand side of a table; contains line captions listing those units to be discussed in the columns.

suppressed zero   a graph beginning with a larger number when it would be impossible or impractical to start plotting at zero.

table   a visual in which statistical data or verbal descriptions are arranged in rows or columns.

templates   clear plastic sheets containing a variety of symbols, shapes, and designs that can be traced on paper.

tick marks   equally spaced marks drawn on the vertical or horizontal scale of a graph to show units of measurement.

Exercises

1. Record the highest temperature reached in your town for the next five days. Then collect data on the highest temperature reached in three of the following cities—Boston, Chicago, Dallas, Denver, Los Angeles, Miami, New Orleans, New York, Philadelphia, Phoenix, Salt Lake City, San Francisco, Seattle—over the same five days. (You can get this information from a newspaper.) Prepare a table showing the differences for the five-day period.

2. Go to a supermarket and get the prices of four different brands of the same product (hair spray, aspirin, a soft drink, a box of cereal). Put your findings in the form of a table.

3. One government agency supplied the following statistics on the world production of oranges (including tangerines) in thousands of metric tons for the following countries during the years 1987–1990: Brazil, 2,005, 2,132, 2,760, and 2,872; Israel, 909, 1,076, 1,148, 1,221; Italy, 1,669, 1,599, 1,766, 1,604; Japan, 2,424, 2,994, 2,885, 4,070; Mexico, 937, 1,405, 1,114, 1,270; Spain, 2,135, 2,005, 2,179, 2,642; and the United States, 7,658, 7,875, 7,889, 9,245. Prepare a table with this information and then write a paragraph in which you introduce the table and draw conclusions from it.

4. Keep a record for one week of the number of miles you walk, ride, or drive each day. Then prepare a line graph depicting this information.

5. Prepare a table to show the following statistical data: According to the 1980 Census, the town of Ardmore had a population of 34,567. By the 1990 Census the town had decreased its population by 4,500. In the 1980 Census the town of Morrison had a population of 23,809, but by the 1990 Census the population had increased by 3,689. The 1990 Census figure for the town of Berkesville was 25,675, which was an increase of 2,768 from the 1980 Census.

6. Prepare a line graph for the information in Exercise 5.

7. Prepare a bar graph for the information in Exercise 5.

8. Write a paragraph introducing and interpreting the table printed below.

Year	Soft drink companies	Bottling plants	Per capita consumption (gallons)
1935	750	750	10.3
1940	578	611	12.5
1945	457	466	18.6
1950	380	407	17.2
1955	231	292	15.9
1960	171	229	15.4
1965	118	197	16.0
1970	92	154	18.7
1975	54	102	21.1
1980	43	88	23.1
1985	45	82	25.3
1990	37	78	27.6

9. Prepare a circle chart showing the breakdown of your budget for one week or one month.

10. According to a municipal study in 1993 the distribution of all companies classified in each enterprise industry in that city was as follows: minerals, 0.4%; selected services, 33.3%; retail trade, 36.7%; wholesale trade, 6.5%; manufacturing, 5.3%; and construction, 17.8%. Make a circle chart to represent this distribution and write a one- or two-paragraph interpretation to accompany (and explain the significance of) your visual.

11. Construct a segmented-bar chart to represent the kinds and numbers of courses you took in a two-semester period or during your last year in high school.

12. Prepare a bar chart for the different brands of one of the products in Exercise 2. Write a paragraph introducing this illustration.

13. Find a pictogram in a math or business textbook or in a magazine (try *Newsweek* or *U.S. News & World Report*) and make a bar graph from the information contained in it. Then write a paragraph introducing the bar graph and drawing conclusions from it.

14. Make an organizational chart for a business or agency you worked for recently. Include part-time and full-time employees, but indicate employees' status with different kinds of shapes or lines. Then write a brief letter to your employer explaining why this kind of organizational chart should be distributed to all employees.

15. Prepare a flow chart for one of the following activities.
   a. jumping a "dead" car battery
   b. giving an injection

    c. crocheting an afghan

    d. painting a set of louvered doors

    e. making an arrest

    f. putting out an electrical fire

    g. calling up a computer program

    h. preparing a visual using a graphics software package

    i. any job you do

16. Make a map representing at least two blocks of your neighborhood. Include with appropriate symbols any stores, police or fire stations, houses of worship, parks, or schools. Supply a legend for your readers.

17. Draw a map for a visitor who wants to know how to get from your college library to the downtown area of your city. Supply a distance scale.

18. Draw an interior view of a piece of equipment you use in your major; then identify the relevant parts using callouts.

19. Prepare a drawing of one of the following simple tools and include appropriate callouts with your visual.

    a. golf club   **f.** computer terminal, keyboard, and printer

    b. hammer   **g.** ballpoint pen

    c. pliers   **h.** soldering iron

    d. stethoscope   **i.** table lamp

    e. swivel chair   **j.** pair of eyeglasses

20. Prepare appropriate visuals to illustrate the data listed below. In a paragraph immediately after the visual explain why the type of visual you selected is appropriate for this information.

    a. Life expectancy is increasing in America. This growth can be dramatically measured by comparing the number of teenagers with the number of older adults (over age 65) in America during the last few years and then by projecting these figures. In 1970 there were approximately 28 million teenagers and 20 million older adults. By 1980 the number of teenagers climbed to 30 million and the number of older adults increased to 25 million. In 1990 there were 27 million teenagers and 31 million older adults. By the year 2000 the number of teenagers will level off to 23 million, but the number of older adults will soar to more than 36 million.

    b. The percentage of women in the work force is steadily increasing. According to the U.S. Department of Labor, of all women sixteen years and older, 37.7 percent of them were employed in the work force in 1960. In 1965 there were 38.9 percent; by 1970 43.3 percent; by 1975 46.3 percent; by 1980 51.5 percent; by 1985 55.2 percent; and by 1990 58.4 percent.

    c. Researchers estimate that for every adult in America 3,985 cigarettes were purchased in 1970; 4,100 in 1975; 3,875 in 1980; 3,490 in 1985; and 3,210 in 1990.

21. Find a photograph that contains some irrelevant clutter. Write a letter to the photography department of a company for which you presumably work that wants to use the photograph. Tell the department what to delete and why.

22. Make a simple line drawing of only the relevant portions of the photograph in Exercise 21. Explain in two paragraphs why the drawing is better than the photograph.

23. You work for a large manufacturer of industrial heat pumps and have been asked to help write a section of a report on the increased business your firm has been doing overseas. Based on the sales figures below for the years 1991, 1992, and 1993 (listed in that order) for each of the following countries, prepare two different yet complementary visuals. Also, supply a one-page description and interpretation of the statistics represented in your visuals. You may work collaboratively with one or more students in your class to prepare the visuals as well as to write the section of the report on international sales.

Argentina, 45, 53, 34; Australia, 78, 90, 115; Bolivia, 23, 43, 52; Brazil, 29, 34, 35; Canada, 116, 234, 256; Denmark, 65, 54, 87; England, 256, 345, 476; France, 198, 167, 345; Germany, 234, 398, 429; Holland, 65, 80, 89; Italy, 49, 52, 97; Japan, 67, 43, 29; New Zealand, 12, 69, 114; Norway, 33, 92, 104; Switzerland, 164, 266, 306; Sweden, 145, 217, 266; People's Republic of China, 7, 100, 296; Korea, 55, 43, 28.

In your written report, take into account trends, shifts in sales, and possible consequences for further marketing, and conclude with a specific recommendation to your employer.

24. Prepare an appropriate visual and an accompanying description and analysis of it, either to encourage or discourage your employer to lease rather than buy a company car. After studying the market, you have found the following information about the particular model your company uses: down payment for a new car is $1,500; security deposit for a leased vehicle is equivalent to two month's lease payments or $698; resale value for a new car is $7,100 after four years; total payments on a car leased for four years add up to $16,752; the principle financed for a new car is $21,999; sales tax on a new car is $1,410; finance charges for a four-year loan on a new car are $5,782; with both the leased vehicle and the purchased car you are responsible for all maintenance costs—tires, gas, oil, etc.; you are allowed up to 10,000 miles per year on the leased car—anything over that will cost .18 a mile; on the average, your company will use the car for about 20,000 miles a year; insurance coverage will cost your company $630 more a year for the owned vehicle as opposed to the leased one.

25. Working with one or two classmates, develop a brief orientation brochure for new students on your campus. Decide what visuals to use in your brochure (for instance, a simplified campus map, a table of useful campus phone numbers, or a graph showing the change in enrollment on your campus in recent years). Then break the project down into tasks for individual team members to complete, such as collecting data, drafting and revising text, finding or creating visuals, and editing the final copy. As you draft the text for your brochure, be sure to provide references to and interpretations of the visuals. Invite several classmates outside your team to critique your brochure, and then revise it in light of their comments. Submit the final copy of your brochure with visuals to your instructor.

Instructions, Proposals, and Reports

IV

Writing Clear Instructions

Clear and accurate instructions are essential to the world of work. Whether given orally or in writing, they make a business run economically, effectively, and safely. In fact, no work could be done at all if employees did not have clear instructions to follow; and customers would not purchase a product or service if they could not understand how to use it properly and safely. Instructions determine how carefully products are made, how efficiently a service or procedure is implemented, and how quickly customers are satisfied. Perhaps no other type of occupational writing demands more from the writer than do instructions because so much is at stake. You cannot afford to be unclear or inaccurate.

To prepare effective instructions you will have to use all your resources for analyzing your audience (pages 4-10) and following other parts of the writing process (pages 29-39). You will have to anticipate your readers' questions and problems, making absolutely sure they can understand and carry out all of your steps; you will have to organize your instructions so that nothing is missing or out of place; and you will have to select the most clear and precise words possible to help readers get the job done.

The Importance of Instructions

Instructions tell, and frequently show, how to do something. They indicate how to perform a procedure (draw blood); operate a machine (run a forklift); assemble, maintain, or repair a piece of equipment (a photocopier; a carburetor); or locate an object (coils in a circuit). Readers use instructions for reasons of safety, efficiency, convenience, and economy. Product labels in a medicine chest, for example, inform users when and why to take the medications and how much to take. Owners' manuals instruct buyers on how to avoid the inconvenience of a product breakdown by keeping the product in good working order. Magazines such as *Popular Mechanics, Popular Photography,* and how-to books offer consumers money-saving instructions on topics ranging from repairing their homes to training guard dogs. You might want to read some of these how-to publications and manuals to see how they identify and meet the needs of the reader trying to perform a certain procedure.

As part of your job, you may be asked to write instructions, alone or with a group, for your coworkers as well as for the customers who use your company's services or products. For long, complex instructions you will certainly be part of a team of illustrators, technicians, and marketing specialists. But whether the instructions are brief or lengthy, your employer stands to gain or lose much from the kinds of instructions you write. Clearly written instructions help employees to work efficiently. Imagine how costly it would be if employees had to stop their work each time they could not understand a set of instructions, or if they made a number of serious mistakes because of confusing directions. Thorough, carefully written instructions found in guides and manuals are an important part of "service after the sale." If your customers, especially ESL readers, cannot follow your instructions easily, they will not use your company's products or services again. Even more important, poorly written instructions may result in injury to the person trying to follow them and thus lead to damage claims or even lawsuits.

The Variety of Instructions: A Brief Overview

Instructions vary in length, complexity, and format. Some instructions are one word long: *stop, lift, rotate, print, erase.* Others are a few sentences long: "Insert blank diskette in external disk drive"; "Close tightly after using"; "Store in an upright position." Short instructions are appropriate for the numerous, relatively nontechnical chores performed every day. For more elaborate procedures, however, detailed instructions may be as long as a page or a book. When your firm purchases a new mainframe computer or a piece of earth-moving equipment, it will receive an instruction pamphlet or book containing many steps, cautionary statements, and diagrams. Many businesses prepare their own training manuals containing instructions for 200 or 300 different procedures.

Instructions can be given in paragraphs or in lists, and you will have to determine which format is most appropriate for the kinds of instructions you write. Figures 14.1 and 14.2 show two sets of brief instructions written in paragraph format. In Figure 14.1 hospital employees are told how to prepare and administer a sitz bath; in Figure 14.2 park rangers are given instructions on how to repair a halyard, or tackle, used to raise a flag or move a pulley.

The instructions shown in Figures 14.3 (p. 526) and 14.4 (p. 527) are printed in list form. In Figure 14.3 readers will find directions on how to change a type-

FIGURE 14.1   Instructions on how to prepare and administer a sitz bath.

First, adjust water temperature dial to 105–110°F. Then turn on the faucet and fill sitz tub with enough water to cover the patient's hips. Before assisting the patient into the tub, place bath towel in the bottom of the tub. Allow the patient to sit in the tub for 15–20 minutes. At the end of this time, help the patient out of the tub. Then dry the patient thoroughly.

FIGURE 14.2   Instructions on how to repair a halyard.

Easy Temporary Join for Synthetic Ropes

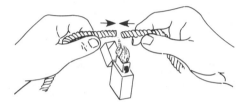

If you are faced with the problem of reeving a new halyard on a flagpole or mast, or through a block or pulley in an inaccessible location, the solution can be easy if both old and new lines are made of nylon or polyester (Dacron, Terylene, etc.). Simply join the ends of the old and new lines temporarily by melting end fibers together in a small flame (a little heat goes a long way). Rotate the two lines slowly as the fibers melt. Withdraw them from the flame before a ball of molten material forms, and if the stuff ignites, blow out the flame at once. Hold the joint together until it is cool and firm.

R. I. Standish, *Parks* 51 (Apr.–June 1980): 21.

style font (all the letters and symbols of a specific size of typeface) on an IBM "Quietwriter" printer; the directions in Figure 14.4 (page 527) give details on how to assemble an outdoor grill.

Assessing and Meeting Your Audience Needs

Regardless of their format (paragraphs or lists), instructions must be clear, complete, and easy to follow. In most instances you will not be available for readers to ask you questions when they do not understand something. Consequently, they will have to rely on your written instructions. Your purpose in writing those instructions is to get readers to perform the same steps you followed and, most important, to obtain the same results you did. Writing instructions is like teaching.

· FIGURE 14.3 Instructions on how to replace a typestyle font on an IBM "Quietwriter" printer.

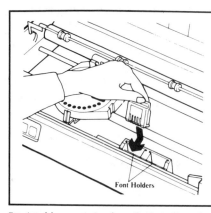

Replacing a Typestyle Font

1. Place the font in the font holder.

2. Place your finger on top of the font.

3. Press down and toward you until the font is securely latched into the font holder. (If this is your active font, the **font** light will go off. This is also normal.)

4. Close the printer cover.

Font Holders

Reprinted by permission from *Guide to Operations for the IBM "Quietwriter" Printer* by International Business Machines Corporation.

You must understand the material yourself and know the best way of presenting it. You have to set goals for your readers the way a teacher sets goals for students in a course.

The best way to establish those goals is to ask yourself the following questions about the intended audience for your instructions.

1. How and why will readers use my instructions? (Engineers have different job expectations than do office personnel. And customers have different expectations still.)

2. How much do readers know about the procedure they have to follow?

3. How much essential background (introductory) information will I have to give readers?

4. Where will my audience most likely be following my instructions—in the workplace with all types of sophisticated equipment and likely help from coworkers, or alone in their homes?

5. How many resources will my readers need to perform my instructions successfully? Equipment? Power sources? Safety precautions?

To make sure that your instructions are clear and accurate for your readers, plan them carefully. You must first completely understand the job or procedure that you are asking someone else to perform. Make sure you know the reason for doing something, the parts or tools required, the steps to be followed to get the job done, and the results of that job. If you are not completely sure about the procedure, watch an expert perform it. If you work in a group, everyone in the group needs to understand the procedure, start to finish. An uneven level of expertise among group members spells trouble; some steps of your instructions will be complete and accurate while others may not.

Next, actually perform the procedure (assembling, repairing, maintaining, ordering, dissecting) yourself or with all of your writing team present. If possible,

FIGURE 14.4   Instructions on how to assemble an outdoor grill.

ASSEMBLY INSTRUCTIONS

The instructions shown below are for the basic grill with tubular legs. If you have a pedestal grill, or a grill with accessories, check the separate instruction sheet for details not shown here.

NOTE: Make sure you locate all the parts before discarding any of the packaging material.

TOOLS REQUIRED . . . A standard straight blade screwdriver is the only tool you need to assemble your new Meco grill. If you have a pedestal grill, you will need a 7-16 wrench or a small adjustable wrench.

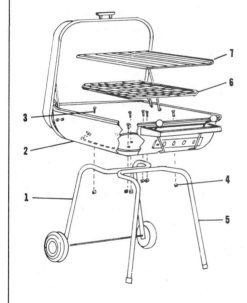

1. Before you start, take time to read through this manual. Inside you will find many helpful hints that will help you get the full potential of enjoyment and service from your new Meco grill.

2. Lay out all the parts.

3. Assemble roller leg (1) to bottom rear of bowl (2) with 1¼" long bolts (3) and nuts (4).

4. Assemble fixed leg (5) to bottom front of bowl (2) with 1¼" long bolts (3) and nuts (4).

5. Place fire grate—ash dump (6) in bottom of bowl (2) between adjusting levers.

6. Place cooking grid (7) on top of adjusting levers. Make sure top grid wires run from front to back of grill.

Meco Assembly Instructions and Owners Manual, Metals Engineering Corp., P.O. Box 3005, Greenville TN 37743. Reprinted by permission.

go through a number of trial runs. Take notes as you go along and be sure to divide the procedure into simple steps for readers to follow. You should not give the reader too much to do in one step. Each step has to be complete, sequential, reliable, straightforward, and easy for your audience to identify and perform.

Then transform your notes into a draft (or drafts) of the instructions you want readers to follow. To test your draft(s), ask someone from the intended audience (consumers, technicians) who may never have performed the procedure before to follow it to complete the task. Ask this individual to identify any places in your instructions that are vague, hard to follow, inconsistent (steps bunched up or out of order), or incomplete. Then revise your draft(s) and edit the final copy of the instructions that you will give to readers.

As you revise, pay special attention to the technical language and the amount of detail you include. Analyzing the needs and background of your audience will help you to determine which words and details to include. A set of instructions accompanying a chemistry set would be much different in terminology, abbreviations, and detail from a set of instructions a professor gives a class in organic chemistry.

> **General Audience:** Place 8 drops of vinegar in a test tube and add a piece of limestone about the size of a pea.
> **Specialized Audience:** Place 8 gtts of $CH_3 COOH$ in a test tube and add 1 mg of CO_3.

Do not assume that your readers have done the procedure or have operated the equipment as many times as you have. (If they had, there would be no need for your instructions.) No writer of instructions ever disappointed readers by making directions too clear or too easy to follow. Use language and symbols that will be readily understood. If someone is puzzled by your directions, you defeat the reasons for writing them.

Selecting the Right Words

To write instructions that readers can understand and turn into effective action, follow these guidelines.

1. Use verbs in the imperative mood. Imperatives are commands that have deleted the pronoun "you." Almost all the sentences in Figures 14.1–14.4 contain imperatives: "adjust water temperature" for "you adjust water temperature"; "fill the sitz tub with enough water" for "you fill the sitz tub with enough water"; "lift the cover" for "you lift the cover." Deleting the "you" is not discourteous, as it certainly would be in a business letter, a memo to a coworker, or a report. Instructions are best expressed as commands to show that the writer speaks with authority. Instructions reassuringly say, "These steps work, so do it exactly this way." Imperatives also get the reader to do something specific without hesitation. Don't water down your directions with statements such as "Please see if you can remove the outside panel"; "Try to allow the mixture to cool for five minutes"; or "If at all possible, adjust the thermostat to 78°." Wishy-washy statements may lead the reader to believe that there are some choices involved, when in fact there are none. For this reason, avoid *might, could, should:* "You might want to ignite the fire next" does not have the force of "ignite the fire next." Instead, choose action verbs such as those included in Table 14.1.

2. Write clear, short sentences. Since readability is especially important in instructions, keep sentences short and uncomplicated. This advice is especially important when you are writing for ESL readers. Sentences under twenty words (and preferably under fifteen) are easy to read. Note that the sentences in Figures 14.1–14.4 are, for the most part, under fourteen words. Avoid the passive voice. In place of "The air blower is to be used last," write "Use the air blower last." Also avoid addressing the reader as "one" or "the user": "The user should apply the air blower last" and "One must use the air blower last" are, again, best expressed as "Use the air blower last."

TABLE 14.1   Some Imperative Verbs Used in Instructions

adjust	dig	loosen	pull	slip
apply	drain	lower	push	spread
blow	drill	lubricate	raise	start
boot up	drop	measure	release	switch
call up	ease	mount	remove	tear
change	eliminate	move	review	tie
check	enter	notify	roll	tighten
choose	freeze	oil	rotate	trim
clean	hold	open	rub	turn
close	increase	point	save	twist
connect	insert	pour	saw	type
cut	inspect	press	shift	unplug
delete	lift	prevent	shut off	verify
determine	load in	print	slide	wipe

You can keep your sentences clear by avoiding ambiguity. Do not write a sentence that sends the reader a message opposite from what you intend. A direction such as "Before using the soldering iron on metal, clean it with Freon" may mislead the inexperienced welder to put Freon on the iron rather than on the metal that is to be cleaned. Similarly, "Perform venipuncture with the arm in a downward position" does not clearly specify whose arm is to be in that position; appropriately revised, the instruction reads "Put the patient's arm in a downward position."

3. Use precise terms for measurements, distances, and times. Indefinite, vague directions leave users wondering if they are doing the right thing. (Review pages 127–129 in Chapter 5.) The following imprecise directions are better expressed through the revisions listed in parentheses: "Turn the distributor cap a little." (How much is "a little"? "Turn the distributor cap three-quarters of an inch."); "Let the contents stand for a while." (How long? "Let the contents stand for ten minutes.") Precise measurement and timing are essential to the success of many kinds of instructions ranging from baking a cake to completing an experiment in a chemistry laboratory.

4. Use connective words as signposts to specify the exact order in which something is to be done (especially when your instructions are written in paragraphs). Words such as *first, then, before* in Figure 14.1 help readers stay on course, telling them how and why the various procedures are connected to produce the desired results.

5. Label each step with a number when you present your instructions in a list (as in Figure 14.4). You may also use bullets, as shown in Figure 14.12 on page 539. Plenty of white space between steps also distinctly separates them for the reader. If circumstances permit the use of color, employ it sparingly to set off important elements of your instructions. Color is especially effective for safety notices (see page 545).

Using Visuals Effectively

Readers welcome visuals in almost any set of instructions. Visuals are graphic and direct, helping readers to understand what they must do. A visual can simplify a process, reinforce or even save words, and help readers get the job done faster and with more confidence. For example, the illustration in Figure 14.2 reinforces the process of joining the two parts of the halyard by fire, and the sketch in Figure 14.3 shows the printer parts that the users must understand if they are to replace a typestyle font. Another frequently used visual in instructions is the exploded drawing, such as the one shown in Figure 14.4, to help consumers see how the various components of the grill fit together for easy assembly.

The number and types of visuals you include will of course depend on the procedure or equipment you are explaining. Some instructions, such as those in Figures 14.5 and 14.6, use a visual to illustrate each step. Others may require only one or two (such as in Figures 14.2–14.4). Instructions for computer programs sometimes show users what they can expect to see on a screen—either to make

FIGURE 14.5   Instructions on inserting and removing videocassettes.

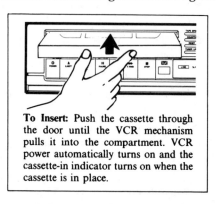

To Insert: Push the cassette through the door until the VCR mechanism pulls it into the compartment. VCR power automatically turns on and the cassette-in indicator turns on when the cassette is in place.

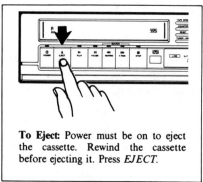

To Eject: Power must be on to eject the cassette. Rewind the cassette before ejecting it. Press *EJECT.*

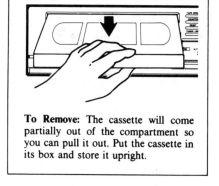

To Remove: The cassette will come partially out of the compartment so you can pull it out. Put the cassette in its box and store it upright.

RCA / Thomson Consumer Electronics.

FIGURE 14.6   Instructions on using a vacuum cleaner with accompanying visuals.

How to use

ON-OFF switch

To turn cleaner ON, push switch down. To turn cleaner OFF, push switch up.

Some models are equipped with a two-speed Power Surge™ switch. When switch is pushed up as far as possible, it is in the OFF position.

Normal Speed is to be used for regular cleaning of carpet and rugs and when using cleaning tools. Slide switch down one notch from OFF to NORMAL speed.

'Power Surge' Speed is to be used for extra cleaning power on heavily soiled areas of carpet. Slide switch down as far as possible and hold it in that position to engage the "POWER SURGE" speed. When switch is released, it will return to the NORMAL speed position.

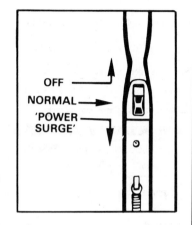

To operate

Plug cord into electrical outlet. Your cleaner is now ready to operate. Turn cleaner "ON" and, with handle in upright position, pull back on handle until the front of cleaner is lifted off the carpet. This insures that the throw away bag is inflated.

Handle positions

The handle of your cleaner has three positions: **Upright** for storage and for using attachments; **Operating** for general operation on carpet and floors; **Low** for reaching under low furniture. Step on handle release lever to lower the handle.

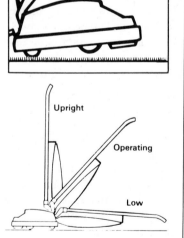

Reprinted by permission of The Hoover Company, 1988.

FIGURE 14.7   Instructions on using a computer program.

Changing Screen Colors

There are several color schemes available for MS–DOS Shell.

To choose a color scheme:

1. From the Options menu, choose Colors. The Color Scheme dialog box appears.

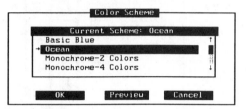

2. Click the scroll arrows until the color scheme you want comes into view, and then click that color scheme. Or use the UP ARROW or DOWN ARROW key to select the color scheme you want.

3. To preview the new color scheme, choose the Preview button. Choose the OK button to implement the color scheme.

Microsoft MS-DOS User's Guide and Reference for the MS-DOS Operating System Version 5.0 © 1991. Phoenix Technologies. Reprinted by permission.

choices, as in Figure 14.7, or to identify problems. Gear the type of visual you include to the task you want the reader to perform and to the reader's knowledge of that task. Note in Figure 14.8 how symbols (triangle, square, circle) graphically portray the proper use of fire extinguishers.

Guidelines for Using Visuals with Your Instructions

Regardless of the number and type of visuals you include, follow these guidelines to use them effectively.

1. Whenever possible, place the visual next to the step the reader is to perform, not on another page or buried at the bottom of the page. To gain the most from visuals, readers must be able to see the illustrations or diagrams immediately before and after reading the directions they clarify.
2. If you are using many visuals, assign each one a number (Figure 1, Figure 2, etc.) and in your directions tell readers where those visuals can be found ("to the left of these instructions"; "see the sketch at the right").
3. Make sure that the visual looks like the object the user is trying to assemble, maintain, run, or repair.
4. Wherever necessary, label parts of the visual. The drawing in Figure 14.3 does this very carefully for readers.
5. Inform readers if a part of an object is missing or reduced in size in your visual.
6. Set each visual off with white space so it is easy to find, read, and reread.

FIGURE 14.8   Instructions on the proper use of fire extinguishers.

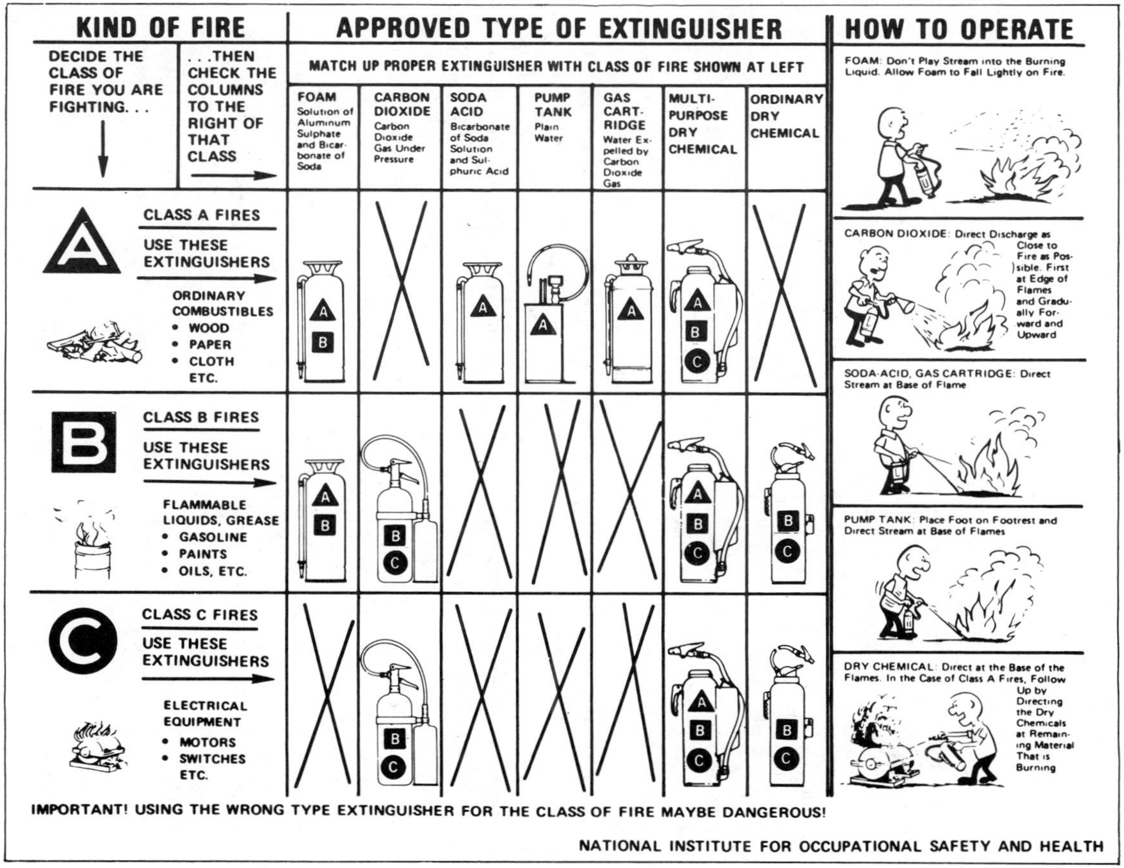

National Institute for Occupational Safety and Health.

The Four Parts of Instructions

Except for very short instructions, such as those illustrated in Figures 14.1–14.4, a set of instructions generally contains four main parts: (1) an introduction, (2) a list of equipment and materials, (3) the actual steps to perform the process, and (4) a conclusion (when necessary).

The Introduction

Whether you need an introduction depends on the particular process or machine you are describing. Short instructions require no introduction or only a brief one- or two-sentence introduction, such as the one in Figure 14.4. More complex instructions require lengthier introductions. For instance, a ninety-page manual may contain a two- or three-page introduction. An introduction should be proportional to the kinds of instructions that will be given. For example, instructions on how to sand a floor will not need a one-page introduction on how friction works.

The function of an introduction is to provide readers with enough *necessary* background information to understand why and how your instructions work. An introduction must make readers feel comfortable and well prepared before they turn to the actual steps. Accordingly, you can do one or all of the following in your introduction.

1. State why the instructions are useful for a specific audience. Here is an introduction from a safety procedure describing the protective lockout of equipment: "The purpose of this procedure is to provide plant electrical technicians with a uniform method of locking out machinery or equipment. This will prevent the possibility of setting moving parts in motion, energizing electrical lines, or opening valves while repair, set-up and adjustment, or cleaning work is in progress." Many instructions in training manuals contain introductions that stress the educational benefits to the user: "These instructions will serve as a valuable training tool for the beginning draftsperson, showing him or her the proper ways of preparing detailed drawings that will be useful in woodwork manufacturing today."

Figure 14.9 contains the introduction to a guide for nurses who have to be familiar with the features "Set-up, Operation, and Response to Alarms" for an infusion pump. Note how this "Overview Orientation" stresses the safety and convenience of this piece of equipment for the nursing staff as they meet patients' needs.

2. Indicate how a particular machine, procedure, or process works. A brief discussion of the "theory of operation" will help readers understand why something works the way your instructions say it should. Such discussion sometimes describes a scientific law or principle. The introduction to instructions on how to run a machine begins by stressing the function of the machine: "These instructions will teach you how to operate an autoclave. The autoclave is used to sterilize surgical instruments through live additive-free steam." An introduction to

FIGURE 14.9 Introduction to a guide for using an infusion pump.

1 Overview Orientation

The LifeCare PROVIDER 5500 System is a portable infusion pump, specially designed to deliver analgesic drugs, antibiotics, and chemotherapeutics.

The pump can be programmed in either milligrams or cubic centimeters, and in four different delivery configurations for greater nursing convenience and to tailor precisely the most effective regimen for each patient.

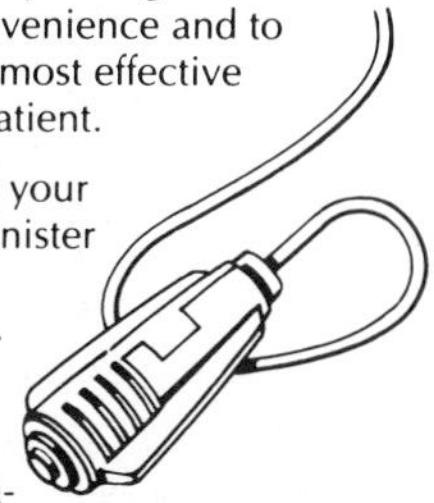

Bolus Mode allows your patient to self-administer analgesia within programmed limits.

This is the traditional PCA delivery, "analgesia-on-demand," based on the patient's need.

Continuous Mode delivers a continuous "background" infusion with no additional PCA doses permitted.

Continuous-plus-Bolus Mode allows the patient to self-administer a Bolus dose in addition to receiving a simultaneous Continuous dose infusion.

Intermittent Mode delivers a specific dose (in cc or mg) at intermittent intervals over 24 hours.

You can also establish the "lockout" interval, the frequency with which a patient may receive a Bolus dose of analgesic drug.

The PROVIDER 5500 System records all settings in memory and can be quickly re-programmed to save nursing time when repeating established protocols or changing fluid reservoirs.

The portable system operates on battery power.

To minimize tampering and discourage theft, there is an optional locking security lockbox that also secures the system to an IV pole.

The audible alarm signals in the event of a malfunction, and the digital readout describes the malfunction.

- Compact and lightweight.
- Delivery rates between 0.1 cc and 250 cc per hour, in 0.1-cc increments.

Display Panel

- Individual display indicators appear only during programming and operation.
- Only on a *selective* basis.
- Tone sounds when activated.
- Runs on BATTERY POWER ONLY.
- Disposable Primary IV set with integral infusion cartridge.

Reprinted by permission of Abbott Laboratories Hospital Products Division.

laboratory experiments usually begin with a discussion of reasons why a particular effect will occur or how something develops under certain circumstances. For example, the following paragraph introduces an experiment on osmosis, the process by which fluids flow from one cell to another.

> The distribution of water among the various fluid compartments of the body is determined in part by the solute [dissolved substance] content of these fluids. Since most solutes penetrate cell membranes relatively slowly, water, because of its abundance and permeability, plays an important role in establishing osmotic equilibrium between cells and their environment. When placed in a solution whose water concentration is different from that in its own protoplasm, a cell either gains or loses water. The process of direct migration of solvents through membranes is called osmosis. This experiment will demonstrate the movement of water across a membrane because of differences in solute concentration across the two sides.[1]

Figure 14.10 contains a description of a piece of exercise equipment from the owner's instructional manual. Note how precise yet clear the description of the StairMaster is for users. This description focuses on what the equipment does and how it accomplishes it for readers.

FIGURE 14.10   Introduction to an owner's manual for a piece of exercise equipment.

WHAT IS THE STAIRMASTER 4000 PT EXERCISE SYSTEM?

The StairMaster 4000 PT Exercise System is a vertical climbing machine that provides an aerobic workout equivalent to climbing stairs, without the inertial loads and skeletal trauma common to most aerobic activities.

The 4000 PT Exercise System is computer controlled to offer automated, timed workouts from 5 to 45 minutes, as selected by the user. There is a choice of eight preprogrammed workouts, each with ten levels of intensity. In addition, there is also a nonprogrammed (manual) workout that allows you to pace yourself or experiment with the various speeds. Also, users have the option of designing up to ten "customized" workouts that can be created and stored in the computer.

All of the workout programs on the StairMaster 4000 PT Exercise System feature computer-controlled speeds from 26 steps / minute to 138 steps / minute, based on 8-inch steps. The faster the speed, the greater the intensity level at which you are working. At the conclusion of your completed workout, the computer console displays the number of calories you burned while exercising, the equivalent number of floors you climbed, and the equivalent number of miles that you ran. If your machine has Revision 2.1 or 2.2 software, you can request this information and also request elapsed time, KGMs, and watts at any time during your workout and then return to the standard workout display.

From *Owner's Instructional Manual for the StairMaster 4000 PT Exercise System.*

---

[1] Byron A. Schottelius, John D. Thomson, and Dorothy D. Schottelius. *Physiology: Laboratory Manual,* 4th ed. St. Louis: C. V. Mosby, 1978: 11. Reprinted by permission.

3. Establish how long it should take the user to complete all steps of the instructions. If users know how long a procedure should take, they will be better able to judge whether they are doing it correctly—if they are waiting too long or not long enough between steps or if they are going too slowly or too quickly: "It should take about three and one-half hours from the time you start laying the floor tiles until the time they dry well enough to walk on." You may also have to advise readers when a certain procedure must be monitored or performed. Instructions for the EPS premium cartridge for laser printers, for example, tell purchasers that they must clean their cartridge corona at the time of installation and after every thousand copies.

4. Stress any advantages or benefits the reader will gain by performing the instructions. Make the reader feel good about buying or using your product by explaining how it will make a job easier to perform, save the reader time and money, or allow the reader to accomplish a job with fewer mistakes or false starts. Note how the following introduction to a set of instructions on using an auto dial/auto answer modem encourages the reader to want to learn how to operate this computer-based telephone system.

> Welcome to high-speed telecommunications and congratulations on choosing the Signalman EXPRESSi. You've made an excellent choice. The EXPRESSi is the ideal link between your computer and the ever-expanding world of information utilities, databases, electronic mail, bulletin boards, computer time sharing, and more.
>
> The EXPRESSi can be used in the IBM Personal Computer, PC XT, PC AT, and other PC-bus compatible computers. And because the EXPRESSi fits inside your PC, it saves valuable desk space and eliminates expensive, bulky cables.[2]

5. Inform the user about any special circumstances to which the instructions apply. Some instructions precede others or are used only on special occasions. Readers must be informed about those changes or emergency situations. A supervisor of a large chemical plant sent employees the memo contained in Figure 14.11 to describe operating procedures to be followed during energy shortages. Note the brief introduction emphasizing the special circumstances.

The instructions contained in the memos in Figures 14.11 (p. 538) and 14.12 (p. 539) are addressed to two different audiences, each with separate needs. The Hercules memo in Figure 14.11 was sent to a specific, technical audience—firefighters and supervisors—who needed instructions on a special process. Cliff Burgess's memo in Figure 14.12, on the other hand, went out to all Burton employees, a more diverse, rather than technical, group of readers. His helpful instructions do not require a list of equipment or materials or a description of steps in a process. Instead, his memo consists of an introduction, three bulleted instructions, and a conclusion. Study the annotations to Figure 14.12 to see how Cliff Burgess met the needs of his general, diverse audience.

---

[2] Courtesy of Anchor Automation, Inc., Chatsworth, CA.

FIGURE 14.11   Instructions alerting a technical audience to special circumstances.

TO: All Shift Supervisors
             All Firefighters

FROM: Robert A. Ferguson   *R. F.*

SUBJECT: Operating Procedures During Energy Shortages

DATE: October 10, 1994

The following policy has been formulated to aid in maintaining required pressures during periods of low wood flow and severe natural gas curtailment.

All boilers are equipped with lances to burn residue or no. 6 fuel oil as auxiliary fuels. When wood is short, no. 6 oil should be burned in no. 2 and no. 3 boilers at highest possible rate consistent with smoke standards. To do this, take these steps:

1. Put no. 6 oil on no. 3 boiler lances.

2. Shut down overfire air.

3. Shut down forced draft.

4. Turn off vibrators.

5. Keep grates covered with ashes or wood until ash cover exists.

These steps will result in an output of 25,000 to 35,000 lbs./hr. steam from no. 3 boiler and will force wood on down to no. 4 boiler.

If required, the same procedure can be repeated on no. 2 boiler.

Used by permission of Hercules, Inc.

FIGURE 14.12   An instructional memo listing safety precautions for a general audience.

 BURTON MANUFACTURING SYSTEMS
St. Louis, MO 63174

TO: All Burton Employees

FROM: Cliff Burgess, Environmental Safety Director *C.B.*

RE: Video Display Terminal (VDT) Safety Precautions

DATE: September 2, 1994

Introduction emphasizes reasons for instructions, gives non-technical explanation, and offers an analogy

You may experience some possible health risks in using your computer video display terminal (VDT). These risks include sleep disorders, behavioral changes, danger to reproductive system, and cancer. The source of any risk comes from the electromagnetic fields (EMFs) that surround anything that carries an electric current—for example, photocopiers, circuit breakers, and especially VDTs. Your computer monitor is a major source of EMFs. Magnetic fields go through walls as easily as light goes through glass.

Although EMFs can affect your health, you can considerably reduce your exposure to these fields by following these three simple steps:

Explains how to use equipment. Steps stand out through use of bullets, boldface, and spacing

- **Stay at least three feet (an arm's length) away from the front of your VDT.** (The magnetic field is reduced greatly with this amount of distance.)

- **Stay at least four feet away from the sides and back of someone else's VDT.** (The fields are weaker in the front of the **VDT** but much stronger everywhere else.)

- **Switch your VDT / computer off when you are not using it.** (If the computer has to remain on, be sure to switch off the monitor; screen savers do not affect the exposure to **EMFs**.)

Conclusion reassures readers they are acting safely by following instructions

Although there may be some health problems, they are not widespread. In any case, our environmental safety team will continue to monitor and investigate them. Observing the guidelines above, however, will help you to take all the necessary precautions in order to minimize your exposure to EMFs.

If you have any questions about these procedures or your exposure to EMFs, please call me for an appointment at Ext.–4311.

Not every introduction to a set of instructions will contain facts on all the categories of information listed on pages 534–537. Some instructions will require less detail. You will have to judge how much background information to give readers for the specific instructions you write.

List of Equipment and Materials

Immediately after the introduction, inform readers of all equipment or materials they will need. This list should be complete and clear. Do not wait until the readers are actually performing one of the steps in the instructions to tell them that a certain type of drill or a specific kind of chemical is required. They may have to stop what they are doing to find this equipment or material; moreover, the procedure may fail or present hazards if users do not have the right equipment at the specified time.

Do not expect your readers to know exactly what size, model, or quantity you have in mind. Tell them precisely. For example, if a Phillips screwdriver is necessary to complete one step, specify this type of screwdriver under the heading **"Equipment and Materials"**; do not just list "screwdriver." Here are some additional examples of unclear references to equipment and materials, with more helpful alternatives listed in parentheses after them: solution (0.7% NaCl solution); pencils (two engineering pencils); electrodes (four short platinum wire electrodes); file (cheese-grater file); sand (10-lb. bag of sand): needle (butterfly needle); water (2 gallons untreated sea water).

If you are concerned that readers will not understand why certain equipment or materials are used, give the explanation in parentheses after the item. For example, listing alcohol and cotton as materials needed to take a blood pressure might confuse readers not familiar with the uses of these materials. A clarifying comment after the materials such as "used to clean stethoscope headphones" would help. The following example, "Instructions for Absentee Voters," contains such helpful comments.

This absentee ballot package has been sent to you at your request. It contains the following items:

1. sample paper ballot (for information only)
2. official ballot (this is a punch card)
3. punching tool
4. envelope with attached declaration
5. addressed return envelope

Voters will know that the punch card is their official ballot and that it does not look like the sample ballot because of the parenthetical information in numbers 1 and 2. The point is reinforced later in the directions by this statement.

IMPORTANT

- Punch only with tool provided, never with a pencil or pen.
- Your vote is recorded by punching this ballot card, not by marking the paper ballot.
- Do not return the sample paper ballot.

Read the following instructions on refinishing a piece of wood, which provide a very detailed list of materials used to clean and smooth wood surfaces.[3]

Preparing the Surface

Before you attempt to refinish a wood item, be sure the surface is smooth and free from dirt, dust, and grease.

Materials
The following materials are suitable for cleaning and smoothing wood surfaces:

Abrasives

- *Sandpaper.* Sandpaper is not made of sand as the name suggests. It is made of various kinds of abrasive material applied to paper or cloth backing and is made in sheet, drum, belt, and other forms. Sandpaper comes in various grades ranging from No. 4/0 to No. 1. No. 4/0 is used when an extra fine finish is required; No. 2/0 for a fine finish; No. 1/2 for rubbing down undercoats of paint and varnish in preparation for final finish; and No.1 to No. 3 for sanding down old coats of paint too badly chipped to repaint.
- *Sanding disks.* Sanding disks are flat, circular pieces of sandpaper of various types, sizes, and coarseness for use on a power sander. These disks can also be used either on a disk or rotary hand sander.
- *Commercial steel wool.* Steel wool is a fluffy or wool-like mass of steel turnings. It is made in grades No. 00, 0, 1, and 3, ranging from extra fine to coarse. It is a mild abrasive for rubbing down and smoothing wood and is well suited for removal of light rust from metal prior to repainting.

Cloth and Sponges

- *Jute burlap.* Jute burlap is a coarse, heavy, loose-woven material, used for all general purpose cleaning.
- *Osnaburg cotton cloth.* Osnaburg cloth is coarse and heavy, used as a substitute for jute burlap and serves the same purposes.
- *Cotton wiping cloth.* This cloth is relatively free from lint. It is used as a substitute for cotton waste, especially when lint deposits are undesirable, and as a substitute for sponges when washing wood and metal work. It can be used to apply strong soap, lye, soda ash, or other solutions, which destroy sponges quickly.
- *Cellulose sponge.* This is a synthetic material. It *cannot* be used with solutions

---

[3] U.S. Army Manual FM 43-4, *Repair of Wood Items.*

The Steps in Instructions

The heart of your instructions will consist of clearly distinguished steps that readers must follow to achieve the desired results. To make sure that you help your readers understand your steps, observe the following rules.

1. Put the steps in their correct order. If a step is out of order or is missing, the entire set of instructions can be wrong or, worse yet, dangerous, as the cartoon in Figure 14.13 humorously illustrates. Double-check your steps before you write them down. Each step should be numbered to indicate its correct place in the sequence of events you are describing. Never put an asterisk (*) before or after a step to make the reader look somewhere else for information. If the information is important, put it in your instructions; if it is not, delete it.

FIGURE 14.13   A cartoon emphasizing the importance of putting instructions in proper order.

2. Group closely related activities into one step. Sometimes closely related actions are grouped into one step to help the reader coordinate activities and to emphasize their being done at the same time, in the same place, or with the same equipment. Study the following instructions listing the receptionist's duties performed by the unit secretary in a hospital.

1. Greet patients warmly and make them feel welcome. Never fall into the trap of groaning and saying "not another one." Remember the patient probably did not want to come to the hospital in the first place.
2. Check the identity bracelet against the summary sheet and addressograph plate. If the bracelet is not on the patient's wrist, place it there immediately. Set about correcting any errors you may find in any of this information at once.
3. If asked, escort the patient to his or her room. Explain the signal light, answer any questions, and introduce the patient and roommate, if any.
4. Notify the head nurse and/or the nurse assigned to that room of the patient's arrival.
5. Notify the admitting physician by phone of the patient's arrival and room. If the patient lacks admission orders, mention this to the physician's secretary at this time.[4]

Note how step 3 contains all the duties the unit secretary performs once patients are taken to their rooms. It is easier to consolidate all the activities that take place in the room—explaining the signal light, answering questions, making introductions—than to list each as a separate step. But be careful that you do not overwork a single step. To combine steps 4 and 5 would be wrong (and impossible) because those two distinct steps require the unit secretary to speak to someone in person and to make a phone call. These two actions are two separate stages in a process.

Similarly, instructions on how to use a fax machine are clearer when distinct steps are stated separately. The first set of instructions below incorrectly tells users how to transmit a fax by combining steps that must be performed separately. Step 2 asks users to pick up the phone and then dial the number—two separate actions. Step 3 asks users to press the button and return the handset, again two actions that cannot be performed simultaneously.

Incorrect:
Step 1. Load the paper into the outgoing document slot, adjusting the paper guides to the appropriate width.
Step 2. Pick up the telephone handset and listen for a dial tone. When you hear the dial tone, dial the number of the receiving fax machine.
Step 3. When the receiving fax machine answers the ring, press the start button. After the transmission is completed, return the handset to its cradle.

Correct:
Step 1. Load the paper into the outgoing document slot, adjusting the paper guides to the appropriate width.
Step 2. Pick up the telephone handset and listen for a dial tone.
Step 3. When you hear a dial tone, dial the number of the receiving fax machine.
Step 4. When the receiving fax machine answers the ring, press the start button.
Step 5. After the transmission is completed, return the handset to its cradle.

---

[4] Myra S. Willson, *A Textbook for Ward Clerks and Unit Secretaries.* St. Louis: C. V. Mosby, 1979: 70. Reprinted by permission.

Don't divide an action into two steps if it has to be done in one. For example, instructions showing how to light a furnace would not list as two steps actions that must be performed simultaneously to avoid a possible explosion.

Incorrect: **Step 1.** Depress the lighting valve.
               Step 2. Hold a match to the pilot light.

Correct: **Step 1.** Depress the lighting valve while holding a match to the pilot light.

Similarly, do not separate two steps of a computer command that must be performed simultaneously.

Incorrect: **Step 1.** Press the CONTROL key.
               Step 2. Press the BREAK key.

Correct: **Step 1.** While holding down the CONTROL key, press the BREAK key.

3. Give the reader hints on how best to accomplish the procedure. Obviously, you cannot do this for every step, but if there is a chance that the reader might run into difficulties or may not anticipate a certain reaction, by all means provide assistance. For example, telling readers that a certain aroma or color is to be expected in an experiment will reassure them that they are on the right track. Particular techniques on how to operate or service equipment are also helpful: "If there is blood on the transducer diaphragm, dip the transducer in a blood solvent, such as hydrogen peroxide, Hemosol, etc." If readers have a choice of materials or procedures in a given step, you might want to list those that would give the best performance: "Several thin coats will give a better finish than one heavy one."

4. State whether one step directly influences (or jeopardizes) the outcome of another. Because all steps in a set of instructions are interrelated, you could not (and should not have to) tell readers how every step affects another. But stating specific relationships is particularly helpful when dangerous or highly intricate operations are involved. You will save the reader time, and you will stress the need for care. Forewarned is forearmed. Here is an example.

    Step 2: Tighten fan belt. Failure to tighten the fan belt will cause it to loosen and come off when the lever is turned in step 5 below.

Do not wait until step 5 to tell readers that you hope they did a good job in tightening the fan belt. That information comes after the fact.

Insert Warning, Caution, and Note Statements Where Necessary

A warning statement tells readers that a step, if not prepared for or performed properly, can endanger their safety.

WARNING: UNPLUG THE MONITOR BEFORE CLEANING ANY
PART WITH DAMP CLOTH.

DO NOT APPLY PRESSURE UNTIL SAFETY VALVE IS
COMPLETELY SEALED.

A caution statement tells readers to take certain precautions: wear protective clothing, check an instrument panel carefully, use special care in running a machine, measure weights or dosages exactly, save a document on a computer.

CAUTION
MAKE SURE BRAKE SHOES WON'T RUB TIRE AND THAT
SHOES MATE WELL WITH RIM WHEN BRAKES ARE APPLIED.

BE SURE TO ENTER CORRECT CODE FOR **WORD SMART.**
KEYBOARDING THE WRONG CODE WILL ERASE DOCUMENT.

Warning and caution statements are very important for legal and safety reasons. Including them is more than a courtesy for readers and is *not* optional. They are necessary to protect lives and property. In fact, you and your company can be sued if you fail to notify users of your product or service of potentially dangerous conditions. Follow these three guidelines in using warning and caution statements in your instructions.

1. **Put warning and caution statements in the right place.** Place them immediately before the step to which they pertain. When they are out of place you risk placing your readers and/or their equipment in danger. If you insert a warning or caution statement too early, the reader may overlook it by the time he or she comes to the step to which it applies. And if you put the notification too late, you almost certainly expose the reader to danger and the equipment to breakdown.
2. **Put warning and caution statements in the right format.** Because of the extremely important information they impart, warning and caution statements should be graphically set apart from the rest of the instructions. There should be no chance that readers will overlook them. Put these statements in capital letters, in boldface type, in boxes, in different colors (red is especially effective for warnings, yellow for caution). Use one or all of these devices. Distinc-

tive symbols, such as a skull and crossbones or an exclamation point inside a triangle, often precede a warning notation.

3. **Include enough explanation to help readers know what to watch out for and what precautions they must take.** Do not just insert the word WARNING or CAUTION. Explain what the dangerous condition is and how to avoid it. Look at the examples of warnings and cautions in Figures 14.14 and 14.15 (p. 549).

Warning and caution statements should not be used just because you want to emphasize a point. Putting too many of these statements in your instructions will decrease the dramatic impact they should have on readers. Use them sparingly— only when absolutely necessary—so readers will not be tempted to bypass them.

Unlike warnings and cautions, a *note* statement simply adds a comment to clarify instructions.

Note: All models in 3500 series have a hex nut in the upper right, not left, corner.

 Drive B disk indicator will glow and the drive will make a few clicking sounds as the disk is formatted.

 At 20 degrees F, a battery uses about 68 percent of its power.

The instructions in Figure 14.14 on how to paint a garage floor contain steps that offer hints on how best to do the job, comment on how one step affects another, and issue warning, caution, and note statements. Not every instruction requires this amount of detail. Use such comments and signals only when the procedure you are describing calls for them and when they will help your readers.

The Conclusion

Not every set of instructions requires a conclusion. For short instructions containing a few simple steps, such as those in Figures 14.1–14.4, no conclusion is necessary. These instructions usefully end with the last step the reader must perform. For longer, more involved jobs, a conclusion can help readers finish the job with confidence and accuracy. For example, a short conclusion like the following might help users who have just followed the step-by-step instructions on painting a garage floor given in Figure 14.14.

With proper care this procedure should have to be repeated only once every three years. To keep the floor in top shape, sweep it at least twice a month to prevent gritty materials such as sand from scaling the painted surface. If possible, wipe up grease and oil immediately to prevent them from soaking into the paint. Make sure you dispose of rags properly to avoid chance of fire.

FIGURE 14.14   Instructions on how to paint a garage floor.

Cleaning the Floor

1. Remove all objects from the floor.
2. Scrape areas where there is old chipped paint with a metal scraper. For hard-to-reach places such as corners or underneath pipes, use a 3-inch wire brush. New paint will not stick to the floor if old paint is not first removed.
3. Sweep the floor first with a broom; then to make sure that all particles of dust and dirt are removed, use a vacuum sweeper.
4. Open all windows for proper ventilation. Fumes from cleaning solution used in Step 5 should not be inhaled.

CAUTION: USE PROTECTIVE EYEWEAR AND RUBBER GLOVES FOR NEXT STEP TO PROTECT SKIN FROM IRRITATION.

 WARNING: DO NOT USE DETERGENTS CONTAINING AMMONIA. AMMONIA ADDED TO THESE INGREDIENTS WILL CAUSE AN EXPLOSION.

5. Mop the entire floor with a solution composed of the following ingredients:
   1/3 box of Floorex
   1 quart of bleach
   10 quarts of water
   1 cup powdered detergent
   Note: Do not worry if the mixture does not appear soapy; it does not need suds to work.
6. For any grease spots that remain, sprinkle enough dry Floorex powder to cover them entirely. Scrub these spots with a 5-inch wire brush.
7. Rinse the entire floor thoroughly with water to remove cleanser. Allow floor to dry (**30** min.) before painting.

Painting the Floor

8. Mix the paint with a stirrer ten or fifteen times until the color is even.
   Note: If the paint has not already been shaken by machine before being opened, shake the can for about three minutes, open, and stir the contents for about five to ten minutes or until the paint is mixed.
9. Pour the paint into the paint tray.
10. With the 3-inch paint brush, paint the floor around the baseboard. Come out at least two to three inches so that roller used in the next step will not touch the baseboard.
11. Paint the rest of the floor with a roller attached to an extension handle. A roller handles much more easily than a brush and distributes the paint more smoothly. Move the roller in the same direction each time. Overlap each row painted by one-half inch to avoid spaces between rows of paint.

FIGURE 14.14 **(Continued)**

> 12. Allow two hours to dry. The floor will be ready to walk on.
>
> > **CAUTION:** DO NOT DRIVE VEHICLES ONTO FLOOR FOR 24 HOURS. TIRES WILL PICK UP NEW PAINT.

When they are necessary, conclusions can help the reader in a variety of ways. They might either provide a succinct wrap-up of what the reader has done or end with a single sentence of congratulation, or they can reassure readers as the conclusion in Cliff Burgess's memo (Figure 14.12) does. A conclusion might also tell readers what to expect once a job is finished, describe the results of a test, or explain how a piece of equipment is supposed to operate. Furthermore, conclusions can also give readers practical advice on how to maintain a piece of equipment or how to follow a certain procedure, as the conclusion for painting a garage floor does on page 546.

Instructions: Some Final Advice

Perhaps the most important piece of advice to leave you with is this: Do not take *anything* for granted when you have to write a set of instructions. It is wrong and on occasion dangerous to assume that your readers have performed the procedure before, that they will automatically supply missing or "obvious" information, or that they will easily anticipate your next step. No one ever complained that a set of instructions was too clear or too easy to follow.

To make sure that your instructions are clear and complete, draft, revise, edit, proofread, and test them with your reader in mind. Give the reader all the appropriate information needed for the task—and in the right order. Make sure your instructions have all the parts the reader must have to do the job safely and accurately: introduction, list of materials, the steps, and conclusion. Use visuals to clarify a tricky step or to simplify a procedure, and always insert warning, caution, or note statements where needed.

Figure 14.15 contains the final example of instructions in this chapter. Sent to "concerned residents," or a nontechnical audience, these instructions explain the possible safety hazards of a pipeline leak and clearly outline the precautionary measures residents need to take if they recognize such a danger. These instructions—in both content and format—illustrate many of the guidelines this chapter has emphasized. Study Figure 14.15 to review these guidelines and to prepare for writing similarly clear and helpful instructions for your audience.

FIGURE 14.15   Instructions on pipeline safety for a nontechnical audience.

ENTERPRISE PRODUCTS COMPANY
Houston, Texas

Dear Resident:

We operate pipelines through your area and we work hard to keep them safe and secure. Our pipelines are designed, installed, tested, operated, patrolled, and maintained to promote your safety and to prevent hazards.

Unforeseen damage can cause any pipeline to leak. That is why we want you, our neighbors, to know how to recognize a pipeline leak, what to do if you ever notice a leak, and how to report it quickly so it can be repaired. Our aim is to prevent any hazard to you and your property.

You can help by **first immediately contacting your local police and fire departments.** Then contact us at the **phone number listed below (and on the handy emergency sticker enclosed).**

You have probably seen signs like the one pictured on this page. They mark our pipeline route. Please remember that pipelines normally are buried and usually are not visible, so it is easy to forget that they are present.

Our pipelines operate around the clock, carrying vital products to markets for treatment and distribution. Their uninterrupted operation is important to all of us. If our pipelines are damaged, or if leaks go unreported, a very real hazard may exist. Your attention and assistance will help us protect your safety and our country's energy supplies.

Report any pipeline leak to:

Enterprise Products Company
P. O. Box 4324
Houston, Texas 77210
In Texas phone: 1-800-392-2880
Out of Texas phone: 1-800-231-2809
Chemtrec phone: 1-800-424-9300

<u>Pipeline Markers (Signs)</u>

Take a close look at the sign pictured above. These signs mark our pipeline route and stand either on top of or very near the underground pipeline. They are there to warn the public and to help our company patrol and monitor the pipelines.

FIGURE 14.15   (Continued)

How to Recognize a Pipeline Leak

Often you can **see** a pipeline leak, but unless our product has been odorized—and many are not—you cannot usually smell the leak. You can detect a leak if **you** notice:

1. A blowing or hissing sound
2. A white vapor cloud
3. Dust blowing from a hole in the ground
4. Continued bubbling in wet or flooded areas
5. Patches of dead vegetation (grass, bushes, trees, etc.)
6. Areas of abnormally hard or dry soil (discolored, cracked, or "different" looking)
7. A gas or "smelly oil" odor
8. Vapors or "clouds" that look like ground fog (pipeline gases are heavier than air, and they hug the ground)
9. Fire burning on or above the ground
10. A rainbow-colored sheen on the surface of water

What to Do

1. Shut off and abandon all equipment you are operating that cause any sparks, including motor vehicles, electric motors, and any engine in or near the area.
2. Avoid open flames, and do not smoke.
3. Evacuate the area immediately and guard against entry by unsuspecting parties. **Secure the aid of local law enforcement officials to isolate the area, if necessary,** and telephone us at the toll-free numbers given on the previous page RIGHT AWAY. **These numbers are also listed on the warning signs that mark our pipeline.**

Tell us where you are and what you have noticed. We need this information to locate and repair the leak. Do not worry about "getting in trouble" when you phone. We intend to repair the leak, not blame anybody.

What **NOT** to Do

1. **Do not** try to "put out" a pipeline fire or "plug" a leak. All products are under pressure and require specially trained people to handle situations such as this.
2. **Do not** try to turn or operate any pipeline valves.
3. **Do not** attempt to extinguish a gas fire. **Secure the aid of firefighters to protect adjacent property,** if necessary.

The worst thing you could do is . . . nothing. A pipeline leak can be hazardous if not controlled in a timely fashion by professionals. For your safety, be aware that serious personal injury and property damage can result from your disregarding warnings and failing to follow instructions. People who are specifically trained to handle pipeline leaks are on 24-hour alert to deal with potential pipeline problems and are prepared to respond safely and quickly.

We want to be good neighbors, and we are confident that you feel the same way.

FIGURE 14.15   (Continued)

Who Should Report?

ANYONE observing indications of a pipeline leak should report the leak by calling the appropriate toll-free telephone number provided on page 1 of this letter. Property owners, home owners, tenants, law enforcement agencies, fire departments, contractors, hunters, or anyone can promote safety by reporting any of the indications. That's what good neighbors do.

Excavating or Blasting?

If you plan digging, probing, blasting, or any other activity that you suspect could damage our pipeline (or any marked pipeline), please phone **first,** before you begin. Any such activity near or on pipeline routes can be dangerous and can cause damage and injury unless proper precautions are taken. For a safer operation, check before you dig.

Even if you should cause what seems like only minor damage to a pipeline, notify us immediately. A gouge, scrape, dent, crease, or other damage to a pipeline or coating may one day cause a break or leak. So it is imperative that we evaluate and repair any damage to our pipeline.

A Word to the Wise

Tampering with pipelines carries severe penalties. Pipelines are safe, but nothing in this world is immune from "curious" people. Exercise caution and use common sense. Encourage others to do the same. Ask your local sheriff about the legal consequences of tampering with pipelines. If our pipelines are damaged, you, the public, or your employees may suffer injury, equipment may be destroyed, or available energy supplies may be lost. Thank you very much for your cooperation.

For More Information

Write or call:
Associate Administrator for Pipeline Safety
Department of Transportation
Washington, D. C. 20590
(202) 366-4595

Reprinted by permission of Enterprise Products Company.

✓ Revision Checklist

Careful revision is especially important in the preparation of safe and effective instructions. Use the following questions to help you revise your instructions.

1. Have I effectively analyzed my intended audience's background, especially why and how they will use my instructions?
2. Have I tested my instructions to make sure they include all necessary steps in their proper chronological sequence?
3. Have I made sure all measurements, distances, times, and relationships are precise and correct?
4. Is the language of my instructions appropriate for my audience? Have I made sure that I avoided technical terms if my audience is not a group of specialists in my field?
5. Have I used the imperative mood throughout my instructions? Have I made each of my sentences clear and short?
6. Have I made sure I eliminated ambiguity or anything unclear from my instructions?
7. Have I used numbers or bullets to label each step? Have I used connective words—*first, then, next*—to indicate the order in which each step is done?
8. Have I chosen or created effective visuals where necessary? Are these visuals clearly labeled and placed next to the step(s) to which they apply?
9. If an introduction is necessary, is it proportionate to the length and complexity of my instructions and does it meet my readers' needs?
10. If necessary, have I included a complete list of tools and materials my audience needs to carry out the instructions?
11. Did I use warning, caution, and note statements where necessary? Have I set warning and caution statements apart so that they are easily seen and read?
12. Did I supply a conclusion that summarizes what readers should have done or reassures them that they have completed the job satisfactorily?

Exercises

1. Bring to class two examples of short directions that require no introduction, list of materials and equipment, or conclusion. Look for these two examples on labels, carton panels, or backs of envelopes. Evaluate the effectiveness of these instructions by commenting on how precise, direct, and useful they are.

2. Find at least one example of long instructions containing an introduction, list of materials and equipment, statements of warning, caution, or note, and a conclusion. Bring this example to class and be prepared to show how the various steps in this set of instructions follow the principles outlined on pages 542–546 in this chapter. You can find a set of full instructions in many technical manuals and in some manuals to help consumers assemble or maintain large or complex home appliances.

3. Find a set of instructions that does not contain any visuals, but which you think should have some graphic material to make it clearer. Design those visuals yourself and indicate where they should appear in the instructions.

4. From a technical manual in your field or from an owner's manual, locate a set of instructions that you think are poorly written and illustrated. In a memo to your instructor, explain why those instructions are unclear, confusing, or badly formatted. Then revise the instructions to make them easier for the reader to carry out. Submit the poor instructions with your revision.

5. Write a set of instructions in numbered steps (or in paragraph format) on one of the following relatively simple activities.
   a. tying a shoe
   b. brushing your teeth
   c. unlocking a door with a key
   d. making a long distance collect telephone call
   e. planting a tree or shrub
   f. logging on to a computer
   g. removing a stain from clothing
   h. pumping gas into a car
   i. building a campfire
   j. checking a book out of the library
   k. parallel parking a car
   l. shifting gears in a car
   m. photocopying a page from a book

6. Working alone or as part of a collaborative writing team, write a set of full instructions on one of the following more complex topics. Identify your audience. Include an appropriate introduction, a list of equipment and materials, numbered steps with necessary warning, caution, and note statements, and an effective conclusion. Also include whatever visuals you think will help your audience.
   a. outfitting a kayak for a sea expedition
   b. changing a flat tire
   c. designing a computer program
   d. developing black-and-white film
   e. shaving a patient for surgery
   f. changing the oil and oil filter in a car
   g. making a blueprint
   h. installing a wind turbine on a roof

    i. filling out an income tax return

    j. surveying a parcel of land

    k. pruning hedges

    l. jumping a dead car battery

    m. using the Heimlich maneuver to help a choking individual

    n. filleting a fish

    o. arranging a footlocker for inspection

    p. taking someone's blood pressure

    q. changing a cash register tape

    r. finding and plugging a leak in a tire

    s. taking reservations at a hotel/motel

    t. painting a car

    u. cooking a roast

    v. flossing a patient's teeth after cleaning

    w. sewing on a button

7. Write an appropriate introduction and conclusion for the set of instructions you wrote for either Exercise 5 or Exercise 6 on p. 553.

8. The following set of instructions is confusing, vague, and out of order. Rewrite these instructions to make them clear, easy to follow, and correct. Make sure that each step follows the guidelines outlined in this chapter.

Reupholstering a Piece of Furniture

(1) Although it might be difficult to match the worn material with the new material, you might as well try.

(2) If you cannot, remove the old material.

(3) Take out the padding.

(4) Take out all of the tacks before removing the old covering. You might want to save the old covering.

(5) Measure the new material with the old, if you are able to.

(6) Check the frame, springs, webbing, and padding.

(7) Put the new material over the old.

(8) Check to see if it matches.

(9) You must have the same size as before.

(10) Look at the padding inside. If it is lumpy, smooth it out.

(11) You will need to tack all the sides down. Space your tacks a good distance apart.

(12) When you spot wrinkles, remove the tacks.

(13) Caution: in step 11 directly above, do not drive your tacks all the way through. Leave some room.

(14) Work from the center to the edge in step 11 above.

(15) Put the new material over the old furniture.

P.S. Use strong cords whenever there are tacks. Put the cords under the nails so that they hold.

Proposals

A proposal is a detailed plan of action that a writer submits to a reader or group of readers for approval. These readers are usually in a position of authority—supervisors, managers, department heads, company buyers, elected officials, civic leaders—to endorse or reject the writer's plan. Proposals are among the most important types of job-related writing. Their acceptance can lead to improved working conditions, a more efficient and economical business, additional jobs and business for a company, or a safer and more attractive environment.

Writing Successful Proposals

Proposals are written for many purposes. You might write a proposal to your boss seeking authorization to purchase a new piece of equipment for the office; for example, a copier with a reduction mode to handle the special printing needs you see on the job. William Tisch's memo in Figure 2.5 (page 36) is a proposal persuading his boss to purchase a fax machine. Proposals also routinely go to potential customers offering a product or a service. For instance, you might write a proposal to a manager of a high school cafeteria to convince her to stock your company's brand of potato chips or to a fire chief offering to supply special firefighting gear. Government agencies (e.g., Department of the Interior, Department of Health and Human Services) regularly request and receive proposals from individuals hoping to gain funding for research projects that might study the mating and feeding habits of a particular species or determine the mercury levels at a certain lake.

Depending on the job, proposals can vary greatly in size and in scope. A proposal to your employer could easily be conveyed in a memo of a page or two. A proposal to do a research project for a class assignment can also be successfully completed in a brief memo. To propose doing a small job for a prospective client—redecorating a waiting room in an accountant's office—a letter with information on costs, materials, and a timetable might suffice. But for an extremely large and costly job—constructing a ten-story office building, for example—the customer would require a detailed report hundreds of pages long together with appendixes containing sections on engineering specifications, detailed budgets, and even résumés of all key personnel working on the project.

A discussion of long, elaborate proposals is beyond the scope of this chapter. But the principles and techniques of audience analysis, organization, and drafting that this chapter does cover apply equally well to any longer project you may be called on to prepare individually or as part of a team.

Proposals Are Persuasive Plans

Proposals, whether large or small, have one thing in common. They must be highly persuasive to succeed. Without your audience's approval, your plan will never go into effect, however accurate and important you think it is. Through the details of your proposal you must convince readers that your plan will help them either improve their businesses or generally make their jobs easier. The tone of your proposal should be "Here is what I can do for you." Stress the precise benefits your plan has for the reader. Show readers how approving your plan will save them time and money or will improve their employees' morale or their customer relations.

Competition is fierce in the world of work, and a persuasive proposal frequently determines which company receives a contract. Demonstrate to your reader why your plan is better—more efficient, practical, economical—than a competitor's. In a sense, a proposal combines the persuasiveness of a sales letter (see Chapter 7), the documentation of a report (see Chapters 16 and 17), and the binding power of a contract, for if the reader accepts your proposal, he or she will expect you to live up to its terms to the letter.

Proposals Frequently Are Collaborative Efforts

Like many other types of business and technical writing, proposals often are the product of teamwork and sharing. Even a short internal proposal (p. 561-568) such as that found in Figure 15.3 (pp. 562-565) is often researched and put together by more than one individual in a company or agency. Before looking at the specific types of proposals, we might find it useful to see how collaboration is a vital part of the evolution of a proposal. Figure 15.1 describes the behind-the-scenes joint effort that went into Joycelyn Woolfolk's preparation of a memo proposal for her boss about starting a professional journal. Woolfolk wanted her employer to authorize this new journal, which would incorporate a newsletter

FIGURE 15.1   An account of how one proposal originated and was collaboratively prepared.

The idea to start a regional magazine was first expressed in passing by our vice president, a member of our senior management, who is interested in getting more and higher-level visibility for our regional office. Several other regional offices in our company have recently put out fairly attractive magazines, and one office in particular has earned a lot of good publicity.

The public affairs manager (my boss) and I quickly picked up on the vice president's hint and began to formulate ways to investigate the need for such a publication and ways to substantiate our recommendation. For several weeks the public affairs manager and I had a number of conversations addressing specific points, such as the kind of documentation our proposal would need, what our resources for researching the question were, what our capabilities would be for producing such a publication, and so on. We were guided by the twofold goal of getting the vice president's approval and, ideally, meeting a genuine market need.

After discussions with the public affairs manager, I met with members of my staff to ask them to do the following tasks:

1. review existing HMO publications and report on whether there was already a regional magazine for the Northwest
2. develop, administer, and analyze a readership survey for current subscribers to our newsletter, which would potentially be incorporated into the new magazine
3. formulate general design concepts for the magazine that we can implement without increasing staff, while still producing the quality magazine the vice president wants
4. prepare a budget for projected costs
5. consult with experts (actuaries, physicians, nurses) on our staff about topics of interest

I requested memos and other written documentation from my staff members about most of these tasks, and I then used that information to draft the proposal that eventually would go to the vice president, and perhaps even to the president's office.

I revised my draft several times and, as a courtesy, had my staff look over each draft for feedback and proofreading. Based on their comments, I made further revisions and did careful editing. My boss (the public affairs manager) reviewed my proposal and also revised and edited it in minor ways innumerable times. Ultimately, the proposal will go out as a memo from me to my boss, who will then send it under her name to the vice president.

The copy of my proposal may be further revised in response to the vice president's comments when she gets it. She may use some portion or all of it in another memo from her to the president, or she may write her own proposal to the president supporting her argument with the specifics from my proposal. The vice president will word the proposal to fit the expressed values and mission of our regional office as well as to provide information that addresses budgetary and policy concerns for which her readers (our company president and board members) have final responsibility.

This is how a proposal started and where it will eventually end.

her office currently prepares. A publications coordinator for a large, regional health maintenance organization (HMO), Woolfolk supervises a small staff and reports directly to the public affairs manager, who in turn is responsible to the vice president of the regional office. The vice president is ultimately accountable to the president and board of directors. As you will see from reading Woolfolk's scenario, communication moves up and down the chain of command, with participation at all levels.

Often, individual employees will pull together information from their separate areas (such as finance, marketing, sales, and transportation) and put it into a proposal that each team member then reads and revises until the team agrees that the document is ready to be released.

Types of Proposals

Proposals are classified according to how they originate and where they are sent after they are written. Distinctions are made between *solicited* and *unsolicited* proposals based on how they originate and between *internal* and *external* proposals based on where they are sent. Depending on your audience and your purpose, you may write an internal solicited or unsolicited proposal; or you may write an external solicited or unsolicited proposal.

Solicited and Unsolicited Proposals

When a company has a particular problem to be solved or a job to be done, it will solicit, or invite, proposals. The company will notify you and other competitors by preparing a Request for Proposals (an *RFP*), which is a set of instructions that specify the exact type of work to be done along with guidelines on how and when the company wants the work completed. Some RFPs are long and full of legal requirements and conditions. Others, like the example in Figure 15.2, are more concise. RFPs are mailed to firms with track records in the area the company wants the work done. RFPs are also printed in trade publications to attract the highest number of qualified bidders for the job. The U.S. government publishes RFPs in the *Federal Register,* while private companies sometimes send their RFPs to *Business Daily.*

An RFP helps you to know what the customer wants. It is often extremely detailed and even tells you how the company wants the proposal prepared; for example, what information is to be included (on backgrounds, personnel, equipment, budgets), where it needs to appear, and even how many copies of the proposal you have to submit. Your own proposal will be judged according to how well you fulfill the terms of the RFP. For that reason, follow the directions in the RFP exactly. (Note how the solicited proposal in Figure 15.4 [p. 569] directly refers to the terms of the RFP.)

With an unsolicited proposal, you—not the reader—make the first move. You identify a problem for readers and prepare a proposal to solve it. Doing that is not as difficult as it sounds. See how the writers of the unsolicited proposals in Figures 15.3 and 15.5 (pp. 572-574) identify a problem for their readers.

FIGURE 15.2   A sample RFP.

REQUEST FOR PROPOSALS

Mesa Community College solicits proposals to construct and to install fifty individual study carrels in its Holmes Memorial Library. These carrels must be highly serviceable and conform to all specification standards of the ALA. Proposals should include the precise measurements of the carrels to be installed, the specific acoustical and lighting benefits, and the types and amount of storage space offered. Work on constructing and installing the carrels must be completed no later than the start of the Fall Semester, August 29, 1994. Proposals should include a schedule of when different phases of work will be completed and an itemized budget for labor, materials, equipment, and necessary tests to ensure high quality acoustical performance. Contractors should state their qualifications, including a description of similar recent work and a list of references. Proposals should be submitted in triplicate no later than May 16, 1994, to:

> Mrs. Barbara Feldstein-Archer
> Director of the Library
> Mesa Community College
> Mesa, NV 89203-0996

Before you write an unsolicited proposal, though, you may want to speak with an appropriate manager at the company or write an inquiry letter to that individual to determine if he or she would be interested in receiving your proposal. Many times a company is eager to learn about a problem and how the writer proposes to solve it for the company. Sometimes the company will even help by giving you information through an interview or a tour. If so, acknowledge that assistance in your proposal.

Unlike a solicited proposal in which the company knows about the problem, an unsolicited proposal has to convince readers in the first place that there is a problem and in the second place that you and your firm are the ones to solve it. Accordingly, your unsolicited proposal has to document the existence of the problem and demonstrate how solving it is in the best interest of the readers. If they accept your identification of the problem, you have greatly increased your chances of their accepting your plan to solve it. On the other hand, if you do not convince readers that a problem exists, your solution, and hence your proposal, will be rejected or ignored.

Internal and External Proposals

An internal proposal is written to a decision maker within your own organization. As you will see on pages 562–565, this type of proposal can deal with a variety of topics, including changing a policy or procedure or requesting additional personnel or equipment.

An external proposal is sent to a decision maker outside of your company. It might go to a potential client you have never worked for or to a previous or current client. An external proposal can also be sent to a government funding agency such as the Department of Agriculture. External proposals tend to be more formal than internal ones.

Guidelines for Writing a Successful Proposal

Regardless of the type of proposal you are called on to write, the following guidelines will help you to persuade your audience to approve your plan. Refer to these guidelines both before and while you formulate your plan.

1. Approach writing a proposal as a problem-solving activity. Your goal is to solve a problem that affects the reader. Do not lose sight of the problem as you plan and write your proposal. Everything in your proposal should relate to the problem, and the organization of your proposal should reflect your ability as a problem-solver. Psychologically, make the reader feel confident that you can solve the problem.

2. Regard your audience as skeptical readers. Even though you offer a plan that you think will benefit readers, do not be overconfident that they will automatically accept it as the best and only way to proceed. To determine the feasibility of your plan, readers will question everything you say. They will withhold their approval if your proposal contains errors, omissions, or inconsistencies. Consequently, try to examine your proposal from the readers' point of view. Note how Joycelyn Woolfolk considers her multiple audience's needs and possible objections in Figure 15.1.

3. Research your proposal carefully. A winning proposal is not based only on a few well-meaning, general suggestions. All your good intentions and enthusiasm will not substitute for the hard facts readers will demand. Concrete examples persuade readers; unsupported generalizations do not. To make your proposal complete and accurate, you will have to do a lot of homework; for example, reading previous correspondence or research about the problem, doing comparative shopping for the best prices, verifying schedules and timetables, interviewing customers and/or employees, making site visits. Again, refer to Woolfolk's description in Figure 15.1 of the steps she and her coworkers took to make sure they gathered the right and most appropriate information.

4. Prove that your proposal is workable. The bottom-line question from your reader is "Will this plan work?" Your proposal should be well thought out. It should contain no statements that say "Let's see what happens if we do X or Y." By analyzing and, when possible, by testing each part of your proposal in advance, you can eliminate any quirks and revise the proposal appropriately before readers evaluate it. What you propose should be consistent with the organization and capabilities of the company. It would be foolish to recommend, for example, that a small company (fifty employees) triple its work force to accomplish your plan.

5. Be sure that your proposal is financially realistic. This point is closely associated with and follows from guideline 4. "Is it worth the money?" is another bottom-line question you can expect from readers. Do not submit a proposal that would require an unnecessarily large amount of money to implement. For example, it would be unrealistic to recommend that your company spend $20,000 to solve a $2,000 problem that might not ever recur. Study the economic climate, too—are you in an economic slump or in a boom time?

6. Package your proposal attractively. Make sure your proposal is letter-perfect, inviting, and easy to read (e.g., use plenty of headings and other visual devices discussed on pages 16-17). The appearance as well as the content of your proposal can determine whether it is accepted or rejected. Remember that readers, especially those unfamiliar with your work, will evaluate your proposal as evidence of the type of work you want to do for them. Take advantage of any software programs dealing with desktop publishing (see pages 424-425) that may be available to you. This software will allow you to prepare a proposal that looks as if it were done by a professional printer.

Internal Proposals

The primary purpose of an internal proposal, such as the one included in Figure 15.3, is to offer a realistic and constructive plan to help your company run its business more efficiently and economically. On your job you may discover a better way of doing something or a more efficient way to correct a problem. In the world of work, typical problems for which proposals are written focus on money, personnel, outdated technology, health concerns, and organizational communications. You believe that your proposed change will save your employer time, money, or further trouble. (Tina Escobar and Oliver Jabur in Figure 15.3 have identified and researched a more effective and less costly way for Community Federal Bank to do business and to satisfy its customers.) You decide to notify your department head, manager, or supervisor, or your employer may ask you for specific suggestions to solve a problem he or she has already identified. Mike Gonzalez's memo in Figure 7.4 (page 193) responds to such a request from his employer.

Generally speaking, your proposal will be an informal, in-house message, so a brief (usually one- or two-page) memo should be appropriate.

An internal proposal can be written about a variety of topics, such as:

- purchasing new or more advanced equipment: word processors, transducers, automobiles
- hiring new employees or training current ones to learn a new technique or process
- eliminating a dangerous condition or reducing an environmental risk to prevent accidents—for employees, customers, or the community at large
- improving communication within or between departments of a company or agency

FIGURE 15.3 An internal unsolicited proposal.

EQUAL HOUSING
LENDER

FDIC/DIFM

COMMUNITY FEDERAL BANK

Powell	*Monroe*	*Langston*
584-5200	*413-6000*	*796-3009*

TO: Michael L. Sappington, Executive Vice President
         Dorothy Woo, Langston Regional Manager

FROM: Tina Escobar, Oliver Jabur, ATM Services

DATE: June 2, 1994

RE: A Proposal to Install an ATM at the Mayfield Park Branch

PURPOSE

Clearly states why proposal is being sent

We are writing to propose a cost-effective solution to what is a growing problem at the Mayfield Park branch in Langston: inefficient servicing of customer needs and rising personnel costs. We recommend that you approve the purchase and installation, within the next three to four months, of an ATM at Mayfield. Such action is consistent with Community's goals of expanding electronic banking services and promoting our image as a self-serve yet customer-oriented institution.

THE PROBLEM WITH CURRENT SERVICES AT MAYFIELD PARK

Identifies problem by giving reader necessary background information

Currently, we employ four tellers at Mayfield. However, we are spending too much on personnel/salary for routine customer transactions. In fact, as determined by teller activity reports, nearly 25 percent of the 4 tellers' time each week is devoted to routine activities easily accommodated by ATMs. Here is a breakdown of teller activity for the month of May:

Teller #	Total Transactions	Routine Transactions
1	6,205	1,551
2	5,989	1,383
3	6,345	1,522
4	6,072	1,518
	24,611	5,974

FIGURE 15.3   (Continued)

page 2

Divides problem   Clearly, we are not fully using our tellers' sales abilities when they are
into parts—   kept busy with routine activities. To compound the problem, we
volume,   expect business to increase by at least 25 percent at Mayfield in the
financial,   next few months, as projected by this year's market survey. If we do
personnel,   not install an ATM, we will need to hire a fifth teller, at an annual cost
customer   of $20,800 ($15,500 base pay plus approximately 30 percent for
service   fringes), for the additional 6,000 transactions we project.

Verifies that   Most important, customer needs are not being met efficiently at
problem is   Mayfield. Recent surveys done for Community Federal by Watson-
widespread   Perry demonstrate that customers are dissatisfied about not having
          the convenience of an ATM at Mayfield. Seventy-seven percent of
          the respondents to the Watson-Perry questionnaire pointed to the
          lack of an ATM as Mayfield's biggest drawback. Customers are
          unhappy about long waits in line to do simple banking business,
          such as deposits, withdrawals, and loan payments, and about having
          to drive to other branches to do their after-hours banking. Conversa-
          tions we had with manager Rachael Harris-Ignara at Mayfield
          confirm that customers regularly complain to tellers and loan officers
          about not having an ATM.

          Ultimately, the lack of an ATM at Mayfield Park hurts Community's
          image. With ATMs available to Mayfield residents at local stores and
          other banks, our institution risks having customers and potential
          customers disassociate Community from their banking needs. We
          not only miss the opportunity of selling them on our other services
          but also risk losing their business entirely.

          A SOLUTION TO THE PROBLEM

Relates   The purchase and installation of an ATM at Mayfield Park will initially
solution to   result in significant savings in personnel costs and time. We will not
individual   have to hire a fifth teller at $20,800 for the anticipated increase in
parts of the   transactions. Thanks to an ATM, we will also be able to allocate more
problem   effectively the talents of the four existing tellers at Mayfield. These
          tellers will then be able to assist customers with questions and
          transactions that cannot be handled through an ATM, such as
          purchase of savings bonds, traveler's checks, or foreign currency.
          Mayfield tellers, therefore, will have more opportunities for greater
          involvement in customer services and can spend more time
          cross-selling our services. As a result, we will get additional
          personnel achievements without reducing the level of customer
          service. In fact, we will be improving that service.

          The increase in teller availability will inevitably lead to greater
          customer satisfaction. An ATM will allow customers the option of
          meeting their banking needs electronically or through a teller.
          Customers in a hurry can easily make a withdrawal with their

FIGURE 15.3 **(Continued)**

ATM cards, while those who need more personal attention can take advantage of window service. As customer frustration is eased, so too will be the stress on tellers because of shorter lines and fewer complaints.

Shows problem can be solved and stresses how

It is feasible to install an ATM at Mayfield. This location does not pose the difficulties we faced at some older branches. Mayfield offers ample room to install a drive-up ATM in the stubbed-out fourth drive-up lane. This location is away from the heavily congested area in front of the bank, yet it is easily accessible from the main driveway and the side drive facing Cornith Avenue.

Judging from the ATM vendor's past work, the ATM could be installed and operational within three to four months. That is the amount of time it took to install ATMs at the first two locations in Powell and for Archer Avenue in Langston. Moreover, by authorizing the expenditure at Mayfield within the next month, you will ensure that ATM service is available before the Christmas season.

COSTS

Itemizes costs

The costs of implementing our proposal are as follows:

Diebold Drive-up ATM	$28,000.00
Installation fee	2,000.00
Maintenance (1 year)	1,500.00
	$31,500.00

Interprets costs for reader

This $31,500.00, however, does not truly reflect into our annual costs. We would be able to amortize, for tax purposes, the cost of installation of the ATM over five years. Our annual expenses would, therefore, look like this:

$30,000 (28,000 + 2,000) ÷ 5 years =
$6,000.00 + 1,500 (maintenance) or <u>$7,500 per year</u>.

Compared with the $20,800 a year the bank would have to expend for an additional fifth teller at Mayfield, the annual depreciated cost for the ATM ($7,500) reduces by nearly two-thirds the amount of money the bank will have to spend for much more efficient customer service.

FIGURE 15.3   (Continued)

---

page 4

CONCLUSION

Stresses
benefits for
reader and
bank as a
whole

Authorizing an ATM for the Mayfield Park branch is both feasible and cost-effective. Adoption of this proposal will save our bank more than $13,000.00 in teller services annually, reduce customer complaints, and increase customer satisfaction and approval. We will be happy to discuss this proposal with you anytime at your convenience.

- revising a policy to improve customer relations (eliminating an inconvenience, speeding up a delivery) or employees' morale (offering vanpooling; adding more options for a schedule).

As this list shows, internal proposals cover almost every activity or policy that affects the day-to-day operation of a company or agency.

Your Audience and Office Politics

Writing an internal proposal requires you to be aware of and sensitive to office politics. To be successful, your internal proposal should be written with the needs and likes of your audience in mind. Remember that your boss will expect you to be very convincing about both the problem you say exists and the solution you propose to correct it. You cannot assume that your reader will automatically agree with you that there is a problem or that your plan is the only way to solve it.

Your reader in fact may feel threatened by your plan. After all, you are advocating a change. Some managers regard such changes as a challenge to their administration of an office or department. Or your reader may be indifferent, not even wanting to give your work serious consideration. Or your manager-reader may have certain "pet" projects or ways of doing things that you must take into account. To surmount these and other obstacles, show that the change you propose is in everyone's best interest. Do not overlook the possibility that your boss may have to take your proposal up the organizational ladder for commentary and, eventually, approval. Again, refer to Joycelyn Woolfolk's description of the chain of command at her agency (Figure 15.1). Writing a proposal may mean working as a team with your boss—putting his or her name on the document, too, to get notice and credit.

Before you write an internal proposal, consider the implications of your plan for your boss and for other offices or sections in your company. A change you propose for your department or office (transfers; new budgets or schedules) may have sweeping and potentially disruptive implications for another office or division within your company. It is wise to discuss your plan with your boss before you put it in writing. Then you might provide your boss with a draft, asking for his or her revisions or feedback, as Joycelyn Woolfolk did in Figure 15.1.

Never submit an internal proposal that offers an idea you think will work but relies on someone else to supply the specific details on *how* it will work. For example, do not write an internal proposal that says the payroll, community relations, maintenance, or advertising department can give the reader the details and costs he or she needs about your proposal. That pushes the responsibility onto someone else, and your proposal could be rejected for lack of concrete evidence.

The Organization of an Internal Proposal

A short internal proposal follows a relatively straightforward plan of organization, from identifying the problem to solving it. Internal proposals usually contain four parts, as shown in Figure 15.3. Refer to this proposal as you read the following discussion.

The Introduction

Begin your proposal with a brief statement of why you are writing to your boss: "I propose that . . ." State why you think a specific change is necessary now. Then succinctly define the problem and emphasize that your plan, if approved by the reader, will solve that problem. Where necessary, stress the urgency to act—within the next week? month?

Background of the Problem

In this section prove that a problem does exist by documenting its importance for your boss and your company. As a matter of fact, the more you show how the problem affects the boss's work (and area of supervision), the more likely you are to persuade him or her to act. And the more concrete evidence you cite, the easier it will be to convince the reader that the problem is significant and that action needs to be taken now.

Avoid vague (and unsupported) generalizations such as "we're losing money each day with this procedure (or piece of equipment)"; "costs continue to escalate"; "the trouble occurs frequently in a number of places"; "numerous complaints have come in"; "if something isn't done soon, more difficulty will result."

Instead, provide readers with quantifiable details about the number of dollars a company is actually losing per day, week, or month. Emphasize the financial trouble so that you can show how your plan (described in the next section) offers an efficient and workable solution. Indicate how many employees (or work-hours) are involved or how many customers are inconvenienced or endangered by a procedure or condition. Notice how Escobar and Jabur include this information in their proposal in Figure 15.3. Verify how widespread a problem is or how frequently it occurs by citing specific occasions. Rather than just saying that a new word processor would save the company "a lot of money," document how many work-hours are lost using other equipment for the routine jobs your company now has employees perform.

The Solution or Plan

In this section describe the change you want approved. Tie your solution (the change) directly to the problem you have just documented. Each part of your plan should help eliminate the problem or should help increase the productivity, efficiency, or safety you think is possible.

Your reader will again expect to find factual evidence. Do not give merely the outline of a plan or say that details can be worked out later. Supply details that answer the following questions: (1) Is the plan workable—can it be accomplished here in our office or plant? and (2) Is it cost-effective—will it really save us money in the long run or will it lead to even greater expenses?

To get the boss to say yes to both questions, supply the facts that you have gathered as a result of your research. For example, if you propose that your firm buy a new piece of equipment, do the necessary homework to locate the most efficient and cost-effective model available, as Tina Escobar and Oliver Jabur do in Figure 15.3. Supply the dealer's name, the costs, major conditions of service and training contracts, and warranties. Describe how your firm could use this equipment to obtain better results in the future. Cite specific tasks the new equipment can perform more efficiently at a lower cost than the equipment now in use.

It is also wise to raise alternative solutions, before the reader does, and to discuss their disadvantages. Notice how Tina Escobar and Oliver Jabur do this in Figure 15.3, in their discussion of the solution to the bank's customer-service problem. They show why installing an ATM is more necessary than hiring a fifth teller. Their discussion is based on a strong persuasive strategy, demonstrating to their readers that they have examined all alternatives and chosen the best.

If you are proposing that your company hire or reassign employees, indicate where these employees will come from, when they will start, what they will be paid, what skills they must have, where they will work and for how long. If you propose to assign current employees to a job, keep in mind that their salary will still have to be paid by your company. Just because they are coworkers does not mean they will work for nothing. Note again in Figure 15.3 how Tina Escobar and Oliver Jabur raise and resolve the problem of new and profitable responsibilities for the tellers at Community Federal Bank.

A proposal to change a procedure must include the following details:

1. how the new (or revised) procedure will work
2. how many employees or customers will be affected by it
3. when it will go into operation
4. how much it will cost the employer to change procedures
5. what delays or losses in business might be expected while the company switches from one procedure to another
6. what employees, equipment, or locations are available to accomplish this change

As these questions indicate, your boss will be concerned about schedules, working conditions, employees, methods, locations, equipment, and the costs involved in your plan for change. The costs, in fact, will be of utmost importance. Make sure that you supply a careful and accurate budget so that your reader will know what the change is going to cost. Moreover, make those costs attractive by emphasizing how inexpensive they are as compared to the cost of not making the change, as Escobar and Jabur do in the section labeled "Costs." Double-check your math.

The Conclusion

The conclusion to your internal proposal should be short—a paragraph or two at the most. Your intention is to remind the reader that the problem is serious, that the reason for change is justified, and that you think the reader needs to take action. Select the most important benefits and emphasize them again. In Figure 15.3, Escobar and Jabur again emphasize the savings that the bank will see by following their plan as well as the increase in customer satisfaction. Also indicate that you are willing to discuss your plan with the reader.

Sales Proposals

A sales proposal is the most common type of external proposal. Its purpose is to sell your company's products or services for a set fee. Whether short or long, a sales proposal is a marketing tool that includes a sales pitch as well as a detailed description of the work you propose to do. Figures 15.4 and 15.5 contain sample sales proposals.

The Audience and Its Needs

Your audience will usually be one or more business executives who have the power to approve or reject a proposal. Unlike readers of an internal proposal, your audience for a sales proposal may be even more skeptical since they may not know you or your work. Your proposal may also be evaluated by experts in other fields employed by your prospective customer. Readers of a sales proposal will evaluate your work according to (1) how well it meets their needs and (2) how well it compares with the proposals submitted by your competitors. Your proposal must convince readers that you can provide the most appropriate work or service and that your company is more reliable and efficient than any other firm.

The key to success is incorporating the "you attitude" (see pages 164–169) throughout your proposal. Relate your product, service, or personnel to the reader's exact needs as stated in the RFP for a solicited proposal or through your own investigations for an unsolicited proposal. You cannot submit the same proposal for every job you want to win and expect to be awarded a contract. Different firms have different needs. The most important question the reader will raise, therefore, about your work is "How does this proposal meet our company's special requirements?" Some other fairly common questions readers will have as they evaluate your work include the following.

- Does the writer's firm understand our problem?
- Can the writer's firm deliver what it promises?

FIGURE 15.4   An external solicited proposal.

REYNOLDS INTERIORS
250 Commerce Avenue, S.W.
Portland, OR 97204-2129

503-555-8733   FAX 503-555-1629

January 21, 1994

Mr. Floyd Tompkins, Manager
General Purpose Appliances
Highway 41, South
Portland, OR 97222

Dear Mr. Tompkins:

In response to your Request 7521 for bids for an appropiate floor covering at your
new showroom, Reynolds Interiors is pleased to submit the following proposal. After
carefully reviewing your specifications for a floor covering and inspecting your new
facility, we believe that the Armstrong Classic Corlon 900 is the most suitable choice.
I am enclosing a sample of the Corlon 900 so that you can see how it looks.

Corlon's Advantages

Guaranteed against defects for a full three years, Corlon is one of the finest and most
durable floor coverings manufactured by Armstrong. It is a heavy-duty commercial
floors 0.085-inch thick for protection. Twenty-five percent of each tile consists of
interface backing; the other 75 percent is an inlaid wear layer that offers exceptionally
high resistance to everyday traffic. Traffic tests conducted by the Independent Floor
Covering Institute repeatedly proved the superiority of Corlon's construction and
resistance.

Another important feature of Corlon is the size of its rolls. Unlike other leading brands
of similar commercial flooring—Remington or Treadmaster—Corlon comes in
12-foot-wide rather than 6-foot-wide rolls. This extra width will significantly reduce
the number of seams in your floor, thus increasing its attractiveness and reducing the
danger of tile split.

Installation Procedures

The Classic Corlon requires that we use the inlaid seaming process, a technical
procedure requiring the services of a trained floor mechanic. Herman Goshen, our
floor mechanic, has over fifteen years of experience working with the inlaid seam
process. His professional work has been consistently praised by our customers.

Installation Schedule

We can install the Classic Corlon on your showroom floor during the first week of
March, which fits the timetable specified in your request. The tile will take three and
one-half days to install and will be ready to walk on immediately. We recommend,
though, that you not move equipment onto the floor for twenty-four hours after
installation.

FIGURE 15.4   (Continued)

---

page 2

Costs

The following costs include the Classic Corlon tile, labor, equipment, and tax:

750 sq. yards of Classic Corlon at $12.50/yard	$ 9,375.00
Labor (28 hr. @ $15.00/hr.)	420.00
Sealing fluid (10 gal. @ $10.00/gal.)	100.00
Total	9,895.00
Tax (5 percent)	494.75
GRAND TOTAL	**$10,389.75**

Our costs are $250.00 under those you specified in your request.

Reynolds's Qualifications

Reynolds Interiors has been in business for more than twenty-eight years. In that time, we have installed many commercial floors in Portland and its suburbs. In the last year, we have served more than sixty customers, including the new multi-purpose Tradex plant in Portland.

Conclusion

Thank you for the opportunity to submit this proposal. We believe you will have a great deal of success with an Armstrong floor. If we can provide you with any further information, please call us.

Sincerely yours,

Sharon Scovill

Sharon Scovill
Sales Manager

Jack Rosen

Jack Rosen
Installation Supervisor

- Can the job be completed on time?
- What assurances does the writer offer that the job will be done exactly as proposed?

Answer each of these questions by demonstrating how your product or service is tailored to the customer's needs.

Organizing a Sales Proposal

A sales proposal can have the following parts: introduction, description of the proposed product or service, timetable, costs, qualifications of your company, and conclusion.

Introduction

The introduction to your sales proposal can be a single paragraph in a short sales proposal or several pages in a more complex one. Basically, the introduction should prepare readers for everything that follows in your proposal. The introduction itself may contain the following sections, which sometimes may be combined.

1. Statement of purpose and subject of proposal. Tell readers why you are writing and identify the specific subject of your work. If you are responding to an RFP, use specific code numbers or cite application dates, as the proposal in Figure 15.4 does. If your proposal is unsolicited, indicate how you learned of the problem, as Figure 15.5 does. Briefly define the solution you propose.

2. Background of the problem you propose to solve. Show readers that you are familiar with their problem and that you have a firm grasp of the importance and implications of the problem. In a solicited proposal, such as the one shown in Figure 15.4, a section outlining the problem is usually unnecessary, because the potential client has already identified the problem and just wants to know how you would handle it. In that case, just point out how your company would solve the problem, mentioning your superiority over your competitors (see the third paragraph of Figure 15.4). In an unsolicited proposal, you need to describe the problem in convincing detail, identifying the specific trouble areas. However, if it is an external proposal to a current customer, such as the one in Figure 15.5, it would be unwise to point out past problems your client may have had with your company's service or products. In Figure 15.5, note how the problems of the Piko 2500 model are described mainly as a way to sell the advantages of the Piko 4000.

Description of the Proposed Product or Service

This section is the heart of your proposal. Before spending their money, customers will demand hard, factual evidence of what you claim can and should be done. Here are some points that you should cover.

1. Carefully show your potential customers that your product or service is right for them. Stress specific benefits of your product or service most relevant to your reader. Blend sales talk with descriptions of hardware.

FIGURE 15.5   **An external unsolicited proposal.**

National Business Equipment
470 Rodgers Rd. ■ Camden, NJ 08104-0826 ■ (201) 555-1100

September 20, 1994

Ms. Denise Taylor
Business Manager
Madison Tool and Die Company
3400 Veterans Boulevard
Camden, NJ 08104

Dear Ms. Taylor:

While we were servicing your Piko 2500 copier last week, it occurred to me that you might be interested in purchasing a newer model that will give you state-of-the-art features to make your copying work more efficient and reliable. In the past three years since you purchased your 2500, copier technology has advanced tremendously, giving users many benefits at surprisingly low cost.

Based on our assessment of Madison Tool and Die Company's needs for the most reliable office equipment available, we recommend that you purchase the Piko 4000. We believe that this copier will satisfactorily meet all of your copying needs for the present and well into the future.

ADVANTAGES OF THE PIKO 4000

With the Piko 4000, your cost per single copy will be reduced to only $1\frac{1}{2}$ cents, compared with approximately 3 cents per copy with your present machine. The 4000 model is designed to make as many as **75,000 copies per month**, almost double the recommended work load of your current copier. The following description of the main features of the Piko 4000 will show you its other advantages over your current copier.

Printing Technology

The Piko 4000's **printing rate of 80 copies per minute** will save you valuable time. The automatic duplexing capability allows you to turn single-sided documents into double-sided ones, thus reducing paper costs. In addition to the standard paper sizes--$8\frac{1}{2}$ x 11, $8\frac{1}{2}$ x 14, and 11 x 17--the **4000 functions effectively with other paper sizes and shapes**, including heavyweight sheet stock suitable for specifications and drawings. The Piko 4000 has original-size sensing, which can copy varying sizes automatically.

FIGURE 15.5   (Continued)

Copier Control Security System

The Piko 4000's **electronic ID keypad** allows only authorized users, with individual entry codes, to run the copier. This keypad can control access, limit copies, and provide tabulated records of use for your accounting purposes.

Feeding/Sorting Capacity

The 4000 includes as standard equipment both a recirculating automatic document feeder and an automatic sorter/stapler. These features **can reduce the time spent on large copying jobs by as much as 50 percent.**

Printing Quality

The new Piko 4000 offers top-quality, high resolution reproduction **in four colors** in addition to black and white. Since seeing is believing, I am enclosing a copy of this proposal made on the 4000 as well as a copy of a blueprint to show you how both copied documents look.

Reduction/Enlargement Function

The Piko 4000's zoom capability allows you to increase or decrease the size of your copy within a range of 50–200 percent. Since these changes are made in increments of 1 percent, your copy is always the exact size you want.

Size

The Piko 4000 measures 4' × 3' × 4', **occupying one-quarter less space** than your present copier. Once the machine is installed, you will find this extra space useful for your storage needs.

INSTALLATION, TRAINING, AND SERVICE

We will deliver and install your new Piko 4000 within one week of receiving your purchase order. The installation requires approximately forty-five minutes.

Our local sales representative, Darlene Simpson, is available to instruct your employees in the operation and routine maintenance of the 4000. A phone call will allow us to set up a mutually convenient date for such instruction. If a problem occurs, **we offer customers the latest in remote diagnostics**. A modem installed in the Piko 4000 allows us to diagnose specific problems (and needed parts) before dispatching a service representative. We save time, so you save time. In addition, our "hot line" is

FIGURE 15.5   (Continued)

page 3

available to you on business days from 8:00 A.M. to 5:00 P.M. We guarantee that a service representative will arrive at your office **within two business hours** from the time of your call.

COSTS

Below is the price of the Piko 4000 and appropriate initial supplies:

Piko 4000	$18,295.00
Toner (tube)	23.00
Paper (5,000 sheets of medium grade 8½ x 11)	25.00
Service contract--optional	
(per year, parts and labor included)	2,300.00
Total	$20,643.00

We install your new Piko 4000 **free of charge.**

NATIONAL'S REPUTATION

Over the past 22 years, National has supplied copiers to more than 90 companies in the greater Camden area, including Biscayne Industries, Northeast Manufacturing, and Teunissen Accounting, Inc. In addition to providing quality products, we are **dedicated to giving our customers fast and efficient service long after a sale.**

We appreciate your using **National Business Equipment** for your repair needs and hope that you will decide to purchase the new Piko 4000. Please call me if you have any questions about the Piko 4000 or National.

If this proposal is acceptable, please sign and return a copy of this letter.

Sincerely yours,

Marion Copely

Marion Copely

Encls. Copier samples

I accept this proposal made by National Business Equipment.

_____

for Madison Tool and Die Company

2. Describe your work in suitable detail—what it looks like, what it does, and how consistently and well it will perform in the readers' office, plant, hospital, or agency. You might include a brochure, picture, or, as the writers of the proposals in Figures 15.4 and 15.5 do, a sample of your product for customers to study. Convince readers that your product is the most up-to-date and efficient one they could select. Note how the proposals in Figures 15.4 and 15.5 emphasize this.

3. Stress any special features, maintenance advantages, warranties, or service benefits. Highlight features that show the quality, consistency, or security of your work. For a service, emphasize the procedures you use, the terms of that service, and even the kinds of tools you use, especially any "state-of-the-art" equipment. Be sure to provide a step-by-step outline of what will happen and why each step is beneficial for readers.

Timetable

A carefully planned timetable shows readers that you know your job and that you can accomplish it in the right amount of time. Your dates should match any listed in an RFP. Provide specific dates when the work will begin, how long it will continue, and when you will be finished installing equipment, testing equipment, or training employees to use equipment. For proposals offering a service, specify how many times—by the hour, week, month—customers can expect to receive your help; for example, spraying three times a month for an exterminating service or making deliveries by 10:00 A.M. for a trucking company. Indicate whether follow-up visits or service calls will be provided.

Costs

Make your budget accurate, complete, and convincing. Accepted by both parties, a proposal is a binding legal agreement. Don't underestimate costs in the hope that a low bid will win you the job. You may get the job but lose money doing it, for the customer will rightfully hold you to your unrealistic figures. Neither should you inflate prices; competitors will beat you in the bidding.

Give customers more than the bottom-line cost. Show exactly what readers are getting for their money so they can determine if everything they need is included. Itemize costs for specific services, equipment, labor (by the hour or by the job), transportation, travel, or training you propose to supply. If something is not included or is considered optional, say so—additional hours of training, replacement of parts, and the like. If you anticipate a price increase, let the customer know how long current prices will stay in effect. That information may spur them to act favorably now.

Qualifications of Your Company

Emphasize your company's accomplishments and expertise in using relevant services and equipment. You might list previous work you have done that is identical or similar to the type of work you are proposing to do for the customer. You may even want to mention the names of a few local firms for whom you have worked that would be pleased to recommend you. Never misrepresent your qualifications or those of the individuals who work with or for you. Your prospective client may verify if you have in fact worked on similar jobs for the last five to six years.

Conclusion

This is the "call to action" section of your proposal. As with the conclusion in an internal proposal, encourage your reader to approve your plan. Stress the major benefits your plan has for the customer. Notice how the last paragraphs of Figures 15.4 and 15.5 do this effectively. Offer to answer any questions the reader may have. Some proposals end by asking readers to sign and return a copy of the proposal thus indicating their acceptance of it, as the proposal in Figure 15.5 does.

Proposals for Research Papers and Reports

You may have to write a proposal like the one in Figure 15.6 when your instructor asks you to submit a report or research paper, a topic for an independent study, or some other type of major term project.

Writing for Your Teacher

The principles guiding internal and sales proposals also apply to research proposals. As with internal and sales proposals, you will be writing to convince your reader—the teacher—to approve a major piece of work. But otherwise the goals of your teacher/reader will be considerably different from those of other proposal readers. A teacher will read your proposal to help you write the best possible paper or report. In examining your proposal, the teacher will want to make sure of four things:

1. that you have chosen a significant topic
2. that you have a sufficiently restricted topic
3. that you will investigate important sources of information about that topic
4. that you can accomplish your work in the specified time

Your proposal gives your teacher an opportunity to spot omissions or inconsistencies and to provide helpful suggestions.

To prepare an effective proposal for a research project, you must do some preliminary research. You cannot pick any topic that comes to mind, or guess about procedures, sources, or conclusions. As other proposal readers do, your teacher will want convincing and specific evidence for your choice of topic and your approach to it. Be prepared to cite key facts to show that you are familiar with the topic and that you can handle it successfully.

Organization of a Proposal for a Research Paper

Your proposal for a school research project can be a memo divided into five sections, as illustrated in Figure 15.6: introduction (or purpose), scope of the problem or topic to be investigated, methods or procedures, timetable, and request for approval. However, be ready to reverse or expand these sections if your teacher wants you to follow a different organizational plan.

FIGURE 15.6   **A proposal for a research paper.**

TO: Professor Barbara Felton-Parks
           Business Management 200

FROM: James Salinas

DATE: February 5, 1993

SUBJECT: Proposal for a report on the advantages and
           disadvantages of electronic mail

Purpose

For my term project, I propose to research and write a report on the advantages
and disadvantages for an office in switching to an electronic mail system.

Electronic mail has been used increasingly by many private companies and
government agencies. It has been estimated that more than fifteen million
workers today use electronic mail through the services of such vendors as AT&T
(EasyLink), MCI Communications (MCI Mail), or BT North America (Dialcom). Eric
Arnum, editor of Electronic Mail & Micro Systems, has enthusiastically
predicted that electronic mail will in time become "as universal and simple to
use as the telephone" (Sales & Marketing Management [Jan. 1991]: 72).

Although electronic mail has brought many companies closer to the paperless
office of the future, it also poses some major problems. The United States Postal
Service discontinued its express E-COM service, as did Federal Express its
ZapMail and the American Medical Association its AMA/Net. An understanding of
the benefits as well as the drawbacks of electronic mail is important for any
office manager thinking of converting to it. My paper will serve as a background
report for an office manager considering electronic mail.

Problems to Be Investigated

At this stage of my research, I think my report needs to answer the following
questions:

1. How does electronic mail work as compared to conventional communication
   methods?
2. What kinds of special applications does it offer users in preparing and
   sending routine messages (invoices, monthly sales reports) or special ones?
3. Will electronic mail provide the same level of security and confidentiality
   as conventional mail?
4. Do the costs of switching to electronic mail--keyboarding problems, terminal
   modems, hookups--offset the costs of conventional preparation, forwarding,
   and storing of mail?

FIGURE 15.6 **(Continued)**

I propose, therefore, to divide the body of my paper according to the four key issues of **operation, application, security,** and **costs.**

Methods of Research

I will rely heavily on literature dealing with electronic mail. Judging from the number of entires on this topic in the Business Periodicals Index from 1985 to early 1993, the subject is popular and significant. For these years, I located more than 200 entries. Of course, not all of them focus on benefits versus disadvantages of E-mail, the proposed subject of my report. But from a preliminary check of some articles available in our library, I think the following may be most useful to me:

Avari, Brenda. "Can You Depend on Electronic Mail?" Office Systems Review 21 (Apr. 1989): 61+.

"Bidirectional Electronic Mail System Helps Account for Firm's Increased Productivity." Communication News 21 (Feb. 1991): 54.

Childs, Ronald G. "Seven Steps to Successful E-Mail." Datamation 15 Sept. 1991: 56–58.

Churbuck, David. "Prepare for E-Mail Attack." Forbes 23 Jan. 1989: 82–87.

Fiedler, David. "E-Mail for Power Users." Byte 16 (Dec. 1991): 95–98.

Foley, M. J. "Hardware Vendors Adapt to Changing E-Mail Market." Electronic Business 1 May 1988: 40+.

Getts, Judy. "How Private Is E-Mail?" PC World 7 (Feb. 1989): 64–66.

Kroeger, Lin. "E-Mail: Cost-Effective or Just Costly?" Corporate Controller (Sept./Oct. 1991): 54–55.

"Limitations of E-Mail Systems." Office Electronics 39 (June 1985): 10.

Meeks, Brock N. "E-Mail Economics." Byte 14 (Apr. 1989): 151–55.

Nall, Roger. "How to Use Electronic Mail Successfully." Supervisory Management 37 (Jan. 1992): 11.

Stevens-Renfrow, Patricia. Telecommunications: An Introduction. Pittsburgh: Data Processing Press, 1992.

FIGURE 15.6   (Continued)

---

page 3

Sussman, Lyle, Peggy Golden, and Renée Beauclair. "Training for E-Mail."
  Training & Development Journal 45 (Mar. 1992): 70–73.

Walker, Philip M. "Electronic Mail Offers Growing Range of Uses." The Office 106
  (Jan. 1988): 120.

Wiegner, Kathleen. "The Trouble with E-Mail." Working Woman 17 (Apr. 1992): 46.

I intend to interview two office managers in Springfield whose companies
switched to electronic mail in the last year. My choices right now are Alice
Phillips at Dodge & Spenser Hydraulic Systems and Keith Wellbridge at General
Dynamics. But because of their possible schedule conflicts, I may have to
interview two other individuals.

Timetable

I hope to complete my library research by April 2 and my interviews by April 8.
Then I will spend the following two weeks working on a draft, which I will submit
by April 19, the date you specified. After receiving your comments on my draft, I
will work on revisions and the final copy of my paper and turn it in by May 12, the
last day of class. I will submit two progress reports--one when I finish my
research and another when I decide on the final organization of my paper.

Request for Approval

I ask that you approve my topic and my approach to it. I would appreciate any
suggestions on how you think I might best proceed. Thank you.

The Introduction

Keep your introduction short—a paragraph, maybe two, pinpointing the subject
and purpose of your work.

> I propose to research and write a report about the
> "hot knife" laser used in treating port wine stain and
> other birthmarks.

> I intend to investigate the relationship that exists
> in today's office between office design and the
> employee's need for "psychological space."

Then briefly indicate why the topic or the problem you propose to study is significant. In other words, be prepared to explain why you have chosen that topic and
why research on it is relevant or worthwhile for a specific audience or course
objective. Note how James Salinas in Figure 15.6 states how and why his paper
will be useful to an office manager.

Supply your teacher/reader with a few background details about your topic; for example, the importance of using a laser as opposed to conventional ways of treating birthmarks or why psychological space plays a crucial role in employee productivity and morale. Prove that you have thought carefully about a suitable topic.

The Scope of the Problem or Topic to Be Investigated

The second section, which might be entitled "Problems to Be Investigated" or "Areas to Be Studied," shows how you propose to break the topic into meaningful units. Tell your reader what specific issues, points, or areas you hope to investigate. Doing this, you show how you will limit your topic to establish the appropriate scope for your work.

Some instructors ask students to formulate a list of questions their research paper or report intends to answer. The topics included in these questions, or a list of areas or problems to be covered, might later become major sections of your paper. Make sure that the issues or questions do not overlap and that each relates directly to and supports your restricted topic. Note how the student in Figure 15.6 hopes to divide his study of electronic mail into four distinct and useful areas.

Methods or Procedures

In the third section of your proposal inform your teacher how you expect to find the answers to the questions you raised in the previous section, or how you intend to locate information about your list of subtopics. It's not enough to write, "I will gather appropriate information and analyze it." Specify what data you hope to include, where they are located, and how you intend to retrieve them.

Most students gather data from literature published about their topics. (In fact, many research papers are based exclusively on library work.) This literature can include books, encyclopedias or other reference materials, articles in professional publications, newspapers, bulletins, manuals, or audiovisual materials. Inform your teacher what indexes, abstracts, or even computer searches you intend to use (review pages 321-339) as part of your literature search. To document your preliminary library work, provide your instructor with a list of a few appropriate titles on your topic following the style of documentation used for a Works Cited page (discussed on pages 360-366).

In addition to library materials, you might collect information from experiments you will perform in a laboratory or from a field test, interviews with experts, replies to letters of inquiry, questionnaires, or a combination of any of these sources.

Timetable

Your proposal should indicate when and in what order you expect to complete the different phases of your project. Your teacher needs this information to keep track of your progress and to make sure that you will turn in an assignment on time. Specify tentative dates for completing your research, draft(s), revisions, and final copy.

Some instructors also ask students to turn in progress reports at regular intervals. If you are asked to do this, indicate when those progress reports will be submitted, as James Salinas does in Figure 15.6.

Request for Approval

End your proposal with a request for approval of your topic. You might also indicate that you would appreciate any suggestions from your teacher on how you might restrict, research, organize, or write about your topic.

Preparing Proposals: A Final Reminder

This chapter has given you some basic information and specific strategies for writing proposals. Keep in mind that a proposal presents a plan to a decision maker for his or her approval. To win that approval, your proposal must be *realistic, carefully researched,* and *highly persuasive.* These essential characteristics apply to internal proposals in memo format written to your employer, more formal sales proposals sent to a potential customer, and research proposals submitted to your instructor.

✓ Revision Checklist

As you revise your proposal, ask yourself these questions to make sure that you have written a complete and convincing document for your readers. If your proposal is a team effort, you might ask one team member to serve as an editor. The editor would then make sure that these questions are answered by the individuals responsible for the different sections of the proposal to which the questions pertain. For some questions (such as 1, 2, 5, and 17), however, response from the entire team would be helpful.

1. Have I identified a realistic problem, one that is restricted and relevant to my audience?
2. Have I effectively tried to convince my reader that the problem exists and needs to be solved?
3. Does my description of the problem involve quantifiable details that show precisely how much money, time, and so on, are being lost or wasted?
4. Is my proposal persuasive? Have I emphasized the benefits of solving the problem—in time, money, personnel, technology? Have I incorporated the "you attitude" throughout?

5. Can my proposal be realistically implemented? Is my solution both appropriate for my audience and feasible? Will my audience clearly see how and why my solution works?

6. Have I researched the background of the problem to make sure it squares with my proposed solution?

7. Have I used specific figures and concrete details to show my audience how my proposal will save both time and money?

8. Have I given my readers all the information they will need to make a decision in my favor?

9. Have I double-checked my proposal to catch errors, omissions, and inconsistencies?

10. Have I made sure that I did not overextend myself or exaggerate what I or my plan can actually do for my readers?

11. Is my proposal clearly organized, with appropriate headings, and is it easy to read? Have I made sure that my proposal is written in concise and clear language?

12. For an internal proposal, have I demonstrated how my proposal is in my company's best interest? Have I taken into account any "office politics" in describing the problem and the solution? Did I discuss my proposal with coworkers or supervisors who may be affected by my proposal?

13. In a sales proposal, have I related my product or service to my buyer's needs? Have I shown my audience that I have a clear understanding of these needs?

14. Is my budget comprehensive and realistic? Can my proposal actually be implemented with this budget? Have I accounted for all expenses? Have I itemized costs of products and services in my sales proposal?

15. Have I provided a timetable with exact dates for implementing my proposal?

16. Have I shown my company's credibility by citing other successful jobs and satisfied clients?

17. Does my conclusion reiterate the most important benefit(s) for my readers and include a call for action?

Exercises

1. In two or three paragraphs identify and document a problem (in services, safety, communication, traffic, scheduling) you see in your office or plant or at your school. Make sure that you give readers—a school official (chairperson; dean) or employer (section or department head; manager)—specific evidence that a problem does exist and that it needs to be corrected.

2. Write a short internal proposal, modeled after Figure 15.3, based on the problem you identified in Exercise 1.

3. Write a short internal proposal, similar to Tina Escobar and Oliver Jabur's in Figure 15.3, recommending to a company or a college a specific change in procedure, equipment, training, safety, personnel, or policy. Make sure that you provide an appropriate audience (a college administrator or department manager or section chief) with specific evidence about the existence of the problem and your solution of it. Here are some possible topics:

- providing more and safer parking
- extending the bookstore or company credit union hours
- purchasing new office or laboratory equipment or computer software
- hiring more faculty, student workers, or office help
- reorganizing or redesigning the school yearbook or company annual report or sales catalog
- changing the decor/furniture in a student or company lounge
- expanding the number of weekend or night classes in your major
- adding more offerings to a school or company cafeteria menu
- altering the programming on a campus radio station
- improving access for handicapped students or employees
- decreasing waiting time at school registration or in a computer lab

4. Rewrite the following vague and unconvincing internal proposal to make it more effective. Supply any details you think necessary.

TO: Holly Gordon   SUBJECT: Changes at Acme Corp.

FROM: K. T. Smith   DATE: April 14, 1994

For some time now I have noticed a problem with the way the office handles information. Things are often out of place and sometimes hard to find. I know that it took me more than 15 minutes one day to find an important report for Mr. Swanson. Others in the office too have been complaining about this problem. I propose that we do something about the way information is conveyed in our department.

Having the right kind of equipment would save us hours and money. I suggest that we call a few of the office equipment supply offices for their opinion about the kinds of changes we need to make.

We should also call one of the new assistant managers in the engineering department to find out how that office is run. I have been there a number of times and things seem to be going very smoothly. Clearly

---

they do not have the organizational problems we do.

Along with these investigations, I suggest that we have someone from accounting give us an estimate about how much we could afford to spend this year.

As for costs, though, I don't think the investment would be bad and the company would be getting a lot for its money, more than they are now with our outmoded communication system in this office.

Please let me know what you think of my idea. I think it is worth pursuing.

5. Write an unsolicited sales proposal, similar to the one in Figure 15.5, on one of the following services or products you intend to sell, or on a topic your instructor approves.

   - providing exterminating service to a store or restaurant
   - supplying a hospital with rental television sets for patients' rooms
   - typing or word processing for students
   - offering temporary office help or nursing care
   - providing landscaping and lawn care work
   - testing for noise, air, or water pollution in your community or neighborhood
   - furnishing transportation for students, employees, or members of a community group
   - providing consulting service to save a company money
   - designing business forms for a local bank or hospital
   - digging a septic well for a small apartment complex
   - supplying insurance coverage to a small (five to ten employees) firm
   - cleaning the parking lot and outside walkways at a shopping center
   - selling a piece of equipment to a business
   - making a work area safer
   - offering a training program for employees
   - increasing donations to a community or charitable fund

6. Write a solicited proposal for one of the topics listed in Exercise 5 or for a topic that your instructor approves. You might want to review Figure 15.4.

7. Write an appropriate proposal—internal or solicited or unsolicited sales—based on the information contained in one of the following three articles. Assume that you or your prospective customer's company or community faces a problem similar to one discussed in one of these articles. Use as much of the information in these articles as you need and add any details of your own that you think are necessary.

Turning Schoolgrounds Green

"If our conservation district doesn't take the initiative to show our children and school leaders how to stop erosion on their playgrounds, then who will?" said Bobby Joe Ganey, Chair of the Lasalle Soil and Water Conservation District in Lasalle Parish, Louisiana.

Ganey, along with other conservation district board members, was tired of seeing bare, eroded soil outside classroom doors, so the district board initiated a project to put a cover on the schoolgrounds.

The district board members talked with school principals in the parish about erosion problems on their school campuses. The district board determined that six school campuses were suffering from a lack of vegetative cover, and erosion was keeping their playgrounds bare. Board members asked the Soil Conservation Service to prepare a plan for the schools.

"School grounds get a lot of foot traffic from the students, so it was necessary for us to establish a species of grass that could withstand this traffic," Ganey said.

The Lasalle Soil and Water Conservation District supplied the funds to buy bermuda grass seed and fertilizer.

"It was our intention from the beginning to have the students take an active part in establishing vegetative cover on the playgrounds," said Ganey. "In this way not only could they see the value of erosion control at their school but they also could learn how erosion is bad for the community and for their futures."

The district board and Soil Conservation Service introduced the students to erosion problems through a slide show. More than 650 students from the six elementary schools participated in the erosion control work on their campuses. They helped till, seed, and fertilize the eroding areas.

To be sure that the newly established grass would be properly maintained, the plan included information and training on cutting height and fertilizer requirements.

Soil and Water Conservation News (Oct. 1984): 9.

Self-illuminating Exit Signs

The Marine Corps Development and Education Center (MCDEC), Quantico, Virginia, submitted a project recently, to replace incandescent illumination exit signs with self-illuminating exit signs for a cost of $97,238. The first-year savings were anticipated to be about $37,171 with an anticipated payback time of 2.6 years—an excellent prospect. The contractor bid much lower, however, and the actual payback will be about 1.5 years.

What are the benefits of these self-illuminating exit signs? The primary benefit is that virtually all operation and maintenance expense is eliminated for the life of the device, normally from 10 to 12 years. Power failures or other disturbances will not cause them to go out.

In new construction, expensive electrical circuits can be totally eliminated. In retrofits, the release of a dedicated circuit for other use may be of considerable benefit. Initial total cost of installing circuits and conventional devices approximately equals the cost of the self-illuminating signs. Installation labor and expense for the self-illuminating signs is about that of hanging a picture.

The amount of electricity saved varies and depends on whether your existing fixtures are fluorescent (13 to 26 watts) or incandescent (50 to 100 watts). Multiply the number of fixtures × wattage/fixture × hours operated/day × days/year = KWH/year savings. For example assume:

400 incandescent fixtures

0.08 $/KWH 0.05 KW/fixture

24 hours/day 365 day/year operation

400 × 0.1 × 365 = 350400 KWH/year

350400 × 0.08 = $28,032/year for electricity

Now add in savings achieved from:

- reducing labor to change bulbs
- avoiding bulb material, stocking, and storage costs
- avoiding transportation costs involved in bulb changes
- reusing existing bulbs

The above savings can be significant. For the MCDEC Quantico project, estimates of bulb change interval and savings were 700 hours (29 days) and $13,512/year when all factors were considered.

The cost of a self-illuminating sign depends on whether one or two faces are illuminated primarily and varies between different suppliers. Single-face prices will likely be $100 to $150 while double-face prices may be $250 to $330. The contractor at Quantico found better prices than these ranges indicate. The labor cost should be about $10 per sign.

If you can use an exit-sign system with high dependability, no maintenance, and zero operations cost in your retrofit on new construction projects, try a self-illuminating exit-sign system in your economic analysis today. "Isolite" signs, by Safety Light Corp., are listed as FSC (Fire Safety Code) Group 99, Part IV, Section A, Class 9905, signs and are available through GSA contract. Contact Gerald Harnett, Safety Light Corp., P.O. Box 266, Greenbelt, MD 20070 for more information.

Lt. James F. McCollum, CEG, USN. "Self-illuminating Exit Signs Equal High Payback." *Navy Civil Engineer* (Summer 1983): 30–31.

Wheelchair-Lift Switch Covers

In order to ensure year-round access to the Springfield Armory National Historic Site (Massachusetts) museum, Michael C. Trebbe designed the cover for switches on wheelchair lifts. During the extreme New England winters, the switch buttons would freeze, thus making the lift inoperable, which in turn required several hours to thaw. The installation of these covers prevented the freezing of the switch buttons and, therefore, allowed maintenance personnel to attend to matters such as snow removal.

The covers were made of materials found on site, which resulted in the covers being almost cost free. The covers can be quickly built, and they are mounted with the same mounting screws as the switch boxes so as to not destroy any original fabric (in the case of Springfield Armory NHS, brownstone). The materials used included:

- 1/8-in. by 4 1/2-in. by 12-in. piece of rubber mat
- 3 1/2-in. by 6 1/2-in. piece of sheet metal
- three aluminum pop rivets
- primer for the sheet metal

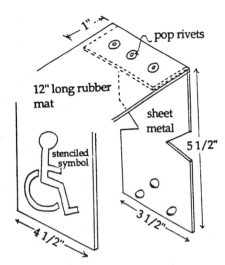

- wheelchair symbol
- white paint for the symbol

The sheet metal is bent to a 90-degree angle at the 5 1/2-inch point. The lowest two holes (see diagram) are drilled to mount the screws of the switch box, which also secure the cover. Triangular cutouts and other holes are drilled for the clearance of the housing screws on the rear of the switch box (see diagram).

The handicap symbol is stenciled on the front of the piece of rubber mat using white paint.

Michael C. Trebbe, *Grist*, Vol. 36, No. 1 (Winter 1992). U.S. Department of the Interior, National Park Service.

8. Write a suitable research proposal on which the research paper on "Stress and the Computer Programmer" (pages 373–386) could have been based.

9. Write a research proposal to your instructor seeking approval for a major term project. Do the necessary preliminary research to show that you have selected a suitable topic, that you have narrowed it, and that you have identified the sources of information you have to consult. Identify at least six or seven relevant articles and one or two books on your topic.

16

Short Reports

This chapter will show you how to write short reports, also called informal, semi-formal, or semi-technical reports. You may be asked to write them on your own or in collaboration with coworkers. Short reports, which emphasize factual details, provide coworkers, employees, and clients with needed information. The skills necessary for writing them are among the most important ones you can develop, because you will be expected to prepare short reports often on your job. A large part of your own annual evaluation for raises and promotions will depend on your ability to write effective short reports. Even though these reports are brief, you must allow time for careful planning, drafting, revising, and editing to say what you need to say without wasting your readers' time. Writing concisely—to the point and clearly—takes effort and time. You may want to review relevant sections of Chapters 4 and 5 (pages 110; 129-133) about avoiding wordiness. In Chapter 17, you will learn how to write a long report.

Why Short Reports Are Important

Business and industry cannot function without short written reports. A report may be defined as an organized presentation of relevant data on any topic—money, travel, time, personnel, equipment, management—that a company or agency must keep track of in its day-to-day operations. Reports tell whether schedules are being met, costs contained, sales projections met, clients and patients efficiently served. Reports also are likely to be required if unexpected problems occur.

You may write an occasional report in response to a specific question, or you may be required to write a daily or weekly report on routine activities about which your readers expect detailed information. Many organizations—businesses, clinics, mass transportation systems, schools—must submit regularly scheduled reports in order to maintain their accreditation or funding by state or federal agencies.

Types of Short Reports

To give you a sense of some of the topics that you may be required to write about, here is a list of various types of short reports that are found in business and industry.

appraisal report	medicine/treatment error report
audit report	operations report
construction report	periodic report
design report	production report
evaluation report	progress report
experiment report	recommendation report
incident report	research report
investigative report	sales report
laboratory report	status report
library report	test report
manager's report	trip report

Discussing each of these reports is too large a task for one chapter. Instead, Chapter 16 will concentrate on six of the most common types of reports you are likely to encounter in your professional work:

1. periodic reports
2. sales reports
3. progress reports
4. trip reports
5. test reports
6. incident reports

The first five reports can be called *routine reports* because they give information about planned, ongoing, or recurring events. *Incident reports* describe events that writers did not anticipate—accidents, breakdowns, environmental mishaps, delivery delays, or work stoppages. All six, however, may be termed "short" reports. They deal with current happenings rather than with long-range forecasts. Short reports focus on the "trees," not the "forest."

How to Write Short Reports

The most important point to keep in mind is that reports are written for readers who need information so that they can get a job accomplished. Never think of the reports you write as a series of short notes jotted down for *your* own convenience. And also do not believe that because they are short you can dash these reports off quickly.

An effective short report needs the same careful planning that goes into other types of on-the-job writing. You should expect to do some necessary research, which may involve checking a client's file, reading background material, searching a computer database, or performing an experiment or test. You also should expect to take notes, compile statistics, or describe a location or piece of equipment. Spreadsheet and executive information systems (EIS) software can help you process data and can assist you in creating your short report. Equipped with all this information from your research, you can prepare a brief outline or a preliminary draft first to make sure you get all your ideas down and in the most useful order for your audience. Then you need to do some additional drafting and revising to make sure your report is clear and concise. Finally, you will have to edit and proofread carefully.

If you work with a team to prepare your short report, make sure you clarify each individual's responsibility and that you confer with one another about progress and any problems. This communication can be as simple as making a phone call or sending a message through E-mail or a fax. Scientific reports—such as that in Figure 16.12 (pp. 613–615)—are frequently the product of a collaborative effort.

Some General Guidelines

Under each of the following categories you will find specific guidelines applicable to writing any short report you encounter. More specific information pertinent to particular types of reports is given within a discussion of those reports later in this chapter.

   1. Audience. Short reports are written to coworkers, employers, and customers. The needs of each audience will vary. Consider how much your audience knows about your project and its reason for reading your report before writing it. While it is likely that coworkers in your department will be familiar with your project, readers in another department or section of your company may not be. You will have to define or avoid using terms that people who are not specialists in your field would fail to understand. Also, you may have to explain (and interpret) the implications and significance of statistical or scientific information you are including. Even employers, who will constitute the largest group of readers for your short reports, may not always know about the details of your work. These managers will use your reports to help them make decisions. Always give readers the details most relevant for their job.

   Try to anticipate how your audience will use your report. For instance, in a report for a business manager about equipment failure, your reader will be less concerned with the technical details about what went wrong than with the costs of parts replacement or the amount of lost work time.

   Many times a short report is sent to an overseas client, coworker, or manager to inform him or her and to get his or her ongoing approval. Writing such a report requires even closer attention to the kinds of writing outlined on pages 175–180 on international English. You should avoid jargon, excessively detailed and long sentences, or idioms ("the ball is in your court") in short reports for ESL audiences.

   2. Length. Short reports are brief—one paragraph to two or three pages—and get right to the point. Nothing angers busy readers in the world of work more than having to wade through extra pages that merely repeat information or that are filled with long-winded, unnecessary comments. The purpose of your short report will determine its length. Some test reports ask for nothing but numbers; for example, the glucose level on a blood test. A progress report, however, calls for written evaluations.

3. Format. Since so many short reports are done within a company, the memo is the most frequently used format. Review pertinent sections of Chapter 7 dealing with memos (pages 190-197). When you are writing to individuals outside your business, you will generally use a letter format. Prepared forms can also be used (or may be required) for reports. Regardless of format—letter or memo—be sure that you use headings to help readers follow your work and also help you classify information into easily understood and labeled categories. Most of the examples in this chapter employ headings to highlight and preview information for readers.

4. Content. The emphasis is on the objective reporting of the facts: costs, sales figures, eyewitness accounts, observations, statistics, test measurements, accurate descriptions. Impressions, unsupported personal opinion, and guesswork are inappropriate. Readers want a straightforward account of current events. Past activities should be mentioned for necessary background information to help readers understand the context of your report, but only to clarify the present and to help readers follow current details. Some numbers are more readily understood in tabular or graph form. If you are using a computer to prepare these visuals, experiment with different types of graphic presentations.

Always give dates and specify the exact period the report covers and indicate A.M. or P.M. Just listing "Thursday" is often not enough. Give the date. To record time in compact and specific terms, some employers may use a twenty-four-hour clock: 1:00 A.M. is 0100 hours; 1:00 P.M. is 1300 hours. An event occurring on February 19, 1994 at 2:30 P.M. is written 94/2/19/1430—year, month, day, time (hours/minutes). Give precise locations as well. "Highway 30" is not as helpful as "Highway 30, three miles southeast of the Morton exit." Call a machine by its precise technical name. Never use "thing," "gizmo," or "contraption" to refer to parts or tools. Keep any appropriate manuals or other reference materials handy to check on technical names, serial numbers, or codes. Refer to individuals by their proper names, not nicknames (Buddy, Red, Dee Dee).

5. Organization. Organization means order. And order means making your work easy for readers to follow and understand. Effective organization of a short report also means that you include the right amount of information in the most appropriate places for your audience. The organization of a short report will not be as elaborate as that for a long report. Many times a simple chronological or sequential organization will be acceptable for your readers' needs. Or you may follow one of the patterns of organization discussed in Chapter 3, pages 80-86.

Here is a fairly standard outline to follow when you are not required to submit a specially prepared form.

Purpose. Always begin with a statement of purpose. Tell readers why you are writing to them and alert them to what you will discuss. When you establish the scope (or limits) of your report, you help readers zero in on the specific times, places, procedures, or problems you will discuss. Depending on your exact purpose and audience, you may have to start with a clear explanation or description of the problem to be studied or solved. You may also need to provide necessary background information (e.g., a summary of an earlier report or occurrence) to assist readers.

Findings. The data that you collected go under the section on findings. Data include the facts you have gathered about prices, personnel, equipment, events, locations, incidents, or experiments. Gather these data from your research, personal observations, interviews, or conversations with clients, coworkers, or employers. Many times you will find it convenient and helpful to readers to list your data in an appropriate visual, especially a table or graph. See how visuals are used in the reports contained in Figures 16.3, 16.9, and 16.12. Some short reports even attach a computer printout with statistical data, as in Figure 16.2.

Conclusion. The conclusion can be a brief summary of what has happened or a review of what actions were taken. In a conclusion you might also explain the outcome or results of a test, a visit, or a program. The conclusion tells readers what your data mean.

Recommendations. A recommendation tells readers what specific actions need to be taken: when, where, what, why, and how. Recommendations must be based on the data you have collected and the conclusions you reached. The placement of recommendations in a short report can vary. Some employers prefer to see recommendations at the beginning of a report; others want them listed last. Some short reports (e.g., those included in Figures 16.1, 16.2, 16.5, 16.8) do not require a recommendation. Be sure to find out if your reader will expect you to make one.

Periodic Reports

Periodic reports, as their name signifies, provide readers with information at regularly scheduled intervals—daily, weekly, bimonthly (twice a month), monthly, quarterly. They help a company or agency keep track of the quantity and quality of the services it provides and the amount and types of work done by employees. Today much information contained in periodic reports is tracked by computer. Information in periodic reports helps managers make schedules, order materials, assign personnel, budget funds, and, generally speaking, determine agency or corporate needs.

You may already be familiar with some kinds of periodic reports. For example, if you have ever punched a timecard and turned it in at the end of the week, or if you have ever taken inventory in a stockroom, you have prepared a periodic report.

Periodic reports are used for numerous jobs. Delivery services require drivers to keep a daily record documenting the number of packages delivered, the time, and the location. *A log,* another kind of periodic report, is shown in Figure 16.1.

FIGURE 16.1   A log, a type of periodic report.

DENVER POLICE DEPARTMENT
DAILY ACTIVITY LOG
Page ____ of ____ pages

Name					Ser. No.		Name			Ser. No.

| Date | Mo. | Day | Yr. | Unit No. | | Unit No. | | Class 1 Actions | No. | Min. | ON DUTY TIME Assgnd. & O'time : | | Sgt. Approved : | Ser. No. |

Detail — Mileage Off — Mileage Off — Class 2 Actions — Total Time Used : All Action Classes — Clerk Recapped : — Ser. No.

From: To — Mileage On — Mileage On — Class 3 Actions — Captain Approved : — Ser. No.

Dist. & Precinct / — Total — Total — Total Class Actions — Patrol Time

Act. Cl.	Call Code	Time Out	Time In	Time Used	LOCATION, KIND OF ACTION AND DISPOSITION: Names, License, Citation No., etc.

CLASS 1 Felony Arr.
CLASS 1 Misc. Arrests
CLASS 2 Felony Arrests
CLASS 2 Misc. Arrests
CLASS 2 DUI Arrests
CLASS 2 Open Door
Recovered Units
Contact Cards
Offense Reports
Other Reports
Moving Violations
Parking Violations
Warning Violations
Accident Violations
Accident Reports

UNIT INSPECTION RECORD

Date	Unit No.	Car No.	Speedometer Reading	Old DAMAGE New	Officer	Ser. No.	Officer	Ser. No.	Supervisor

COMMENTS OR DEFECTS:

Right Side   Left Side   Front   Rear

Reprinted courtesy of the Denver Police Department.

At the end of a tour of duty, for example, law enforcement officers submit a daily activity log showing hours worked and actions taken. Often information from these daily logs is stored in a computer to allow for easy retrieval. Employees at television and radio stations may have to keep weekly reports of calls received by the station to aid management in determining the types of programming to offer.

Periodic reports follow no single format. Employers often supply routine forms on which to list information. These forms, such as the one illustrated in Figure 16.1, are relatively easy to complete. They ask for numbers, dates, codes, and expenses; occasionally a few clarifying or descriptive comments have to be added. Clearly distinguished categories on routine forms help to organize information for readers.

Other kinds of periodic reports may require more writing. You may be responsible for compiling a report based on individual periodic reports. Figure 16.2, a report submitted to a police captain, summarizes, organizes, and interprets the data collected over a three-month period from individual activity logs similar to the one in Figure 16.1. Such a report answers the reader's questions about the frequency and types of crimes committed and the work of the police force in the community. Because of this report, Captain Alice Martin will be better able to plan future protection for the community and to recommend changes in police services.

Sales Reports

Sales reports provide businesses with a necessary record of accounts, purchases, and profits over a specified period of time. Sales reports might be considered a special type of periodic report, but because of their importance in the world of business they deserve a separate category here. They are important at various levels of business. Retail stores require a daily sales report in which purchases, classified by bar code scanners, are arranged into major categories. Salespersons often submit weekly reports on the types and costs of products sold in a given district. Branch managers write monthly reports based on the figures given to them by their sales force. Higher up the business ladder, the president of a company sends stockholders an annual report assessing the financial health of the business. A report sent to someone at the same level of management as the writer (branch manager to branch manager) is known as a *lateral report*. A report sent to a higher executive level than the level of the writer (branch manager to vice president of marketing) is known as a *vertical report*.

Sales reports help businesses assess past performance and plan for the future. In doing this they fulfill two functions: financial and managerial. As a financial record, sales reports list costs per unit, discounts or special reductions, and subtotals and totals. Like an accountant's ledger or spreadsheet, sales reports show gains and losses. They may also provide statistics for comparing two quarters' sales. The method or origin of a sale, if significant, can also be recorded. In selling

FIGURE 16.2   A quarterly periodic report.

GREENFIELD POLICE DEPARTMENT
"To Serve and To Protect"
Greenfield, TX 77003

Administration 555-1000   Traffic 555-1001   Drug Enforcement 555-1002

TO: Captain Alice Martin

FROM: Sergeants Daniel Huxley, Jennifer Chavez, and Peter Kellogg

SUBJECT: Crime rate for the first quarter of 1993

DATE: April 11, 1994

From January 1 to March 31, 1,276 crimes were committed in Greenfield, representing a 25 percent increase over the 1,021 crimes recorded during the previous quarter.

The following report, based on the enclosed computer printout, discusses the specific types of crimes, organized into three categories: felonies, traffic, and misdemeanors.

FELONIES

The greatest increase in crime was in robberies, 20 percent higher than last quarter's figure (126 robberies). Downtown merchants reported 75 burglaries totaling more than $850,000. The biggest theft occurred on January 21 at Weisenfarth's Jewelers when three armed robbers stole more than $97,000 in merchandise. (These suspects were apprehended three days later.) Home burglaries accounted for 43 crimes, though the thefts were not confined to any one residential area. We also had 39 car thefts reported and investigated.

The number of homicides decreased from last quarter. During the first quarter, we had 8 homicides as opposed to 9 last quarter. Charges for battery, however, increased to 92--15 more than we had last quarter. There were 5 charges for arson, 11 for carrying a concealed weapon, and 47 for possession of a controlled substance. The number of rapes for this quarter was 8, fewer than last quarter (9). Three of those rapes happened within one week (February 6–12) and have been attributed to the same suspect, now in custody.

FIGURE 16.2   (Continued)

Captain Martin
April 11, 1994
Page 2

TRAFFIC

Traffic violations for this period were lower than last quarter's
figures. The 319 citations for moving violations for the first quarter
represent a 5 percent decrease over last quarter's 335 violations. Most were
issued for speeding (158) or for failing to observe signals (98). Officers
issued 45 citations to motorists for DUI. These citations point to an
impressive decrease over the 78 issued last quarter. The new state penalty
of withholding for six months the driver's license of anyone convicted of
driving while under the influence appears to be an effective deterrent.

MISDEMEANORS

The largest number of arrests in this category were for disturbing the
peace--53. Compared to last quarter, this is an increase of 10 percent.
There were 48 charges for vagrancy and public drunkenness, a decrease from
the 59 charges brought last quarter. We issued 32 citations for violation of
leash laws, which represents a sizable increase over last quarter's 21
citations. Fifty citations were issued for violations of city codes and
ordinances; 37 of those 50 citations were issued for dumping trash at the
Mason Reservoir.

Encl. computer printout

books, for example, a publisher keeps a careful record of where sales originate—
direct orders for single copies from readers, adoptions for classroom use, purchases at bookstores, or orders from wholesale distributors handling the book.

Sales reports are also a managerial tool, because they help businesses make
both short- and long-range plans. By indicating the number of sales, the report
alerts buyers and managers about which items or services to increase, modify, or
discontinue. The sales report illustrated in Figure 16.3 guides the restaurant owners in menu planning. Knowing which popular dishes to highlight and which
unpopular ones to delete, the owners can increase profits. Note how the recommendations follow from the figures Sam Jelinek gives to Gina Smeltzer and Frank
Drew, the owners of the Palace Restaurant.

To write a sales report, keep a careful record of order forms, invoices, and
production figures. Sales information might be arranged in list form, as in Figure

FIGURE 16.3   A sales report in tabular form.

The Palace
Dayton, OH 43210
(813) 555-4000

TO: Gina Smeltzer   DATE: June 27, 1994
       Frank Drew, Owners

FROM: Sam Jelinek *S.J.*   SUBJECT: Analysis of entrée
       Manager   sales, June 12–25

As we agreed at our monthly meeting on June 3, here is my analysis of entrée sales for two weeks to assist us in our menu planning. Below is a record of entrée sales for the weeks of June 12–18 and June 19–25 that I have compiled into a table for easier comparisons.

	Portion Size	June 12–18 Amount	June 12–18 Ratio	June 19–25 Amount	June 19–25 Ratio	2 weeks combined Amount	2 weeks combined Ratio
Cornish Hen	6 oz.	238	17%	307	17%	545	17%
Stuffed Young Turkey	8 oz.	112	8	182	10	294	9
Broiled Salmon Steak	8 oz.	154	11	217	12	371	12
Brook Trout	12 oz.	182	13	252	14	434	13
Prime Rib	10 oz.	168	12	198	11	366	11
Lobster Tails	2–4 oz.	147	10	161	9	308	10
Delmonico Steak	10 oz.	56	4	70	4	126	4
Moroccan Chicken	6 oz.	343	25	413	23	756	24
		1,400	**100%**	**1,800**	**100%**	**3,200**	**100%**

Recommendations

Based on the figures in the table above, I recommend that we do the following:

1. order at least one hundred more pounds of prime rib each two-week period to be eligible for further quantity discounts from the Northern Meat Company
2. delete the Delmonico steak entrée because of low acceptance
3. introduce a new chicken or fish entrée to take the place of the Delmonico steak; I would suggest grilled lemon chicken. This addition would help us to further meet the needs of those of our patrons interested in tasty, low fat, lower cholesterol entries.

Please give me your reactions within the next week. It shouldn't take more than two weeks to implement these changes.

FIGURE 16.4   A narrative sales report.

HAMILTON COIN SHOP
Erie, PA 17321-3636
555-1228

TO: Harry T. Udall   DATE: September 8, 1994
       Owner

FROM: Jessica Alonzo   SUBJECT: Favorable August sales
      Manager   J.A.

ROUTINE SALES

Our sales were brisk during August. Sales of **mint sets** and **proof sets** totaled **$2,043**. The sale of individual coins came to $2,925. **Commemorative coin** sales were **$651**. These sales total **$5,619**.

SPECIAL SALES

The most impressive sales came from our offer to sell pennies by the pound. We placed ads in the **Erie Times-News** and in **Coin World Today**. Our ads over WTOR AM may also have helped sales. Although it is hard to determine what portion of our walk-in business came from the radio announcements, possibly it was as much as a third. The total sales for the **pennies by the pound** were **$7,413**.

OVERALL SALES ACTIVITY

Sales for the month of August come to **$13,032**. Detailed breakdowns of these figures will appear in my September 30 quarterly report.

16.3, or in narrative form, as in Figure 16.4. If you use the narrative format, make sure you do not overload your readers with numbers. Underlining key numbers or putting them in boldface, as Jessica Alonzo does in Figure 16.4, will emphasize them for a reader.

Progress Reports

A *progress report* informs readers about the status of an ongoing project. It lets them know how much and what type of work has been completed by a particular date and how close the entire job is to being completed. A progress report emphasizes whether you are (1) keeping on schedule, (2) staying within a budget, (3) using the proper equipment, (4) making the right assignments, and (5) completing the job efficiently and correctly. Almost any kind of ongoing work can be described in a progress report—research for a paper, construction of an apartment complex, preparation of a fall catalog, documentation of a patient's rehabilitation.

A progress report is intended for people who generally are not working alongside you, but who need a record of your activities to coordinate them with other individuals' efforts and to learn about problems or changes in plans. For example, since local management or supervisors at the home office cannot be in the field or branch office or at the construction site, they will rely on a progress report for much of their information. Customers, too, will expect a report on how carefully their money is being spent. That way they can make any alterations in schedules or decide whether to change something in order not to go over a budget.

The length of the report will depend on the complexity of the project. A short memo about organizing a time management workshop, such as that in Figure 16.5, might be all that is necessary. A report to a teacher about the progress a

FIGURE 16.5   A one-time progress report.

R **REPUBLIC INDUSTRIES**	P.O. Box 5073 Trenton, NJ 08542-5073 609-555-9000 FAX 609-555-9876

TO: Kathy Sands, Trenton   DATE: September 14, 1994

FROM: Philip Javon   SUBJECT: Preparations for the
                                                 Time Management
                                                 Workshop

As you requested last week, I sent E-mail and Telex messages to the managers of all departments in both our Trenton and Frankfurt, Germany, offices on Thursday, September 8, to remind them of the time management workshop we will offer on October 8–9. I also confirmed travel arrangements for out-of-town managers today.

I have reserved the corporate conference center for both October 8 and 9 and ordered all the supplies we will need. The management kit will have the company brochures on organization policies, the time sheets used in the plants, the report forms we used last March, and the research department's report on improved time management and sales projections. I have also arranged with Carmen Suarez in the audiovisual department to set up the audiovisuals on the morning of October 8. By tomorrow I hope to complete a list of all those who will participate in the workshop.

Plans are going according to schedule.

cc: Hans Kohl, Frankfurt

student is making on a research paper could easily be handled in a one-page memo, such as James Salinas's progress report in Figure 16.6 for his research paper proposed on pages 577–579. Similarly, Dale Brandt's assessment of the progress his construction company is making in renovating Dr. Burke's office is given in a two-page letter in Figure 16.7 (pages 602–603).

Progress reports should contain information on (1) the work you have done, (2) the work you currently are doing, and (3) the work you will do.

They can be written daily, weekly, monthly, quarterly, or annually. Your specific job and your employer's needs will dictate how often you have to keep others informed of your progress. Nurses have to write progress notes for each eight- or twelve-hour shift; management trainees may have to submit a weekly report of their accomplishments. A single progress report is sufficient for Philip Javon's purpose in Figure 16.5. James Salinas has been asked to submit two progress reports, the first of which is in Figure 16.6. Contractor Brandt in Figure 16.7 has found that three separate reports, spaced four to six weeks apart, are needed to keep Dr. Burke posted.

How to Begin a Progress Report

In a brief introduction, indicate why you are writing the report. Provide any necessary project titles or codes and specify dates. Help readers recall the job you are doing for them. If you are writing an initial progress report, supply background information. Philip Javon's first two sentences in Figure 16.5 quickly establish his purpose by reminding Kathy Sands of their discussion last week. Similarly, James Salinas in Figure 16.6 reminds his teacher of the purpose and scope of his work in the first paragraph. If you are submitting a subsequent progress report, show where the previous report left off and where the current one begins. Make sure that the period covered by each report is clearly specified. Notice how Dale Brandt's first paragraph in Figure 16.7 calls attention to the continuity of his work.

How to Continue a Progress Report

The body of the report should provide significant details about costs, materials, personnel, and times for the major stages of the project. Emphasize completed tasks, not false starts. If you report that the carpentry work or painting is finished, readers do not need an explanation of paint viscosity or geometrical patterns. Omit routine or well-known details ("I had to use the library when I wanted to read the back issues of *Safety News*") in your progress report. Describe in the body of the discussion, too, any snags you encountered. See Dale Brandt's section on electrical problems in Figure 16.7. It is better for the reader to know about trouble early in the project, so that appropriate changes or corrections can be made.

How to End a Progress Report

The conclusion should give a timetable for the completion of duties or when the next progress report can be expected. Give the date by which work will be completed; be realistic. Do not promise to have a job done in less time than you know

FIGURE 16.6   **A progress report from a student to a teacher.**

TO: Professor Barbara Felton-Parks

FROM: James Salinas

DATE: April 8, 1993

SUBJECT: First Progress Report on Research Paper

This is the first of two progress reports that you asked me
to submit about my research paper on the advantages and
disadvantages of electronic mail.

From March 8 until April 6, I gathered information from
library materials and from an interview. Of the fifteen
references listed on my proposal, I found only nine.
Stevens-Renfrow, Telecommunications: An Introduction, the
articles by Foley ("Hardware Vendors Adapt to Changing E-Mail
Market") and Nall ("How to Use Electronic Mail Successfully"),
as well as "Bidirectional Electronic Mail . . ." (Communication
News) are not in our library. I have ordered them through
interlibrary loan.

On February 23, I had an extended interview (1-1/2 hours)
with Mr. Keith Wellbridge of General Dynamics, who gave me
some brochures as well as a copy of a report on electronic
mail he wrote for General Dynamics--materials I hope to
incorporate in my paper.

Because of a long business trip to Denver, Ms. Alice Phillips
of Dodge & Spenser could not meet with me. At her suggestion,
I am trying to schedule an interview with Ms. Gloria Sirkin,
the office manager at Mid-Atlantic Power Company. Her firm
has recently switched to electronic mail.

Even if Ms. Sirkin cannot meet with me, I believe that Mr.
Wellbridge gave me enough information about a business
manager's view of electronic mail systems. However, not
having the Stevens-Renfrow book and the articles cited above
may slow, but not stop, my work a little.

Starting tomorrow, I will begin organizing my paper. I will
be able to submit a draft by April 27. You will receive my
second progress report on the organization of my paper by
April 20.

FIGURE 16.7 **The second of three progress reports from a contractor to a customer.**

BRANDT CONSTRUCTION COMPANY
Halsted at Roosevelt
Chicago, Illinois 60608-0999

312-555-3700   **FAX 312-555-1731**

April 28, 1994

Dr. Pamela Burke
1439 Grand Avenue
Mount Prospect, IL 60045-1003

Dear Dr. Burke:

Here is my second progress report about the renovation work at your new
clinic at Hacienda and Donohue. Work proceeded satisfactorily in April
according to the plans you had approved in March.

REVIEW OF WORK COMPLETED IN MARCH

As I informed you in my first progress report on March 31, we had torn
down the walls, pulled the old wiring, and removed existing plumbing
work. All the gutting work was finished in March.

WORK COMPLETED DURING APRIL

By April 8, we had laid the new pipes and connected them to the main
sewer line. We had also installed the two commodes, the four standard
sinks, and the utility basin. The heating and air-conditioning ducts
were installed by April 13. From April 18 to 23, we erected soundproof
walls in the four examination rooms, the reception area, your office,
and the laboratory. We had no problems reducing the size of the
reception area by five feet to make the first examination room larger,
as you had requested.

PROBLEMS WITH ELECTRICAL SYSTEM

We had difficulty with the electrical work, however. The number of
outlets and the generator for the laboratory equipment required
extra-duty power lines that had to be approved by both Con Edison and
county inspectors. The approval slowed us down three days. Also, the
wholesaler, Midtown Electric, failed to deliver the recessed lighting
fixtures by April 25 as promised.

FIGURE 16.7 (Continued)

---

page 2

These fixtures and the generator are now being installed. Moreover, the cost of these fixtures will increase the material budget by $568.00. The cost for labor is as we had projected--$89,450.

WORK REMAINING

The finishing work is scheduled for May. By May 9, the floors in the examination rooms, laboratory, washrooms, and hallways should be tiled and the reception area and your office carpeted. By May 13, the reception area and your office should be paneled and the rest of the walls painted. If everything stays on schedule, touch-up work is scheduled for May 16–20. You should be able to move into your new clinic by May 23.

You will receive a third and final progress report by May 13.

Sincerely yours,

Dale Brandt

Dale Brandt

---

it will take. Readers will not expect miracles, only informed estimates. Any conclusion must be tentative. Note that the good news Dale Brandt gives Dr. Burke about moving into her new clinic is qualified by the words "if everything stays on schedule." A recommendation may also find a place in the conclusion. Such a recommendation might advise readers, for example, of a less costly, equally durable siding than the one originally planned, suggest that a joint meeting of two committees would expedite production of a college yearbook, or show that hiring an additional part-time salesclerk would help ease the busy workload over the holiday sales period.

Trip Reports

Reporting on the trips you take is an important professional responsibility. Trips can range from a brief afternoon car ride across town to a one-month long journey across the country. You may travel alone or you may be asked to travel with coworkers and to write reports collaboratively on your findings. These reports inform readers about your activities outside the office, plant, clinic, or agency. In documenting what you did and saw, these *trip reports* help your readers to better understand what has happened and even give them information they can use for later reports. Specifically, a trip report should answer the following questions for your readers.

1. Where did you go?
2. When did you go there?
3. Why did you go there?
4. Whom did you see?
5. What did they tell you?

For a business trip you are likely to have to inform readers how much the trip cost and to supply them with receipts for all your expenses.

Common Types of Trip Reports

Trip reports can cover a wide range of activities and are called by different names to characterize those activities. Undoubtedly, you will encounter the following three types of trip reports.

1. Field trip reports. These reports, often assigned in a course, are written after a visit to a local plant, military installation, garage, hospital, forest, detention center, or other facility. Their purpose is to show what you have learned about the operation of these places. You will be expected to describe how an institution is organized, the equipment or procedures it uses, the ecological conditions present, or the ratio of one group to another. The emphasis in these reports is on the educational values of the trip, as Mark Tourneur's report in Figure 16.8 demonstrates.

2. Site inspection reports. These trip reports are written to inform managers, department heads, or section chiefs about conditions at a branch office or plant, a customer's business, or at an area directly under an employer's jurisdiction. Site inspection reports tell how machinery or production procedures are working or provide information about the physical plant, environment (air, soil, water), and computer or financial operations. A site inspection report will be written for an employer or a customer who wants to relocate or build new facilities (such as a record shop, a halfway house, or a branch office) in order to assess the suitability of a particular location. Accreditation or financial auditing teams prepare site inspection reports to assess the quality or fiscal status of an agency or organization. After visiting the site, you will determine whether it meets your employer's (or customer's) needs. Figure 16.9 (pp. 607–608), which shows a report written to a manager interested in acquiring a new site for a fast-food restaurant, begins with a recommendation.

3. Home health or social work visits. Nurses, social workers, and probation officers report daily on their visits to patients and clients. Their reports describe clients' lifestyles, assess needs, and make recommendations. A report from a social

FIGURE 16.8   A student's field trip report.

TO: Katherine Holmes, RN, MSN   DATE: November 11, 1994
      Director, RN Program

FROM: Mark Tourneur *M. T.*   SUBJECT: Field Trip to
      RN Student   Water Valley
                                         Extended Care
                                         Center

On Tuesday, November 8, I visited the Water Valley
Convalescent Center, 1400 Medford Boulevard, in
preparation for my internship in an extended care facility
next semester.

Philosophy and Organization

Before my tour started, the director, Sue LaFrance,
explained the holistic philosophy of health care at Water
Valley and emphasized the diverse kinds of nursing
practiced there. She stressed that the agency is not
restricted to geriatric clients but admits anyone
requiring long-term care. She pointed out that Water
Valley is a medium-sized facility (150 beds) and contains
three wings: (1) the Infirmary, (2) the General Nursing
Unit, and (3) the Ambulatory Unit.

Primary Client Services

My tour began with the Infirmary, staffed by one RN and
two LPNs, where I observed a number of life-support
systems in operation--IVs, oxygen setups, feeding tubes,
and cardiac monitors. Then I was shown the General Nursing
Unit, a forty-bed unit that is staffed by three LPNs and
four aides. Clients can have private or semiprivate rooms;
bathrooms have wide doors and lowered sinks for patients
using wheelchairs or walkers. The ambulatory section cares
for ninety clients who can provide their own daily care.

Additional Client Services

Before lunch in the main dining room, I was introduced to
Doris Betz, the dietitian, who explained the different
menus she coordinates. The most common are low-sodium and
ADA (American Diabetic Association) restricted-calorie.
Staff members eat with the clients, reinforcing the
holistic concern of the agency.

FIGURE 16.ᶜ (Continued)

After lunch, Jack Tishner, the pharmacist, discussed the
agency's procedures for ordering and delivering medications.
He also explained the kinds of client teaching he does and
the in-service workshops he conducts. I then observed
clients in both recreational and physical therapy. Water
Valley's full-time physical therapist, Tracy Cook, works
with stroke and arthritic clients and helps those with
broken bones regain the use of their limbs. In addition to
a weight room, Water Valley has a small sauna that most
of the clients use at least twice a week. The clients'
spiritual needs are not neglected, either. A small chapel
is located just off the Ambulatory Unit.

Benefits for My Internship

From my visit to Water Valley, I learned a great deal
about the health care delivery system at an extended
care facility. I was especially pleased to have been
given so much information on emergency procedures,
medication orders, and physical therapy programs. My
forthcoming internship will be much more useful, since I
have firsthand knowledge about these available services.

---

worker to a county family services agency can be seen in Figure 16.10
(pp. 609-610). The report begins with the information Jeff Bowman acquired
from his visit with the Scanlons and concludes, not with a recommendation, but
rather with a list of the actions this social worker has taken.

How to Gather Information for a Trip Report

Regardless of the kind of trip report you have to write, your assignment will be
easier and your report better organized if you follow these suggestions.

Before You Leave for the Site

1. Obtain all necessary names, addresses, telephone, and fax numbers.
2. Check the files for previous correspondence, case studies, terms of contracts,
   or agreements.
3. Locate a map of the area or a blueprint of the building.
4. Look for brochures, work orders, instructions, or other documents pertinent
   to your visit.
5. Make sure you have a notebook and a pen with you.
6. Depending on your job, you may also need to bring a camcorder, tape recorder, camera, or calculator. Use these instruments to record important data.

FIGURE 16.9   A site inspection report using a map.

VAIL'S, INC.
Denver, CO 87123
(303) 555-7200

TO: Dale Gandy   DATE: July 1, 1994
        District Manager

FROM: Beth Armando *B.A.*   SUBJECT: New Site for Vail's #8
        Development Department

RECOMMENDATION

The best location for the new Vail's Chicken House is the vacant Dairy
World shop at the northeast corner of Smith and Fairfax Avenues--
1701 Fairfax. I inspected this property on June 21 and 22 and also
talked with Marge Bloom, the broker at Crescent Realty representing the
Dairy World Company.

THE LOCATION

Please refer to the map below. Located at the intersection of the two
busiest streets on the southeast side, the property allows us to take
advantage of the traffic flow to attract customers. Being only one block
west of the Cloverleaf Mall should also help business. Customers have easy
access to our location.

FIGURE 16.9   (Continued)

Dale Gandy
July 1, 1994
Page 2

They can enter or exit the Dairy World from either Smith or Fairfax, but
left turns on Smith are prohibited from 7 A.M. to 9 A.M. However, since most
of our business is done after 11 A.M., the restriction poses few problems.

AREA COMPETITION

Only two other fast-food establishments are in a one-mile vicinity.
McGonagles, 1534 South Kildare, specializes in hamburgers; Noah's, 703
Zanwood, serves primarily fish entrées. Their offerings will not directly
compete with ours. The closest fast-food restaurant serving chicken is
Johnson's, 1.8 miles away.

PARKING FACILITIES

The parking lot has space for 45 cars. The area at the south end of the
property (38 feet x 37 feet) can accommodate another 14 to 15 cars. The
driveways and parking lot were paved with asphalt last March and appear to
be in excellent condition. We will be able to make use of the drive-up
window on the north side of the building.

THE BUILDING

The building has 3,993 square feet of heated and cooled space. The
air-conditioning and heating units were installed within the last fifteen
months and seem to be in good working order; nine more months of
transferable warranty remain on these units. The only major changes we would
have to make are in the kitchen. To prepare items on the Vail's menu, we
would have to add three more exhaust fans (there is only one now) and expand
the grill and cooking areas. The kitchen also has three relatively new sinks
and ample storage space in the sixteen cabinets.

The restaurant has a seating capacity of up to 54 persons; ten booths are
covered with red vinyl and are comfortably padded. A color-coordinated
serving counter could seat 8 to 10 patrons. The floor does not need to be
retiled, but the walls will have to be painted to match Vail's color decor.

FIGURE 16.10   A social worker's visit report.

Green County
Family Services
FAX 703-555-4004

Randall, VA 21032
703-555-4000

TO: Margaret S. Walker, Director
           Green County Family Services

FROM: Jeff Bowman, Social Worker   *J.B.*

SUBJECT: Visit to Mr. Lee Scanlon

DATE: October 14, 1994

PURPOSE OF VISIT

At the request of the Green County Home Health Office, I visited Mr.
Lee Scanlon at his home at 113 West Diversy Drive on Tuesday, October 11.
Mr. Scanlon and his three children (ages six, eight, and eleven) live in a
two-bedroom apartment above a garage. Last week, Mr. Scanlon was discharged
from Lutheran General Hospital after leg surgery and has asked for financial
assistance.

DESCRIPTION OF VISIT

Mr. Scanlon is a widower with no means of support except unemployment
compensation of $984 a month. He lost his job at Baymont Manufacturing when
the company went out of business four weeks ago and wants to go back to
work, but Dr. Canning-Smith advised against it for six to seven weeks. His
oldest child is diabetic, and the six-year-old daughter must have a
tonsillectomy. Mr. Scanlon also told me the problems he was having with his
refrigerator; it "was off more than it was on," he said.

Mrs. Alice Gordon, the owner of the garage, informed me that Mr.
Scanlon had paid last month's rent but not this month's. She also stressed
how much the Scanlons need a new refrigerator and that she had often let
them use part of hers to store their food.

Here is a breakdown of Mr. Scanlon's monthly bills:

Expenses	Income
$ 550 rent	$984 unemployment compensation
150 utilities	
350 food	
120 drugs	
80 transportation	
$1,150	

FIGURE 16.10   (Continued)

Margaret S. Walker
October 14, 1994
Page 2

ACTION TAKEN

To assist Mr. Scanlon, I have done the following:

1. Set up an appointment (10/20/94) for him to apply for food stamps.
2. Talked with Blanche Derringo regarding Medicaid assistance.
3. Asked the State Employment Commission to aid him in finding a job as
   soon as he is well enough to work. My contact person is Wesley Sahara.
4. Visited Robert Adkins at the office of the Council of Churches to obtain
   food and money for utilities until federal aid is available; he also
   will try to find the Scanlons another refrigerator.
5. Telephoned Sharon Muñez at the Green County Health Department to have
   Mr. Scanlon's diabetic daughter receive insulin and syringes gratis.

When You Return

1. Write your report promptly. If you put it off, you may forget important items.
2. When a trip takes you to two or more widely separated places, note in your report when you arrived at each place and how long you stayed.
3. Do not include in your report everything you saw or did on the trip. Exclude irrelevant details, such as whether the trip was enjoyable, where you stayed overnight, what you ate, or how delighted you were to meet people.
4. As you edit the final copy of your report, check to make sure that you have correctly transcribed names and figures from your notes.

Test Reports

Much physical research (the discovery of facts) is communicated through reports. These reports have various names. Depending on your profession's terminology, they may be called *experiment, investigation, laboratory, operations,* or *research reports.* They all record the results of tests, whether the tests were conducted in a forest, computer center, laboratory, parking lot, shopping center, or soybean field.

No doubt you have already written a *test report* (or laboratory report) after performing an experiment in a science class. Writing an effective test report involves specific training in a scientific or technological field.

Objectivity and accuracy are essential ingredients in a test report. Readers want to know about your empirical research (the facts), not about your feelings (the "I"). Record your observations without bias or guesswork in a laboratory journal or log book and always include precise measurements. When you draft and revise your report, tell readers why the test was made, under what circumstances (or controls) it was made, and what the outcome was. When you sign the final copy of your test report, you are certifying that things happened exactly when, how, and why you say they did.

Figure 16.11 (p. 612) contains a relatively simple and short test report in memo format regarding sanitary conditions at a hospital psychiatric unit. This report follows a direct and useful pattern of organization:

- statement of purpose
- findings
- recommendations

Submitted by an infection control officer, the report does not provide elaborate details about the particular laboratory procedures used to determine if bacteria were present; nor does it describe the pathogenic (disease-causing) properties of the bacteria. Such descriptions are unnecessary for the audience (the housekeeping department) to do its job.

A more complex example of a short test report is found in Figure 16.12 (pp. 613–615); it studies the effects of four light periods on the growth of paulownia (a flowering tree cultivated in China) seedlings. This report, published in a scientific journal, is addressed to specialists in forestry. To meet the needs of this expert audience, the writers had to include much more detailed information than Janeen Cufaude did about the way the test was conducted and about the types of data the audience would need to confirm and use the scientific data from the authors' tests. The researchers did not have to define technical terms for their audience, and they can confidently use scientific symbols and formulas as well. Such a test report follows a different pattern of organization than the one in Figure 16.11 and includes the following parts:

- **informative abstract** (see pages 413–414)
- **introduction** to provide background information about the importance of the test and perhaps to review previous research on the topic
- **materials and methods section** to describe the exact scientific procedures and equipment the author(s) used to conduct the test
- **results and discussion section** (sometimes separated into two sections) to record the data obtained from the test and to explain the significance of the data. Many times a test report will conclude by confirming previous studies, emphasizing the need for further tests, or offering researchers new interpretation of the evidence
- **list of references cited** in the study

Notice how the needs of two different audiences as well as the authors' purpose control the way each report is organized and how much and what type of information is included. Janeen Cufaude's reader is a nonspecialist, less interested in scientific theory than in the practical application of that theory; Immel, Tackett,

FIGURE 16.11   A test report with recommendations.

CHARLESTON CENTRAL HOSPITAL
CHARLESTON, WV 25324-0114

HOSPITAL

TO: James Dill, Supervisor   DATE: December 6, 1994
          Housekeeping

FROM: Janeen Cufaude *J. C.*   SUBJECT: Routine sanitation
          Infection Control Officer   inspection

As part of the monthly check of the psychiatric unit (11A), the following areas
were swabbed and tested for bacterial growth. The results of the lab tests of
these samples are as follows:

AREA   FINDINGS

1. cabinet in patients' kitchen   1. positive for 2 colonies of strep germs

2. rug in eating area   2. positive for food particles and yeasts
                                     and molds

3. baseboard in dayroom   3. positive for particles of dust and fungi

4. medicine counter in nurses'   4. negative for bacteria--no growth after
   station   48 hrs.

5. corridor by south elevator   5. positive for 4 colonies of staph germs

ACTIONS TO BE TAKEN AT ONCE

1. Clean the kitchen cabinet with K-504 liquid daily, 3:1 dilution.

2. Shampoo rug areas bimonthly with heavy-duty shampoo and clean visibly soiled
   areas with Guard-Pruf as often as needed.

3. Wipe all baseboards weekly with K-12 spray cleanser.

4. Mop heavily traveled corridors and access areas with K-504 cleanser daily, 1:1
   dilution.

and Carpenter's readers are experts demanding scientific documentation and commentary. As these two reports show, you should always determine how much technical knowledge an audience has about your field and how they will use your report to accomplish *their* specific job.

FIGURE 16.12   A short test report published in a scientific journal.

Paulownia Seedlings Respond to Increased Daylength

M. J. Immel, E. M. Tackett, and S. B. Carpenter

Abstract

Paulownia seedlings grown under four photoperiods were evaluated after a growing period of 97 days. Height growth and total dry weight production were both significantly increased in the 16- and 24-hour photoperiods.

Introduction

Paulownia (*Paulownia tomentosa* [Thunb.] Steud.), a native of China, is a little-known species in the United States. Recently, however, there has been increased interest in this species for surface mine reclamation (*1*).* Paulownia seems to be especially well adapted to harsh micro-climates of surface mines; it grows very rapidly and appears to be drought-resistant. In Kentucky and surrounding states, paulownia wood is actively sought by Japanese buyers and has brought prices comparable to black walnut (*2*).

This increased interest in paulownia has resulted in several attempts to direct seed it on surface mines, but little success has been achieved. The high light requirements and the extremely small size of paulownia seed (approximately 6,000 per gram) may be the limiting factors. Planting paulownia seedlings is preferred; but, because of their succulent nature, seedlings are usually produced and outplanted as container stock rather than bareroot seedlings. Daylength is an important factor in the production of vigorous container plants (*5*). Our study compares the effects that four photoperiods—8, 12, 16, and 24 hours—had on the early growth of container-grown paulownia seedlings over a period of 97 days.

Materials and Methods

Seeds used in this study were stratified in a 1:1 mixture of peat moss and sand at 4° C for 2 years. Following cold storage, seeds were placed on a 1:1 potting soil-sand mix and mulched with cheesecloth. They were then placed under continuous light until germination occurred. Germination percentages were high, indicating paulownia seeds can survive long periods of storage with little loss of viability (*3*). Thirty days after germination, 3- to 4-centimeter seedlings were transplanted into 8-quart plastic pots filled with an equal mixture of potting soil, sand, and peat moss. Seventy-five seedlings were randomly assigned to each of the four treatments. Treatments were for 4 photoperiods—8, 12, 16, and 24 hours—and were replicated three times in 12 light chambers. Each chamber was 1.2- by 1.2-meters with an artificial light source 71 centimeters above the chamber floor.

The light source consisted of eight fluorescent lights: four 40-watt plant growth lamps alternated with four 40-watt cool white lamps. Light intensity averaged 550 foot-candles (1340μ einsteins/m²/sec) at the top of each pot and the temperature averaged 23° C ($\pm$ 2°C).

---

*All actual references in the Works Cited section have been omitted to save space.

FIGURE 16.12   (Continued)

TABLE 1.   Height, Diameter, Root Length, Total Dry Weight, and
R/S Ratio for Paulownia Seedlings Grown Under Four Photoperiods
after 97 Days

Photo period (brs.)	Height (cm)	Diameter (cm)	Root length (cm)	Total dry weight (gm)	R/S ratio
8	13.1b	0.48	16.0	1.65c	0.18
12	17.8b	0.67	34.7	7.27b	0.32
16	27.3a	0.93	31.1	15.92a	0.39
24	29.2a	0.90	43.9	18.56a	0.33

Seedlings were kept watered and were fertilized after transplanting with a 6-gram 14-4-6 agriform container tablet. Beginning 1 month after transplanting, two seedlings were randomly selected and harvested from each chamber for a total of 24 trees. Height, root collar diameter, length of longest root, and oven-dry weight (at 65° C) were determined for each seedling. Harvests continued every week for 5 additional weeks.

Results and Discussion

Results indicate that early growth of paulownia is influenced by photoperiod, as shown in Table 1. Expanding the photoperiod from 8 to either 16 or 24 hours increased height growth by 100 percent. Height growth in the 12-hour treatment also increased, but did not differ significantly from the 8-hour treatment. Heights under photoperiods of 8, 12, 16, and 24 hours were 13.1, 17.8, 27.3, and 29.2 centimeters, respectively.

Previous studies have also shown that photoperiod affects the growth of paulownia seedlings (4, 6). Sanderson (6), for example, found that paulownia seedlings grown under continuous light averaged 27.2 centimeters in height after 101 days compared with 29.2 centimeters for our 24-hour seedlings. Other corresponding photoperiods were equally comparable. Downs and Borthwick (4) also concluded that height growth of paulownia was affected by extending the photoperiod.

The greatest treatment differences were shown in total dry weight production. Refer again to Table 1. The mean weight of 1.65 grams for seedlings in the 8-hour treatment was significantly less than that of any of the other photoperiods. The 16- and 24-hour treatments did not differ significantly. In fact, they more than doubled the average weight for seedlings in he 12-hour treatment.

Root-to-shoot ratio (R/S) indicates the relative proportion of growth allocated to roots versus shoots for the seedlings in each photoperiod. In this study, shoots were developing at nearly three times the rate of the roots for seedlings in the 12-, 16-, and 24-hour photoperiods. The 0.18 R/S ratio for seedlings in the 8-hour treatment was much lower, indicating that relative growth of the shoot is approximately five times that of the root. The shorter photoperiod therefore decreased root development relative to shoot development as well as significantly reduced total dry weight production.

FIGURE 16.12   (Continued)

> Although root collar diameter and root length did not significantly differ under the different photoperiods after 97 days, there was a trend for greater diameter and root growth with longer photoperiods.
>
> **Conclusions**
>
> Results indicate that the growth of paulownia seedlings is affected by changes in the photoperiod. Increasing the photoperiod significantly increased height growth and total dry matter production. The distribution of dry matter (R/S ration) was altered by increasing the photoperiod; the ratio was larger in the longer photoperiods. In contrast to earlier studies (4), we found paulownia seedlings subjected to extended photoperiods were still growing after 97 days.

Tree Planters' Notes 31 (Winter 1980): 3–5.

Incident Reports

The reports discussed thus far in this chapter have dealt with routine work. They have described events that were anticipated or supervised. But every business or agency runs into unexpected trouble that delays routine work. Employers, and on some occasions government inspectors, insurance agents, and attorneys, must be informed about those events that interfere with or threaten normal, safe operations. A special type of report known as an *incident report* is submitted when there is an accident, law enforcement offense, environmental danger, machine breakdown, delivery delay, cost overrun, or production slowdown.

Protecting Yourself Legally

The incident report can be used as legal evidence. It frequently concerns the two topics over which powerful legal battles are waged—health and property. The report can sway the outcome of insurance claims, civil suits, or criminal cases and therefore requires careful planning and revision. To ensure that what you write is legally proper, follow these three guidelines:

1. Be accurate, objective, and complete. Never omit or distort facts; the information may surface later, and you could be found guilty of a cover-up. Do not just write "I do not know" for an answer. If you are not sure, state why. Also be careful that there are no discrepancies in your report.

2. Give facts, not opinions. Provide a factual account of what actually happened, not a biased interpretation of events. Indirect words, such as "I guess," "I wonder," "apparently," "perhaps," or "possibly," weaken your objectivity. Stick to details you witnessed or that were seen by eyewitnesses. Identify witnesses or victims by giving names, addresses, place of employment, and so on. Indicate who saw what. Keep in mind that stating what someone else saw will be regarded as hearsay, and therefore not be admissible in a court of law. State only what *you* saw or heard. When you describe what happened, avoid drawing uncalled-for conclusions. Consider the following statements of opinion and fact:

Opinion   The patient seemed confused and caught himself in his IV tubing.
Fact   The patient caught himself in his IV tubing.

Opinion   The equipment was defective.
Fact   The bolt was loose.

Be careful, too, about blaming someone. Statements such as "Baxter was incompetent" or "The company knew of the problem, but did nothing about it" are libelous remarks.

In law enforcement work, identify a suspect by his or her alias and by any distinctive characteristics, for example "jagged 4-inch scar on left forearm."

3. Do not exceed your professional responsibilities. Answer only those questions you are qualified to answer. Do not presume to speak as a detective, inspector, physician, or supervisor. Do not represent yourself as an attorney or claims adjuster in writing the report.

Parts of an Incident Report

You will use either a memo or a specially prepared form with spaces for detailed comments. Figure 16.13 contains an incident report written in memo format; Figure 16.14 (p. 618) shows a typical incident report form used to report an accident. Regardless of the format used, all incident reports will ask for the following information.

1. Personal details. Record titles, department, and employment identification numbers. Indicate if you or your fellow employees were working alone. For customers or victims, record home addresses, phone numbers, and places of employment. Insurance companies will also require policy numbers. Note that the first four questions in Figure 16.14 request this kind of information.

2. Type of incident. Briefly identify the incident—personal injury, fire, burglary, delivery delay, equipment failure. In the case of injury, identify the part(s) of the body precisely. "Eye injury" is not enough; "injury to the right eye, causing bleeding" is better. "Dislocated right shoulder," "punctured left forearm," and "twisted left ankle" are descriptive and exact phrases. A report on damaged equipment should list model numbers. Note how Ned Roane's report (Figure 16.13) specifies the grain car numbers. For thefts, supply colors, brand names and/or manufacturer, model names, serial numbers, and quantities. "A stolen watch" will not help detectives locate the right object; "a seven-jewel lady's Benrus" will.

3. Time and location of the incident. Follow the advice given at the beginning of this chapter, page 591.

4. Description of what happened. This section is the longest part of the report. Some forms ask you to write on the back, to attach another sheet, or to add a photograph or diagram. Put yourself in the reader's position. If you were not

FIGURE 16.13   An incident report in memo format.

 THE GREAT HARVESTER RAILROAD
P.O. Box 4005
Des Moines, IA 50306-4005

TO: Angela O'Brien   DATE: March 3, 1994
        District Manager
        James Day
        Safety Inspector

FROM: Ned Roane *N.R.*   SUBJECT: Derailment of Train 28 on
        Engineer   March 3, 1994

DESCRIPTION OF INCIDENT

    At 7:20 A.M. on March 3, 1994, I was driving Engine 457 traveling north
at a speed of fifty-two miles an hour on the single main-line track four
miles east of Ridgeville, Illinois. Weather conditions and visibility were
excellent. Suddenly the last two grain cars, 3022 and 3053, jumped the
track. The train automatically went into emergency braking and stopped
immediately. There were no injuries to the crew. But the train did not stop
before both grain cars turned at a 45° angle. After checking the cars, I
found that half the contents of their load had spilled. The train was not
carrying any hazardous chemical shipments.

    I notified Supervisor Bill Purvis by AMAX telephone at 7:40 A.M., and
within forty-five minutes he and a section crew arrived at the scene with
rerailing equipment--a bulldozer and a derrick. The section crew removed the
two grain cars from the track, put in new ties, and made the main-line track
passable by 9:25. At 9:45 a vacuum car arrived with Engine 372 from
Hazlehurst, Illinois, and its crew proceeded with the cleanup operation. By
10:25 A.M. all the spilled grain was loaded onto the cars brought by the
Hazlehurst train. Bill Purvis called Barnwell Granary and notified them that
their shipment would be at least three hours late.

CAUSES OF INCIDENT

    Supervisor Purvis and I checked the stretch of train track where the
cars derailed and found it to be heavily worn. We believe that a defective
fisher joint slipped when the grain cars hit it, and the track broke.

RECOMMENDATIONS

    We made the following recommendations to the switch yard in Hazlehurst
to be carried out immediately:

1. Check the section of track for ten miles on either side of Ridgeville for
   defective fisher joints.

2. Repair all such defective joints at once.

3. Instruct all engineers to slow down to five to ten mph over this section
   of the road until the rail check is completed.

FIGURE 16.14 An accident report form.

DIVERSIFIED INDUSTRIES, INC.
Baltimore, Maryland

(301) 555-4656   FAX (301) 555-4603

ACCIDENT REPORT

1. Name of the employee (last, first, middle) _____
2. Employee identification number _____
3. Social Security number _____
4. Home address and telephone number _____
5. Time of injury _____ A.M. Location _____
   P.M.
6. Type of injury (specify exact body part[s]) _____
   _____

7. What kind of treatment did injured party receive? Where was treatment given?
   _____
   _____

8. Describe what happened (give a narrative of events before, during, and after; describe any materials or tools involved in accident):

9. Provide names and addresses of eyewitnesses:

10. What caused the accident?

11. What action should be taken to prevent similar accidents from occurring in the future?

12. Which company employees (e.g., supervisor, union representative) were notified?

Signature of person filling out form _____

Date form is filled out _____

Send white copy to Home Office records; green copy to Safety Department; and yellow copy to Personnel Department.

---

present or did not speak directly to witnesses, would you know by reading the report what happened exactly and why, how it occurred, who and what were involved, and what led up to the incident?

The two most common errors writers make are that they do not give (1) enough information or (2) the right kinds of information. Recount what happened in the order in which it took place. What you (or eyewitnesses) saw, heard, felt, and smelled are the essentials of your description. Describe what happened before the incident, if that is relevant—for example, environmental or weather conditions for storm damage or an automobile accident, or warning signals for a malfunctioning machine. If you are depending on an eyewitness account, use quotation marks to set off statements by the witness. But delete any emotional reactions of eyewitnesses—how much an object meant or how surprised they were to see something happen. Filter out other irrelevant details. If you are reporting a work stoppage, it is unnecessary to indicate what the employees did while waiting for machinery to be repaired. Do not duplicate information found elsewhere in the report—license numbers, times, employee identification numbers. Finally, if necessary, give information about expenses.

5. What was done after the incident. After describing the incident, describe the action you took to correct conditions, to get things back to normal. Readers will want to know what was done to treat the injured, to make the environment safer, to speed delivery of goods, to repair damaged equipment, or to satisfy a customer's demands.

6. What caused the incident. Make sure that your explanation is consistent with your description in number 4. Pinpoint the trouble. In Figure 16.13, for example, the defective fisher joint is discussed under the heading "Causes of Incident." In the following example, the two causes cited in a report of an accident involving a pipe falling from a crane are exact and helpful.

1. The crane's safety latch had been broken off and was never replaced.
2. A tag line was not used to guide the pipe onto the truckbed.

7. Recommendations. Readers will be looking for specific suggestions to prevent the incident from happening again. Recommendations may involve discussing the problem at a safety meeting, asking for further training from a manufacturer, adapting existing equipment to meet customers' needs, doing some emergency planning for the next storm damage, modifying schedules, or cutting back on expenses. In the example of the falling pipe in number 6 above, the writer of the incident report listed the following two appropriate recommendations.

1. Order safety latches to replace the broken latch and have additional spare latches on hand.
2. Have a pipeshop supervisor conduct a safety meeting for employees and use a representative drawing of the incident as an aid.

Main Points to Remember About Short Reports

Before considering long reports, the subject of the next chapter, let's review the main points about short reports.

1. They are a few pages at most and get to the point quickly and concisely.
2. They can be prepared in a variety of formats—memo, letter, or special form.
3. Their content will vary with the type of report—periodic, sales, progress, trip, test, or incident. In all types of short reports, however, the emphasis is on facts and objectivity. You need to anticipate the types of information your readers will need and how they will use it.
4. They are generally organized to include information on purpose, data, conclusions, and recommendations.

✓ Revision Checklist

Preparing short reports requires the same attention to your audience's needs as do your letters. To make sure you meet those needs, ask yourself the following questions as you revise your work. Keep in mind that the revision stage gives you another opportunity to make your short report easy to read and more effective.

1. Do I have a clear sense of how my readers will use my report?
2. Have I done sufficient research to meet my readers' needs? Have I consulted appropriate sources to give my audience enough details to help them make informed decisions?
3. Is my report objective? Have I provided significant information about costs, materials, personnel, and times so my readers will know that my work is factual and not impressionistic?
4. Have I double-checked all my data—figures, dates, places, and equipment numbers? Have I verified necessary sales figures, dates, costs, and references so that my work is thorough and accurate?
5. Is my report concise and to the point? Have I digressed anywhere or included more information than my readers need or want?
6. Have I used headings whenever feasible to organize and categorize information for my readers? Have I used underlining, boldface, or italics to set these headings apart or to emphasize key ideas in my report?
7. Have I begun my report with a statement of purpose that clearly limits the scope and significance of my work?
8. Have I used tables and other pertinent visuals to display data whenever appropriate?
9. Does my conclusion clearly explain what the data mean?

10. If my readers expect a section providing recommendations, have I placed that section appropriately in my report? Do the recommendations logically follow from the data I have presented? Are my recommendations realistic and distinct? Will my readers know how to act on them?

Exercises

1. Bring to class an example of a periodic report from your previous or present job or from any community, religious, or social organization to which you belong. In an accompanying memo to your instructor, indicate who the audience is and why such a report is necessary, stressing how it is submitted and organized and what kinds of factual data it contains.

2. Assume that you are a manager of a large apartment complex (200 units). Write a periodic report based on the following information—there are 26 units vacant, 38 ready to become vacant, and 27 soon to be leased (by June 1). Also add a section of recommendations to your boss (the head of the real estate management company for which you work) on how vacant apartments might be leased quickly.

3. Assume you work for a household appliance store. Prepare a second-quarter sales report based on information contained in the following table.

	Numbers Sold	
Product	1st Quarter	2nd Quarter
Kitchen appliances		
Refrigerators	72	103
Dishwashers	27	14
Freezers	10	36
Electric Ranges	26	26
Gas Ranges	10	3
Microwave Ovens	31	46
Laundry appliances		
Washers	50	75
Dryers	24	36
Air treatment		
Room Air-conditioners	41	69
Dehumidifiers	7	2

4. Write a progress report on the wins, losses, and ties of your favorite sports team for last season. Address the report to the Director of Publicity for the team and stress how the director might use these facts for future publicity.

5. Submit a progress report to your writing teacher on what you have learned in his or her course so far this term, which writing skills you want to develop in greater detail, and how you propose doing so. Mention specific memos, letters, instructions, reports, or proposals you have written or will soon write.

6. Compose a site inspection report on any part of the college campus or plant, office, or store in which you work that might need remodeling, expansion, or new or additional air-conditioning or heating work.

7. You have been asked to write a short preliminary inspection report on the condition of a historic building for your state historical society. Inspecting the building, the home of a famous late nineteenth-century governor, you discover the following problems. Include all these details in your report. Also supply recommendations for your readers—a director of the state historical society, a state architect, and four representatives of the subcommittee on finance from your state legislature.

   - Eight front columns are all in need of repair; two of them in fact may have to be replaced.
   - The area below the bottom window casements needs to be excavated for waterproofing.
   - The slate tile on the roof has deteriorated and needs immediate replacement.
   - The front stairs show signs of mortar leaching requiring attention at once.
   - Sections of gutter on the northwest and northeast sides of the house must be changed; other gutters are in fair shape.
   - Wood louvers need to be repainted; four of the twelve may even need to be replaced.
   - All trees around the house need pruning; an old elm in the backyard shows signs of decay.
   - The siding is in desperate need of preparation and painting.
   - The brick near the front entrance is dirty and moss-covered.

8. Assume that you are a social worker, law enforcement officer, or youth counselor. Write an appropriate trip report based on the following information. Make sure to include your reasons for the visit, a description of the visit, and some appropriate recommendations based on your visit.

   George Morrow, age 15, was put on probation last August for stealing. He has missed a number of school days this term. The principal at his high school said he also got into some trouble about library books—defacing them or not returning them. George's parents were recently divorced, and he lives with his mother. His mother has requested some help and wants to know what kinds of programs are available. George is very eager to go to technical school and become an electrician. He feels as though his misdeeds will hurt him. George has to report to the court at least once a month for the next year.

9. Write a report to an instructor in your major about a field trip you have taken recently. Indicate why you took the trip, name the individuals you met on the trip, and stress what you learned and how that information will help you in course work or on your job.

10. Submit a test report on the purpose, procedures, results, conclusions, and recommendations of an experiment you conducted on one of the following subjects:

a. soil	**h.** computers
b. machinery	**i.** forests
c. water	**j.** food
d. automobiles	**k.** air quality
e. textiles/clothing	**l.** transportation
f. animals	**m.** blood
g. recreational facilities	**n.** noise levels

11. Write an incident report about a problem you encountered in your work in the last year. Use the memo format or the form reprinted in Figure 16.14.

12. Write an incident report about one of the following problems. Assume that it has happened to you. Supply relevant details in your report. Identify the audience for whom you are writing and the agency you are representing or trying to reach.

a. After hydroplaning, your company car hits a tree and has a damaged front fender.

b. You have been the victim of an electrical shock because an electrical tool was not grounded.

c. You twist your back lifting a bulky package in the office or plant.

d. Your boat capsizes while you are patrolling the lake.

e. The crane you are operating breaks down and you lose a half day's work.

f. The supplier shipped the wrong replacement part, and you cannot complete a job without renting an expensive tool.

g. An electrical storm knocked out your computer; you lost 1,000 mailing labels and will have to hire additional help to complete a mandatory mailing by the end of the week.

13. Choose one of the following descriptions of an incident and write a report based on it. The descriptions contain unnecessary details, vague words, insufficient information, unclear cause-and-effect relationships, or all of these errors. In writing your report, correct the errors by adding or deleting whatever information you believe is necessary. You may also want to rearrange the order in which information is listed. Use the form in Figure 16.14 or a memo format to write the report.

a. After sliding across the slippery road late at night, my car ran into another vehicle, one of those fancy imported cars. The driver of that car must have been asleep at the wheel. The paint and glass chips were all over. I was driving back from our regional meeting and wanted to report to the home office the next day. The accident will slow me down.

b. Whoever packed the glass mugs did not know what he or she was doing. The string was not the right type, nor was it tied correctly. The carton was too flimsy as well. It could have been better packed to hold all those mugs. Moreover, since the bus had to travel across some pretty rough country, the package would have broken anyhow. The best way to ship these kinds of goods is in specially marked and packed boxes. The value of the box was listed at $350.

Long Reports

This chapter will introduce you to long reports—how they differ from short reports, how they are written, and how they are organized. It is appropriate to discuss long reports in one of the last chapters of *Successful Writing at Work*. The long report is often assigned last in class because writing one gives you an opportunity to use and combine many of the writing skills and strategies you have already learned. In business, a long report is the culmination of many weeks or months of hard work on an important company project.

The following skills and strategies will be most helpful to you as you prepare to study long reports; appropriate page numbers appear below where these topics have already been discussed.

- assessing and meeting your audience's multiple needs (pages 4-13)
- gathering and summarizing information, especially from reference works (pages 312-352; 393-404)
- generating, drafting, revising, and editing your ideas (pages 28-43)
- reporting the results of your research accurately and concisely (pages 454-464; 589-592)
- writing a variety of paragraph patterns and sentence types (pages 80-86; 96-112)
- creating and introducing visuals (pages 473-514)
- using an appropriate method of documentation (pages 356-372)
- preparing an informative abstract (pages 413-414)

Having improved these skills, you should be ready to write a successful long report.

How a Long Report Differs from a Short Report

Both long and short reports are invaluable tools in the world of work. They provide essential information to help a company or agency function. Both should be written in formal, standard English and have an objective, professional tone. Basic differences exist, though, between these two types of reports. A short report is not a watered-down version of a long report; nor is a long report simply an expanded version of a short one. These reports differ in purpose, scope, format, and, many times, audience. The following section explains some of the key differences between these two reports. By understanding these differences, you will be better able to follow the rest of Chapter 17 as it covers the process of writing a long report and the organization and parts of such a report. A model long report is included in Figure 17.3.

1. Scope. A long report is a major study that provides an intensive and in-depth view of the problem or idea. For example, a long report written for a course assignment may be eight to twenty pages long; a report for a business or industry may be that long or, more likely, much longer, depending on the scope of the subject. The implications of a long report are wide-ranging for a business or industry—relocating a plant, adding a new line of equipment, changing a computer programming operation. While the long report examines a problem or idea in detail, the short report covers just one part of the problem. Unlike a short report, a long report may discuss not just one or two current events, but rather a continuing history of a problem or idea (and the background information necessary to understand it in perspective). For example, the short test report on paulownia in Figure 16.12 (pp. 613–615) would be used with many other test reports for a long report for a group of industrialists or a government agency on the value of planting these trees to prevent soil erosion at mine sites.

The following titles of some typical long reports further suggest their extensive (and in some cases exhaustive) coverage:

- A Master Plan for the Recreation Needs of Syracuse, New York
- The Transportation Problems in Kingford, Oregon, and the Use of Monorails
- Building and Equipment Needs for Rivera Plastics Over the Next Five Years
- The Revolutionary Advances in the Manufacture and Use of the Compact Disc Player
- Public Policy Implications of Expanding Health Care Delivery Systems in Tate County

2. Research. A long, comprehensive report requires much more extensive research than a short report does. The research provides writers with the detailed documentation that readers of a long report expect and need. Such research can be gathered over time from questionnaires, laboratory experiments, library research, on-site visits and tests, interviews, and the writer's own observations. For a course report, you will have to do a great deal of library research and possibly interviewing to identify a major problem or topic, to track down the relevant background information, and to discover what experts have said about the subject and what they propose should be done.

Information gathered over many short reports can also be used to help prepare a long report. In fact, as the example of paulownia shows, a long report can use the experimental data included in a short report to arrive at a conclusion. Also for a long report writers often supply one or more progress reports (one type of short report—review pages 598–603).

Finally, preparing a proposal can lead to writing a long report. You might suggest a change to an employer, who then would request you to write a long report containing the research necessary to implement that change. Your instructor may ask you to write a proposal on doing a long report for a class project, as James Salinas did in Figure 15.6.

3. Format. Another significant difference between a long and short report is in format. Because a long report contains extensive documentation, it is too detailed and complex to be adequately organized in a memo or letter format. The product of thorough research and analysis, the long report gives readers detailed discussions of large quantities of data. To present this information in a logical and orderly fashion, the long report contains more parts, sections, headings, subheadings, and supplements (appendixes) than would ever be included in a short report. The long report often includes many graphs, spreadsheets, charts, and tables to provide readers with extensive background information and documentation. The long report also incorporates many summaries of data at the beginning, at the end, and at key points in between for readers' convenience.

4. Timetable. The two types of reports also differ in the time it takes to prepare them and in the way in which they are written. Writers of these two types of reports are working under different expectations from their readers and under different kinds of deadlines. A long report is generally commissioned by a company or agency to explore in detail some subject involving personnel, locations, costs, safety, or equipment. Many times a long report is required by law; for example, investigating the feasibility of a new missile system or a change in the ecosystem. The long report is so important that it becomes a record a company will keep on file for executives and employees to consult. A short report is often written as a matter of routine duty where the writer is given little or no advance notice. The long report may take weeks or even months to write. Over this period the researchers have to gather the extensive documentation readers will expect. When you prepare a long report for a class project, make sure that you select a topic that really interests you, for you will spend a good portion of the term working on it.

5. Audience. The audience for a long report is generally broader—and goes higher in an organization's hierarchy—than that for a short report. Your short report may be read by coworkers, a first-level supervisor, and possibly that person's immediate boss, but a long report is always intended for people in the top levels of management—presidents, vice presidents, superintendents, directors— who make long-range financial and organizational decisions. These individuals are responsible for long-range planning and for always seeing the big picture, so to speak. In addition, copies of long reports may be sent to appropriate department heads for their information and commentary. A long report written about a campus issue or problem may at first be read by your teacher and then sent to an appropriate decision maker, such as a dean of students, a business manager, a director of athletics, or the head of campus security.

6. Collaborative Effort. Unlike many short reports, the long report in the business world and industry quite often is not the work of one employee. Rather, it may be a collaborative effort, the product of a committee or group whose work is reviewed by one main editor to make sure that the final copy is consistently and accurately written. Individuals in many departments within a company—art, computer programming, engineering, public relations, industrial safety—may cooperate in planning, researching, drafting, revising, and formatting a long report, which may reflect their various skills: graphics production, statistical analysis, interviewing. Your instructor may ask you to work in a group (or alone) in preparing your long report.

If you are responsible for setting up a collaborative team, you will have to coordinate the schedules and duties of coauthors to determine who will write what and how revisions will be handled. Collaboration, especially on long reports, almost always involves more time to allow for sufficient participation by the group. Collaboration, too, can involve many forms—one person can draft the report; another (often a manager or supervisor) adds, deletes, or points out weak spots; and still another may make the changes as directed. Or two or more people may write separate parts of a long report and then put them together. Collaboration is very common in the world of work and will require you to be an effective team member, so you may find it helpful to review pages 39-43.

The Process of Writing a Long Report

As we just saw, writing a long report requires a lot of time and effort. Your work will be spread over many weeks, and you need to see your report not as a series of static or isolated tasks but as an evolving and accomplishable project. Before you embark on that project, review the information on the writing process found in Chapter 2. You may also want to study the flow chart found on page 497, illustrating the different stages in writing a research paper.

The first steps involve identifying a broad yet significant subject area to explore. You can accomplish this by doing some preliminary research—general reading, consulting relevant indexes, talking to experts about the subject. From this preliminary research you are better able to arrive at a restricted topic, the second major step in the process. After that, you need to assemble information (the documentation) on that topic and read and think about it carefully. From this information and your analysis of it you can prepare one or more outlines. Then you may want to start drafting, though you may return to outlining later on. Through revisions and editing, your work will ultimately lead to the final copy of your report. (Some writers find it helpful to outline and draft at the same time, moving back and forth between drafting and outlining.)

In the business world, you are likely to be assigned a given subject area. Of course, you will need to do a great deal of research on it, but you will also be expected to confer regularly with your supervisor and to ask a lot of questions in order to pin down exactly what you boss wants. Your questions will focus on the company's use of your report, how the company wants you to express certain ideas, and the amount of information it wants you to present. Your supervisor may want you to submit an outline before you draft the report, and may expect you to submit a certain number of drafts for his or her approval before you proceed.

In the process of writing the long report, expect to revise your work often—and sometimes extensively—depending on what your boss, teacher, or collaborative team recommends. You will have to reexamine and rethink your ideas. While you do this, your organization and analysis may change. You may have to consult new sources and arrive at a *new interpretation* of those sources. Be sure to share major changes in your thinking with coauthors or the supervisor who assigned the project. Not everything you need will be available to you right away. You may have to order materials from a company or through interlibrary loan, or you may have to reschedule an interview. Also, as you narrow your purpose and scope, you may find yourself deleting information or modifying its place in your work. You may even substitute a better source for a weaker one. At the earlier stages of outlining and preparing rough drafts, you may move material around a great deal to avoid unnecessary duplications and to ensure adequate coverage. At the later stages, you will be revising and editing sentences and paragraphs to make them read more smoothly and logically. At this stage you should also pay increasing attention to the transitions between and among sentences and paragraphs.

Keep in mind, even as you work on your drafts and revisions, that a long report is not written in the order in which the parts will finally be assembled. You cannot write in "final" order—abstract to appendix. Instead, you will write in "loose" order to reflect the order in which you gathered information and assembled it for the final copy of the report. Accordingly, the body section is usually written first, for authors must obtain material included here in order to construct the rest of the report. However, you may want to sketch in parts of your introduction first as a way of establishing guideposts for later sections of the report. But keep in mind that introductions usually are written later because authors then can make sure they have not left anything out. The abstract, which appears very early in the report, is always written last, after all the facts have been recorded and the recommendations made or the conclusions drawn. The title page and table of contents, too, are always prepared after you write the body of the report.

To keep track of your work, prepare both a work calendar and a checklist. Keep both posted where you do your work—above your desk, typewriter, or word processor. Make sure that every member of your collaborative team is following the same calendar and using the same checklist so there are no problems with goals and deadlines. The calendar should mark the dates by which each stage of your work must be completed. Match the dates on your calendar with the dates your instructor or employer may have given you for a copy of the outline, for progress reports, for the final copy. Your checklist should present the major parts of your report. As you complete each section, check it off. Before assembling the final copy of your report for readers, use the checklist to make sure that you do not accidentally omit something.

Parts of a Long Report

A long report may include some or all of the following twelve parts, which form three categories: *front matter,* the *text of the report,* and *back matter.* The entire report may be placed in a clear plastic folder or other suitable cover.

Front Matter

As the name implies, the front matter of a long report consists of everything that precedes the actual text of the report. Such elements introduce, explain, and summarize to help the reader locate various parts of the report.

1. Letter of transmittal. This three- or four-paragraph letter states the purpose, scope, and major recommendation of the report. If written to a teacher, the letter should additionally note that the report was done as a course assignment. Sometimes the letter of transmittal is bound with the report as part of it; most often it comes before the report, serving as a cover letter. Figure 17.1 (p. 630) is a sample letter of transmittal for a business report; Figure 17.3 (p. 638) contains a letter of transmittal for a student's long report.

2. Title page. The title, which should be listed in all capital letters, indicates a specific subject and how or why you studied it. Select your title carefully so that it clearly tells the reader what your topic is and how you have restricted it in time, space, or method of research. Your title says that the topic of your report is focused and significant. The title page also gives the name of the company or agency preparing the report, the name(s) of the report writer(s), the date, any agency or order numbers, and the name of the firm for which the report was prepared. For a report for a class, you will indicate your instructor's name and the specific course for which you prepared the report.

It is important that your title page look professional. Center your title and logically and graphically subordinate any subtitles. If you are using a word processor, experiment with different type sizes and styles. Figure 17.3 shows a typical title page for a long report.

3. Table of contents. The contents page tells readers on which pages they can find different parts of your report and shows how you organized your report. By looking at the table of contents in Figure 17.2 (p. 631), for example, the reader sees at a glance how the report, "A Study to Determine New Directions in Women's Athletics at Coastal College," is divided into four chief parts (Introduction, Discussion, Conclusion, and Recommendations). A table of contents emerges from the many outlines and drafts based on the outlines that you prepared for your report. The items on these outlines frequently expand, shrink, and move around until you decide on the formal divisions and subdivisions of your report. When preparing a table of contents, use lower-case roman numerals for front matter elements as in Figures 17.2 and 17.3. Never list the contents page

FIGURE 17.1   A letter of transmittal for a long report.

α

ALPHA CONSULTANTS
1400 Ridge
Evanston, California 97213-1005
805-555-9200
FAX 805-555-9221

August 1, 1994

Dr. K. G. Lawry, President
Coastal College
San Diego, California 93219-2619

Dear Dr. Lawry:

We are happy to present to you the enclosed report, "A Study
to Determine New Directions in Women's Athletics at Coastal
College," that you asked us to prepare. The report contains
our recommendations about strengthening existing sports
programs and creating new ones at Coastal College.

After studying Coastal's sports facilities and the College's
plans for expansion, we interviewed the coaching staff and
many of Coastal's women athletes. We also polled the coaching
staffs and 100 women athletes at three local colleges--
Baystown Community College, California State University of
Arts and Sciences, and Central Community College.

Our recommendation is that Coastal should engage in more
active recruitment to establish a competitive women's baseball
team, start to offer athletic activities in women's track and
field by August 1995, and create a new interdisciplinary
program between the Athletic Department and the Women's
Studies Program.

We hope that you find our report useful in meeting students'
needs at Coastal College. If you have any questions or if you
would like to discuss any of our recommendations, please
call us.

Sincerely yours,

Barbara Gilchrist

Barbara Gilchrist

Lee T. Sidell

Lee T. Sidell

Encl. Report

FIGURE 17.2   A table of contents for a long report.

CONTENTS

LIST OF ILLUSTRATIONS iii

ABSTRACT iv

INTRODUCTION 1
  Background 1
  Problem 1
  Purpose of Report 4
  Scope of Report 5

DISCUSSION 6
  Women's Athletics at Area Colleges 7
    Baystown Community College 7
    California State University of Arts and Sciences 9
    Central Community College 10
  Coastal's Sports Facilities 12
    North Campus 12
    South Campus 14
  Coastal's Coaching Staff 16
    First-Year Teams 16
    Varsity Teams 18
  Performance of Coastal's Women Athletes 19
  Coastal's Recruitment Strategies 20
  Women's Athletics and the Curriculum 22
    Interdisciplinary Women's Studies Program 23
    Physical Education Program 25

CONCLUSION 28
  Views of the Students 29
  Views of the Coaches 31

RECOMMENDATIONS 32

REFERENCES CITED 34

APPENDIXES 37
  A. Sample Questionnaire for Coaches 38
  B. Sample Questionnaire for Athletes 39
  C. Profile of Women Athletes' Achievements 42
  D. Cost Estimates for Physical Plant Additions 57

itself, the letter of transmittal, or the title page in your table of contents, and never have just one subheading under a heading. You cannot divide a single topic by one.

Incorrect   EXPANDING THE SPORTS PROGRAM
        Basketball
    BUILDING A NEW ARENA
        The West Side Location

Correct   EXPANDING THE SPORTS PROGRAM
        Basketball
        Track and Field
    BUILDING A NEW ARENA
        The West Side Location
        Costs

4. List of illustrations. This list of all the visuals indicates where they can be found in your report. Figure 17.3 shows a list of illustrations.

5. Abstract. As discussed in Chapter 11 (pages 413–415), an abstract presents a brief overview of the problem and conclusions; it summarizes the report. An informative abstract is far more helpful to readers of a report than is a descriptive one, which gives no conclusions or results.

Not every member of your audience will read your entire report. But almost everyone will read the abstract of your long report. For example, the president of the corporation or the director of an agency may use the abstract as the basis for approving the report and passing it on for distribution. Thus the abstract may be the most important part of the report.

Abstracts may be placed at various points in long reports. They may be placed on the title page, on a separate page, or on the first page of the report text.

Text of the Report

6. Introduction. The introduction may constitute as much as 10 or 15 percent of your report but should not be any longer. If it were, the introduction would be disproportionate to the rest of your work, especially the body section. The introduction is essential because it tells readers why your report was written and thus helps them to understand and interpret everything that follows. Do not regard the introduction as one undivided block of information. It includes the following related parts, which should be labeled separately in the introduction with subheadings. Keep in mind, though, that your instructor or employer may ask you to list these parts in a different order.

a. Background. To understand why your topic is significant and hence worthy of study, readers need to know about its history. This history may include information on such topics as who was originally involved, when, and where; how someone was affected by the issue; what opinions have been expressed on the issue; what the implications of your study are. See how the long report on robots (Figure 17.3) provides useful background information on when and where robots were first used in industry and why.

b. Problem. Identify the problem or issue that led you to write the report. Since the problem or topic you investigated will determine everything you write about in the report, your statement of it must be clear and precise. That statement may be restricted to a few sentences. Here is a problem statement from a report on how construction designs have not taken into account the requirements of a growing number of older and disabled Americans.

> The construction industry has not satisfactorily met the needs for accessible work-places and homes for all age and physical ability groups. The industry has relied on expensive and specialized plans to modify existing structures rather than creating universally designed spaces that are accessible to everyone.

c. Purpose statement. The purpose statement, crucial to the success of the report, tells readers why you wrote the report and what you hope to accomplish or prove. In explaining why you gathered information about a particular problem or topic, indicate how such information might be useful to a specific audience, company, or group. Like the problem statement, the purpose statement does not have to be long or complex. A sentence or two will suffice. You might begin simply by saying, "The purpose of this report is . . . ."

d. Scope. This section informs readers about the specific limits—number and type of issues, times, money, locations, personnel, and so forth—you have placed on your investigation. The long report on robots in Figure 17.3 concentrates on the economic and safety benefits of robots in industry, not on the technology of robot construction or on disadvantages of using robots—two completely different topics. To cite another example, a report on waste disposal might include a scope statement such as, "This report examines the recent techniques involved in the disposal of liquid and solid wastes; gaseous wastes are not discussed in this report." In your report, you may not have studied individuals in an adjacent town or county because of time or may not have reviewed certain types of electronic equipment because of their costs or availability. If so, indicate this in your scope section. You also might limit your report by directing it to a particular audience or by writing at a particular technical level for that audience. "This report is intended for nonengineering managers to acquaint them with recent investigations in unit mechanization design." A careful statement of the scope should tie in with the purpose of your report.

7. The body. Also called the *discussion,* this section is the longest part, possibly making up as much as 70 percent of your report. Everything in this and all the other sections of your report grows out of your purpose and how you have limited your scope. The body of your report should supply readers with statistical information, details about the environment, and physical descriptions, as well as the various interpretations and comments of the authorities whose work you consulted as part of your library research. (Follow the method of documentation discussed on pages 360–366.)

The body of your report should be carefully organized to reveal a coherent and well-defined plan. Your goal is to impose a rational order on your material to help readers understand it easily and accurately. To do that, you have to separate the material in the body of your report into meaningful parts. Make sure that you identify the major issues as well as subissues in your report. These must be clearly related to each other. Headings help your reader identify major sections more quickly.

Your organization should be carefully reflected in the different headings (and maybe even subheadings) included in your report. Use them throughout your report to make it easy to follow. These organizational headings will also enable someone skimming the report to find specific information quickly. These headings, of course, will be included in the table of contents page.

The order in which you present these sections is equally important for your readers. Divide your information based on the categories into which it logically falls. For example, in tracing an idea or a program through various stages, you might follow a straight chronological order. If you were writing a feasibility report, one in which you study and weigh conflicting options (locations, equipment, programs) for readers, you would devote a section of the body to each one of the options being studied. If you were investigating the usefulness of a piece of equipment, you might divide your discussion according to the value of each major part of that equipment. An investigation of the public transportation of a community might be divided into the modes of transportation you have investigated: "Rail," "Buses," "Cabs," "Van- and Carpooling," and "Private Automobiles." Study the way in which the body of the model report included in Figure 17.3 is organized.

In addition to headings, use transitions to reveal the organization of the body of your report. At the beginning of each major section of the body, tell readers what they will find in that section and why. Summary sentences at the end of a section will tell readers where they have been and prepare them for any subsequent discussions. The report in Figure 17.3 does an effective job of providing these internal summaries.

8. Conclusion. The conclusion should tie everything together for readers by presenting the findings of your report. These findings need to explain to readers what the data you have gathered mean. Findings, of course, will vary depending on the type of research you engage in. For a library research report, the conclusion should summarize the main viewpoints of the authorities whose works you have cited. Perhaps your instructor will ask you to assess in your conclusion which resource materials were most thorough and helpful, and why. For a marketing report done for a business or industry, you must spell out the implications for your readers in terms of costs, personnel, products, location, and so forth.

Regardless of the type of research you do, your conclusions should be based on the information and documentation you presented in the body of the report. Be careful that your conclusions do not contradict the evidence/information you gave in the body of your report. Also, make sure that your conclusions do not go into areas that your report did not cover. In essence, to write an effective conclusion, you will have to summarize carefully a great deal of information accurately and concisely.

Notice how the following conclusion of a long report on well casing materials concisely summarizes the findings of the report by reviewing the literature at this crucial stage of the report.

Conclusions

Presently, there are many materials available for coating monitoring wells. The potential for these casing materials to interact with ground water is affected by many factors, including pH and composition of the ground water and the casing-ground water contact time. The complex and varied nature of ground water makes it difficult to predict the sorption and leaching potential of the various casing materials. Consequently, selecting the proper casing material for a particular monitoring application is difficult. Researchers disagree about which is the best material.

The two main classes of casing materials are metals and synthetics. SS304 and SS316 are the preferred metals, whereas PTFE and PVC are the two preferred synthetic polymer casing materials.

Researchers have offered no clear choice as to which material is best for sampling organic or inorganic material; however, we can draw the following conclusions from our review of the literature:

1. If metals are to be tested, metallic casing of any type should **not** be used.
2. If organic materials in high concentrations are to be tested, SS metals are preferred, since PVC and PTFE are questionable.
3. If metals and low levels of organic materials or compounds are to be tested, PVC and PTFE are acceptable.[1]

---

[1] Adapted from *Ground-Water Issue: The Effects of Well Casing Material on Ground-Water Quality,* Oct. 1991, p. 12, U.S. Environmental Protection Agency, Office of Solid Waste and Emergency Response.

Let's look at another effective example of a conclusion. The following conclusion to a long report on the Japanese tuna market clearly summarizes the market opportunities explained in the report.

Conclusion

A huge consumption market in Japan offers an opportunity for the U.S. tuna industry to expand its role in the Japanese market. This market, presently 400,000 tons a year and growing rapidly, is already being supplied by imports totaling about 35 percent of sales. Our report has indicated that not only will this market expand but the share of imports will continue to grow. The trend is alarming to Japanese tuna industry leaders, because this important market, close to a billion dollars a year, is increasingly subject to the influence of foreign imports. Declining catches by Japan's own tuna fleet, as well as a sharp upward turn in food preference by affluent Japanese consumers, have contributed to this trend.[2]

---

[2] Adapted from Sunee C. Sonu, *Japan's Tuna Market,* Sept. 1991, U.S. Department of Commerce, NOAA Technical Memorandum NMFS.

9. Recommendations. A research report for a course may not require a recommendation section. But for a business or scientific report, the most important part of the report, after the abstract, is the recommendation(s) section, which tells readers what should be done about the findings recorded in the conclusion. Your recommendation section shows readers how you want them to solve the problem your report has focused on. Review the principles of writing effective recommendations in Chapter 12 (pages 454–464).

Consider how the report on the Japanese tuna market, discussed on p. 635, uses a numbered list to make its recommendations.

Recommendations

Based on our analysis, we recommend five marketing strategies for the U.S. tuna industry:
1. farm greater supplies of bluefin tuna to export
2. market our own value-added products
3. sell fresh tuna directly to the Tokyo Central Wholesale Market
4. sell to other Japanese markets also
5. make direct sales to Japanese supermarket chains[3]

---

[3] Adapted from Sonu, *Japan's Tuna Market*.

Back Matter

Included in this section of the report are all the supporting data that, if included in the text of the report, would bog the reader down in details and cloud the main points the report makes.

10. Glossary. An alphabetical list of the specialized vocabulary with its definitions appears in the glossary (see pages 515–516). A glossary might be unnecessary if your report does not use highly technical vocabulary or if all members of your audience are familiar with the specialized terms you do use.

11. References cited. Any sources cited in your report—books, articles, television programs, audiovisual materials, questionnaire surveys, interviews, and reviews—are usually listed in this section (see Chapter 10, pages 360–366, on preparing a Works Cited page). Also, ask your instructor or employer about how he or she wants information to be documented. Sometimes, in the world of work, employers prefer all information to be documented in footnotes or cited parenthetically in the text (without a formal Works Cited page).

12. Appendix (plural Appendixes). The appendix contains all the supporting materials for the report—tables and charts too long to include in the discussion, sample questionnaires, budgets and cost estimates, correspondence about the preparation of the report, case histories, transcripts of telephone conversations. Group like items together in the appendix, as the examples under "Appendixes" in Figure 17.2 show.

The Model Long Report in This Chapter

The long report in Figure 17.3 is a research report written by a student for a communications class. It deals with robots in American industry, a popular topic about which the student gathered relevant data primarily through library work. It contains all the parts of a long report discussed on pages 629–636 except a recommendation, glossary, and appendix. Intended for a general audience unfamiliar with robot technology, the report consequently avoids the technical terms and descriptions for which a glossary might be necessary. Because the student is surveying authorities' opinions, he does not supply a recommendation section of his own.

The student's main task is to investigate what has been said about robots in American industry and to report the results of his research in a logically organized discussion. Notice how the body section of his report is divided into four closely related areas—employment, safety in the workplace, benefits to employers, and future advances from robot technology. A number of these areas are further subdivided, as you will see from the table of contents and the subheadings in the report.

This report shows how one writer researched, organized, and discussed a major problem (or topic) suitable for a long report.

FIGURE 17.3   A long report.

345 Spruce Lane
Apt. 34-C
Gunderson, NE 68345

May 18, 1992

Professor Dorothy Ridgely
Communications Department
Fairmont Central College
Fairmont, NE 68339-6717

Dear Professor Ridgely:

With this letter I am enclosing my research report on the
robotics topic you approved six weeks ago. My report discusses the various contributions robots can make to American
industry, both for workers and for employers.

Robotization offers significant and widespread technological
benefits. Contrary to some views, robots will not take jobs
away from American workers but instead will increase employment opportunities. Robots will also make the work environment
safer and offer employers many financial benefits. Finally,
robots of the future will radically improve American industry
and the life-style of workers.

I hope that you will find this report interesting and carefully researched. If you should need to discuss it with me,
I can be reached at 678-3400 during the day and at 456-8294
after 6:00 P.M.

Sincerely yours,

John Mark Russell

John Mark Russell

Enclosure

FIGURE 17.3   **(Continued)**

THE POSITIVE EFFECTS OF ROBOTS IN AMERICAN INDUSTRY

John Mark Russell

May 18, 1992

Communications 102

Professor Dorothy Ridgely

FIGURE 17.3   **(Continued)**

Table of Contents

LIST OF ILLUSTRATIONS iii

ABSTRACT iv

INTRODUCTION 1

Background 1

Problem 2

Purpose of Report 2

Scope 2

DISCUSSION 3

Robots Will Encourage, Not Threaten, Employment 3

Unjustified Fears About Unemployment 3

Fewer Robots Mean Fewer Jobs 4

Increased Employment Because of Robots 5

Robots Provide Efficiency and Safety in the Workplace 6

Robots Can Improve Workers' Efficiency 6

Robots Will Make the Workplace Safer 7

Robots Offer Employers Benefits 8

Robots Can Increase Output and Quality 9

Robots Can Decrease Manufacturing Costs 10

What Robots Will Do in the Future 12

CONCLUSION 14

WORKS CITED 15

FIGURE 17.3   (Continued)

LIST OF ILLUSTRATIONS

Table 1: Estimated Number of New Robot-related Jobs,
1990—1998 6

Figure 1: Costs for Robot and Human Workers as
of 1995 11

ABSTRACT

After thirty years of rather slow growth, the robot worker
in American industry is finally becoming an indispensable
part of our technology. This robot revolution has created
fears that many human workers will lose their jobs. Most
industry experts agree, however, that only a small
displacement of human workers will occur and that most of
these workers will be transferred to related or upgraded
jobs. Through their greater productivity, robots are
expected to create more jobs than they eliminate. They will
also make the workplace safer for human employees and
improve their effectiveness. Robots will reward employers by
giving them improved efficiency and productivity at lower
costs. Moreover, robots will bring even greater benefits to
workers through better jobs and a higher standard of living.

FIGURE 17.3   (Continued)

INTRODUCTION

Background

For centuries people have been fascinated by amazing stories of machines that could be programmed through remote control to do superhuman feats. However, we have seen less enthusiasm about robots in such places as an assembly line or a chemical plant. The name *robot* itself (from the Czech word meaning "compulsory labor, drudgery") symbolizes the reaction many people have to mechanical devices that perform human jobs in the workplace.

The first industrial robot was used in 1959, and shortly afterwards, in 1962, General Motors installed its first Unimation robot (Ayres and Miller 4). But the growth of robots in American industry was slow. By 1970 only a few hundred robots were found in American plants. It was not until the 1980s that industry readily accepted them (Krepchin 46). The successful introduction of robots by several major companies, especially Detroit automakers, encouraged other industries to make the same investment (Aronson 22–23). In the early 1980s, more than 5,000 robots were at work in the United States, with a growth rate projected by the firm of Bache Investments to be 35 percent annually (Ayres and Miller 5). Unfortunately, that growth rate has not been fully realized. In the 30 years or so

FIGURE 17.3   **(Continued)**

2

since robots were introduced, only 10 percent of U.S.
manufacturing firms have begun using them. Yet
according to Eric Mittelstadt, President and CEO of
GMFanuc Robotics, automation, which has long been
viewed as a luxury by many American companies, "is now
essential to maintaining manufacturing competitiveness"
(84).

Problem

Robotics technology is not universally understood or
accepted. Although this technology will certainly shape
American industry in the future, many workers and some
managers fear it and do not understand its benefits.

Purpose of Report

The purpose of this report is to discuss the benefits
robots offer American industrial workers and their employers.

Scope

This report includes information on how robots can
establish new jobs, make the workplace safer for
employees, improve production for employers, and create a
better future for American workers through advanced
technology.

FIGURE 17.3 (Continued)

3

DISCUSSION

Robots Will Encourage, Not Threaten, Employment

Unjustified Fears About Unemployment

A recurrent fear about the widespread use of robots is that they may put American workers out of a job. Some industrialists predict that in the near future, most assembly and packaging lines will be completely automated, replacing millions of human operators with robots (Spaulding 35). According to Barbara Rice, each robot installed in the early 1980s displaced about two workers a day, but as robot capabilities increase, they may displace more than three workers a day (interview).

These statistics are misleading, however. Most industry experts, including officials of the United Auto Workers, consider these projections to be excessively high. These and other experts "predict that robots will never displace more than 5 percent of the work force" (Aronson 26). In a 1991 survey of Fortune 500 firms that use robots, only 7.8 percent of the respondents reported a decline in employment, while 84.3 percent reported no change at all (Alkhafaji 50). Furthermore, some experts believe that by 1998 less than 1 percent of the American work force may be laid off because of robots (Koelsch 49—50; Jones 22). To date, robots have displaced only about 15,000 workers in America, most of whom have been shifted into related or more technologically advanced positions.

FIGURE 17.3   (Continued)

4

Fortunately, nearly all of these workers should be "retrained for new jobs within their companies" ("Robots to Create" 15). This occupational relocation, together with a declining birthrate over the next few decades, should remove any fears of widespread unemployment caused by robots (Aronson 26—27; Jones 26). Ironically enough, it is the outmoded robots that most likely will be laid off as sophisticated, newer models take their places (Williams 23).

Fewer Robots Mean Fewer Jobs

When American companies do **not** use robots, they jeopardize the jobs of American workers. Less than ten years ago, James Albus, an expert in industrial systems and robotics, precisely identified the cause-and-effect relationship between advanced technology, such as robotics, and employment:

> It is in the industries that fall behind in productivity where job layoffs are prevalent. Inefficient industries lose market-share to competitors, shrink, and eventually die. Thus, the biggest threat to jobs is not in industries that adopt the fastest robot technology but in those that do not. (27)

To illustrate this principle on an international scale, consider that today "more than 200,000 industrial robots are in use in Japan, making everything from VCRs to sushi. Compare this figure with the 37,000 robots working in the U.S. factories" (Spaulding 35). Applying

FIGURE 17.3   (Continued)

this principle closer to home, some economic forecasters
predict that United States automakers will lose 400,000
jobs to foreign competitors by trailing them in the use
of robots (Jones 23). American workers are unemployed
because of the robots in Japan, not the robots in
Detroit (Albus 27). In fact, most experts predict that
by failing to use robots, certain industries will become
obsolete and that workers in these industries will
suffer.

Increased Employment Because of Robots

   Not only will the robot boom help to prevent
unemployment but it may, in all likelihood, increase
employment. Georgia Scapelli of the United Technology
Workers sees "new types of jobs created" because of
robots (qtd. in Ayres and Miller 42). Robotics should,
like earlier automation in industry, create more jobs
than it eliminates through increased production (Aronson
26). Greater industrial productivity means more human
involvement in the decision-making, manufacturing, and
marketing processes. Moreover, robot technology will
create new opportunities for workers in maintaining and
repairing these machines (Krepchin 49; Toepperwein et
al. 308) as well as in constructing them. Additional
human supervisors will be needed to troubleshoot
problems on the assembly or transportation line (Dodd
694). As Table 1 on the following page indicates, the
Robotics Alpha Report estimates that more than 45,000
new jobs will be available by 1998 because of robots.

FIGURE 17.3   (Continued)

6

Table 1. Estimated Number of New Robot-related Jobs			
	1990	1994	1998
ROBOT INDUSTRY	1300	2300	3050
SUPPLIER INDUSTRIES	1000	2200	4500
USERS			
MAINTENANCE	5500	18,000	25,300
PROGRAMMING	3700	6000	12,650
TOTAL EMPLOYMENT ASSOCIATED WITH USE OF ROBOTS	11,500	28,500	45,500
From *Robotics Alpha Report*, 1989.			

Source: Nagler 59.

Thus, it seems safe to conclude that robots "will complement, not compete with, humans" (Albus 27).

Robots Provide Efficiency and Safety
in the Workplace

Some authorities believe that the robot revolution will, in the long run, provide vast improvements and benefits for Americans in their workplaces. Not only will new and better jobs result because of robots but they will enhance many existing jobs. Vary T. Coates, an expert on technology assessment, speculates that many companies will purchase robots to help improve working conditions especially in those environments that "may be inefficient, unsafe, and inhospitable for human workers" (qtd. in Coates and Coates 32).

FIGURE 17.3   (Continued)

7

Robots Can Improve Workers' Efficiency

Coates's first area of concern—inefficiency—is one
in which robots on the job site can be of great help. A
robot can assist a human worker to accomplish specific
duties much more carefully and precisely. For example,
robots can be designed to reach into very small or
awkward places that would be impossible or extra-
ordinarily difficult for human workers. A robot can also
precisely measure the insides of a pipeline or test the
interior components of a machine without disassembling
the machine. Robots can also sample products (such as
Coca-Cola) for uniformity, thus "eliminating the
monotony experienced by technicians performing [such]
routine analyses" ("Robot and Weighing System" 15). With
robots performing repetitive tasks in medical
laboratories, technologists can spend more time
providing information to physicians and nurses and
developing new tests and procedures (Hard 56).

Robots Will Make the Workplace Safer

Perhaps the ultimate contribution of robots will be
in making the workplace safer for human beings. Thanks
to robots, human workers may not have to be exposed to
occupational environments that threaten their health.
Robots do not have lungs, skin, ears, or eyes to
protect. Nor do they have to worry about noise levels,
dust or asbestos particles, or eyestrain and headaches
from uninterrupted work. Robots on hazardous work sites

FIGURE 17.3   **(Continued)**

8

will, therefore, significantly help to decrease
employment-related injuries and illnesses (Alkhafaji 53).

Robots can be invaluable in providing safety nets in
potentially dangerous industries such as nuclear power
plants. Countless human lives could be spared because of
robots in this industry. For example, if there were a
leak of lethal radioactive material, robots rather than
human beings would be exposed at the power plant. At the
beginning of the next century, the U.S. nuclear industry
is scheduled to use a small army of robots to
decommission and mothball some 100 aging power plants
(Rice interview).

Similarly, robots can reduce hazards to human
workers at factories that produce toxic chemicals or
explosives. Robots can also safely load and transport
toxic materials (Coates and Coates 31–32; Toepperwein et
al. 207). In addition, "Robots can be important in
assisting individuals who work in mines, one of the most
dangerous occupational sites in America" (Rice
interview). Robots have even started "to perform such
tasks as . . . putting out fires, disposing of terrorist
bombs, and spotting drug smugglers" (Miles 92).

Robots Offer Employers Benefits

Robots also offer employers numerous benefits. They
improve the quality and output of the employer's plant,
and they can significantly reduce the cost of materials.

FIGURE 17.3   **(Continued)**

9

Robots Can Increase Output and Quality

     An important benefit of robotization is the
increased output and amazingly high quality that a robot
can provide. While human welders can keep their torches
on the job only 30 percent of the time, robot workers
can keep going 90 percent of the time. Robots used for
welding also have the capability of correcting errors
during a job, saving time, and increasing production.
Since Westinghouse Electric Corporation put the first
Rosa model robot to work in the early 1980s, "the robots
have slashed power plant downtime, saving Westinghouse's
utility-company customers at least $500,000 each time
the robots finish a chore one day sooner than humans
can" (Miles 94). By the late 1980s, robots at the
Garrett Turbine Engine Company in Phoenix could measure
noise levels at eighty locations in a power turbine unit
in fourteen minutes, a job that normally takes nine hours
for human workers (Tolman 6).

     Robots on the job also improve the quality of work
done for an employer. T. E. Baker of General Electric
convincingly describes one of the robot's chief virtues:

          The robot is a maddeningly demanding and consistent
          machine. . . . If materials fed to it are not
          completed, uniform, and reasonably flawless, it will
          either correct the problem itself, summon its human
          supervisor with a bell or whistle, or just quit.
          (qtd. in Dodd 689)

A robot can deliver high quality by also being extremely
accurate. It is capable of drilling sets of holes within

FIGURE 17.3   **(Continued)**

10

.005 inch of error and can machine 250 different parts.
A human worker on the job produces 6 parts per shift
with 10 percent rejections, while a robot in the same
job makes 24 to 30 parts with zero rejections (Dodd
691). Used in the electronics industry, robots can
insert microchips without "deviating so much as a
millimeter's space" (Jones 27).

Every aspect of our economy benefits from the
increased production and improved quality of American-
made products. Certainly two of the most welcome
advantages of using robots will be more orders for
American goods and increased employment for American
workers. Robots will enable America to compete more
successfully in the world market.

Robots Can Decrease Manufacturing Costs

As the initial price of purchasing a robot falls
with improved technology, lower labor cost becomes a
principal argument for the robotization of American
factories. Dale Vandervort of PLS International, a
manufacturer of pipe-crawling robots, has said that
"while an average natural gas utility may spend $10,000
digging a single hole looking for a leak . . . [a] robot
can search 600 feet of pipe for only $1,000 a hole"
(qtd. in Greenberger 37). Joseph Engleberger, former
president of the largest U.S. robot manufacturer,
estimated that the cost per hour of a medium-priced
hypothetical robot is $9.00. This figure represents only
a 50 percent increase since 1967, while hourly rates for

FIGURE 17.3   (Continued)

Figure 1. Costs for Robot and Human Workers as of 1995.

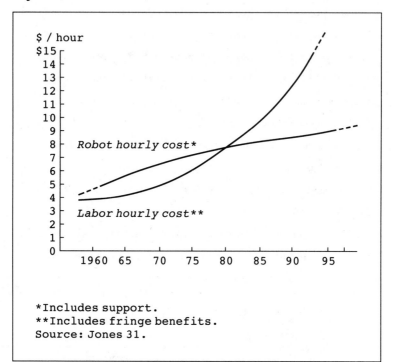

*Includes support.
**Includes fringe benefits.
Source: Jones 31.

human laborers have increased by 250 percent over the same period (Ayres and Miller 72). The graph in Figure 1 records the differences in labor costs between human and robot workers up to 1995. Moreover, as the production of robots increases, the cost per unit will surely decrease (Jones 33). In addition, businesses can expect to pay less for their robots, thanks to a number of recent tax incentives and low-interest government loans (Farnum 56; Nagler 60).

Significant savings can also result from a robot's efficient use of materials. At one General Electric

FIGURE 17.3   (Continued)

12

factory, a robot used for painting saved $19,000 worth
of paint in one year while improving coverage and finish
(Ayres and Miller 77). Because of their mechanical
capabilities, robots waste fewer parts and less
materials (such as die, plastic for moulding, bolts) and
energy in any manufacturing process (Toepperwein et al.
107—8). This increased cost efficiency may be the chief
method of protecting American industry from foreign
competitors.

What Robots Will Do in the Future

So far this report has emphasized the current
advantages robots offer industrial workers and
employers. Compared to what robots will do for us in the
future, these benefits are relatively small. Brian
Carlisle, President of Robotic Industries Association,
predicts that by the year 2000, "we'll see applications
we can't even imagine today" (qtd. in Krepchin 49). In
the 1970s and early 1980s, robots admittedly had limited
capabilities and applications. For the most part they
were restricted to performing pick-and-place operations
(Aronson 26). But new markets opened up in the late
1980s and early 1990s for robots outside of auto
assembly lines and manufacturing.

Although experts say that we are many years away
from taking daily advantage of highly skilled robots
(Albus 22—23; Dodd 692), experimental laboratories are
already using robots that have extraordinary vision and

FIGURE 17.3   (Continued)

13

tactile sensory systems (Jones 24—25). The next
generation of robots will have sensory capabilities
unmatched by their human counterparts. Like the Bionic
Woman, the Six Million Dollar Man, and Superman, they
will be able to see, touch, smell, and hear perfectly
and do so under extremely dangerous conditions. A
growing number of robots are already equipped for voice
recognition. Robots in the medical field, which now
perform service duties and laboratory testing, soon will
be used for surgical procedures (Zipser 18; Hard 57;
Krepchin 45). And in the near future, astrorobots will
be employed for "assembling and servicing the planned
U.S. space station" (Miles 92).

    This growth in robot capabilities will be matched by
the increase in the number of robots in industry. Robots
will be found in almost every manufacturing process in
the mid-1990s and early 2000s, and by the year 2000,
Barbara Rice predicts, there will be 37 percent more
robots in America than today (interview). With such
large corporations as Martin Marietta, Corning Inc.,
General Motors, IBM, and Texas Instruments entering the
robotics field, these estimates may not be unreasonable
(Ayres and Miller 8).

    All of these technological advances will translate
into a better life for workers. Amy Waterstein,
automation director for Southeast Industries, predicts
that robots will soon give workers "shorter hours,
longer vacations, and higher wages" (qtd. in Jones 25).
Looking further into the future, James Albus predicts

FIGURE 17.3   (Continued)

14

that "if all humans could own the equivalent of one or
two robots, they would be financially independent,
regardless of whether they were employed or not" (27).
Robots may not make everyone rich, but if Joseph
Engleberger is correct, robots will one day "clean
bathrooms, scrub floors, cook meals, cut the grass, and
shovel snow" (qtd. in Miles 97). As Jones points out,
robots will join the computer as "the two most essential
tools of the late 21st century" (32).

CONCLUSION

The steadily increasing use of robots in American
industry will benefit workers and employers, not hurt
them. Although some individuals have worried about
potential jobs being lost to robots, many industrialists
and union leaders maintain that robots will create more
jobs in the 1990s than they eliminate. Previous
successes with automation confirm this assessment.
Despite a temporary displacement of a small percentage
of the work force, industrial robots can improve overall
working conditions for employees. Robots help human
workers to perform more efficiently and to escape
hazardous jobs and work sites. Employers find robots
desirable because they will make it possible to cut
costs, to reduce errors, and to improve quality and
output. As robot technology improves, it certainly will
offer numerous future benefits, including a higher
standard of living for the American industrial worker.

FIGURE 17.3   (Continued)

15

Works Cited

Albus, James. "Robots in the Workplace." *The Futurist*
17 (1983): 22—27.

Alkhafaji, Abbass F.   "Strategic Applications of
Robotics Technology." *Management Decision* 29.4
(1991): 49—54.

Aronson, Robert. "The Robot Boom Is On." *Machine
Design* 52 (1980): 22—28.

Ayres, Robert, and Steven Miller. *Robotics Applications
and Social Implications.* Cambridge, MA: Ballinger,
1988.

Coates, Vary T., and J. F. Coates.   "The Potential Impacts
of Robotics." *The Futurist* 17 (1983): 28—32.

Dodd, John. "Robots: The New Steel-Collar Worker."
Personnel Journal 60 (Sept. 1985): 688—95.

Farnum, Gregory T.   "Industrial Robots--The Next Ten Years."
Manufacturing Engineering 95 (Dec. 1985): 55—56.

Greenberger, Leonard S.   "To Boldly Go Where No One
Wants to Go." *Public Utilities Fortnightly* 1 (Dec.
1991): 37—39.

Hard, Rob. "Robots: Can They Help Solve the Technologist
Shortage?" *Hospitals* 20 (June 1991): 56—58.

Jones, Sue-Ellen. "The Social and Economic Impact of
Robots in the American Workplace." *Journal of
Business and Engineering Technology* 9 (1990): 22—37.

Koelsch, James R.   "The Steel-Collar Worker: Friend or
Foe?" *Product Engineering* 33 (1986): 48—50.

FIGURE 17.3 (Continued)

16

Krepchin, Ira P. "Robots: The Once and Future Technology."
    Modern Materials Handling 45 (May 1990): 44—49.

Miles, Gregory L. "Robotics: It's a Dirty Job, But
    Somebody's Gotta Do It." *Business Week* 20 (Aug.
    1990): 92—97.

Mittelstadt, Eric. "What We Must Do to Compete in the
    1990s." *Controls & Systems* 39 (Jan. 1992): 84.

Nagler, Ben. "Career Paths in Robotics." *Manufacturing*
    Engineering 99 (Dec. 1989): 59—60.

Rice, Barbara. Industrial Technology Professor,
    Fairmont Central College. Personal interview,
    30 Mar. 1992.

"Robot and Weighing System Reduce Sample Testing Costs
    50% at Coca-Cola." *Chilton's Food Engineering* 57
    (Dec. 1985): 115.

"Robots to Create 44,500 Jobs by 1995." *Modern*
    Materials Handling 42 (1987): 15—17.

Spaulding, Mark. "The Zero-Man Option." *Packaging* 36
    (Dec. 1991): 35—36.

Toepperwein, L. L., et al. *Robotics Applications for*
    Industry: A Practical Guide. Park Ridge, IL: Noyes
    Data Co., 1989.

Tolman, Alan G. "Sound Intensity Measurements in
    Hazardous Areas." *Sound and Vibration* 21 (1987): 6.

Williams, David. "Steel Collar Layoffs as Robots
    Decline." *Automotive Industries* 166 (Oct. 1986): 23.

Zipser, Andy. "Foot in the Door: Robots Are Just
    Starting to Realize Their Promise." *Barron's* 8
    (Oct. 1990): 18+.

A Final Word About Long Reports

Perhaps no piece of writing you do on the job—or as a course assignment for your instructor—carries more weight than your work on a long report. Your readers will inevitably place a great deal of emphasis on your work. As we have seen, these reports deal with major issues affecting long-range planning and decision making. The long report asks you to use all the researching and writing skills you have learned. The preparation of a long report may appear at first to be a formidable task. But you can simplify your job and increase your chances for success by following the guidelines offered in this chapter. Among those guidelines, always keep these four points in mind:

1. Plan and work early—do not postpone work on identifying, researching, and drafting until a deadline draws near.
2. Divide your work load into meaningful units—reassure yourself that you do not have to write the report or even an entire section of a report in a day or two.
3. Set up mini-deadlines for each phase of your work and then meet them.
4. If you are preparing the report as part of a team, confer often and carefully with others on your team.

✓ Revision Checklist

Below are some central questions to ask as you revise your long report. But keep in mind that since you will have to rely on a number of writing skills to complete a successful long report, you also may want to refer to the revision checklists in earlier chapters for such topics as writing summaries, supplying correct documentation, and organizing your work.

1. Does my report concentrate on a major problem? That is, does the problem or issue that I am writing about have significant implications for my major, my neighborhood, my city, or my employer?
2. Have I clearly identified and explained the significance of the main problem as opposed to a minor side issue?
3. Have I done sufficient research—in the library, through interviewing, from personal observation and/or testing—to convince my readers that I am knowledgeable about this problem, its scope and effects, and likely solution? Does my report prove to readers that I am familiar with key terms, major researchers in the field, major changes, trends, and accomplishments?

4. Have I anticipated how various readers will use and profit from my report for their long-range planning? Do I know what my employer/teacher/reader is looking for?

5. Have I followed my company's/instructor's guidelines for the format and documentation of my work?

6. Have I followed my company's/instructor's schedule for completing various stages of my long report?

7. Have I clearly divided and labeled the parts of my long report to make it easy for readers to follow and to show my careful plan of organization?

8. Did I supply an abstract that leaves no doubt in my readers' minds about what my report deals with and why?

9. Is my title page attractively presented, and does it contain all the basic information—title, date, for whom the report is written, my name—that my readers require?

10. Does the introduction to my report give readers all the necessary information about the background, the problem, the purpose of my report, and its scope? Have I made sure that my introduction is neither too long nor too short?

11. Is the body of my report the longest part of my work? Have I included in this section the weight of all my research—the facts, statistics, and descriptions—that my readers need in order to know that I have done my homework on the topic well? Have I included subheadings to reflect the major divisions into which I have organized the research that forms the nucleus of the body of my report?

12. Does my conclusion succinctly wrap up my report? Does it tell readers what the findings of my research are? That is, does it accurately interpret all the data I have gathered? Does my conclusion square with the body of my report so that it neither contradicts nor omits major points that I have made in the body?

13. If required, have I supplied a recommendation section that tells readers concretely how they can respond to the problem using the data I have given them? Do my recommendations make sense—are they realistic and practical, and do they relate directly to the research and topic I have been studying and not verge on a different topic or side issue? Are my recommendations persuasive?

14. Have I included in the final copy of my report all the parts listed in my table of contents?

15. Did I supply a one-page letter of transmittal or cover letter specifically informing my readers why the report was written and indicating its scope and findings?

Exercises

1. Write a memo to your instructor on how one of the short reports in Chapter 16 could be useful to someone who has to write a long report.

2. Using the information contained in Figures 17.1 and 17.2, write an introduction for the report "A Study to Determine New Directions in Women's Athletics at Coastal College." Add any details you think will be relevant.

3. What kinds of research did the student do to write the long report in Figure 17.3? As part of your answer, include the titles of any specific reference works you think the writer may have consulted. You may want to review Chapter 9.

4. Study Figure 17.3 and answer the following questions based on it.
   a. Why can the abstract be termed informative rather than descriptive?
   b. How has the writer successfully limited the scope of the report?
   c. Where does the writer use internal summaries especially well? (See page 634 for a discussion of the values of such summaries.)
   d. What visual devices does the writer employ to separate parts of the report and divisions within each part?
   e. How does the writer introduce, summarize, and draw conclusions from the expert opinions he cites in order to substantiate the main points?
   f. What are the ways in which the writer documents information he has gathered?
   g. What functions does the conclusion serve for readers? Cite specific examples from the report.

5. Come to class prepared to discuss at least two major problems that would be suitable topics for a long report. Consider an important community problem—traffic, crime rate, air and water pollution—or a problem at your college. Then write a letter to a consulting firm or other appropriate agency or business, requesting a study of the problem and a report.

6. Write an outline of the report appropriate for one of the problems listed in Exercise 5. Use major headings and include the kinds of information listed on pages 629–632.

7. Have your instructor look at and approve the outline you prepared for Exercise 6. Then write a long report based on the outline.

Oral Reports

Every job requires employees to have carefully developed speaking skills. In fact, to get hired, you have to be a persuasive speaker at your job interview. On the job you will have oral communication responsibilities that will vary in the amount of preparation you have to do for them, the time they last, and the audience and occasion for which they are intended. You may have to brief your collaborative writing team, report to a group of supervisors about your job accomplishments, or make a sales presentation before a group of potential customers. Or you may need to meet with your boss alone to fill him or her in on some aspect of your work. Whatever your oral communication responsibilities, this chapter offers practical advice on how to become a better, more assured communicator in informal briefings and formal speeches.

Informal Briefings

If you have ever given a book report or explained laboratory results in front of a class, you have given an informal briefing. Such semi-formal reports are a routine part of many jobs. Nurses and law enforcement officers, for example, give their colleagues or supervisors end-of-shift reports, summarizing major activities for the previous eight or twelve hours.

Another kind of briefing involves explaining a new procedure or policy to other departments. As a personnel officer, you may have to inform plant employees of extended coverage in an insurance policy. If your company has just purchased a new piece of equipment, you may have to demonstrate it. Or you may introduce a speaker, a visitor to your agency, or a new employee or report on a convention you attended. Finally, you may give a brief report at a meeting—before a school board, group of county supervisors, or government agency.

These informal reports are usually short (one to seven minutes, perhaps), and you always will be given advance notice. Make your comments brief and to the point. When the boss tells you to "say a few words about the new Minivac (or the new parking policy)," you are not expected to give a lengthy formal speech. For example, the personnel officer informing employees about extended insurance coverage should not read the fine print in the policy, but rather cover its key points, saving detailed questions for private conferences.

Rather than writing down all your comments in full sentences, make a few rough notes and jot them down on a three-by-five note card you can easily hold in the palm of your hand. Your notes should consist of only the major points you want to mention, preferably in chronological order or from cause to effect (see pages 81–82; 84). A note card with key facts used by an employee who is introducing Ms. Rizzo, a visiting speaker, to a monthly meeting of safety directors might include the following items.

- Diana J. Rizzo, Chief Engineer of the Rhode Island State Highway Department for twelve years.

- Experience as both a civil engineer and safety expert.

- Consultant to Secretary Habib, Department of Transportation.

- Member of the National Safety Council and author of "Field Test Procedures in Highway Safety Construction."

- Designed specially constructed aluminum posts used on Rhode Island highway system.

- Received "Award for Excellence" from the Northeastern Association of Traffic Engineers in May, 1994.

Similarly, a note card used by a personnel officer to inform employees about new insurance coverage might list the following major points.

- American Democratic Insurance has changed some of the coverage on employees' policies.
- If you are hospitalized, American Democratic will pay up to $221.75 per day on your room. This is an increase of $38.35 per day from the old policy.
- Outpatient lab benefits are also increased. American Democratic will now pay $500 a year rather than the $375 under the old policy.
- Premiums will also increase by about $3.40 a week, but Tramco, the employer, will pay $1.40 of that increase, meaning employees will have $2.00 more deducted from weekly checks.
- Currently we are exploring a dental rider on the American Democratic policy.
- If you have any questions, call me or Mr. Blackwell at extension 3452 or drop by the Personnel Office in the Administration Building.

Formal Speeches

Whereas an informal briefing is likely to be short, generally conversational, and intended for limited numbers of people, a formal speech is likely to be longer, less conversational, and intended for a wider audience. Therefore, it involves more preparation and less interaction between speaker and audience; it is, in other words, more "formal."

Most of us are uncomfortable in front of an audience because we feel frightened or embarrassed. Much of this anxiety can be eased, though, if you know what to expect. The two areas you should investigate thoroughly before you begin to prepare your speech are (1) who will be in the audience and (2) why they are there.

Analyzing Your Audience

The more you learn about your audience, the better equipped you will be to give them what they need. First, determine what unites them as a group. For example, are they all members of one profession (computer programming or mechanical engineering) or do they have similar professional interests (court reporters, paralegals, and legal secretaries)? Or your audience may be linked by place of employment; for instance, all the employees—mechanics, bookkeepers, salespeople—in a car dealership. Other bonds, too, may unite an audience—ethnic background, hobbies, membership in clubs, age, sex, or religion. Your audience may also be united in their emotional response to a given topic—pro or con. In order to diminish any potential reservations they may have, try to anticipate how they may respond to your subject matter as well as to the approach you take.

Once you have defined your audience, assess how much they will know about your topic. Everything depends on what your audience will understand and need—the terms you use, how many details you have to give, the number of explanations and definitions you supply, and the amount of background information required. Terms taken for granted by one group must be explained or omitted for another group.

If you are at a conference or other type of meeting, mingle with the audience beforehand to learn more about them. Listen for comments. You might pick up information that you can work into your talk.

Speaking for the Occasion

Understanding why your audience is there will help you deliver a successful speech. An audience may be present for a variety of reasons—for a social gathering, a business meeting, or an educational forum. Shape your remarks to fit the occasion.

Consider also how much time is allotted for your speech and whether you are the only speaker scheduled. It makes a big difference in your preparation if you are the first speaker at an 8:00 A.M. breakfast meeting or the last of four speakers at an evening meeting. Are you speaking on Monday morning or Friday afternoon? Take into account your audience's interest level and attention span at various times of the day or week. Also find out if someone will introduce you or if you will begin on your own. If someone introduces you, it would be embarrassing to repeat the identical information from that introduction in your speech.

The number of people in your audience is also significant. A formal presentation to a small group—five or six supervisors or buyers—seated around a conference table can nonetheless be made more personal; you can walk around the table or stop your talk a few times to ask if there are any questions. You will obviously have much less flexibility when addressing a large group—seventy or eighty people—in an auditorium.

Ways of Presenting a Speech

Your effectiveness depends directly on the extent of your preparation. Of the four approaches below, the extemporaneous is best suited to most individuals and occasions. But first we will examine three other possibilities and their advantages and disadvantages.

1. Speaking off-the-cuff. The professional speechmaker may be comfortable with an off-the-cuff approach, but for most of us, the worst way to deliver a speech is to speak without any preparation whatsoever. You may know a subject very well and think that your experience qualifies you for an on-the-spot performance. But you will only be fooling yourself if you think you have all the details and explanations in the back of your head. It is equally dangerous to believe that once you start talking, everything will fall into place smoothly. The "everything works out for the best" philosophy, unaided by a lot of hard work, does not operate in public speaking. Without preparation, you are likely to forget or to confuse important points entirely. Mark Twain's advice is apt here: "It takes three weeks to prepare a good impromptu speech."

2. Memorizing a speech. The exact opposite of the off-the-cuff approach, a memorized speech does have some advantages for certain individuals—tour bus drivers, guides, or salespeople—who must deliver the same speech many times over. But for the individual who has to deliver an original speech just once, a memorized speech contains pitfalls. First, the hours spent memorizing exact words and sentences would be better devoted to organizing your speech or gathering information for it. Second, if you forget a single word or sentence, you may lose the rest of the speech. Third, a memorized delivery can make you appear mechanical. Rather than adjusting to an audience's reactions, you will be obligated to speak the exact words you wrote before you saw your audience.

3. Reading a speech. Reading a speech may be appropriate if you are presenting information on company policy or legal issues on which there can be no deviation from the printed word. Most speeches, however, will not require this rigid adherence to a text. Your speeches will be more acceptable, socially and professionally, when you interact with the audience. In reading, you set up a barrier between yourself and the audience. You will not establish eye contact with your audience for fear of losing your place.

4. Delivering a speech extemporaneously. An extemporaneous delivery is best for the widest variety of occasions. Unlike a speaker using a memorized or written speech, you do not come before your audience with the entire speech in hand. *By no means, though, is an extemporaneous delivery an off-the-cuff performance.* It requires a great deal of preparation. But what you prepare is an outline of the major points of your speech, as discussed later in this chapter. You will rehearse using that outline, but the actual words you use in your speech will not necessarily be those you have rehearsed. Stand confidently in front of the audience with your outline reminding you of major points but not the precise language to express them. In this way you can establish contact with the audience.

The rest of this chapter will discuss various effective ways of preparing and delivering an extemporaneous speech.

Preparing the Parts of a Speech

The Introduction

The most important part of a speech, your introduction should capture the audience's attention by answering these questions: (1) Who are you? (2) What are your qualifications? (3) What topic are you speaking about, and how is that topic restricted? and (4) How is that topic relevant to us? An effective introduction is proportional to the length of your speech. A ten-minute speech requires no more than a sixty-second introduction; a twenty-minute speech needs no more than a two-minute introduction.

You can begin by introducing yourself, emphasizing your professional qualifications. (This self-introduction may be unnecessary if someone else introduces you or if everyone in the room knows you; always thank the person introducing you.) Never apologize for taking up your audience's time or for your limitations as a professional speaker. And do not criticize the circumstances surrounding your speech—for example, "I know it is late (or early) and we're all tired"; or "This is a very bad location; this room is stuffy and not well lighted."

Thank the audience for the opportunity of addressing them and indicate at once what your topic is and how it is divided. The most interesting speeches are the easiest to follow. Restrict your topic to ensure that it will be organized carefully. Focus on one major (and restricted) idea, such as a tasty diet under 1,000 calories a day or a course in canoeing.

Give listeners a "road map" at the beginning of your talk so that they will know where you are, when you are there, and what they have to look forward to or to recall: "Tonight I will discuss the three problems a foodstore manager faces when deciding to stock inventory: (1) the difficulty in predicting needs, (2) the inability of the production department to record current levels of stock accurately, and (3) the uncertainty of marketplace conditions."

Moving from your announcement of the topic to your presentation of it requires skill at inducing an audience to listen. Use a variety of tactics to get the audience to "bite on the hook." The simplest is to ask a question: "Do you know how much actual meat there is in a hot dog?" "How many of you have taken Graphics 201?"

Another often used technique is to cite some interesting statistics. Listeners' curiosity should be so piqued that they will stay tuned in for an explanation or description: "In 1994 two million heart attack victims in America lived to tell about it." "By 1993, more than half of America's population was over thirty-five." Notice how Julie Webster uses this technique in her speech on voice mail systems outlined in Figure 18.2 (p. 671). The introduction to her speech contains pertinent— and frightening—statistics on the high cost of a business call, as well as on the number of phone calls that do not go through.

You might also begin with an anecdote, or brief story, that illustrates the main points of your speech. Sometimes effective speakers start with something humorous. But be careful about using jokes to get the audience in a good mood. Some may not find your joke amusing, in good taste, or relevant. Make your audience feel at ease and friendly toward you by establishing a bond with them. Include some local history or local events in your introduction; find some way to compliment your audience (or someone prominent in that audience).

The Body of the Speech

The body is the longest part of your speech just as it is in a long report. It supplies the substance of your speech by (1) explaining a process, (2) describing a condition, (3) telling a story, (4) arguing a case, or (5) doing all of the above. See how the body of Julie Webster's speech (Figure 18.2, pages 671–674), is organized around the customer benefits of the three main functions of voice mail—messaging, response, and the automated attendant.

To get the right perspective, recall your own experiences as a member of an audience. How often did you feel bored or angry because a speaker tried to overload you with details? The Peanuts cartoon in Figure 18.1 below points out the consequences of boring an audience.

When you prepare the body of your speech, consider your audience as a group of listeners, *not* readers. Readers have more time to digest the ideas in your work. They can read as slowly or as quickly as they want, reread and double-check details, or skim wherever they want. Listeners, however, cannot absorb as much as readers can. The speaker's audience has a shorter attention span. You cannot include every fact you gathered in preparing the speech.

Most important of all, do not forget that your speech is being delivered for the benefit of your audience. Relate everything in your talk to them. Do this by

FIGURE 18.1   How to find out if you are a boring person.

© 1980 United Features Syndicate, Inc.

selecting only details that are relevant to your audience and your purpose. Choose concrete (not abstract or general) examples; look for memorable stories, analogies, or events that an audience can carry away with them *after* your speech is completed. Ask yourself such key questions as the following.

- Have I given my audience the interest-level details they deserve to have?
- Have I loaded my speech with too many details, or details that are too complex or technical for my audience's needs or background?
- Have I stuck to my main topic without wasting my audience's time on an irrelevant tangent?

Here are a few helpful ways you can present and organize information in the body of your speech. In writing a report, you assist readers by supplying headings, underscorings, and bullets. In a speech, switch from purely visual devices to aural ones, as in the following.

1. Give signals (directions) to show where you are going or where you have been. These signals will convince an audience that your speech does not ramble. Enumerate your points: "first," "second," "third." When you tell a story, follow a chronological sequence and fill your speech with signposts: *before, following, next, then.*

2. Comment on your own material. Tell the audience if some point is especially significant, memorable, or relevant. "This next fact is the most important one in my speech." "The best determiner of pressure is the amount of liquid present in the chamber."

3. Repeat key ideas. You can repeat a sentence or a word for emphasis and to help the audience remember it. But do this sparingly; repeating the same point over and over again bores an audience.

4. Provide internal summaries. Spending a few seconds to recap what you have already covered will reassure your audience and you as well. For example, "We have already discussed the difficulties in establishing a menu repertory, or the list of items that the food-service manager wants to appear on the menu. Now we will turn to ways of determining which items should appear on a menu and why."

The Conclusion

Plan your conclusion as carefully as your introduction. Stopping with a screeching halt is as bad as trailing off in a fading monotone. An effective conclusion leaves the audience feeling that you have come full circle and accomplished what you promised. Conclusions, even for long speeches (twenty minutes), should never run more than sixty to ninety seconds. Moreover, you should clearly inform your audience when you are approaching the end of your speech: "finally," "in conclusion," "to wrap up."

When you tell your audience that you are concluding your talk, make sure that you mean it. An audience will get angry with a speaker who gives them a false ending. Saying, "In conclusion," and then talking for another ten minutes will only frustrate your listeners and make them less receptive to your message.

A conclusion should contain something lively and memorable. Do not introduce a new subject or simply repeat your introduction. A conclusion contains a restatement and reemphasis of your most important points (or the conclusions you reached about them). For example, "The installation of the stainless steel heating tanks has, as we have seen, saved our firm 32 percent in utility costs, since we do not now have to run the heating system all day." If you are delivering a persuasive speech, issue a call for action, just as in a sales letter (see pages 201–211). Stress what you want your listeners to do and why it is beneficial for them to do it or harmful (or less desirable) if they do not follow your advice. Once again, notice how Julie Webster ends her speech (Figure 18.2) with a concise summary of her main points and urges her listeners to act by telephoning her company to arrange for a demonstration on how a voice mail system works.

The Speech Outline

Construct a speech outline to represent the introduction, the body, and the conclusion. As we saw, in an extemporaneous speech you do not write out the entire speech you are going to deliver. Instead, you will have a speech outline to guide you. The speech outline has great psychological value in that it gives you enough facts to handle your speaking engagement confidently, yet it is not so detailed that it places you in a straitjacket.

The speech outline illustrated in Figure 18.2 contains the appropriate amount of detail to represent the introduction, body, and conclusion of a speech given by Julie Webster, a sales representative at Madisonville Telecommunications. A roman numeral designates each major point; capital letters indicate appropriate supporting facts. Be careful about crowding too much into a speech outline. You do not need an outline as highly structured as the following.

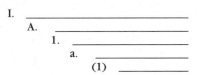

Not every point will require four or five capital letters. But each point, whether indicated by a roman numeral or a capital letter, should be written as a complete sentence. Since your outline must be easy to read and follow, leave wide margins and double-space between your points. Mark, perhaps with a red pen or in capital letters, where visuals appear in your speech. That way, you won't forget them.

Using Visuals

Visuals have numerous benefits for speakers and their audiences. A visual can arouse an audience's interest, summarize a great deal of information quickly, and reinforce the main points of your talk.

You may use a variety of visuals during your talk: photographs, maps, chalk-boards, models, pasteboards (large, two-by-three-foot, stiff pieces of white card-board), diagrams, transparencies, or slides. Visuals are used in a speech for the same reasons as in a report—to explain quickly, condense information, and add interest and variety. But visuals in an oral presentation must be constructed even more carefully than for a written report. Unlike a reading audience, a listening audience cannot refer to a visual again and may not have time to study the visual in detail.

The size and shape of your visuals are important. Make sure that they are large and easy to read, even from the back row or from the far corner of a long confer-ence table. If they cannot be seen clearly from a distance and understood at once, they are not very useful. If possible, before using any visual, mount it in the front of the room and sit in the last row of chairs in the room in which you will speak to see if your audience will be able to decipher it. You might decide to hold your visual up higher and show it to different sections of your audience by walking from one side of the room to another. Or you might want to increase its size (enlarge a photograph, for example). All photocopy machines have enlargement features, and various computer software programs also allow you to blow up a fig-ure or a table.

In addition to making your visuals large enough for your audience to see, make sure that each visual is easy to understand the very first view an audience has of it. If you suspect that your audience may have trouble, even momentarily, knowing what the visual is or why and how it works in your presentation, redesign it or delete it from your talk. For example, using technical (or excessive) computer flow charts may detract from rather than add to your talk if an audience does not readily know what these flow charts mean. And don't make the mistake of taking five minutes to explain what a visual is; use that time more profitably to deliver your talk.

Also, be careful that a visual does not interfere with your message. Will it lead an audience astray on a tangent? Will it contradict the message you are attempting to deliver? If so, delete or revise it.

Follow this cardinal rule: keep all visuals clear, simple, and large so they work for you in communicating with your audience.

Determining How Many Visuals to Use

Use visuals sparingly. A brief speech may not require any visuals, and even a very long speech may need only two or three visuals. Their purpose is to clarify (or supplement), not to compete with, what you say. (Note Julie Webster's limited use of visuals in Figure 18.2.) Too many visuals will distract your audience.

FIGURE 18.2   An outline for a speech on voice mail.

Madisonville
TELECOMMUNICATIONS

Julie Webster, President

AUDIENCE: Madisonville Business Association

PURPOSE: To convince businesses to install a voice mail
system

INTRODUCTION

  I. Voice mail can solve telephone communication problems
efficiently and economically.

    A. Seventy-five percent of all business calls cannot be
completed on the first attempt.

    B. When a business call does go through, it can cost up
to $20.

    C. Voice mail is solving these and other problems by
changing the way people in organizations are
communicating with each other and their customers.

    D. Voice mail is an electronic messaging system accessed
through a company's network of push-button phones
linked to a computer.

    E. Voice mail turns your phone into a post office that
delivers messages almost immediately--24 hours a day--
and never makes a mistake.

    F. Madisonville Telecommunications can show you how to
improve your communications using voice mail's three
key functions. SHOW POSTER WITH WORDS "MESSAGING,"
"RESPONDING," "ATTENDING."

FIGURE 18.2   (Continued)

2

<u>BODY</u>

II. All businesses benefit from voice mail's **messaging functions.**

    A. Voice mail contributes to today's efficient paperless office.

        1. You will never again have to battle those pink message slips and worry that they contain a wrong or incomplete message.

        2. Unlike those written messages, with voice mail you actually hear the caller directly and get helpful clues from the tone and inflection of the caller's voice.

        3. Since receptionists no longer have to stop what they're doing to take messages, they have more time to devote to other duties.

    B. Voice mail systems automatically forward messages to your company's telephones or radio pagers.

        1. Executives--even at remote sites--will not miss important client calls while they're away from the office.

        2. Voice mail will free you from the inconvenience of time zones because your message can be sent at any hour and received at the recipient's most convenient time.

    C. Voice mail allows you to screen incoming calls.

        1. Executives working on major projects with stringent deadlines have the option of accepting only top-priority calls.

FIGURE 18.2   (Continued)

3

   2. Other callers have the option of leaving a
      message.

   D. Voice mail also calls users with reminders.

      1. Clients and customers can be reminded about
         appointments, sales, and new schedules.

      2. Employers can remind employees--scattered across
         town or throughout the country--of meetings,
         deadlines, or procedures.

III. Businesses benefit from voice mail's **response function**.

   A. Employees can access recorded company information
      through voice mail.

      1. Each employee can easily access a voice mail
         "mail box" to receive interoffice memos and
         customer communications.

      2. Special password functions protect privileged
         information in your company.

   B. From all over the world, clients and customers can
      access information on your merchandise and services
      through voice mail.

      1. One system can provide several different pre-
         recorded messages.

      2. Step-by-step voice "prompts" make access easy for
         clients.

      3. Callers can use this service even outside of
         business hours.

FIGURE 18.2   (Continued)

4

IV. Businesses profit from voice mail's **automated attendant function.**

    A. The automated attendant directs callers on how to reach a certain department or person simply by using a touch-tone pad.

        1. Receptionists save time by not having to answer and route calls.

        2. Easy menu options make voice mail "user friendly" for your callers.

        3. Customers save time by having their calls promptly answered and routed.

    B. If the party is unable to answer, the automated attendant will activate your voice messaging system.

        1. If there is no answer, the caller may leave a recorded message.

        2. If the line is busy, voice mail tells the caller how many calls are ahead of him or her and offers the option of leaving a message or waiting on hold.

CONCLUSION

  V. Let Madisonville Telecommunications help you to select the most successful voice mail system for your business.

    A. The three services of a voice mail system--**messaging, responding, attending**--are interrelated. SHOW TRIANGLE DEPICTING RELATIONSHIP.

    B. Voice mail will help you to receive more messages more efficiently and accurately.

    C. Madisonville Telecommunications can show you how to improve your business communications around the clock.

    D. Please give us a call for your free demonstration.

Getting the Most from Your Visuals

The following practical suggestions will help you get the most from your visuals.

1. Do not set up your visuals before you begin speaking. The audience will try to determine how you are going to use them and so will not give you full attention. When you are finished with a visual, put it away. Your audience will not be distracted by it or tempted to look at it instead of listening to you.

2. Firmly anchor any maps or illustrations. Having a map roll up or a picture fall off a stand during your presentation is embarrassing.

3. Never obstruct the audience's view by standing in front of the visuals you are explaining. Use a pointer or a laser pointer (a pen-sized tool that projects a bright red spot up to 150 feet) to direct audience attention to your visual.

4. Avoid crowding three or four visuals onto one pasteboard to save space or time. Use different pasteboards instead.

5. Do not put a lot of writing on a visual. Elaborate labels or descriptions defeat your reason for using the visual. Your audience will spend more time trying to decipher the writing than attempting to understand the visual itself. If any writing must appear on one of your visuals, enlarge it so your audience can read it quickly and easily.

6. Be extra cautious with a slide projector. Check beforehand to make sure that all your slides are in the order in which you are going to discuss them and that they are right side up. Most important, make sure the projector works.

Using Videos in Your Talk

Many business presentations rely on video players and large-screen televisions to sell a product, service, or idea. Camera, lights, sound, and action—all can arouse an audience's interest. There is no doubt that a film (or video) can show things that could never be duplicated in a conference room or that could never be described in such detail so quickly. If you intend to show a film or video to your audience, follow these guidelines:

1. Prepare your audience for viewing the video. Don't just walk into the room and turn on the VCR. Also, don't stop your talk and say, "Now let's view this." Help your audience by telling them why you are going to show them the video, what they should look for, and how long the video will last.
2. Never make the video substitute for your talk. Don't show a 20- or 30-minute film or video and think that it alone will sell your product or make all the points for you. Preview the video or film and show only those sections that are essential to your talk. The film or video should become a *selected* part of your presentation, not the presentation itself. For a 12- to 15-minute talk, plan on devoting no more than a few minutes of your time to showing a video.
3. Always identify the source of the video (where it comes from, even if from your own company), and indicate whether your audience can obtain a copy of the edited or full video, if they wish.

Rehearsing a Speech

An efficient writer never submits a rough draft of a paper or report as final copy to an employer. Rather, the draft is revised, edited, and carefully checked before it is keyboarded to produce the final copy. Similarly, a careful speaker does not write a speech and march off to deliver it. Between the time you write a speech and deliver it, rehearse it several times. Going over your ideas aloud may help you to spot poor organization and to correct insufficient or inaccurate content.

Rehearsing will also help you to acquire more natural speech rhythms, pitch, pauses, and pacing. Try speaking in front of a full-length mirror for at least one of your rehearsals to see how an audience might view you. At another time, speak into a tape recorder to determine if you sound friendly or frantic, poised or pressured. You can also catch and correct yourself from going too quickly or too slowly. Time yourself so that you will have a fairly accurate idea if your talk falls within the time allotted you. Practice with the visuals or equipment you intend to use in your speech for valuable "hands-on" experience.

Delivering a Speech

A poor delivery can ruin a good talk. When you speak before an audience, you will be evaluated on the image you project by how you look, talk, and move (your body language). Do you mumble into your notes, never looking at the audience? Do you clutch the lectern as if to keep it in place? Do you shift nervously from one foot to another? All these actions betray your nervousness and detract from your presentation.

The following suggestions on how to present a speech will help you to be a well-prepared speaker.

Before You Speak

Your name is called, and within a minute or two you will have to begin addressing the audience. You will be nervous. Accept the fact and even allow a few seconds for a "panic time." But then put the nervous energy to work for you. Chances are, your audience will have no idea how fearful you are; they cannot see the butterflies in your stomach. If you have to go to a lectern, walk slowly so you do not trip.

Once you are before the lectern, remove any pitchers or glasses of water if you are worried about spilling them. Always have a wristwatch with you. Before speaking, lay it on the desk or lectern so that you can occasionally glance down to see how much time you have left. This unobtrusive act is far preferable to reminding the audience that you are running out of time by noticeably raising your arm to look at your watch.

Giving Your Talk

Begin your speech slowly. Give listeners a chance to sit back in their chairs and establish a mental connection with your topic. Rushing into your speech may be startling, causing you to lose the audience from the start. To speak effectively, pay attention to the following four points.

1. Establish eye contact with your listeners to form a special relationship with them. Burying your head in notes signals your lack of interest in the audience or your fear. Some timid speakers think that if they look only at some fixed place or object in the back of the room, the audience will still regard this as eye contact. But this kind of cover-up does not work. Another tactic poor (or frightened) speakers use is to look at only one member of the audience or to focus, with frequent sidewise glances, on the individual next to them on the stage, perhaps the person who has introduced the speakers.

Establish a pattern of gazing at your notes and then looking up at various individuals in the audience. If the group you are addressing is small (five to ten people), look at each person in the course of your talk. When you speak to a large audience (fifty or more individuals), visually divide this group into four or five sections, and look at each section a number of times as you speak.

2. Make the volume, tone, and rate of your delivery a favorable part of your image. Speak in a natural, conversational voice, but avoid such "verbal tics" as "you know" or "I mean" repeated several times each minute. Such nervous habits will make your audience nervous too and make your speech less effective. Be careful to vary the rate of your delivery. Talking in a monotone, never raising or lowering your voice, will surely help to put your audience to sleep. Use your volume and rate to help you emphasize key points and make transitions in your speech. Talk slowly enough for your audience to understand you, yet quickly enough so that you don't sound as if you are emphasizing each word.

Talk loudly enough for everyone to hear, but be careful if you are using a microphone. Your voice will be amplified; if you are speaking loudly, you will boom rather than send messages pleasantly to your audience. Watch out for the other extreme—speaking so softly that only the first two rows can hear you.

As you rehearse your speech, look up in a dictionary the pronunciation of any words you are unsure about. Pay special attention to the pronunciation of individuals' names and company and city names, too. Ask ahead of time to double-check.

3. Watch your posture. If you stand motionless, looking as if rigor mortis has set in, your speech will be judged as cold and lifeless, no matter how lively your words are. Be natural; move, and let your body react to what you are saying. Smile, nod your head, move your arms, point your fingers at an object, stand back a little from the lectern. This is not to say that you should be a moving target. Never sit on a desk or lean on a lectern in front of your audience. Listeners will be waiting to see if you fall off your newly discovered perch.

4. Let your gestures be a help, not a hindrance. Be natural and consistent. Do not startle an audience by suddenly pounding on the lectern for emphasis. Any quick, unexpected movement detracts from what you are saying. Let your material suggest appropriate movements. If you are itemizing two or three points, hold up the appropriate number of fingers to indicate which point you are discussing. Using your hands and arms to indicate direction, size, or relationships is also a way to use body language to comment on your material.

Avoid any gesture that will distract your audience; do not provide your own sideshow. The following nervous habits, engaged in frequently during a speech, can divert the audience's attention: scratching your head, rubbing your nose, twirling your hair, pushing up your glasses, fumbling with your notes, or tapping your foot.

When You Have Finished Your Speech

Don't just smugly sit down, walk back to your place on the dais or in the audience, or, worse yet, march out of the room. Thank your listeners for their attention, and stay at the lectern for them to applaud, ask questions, or perhaps give the person who introduced you a chance to thank you while you are still in front of the group. If a question-and-answer session is to follow your speech, give your audience a time limit for questions. For example, you might say, "I'll be happy to answer any questions you may have now before we break for lunch in ten minutes," or "I have set aside the next ten minutes for questions." By setting limits, you reduce the chances of engaging in a lengthy debate with members of the audience, and you also can politely leave after your time elapses.

Speech Evaluation Form

A large portion of Chapter 18 has given you information on how to construct and deliver a formal speech. As a way of reviewing that advice, study Figure 18.3, an evaluation form similar to those used by instructors in speech classes. Note that the form gives equal emphasis to the speaker's performance and to the organization and content of the speech.

FIGURE 18.3   A speech evaluation form.

Name of speaker _____   Date of speech _____

Title of speech _____   Length of speech _____

PART I: THE SPEAKER (circle the appropriate number)

1. Appearance:	1 sloppy	2	3	4	5 well groomed
2. Eye contact:	1 poor	2	3	4	5 effective
3. Voice:	1 monotonous	2	3	4	5 varied
4. Posture:	1 poor	2	3	4	5 natural
5. Gestures:	1 disturbing	2	3	4	5 appropriate
6. Self-confidence:	1 nervous	2	3	4	5 poised

PART II: THE SPEECH (circle the appropriate number: 1 = poor; 5 = superior):

A. Overall performance

    1. Speaker's knowledge of the subject—carefully researched; factual errors; missing details:

           1   2   3   4   5

    2. Relevance of the topic for audience—suitable for this group:

           1   2   3   4   5

    3. The speaker's language—too technical; filled with cliches or slang expressions; or crisp and descriptive:

           1   2   3   4   5

FIGURE 18.3   (Continued)

4. Use of visuals—too many or too few; well placed; appropriate size; handled with care; interfered with speech:

       1   2   3   4   5

B. Parts of the speech

1. The introduction—brief and attention-getting; informative about division and presentation of topic:

       1   2   3   4   5

2. The body—carefully organized and easy to follow; appropriate amount of information; message developed and conveyed clearly:

       1   2   3   4   5

3. The conclusion—brief, effective summary of the main points:

       1   2   3   4   5

PART III: YOUR FINAL REACTIONS (briefly complete the following statements)

1. Of all the speakers on the platform today, this speaker should be ranked:

_____

2. The speaker's main strengths were: _____

_____

_____

_____

3. The speaker needs to improve on: _____

_____

_____

✓ Revision Checklist

Use the questions in this checklist to revise your speech outline and to improve your delivery during the rehearsal process.

1. In my speech, have I anticipated my audience's background, interest, or even potential reluctance to my message?
2. Does my introduction arouse my audience's interest and encourage them to receive and accept the rest of my message?
3. Did I start with interesting and relevant statistics, a question, or an anecdote to gain my audience's attention?
4. Have I limited the body of my speech to three or four main points?
5. Have I arranged these main points logically, and do I make connections between or among them?
6. Have I used supporting examples and illustrations that can be readily understood by my listening audience?
7. Does my conclusion contain a summary of the main points of my speech and/or a specific call for action?
8. As I rehearsed my speech, did I notice any weak or redundant areas in the outline and have I eliminated them?
9. Are my visuals clear and easy to see, even from the back of the room?
10. Have I double-spaced my speech outline and left wide margins to make it easier to read?
11. Have I rehearsed my speech well enough so that I am familiar with its organization and am comfortable using visuals?
12. Have I monitored appropriately my volume and tone to vary my delivery and emphasize major points?
13. Are my gestures relevant and nonintrusive?
14. Have I timed my speech, complete with visuals, so that I won't run under or over my allotted time?

Exercises

1. Prepare a three- to five-minute talk explaining how a piece of equipment that you use on your job works. If the equipment is small enough, bring it with you to class. If it is too large, prepare an appropriate visual or two that you can use in your talk.

2. You have just been asked to talk about the students at your school. Narrow this topic and submit a speech outline to your instructor, showing how you have limited the topic and supplied appropriate evidence. Use two or three appropriate visuals (tables, photographs, etc.). Follow the format of the outline in Figure 18.2 (pages 671–674).

3. Prepare a ten-minute talk on a controversial topic that you would present before some civic group—a local PTA, a local chapter of an organization, a post of the Veterans of Foreign Wars, a synagogue or church club. Submit a speech outline similar to that in Figure 18.2 to your instructor, together with a one-page statement of your specific call to action and its relevance for your audience.

4. Using the information contained in the research paper in Chapter 10 (pages 373–386) or the long report in Chapter 17 (pages 638–657), prepare a short speech (five to seven minutes) for your class.

5. Using the evaluation form contained in Figure 18.3, evaluate a speaker; this person can be someone in a speech class, a local politician, or perhaps someone delivering a report at work. Specify the time, place, and occasion of the speech.

Index

Abbreviations, 123, 136-37
    for states and provinces, 157, 158
    when not to use, 136-37
Abstracts
    descriptive, 414
    informative, 390-404, 413-14
    for long reports, 628, 632
    of specific reference works, 327, 328,
        332-33, 350-52
    for test reports, 611
Acceptance letters, for a job, 299-300
Accident reports, 589, 615-19
Achtert, Walter S., 358
Action verbs (in résumés), 261
Active voice, 100-2
Adjustment letters, 226-30
    saying "no," 230, 233
    saying "yes," 227, 230
Administrative Management Society (AMS)
        letter format, 151, 153, 154, 157,
        159, 198
Advertisements, for jobs, 256
Alphabetizing, 314-15
    references in Works Cited list, 365-66
American Heart Association, 4-7
Apostrophes, use of, 122-23
Appendix, for long reports, 628, 636
Application forms, for jobs, 290-92
Application letters, 281-90
Applied Science & Technology Index,
        324, 325
Artist's tools, for visuals, 478-79
Asterisks, 17, 542
ATMs (automatic teller machines), 562-65
Attention line, on envelopes, 163
Audience analysis, 4-10, 110
    for application letters, 281-83
    for ESL (English as a second language)
        readers, 6-7, 175-80, 524, 528, 590

for formal speeches, 663-64
for instructions, 525-26
for letters, 148-49, 163-69, 197, 201,
        204, 206-9, 211-15, 223, 226, 233
for long reports, 626-27
for memos, 195-96
in office politics, 565-66
for proposals
    internal, 565-66
    research, 576
    sales, 568, 571
for questionnaires, 428-29, 438
questions to ask about, 6-8
for résumés, 259-60
for short reports, 590
Audiovisual materials, 337-39
Author card, 315
Author-date method of documentation,
        371-72

Back matter, in long report, 636
Bar codes, 161, 421, 594
Basic English. *See* International English
Bibliographic Retrieval Service (BRS), 329
Bibliography cards, 340-41
Blind ads, for jobs, 256, 283
Body of a work
    of business letters, 159
    of formal speeches, 667, 668
    of long reports, 633-34
Body language, 676-78
Boldface type, 17
Book reviews, 406, 408
Brainstorming, 31, 69, 259, 429
Bullet résumé, 271
Bullets, 17, 271, 461, 529
Business Periodicals Index, 282,
        324-26, 327

Call numbers, for books, 316, 319-20
Capitalization, 17, 155, 265
Card catalog, 313-19
Career objective statement, 265-66
Case studies
    of collaboratively written paragraph
        revision, 60-64
    of collaboratively written proposal,
        556-58, 562-65
    of instructions, 537, 539
    of long report, 638-57
    of paragraph revision, 57-60
    of questionnaires and questionnaire
        reports, 455-58, 462-66
    of research paper, 372-86
    of summary, 396-404
    of the writing process, 28-37
Caution statement, 544-46
CD-ROM, 327-28, 420
Charts, 489-94, 496-99
*CIS/Index to Publications of the United
    States Congress*, 335
Clauses, 96-100
    definition of, 96
    dependent and independent, 96-97
    relative, 106
    subordinate, 96-98
Clip art, computer, 510-11
Clustering, 29-30, 259
Code words, on note cards, 342
Collaborative writing
    benefits of, 21
    with computers, 46-47
    definition of, 20
    of instructions, 524, 526
    of long reports, 627, 637
    of memos, 195
    organizational models for, 39-41
        functional, 40
        integrated, 40
        sequential, 40
    of paragraphs, 60-64
    problems to avoid in, 42-43
    process of, 39-43
    of proposals, 556-58, 565
    of questionnaire reports, 454, 455-58
    responsibilities in, 41-42
    of short reports, 588, 590
    in the workplace, 20-21, 661
Collection letters, 237-42

College Placement Annual, 256-57
Comma splice, 98-100
    four ways to correct, 99-100
    how *not* to correct, 100
Complaint letters, 223-26
Complimentary close, 159
Computer graphics, 473, 479, 508-13
    advantages of, 513
    capabilities of, 512-13
    drawing software, 512
    presentation graphics, 510-12
Computer hardware, 44, 508-9
Computer programming flow chart, 499
Computer software, 44, 510-12
Computerized bibliographic searches,
    326-30
    compact disks (CD-ROM), 327-28
    online searches, 328-29
Computerized library catalog, 314-19
Computers
    to check spelling, 46, 118-19
    clip art, 510-11
    in collaborative writing, 46-47
    in the electronic office, 418-19
    for E-mail transmission, 188-90
    in formatting résumés, 265, 277
    in the job search, 257
    in letter writing, 149-50
    in library searches, 45, 314-19,
        326-30, 420
    in note-taking, 340-42
    in preparing questionnaires, 443, 444
    in preparing visuals, 484, 508-13, 591
    to tally questionnaires, 451, 453
    in the writing process, 43-49, 129, 394,
        395, 590, 629
Conciseness, 129-33
    of reports, 590-91
Conclusions
    in adjustment letters saying "no," 233
    in adjustment letters saying "yes," 230
    in formal speeches, 668-69
    in long reports, 634-35
    in memos, 196
    in progress reports, 600, 603
    in sales letters, 211
    in short reports, 592
    after speeches, 678
Concrete language, 14, 128-29, 206
Congratulation letters, 216, 218-19

Conjunctions, 96-97, 99
  coordinating, 99-100
  subordinate, 96-97, 99
Conjunctive adverbs, 100
Contemporary language, in letters, 171-74
"Copyrights Approved for Colorization,"
  391
Correspondence. *See* Letters
"Counting on the Census," 396-401
Cover letters, 448-50
Cultural traditions, of ESL readers, 175,
  177 180
Customer relation letters, 211-42
  direct approach, 212-15
  indirect approach, 212-15

Dangling modifiers, 106
Data sheet. *See* Résumé
Date line, 155, 195
Delivery of speeches, 676-78
Dependent clause, 96-97
Dewey decimal system, 316, 319-20
DIALOG, 329
Dictionaries
  English language, 331-32
  specialized, 349-50
Direct quotations, 357
  on note cards, 342-44
  in questionnaire reports, 460
Directory of Corporate Affiliations, 282
Discrimination, laws prohibiting in job
  hiring, 270, 297
Documentation
  author-date method, 371-72
  importance of, 357
  material to document, 357
  MLA guidelines for, 358-70
  ordered references method, 372
  parenthetical vs. footnoting, 358-60
  preparing Works Cited page, 360-66
  within the text, 366-70
Dossier, 252-56
Double consonants, 119
Dow Jones News/Retrieval, 329
Drafting
  in business letters, 147, 149, 167-72, 212
  in collaborative writing, 42-43
  with computers, 45
  in instructions, 527, 548

in letters of application, 283-84
in long reports, 627-28
in memos, 196
in paragraphing, 56-64
sentences, 94
in short reports, 590
in summaries, 395, 402
in the writing process, 32-37
Drawings, 504-8
  in instructions, 530-32
Dummy subject, 109

Editing
  with computers, 46
  in collaborative writing, 42-43
  general principles of, 38-39
  in instructions, 527, 548
  in letters, 147, 150
  in letters of application, 259
  in long reports, 628
  as part of research process, 357
  in questionnaires, 431
  in résumés, 279
  sentences, 95, 105
  in short reports, 590
  in summaries, 396
  words, 117
Electronic office, 417-22
"Electronic Publishing: The Next Great
  Office Revolution," 422-25
Ellipsis, 343-44
E-mail, 188-90, 577-79
"Emergency Preparedness via Cable TV,"
  91-93
Employment agencies, 257, 258
Employment evaluations, 301-2
Enclosure line, in letters, 160
Encyclopedia of Associations, 256
Encyclopedias, 331, 347-49
Envelope format, 161-63
ESL (English as second language) readers,
  6-7, 175-80
  guidelines for communication with,
  175-76
  refusal of credit to, 234-36
  respecting cultural traditions of, 177,
  180
  writing instructions for, 524, 528
  writing reports for, 590

Evaluations
  of employment, 301-2
  of formal speeches, 678-80
  of résumés, 279-80
Exploded drawings
  as visuals, 507-8
  in instructions, 530
Extemporaneous speeches, 665
Eye contact, 665, 677

Facts on File, 391
False plurals, 121-22
"Fatal assumptions," of job seekers,
  251-52
Fax machines, 32-34, 36, 147, 188-90,
  58, 543
Federal Job Register, 258
Figures, 485-508
  part of long report, 624, 626
  usefulness in occupational writing,
    15-16
Findings in short reports, 592
Flex time, 30, 83
Flow charts, 498-500
Follow-up letters, 297-98, 219-22
Footnotes, 358-59
Forbes, 282
Formal speeches
  delivery of, 676-78
  evaluation of, 678-80
  forms of presentation
    extemporaneous, 665
    memorized, 665
    off-the-cuff, 664-65
    read, 665
  outlining, 669
  preparation of
    body, 667-68
    conclusion, 668-69
    introduction, 665-66
    rehearsal of, 676
    visuals in, 669-70. 675
Fortune, 282
Forwarding instructions, on envelopes,
  163
Fragments, of sentences, 97-98
Freewriting, 31
Front matter, in long reports, 629, 632
Full block format, for letters, 151, 154, 156
Gallup, George, 446

Gestures. *See* Body language
Gibaldi, Joseph, 358
Glossary
  for long reports, 636
  of terms to describe visuals, 515-16
Goodwill, in business correspondence,
  148, 163-69, 207, 211, 215, 216, 218,
  219, 233
Government documents, 333-35
Graphs, 485-88
Group writing. *See* Collaborative writing

Handbooks, manuals, almanacs, 333
Harris, Lou, 446
Headings
  importance of
    in long reports, 633-34
    in memos, 191, 195
    in proposals, 561
    in short reports, 591
    in writing, 16
  for tables, 484
Heparin, descriptions of, 12-13
Horizontal axis, of a graph, 485-86
"How to Outfit the High-Tech Office,"
  417-22

Idiomatic expressions, avoiding for ESL
  readers, 176
Illustrations list, for long report, 632
Imperatives, in instructions, 528, 529
Incident reports, 615-19
Independent clause, 96-97
Index to Government Periodicals, 333
Indexes, reference works, 321-26, 346-47
Informal briefings, 661-63
InfoTrac, 328
Initials, use of
  in "From" lines in memos, 191
  in letters (for reference initials), 160
Inside address, 155, 157
Instructions
  guidelines for writing, 528-29
  importance of, 523-24
  parts of
    actual steps, 542-46
    conclusion, 546-48
    introduction, 534-40
    list of equipment and materials,
      540-41

for questionnaires, 443-44
variety of, 524-25
visuals in, 530-33
before writing, 525-27
International English, 6-7, 175, 234-35,
    590
International readers. *See* ESL readers
Interviews, for jobs, 292, 295-97
Introductions
    to formal speeches, 665-66
    to instructions, 534-40
    to long reports, 632
    to progress reports, 600
    to proposals, 566, 571, 579-80
    to a test report, 611
    of visuals, 480-81
Italics, use of, 17

Jargon, 135-37, 394
Job hunting
    application forms, 290-92
    dossier, 252-53, 256
        letters of recommendation in, 253
        where stored, 252
    identifying qualifications for, 251-52
    interviews, 292, 295-97
    letters of application, 281-90
    placement offices, 252, 256-57
    restricting job search, 251-52
    résumés, 258-80
    sources for jobs, 256-58
Journals, as opposed to magazines, 321

Landers, Ann, 137
Legal notification for collection letters,
    237, 242
Legal significance of long report, 626
Legally proper writing, 524, 615-16, 619
Legibility, 340
Letterhead, 154, 155
Letters
    of acceptance and refusal, 299-301
    adjustment, 226-33
    of application, 281-90
    of assessment, 301-2
    collection, 237-42
    complaint, 223-26
    of congratulation, 216, 218-29
    cover letter for questionnaires, 448-50
    customer relations, 211-42

definition of, 147
effective language in, 169-74
follow-up, 219-22, 297-98
formats, 150-54
functions of, 147-48
general content, 163-69
of inquiry, 199
order, 197-99
    external, 198
    internal, requisition, 199
parts of
    body, 159
    complimentary close, 159
    copy distributed notation, 160
    date line, 155
    enclosure line, 160
    inside address, 155, 157
    reference initials, 160
    salutation, 157
    signature, 159-60
    subject line, 157
of recommendation, 252, 253, 256
refusing credit, 233-36
request for letter of recommendation,
    253, 254
sales, 201, 203-11
    the "four A's," 206-11
special request, 199, 201
thank-you, 215-16
thank-you, after job interview, 297-98
of transmittal, 629, 630
Libraries
    circulation desk, 313
    library catalog, 313-19
        author card, 315
        subject card, 317-19
        title card, 315, 317
    the stacks, 319-21
        call numbers, 319-20
        shelves, 320-21
Library of Congress classification system,
    319-20
Library research
    note taking, 339-44
    quoting and paraphrasing, 342-44
    reference works, 45, 321-33, 346-52
Long reports
    back matter
        appendix, 636
        glossary, 636

Long reports *(Continued)*
    works cited, 636
    collaboration in, 627
    differences from short reports, 625–27
    documentation in, 636
    format for, 626
    front matter
        abstract, 632
        letter of transmittal, 629
        list of illustrations, 632
        table of contents, 629, 631, 632
        title page, 629
    model of, 638–57
    process of writing, 627–28
    purpose of, 625
    text of
        body, 633–34
        conclusion, 634–35
        introduction, 632–33
        recommendations, 635–36

Magazines. *See* Reference works:
    periodicals; popular press
Mail questionnaires, 427–28, 448, 450
Maps, 500–2
Margins, use of, 149, 277, 444, 482, 484,
    488
Measurements, significance of, 17, 529,
    591, 611
Melville, Herman, 136
Memorized speeches, 665
Memos, 190–97
    definition of, 190
    formats for, 190–95
    function of, 190
    protocol for, 195
    strategies for organization, 196–97
    style and tone, 195–96
    suggestions on writing, 195–97
    used for proposals, 556, 561
    used for short reports, 591
    versus letters, 190–91
Message, 11–12, 147, 159, 212, 284,
    287, 290, 393, 526, 591
Microfiche, 339
Microfilm, 338
"Microwaves," 25–26
Million Dollar Directory, 282
Minutes of meetings, 408–12
Misplaced modifiers, 106–7

MLA Handbook, 358
Modifiers, 106–7, 111
    dangling, 106
    misplaced, 106–7
Money, 282
*Monthly Catalog of U.S. Government
    Publications*, 333
Multiple-bar charts, 492–93, 494
Musty expressions, 171–74

NewsBank, 337
Newspapers. *See* Reference works:
    popular press
Note cards, 341–44
    for formal speeches, 662–63
Numbers
    percents, 454, 458–59
    in questionnaire reports, 454, 458–60
    rules for writing out, 454, 458
    significance in reports, 17
    in table of contents, 629

Objectivity, importance of, 14–15, 206,
    393–94, 409, 435–37, 591, 611,
    615, 620
Office politics, audience analysis in,
    565–66
Omissions, in incident report, 615
Oral reports
    formal speeches, 663–80
    informal briefings, 661–63
Order letters, 197–99
Ordered references method of
    documentation, 372
Organization
    of headings, in long reports, 633–34
    of memos, 196–97
    of steps, in instructions, 542–46
    of *Successful Writing at Work*, 22
    of summaries, 393
Organizational charts, 496–98
Outlines
    for business correspondence, 212
    for formal speeches, 669, 671–74
    importance in the writing process, 31,
        33, 627, 628
    for long reports, 627, 628

Pagination
    second or subsequent pages, 154

table of contents, 629, 632
title page, 632
Paragraphs
    appearance of, 78-80
    coherence in, 73-76
    completeness of, 76-78
    definition of, 55
    importance of, 55-56
    length of, 77-78, 80
        in application letters, 284, 287, 290
        in business letters, 159
        job acceptance letters, 299-300
        in letters of congratulations, 218
        in proposals, 568, 571, 576, 579
        in questionnaire reports, 461
        in sales letters, 207
        in short reports, 590-91
    order in letters of application, 284, 287, 290
    patterns of organization
        cause-to-effect, 84
        classification, 83-84
        combined, 85-86
        comparison/contrast, 82-83
        definition, 83
        description, 81
        effect-to-cause, 85
        examples, 81
        space, 82
        time, 81-82
    topic sentences
        finding one, 69
        importance of, 66
        placement in paragraph, 70
        restricting them, 70-71
    transitional devices in
        parallelism, 76
        repetition of key ideas, 75
        transitional words, 73-75
        use of pronouns, 75-76
    T-shaped, 67
    types of
        concluding, 68-69
        introductory, 67-68
        supporting, 64, 66-67
        transitional, 68
    unity in, 71-73
Parallelism
    to achieve coherence in paragraphs, 76
    in sentences, 103-4

Paraphrases, 344
Passive voice, 100-2
"Paulownia Seedlings Respond to
    Increased Daylength," 613-15
Periodic reports, 592-94
Periodical holdings and indexes, 321-26
Personal interview questionnaire,
    427-28
Persuasion
    in proposals, 556, 567, 571, 575-76
    in sales letters, 201, 206-9, 211
    use of, in occupational writing, 18-20
Photographs, 502-4
Phrases, 96
    definition of, 96
    prepositional, 98, 100, 104, 132
Pie charts. *See* Visuals
Placement file. *See* Dossier
Placement office, for job information,
    252, 256-57
Plagiarism, 357, 480
Plurals, 121-22
"Positive Effects of Robots in American
    Industry," 638-57
Precise words, 127-29
Preliminary screening, for questionnaires,
    448
Prepositional phrases, 98, 100, 104, 132
Presentation software, 420
Prewriting
    with computers, 45
    of résumés, 259, 274
    strategies of, 29-31
Principal International Businesses, 282
Process of writing
    for business letters, 148-49
    with computers, 43-49
    general guidelines, 28-39
    for letters of application, 283-84
    for long reports, 627-28
    for paragraphs, 56-64
    for progress reports, 600, 603
    restricting a topic, 429-30
    for résumés, 258-61
    for sentences, 94-95
    for short reports, 589-92
    for summaries, 394-404
    for topic sentences, 69
Progress reports, 598-603
Pronouns, misplaced or faulty, 107

Pronunciation, in a speech, 677
Proofreading
    letters, 149–50
    résumés, 260, 279
Proposals
    appearance, 561
    audiences for
        internal proposals, 565–66
        research papers, 576
        sales proposals, 568, 571
    as collaborative efforts, 556–58
    cost sections in, 567–68, 575
    definition of, 555
    formats of, 566–68, 571, 575–76,
        580–81
    guidelines for writing, 560–61
    as persuasive plans, 556
    purposes of, 555–56
    qualifications of writer/company,
        575–76
    request for proposals (RFP), 558, 559
    statement/solution of problem, 566,
        567, 571, 580
    timetables in, 575, 580–81
    types
        external, 560
        internal, 559, 561–68
        for research papers, 576, 579–81
        sales, 568, 571–76
        solicited, 558
        unsolicited, 558–59
Punctuation
    apostrophe, 122–23
    colon, 157, 160
    comma, 97, 98, 100, 157, 159
    in a letter, 155, 157, 159, 160
    period, 97, 99–100
    semicolon, 97, 99–100
Purpose
    of instructions, 523–24, 525
    of proposals, 555–56
    of résumés, 258
    of sales letters, 201, 206
    of short reports, 591–92
    in summaries, 393
    in writing on the job, 10–11
    in writing questionnaires, 426–27

Questionnaires
    cover letter for, 448–50
    definition of, 426

distribution of, 448–50
    restricting topics for, 429–30
    selecting respondents for, 446–48
    tabulating responses from, 450–53
    usefulness of, 426–27
    writing instructions for respondents,
        443–44
    writing questions for, 430–41
    writing reports based on, 454–61
Questions
    about audiences, 6–8
    closed, 433–34
    open-ended, 432
    in sales letters, 207
Quota sampling, 447–48

Reader's Digest, 391
Readers' Guide to Periodical Literature,
    321–23
Reading a speech, 665
Recommendations
    in incident reports, 619
    in long reports, 635–36
    in job-related writing, 19–20
    in questionnaire reports, 454, 460–61
    in short reports, 592
    in summaries, 393, 405
    in test reports, 611
    in trip reports, 604
Recommendations, securing for a job,
    252–56
Redundancy, 131–32
Reference, pronoun, 107
Reference works
    abstracts, 332–33, 350–52
    audiovisual materials, 337–39
    computerized, 45, 326–30
    dictionaries, 331–32, 349–50
    encyclopedias, 331, 347–49
    government documents, 333–35
    handbooks, manuals, almanacs, 333
    periodicals and indexes, 321–26, 330,
        346–47
    for popular press, 335–37
Refusal letter, for a job offer, 300–1
Rehearsing a speech, 676
Reliability, of questions, 435–41
Reports
    accident (*see* Incident reports), 589,
        615–19
    collaborative, 590

field trip, 604
home health visits, 604, 606
incident, 589, 615–19
lateral, 594
periodic, 592–94
progress, 598–603
questionnaire survey, 454–61
routine, 589
sales, 594–98
site inspection, 604
social work visits, 604, 606
test, 610–15
trip, 603–10
unusual occurrence (*see* Incident
  reports) vertical, 594
Request for proposals (RFP), 558, 559
Research. *See also* Library research
importance in writing process, 28–29
for long reports, 625–26, 627–28
for proposals, 560, 580
for short reports, 589–90
for test reports, 610–11
Responsibility
of readers, 18
of writers, 18
Résumés
appearance of, 274, 277, 279
audience for, 258
by chronology, 266, 268–69, 271
color of, 277
in job search database, 257
difference from letters of application,
  281
by function or skill areas, 271, 274
organization of, 265–71, 274
parts of
  career objective statement, 265–66
  education, 266, 268
  experience, 268–70
  headings, 265, 274
  hobbies and interests, 270
  personal data, 270
  references, 270–71
  "selling clauses" in, 259–60, 269
  skill areas, 271
techniques for writing, 259–60
on video, 257–58
what to exclude, 263
what to include, 261, 263
Revision
for clarity, 170

with computer, 129
for content, 37
importance of, 37
of long reports, 627–28
for organization, 38
of paragraphs, 56–64
of résumés, 260
of sentences, 94–95
for tone, 38
for words, 117, 132
in the writing process, 37–38
Revision Checklists
for business correspondence,
  242–43
for documentation, 387
for instructions, 552
for a job search, 302–3
for letters, 180–81
for long reports, 658–59
for paragraphs, 86–87
for proposals, 581–82
for questionnaires, 467–68
for research, 345
for sentences, 112–13
for short reports, 620–21
for speeches, 681
for summaries, 416
for visuals, 514
for words, 138
for the writing process, 49–50
Robert's Rules of Order, 409

Sales reports, 594–98
Salutation, 157
avoiding sexist use of, 135, 157
Sampling
quota, 447–48
stratified random, 447
systematic random, 446–47
Scanners, 421, 478, 509
Scripting, as visual device, 17
"See also" card, 317–18
"Self-illuminating Exit Signs," 585–86
Semiblock format, for letters, 151, 152,
  154
Sentences
active verbs in, 111, 260–61
appropriate context for, 105–6
avoiding *that/which* clauses, 112
in business letters, 170–71

Sentences *(Continued)*
  definition of, 96
  in descriptive abstracts, 414
  for ESL readers, 176
  fragments, 97-98
  graceful and positive, in letters, 169
  guidelines for writing, 108-12
  imperative, 528, 529
  in instructions, 528-29
  lead-in, for visuals, 480-81
  length of, 110-11, 176
  logic within, 105, 109-10
  in sales letters, 206
  subject-verb-object pattern, 108-9
  for summary in long report, 634
Sexist language
  ways to eliminate, 134-35, 155, 157
Short reports. *See also* Reports
  definition of, 588-89
  how to write, 589-92
Signature, 159-60
Simplified English. *See* International
    English
"Size Standards for Domestic Mail," 11,
    161
Slang, 137-38
Slide projectors, use of, 675
Spacing, varied, 17
Speaking off-the-cuff, 664-65
Special mailing instructions, 163
Speech outline, 669, 671-74
Spell-checking programs, 46, 118-19
Spelling correctly, rules for, 113-23
*Standard and Poor's Corporation
    Register*, 282, 283
Stratified random sampling, 447
"Stress and the Computer Programmer,"
    373-86
Stub, part of table, 484
Style
  definition of, 12
  nontechnical, 13
  technical, 12-13
Stylus, 509
Subheadings, 16
Subject card, 317-19
Subject line, 157, 159, 195
Summaries. *See also* Abstracts
  contents of, 393-94, 405-6, 408
  definition of, 390

evaluative, 405-8
  internal, in formal speech, 668
  length of, 390, 393, 405
  preparation of, 394-404
  of questionnaire reports, 454
  usefulness of, 390-92, 415
Suppressed zero, 487, 488
Systematic random sampling, 446-47

Table of contents page, 629, 631, 632
Tables, 482-85
Taking notes, 339-44
Talks. *See* Oral reports
Tape recorder
  in rehearsing a speech, 676
  for trip reports, 606
Technical audience, 7, 12-13, 611-12
Technical language, 7, 12-13, 438, 527-8,
    611-12, 636
  for ESL readers, 175-76
Telephone interviews, 428
Templates, 479
Test reports, 610-15
Thank-you letters, 215-16, 297-98
*Thomas Register of American
    Manufacturers*, 282
Tick marks, 486
Title card, 315, 317
Title page, for long reports, 629
Titles, underscoring, 284
Tone
  in adjustment letters, 226-27, 230
  in complaint letters, 223
  definition of, 12
  in test reports, 611
Tools, artist's, 478-79
Transmittal letter, for long reports, 629,
    630
Trip reports, 603-10
"Turning Schoolgrounds Green," 585
"Two Mixtures Could Replace Banned
    Refrigerant," 392
Typing
  of business letters, 149-50
  of envelopes, 161-62
  of résumés, 277

Underscoring, 17, 284

Vague pronoun reference, 107

Vague words, avoiding them, 107, 128-29
Validity
    of questionnaires, 461
    of questions, 435
Verbs, selecting graphic, 129
Vertical axis, of graph, 485-86
Vertical files in library, 336
Visuals
    charts, 489-94, 496-99
    bar, 490-94
    circle, 489-90
    flow, 498-500
    organizational, 496-98
    computer graphics, 420-21, 508-13
    criteria for using, 475-78
    definition of, 473
    drawings, 504-8
    for formal speeches, 669-70, 675
    glossary for, 515-16
    graphs, 485-88
    in instructions, 530-33
    maps, 500-2
    photographs, 502-4
    pictograms, 494-96
    tables, 482-85
    use in long reports, 624, 626
    usefulness of, 15-17, 573-75
    writing about, 479-82
Vita. *See* Résumé
Voice
    active, 100-2
    passive, 100, 102
Voice mail, 671-74

Wall Street Journal, 282
Warning statement, 544-46
"Wheelchair-Lift Switch Covers," 586-87
WILSONLINE, 329
Word processors. *See* Computers
Wordiness, 129-33
Words
    contextually appropriate, 105-6
    general, 128-29
    homonyms, 123-27
    precise, 127-29
    selection for instructions, 528-29
    sexist, 134-35
    specific, 128-29
    spelling of, 118-23
    unnecessary, 129-33
Working bibliography, 340-41
Writing, job related
    characteristics of, 14-20
    importance of, 3-4
    measurements in, 17
    responsibilities for, 18
Writing process. *See* Process of writing
Writing process and the computer, 43-49

"You attitude," 164-69, 206, 223, 284, 568

Zip codes, 162